Contemporary Moral Problems

Contemporary Moral Problems

JAMES E. WHITE
St. Cloud State University

WEST PUBLISHING COMPANY
St. Paul   New York   Los Angeles   San Francisco

COPYRIGHT © 1985   By WEST PUBLISHING CO.
                    50 West Kellogg Boulevard
                    P.O. Box 43526
                    St. Paul Minnesota 55164

Printed in the United States of America

Library of Congress Cataloging in Publication Data

Main entry under title:

Contemporary moral problems.

Includes bibliographies.
1. Ethical problems—Addresses, essays, lectures.
2. Civilization, Modern—1950-   —Addresses, essays, lectures.   I. White, James E.
BJ1031.C6 1985   170   84–17293
ISBN 0–314–85310–3

Contents

Preface

The choice of topics for this text was mostly dictated by student interest. Students were surveyed to see what moral issues they wished to discuss, and at the top of the list were issues about killing—abortion, euthanasia, the death penalty, and nuclear war. All of these are included in the text. Next on the list of popular topics was sexual morality, followed by discrimination against women. There is a chapter on each of these topics.

Student interest was not the only consideration however. Two topics were added because of their logical connection to the six topics of greatest interest. It seemed appropriate to follow the chapters on abortion and euthanasia with a chapter on hunger and starvation because it involves further questions about the right to life and letting people die. Writers on abortion often insist that unborn human beings have a right to life. If so, then why don't distant people also have this right? And why doesn't this right include a welfare right to have basic needs satisfied? Furthermore, if one agrees that there is no moral difference between killing and letting die, as some writers on euthanasia contend, then it seems to follow that

letting people die of starvation, even distant people, is in the same moral category as killing people.

A chapter on animals and the environment was added after the chapter on sexual equality because it raises more questions about discrimination and equal treatment, and it prevents the book from having an overemphasis on killing and letting die. If it is unfair to discriminate against women because of their sex (and thus accept sexism), then why isn't it also unjust to discriminate against animals because of their species (and thus accept what Singer calls "speciesism")? The argument of Peter Singer and others who defend animal rights is that speciesism is analogous to sexism, and if one rejects sexism as unjust, then one should also reject speciesism.

But why should our moral concern end with animals? Isn't it morally arbitrary to draw the line at sentience, and have moral concern only for conscious or sentient beings? This is still another form of discrimination, called "sentientism," the discrimination against nonsentient things such as forests and lakes. The view of Aldo Leopold and his follower William Godfrey-Smith is that the natural environment should be an object of moral concern too.

The chapter on nuclear war was placed at the end of the book. It seemed best to end with a topic that is one of the most important and pressing issues of our time. Furthermore, it is both an issue about killing and letting die on a massive scale, and an environmental issue about large-scale pollution of the environment.

The choice of particular readings on each topic was influenced by a variety of considerations. First and foremost, there was an attempt to find readings of high quality. As a result, many of the articles included are semi-classics such as Judith Jarvis Thomson's "A Defense of Abortion," and none are previously unpublished. Some of the readings were choosen for their historical importance, e.g., the Supreme Court decisions on abortion and the death penalty. Also, there was an attempt to balance the reading, to have different points of view represented. On most of these issues it is possible to discern what might be called, losely speaking, a "conservative view" and a more "liberal view" opposed to it. For example, in the first chapter on abortion, Humber classifies the view he defends as "conservative" and opposes it to the more "liberal view" of Thomson. Whenever possible, a "moderate view," relatively speaking, has been included as well.

Last, and certainly not the least important consideration, was suitability for students. The book is intended to be an introductory textbook that can be read and understood by college students. Most of the readings were assigned in class, and the students were tested for comprehension. It must be admitted that some students had difficulties. To alleviate this problem, several student aids have been provided:

1. *Chapter Introductions.* Each chapter begins with a general introduction that explains the basic concepts or gives background information. Also included is a brief survey of the main philosophical issues, arguments, and theories relevant to the moral issue.

2. *Reading Introductions.* Each reading is preceded by an author biography and a short summary of the author's main arguments and conclusions.

3. *Study Questions.* After each reading there are study questions of two kinds. First, there are pedestrian review questions that test the student's grasp of the main points in the reading. They are directed towards the reader who has had trouble following the text. Second, there are more difficult discussion questions that probe deeper into the reading. They are aimed at the person who has understood the reading and is ready to discuss it.

4. *Problem Cases.* At the end of each chapter, there are problem cases that require the student to apply the concepts, principles, and theories discussed in the chapter to a hard case, either actual or hypothetical. This case-study method (as they call it in law schools and business schools) produces lively discussion and it is a good way to get the students thinking about moral issues from a moral point of view. Moreover, the problem cases can be assigned as short paper topics or used on essay tests.

5. *Suggested Readings.* Specific suggestions are made for further reading. Usually these suggested readings are discussed in the chapter introduction so that the student will have some idea about their relevance to the topic of the chapter. Obviously these suggestions are not intended to take the place of a comprehensive bibliography. Rather they are items that might have been included in the chapter.

In putting the book together (in several different versions), I have benefited from the help and advice of many people. In particular, I want to thank my colleague Myron Anderson, James A. Nelson of St. John's University, Tom Regan of North Carolina State University, my secretary Barbara Seefeldt, the reviewers who made useful suggestions, and my patient and perceptive editor Clark Baxter of West Publishing Co.

ACKNOWLEDGMENTS

Robert Corrington, Penn State
Michael Davis—Illinois State University
Thomas Mayberry, University of Toledo
Dale Jamieson, University of Colorado
William Carter, North Carolina State University

Contemporary Moral Problems

CHAPTER 1

Abortion

Basic Concepts

Abortion is the termination of pregnancy involving the death of the fetus. Strictly speaking, the term fetus refers to the prenatal organism from about the eighth week of pregnancy until birth, and it is preceded by the zygote (the fertilized egg or ovum) and the embryo. But it is convenient to follow the common practice of using the term fetus as a general term covering the organism from conception to birth.

REASONS FOR ABORTION

Why would a woman get an abortion? Various reasons can be given. One obvious one is to save her life. In cases of tubal pregnancy, for example, where the zygote does not descend to the uterus but remains lodged in the fallopian tube, the mother will die if an abortion is not performed and there is no hope for the survival of the zygote. Another reason is rape. If a woman is pregnant due to rape, she may feel justified in getting an abortion. Also incest is often cited as a reason for getting an abortion. Another common reason is to avoid giving birth to a defective child. Or a woman may want to get an abortion because it is inconvenient to be pregnant, for example, because it interferes with her job or career.

PHILOSOPHICAL ISSUES

The basic moral issue, of course, is whether or not abortion is morally wrong. But settling this issue seems to require resolving certain philosophical issues. Debate about abortion has often centered on the nature and status of the fetus. Does it have a full moral status, partial moral status, or none at all? One approach to this problem is "line drawing," that is, an attempt is made to find a morally significant point in the development of the fetus that divides the period in which it is not of moral concern from the period in which it does deserve moral concern. Justice Blackmun and Alan Zaitchik both agree that viability is such a dividing line. Viability is the point at which the fetus is capable of surviving outside the womb; this usually occurs somewhere between the twentieth and twenty-eighth week of pregnancy. Opponents of "line drawing" such as John T. Noonan use "slippery slope arguments" to argue that a line cannot be securely drawn at any point in the development of the fetus. Such a line will inevitably "slide" down the slope of development to conception.

Noonan adopts a different approach to the problem of the moral status of the fetus. He tries to establish that it is a human being with a right to life from the moment of conception. The reason it is a human being, he claims, is that it has human genetic coding. But does human genetic coding by itself make something a human being with a right to life? Critics will object that this is not the case; human cells in the stomach, for instance, have human genetic coding, but they are hardly human beings with a right to life.

Mary Ann Warren argues that the fetus may be a human being in the genetic sense, as Noonan says, but it is not a human being in the moral sense. That is to say, the fetus is not a member of the moral community; it is not a person with rights. But what is a person? This is a difficult question. On Warren's account, a person must be capable of consciousness, communication, reasoning, self-motivated activity, and self-concept formation. The fetus is not a person, she argues, because it does not have all these abilities. But what about infants and comatose people? On Warren's view they are not persons, but critics like James Humber feel strongly that these human beings are persons with a right to life.

An alternative approach to questions about persons is to hold, as Jane English does, that the concept of person has "fuzzy borders," that is, there are borderline cases in which we cannot say whether an entity is a person or not, and the fetus constitutes just such a case.

If we cannot conclusively determine the nature and moral status of the fetus, then how can we decide the moral issue about abortion? The tactic of Judith Jarvis Thomson is to shift the focus of debate from the fetus to the rights of the mother. Even if the fetus is a person with a right to life, it still does not follow, she argues, that abortions are never justified. The rights of the mother, specifically her right to control her own body and her right of self-defense, can still justify abortion.

Thomson's arguments raise new issues: What is a right? How do we resolve conflicts of rights? How are rights established? Who has rights? These questions will be discussed in the chapter on animal rights. For the moment, let us consider Thomson's method. She describes various puzzling cases, e.g., the famous violinist who is plugged into another person, and asks what we would say or think about them. That is to say, she seems to appeal to our moral intuitions. But such an appeal does not always produce agreement. James Humber, for example, does not have the same intuitions about these cases that Thomson does. Another problem with appealing to intuitions, as Hare points out in his criticism of Thomson, is that these intuitions may merely reflect our different backgrounds. If so,

they are not an infallible guide to moral conduct.

In trying to decide if abortion is wrong or not, Hare appeals to the Golden Rule (that we should do to others as we wish them to do to us). He finds that this rule does allow abortions in some cases, e.g., where a person wishes he had been aborted, but not in most cases. In using a general moral rule, Hare is following a respectable tradition of formulating a general moral principle or theory and then applying it to a particular problem. We will not attempt a comprehensive survey of these principles and theories, such as egoism, Kant's theory, utilitarianism, the divine command theory, and so on. (For a good survey, read Frankena's *Ethics,* or see his article in Chapter 8.) Instead we will discuss each principle or theory as it comes up in the course of discussion.

Those who oppose all abortions, and not just some of them, often appeal to the principle that all human life is sacred or intrinsically valuable. But this sanctity of life principle is rejected by Jonathan Glover. He does not think that mere human life is itself intrinsically valuable. It must have some feature or quality besides being human that makes it worthwhile, e.g., pleasure or satisfaction. The utilitarian principle that Glover adopts is that it is wrong to reduce the amount of a worthwhile life. No doubt there are those who will reject this rule. One problem is that the notion of a worthwhile life needs to be defined or explained, and Glover fails to do this. This leaves us with no clear way of distinguishing between worthwhile and worthless lives. More will be said about this problem in the next chapter.

THE SUPREME COURT

Excerpts from *Roe* v. *Wade* (1973)

Harry A. Blackmun is an associate justice of the United States Supreme Court. He is a graduate of Harvard Law School, and he was appointed to the Court in 1970.

Byron R. White is also an associate justice of the United States Supreme Court. He was appointed in 1962, and he is a graduate of Yale Law School.

In the case of Roe v. Wade, a pregnant single woman challenged a Texas abortion law making abortion (except to save the mother's life) a crime punishable by a prison sentence of two to five years. The Court invalidated this law.

The reading includes excerpts from the majority opinion written by Justice Blackmun (concurred in by six other justices), and from the dissenting opinion written by Justice White (concurred in by Justice William H. Rehnquist).

Justice Blackmun argues that the abortion decision is included in the right of personal privacy. But this right is not absolute. It must yield at some point to the state's legitimate interest in protecting potential life, and this interest becomes compelling at the point of viability.

Justice White in his dissenting opinion holds that the Court has no constitutional basis for its decision, and that it values the convenience of the mother more than the existence and development of human life.

MAJORITY OPINION

A recent review of the common law precedents argues . . . that even post-quickening abortion was never established as a common law crime. This is of some importance because while most American courts ruled, in holding or dictum, that abortion of an unquickened fetus was not criminal under their received common law, others followed Coke in stating that abortion of a quick fetus was a "misprison," a term they translated to mean "misdemeanor." That their reliance on Coke on this aspect of the law was uncritical and, apparently in all the reported cases, dictum (due probably to the paucity of common law prosecutions for post-quickening abortion), makes it now appear doubtful that abortion was ever firmly established as a common law crime even with respect to the destruction of a quick fetus. . . .

It is thus apparent that at common law, at the time of the adoption of our Constitution, and throughout the major portion of the 19th century, abortion was viewed with less disfavor than under most American statutes currently in effect. Phrasing it another way, a woman enjoyed a substantially broader right to terminate a pregnancy than she does in most States today. At least with respect to the early stage of pregnancy, and very possibly without such a limitation, the opportunity to make this choice was present in this country well into the 19th century. Even later, the law continued for some time to treat less punitively an abortion procured in early pregnancy . . ..

Three reasons have been advanced to explain historically the enactment of criminal abortion laws in the 19th century and to justify their continued existence.

It has been argued occasionally that these laws were the product of a Victorian social concern to discourage illicit sexual conduct. Texas, however, does not advance this justification in the present case, and it appears that no court or commentator has taken the argument seriously. . . .

A second reason is concerned with abortion as a medical procedure. When most criminal abortion laws were first enacted, the procedure was a hazardous one for the woman. This was particularly true prior to the development of antisepsis. Antiseptic techniques, of course, were based on discoveries by Lister, Pasteur, and others first announced in 1867, but were not generally accepted and employed until about the turn of the century. Abortion mortality was high.

Even after 1900, and perhaps until as late as the development of antibiotics in the 1940s, standard modern techniques such as dilation and curettage were not nearly so safe as they are today. Thus it has been argued that a State's real concern in enacting a criminal abortion law was to protect the pregnant woman, that is, to restrain her from submitting to a procedure that placed her life in serious jeopardy.

Modern medical techniques have altered this situation. Appellants and various *amici* refer to medical data indicating that abortion in early pregnancy, that is, prior to the end of first trimester, although not without its risk, is now relatively safe. Mortality rates for women undergoing early abortions, where the procedure is legal, appear to be as low as or lower than the rates for normal childbirth. Consequently, any interest of the State in protecting the woman from an inherently hazardous procedure, except when it would be equally dangerous for her to forgo it, has largely disappeared. Of course, important state interests in the area of health and medical standards do remain. The State has a legitimate interest in seeing to it that abortion, like any other medical procedure, is performed under circumstances that insure maximum safety for the patient. This interest obviously extends at least to the performing physician and his staff, to the facilities involved, to the availability of aftercare, and to adequate provision for any complication or emergency that might arise. The prevalence of high mortality rates at illegal "abortion mills" strengthens, rather than weakens, the State's interest in regulating the conditions under which abortions are performed. Moreover, the risk to the woman increases as her pregnancy continues. Thus the State retains a definite interest in protecting the woman's own health and safety when an abortion is performed at a late stage of pregnancy.

The third reason is the State's interest— some phrase it in terms of duty—in protecting prenatal life. Some of the argument for this justification rests on the theory that a new human life is present from the moment of conception. . . .

Parties challenging state abortion laws have sharply disputed in some courts the contention that a purpose of these laws, when enacted, was to protect prenatal life. Pointing to the absence of legislative history to support the contention, they claim that most state laws were designed solely to protect the woman. Because medical advances have lessened this concern, at least with respect to abortion in early pregnancy, they argue that with respect to such abortions the laws can no longer be justified by any state interest. There is some scholarly support for this view of original purpose. The few state courts called upon to interpret their laws in the late 19th and early 20th centuries did focus on the State's interest in protecting the woman's health rather than in preserving embryo and fetus. . . .

The Constitution does not explicitly mention any right of privacy. In a line of decisions, however, going back perhaps as far as *Union Pacific R. Co.* v. *Botsford*, 141 U.S. 250, 251 (1891), the Court has recognized that a right of personal privacy, or a guarantee of certain areas or zones of privacy, does exist under the Constitution. In varying contexts the Court or individual Justices have indeed found at least the roots of that right in the First Amendment, . . . in the Fourth and Fifth Amendments . . . in the penumbras of the Bill of Rights . . . in the Ninth Amendment . . . or in the concept of liberty guaranteed by the first section of the Fourteenth Amendment. . . . These decisions make it clear that only personal rights that can be deemed "fundamental" or "implicit in the concept of ordered liberty," . . . are included in this guarantee of personal privacy. They also make it clear that the right has some extension to activities relating to marriage, . . . procreation, . . . contraception, . . . family relationships, . . . and child rearing and education. . . .

This right of privacy, whether it be founded in the Fourteenth Amendment's concept of personal liberty and restrictions upon state action, as we feel it is or, as the District Court determined, in the Ninth Amendment's reservation of rights to the people, is broad enough to encompass a woman's decision whether or not to terminate her pregnancy. . . .

. . . Appellants and some *amici* argue that the woman's right is absolute and that she is entitled to terminate her pregnancy at whatever time, in whatever way, and for whatever reason she alone chooses. With this we do not agree. Appellants' arguments that Texas either has no valid interest at all in regulating the abortion decision, or no interest strong enough to support any limitation upon the woman's sole determination, is unpersuasive. The Court's decisions recognizing a right of privacy also acknowledge that some state regulation in areas protected by that right is appropriate. As noted above, a state may properly assert important interests in safe-guarding health, in maintaining medical standards, and in protecting potential life. At some point in pregnancy, these respective interests become sufficiently compelling to sustain regulation of the factors that govern the abortion decision. The privacy right involved, therefore, cannot be said to be absolute. . . .

We therefore conclude that the right of personal privacy includes the abortion decision, but that this right is not unqualified and must be considered against important state interests in regulation.

We note that those federal and state courts that have recently considered abortion law challenges have reached the same conclusion. . . .

Although the results are divided, most of these courts have agreed that the right of privacy, however based, is broad enough to cover the abortion decision; that the right, nonetheless, is not absolute and is subject to some limitations; and that at some point the state interests as to protection of health, medical standards, and prenatal life, become dominant. We agree with this approach.

The appellee and certain *amici* argue that the fetus is a "person" within the language and meaning of the Fourteenth Amendment. In support of this they outline at length and in detail the well-known facts of fetal development. If this suggestion of personhood is established, the appellant's case, of course, collapses, for the fetus' right to life is then guaranteed specifically by the Amendment. The appellant conceded as much on reargument. On the other hand, the appellee conceded on reargument that no case could be cited that holds that a fetus is a person within the meaning of the Fourteenth Amendment.

All this, together with our observation, *supra,* that throughout the major portion of the 19th century prevailing legal abortion practices were far freer than they are today, persuades us that the word "person," as used in the Fourteenth Amendment, does not include the unborn. . . . Indeed, our decision in *United States* v. *Vuitch,* 402 U.S. 62 (1971), inferentially is to the same effect, for we there would not have indulged in statutory interpretation favorable to abortion in specified circumstances if the necessary consequence was the termination of life entitled to Fourteenth Amendment protection.

. . . As we have intimated above, it is reasonable and appropriate for a State to decide that at some point in time another interest, that of health of the mother or that of potential human life, becomes significantly involved. The woman's privacy is no longer sole and any right of privacy she possesses must be measured accordingly.

. . . We need not resolve the difficult question of when life begins. When those trained in the respective disciplines of medicine, philosophy, and theology are unable to arrive at any consensus, the judiciary, at this point in the development of man's knowledge, is not in a position to speculate as to the answer.

It should be sufficient to note briefly the wide divergence of thinking on this most sensitive and difficult question. There has always been strong support for the view that life does not begin until live birth. This was the belief of the Stoics. It appears to be the predominant, though not the unanimous, attitude of the Jewish faith. It may be taken to represent also the position of a large segment of the Protestant community, insofar as that can be ascertained; organized groups that have taken a formal position on the abortion issue have generally regarded abortion as a matter for the conscience of the individual and her family. As we have noted, the common law found greater significance in quickening. Physicians and their scientific colleagues have regarded that event with less interest and have tended to focus either upon conception or upon live birth or upon the interim point at which the fetus becomes "viable," that is, potentially able to live outside the mother's womb, albeit with artificial aid. Viability is usually placed at about seven months (28 weeks) but may occur earlier, even at 24 weeks. . . .

In areas other than criminal abortion the law has been reluctant to endorse any theory that life, as we recognize it, begins before live birth or to accord legal rights to the unborn except in narrowly defined situations and except when the rights are contingent upon live birth. . . . In short, the unborn have never been recognized in the law as persons in the whole sense.

In view of all this, we do not agree that, by adopting one theory of life, Texas may override the rights of the pregnant woman that are at stake. We repeat, however, that the State does have an important and legitimate interest in preserving and protecting the health of the pregnant woman, whether she be a resident of the State or a nonresident who seeks medical consultation and treatment there, and that it has still *another* important and legitimate interest in protecting the potentiality of human life. These interests are separate and distinct. Each grows in substantiality as the woman approaches term and, at a point during pregnancy, each becomes "compelling."

With respect to the State's important and legitimate interest in the health of the moth-

er, the "compelling" point, in the light of present medical knowledge, is at approximately the end of the first trimester. This is so because of the now established medical fact . . . that until the end of the first trimester mortality in abortion is less than mortality in normal childbirth. It follows that, from and after this point, a State may regulate the abortion procedure to the extent that the regulation reasonably relates to the preservation and protection of maternal health. Examples of permissible state regulation in this area are requirements as to the qualifications of the person who is to perform the abortion; as to the licensure of that person; as to the facility in which the procedure is to be performed, that is, whether it must be a hospital or may be a clinic or some other place of less-than-hospital status; as to the licensing of the facility; and the like.

This means, on the other hand, that, for the period of pregnancy prior to this "compelling" point, the attending physician, in consultation with his patient, is free to determine, without regulation by the State, that in his medical judgment the patient's pregnancy should be terminated. If that decision is reached, the judgment may be effectuated by an abortion free of interference by the State.

With respect to the State's important and legitimate interest in potential life, the "compelling" point is at viability. . . . State regulation protective of fetal life after viability thus has both logical and biological justifications. If the State is interested in protecting fetal life after viability, it may go so far as to proscribe abortion during that period except when it is necessary to preserve the life or health of the mother. . . .

To summarize and repeat:

1. A state criminal abortion statute of the current Texas type, that excepts from criminality only a *life-saving* procedure on behalf of the mother, without regard to pregnancy stage and without recognition of the other

interests involved, is violative of the Due Process Clause of the Fourteenth Amendment.

(a) For the stage prior to approximately the end of the first trimester, the abortion decision and its effectuation must be left to the medical judgment of the pregnant woman's attending physician.

(b) For the stage subsequent to approximately the end of the first trimester, the State, in promoting its interest in the health of the mother, may, if it chooses, regulate the abortion procedure in ways that are reasonably related to maternal health.

(c) For the stage subsequent to viability the State, in promoting its interest in the potentiality of human life, may, if it chooses, regulate, and even proscribe, abortion except where it is necessary, in appropriate medical judgment, for the preservation of the life or health of the mother.

2. The State may define the term "physician," as it has been employed in the preceding numbered paragraphs of this Part XI of this opinion, to mean only a physician currently licensed by the State, and may proscribe any abortion by a person who is not a physician as so defined.

. . . The decision leaves the State free to place increasing restrictions on abortion as the period of pregnancy lengthens, so long as those restrictions are tailored to the recognized state interests. The decision vindicates the right of the physician to administer medical treatment according to his professional judgment up to the points where important state interests provide compelling justifications for intervention. Up to those points the abortion decision in all its aspects is inherently, and primarily, a medical decision, and basic responsibility for it must rest with the physician. If an individual practitioner abuses the privilege of exercising proper medical judgment, the usual reme-

dies, judicial and intraprofessional, are available. . . .

DISSENT

At the heart of the controversy in these cases are those recurring pregnancies that pose no danger whatsoever to the life or health of the mother but are nevertheless unwanted for any one or more of a variety of reasons— convenience, family planning, economics, dislike of children, the embarrassment of illegitimacy, etc. The common claim before us is that for any one of such reasons, or for no reason at all, and without asserting or claiming any threat to life or health, any woman is entitled to an abortion at her request if she is able to find a medical advisor willing to undertake the procedure.

The Court for the most part sustains this position: During the period prior to the time the fetus becomes viable, the Constitution of the United States values the convenience, whim or caprice of the putative mother more than the life or potential life of the fetus; the Constitution, therefore, guarantees the right to an abortion as against any state law or policy seeking to protect the fetus from an abortion not prompted by more compelling reasons of the mother.

With all due respect, I dissent. I find nothing in the language or history of the Constitution to support the Court's judgment. . . . As an exercise of raw judicial power, the Court perhaps has authority to do what it does today; but in my view its judgment is an improvident and extravagant exercise of the power of judicial review which the Constitution extends to this Court.

The Court apparently values the convenience of the pregnant mother more than the continued existence and development of the life or potential life which she carries. . . .

It is my view, therefore, that the Texas statute is not constitutionally infirm because it denies abortions to those who seek to serve only their convenience rather than to protect their life or health. . . .

Review Questions

1. Three reasons have been given to explain the enactment of criminal abortion laws. What is the first reason?
2. The second reason?
3. And the third reason?
4. Are these good reasons for criminal abortion laws?
5. Where does the Constitution guarantee a right of privacy according to Justice Blackmun?
6. Is this right absolute or not?
7. Is the fetus a person in the legal sense according to Justice Blackmun?
8. What is viability? When does it occur?
9. When is the "compelling" point in the State's interest in the health of the mother?
10. And the "compelling" point in the State's interest in potential life?
11. Explain Justice Blackmun's conclusions.
12. What are Justice White's objections?

Discussion Questions

1. What is included in the right of privacy? What is excluded?
2. Does a fetus have any legal or moral rights? Defend your view.
3. Is viability a morally or legally significant point in the development of the fetus? Why, or why not?
4. Should a woman be allowed to get an abortion for the sake of convenience? Defend your position.

ALAN ZAITCHIK

Viability and the Morality of Abortion

Copyright © 1981 by Princeton University Press. *Philosophy & Public Affairs*, vol. 10, no. 1 (Winter 1981). Reprinted by permission of Princeton University Press.

Alan Zaitchik is Senior Lecturer in Philosophy at Ben Gurion University, Beersheva, Israel. He has published articles on moral and political philosophy and the philosophy of mind.

Zaitchik defends the view that viability is a morally significant dividing line in fetal development even though the time at which it occurs is relative to the current state of medical technology. He supports the "liberal view" (as he calls it) that the pre-viable fetus is not a person while the viable fetus is a person.

It is common for fetal "viability" to be dismissed out of hand as a morally arbitrary or problem-ridden criterion for fetal "person- hood." In this essay I want to examine and reject one particular reason often advanced in support of this claim, namely that future medical-technological progress is almost certain to someday render a fetus viable at the earliest stages of pregnancy, perhaps even at conception. Roger Wertheimer writes that "the viability of a fetus is its capacity to survive outside the mother, and *that* is totally relative to the state of available medical technology. In principle, eventually the fetus may be deliverable at any time, perhaps even at conception. The problems this poses for liberals are obvious . . .."[1] But what exactly are these "obvious problems?" I shall argue that no obvious problems, perhaps no problems whatsoever, follow from the *mere* fact that someday even a fertilized ovum may be viable.

First we must clearly understand what is meant by "viability" and why some, including the United States Supreme Court,[2] have thought viability to be morally significant. Only then can we evaluate the force of "the objection from future medical technology" (hereafter called "the Objection").

I

When it is said that around the end of the second trimester of pregnancy a fetus is viable, it is not being said that the fetus could be *delivered* at that point (and then sustained in an incubator). The fact is that, given current medical techniques, it is often impossible to induce labor or surgically remove a fetus without doing it permanent damage, even though it would be possible to sustain it in an incubator if it somehow managed to be maturely born. Viability, then, does not mean deliverability.[3]

Another thing that viability does *not* mean is this: were the fetus somehow ejected intact from its mother's body it *would* be saved and sustained through artificial means. This sense of "viability" depends upon such factors as the fetus' geographical location (is it near a hospital with an incubator or is it in the middle of the desert?) and the fetus' socioeconomic background (would anyone be both interested in and financially capable of providing it with medical care?). Clearly

enough those who want to assign moral significance to viability do not want viability to depend upon morally arbitrary factors such as geography or socioeconomic status. No one would want to say that by flying from Cambridge to Calcutta a woman suddenly gained the right to destroy a formerly "viable" but now "pre-viable" fetus, or that the fetus suddenly ceased to be a person or human, or that it suddenly lost a "right to life." So when we say that a viable fetus is one which could be saved through artificial means, given the current "state of available medical technology" (Wertheimer) we do not mean medical technology *actually available* to the particular fetus in question; we mean medical technology *in principle available*, perhaps only somewhere else in the world and only to the wealthy.

So much for what "viability" means; how is this notion used in the controversy over the morality of abortions? Wertheimer and Noonan both assume that it is the "liberal" who uses the distinction between "pre-viable" and "viable," but in fact we can easily imagine a "conservative" application of the distinction. For unlike the "arch-conservative", the "conservative" might allow abortions to save the mother's life—but only before the fetus reaches viability. Or the conservative might allow abortions where the fetus is expected to die shortly after its (eventual) birth, provided that the diagnosis is made and the abortion is performed before the fetus becomes viable. If the Objection holds against the liberal's use of viability it presumably holds against the conservative's application as well. A quite general characterization of the Objection is thus: "How can you (the liberal, the conservative, and so on) hold that an abortion is permissible (in certain circumstances) if the fetus is not yet viable, but is impermissible (in those same circumstances) if the fetus is viable? For viability is relative to the current state of medical technology and will change in the years to come." Nothing in the Objection depends specifically on the question of whether a liberal or conservative use is being made of viability.

Nonetheless, it is convenient to simplify our discussion by pretending that only the liberal is concerned to defend the moral significance of viability from the thrust of the Objection. It is convenient to make this simplification not only because it saves us from having to write "or the conservative" every time we write "liberal," but also because it proves easiest to formulate just *why* the liberal allows abortions in (almost?) all circumstances before viability—namely, that the liberal does not see the pre-viable fetus as a person—and *why* the liberal denies a woman the right to decide on an abortion after viability—namely, that the liberal does see the viable fetus as a person. Furthermore, the claim that the fetus at this or that stage is or is not a person looks to be a very important judgment, and so we expect the Objection to be strongest when directed against the liberal. For the Objection maintains that viability is a morally insignificant cutoff point upon which no important moral distinctions should rest. So if we can rebut the Objection in the liberal's case we shall be confident that the Objection fails vis-à-vis the conservative as well.

Now I think it is clear that the intuitive basis of the liberal's use of the viability notion is simply this. When a fetus has reached the stage of viability, then even though it is *in fact* still inside and part of a woman's body, and even though it is *in fact* many miles and dollars removed from the nearest incubator—that is, although it *would* in all likelihood not enjoy the benefits of current medical technology even if it were prematurely born—nonetheless we can easily *imagine* it already outside its mother's body doing well in an artificial incubator. It is only due to this particular fetus' "bad luck" that it is still trapped inside the body of a woman who wants it destroyed. So it is natural to view the viable fetus as something more than a mere part of its mother's body; it is natural to view it as a person. *For it is*

only due to this fetus' bad luck that it is not already a person.

None of this can be said about the pre-viable fetus, argues the liberal. If the pre-viable fetus were suddenly born it would die, no matter where the fetus happened to be and no matter what kind of devoted and sophisticated medical care we would then give it. It is not due to the pre-viable fetus' "bad luck" that it is not already a person; it has not yet reached the stage at which it could be a person.

Against this the Objection goes as follows: if this particular pre-viable fetus were conceived in the year 2079 rather than 1979 it would already be viable. So it *is* a matter of "bad luck" that by your (the liberal's) standards this pre-viable fetus is not already a person, for it is a matter of "bad luck" that this pre-viable fetus is not capable of surviving without its mother's help in some incubator of the future. It is at any rate a matter of bad luck for this pre-viable fetus that current medical technology is not already as sophisticated as it will someday be. *If geographical and socioeconomic handicaps play no role in determining viability (and thus personhood), why should historical fortuities be admitted as legitimate?*

The foregoing is the essence of the Objection, but there is an ancillary motif which should be mentioned before we continue any further. For one could also urge against the liberal a related challenge. Viability is, by its very nature, a changing criterion. A liberal who rests his "liberal" pronouncements in favor of abortion throughout early pregnancy upon the viability criterion will, in time, find himself saddled with a very (ultimately, *extremely*) conservative stand, forbidding (or at any rate denying a woman's right to) abortions, from the earliest stages of pregnancy on. (Mutatis mutandis, the conservative proponent of the viability criterion will soon find himself defending what is today the arch-conservative stand.) It may be thought that this alone should make the liberal wary of the viability criterion.

I believe that this "ancillary objection" can be rebutted in one of two ways. The first is obvious; the ancillary objection has force only if directed against a liberal more committed to allowing abortions throughout early pregnancy than to the viability criterion itself. For if the liberal is *genuinely* committed to the viability criterion he will respond quite adequately by promising to someday accept the "conservative" consequences of the viability criterion.

The second possibility is vastly more complex. Surely the liberal will not see a fertilized ovum as a person, no matter what viability it may someday enjoy. And so one expects the liberal to avoid the ancillary objection by modifying his use of the viability notion: viability is a necessary condition for personhood but is not, on its own, a sufficient condition. Just what, according to the liberal, the other conditions are which, together with viability, might constitute a set of necessary *and* sufficient conditions is a question of the utmost difficulty. I shall soon have some suggestions to make on the liberal's behalf, but we must first return to the core of the Objection and see why historical contingencies can be held to differ from geographical and socioeconomic fortuities.

II

It has often been noted that participants in the abortion controversy do not really *infer* the personhood or non-personhood of the fetus (at this or that stage of its development) from a general thesis concerning necessary and sufficient conditions for personhood. Rather they react by *seeing* the fetus (at some stage of its development) *as* a person (or non-person).[4] The visual idiom should not mislead us; we are dealing with more than a conceptual classification prompted by visual stimuli. What the liberal is reacting *to* in "seeing" the viable fetus as a person is a complex set of possible interactions between ourselves and the fetus, and what he is reacting *to* in "not seeing" the pre-viable fetus as

a person is the absence of these interactions, or rather their impossibility.

Consider the prematurely born baby. We know what it is to fondle it, to feed it, to change its diapers, to get up in the middle of the night to see why it is crying, to invite relatives and friends to visit it, and so on. These interactions are not plausibly recast as a set of logically necessary or sufficient conditions (a *criterion*) for personhood. But it is clearly not "arbitrary" or a matter of "caprice" that, given these interactions between ourselves and the prematurely born baby, we see it as "one of us," as a member of the human community, as a person.

Now the liberal is reacting to the viable fetus in much the same way. He *imagines* the viable fetus having been a bit luckier than it was in fact, having escaped from its mother's womb and found refuge in a sophisticated incubator before its mother got a doctor to destroy it. The liberal imagines the very same interactions as mentioned above occurring between us and what is still in fact a viable fetus rather than a prematurely born baby; after all, imagines the liberal, we could at this very moment be fondling it, feeding it, changing its diapers, visiting it, and so on, rather than deliberating over its destruction. And so the liberal's response is a response to possible interactions that, if the fetus were but a little more fortunate, could already be occurring between us and it.

The Objection threatens the liberal with a trivialization of the notion of "possible interactions" which we "can imagine" as occurring. For isn't it *possible*, can't one *imagine*, that this currently pre-viable fetus should exist at some later date at which it would be sustainable (capable of being fondled, fed, changed, visited) in an incubator? Isn't it *possible*, can't one *imagine*, that current medical technology should be sophisticated enough to make possible these interactions? If what is "possible" or "imaginable" is insensitive to geography, socioeconomics, and the fact that even the viable fetus is in actuality still trapped in its mother's body, why should the limits of the "possible" or the "imaginable" be determined by historical accident?

The liberal should reply in the following way. Clearly enough one *can* imagine all sorts of things, from owning the Brooklyn Bridge to teaching philosophy to a pet chimpanzee. All sorts of things are logically possible, too—Lichtenstein's someday being a world power, creatures from Pluto teaching us how to perform brain transplants, and so on. The issue, however, is not the limits of imagination or possibility but rather the moral relevance or moral significance of certain possibilities and of certain imaginable states of affairs. And it is a fact about the way we generally make our moral judgments that only certain possibilities and only certain imaginable states of affairs are allowed to prompt our moral responses. It is important to note that only those possibilities and imaginable alternatives which we either occasionally witness or which we can actually manipulate are usually admitted as relevant.

Two examples will suffice to show what I mean. For all we know it may someday be possible to revive a person hours after all brain and heart activity has "ceased" by today's standards of detection. We do not on that account refuse *today* to see a person as dead immediately upon the "cessation" (as far as we can *today* tell) of brain or heart activity or both. For all we know, someday we shall learn to communicate with porpoises and discover that we can interact with them in many of the ways we interact with each other but with no other species; we may be able to enter into promissory or fiduciary relationships with porpoises. As long as these imaginable possibilities remain nothing more than *logically* imaginable or *logically* possible states of affairs, however, we do not on their account see porpoises as anything more than highly intelligent animals, or see corpses (by our standards) as temporarily incapacitated persons. For we have no experience of the sort imagined; there is nothing we can *do* to realize these logical possibilities in any given actual in-

stance. They are too remote from our actual experience to elicit the conceptual response we would have were they "real possibilities."

Now we do see premature births, and we do know what it is to transport oneself in space; expectant parents often rush off to the hospital in early morning cabs. And we know exactly what we would have to do in order to deliver health services to someone too poor to buy them on his own. All these possibilities are real possibilities for us; we witness them often and can even manipulate them.

But we have no idea how to secure for a twentieth-century fetus the fruits of twenty-first century medical technology. (And we certainly cannot imagine *this* fetus of 1979 being conceived in 2079, for in that case it would have to be some *other* fetus.) The logical possibilities here are as irrelevant to our moral responses, to "how we see things as," as are our logically possible discoveries about porpoises or our logically imaginable ability to "revive the dead."

Is this an "arbitrary" fact? Yes and no. It is "arbitrary" in the way that all of our *basic* moral responses are *"arbitrary,"* that is, it is a non-inferred and non-justifiable general feature of our moral perspectives. But it is *not* an arbitrary judgment (in the genuine sense of "arbitrary") to the effect that some particular type of unfortunate should be excluded from the human community, as would be, for example, the decision to count a black slave as a nonperson.

Historical contingencies, we might say, shape the general framework of "really possible" alternatives that prompt our moral responses, but they do not appear *in* that framework as factors to be manipulated by imagination. The kinds of interactions we may someday see as real possibilities vis-à-vis a fertilized ovum are, like "radically different" scientific theories of years to come, locked away in the future. It may be part of the "arbitrary" natural history of mankind that we shall someday experience them and make our moral responses accordingly, but it is equally part of the natural history of mankind that we dismiss them as incomprehensible and irrelevant in the present.

We can now better see why the "ancillary objection" mentioned above, namely that the liberal surely does not want to *now* commit himself to *someday* seeing the fertilized ovum as a person, is also beside the point. Of course the liberal refuses to commit himself. But he doesn't have to. For viability belongs to a family of features that together determine the response, "That is a person." These considerations include handling, feeding, caring for, talking to, and so on, and it is the supercession of this entire family that is contemplated in the ancillary objection. One may as well ask whether Tooley, who sees personhood as resting upon the possession of a concept of self and of concerns for one's future,[5] would count as a person a creature who had lucid, self-conscious episodes for thirty seconds every 10,000 years but who was as impassive as a rock during the intervals. The experience and praxis which give rise to our conceptual and moral organization of the world around us is simply *too* different from the logically imaginable possibility described to prompt any answer to the question asked. The best we can do is reply that if and when our experience is like that, if and when we interact with such creatures, then we shall know what to say, and what to do.

It turns out, then, that viability is not morally arbitrary just because it is a shifting standard. For relative to the real possibilities we currently have for interacting with a fetus in those ways *generally* used to determine that something is a person, viability guarantees that only *happenstance* has intervened to prevent that judgment. And setting aside happenstance is not morally arbitrary in the least.[6]

Footnotes

1. Roger Wertheimer, "Understanding the Abortion Argument," *Philosophy & Public Affairs* 1, no. 1 (Fall 1971), abridged and reprinted in Joel Feinberg, ed., *The Problem of Abortion* (Belmont, CA: Wadsworth Publishing Co., 1973), p. 43. Since all the references below are found in the Feinberg collection, I shall use the pagination in Feinberg throughout. Wertheimer's objection is echoed by others; see, for example, John Noonan, Jr., "An Almost Absolute Value in History," *Problem of Abortion*, p. 11, excerpted from John T. Noonan, Jr., *The Morality of Abortion: Legal and Historical Perspectives* (Cambridge, MA: Harvard University Press, 1970).

2. See the Majority Opinion in *Roe* v. *Wade* (1973) prepared by Justice H.A. Blackmun, *Problem of Abortion*, pp. 180–187. I accept D. Callahan's interpretation of the court's decision as "a definitive declaration of the nonpersonhood of the pre-viable fetus" (*Problem of Abortion*, p. 195). As we shall see, however, one needn't hold the pre-viable fetus to be a nonperson and the viable fetus to be a person just because one views viability to be "morally significant," that is, to make a difference as regards which abortions are morally permissible and which are not. Incidentally, it must be noted that today abortions are not performed after fetal viability; in a few years this will no doubt change, partly because medical techniques will facilitate safe abortions in later stages of pregnancy and partly because technological progress will "push back" viability into earlier stages of pregnancy.

3. If viability did mean deliverability then the "radical feminist" position, which holds that a woman has a right to an abortion even after viability, would be invalid. For in that case the woman would be credited not with a right to "be rid of" the fetus but with a right to have the fetus "gotten rid of," that is, a right to have the fetus destroyed rather than delivered and adopted and cared for by others. And although some might say that the state (or society) could have a compelling interest or right to destroy rather than deliver and care for certain deliverable fetuses, I think almost no one would want to assign the woman an exclusive decisive right to make this decision. It is clear, therefore, that the term "viability" is used in a sense different from that of "deliverability."

Consequently it is misleading of Wertheimer to formulate the Objection as resting upon the eventual *deliverability* of a fertilized ovum (see the quote from Wertheimer at the beginning of this paper). Noonan, too, makes this mistake: "The perfection of artificial incubation may make the fetus viable at any time: it may be removed and artificially sustained" (*Problem of Abortion*, p. 11). This wrongly suggests that viability is "removability *cum* sustainability."

4. Wertheimer is not alone in making this point, pp. 44–46.

5. Michael Tooley, "Abortion and Infanticide," *Philosophy & Public Affairs* 2, no. 1 (Fall 1972), reprinted in abridged form in *Problem of Abortion*.

6. This setting aside of happenstance bears obvious relations to a "possible worlds" analysis of Kant's notion of universalizability. For further discussion see S. Lappin, "Moral Judgments and Identity Across Possible Worlds," *Ratio* 20 (1978), and Y. Freundlich, "Who Cares about Identity Across Possible Worlds in Moral Deliberation," *Ratio* (forthcoming). I thank Professor Freundlich for letting me read the article in manuscript.

Review Questions

1. What is meant by "viability?"

2. What is the general Objection to saying that viability is morally significant?

3. Explain the intuitive basis of the liberal's use of the viability notion.

4. What is the "ancillary objection" to the liberal's use of viability as a criterion of personhood?

5. Zaitchik replies to this objection in two ways. What is the first way?

6. And the second?

7. Why is it important that the liberal sees the pre-viable fetus as not a person, and the viable fetus as a person?

Discussion Questions

1. Is viability a necessary condition for personhood?

2. Is it a sufficient condition?

3. Can you think of any condition that is both necessary and sufficient for personhood? What is it?

4. Is it true that only those possibilities or alternatives "which we either occasionally witness or which we can actually manipulate" are relevant to moral judgments?

5. Is the fact that the liberal *sees* the viable fetus *as* a person a good reason for saying that it *is* a person?

6. Are all our basic moral responses *"arbitrary?"*

JONATHAN GLOVER

Abortion Reconsidered

© 1977 by Jonathan Glover, *Causing Death and Saving Lives* (London: Pelican Books), pp. 137–149. Reprinted with permission.

Jonathan Glover is a Fellow and tutor in philosophy at New College, Oxford, and has written Responsibility (1970).

Glover discusses the sliding scale assumption that infanticide is worse than abortion which in turn is worse than contraception. As far as direct wrongness is concerned, Glover argues, they are equally wrong because they all involve reducing the amount of a worthwhile life. But when side effects are considered, the sliding scale is vindicated. As for abortion itself, Glover maintains that the harmful side effects of abortion do not outweigh the objections to bringing unwanted children into the world. Consequently he favors abortion on demand, that is, he thinks that there should be no legal restrictions on abortion, and that doctors should perform an abortion when it is requested by the mother.

There is a common assumption that, in terms of direct wrong (that is, irrespective of side effects on other people), killing a new-born baby is worse than abortion, which in turn is worse than the use of contraception. This sliding scale is accepted by many people with very different views about how wrong any one of these acts is. It is accepted by many who think contraception wrong, and by many who think contraception entirely legitimate. It is accepted by many opponents and supporters of legalized abortion on demand.

I shall argue that we should reject this sliding scale when considering whether these acts are *directly* wrong, except insofar as different knowledge is avoidable at different stages. But something like this sliding scale will reappear when side effects are taken into account.

So far two general approaches to abortion have been discussed. One of them involves arguing for (or assuming) some boundary marking the point at which one becomes a person. This rests on some prior assumption that killing persons is intrinsically wrong: a principle of the sanctity of human life or of the rights of persons. The other approach, the "priority" version of the Women's Rights argument, failed to establish the woman's right to an abortion while a sanctity of life principle was retained. But suppose we think that sanctity of life principles should be abandoned, and replaced by a set of principles concerning people's autonomy and the quality of their lives?

ABANDONING THE SANCTITY OF LIFE

It has been argued that there is nothing intrinsically good in a person merely being alive and that the idea of a "right to life" should be rejected. The alternative view proposed is that the objections to killing (apart from side effects and any pain involved) are two: it is wrong to reduce the amount of worthwhile life, and it is wrong to override someone's autonomy when he wants to go on living.

How does this alternative view apply to abortion? The reasons given for the direct wrongness of killing put abortion virtually on a level both with killing a newborn child and with deliberate failure to conceive a child. This is quite out of line with the conventional sliding scale of direct wrong.

Consider the objection to killing that it is wrong to reduce the amount of worthwhile life. Unless one is a supporter of the acts and omissions doctrine, it is clear that deliberate failure to conceive someone who would have a worthwhile life is in this respect on a par with killing a fetus who would have a worthwhile life. In either case the result is one less such person than there might have been. And the same goes for killing a newborn baby. The only relevant differences here can be ones of knowledge of how the potential person will turn out. We normally know more about this potential after birth than we do before birth, and we normally know very little about it before conception. When the greater knowledge we have at the later stages supports the view that the person will be normal, this tends to make infanticide worse than abortion, and abortion worse than nonconception. But where what was an apparently normal fetus turns out to be an abnormal baby, infanticide becomes less (directly) wrong than abortion would have been. And, where a woman has German measles early in her pregnancy, or where amniocentesis detects genetic abnormalities in the fetus, abortion becomes less (directly) wrong than deliberate nonconception.

The claim that killing is directly wrong because it overrides someone's autonomy does not apply to nonconception, abortion, or to the killing of a newborn baby. However much one may regard a newborn baby as a person, it would be absurd to suppose that it has any desire not to die, or even the concepts of being alive or dead on which such a desire depends. There are of course great difficulties in saying at what stage such concepts and desires do start to appear, or even what are the criteria by which we decide whether or not they have appeared. But, although the acquisition of a concept may sometimes be a flickering, gradual affair, and although the phase at which the concepts of life and death develop may be disputed, it cannot plausibly be said that very young babies have a desire to go on living rather than to die. If we accept that they do not have this desire, the second main argument for the direct wrongness of killing provides no reason against either infanticide or abortion. So far as this factor goes, they are both on a par with not conceiving a child.

The third and least of the direct objections to killing is the pain involved. Nonconception and, presumably, very early abortions do not involve painful death. Insofar as later abortions and early infanticide do involve any pain, they are to that extent worse. For simplicity, let us assume that painless abortion and infanticide are possible, bearing in mind that in any actual case where pain *is* involved we must take this into account.

So, on the approach that rejects a "right to life," nonconception, abortion, and the killing of a baby are all on the same level of direct wrong in cases where there is the same expectation of a normal child. Since unfertilized eggs, fetuses, and newborn babies are all without even the capacity for any desire for life, they all fall outside the scope of the principle of autonomy. The only argument for the direct wrongness of failure to conceive, or of these killings, is the "impersonal" one concerned with not reducing the amount of worthwhile life. But, since this is an impersonal principle, there is in its terms nothing wrong with eliminating one potential worthwhile life, provided that another is substituted. (Arguments against abortion that appeal only to the *potential* of the fetus cannot discriminate between abortion and the use of contraceptives.)

In other words, fetuses and babies are, in terms of these principles, replaceable. If a woman knows that to conceive now would result in a handicapped child, while to conceive in three months would probably result in a normal child, many of us would support her her decision to wait. There is nothing special about fertilizing *this* egg, but it is important that the outcome should be a person with a worthwhile life. On the principles I have argued for, we ought (until we consider side effects) to take the same view about the fetus and the baby. If the mother will have other children instead, it is not directly wrong to prevent *this* fetus or *this* baby surviving. If this fetus or baby has a poor chance of having a worthwhile life, it will be directly wrong *not* to replace it with a baby with a better chance. But in many cases these direct considerations will be outweighed by the harmful side effects of such an act.

How Wrong is Deliberate Nonconception?

The impersonal principle that we ought to maximize the amount of worthwhile life commits us to the view that, other things being equal, we ought to conceive as many children as possible who have a good chance of having worthwhile lives. But other things are not equal.

There are the familiar problems of overpopulation. It seems likely that an increase in the population often makes the lives of those already living less worthwhile than they would otherwise be. There may be less food to go round, and greater pressure may be placed on the world's resources of energy and raw materials. People may suffer from a sense of overcrowding. All these factors have to be set against the worthwhile lives of the additional members of the population. I do not know how one should decide what the optimum population would be, either for the world or for a particular country. There are difficult questions about the weight to give to extra people with worthwhile lives as against any reduction in the general quality of life that may result from a larger population. There are also complex factual questions about the possibility of producing more food, of finding new sources of energy, and of dealing with shortages of raw materials. But, however hard it is to decide on an ideal population size, it is reasonable to suggest that sometimes a population can be too large, and that this will then count as a reason against conceiving even someone whose life will probably be well worth living.

There are also special problems of unwanted children and their parents. People will not mind the thought that they ought to have a child where this is what they want anyway. But if they do not want a child, what is the situation then?

Sometimes an unplanned and originally unwanted baby becomes a loved and wanted child. Then no special problems exist. But in other cases the parents continue to feel that it would have been better if the child had not been born. These are the hard-core cases of unwanted children. Such situations are especially likely to arise where the family is already large and the mother already overworked and exhausted, or where the marriage is broken, or where there is poverty, overcrowding, or bad health (mental or physical). An unwanted child is likely to place a great extra strain on both parents, and especially on the mother. Any other children in the family are also likely to suffer from this additional member, either through shortage of money or space or through the psychological pressures on their parents.

An unwanted child is also less likely to have a thoroughly worthwhile life than a wanted child. (A great deal of my argument here rests on this factual assertion, which I do not support with any evidence.) It is also likely that the most antisocial adults are often those who have not been loved enough as children.

For all these reasons, affecting the child, the family, and society at large, it is very undesirable that children who are (and will remain) unwanted should be conceived. Other things being equal, there should be as

many people with worthwhile lives as possible. But where the happiness of a potential unwanted child is so problematic and the diminution of the happiness of others so relatively unproblematic, it seems reasonable to suggest that *there should be as few unwanted children as possible.* The only exception to this would be in the extreme case where a population was so dangerously small that desperate measures were necessary to avoid extinction. This is a case which for practical purposes we can at present ignore. We can take it that, when we consider all relevant factors, including side effects, it is morally justifiable deliberately to prevent conception of a child one does not want.

SIDE EFFECTS OF ABORTION

If the side effects of abortion were the same as those of deliberate failure to conceive a child, the question of its morality would be answered already. There should be as few unwanted children as possible, so nonconception and abortion would be equally justifiable. But there are large and relevant differences.

There are the effects of abortion on the mother. An abortion, especially a late one, can cause emotional distress. Physical and chemical changes during pregnancy, making the mother psychologically adjusted to accept a baby, can lead to great grief after a late abortion. There is also the danger to the mother's fertility and even life. The risk to a mother's life with an early abortion is negligible, but a late abortion is a major operation. Even if these risks are not considered sufficient to cause anxiety, the emotional upheaval often involved is in itself a powerful objection to treating abortion as merely an alternative method of birth control.

There are also the effects, particularly of a late abortion, on the surgeons who perform it and the nurses involved. Some surgeons and nurses object to abortion on principle, but even those who do not are often revolted or distressed by the actual performance of it. And some surgeons understandably feel that the saving of human life is a more satisfying daily activity than its destruction. This provides another reason for saying that late abortion at least is not morally equivalent to birth control.

Then there are the more oblique effects of abortion on society at large. There is the possibility, hard to assess, that increasing numbers of abortions may gradually undermine the general reluctance to kill, with disastrous social consequences. There is the danger, though surely a remote one, that maternal affection for children might be damaged by an easy acceptance of abortion. And, finally, abortions use up the time and equipment of doctors and hospitals, scarce resources that could be used to help others.

All these actual or possible side effects of abortion are sufficient to show that it would be wrong to regard abortion as an equally acceptable alternative to contraception. But abortion at an early stage is very different from late abortion. Early abortion involves little danger to the mother and probably much less distress than late abortion. The early operation, using the suction method, need not be particularly upsetting to surgeons and need not be such a burden on medical resources. And, since many fewer people regard the very early embryo as a person, there is less threat to common attitudes towards killing or towards children.

Some of the harmful side effects of abortion will be eliminated when an "abortion pill" is developed. Once such a pill is safe, without its own harmful effects, a woman will be able to perform her own abortion without anyone else even knowing she has been pregnant.

And some of the distress caused to doctors and nurses could even now be reduced by changing moral and social attitudes. If abortion is widely thought of as a minor kind of murder, this adds to the unpleasantness of it. But we could regard doctors and nurses who perform or help with abortions as especially heroic, doing something intrinsically dis-

tasteful which yet prevents much unhappiness. If this attitude became more widespread, there might be some lessening of the reluctance to perform abortions.

THE MORALITY OF FREELY AVAILABLE ABORTION

I have argued that, in terms of direct wrong, abortion is on a level with deliberate failure to conceive a child. And I have argued that, even given a commitment to maximizing the number of worthwhile lives in the world, there should be as few unwanted children as possible. For this reason, it is legitimate to prevent the conception of a child you believe you will not want.

Abortion differs morally from deliberate nonconception only in its side effects. Because it has worse side effects, it would be wrong to adopt it in preference to contraception. And, since the side effects are worse when the abortion is later, it would be wrong for either a mother or a doctor, deliberately and without a strong reason, to postpone an abortion until late.

But these harmful side effects of abortion do not seem to me to outweigh the objections to bringing unwanted children into the world. For this reason, I think it is always right for a qualified person capable of performing an abortion to do so when requested by the mother. Those who are more optimistic about the happiness of unwanted children and of their families may disagree. But, taking this view, I regard a law which forbids even some cases of abortion as being objectionable on moral grounds. This does not mean (the misleading suggestion in the popular phrase "abortion on demand") that doctors with conscientious objections should have to perform abortions.

One argument against these conclusions, which deserves to be taken seriously, is that put by a couple who wrote a letter to the *New Statesman* in 1972:

We have two adopted children, both attractive, intelligent, and likeable (most of the time). If abortion on demand had been easily available the chances are that the natural mothers would have taken advantage of the facilities and we would never have known our children. At a time when adoption societies are closing through lack of babies to place with clamoring prospective adopters, it must be disheartening for childless couples who have the love and the means to provide a good life for the "unwanted" child to read of fetuses being slaughtered and thrown out with the slops from hundreds of operating theaters.

The possibility of providing children for those who want them but cannot have them naturally or by A.I.D. is not something simply to dismiss. The feelings of deprivation must often be very great. But I doubt whether their elimination justifies forcing women to bear children they do not themselves want and then to give them away. This seems likely to cause more misery than it prevents.

It is sometimes said that few of those who support freely available abortion can really think abortion morally acceptable in all possible cases. Do not even the most liberal feel some disapproval of the mother who has a late abortion because her pregnancy will prevent a holiday abroad? The suggestion is that most of us do not regard the fetus as merely replaceable.

But this suggestion need not be accepted. For it is quite possible to be shocked by the mother's act while still considering the fetus replaceable. The side effects of a late abortion have already been mentioned, and they alone justify criticism. But the central ground for disapproval is tied up with the relationship between a mother and her child. We feel that people who are unenthusiastic about having children are less likely to be good mothers, and a woman who cares more about a holiday abroad than about killing her potential child should not have gotten pregnant or should have had an abortion at once. For all these reasons we can criticize the mother's choice without giving up the view that all unwanted fetuses should be aborted.

WHEN IT IS WRONG
NOT TO HAVE AN ABORTION

One reason for rejecting the claim that the question of abortion is merely a matter of the woman's rights over her own body is that on a utilitarian view it is sometimes wrong to refuse to have an abortion. If tests have established that the fetus is abnormal in a way that will drastically impair the quality of its life, it will normally be wrong of the mother to reject abortion.

Most of us would accept that it would be wrong deliberately to conceive a handicapped child rather than a normal one, if the choice were available. On the moral system defended here, this can be extended to abortion. If aborting the abnormal fetus can be followed by having another, normal one, it will be wrong not to do this. The side effects of abortion will not in general be bad enough to outweigh the loss involved in bringing into the world someone whose life is much less worthwhile than that of a normal person who could be conceived instead.

Some qualifications must at once be made here. There will be cases where the side effects of abortion will be exceptionally bad, perhaps where the mother has had previous abortions and is not in a state to take another. And fetuses can be abnormal to various degrees. To be born with a finger missing may not make much difference to the quality of one's life. On the other hand, some abnormalities are so gross as to make life not worth living at all. There will obviously be different views of how serious an abnormality must be in order to justify abortions causing different degrees of distress. I have no general formula to offer. But it is worth saying that on the whole people recover from abortions after a while, but a handicap normally lasts a lifetime.

Another reservation should be mentioned. In arguing that a woman sometimes has a moral duty to have an abortion, I am not arguing that she should be compelled to perform this duty. Many women will want an abortion if they know the fetus is severely abnormal. Those who do not will sometimes be open to moral persuasion. Where they are not, it seems best to leave them alone. The horrors of some system of compelling women to accept abortion, against their will and perhaps against their moral principles, seem to outweigh the likely advantages of such a policy.

The claim that sometimes one ought to have an abortion has been argued so far in terms of the desirability of aborting an abnormal fetus in order to replace it by a normal one. But there are cases where the possibility of replacement may not exist. Perhaps any child of a particular mother will be abnormal to the same degree. Or perhaps she is at the very end of the childbearing age, or she no longer has a husband.

In cases of this sort, unusually strong reasons are necessary for it to be wrong not to abort. Where the fetus is so abnormal that it cannot have a life worth living it still ought to be aborted. But milder handicaps may make a life less worthwhile without destroying its worth altogether. A blind person has a less favorable start in life than a normal person, but it would be absurd to say that his life is likely not to be worth living. And the same goes for many other severe handicaps, especially when the handicapped person has the support of other people.

HANDICAP AND WORTHWHILE LIFE

I have admitted that I can offer no general formula stating what a worthwhile life is or indicating the point at which a life is not worth living. Obviously people disagree a lot here. There is also a widespread and natural reluctance to consider these questions too closely in the context of handicap and disability. We do not want to hurt handicapped people or those close to them by the suggestion that it would have been better if they had not been born. For the same reason, we are even reluctant to say that people with disabilities have on the whole less worthwhile lives than normal people. There is also the belief in treating all people as our equals, which commits us

to a lack of condescension towards the physically or mentally weak.

But our view of conception and abortion in certain cases should be bound up with our view of the extent to which the potential person will have a worthwhile life. If we are sure that his life will not be worth living, we ought not to conceive him, or, failing that, an abortion should be obtained. It is sometimes morally wrong to evade the question of whether someone's life is likely to be worth living.

And when we think of handicaps such that life is still very clearly worth living, there is some self-deception in not admitting that a handicapped person is likely to have a less worthwhile life than a normal person. Of course this is only a matter of probability: no doubt many individual handicapped people have more satisfying lives than many individual normal people. And it is also true that the quality of such a person's life depends a lot on the attitudes and responses of those close to them and of the wider society. But, despite all this, it remains true that severely handicapped persons stand a less good chance than a normal person in the same situation of an equally worthwhile life. The fact that we recognize this is shown by the choices we would make, if we were able, when conceiving; virtually everyone would think it wrong deliberately to conceive a handicapped child rather than a normal one.

And we can say that a severely handicapped person is likely to have a less good life than a normal person, while treating him as our equal. If someone with a handicap is conceived instead of a normal person, things turn out less well than they might have done. It would have been better if the normal person had been conceived. But things of this sort can be said about almost any of us. If my own conception was an alternative to the conception of someone just like me except more intelligent, or more athletic, or more musical, it would have been better if that person had been conceived. Most of us are ourselves pleased to have been conceived and glad that some other person was not conceived instead. But being glad to have been conceived is quite compatible with the recognition that, from an impartial point of view, it would have been even better if some more gifted or happier person had been conceived instead.

It is true that a severely handicapped person, unlike a normal one, is particularly badly off, with a potential below average. But he is not helped by the pretence that this is not so. Nor does the admission that it is so prevent us from giving his interest equal weight with our own, or make the relationship between us one of inequality. And, if it is better that a normal person should be born rather than a handicapped person, our recognition of this will be important for our beliefs about abortion.

A CONSEQUENCE OF SOME "SANCTITY OF LIFE" VIEWS

Any belief that a fetus is not in moral terms replaceable, and hence that abortion is directly wrong in a way that contraception is not, is in danger of generating socially disastrous consequences. The alternative view outlined here positively encourages abortion of all seriously abnormal fetuses. The view that the fetus has a right to life discourages such abortions, with the result that the proportion of people who are genetically defective is higher than it might be. And, unless we believe in the acts and omissions doctrine, the argument against killing an abnormal fetus also enjoins us wherever possible to save a fetus from spontaneous abortion. Presumably medical technology will one day enable us to save many embryos and fetuses at present spontaneously aborted. A high proportion of these are likely to be grossly abnormal. Acceptance of views about the sanctity of the life of the fetus (unless combined with the acts and omissions doctrine) would in such circumstances commit us to a policy of drastically increasing the proportion of the population who are seriously abnormal.

Review Questions

1. What is the sliding scale assumption about the direct wrongness of killing?
2. Why does Glover reject this assumption?
3. What is the sanctity of life principle?
4. Why doesn't Glover accept it?
5. What are the three direct objections to killing that Glover accepts? Which of these applies to abortion?
6. Why shouldn't we conceive as many children as possible?
7. Why isn't abortion an acceptable alternative to contraception?
8. What is Glover's position on abortion?
9. When it is wrong to not have an abortion?

Discussion Questions

1. Glover does not define or explain "worthwhile life." What is a worthwhile life, and how do we tell if a given life is worthwhile or not?
2. Glover says, "I think it is always right for a qualified person capable of performing an abortion to do so when requested by the mother." Do you agree? Why, or why not?
3. Glover says that (for everyone) "from an impartial point of view, it would have been even better if some more gifted or happier person had been conceived instead." Is this true or not? Defend your position.

JUDITH JARVIS THOMSON
A Defense of Abortion
© 1971 by Princeton University Press. *Philosophy & Public Affairs*, vol. 1, no. 1 (Fall 1971).
Reprinted by permission of Princeton University Press.

Judith Jarvis Thomson is Professor of Philosophy at Massachusetts Institute of Technology. She is the author of numerous articles on issues in ethics and the philosophy of mind.

Thomson assumes, just for the sake of argument, that the fetus is a person from the moment of conception. It does not follow, she argues, that the fetus' right to life always outweighs the mother's rights. Using a series of imaginary examples (such as being plugged into a famous violinist), she tries to convince us that the mother's right to control her own body and her right to self-defense are strong enough to justify abortion in cases of rape, in cases where the mother's life is threatened, and in cases in which the woman has taken reasonable precautions not to get pregnant.

Most opposition to abortion relies on the premise that the fetus is a human being, a person, from the moment of conception. The premise is argued for, but, as I think, not well. Take, for example, the most common argument. We are asked to notice that the development of a human being from conception through birth into childhood is continuous; then it is said that to draw a line, to choose a point in this development and say "before this point the thing is not a person, after this point it is a person" is to make an arbitrary choice, a choice for which in the nature of things no good reason can be given. It is concluded that the fetus is, or anyway that we had better say it is, a person from the moment of conception. But this conclusion does not follow. Similar things might be said about the development of an acorn into an oak tree, and it does not follow that acorns are oak trees, or that we had better say they are. Arguments of this form are sometimes called "slippery slope arguments"—the phrase is perhaps self-explanatory—and it is dismaying that opponents of abortion rely on them so heavily and uncritically.

I am inclined to agree, however, that the prospects for "drawing a line" in the development of the fetus look dim. I am inclined to think also that we shall probably have to agree that the fetus has already become a human person well before birth. Indeed, it comes as a surprise when one first learns how early in its life it begins to acquire human characteristics. By the tenth week, for example, it already has a face, arms and legs, fingers and toes; it has internal organs, and brain activity is detectable.[1] On the other hand, I think that the premise is false, that the fetus is not a person from the moment of conception. A newly fertilized ovum, a newly implanted clump of cells, is no more a person than an acorn is an oak tree. But I shall not discuss any of this. For it seems to me to be of great interest to ask what happens if, for the sake of argument, we allow the premise. How, precisely, are we supposed to get from there to the conclusion that abortion is morally impermissible? Opponents of abortion commonly spend most of their time establishing that the fetus is a person, and hardly any time explaining the step from there to the impermissibility of abortion. Perhaps they think the step too simple and obvious to require much comment. Or perhaps instead they are simply being economical in argument. Many of those who defend abortion rely on the premise that the fetus is not a person, but only a bit of tissue that will become a person at birth; and why pay out more arguments than you have to? Whatever the explanation, I suggest that the step they take is neither easy nor obvious, that it calls for closer examination than it is commonly given, and that when we do give it this closer examination we shall feel inclined to reject it.

I propose, then, that we grant that the fetus is a person from the moment of conception. How does the argument go from here? Something like this, I take it. Every person has a right to life. So the fetus has a right to life. No doubt the mother has a right to decide what shall happen in and to her body; everyone would grant that. But surely a person's right to life is stronger and more stringent than the mother's right to decide what happens in and to her body, and so outweighs it. So the fetus may not be killed; an abortion may not be performed.

It sounds plausible. But now let me ask you to imagine this. You wake up in the morning and find yourself back to back in bed with an unconscious violinist. A famous unconscious violinist. He has been found to have a fatal kidney ailment, and the Society of Music Lovers has canvassed all the available medical records and found that you alone have the right blood type to help. They have therefore kidnapped you, and last night the violinist's circulatory system was plugged into yours, so that your kidneys can be used to extract poisons from his blood as well as your own. The director of the hospital now tells you, "Look, we're sorry the Society of Music Lovers did this to you—we would never have permitted it if we had known. But still, they did it, and the violinist now is plugged into you. To unplug you would be to kill him. But never mind, it's only for nine months. By then he will have

recovered from his ailment, and can safely be unplugged from you." Is it morally incumbent on you to accede to this situation? No doubt it would be very nice of you if you did, a great kindness. But do you *have* to accede to it? What if it were not nine months, but nine years? Or longer still? What if the director of the hospital says, "Tough luck, I agree, but you've now got to stay in bed, with the violinist plugged into you, for the rest of your life. Because remember this. All persons have a right to life, and violinists are persons. Granted you have a right to decide what happens in and to your body, but a person's right to life outweighs your right to decide what happens in and to your body. So you cannot ever be unplugged from him." I imagine you would regard this as outrageous, which suggests that something really is wrong with that plausible-sounding argument I mentioned a moment ago.

In this case, of course, you were kidnapped; you didn't volunteer for the operation that plugged the violinist into your kidneys. Can those who oppose abortion on the ground I mentioned make an exception for a pregnancy due to rape? Certainly. They can say that persons have a right to life only if they didn't come into existence because of rape; or they can say that all persons have a right to life, but that some have less of a right to life than others, in particular, that those who came into existence because of rape have less. But these statements have a rather unpleasant sound. Surely the question of whether you have a right to life at all, or how much of it you have, shouldn't turn on the question of whether or not you are the product of a rape. And in fact the people who oppose abortion on the ground I mentioned do not make this distinction, and hence do not make an exception in case of rape.

Nor do they make an exception for a case in which the mother has to spend the nine months of her pregnancy in bed. They would agree that would be a great pity, and hard on the mother; but all the same, all persons have a right to life, the fetus is a person, and so on. I suspect, in fact, that they would not make an exception for a case in which, miraculously enough, the pregnancy went on for nine years, or even the rest of the mother's life.

Some won't even make an exception for a case in which continuation of the pregnancy is likely to shorten the mother's life; they regard abortion as impermissible even to save the mother's life. Such cases are nowadays very rare, and many opponents of abortion do not accept this extreme view. All the same, it is a good place to begin; a number of points of interest come out in respect to it.

1. Let us call the view that abortion is impermissible even to save the mother's life "the extreme view." I want to suggest first that it does not issue from the argument I mentioned earlier without the addition of some fairly powerful premises. Suppose a woman has become pregnant, and now learns that she has a cardiac condition such that she will die if she carries the baby to term. What may be done for her? The fetus, being a person, has a right to life, but as the mother is a person too, so has she a right to life. Presumably they have an equal right to life. How is it supposed to come out that an abortion may not be performed? If mother and child have an equal right to life, shouldn't we perhaps flip a coin? Or should we add to the mother's right to life her right to decide what happens in and to her body, which everybody seems to be ready to grant—the sum of her rights now outweighing the fetus' right to life?

The most familiar argument here is the following. We are told that performing the abortion would be directly killing [2] the child, whereas doing nothing would not be killing the mother, but only letting her die. Moreover, in killing the child, one would be killing an innocent person, for the child has committed no crime, and is not aiming at his mother's death. And then there are a variety of ways in which this might be continued: (1) But as directly killing an innocent person

is always and absolutely impermissible, an abortion may not be performed. Or (2) as directly killing an innocent person is murder, and murder is always and absolutely impermissible, an abortion may not be performed.[3] Or (3) as one's duty to refrain from directly killing an innocent person is more stringent than one's duty to keep a person from dying, an abortion may not be performed. Or (4) if one's only options are directly killing an innocent person or letting a person die, one must prefer letting the person die, and thus an abortion may not be performed.[4]

Some people seem to have thought that these are not further premises which must be added if the conclusion is to be reached, but that they follow from the very fact that an innocent person has a right to life.[5] But this seems to me to be a mistake, and perhaps the simplest way to show this is to bring out that while we must certainly grant that innocent persons have a right to life, the theses in (1) through (4) are all false. Take (2), for example. If directly killing an innocent person is murder, and thus is impermissible, then the mother's directly killing the innocent person inside her is murder, and thus is impermissible. But it cannot seriously be thought to be murder if the mother performs an abortion on herself to save her life. It cannot seriously be said that she *must* refrain, that she *must* sit passively by and wait for her death. Let us look again at the case of you and the violinist. There you are, in bed with the violinist, and the director of the hospital says to you, "It's all most distressing, and I deeply sympathize, but you see this is putting an additional strain on your kidneys, and you'll be dead within the month. But you *have* to stay where you are all the same. Because unplugging you would be directly killing an innocent violinist, and that's murder, and that's impermissible." If anything in the world is true, it is that you do not commit murder, you do not do what is impermissible, if you reach around to your back and unplug yourself from that violinist to save your life.

The main focus of attention in writings on abortion has been on what a third party may or may not do in answer to a request from a woman for an abortion. This is in a way understandable. Things being as they are, there isn't much a woman can safely do to abort herself. So the question asked is what a third party may do, and what the mother may do, if it is mentioned at all, is deduced, almost as an afterthought, from what it is concluded that third parties may do. But it seems to me that to treat the matter in this way is to refuse to grant to the mother that very status of person which is so firmly insisted on for the fetus. For we cannot simply read off what a person may do from what a third party may do. Suppose you find yourself trapped in a tiny house with a growing child. I mean a very tiny house, and a rapidly growing child—you are already up against the wall of the house and in a few minutes you'll be crushed to death. The child on the other hand won't be crushed to death; if nothing is done to stop him from growing he'll be hurt, but in the end he'll simply burst open the house and walk out a free man. Now I could well understand it if a bystander were to say, "There's nothing we can do for you. We cannot choose between your life and his, we cannot be the ones to decide who is to live, we cannot intervene." But it cannot be concluded that you too can do nothing, that you cannot attack it to save your life. However innocent the child may be, you do not have to wait passively while it crushes you to death. Perhaps a pregnant woman is vaguely felt to have the status of house, to which we don't allow the right of self-defense. But if the woman houses the child, it should be remembered that she is a person who houses it.

I should perhaps stop to say explicitly that I am not claiming that people have a right to do anything whatever to save their lives. I think, rather, that there are drastic limits to the right of self-defense. If someone threat-ens you with death unless you torture some-one else to death, I think you have not the right, even to save your life, to do so. But the case under consideration here is very different. In our case there are only two people involved, one whose life is threat-ened, and one who threatens it. Both are innocent: the one who is threatened is not threatened because of any fault, the one who threatens does not threaten because of any fault. For this reason we may feel that we bystanders cannot intervene. But the per-son threatened can.

In sum, a woman surely can defend her life against the threat to it posed by the unborn child, even if doing so involves its death. And this shows not merely that the theses in (1) through (4) are false; it shows also that the extreme view of abortion is false, and so we need not canvass any other possible ways of arriving at it from the argu-ment I mentioned at the outset.

2. The extreme view could of course be weakened to say that while abortion is per-missible to save the mother's life, it may not be performed by a third party, but only by the mother herself. But this cannot be right either. For what we have to keep in mind is that the mother and the unborn child are not like two tenants in a small house which as, by an unfortunate mistake, been rented to both: the mother *owns* the house. The fact that she does adds to the offensiveness of deducing that the mother can do nothing from the supposition that third parties can do nothing. But it does more than this: it casts a bright light on the supposition that third parties can do nothing. Certainly it lets us see that a third party who says "I cannot choose between you" is fooling him-self if he thinks this is impartiality. If Jones has found and fastened on a certain coat, which he needs to keep him from freezing, but which Smith also needs to keep him from freezing, then it is not impartiality that says "I cannot choose between you" when Smith owns the coat. Women have said again and again "This body is *my* body!" and they have reason to feel angry, reason to feel

that it has been like shouting into the wind. Smith, after all, is hardly likely to bless us if we say to him, "Of course it's your coat, anybody would grant that it is. But no one may choose between you and Jones who is to have it . . .."

3. Where the mother's life is not at stake, the argument I mentioned at the outset seems to have a much stronger pull. "Everyone has a right to life, so the unborn person has a right to life." And isn't the child's right to life weightier than anything other than the mother's own right to life, which she might put forward as ground for an abortion?

This argument treats the right to life as if it were unproblematic. It is not, and this seems to me to be precisely the source of the mistake.

For we should now, at long last, ask what it comes to, to have a right to life. In some views having a right to life includes having a right to be given at least the bare minimum one needs for continued life. But suppose that what in fact *is* the bare minimum a man needs for continued life is something he has no right at all to be given? If I am sick unto death, and the only thing that will save my life is the touch of Henry Fonda's cool hand on my fevered brow, then all the same, I have no right to be given the touch of Henry Fonda's cool hand on my fevered brow. It would be frightfully nice of him to fly in from the West Coast to provide it. It would be less nice, though no doubt well meant, if my friends flew out to the West Coast and carried Henry Fonda back with them. But I have no right at all against anybody that he should do this for me. Or again, to return to the story I told earlier, the fact that for continued life that violinist needs the continued use of your kidneys does not establish that he has a right to be given the continued use of your kidneys. He certainly has no right against you that *you* should give him continued use of your kidneys. For nobody has any right to use your kidneys unless you give him such a right; and nobody has the right against you that you shall give him this

right—if you do allow him to go on using your kidneys, this is a kindness on your part, and not something he can claim from you as his due. Nor has he any right against anybody else that *they* should give him continued use of your kidneys. Certainly he had no right against the Society of Music Lovers that they should plug him into you in the first place. And if you now start to unplug yourself, having learned that you will otherwise have to spend nine years in bed with him, there is nobody in the world who must try to prevent you, in order to see to it that he is given something he has a right to be given.

Some people are rather stricter about the right to life. In their view, it does not include the right to be given anything, but amounts to, and only to, the right not to be killed by anybody. But here a related difficulty arises. If everybody is to refrain from killing that violinist, then everybody must refrain from doing a great many different sorts of things. Everybody must refrain from slitting his throat, everybody must refrain from shooting him—and everybody must refrain from unplugging you from him. But does he have a right against everybody that they shall refrain from unplugging you from him? To refrain from doing this is to allow him to continue to use your kidneys. It could be argued that he has a right against us that *we* shall allow him to continue to use your kidneys. That is, while he had no right against us that we should give him the use of your kidneys, it might be argued that he anyway has a right against us that we shall not now intervene and deprive him of the use of your kidneys. I shall come back to third-party interventions later. But certainly the violinist has no right against you that *you* shall allow him to continue to use your kidneys. As I said, if you do allow him to use them, it is a kindness on your part, and not something you owe him.

The difficulty I point to here is not peculiar to the right to life. It reappears in connection with all the other natural rights; and it is something which an adequate account of rights must deal with. For present purposes it is enough just to draw attention to it. But I would stress that I am not arguing that people do not have a right to life—quite to the contrary, it seems to me that the primary control we must place on the acceptability of an account of rights is that it should turn out in that account to be a truth that all persons have a right to life. I am arguing only that having a right to life does not guarantee having either a right to be given the use of or a right to be allowed continued use of another person's body— even if one needs it for life itself. So the right to life will not serve the opponents of abortion in the very simple and clear way in which they seem to have thought it would.

4. There is another way to bring out the difficulty. In the most ordinary sort of case, to deprive someone of what he has a right to is to treat him unjustly. Suppose a boy and his small brother are jointly given a box of chocolates for Christmas. If the older boy takes the box and refuses to give his brother any of the chocolates, he is unjust to him, for the brother has been given a right to half of them. But suppose that, having learned that otherwise it means nine years in bed with that violinist, you unplug yourself from him. You surely are not being unjust to him, for you gave him no right to use your kidneys, and no one else can have given him any such right. But we have to notice that in unplugging yourself, you are killing him; and violinists, like everybody else, have a right to life, and thus in the view we were considering just now, the right not to be killed. So here you do what he supposedly has a right you shall not do, but you do not act unjustly to him in doing it.

The emendation which may be made at this point is this: the right to life consists not in the right not to be killed, but rather in the right not to be killed unjustly. This runs a risk of circularity, but never mind: it would enable us to square the fact that the violinist has a right to life with the fact that you do not act unjustly toward him in un- plugging yourself, thereby killing him. For

if you do not kill him unjustly, you do not violate his right to life, and so it is no wonder you do him no injustice.

But if this emendation is accepted, the gap in the argument against abortion stares us plainly in the face: it is by no means enough to show that the fetus is a person, and to remind us that all persons have a right to life—we need to be shown also that killing the fetus violates its right to life, i.e., that abortion is unjust killing. And is it?

I suppose we may take it as a datum that in a case of pregnancy due to rape the mother has not given the unborn person a right to the use of her body for food and shelter. Indeed, in what pregnancy could it be supposed that the mother has given the unborn person such a right? It is not as if there were unborn persons drifting about the world, to whom a woman who wants a child says "I invite you in."

But it might be argued that there are other ways one can have acquired a right to the use of another person's body than by having been invited to use it by that person. Sup- pose a woman voluntarily indulges in inter- course, knowing of the chance it will issue in pregnancy, and then she does become pregnant; is she not in part responsible for the presence, in fact the very existence, of the unborn person inside her? No doubt she did not invite it in. But doesn't her partial responsibility for its being there itself give it a right to the use of her body?[6] If so, then her aborting it would be more like the boy's taking away the chocolate, and less like your unplugging yourself from the violinist—do- ing so would be depriving it of what it does have a right to, and thus would be doing it an injustice.

And then, too, it might be asked whether or not she can kill it even to save her own life: If she voluntarily called it into exist- ence, how can she now kill it, even in self- defense?

The first thing to be said about this is that it is something new. Opponents of abortion have been so concerned to make out the independence of the fetus, in order to establish that it has a right to life, just as its mother does, that they have tended to overlook the possible support they might gain from making out that the fetus is *dependent* on the mother, in order to establish that she has a special kind of responsibility for it, a responsibility that gives it rights against her which are not possessed by any independent person—such as an ailing violinist who is a stranger to her.

On the other hand, this argument would give the unborn person a right to its mother's body only if her pregnancy resulted from a voluntary act, undertaken in full knowledge of the chance a pregnancy might result from it. It would leave out entirely the unborn person whose existence is due to rape. Pending the availability of some further argument, then, we would be left with the conclusion that unborn persons whose existence is due to rape have no right to the use of their mothers' bodies, and thus that aborting them is not depriving them of anything they have a right to and hence is not unjust killing.

And we should also notice that it is not at all plain that this argument really does go even as far as it purports to. For there are cases and cases, and the details make a difference. If the room is stuffy, and I therefore open a window to air it, and a burglar climbs in, it would be absurd to say, "Ah, now he can stay, she's given him a right to the use of her house—for she is partially responsible for his presence there, having voluntarily done what enabled him to get in, in full knowledge that there are such things as burglars, and that burglars burgle." It would be still more absurd to say this if I had had bars installed outside my windows, precisely to prevent burglars from getting in, and a burglar got in only because of a defect in the bars. It remains equally absurd if we imagine it is not a burglar who climbs in, but an innocent person who blunders or falls in. Again, suppose it were like this: people-seeds drift about in the air like pollen, and if you open your windows, one may drift in and take root in your carpets or upholstery. You don't want children, so you fix up your windows with fine mesh screens, the very best you can buy. As can happen, however, and on very, very rare occasions does happen, one of the screens is defective; and a seed drifts in and takes root. Does the person-plant who now develops have a right to the use of your house? Surely not—despite the fact that you voluntarily opened your windows, your knowingly kept carpets and upholstered furniture, and you knew that screens were sometimes defective. Someone may argue that you are responsible for its rooting, that it does have a right to your house, because after all you *could* have lived out your life with bare floors and furniture, or with sealed windows and doors. But this won't do—for by the same token anyone can avoid a pregnancy due to rape by having a hysterectomy, or anyway by never leaving home without a (reliable!) army.

It seems to me that the argument we are looking at can establish at most that there are *some* cases in which the unborn person has a right to the use of its mother's body, and therefore *some* cases in which abortion is unjust killing. There is room for much discussion and argument as to precisely which, if any. But I think we should sidestep this issue and leave it open, for at any rate the argument certainly does not establish that all abortion is unjust killing.

5. There is room for yet another argument here, however. We surely must all grant that there may be cases in which it would be morally indecent to detach a person from your body at the cost of his life. Suppose you learn that what the violinist needs is not nine years of your life, but only one hour; all you need do to save his life is to spend one hour in that bed with him. Suppose also that letting him use your kidneys for that one hour would not affect your health in the slightest. Admittedly you were kidnapped. Admittedly you did not give anyone permission to plug him into you. Nevertheless it seems to me plain you *ought*

to allow him to use your kidneys for that hour—it would be indecent to refuse.

Again, suppose pregnancy lasted only an hour, and constituted no threat to life or health. And suppose that a woman becomes pregnant as a result of rape. Admittedly she did not voluntarily do anything to bring about the existence of a child. Admittedly she did nothing at all which would give the unborn person a right to the use of her body. All the same it might well be said, as in the newly amended violinist story, that she *ought* to allow it to remain for that hour—that it would be indecent of her to refuse.

Now some people are inclined to use the term "right" in such a way that it follows from the fact that you ought to allow a person to use your body for the hour he needs, that he has a right to use your body for the hour he needs, even though he has not been given that right by any person or act. They may say that it follows also that if you refuse, you act unjustly toward him. This use of the term is perhaps so common that it cannot be called wrong; nevertheless it seems to me to be an unfortunate loosening of what we would do better to keep a tight rein on. Suppose that box of chocolates I mentioned earlier had not been given to both boys jointly, but was given only to the older boy. There he sits, stolidly eating his way through the box, his small brother watching enviously. Here we are likely to say "You ought not to be so mean. You ought to give your brother some of those chocolates." My own view is that it just does not follow from the truth of this that the brother has any right to any of the chocolates. If the boy refuses to give his brother any, he is greedy, stingy, callous—but not unjust. I suppose that the people I have in mind will say it does follow that the brother has a right to some of the chocolates, and thus that the boy does act unjustly if he refuses to give his brother any. But the effect of saying this is to obscure what we should keep distinct, namely the difference between the boy's refusal in this case and

the boy's refusal in the earlier case, in which the box was given to both boys jointly, and in which the small brother thus had what was from any point of view clear title to half.

A further objection to so using the term "right" that from the fact that A ought to do a thing for B, it follows that B has a right against A that A do it for him, is that it is going to make the question of whether or not a man has a right to a thing turn on how easy it is to provide him with it; and this seems not merely unfortunate, but morally unacceptable. Take the case of Henry Fonda again. I said earlier that I had no right to the touch of his cool hand on my fevered brow, even though I needed it to save my life. I said it would be frightfully nice of him to fly in from the West Coast to provide me with it, but that I had no right against him that he should do so. But suppose he isn't on the West Coast. Suppose he has only to walk across the room, place a hand briefly on my brow—and lo, my life is saved. Then surely he ought to do it, it would be indecent to refuse. Is it to be said "Ah, well, it follows that in this case she has a right to the touch of his hand on her brow, and so it would be an injustice in him to refuse"? So that I have a right to it when it is easy to him to provide it, though no right when it's hard? It's rather a shocking idea that anyone's rights should fade away and disappear as it gets harder and harder to accord them to him.

So my own view is that even though you ought to let the violinist use your kidneys for the one hour he needs, we should not conclude that he has a right to do so—we should say that if you refuse, you are, like the boy who owns all the chocolates and will give none away, self-centered and callous, indecent in fact, but not unjust. And similarly, that even supposing a case in which a woman pregnant due to rape ought to allow the unborn person to use her body for the hour he needs, we should not conclude that he has a right to do so; we should conclude that she is self-centered, callous, indecent, but not unjust if she refuses. The complaints are no less grave; they are just different. However, there is no need to insist on this point. If anyone does wish to deduce "he has a right" from "you ought," then all the same he must surely grant that there are cases in which it is not morally required of you that you allow that violinist to use your kidneys, and in which he does not have a right to use them, and in which you do not do him an injustice if you refuse. And so also for mother and unborn child. Except in such cases as the unborn person has a right to demand it—and we were leaving open the possibility that there may be such cases—nobody is morally *required* to make large sacrifices, of health, of all other interests and concerns, of all other duties and commitments, for nine years, or even for nine months, in order to keep another person alive . . ..

6. My argument will be found unsatisfactory on two counts by many of those who want to regard abortion as morally permissible. First, while I do argue that abortion is not impermissible, I do not argue that it is always permissible. There may well be cases in which carrying the child to term requires only Minimally Decent Samaritanism of the mother, and this is a standard we must not fall below. I am inclined to think it a merit of my account precisely that it does *not* give a general yes or a general no. It allows for and supports our sense that, for example, a sick and desperately frightened fourteen-year-old schoolgirl, pregnant due to rape, may *of course* choose abortion, and that any law which rules this out is an insane law. And it also allows for and supports our sense that in other cases resort to abortion is even positively indecent. It would be indecent in the woman to request an abortion, and indecent in a doctor to perform it, if she is in her seventh month, and wants the abortion just to avoid the nuisance of postponing a trip abroad. The very fact that the arguments I have been

drawing attention to treat all cases of abortion, or even all cases of abortion in which the mother's life is not at stake, as morally on a par ought to have made them suspect at the outset.

Secondly, while I am arguing for the permissibility of abortion in some cases, I am not arguing for the right to secure the death of the unborn child. It is easy to confuse these two things in that up to a certain point in the life of the fetus it is not able to survive outside the mother's body; hence removing it from her body guarantees its death. But they are importantly different. I have argued that you are not morally required to spend nine months in bed, sustaining the life of that violinist; but to say this is by no means to say that if, when you unplug yourself, there is a miracle and he survives, you then have a right to turn around and slit his throat. You may detach yourself even if this costs him his life; you have no right to be guaranteed his death, by some other means, if unplugging yourself does not kill him. There are some people who will feel dissatisfied by this feature of my argument. A woman may be utterly devastated by the thought of a child, a bit of herself, put out for adoption and never seen or heard of again. She may therefore want not merely that the child be detached from her, but more, that it die. Some opponents of abortion are inclined to regard this as beneath contempt—thereby showing insensitivity to what is surely a powerful source of despair. All the same, I agree that the desire for the child's death is not one which anybody may gratify, should it turn out to be possible to detach the child alive.

At this place, however, it should be remembered that we have only been pretending throughout that the fetus is a human being from the moment of conception. A very early abortion is surely not the killing of a person, and so is not dealt with by anything I have said here.

Footnotes

1. Daniel Callahan, *Abortion: Law, Choice and Morality* (New York, 1970), p. 373. This book gives a fascinating survey of the available information on abortion. The Jewish tradition is surveyed in David M. Feldman, *Birth Control in Jewish Law* (New York, 1968), Part 5, the Catholic tradition in John T. Noonan, Jr., "An Almost Absolute Value in History," in *The Morality of Abortion*, ed. John T. Noonan, Jr. (Cambridge, Mass., 1970).

2. The term "direct" in the arguments I refer to is a technical one. Roughly, what is meant by "direct killing" is either killing as an end in itself, or killing as a means to some end, for example, the end of saving someone else's life. See note 5, below, for an example of its use.

3. Cf. *Encyclical Letter of Pope Pius XI on Christian Marriage*, St. Paul Editions (Boston, n.d.), p. 32: "however much we may pity the mother whose health and even life is gravely imperiled in the performance of the duty allotted to her by nature, nevertheless what could ever be a sufficient reason for excusing in any way the direct murder of the innocent? This is precisely what we are dealing with here." Noonan (*The Morality of Abortion*, p. 43) reads this as follows: "What cause can ever avail to excuse in any way the direct killing of the innocent? For it is a question of that."

4. The thesis in (4) is in an interesting way weaker than those in (1), (2), and (3): they rule out abortion even in cases in which both mother *and* child will die if the abortion is not performed. By contrast, one who held the view expressed in (4) could consistently say that one needn't prefer letting two persons die to killing one.

5. Cf. the following passage from Pius XII, *Address to the Italian Catholic Society of Midwives:* "The baby in the maternal breast has the right to life immediately from God. Hence there is no man, no human authority, no science, no medical, eugenic, social, economic or moral 'indication' which can establish or grant a valid juridical ground for a direct deliberate disposition of an innocent human life, that is, a disposition which looks to its destruction either as an end or as a means to another end perhaps in itself not illicit. The baby, still not born, is a man in the same degree and for the same reason as the mother" (quoted in Noonan, *The Morality of Abortion*, p. 45).

6. The need for a discussion of this argument was brought home to me by members of the Society for Ethical and Legal Philosophy, to whom this paper was originally presented.

Review Questions

1. What are "slippery slope arguments?"

2. Why does Thomson reject them?

3. According to Thomson, does the fetus become a human person before birth or not? Does it become a person at conception?

4. Explain the example about the famous violinist.

5. What is "the extreme view?"

6. What argument is used to defend this view?

7. How does Thomson attack this argument?

8. What is the point of the example about the tiny house and the growing child?

9. Why do women say, "This body is *my* body?" (Do they say this?)

10. Explain the example about "Henry Fonda's cool hand on my fevered brow."

11. What is the point of the example about people-seeds taking root in the carpet?

12. In what cases should a woman *not* get an abortion?

13. Explain Thomson's conclusions.

Discussion Questions

1. Does a woman who is pregnant due to rape have a right to get an abortion? Defend your view.

2. Does a woman have a right to have an abortion to save her life? Why, or why not?

3. What are the limits, if any, to the right to self-defense?

4. What obligations, if any, do we have towards people who have a right to life? Do we have an obligation, for example, to take care of them and feed them?

5. Does a woman who gets pregnant accidentally have a right to get an abortion? Why, or why not?

6. In general, how should we resolve conflicts between rights?

JAMES M. HUMBER

Abortion: The Avoidable Moral Dilemma

Reprinted by permission from *The Journal of Value Inquiry* IX, no. 4 (Winter 1975): 284–302.

James M. Humber teaches philosophy at Georgia State University.

Humber assumes that the fetus is a human organism with a right to life, and that abortion is immoral because it is a violation of that right. He proceeds to defend this "conservative" position (as he calls it) from attacks by Hardin, Williams, Thomson, and Brandt. He argues that all these defenses of abortion fail, and that they are merely "after-the-fact rationalizations" resulting from sympathy for the mother rather than for the fetus.

The recent Supreme Court decision in *Roe* v. *Wade* could hardly be said to have solved the problem of abortion.[1] Grave religious and moral issues remain, and until these are settled, there will be continued assaults upon the law as promulgated by the Supreme Court. Now I agree with those who hold that the Supreme Court ruling in *Roe* v. *Wade* gives legal sanction to immoral conduct. At the same time, I would urge those presently engaged in trying to change that law to give up this line of attack. There are two reasons for this. First, at this particular point in time, all avenues for change seem blocked. Given its present constitution, the Supreme Court is not going to modify its ruling; and because the majority of the citizens of this country favor abortion in at least some cases,[2] movements for amendment seem unlikely to succeed. Second, even if the law could somehow be changed, it is quite certain that it would be (as it was in the past) virtually ineffectual. As long as people remain convinced that abortion is both moral and beneficial, they will continue to make use of that procedure, regardless of legal sanctions. To attack the law is to attack a symptom, not the disease; and if

anti-abortionists are to have any hope of eradicating abortion, they must find some way of convincing abortion advocates that this procedure is morally wrong. Now despite the many failures of the past, I think that this can be done. There are several reasons for my optimism here, but primary among them is this: Unless I am mistaken, opponents of abortion have been unable to develop convincing arguments, only because they have failed to discern the true nature of their adversaries' position. Indeed, it is my belief that *no* party to the dispute has ever seen the abortion controversy for what it is, and that once this is done, a much more persuasive case can be made for the immorality of abortion. In order to substantiate this belief, then, I propose to argue in the following way.

First, in sections I and II of this essay, the major defenses of abortion will be examined in detail and shown to be unsound. Further, it will be argued that abortion must always be the taking of a human life, for if we are to take seriously our ordinary ways of speaking, human life must be acknowledged to begin at conception. Next, in section III, a case will be made for the view that the arguments of the pro-abortionists are all so poor that they should not be accepted at face value, but rather should be seen as after-the-fact rationalizations for beliefs held to be true on other grounds. In addition, an attempt will be made to uncover these "other grounds." Finally, in section IV it will be argued that the true basis for the abortion advocates' moral position is such that this view must be rejected out of hand. At the same time, the emotive force of the pro-abortion stance will be recognized, and the present impossibility of assuring moral behavior acknowledged. Taking these facts into consideration, then, a new program for anti-abortion action will be outlined.

I

Most of those arguing for and against abortion see the controversy as being one which can be resolved only by determining the proper use of "human." Those opposed to the procedure, for example, usually offer into evidence biological data which, they say, clearly indicate the fetus' humanity. If prenatal beings are known to be human, they then continue, such organisms must be seen as having the right to life. And since abortion is always the violation of that right, the procedure must be considered immoral.[3] In opposition to this "conservative" position, those favoring abortion use various ploys. Some try to show that "human" is ordinarily being used in such a way that it excludes at least some prenatal beings (e.g., zygotes and/or embryos) from its extension. Unfortunately, all such attempts fail, for with each definition offered, some commonly recognized group of human beings is denied human status.[4] Recognizing this fact, other abortion advocates seek to defend their view by appealing to the arbitrary character of definition. Basically, the argument takes two forms. The most radical position is represented by Mr. Garrett Hardin:

Whether the fetus is or is not a human being is a matter of definition, not fact; and we can define

any way we wish. In terms of the human problem involved, it would be unwise to define the fetus as human.[5]

The difficulty with this view, of course, is all too apparent. That is, if definition is *purely* arbitrary, we may classify any group of persons as nonhuman, just so long as we believe the procedure is warranted by the presence of some "human problem." Alcoholics, the senile, those on welfare, *any* group legitimately may be classed as nonhuman and dealt with as we please. Hardin recognizes the problem, but refuses to acknowledge its force:

This is, of course, the well-known argument of "the camel's nose"—which says that if we let the camel put his nose in the tent, we will be unable to keep him from forcing his whole body inside. The argument is false. It is always possible to draw arbitrary lines and enforce them.[6]

Clearly, Hardin wants prenatal beings *alone* to be arbitrarily classed as nonhuman. But upon what basis can this preference be supported? It is obvious that he could not seriously assert that embryonic organisms constitute the only group of beings posing a "human problem." What we are left with, then, is simply Hardin's "bare feeling" that arbitrary definition is proper if and only if the beings to be classified are *in utero*. But what makes this feeling more proper than the feeling, say, that alcoholics should be classed as nonhuman and exterminated? Hardin gives us no answer.

A less radical version of the arbitrary definition defense of abortion has been developed by Glanville Williams. Sensing Hardin's problem, Williams attempts to give rational support for Hardin's "feeling" that it is with prenatal beings alone that arbitrary nonhuman classification is legitimate:

Do you wish to regard the microscopic fertilized ovum as a human being? You can if you want to. . . . But there are most important social arguments for not adopting this language. Moreover, if you look at actual beliefs and behavior, you will find almost unanimous rejection of it.[7]

In effect, the arbitrary classification of fetuses is now held to be proper, not merely because there are social arguments which make such action desirable, but even more importantly, because society's behavior indicates that the majority does not believe such entities are human anyway (e.g., women do not mourn the loss of a spontaneously aborted zygote as they do the death of a child, etc.).

The first thing which must be noted about Williams' attenuated version of the arbitrary definition defense is that it is not entirely clear. Is Williams claiming that, society's attitudes and behavior being what they are, fertilized ova have *already* been classified as nonhuman, and that it would be improper to disagree with majority opinion? Or is his view merely that the classificatory status of such organisms is in doubt, and that the available "social arguments," together with majority consent, provide us with good reasons for grouping prenatal beings as nonhuman? Let us examine each possibility in turn.

If the first interpretation of Williams' meaning is accepted, his position must be rejected out of hand, for what it amounts to is simply the assertion that the majority is always right. But whether or not the proposition, "x is human," is true or not, it is not something to be resolved by an appeal to majority opinion. In the late Middle Ages, for example, the majority's "actual beliefs and behavior" were such that children were not considered fully human.[8] Would Williams want to admit that one who killed a troublesome child in those days was acting in a morally acceptable manner? And what of the Salem witch hunts? Was witch killing "right for them," but not for us? Surely not; indeed, if the fact that the majority of the residents of Salem thought witch killing proper indicates anything, it is only that the majority of the people of that city were ignorant. The conclusion, then, seems clear:

if Williams wants to show that fertilized ova are nonhuman (i.e., if he wants to prove that it is improper today to disagree with the majority concerning the status of prenatal beings), he must provide us with some reasoned argument which demonstrates that fact. But no such argument is offered. Consequently, this interpretation of his position must be rejected.

Although the second construction of Williams' argument is stronger than the first, there seem to be two good reasons for concluding that it is unsound. First, if Williams takes majority doubt concerning classification plus the availability of "social arguments" as together providing a moral justification for dealing with certain groups of beings as nonhuman, various undesirable consequences follow. In both word and deed, for instance, we every day illustrate that the majority view in this country is that there are at least some criminals who are subhuman. Rapists and murderers are often referred to as "animals" and "mad dogs"; and when these men are caught, they are housed like wild animals in a zoo. Then, too, the social arguments for getting rid of such misanthropes are numerous. Would Williams want to use these insights to develop a new argument for capital punishment?[9]

Although it is not likely that he would do so, it could be that Williams would be willing to accept the logical implications of his argument, and admit that capital punishment, euthanasia, the killing of mentally defectives, etc., are all moral. But even if this were done, Williams' defense of abortion must be rejected as it stands, for unless it is modified in some significant way, it can only be seen as fostering morally irresponsible action. To illustrate: let us say that we were deer hunting with some friends. One of our colleagues sees a movement in the bushes and fires. When we ask him why he acted as he did, he replies: (1) although he was not sure what had moved in the bushes, it was much more probable that it was a deer than a man and (2) if it were a deer he did not want it to get away, for his family needed the food, and the deer in this region had overpopulated and were destroying the crops of local farmers. Now even if we grant the truth of (1) and (2), I doubt that anyone would accept these facts as a justification for our trigger-happy friend's behavior. True, we would not call our hunter immoral; but we *would* think him careless, and insist that he not be allowed to carry a loaded gun. And in the same vein, a woman who was not sure that the fertilized ovum within her was human, and thus decided to have an abortion simply because she wanted no more children, or would be subject to economic and/or psychological hardship given the child's birth, should not be held responsible enough to make that life and death decision.

In order to buttress Williams' argument, defenders of abortion could object to our hunter analogy on two grounds: (a) It could be said that it does not cover two very important cases, to wit, that in which the life of the mother and that in which the lives of the mother and her fetus are endangered; or (b) it could be objected that it fails to note that there is a special relationship between a woman and the organism developing within her. Now both these criticisms appear well founded. Even when modified in the ways suggested, however, Williams' argument must be rejected.

First, *if* it were true that we could never be sure that prenatal beings were human, abortion would have to be considered morally acceptable whenever the conditions of (a) were in evidence. But the reason abortion would be permitted in these two special instances is not what Williams would have us believe. That is to say, in neither case would we arbitrarily define individual fetuses as nonhuman in order to legitimatize particular abortions. On the contrary, if only the mother's life were in jeopardy, we would reason that we *have* to act in order to save her, and that since the fetus is not known to be human, we would be justified in "playing the odds," hoping all the while that our actions were not destructive of a

human being. If, on the other hand, the lives of both the mother and her fetus were endangered, the argument for abortion would be stronger—indeed, abortion in this case would be warranted even if the fetus were known to be human, for the only choice here would be between saving one life, or letting two persons die. If one were to accept Williams' version of the argument, however, he would be led to one of two ridiculous results: either fetuses would be nonhuman (in the two cases mentioned) and not nonhuman (in all other cases) or, because there would sometimes be good reasons for classifying fetuses as nonhuman, it could be argued that they should always be so categorized. Now the first alternative is so inconsistent that I should think even proponents of arbitrary definition would be unwilling to accept it. As for the second, it leads to moral absurdities. For example, an advocate of this view would have to claim that since a *starving* hunter is warranted in arbitrarily classifying a motion in the bushes as nonhuman and shooting, *all* movements in bushes may be though of as being due to nonhuman causes, and all hunters may "fire at will."

Before a proper evaluation of (b) can be made, we must first get clear as to the exact nature of the "special relationship" to which it alludes. Surely it is not simply that of mother to child, for if our hunter analogy is amended so that the careless hunter is a woman who, at the moment of shooting, knew that the motion in the bushes must have been caused either by a deer or her child, we would think her *more* careless rather than less so in firing. If there is anything "special" about the relationship, then, it can only be that the embryonic organism exists as a parasite, and that when an abortion is effected, conditions which are both necessary for the continued life of the fetus and in some sense possessed (or "owned") by the mother, are removed.

Having clarified the nature of the relationship referred to in (b), a second question arises: how could abortion advocates use knowledge of this relationship's existence in order to demonstrate that persons seeking abortions are not morally irresponsible? Two alternatives present themselves. First, it could be argued that the parasitic status of the conceptus shows that it is not a "separate human being endowed with human rights." [10] Now although it may well be true that the fetus' total dependence upon the mother is one factor causing some to doubt its humanity, dependency can hardly be taken to prove that the fetus is nonhuman and without the right to life. To hold otherwise, one should have to accept the contention that it would be morally proper to cut the umbilical cord of a newborn baby who had not yet begun to breathe, and leave the child to die of suffocation and/or starvation. But this is clearly ridiculous. If knowledge of the parasitic status of the fetus is of any importance at all, then, it can only be in helping us to understand why some people doubt prenatal organisms' humanity. But our hunter analogy has all along assumed that the status of fetal beings is dubious, and the reasons for this doubt are (at least at this point in the development of our thesis) of no consequence. As a result, the first interpretation of (b) contains nothing which could allow Williams to avoid the charge of fostering moral irresponsibility.

The second version of (b) is better founded than the first, and it has been defended in detail by Professor Judith Jarvis Thomson.[11] Women have the right to abort, she says, because they have the right to control their own bodies. And *even if the fetus is a human and possessed of human rights,*

> . . . *having a right to life does not guarantee having either a right to be given the use of or a right to be allowed continued use of another person's body—even if one needs it for life itself.*[12]

Because Thomson assumes from the first that prenatal beings are human, I am, by conjoining her argument with that of Williams, strengthening it considerably. In addition, this action gives us a new defense of

abortion—one which, I believe, makes the strongest possible case for abortion's morality. If, as Williams holds, we could never be sure that fetuses were human, and if, as Thomson says, women have a right to control their bodies, then *perhaps* an appeal to the right to control one's body would justify abortion. Quite frankly, I am not sure. Luckily, we need not face this issue, for the combined thesis may be invalidated on other grounds. Specifically, Williams' assumption concerning the uncertain classificatory status of embryonic organisms can be shown to be false; and with this demonstration, the two theses will be separated, Thomson's argument then having to stand or fall on its own.

As previously noted, most of the discussion surrounding abortion has centered upon attempts to determine the proper use of "human." Not only has this procedure been particularly unproductive, it has also failed to explain why those who oppose abortion usually wish to hold that human life begins at conception, rather than at some other point in gestation.[13] Both these failures can be overcome, however, if only one is willing to shift his focus of attention. What, after all, is the meaning of "conception?" As employed in ordinary language, the term appears to have three uses: (1) Sometimes it is used to mean "beginning," "start," or "creation" (as when we say, "The design has been faulty since its conception."). (2) Sometimes it is used to mean "act of conceiving," where "conceiving" means "to imagine" or "to form a notion or idea" (e.g., "Conception of his meaning was possible for me only after he gave an example."). (3) And finally, "conception" is often used to mean "notion" or "idea" (e.g., "I now have a conception of what must have happened yesterday."). Now which of these three uses is being employed when we discuss human conception? Surely it is the first; for when I say (x) "My conception occurred approximately nine months before I was born," I do not mean to say (as with use 2) that I imagined or thought of something at that time. Similarly, I do not mean to hold (as use 3 would require) that someone else—presumably my parents—had an idea or notion of me. Well then, if uses (2) and (3) are excluded, what else could (x) mean than that I had my beginning, start, or creation, about nine months before I was born? And note, it is *I* who got his start at the point thus denominated. This is extremely important, for if it is essential for me to be me that I be human (as surely it is), then what I am asserting when I assert (x) is that my creation *as a human* occurred nine months before my birth. And if this is so, the rationale for the "anti-abortion" position becomes clear: one can deny that human beings are created at conception only by denying that they begin to exist when they begin to exist.

Having demonstrated that from conception on embryonic organisms are human, we can only conclude that Williams is in error when he holds that the classificatory status of these beings is uncertain. This being so, the combined Williams-Thomson argument must be rejected, and we are left with Thomson's argument alone. Now, can that reasoning stand by itself once the humanity of organisms *in utero* is admitted? In arguing that it can, Thomson constructs the following example: Assume, she says, that you are kidnapped by The Society of Music Lovers and connected via some medical equipment to a sick, unconscious, virtuoso violinist. The violinist has a rare, potentially fatal disease, which can be cured only if he remains connected to you for nine months. Only you can perform the lifegiving function because you alone have the proper blood type. Given this as the situation, then, Thomson asks:

Is it morally incumbent on you to accede to this situation? No doubt it would be very nice of you if you did. . . . But do you have to accede to it? What if it were not nine months, but nine years? Or longer still? . . . I imagine you would regard this as outrageous . . . .[14]

The conclusion seems clear: if the right to control one's body justifies "unplugging" the violinist, it must also legitimatize abortion—and this holds true regardless of whether the fetus is human or not.

Although Thomson's argument has immediate appeal, it is a relatively easy matter to show that her reasoning rests upon a confusion.[15] Consider the following counterexample: Let us say that I am involved in a shipwreck. After being thrown overboard, I manage to tie myself securely to a large piece of flotsam. As I am bobbing around in the water, a nonswimmer grabs my arm and asks that I help him get onto the piece of floating debris to which I have tied myself. To this I answer, "having a right to life does not guarantee having either a right to be given the use of or a right to be allowed continued use of another person's body." With that, I shake him loose from my arm and watch him go under for the third time.

Surely no one will doubt that in my example, I acted in an immoral manner. But why does the immorality show up so clearly here, and not in Thomson's paradigm? The answer, I think, lies in the degree of hardship being imposed upon the persons whose bodies are being used. In my example, for instance, it would have required very little effort for the one shipwrecked person to have saved the life of the other. In Thomson's analogy, however, we are asked to consider ourselves bedridden for months, even years. And as Aristotle long ago realized, anyone can "break" under pressure and do something which he realizes is wrong. Now in certain cases (i.e., when the pressure is so great that the average person could not reasonably be expected to withstand it), the man who "breaks" and acts immorally is said to have an excuse for his actions. But to excuse an act is not to say that it is morally right. Indeed, just the opposite is true, for unless an act is wrong, it hardly stands in need of an excuse. And if this is granted, two conclusions seem mandated: First, if Thomson's reasoning has some "convincing power," it is only because the reader has followed her in failing to distinguish between excused acts, and acts which are morally right. Second, if Thomson's argument shows anything at all about abortion, it is only that it is a morally wrong act which, like all other morally wrong acts, may sometimes be excused.

II

Professor Thomson's argument is not the only defense of abortion which proceeds upon the assumption that fetal beings are human. Two others have been constructed along similar lines; and if abortion is to be shown to be immoral, the indefensible character of these theses also must be demonstrated. This will be done. Rather than bringing an end to inquiry, however, our successes here will simply serve to introduce a further question. That is, if abortion advocates' arguments are all as poorly constructed as we will have shown them to be, why is it that proponents of abortion find them convincing? In seeking the answer to this question, evidence will be offered in support of the contention that abortion advocates do not believe as they do for any of the reasons stated in their arguments, and that, as a result, all "formal" defenses of abortion must be seen as after-the-fact rationalizations for beliefs held to be true on other grounds. In addition, once these "other grounds" are uncovered, it will be argued that the nature of the pro-abortion position is such that its rejection is mandatory.

To begin, some of those defending abortion argue that there is a distinction to be made between "human" and "human person," and that as a result, abortion of a human conceptus may be justified.[16] That is, even if human life begins at conception, these people say, no *individual* is present until sometime later in gestation. And if this is so,

> . . . *then under some circumstances the welfare of actually existing persons might supersede the welfare of developing human tissue.*[17]

Now there are two reasons why any defense constructed along these lines must fail.

First, if there are formidable difficulties involved in trying to define "human," these problems must simply rearise in attempts to define "human person." And if this is so, it must be impossible to distinguish a human from a human person. Even if we ignore this apparently irresolvable problem, however, what possibly could serve to justify the belief that an individual's rights may "supersede" those of a human? That is, since the right to life is a human right rather than a personal one, fetuses must be seen as possessing that right even if they are not held to be true individuals. Why, then, do these proponents of abortion feel that a human's right to life may be negated whenever it conflicts with some right or rights possessed by an individual? Clearly there can be only one answer, to wit, these abortion advocates must be assuming that it is more valuable, important, or worthy, to be a human person than to be human. But how could this presupposition be shown to be true? In some circumstances, perhaps (as when the mother-to-be is, say, a doctor on the verge of discovering a cure for cancer), a good case could be made that this woman should be allowed to abort rather than having to risk her life in childbirth. But what if the expectant mother is an alcoholic, on welfare, and a general burden to society? Would the abortion advocate allow us to turn the argument around and insist that this woman should not be allowed to abort her "innocent" fetus, even if her own life were in jeopardy? This seems highly unlikely. But if this is so, the question simply rearises: what is there about being a person which, in itself, makes one better or more worthy than a being who is merely human? The abortion advocate gives us no answer. And this, I suspect, is because there is no answer to be given.

The last defense of abortion to be considered is not only the most philosophically sophisticated, it is also the most complex.[18] Reduced to its barest essentials, Professor Brandt's article presents us with two new defenses of abortion. As a first line of attack, Brandt argues

> . . . *that there is not an unrestricted prima facie obligation not to kill [humans], but only a prima facie obligation not to kill in certain types of cases; and . . . [to] tentatively suggest a general formulation of a restricted principle which would have the effect of not entailing that there is a prima facie obligation not to cause an abortion.*[19]

As an example of a restricted principle which would not entail that it is *prima facie* wrong to have an abortion, Brandt offers the following:

> *It is prima facie wrong to kill human beings, except those which are not sentient and have no desires, and except in reasonable defense of self or others against unjust assault.*[20]

Now, if one accepts Brandt's principle and wishes to justify abortion, there are two avenues of attack open to him, depending upon which part of the principle he wishes to emphasize. First, one could claim that abortion may sometimes be justified as a "reasonable defense of self or others against unjust assault." If this were tried, however, it would have to be rejected, for even if a pregnant woman's life were in danger, a nonsentient fetus could hardly be held responsible for its actions. Further, since the fetus is merely growing without conscious purpose, it makes no sense at all to say that it is attempting to do anything, much less take the life of another human being. But if this is so, no self-defense justification of abortion is possible. After all, how could person (x) seriously hold that his or her killing of another (y) was justified in terms of self-defense, and at the same time admit that (y) was neither responsible for his actions, nor unjustly assaulting (x)?[21]

The second way one could use Brandt's principle to argue for abortion would be to claim that the procedure is justified by the fact that prenatal beings are "not sentient and have no desires." Now if this ploy were used, the reply would be obvious: how can one accept this version of the principle and consistently maintain that it would be wrong to kill a person who was unconscious or in a coma? Brandt realizes that his thesis may be objected to in this way, and he replies that although his principle obviously needs amendment "It seems clear . . . that a restricted principle can be formulated along the suggested line. . . ." Now this statement of confidence is heartwarming, but it offers little in the way of practical help for one who wishes to amend the principle so as to allow for abortion without undesirable side effects. How could the necessary changes be made? Unless I am mistaken, it is a relatively easy matter to show that no amendment is possible.

First, one must get clear as to what Brandt is really trying to do. Rather than holding that all humans have a *prima facie* right to life, and then arguing that to be human one must be sentient (as some have done), Brandt seeks to sidestep the discussion of "human" by using sentience (or the lack of it) as the defining characteristic for a special class of humans—to wit, those to whom the right to life does not apply. But this is clearly illegitimate. After all, the right to life is ordinarily spoken of as a *human* right, i.e., it is not a personal right, nor is it a right which one possesses by virtue of his being a member of a special group or class of humans. To hold otherwise not only makes a mockery of ordinary language, it also undercuts morals completely, potentially justifying all sorts of horrors. In short, one cannot, as Brandt wishes to do, make the question concerning whether or not one has the right to life rest upon a determination of the particular type of human being the person in question is. If one is human he has, by definition, *all* human rights (including the right to life). And this remains true regardless of the *kind* of human being he is.

Brandt seems to sense that an objection of the above sort could be brought against his thesis. Thus, in order to demonstrate that there are "kinds of humans, such that it is not wrong to destroy them," he constructs the following example:

Suppose a human being has suffered massive brain damage in an accident. He is unconscious, and it is quite clear he will never regain consciousness—his brain is beyond repair. His body, however, can be kept alive by means known to science, more or less indefinitely. Is there a prima facie obligation to keep this being alive, or to refrain from terminating its existence? I believe there is no such thing.[22]

Now I have no doubts that most of us believe that we have no *prima facie* duty to keep alive the being described by Brandt. But why is this? Is it because, as Brandt suggests, we see the unconscious being as a human of a special type, one to whom the right to life is no longer applicable? Or is it because we think the unconscious being is, for one reason or another, not fully human? I think the weight of evidence is clearly in favor of the latter view. For instance, do we not refer to beings of the sort Brandt has described as "vegetables?" And do we not say that entities of this kind are "as good as dead?" This being so, there should be nothing mysterious about why we believe that it would be proper to let Brandt's brain-damaged being die. Taking that being's nonhuman status for granted, we reason that there is nothing immoral about letting "it" die, for "it" is not human, and hence does not possess the right to life. If added evidence is needed, one need only refer to Brandt's own example. If it is true, as Brandt believes, that his paradigm illustrates that there are kinds of humans to whom we deny the right to life, why does he end the quoted passage by asking: "Is there an obligation to keep *this being* alive, or to refrain from terminating *its* existence?" I submit that the reasons for this statement are clear, and that they confirm the view that we *never* consider a being to be without the right to life, unless we have sincere doubts concerning his or her humanity.

Brandt's second defense of abortion is double-barreled. First, as an explication of

"A is *prima facie* wrong," he offers the following:

A would be prohibited by a rule of the moral code which would be preferred, as a code to be current in their society, by all persons who

A *expected to live a lifetime in that society,*

B *were rational at least in the sense that their preferences were fully guided by all relevant available knowledge, and*

C *were impartial in the sense that . . . their preference was uninfluenced by information which would specially advantage them as compared with any other person or group.*[23]

Next, he asks, would these impartial choosers opt to prohibit abortion? He believes that they would not, and offers two arguments in support of this view. His first reason for holding as he does is that

. . . we are asked to determine what such an impartial being would choose in a moral system . . . if he did not know whether he was merely a fetus of a living human being. But is such ignorance about one's own status even possible? . . . [I]f a being is able to consider values, alternative biographies, and possible choices among moral systems . . . how could he possibly—assuming he knows the laws of science—be in doubt about whether he is a thinking human adult or merely an unborn fetus which might never be born?[24]

Now, if Brandt's ruminations are true, I would argue that we have a full demonstration of the fact that his explication of "A is *prima facie* wrong" is incorrect. The reasoning is simple. If it is true that the choosers of a moral system would be unable to function because they could not be ignorant of their status (if they could not be impartial in the sense required by C), then, for the same reason, they should not be able to form a sound moral policy on infanticide. Brandt admits as much, for he allows that ". . . there is a difficulty in allowing 'all persons' . . . to include young children, for the intellectual limitations of young children may be such that it is *causally impossible* for them to function in the required way . . . as choosers of a moral code."[25] But if this is true, how could a moral code chooser be in doubt about whether he was an adult or merely a newborn baby? For Brandt to be consistent, then, he must hold that his moral choosers could not decide whether or not infanticide is wrong. And if this is the case, I submit that we have good cause to reject his analysis of "A is *prima facie* wrong."

The second "barrel" of Brandt's argument is even more ingenious than the first. Supposing, for the sake of argument, that his moral code choosers could be impartial in the sense required, he holds that they would not opt to prohibit abortion because

. . . *such a chooser could not know that, even if all fetuses survived birth, he would survive, and hence he would not be motivated to choose the abortion-prohibiting moral system.* . . .[26]

That is to say, it is Brandt's contention that one's personal identity extends back only to the moment of his birth, and that awareness of this fact would cause his impartial choosers to favor abortion. In order to support this view, he offers the following example:

Suppose I were seriously ill and were told that, for a sizable fee . . . my brain would be removed to another body which could provide normal life, but the unfortunate result of the operation would be that my memory and learned abilities would be wholly lost, and that the forming of memory brain traces must begin again from scratch, as a newborn baby. . . . The question is whether I would take an interest in the continued existence of myself in that sense. It seems to me that I would not. . . .[27]

Accepting this analogy, Brandt feels that he has good reason to hold that an impartial moral code selector would choose to permit abortion. His reasoning on this point is as follows:

The thought that the fetus to which he may be attached might issue in a conscious infant would interest him no more than just the thought that somebody will be born. On account of the memory-gap, he will feel no more interest in the birth

of this fetus than I feel in the health and welfare of the body into which my brain is transferred.[28]

Now, if any credence at all is to be given our earlier analysis of "conception," this argument must be rejected; as we have seen, everyday discourse shows clearly that it is conception rather than birth that marks the beginning of each human life. We need not rest our case upon our earlier argument, however, for it is an easy matter to prove Brandt wrong on other grounds. What, after all, is he saying? To be sure, he is in the general tradition of Locke, holding that one's identity extends back as far as his recollections. But this is not all; Brandt goes beyond Locke, assuming that one can remember as far back as his birth. But this is just not true. Try as I may, I cannot remember events before I was one or two years old. (I do not doubt that Professor Brandt has a phenomenal memory, but I still feel certain that even he cannot remember his birth or the events immediately following.) Thus, if Brandt is correct in holding that the existence of a "memory-gap" will cause his moral code choosers to favor abortion, he must also hold that it will lead them to condone infanticide. And unless one is willing to accept the view that the killing of newborn babies is not even *prima facie* wrong, Brandt's analysis must be rejected out of hand.

III

There can be little doubt that none of the major defenses of abortion succeeds in its purpose. Still, in reviewing the literature as we have done, one is struck not so much by the arguments' failures, as by the reasons for those failures. That is, it is not just that the various pro-abortion arguments are unsound, they are unsound for simple, almost foolish reasons. As one reads along, he repeatedly finds himself asking how this or that writer could have made the sophomoric errors exhibited in his work. But this is not the worst of it. Sometimes proponents of abortion are aware of their errors; and whenever this happens, reasoned inquiry simply ends with the abortion advocate dogmatically insisting that although the criticism in question may be, in principle, applicable to his argument, in practice it will never constitute a problem. Now how can these facts be explained? One thing is clear. Unless one is willing to claim that abortion advocates are, to a man, both inconsistent and confused, he must hold that members of this group do not believe as they do for the reasons cited in their arguments. But if this is so, a further question arises: what is the true basis (or bases) for the pro-abortion position? It is this question to which I will now address myself. In doing so, the thesis that I shall argue for is briefly this: although abortion advocates find it impossible to identify or empathize with a fetus, they can and do sympathize with a suffering mother-to-be, and hence simply *feel* that abortion is moral. This view is not without support. Consider the following facts.

First, if our identification hypothesis is accepted, a full explanation can be given for each of the abortion advocate's errors. In general, these errors flow from one of two causes: either the proponent of abortion allows his identifications and sympathies to affect his judgment concerning what is and what is not human, or he tacitly assumes that a human's value or worth is properly determined by another's feelings towards him. In order to see how these causes have been operative in determining abortion advocates' errors, we must briefly reconsider the various pro-abortion arguments discussed above.

Those who defend abortion by trying to show that "human" is ordinarily used in such a way that it excludes prenatal beings from its extension, obviously believe that fetal organisms are nonhuman. Yet, all their attempts to specify the proper use of "human" fail. If consciousness is taken as the touchstone for humanity, persons in a coma may be killed. If abortion is warranted because the fertilized ovum is not "viable,"

then one may kill all those persons being kept alive on heart-lung machines. And so it goes. The failures are legion, but proponents of lexical definition remain undaunted. They "know" that fetuses are not human, and so they continue seeking linguistic support for their views, despite constant frustration. Now how can this be explained? Given our analysis of "conception," we know that the elusive definition they seek will never be found. If their position cannot be given factual support, then, the only possible explanation for the abortion advocate's unwavering belief in the nonhuman status of fetal organisms is that this view is founded, not upon reason or fact at all, but rather upon emotively distorted "fact." Simply put, proponents of lexical definition cannot bring themselves to *feel* that prenatal beings are human. No empathy, no identification, no sympathy for such beings is present; hence, this "developing issue" is considered by them to be nonhuman and without the right to life.

Aside from the above, there is another fact which augurs in favor of our view. That is, if our identification hypothesis is accepted, not only are we able to explain why proponents of lexical definition persist in their efforts despite repeated failure, we can also explain why it is that different abortion advocates have favored different definitions of "human." Those who identify with thinking organisms opt for a definition in terms of sentience or rationality. Those who empathize with beings who look human hold out for a definition in terms of some specific form, etc. In each case, however, the abortion advocate is guilty of confusing the *reason* he has for *feeling* that the term "human" may be applied to a certain being, with the *meaning* of the term itself. But these pro-abortionists should not be judged too harshly; others have fallen victim to the same error. Is it at all surprising, for instance, that the ancient Greeks, enamored of reason, found man's essence in his rationality? And why is it that doctors speak of viability, while anthropologists stress the importance of tool making, family organization, and cultural forms? Why is it not the other way around?

As we have seen, the main problem faced by those defenders of abortion who are proponents of arbitrary definition is to show that their "justification" of abortion cannot be extended so as to make legitimate acts which are commonly recognized as immoral. In order to avoid this trap, then, these proabortionists have argued that arbitrary nonhuman classification should be permitted only in the case of prenatal beings. Try as they will, however, no proponent of arbitrary definition has ever been able to give a reasoned defense of this view. But if this is the case, one can only wonder why it is that fetal organisms alone have been selected for "special" treatment. Accepting our identification hypothesis, a ready answer presents itself: proponents of arbitrary definition believe that fetuses alone should be classified as nonhuman because they cannot help but *feel* that these beings really fall outside the class of things we call human. In short, pro-abortionists of this sort are not truly advocates of arbitrary definition at all; rather, they are continually assuming that one's classificatory status is properly determined by another's feelings towards him. And if this is so, there is no significant difference between the so-called arbitrary definition defenses of abortion, and those which attempt to argue from some ordinary use of "human."

It is not difficult to show that Professor Brandt favors abortion for essentially the same reasons as do proponents of lexical and arbitrary definition. For example, one of the reasons he gives for holding that early abortions (those performed in the first three months of gestation) are moral is that

. . . *there is insufficient reason to suppose that the sympathetic interest of rational and imaginative people would be engaged by the fetus in its early stages.*[29]

Now Brandt holds as he does because he feels that our inability to sympathize with young fetal beings demonstrates that they are humans of a type that do not have the right to life. But as we have seen, the question concerning one's humanity cannot be separated from the question concerning his rights. If a being is human he has, by definition, all human rights. Really, then, the position Brandt is defending is this: Fetuses in their early development may be killed because they are not human and do not, for that reason, possess the right to life. Further, the grounds for declaring these beings nonhuman is simply that they do not "engage the sympathies of rational and imaginative people." Brandt has gone to some pains to discourage this interpretation of his work, but there would appear to be no other way to explain his quite extraordinary and erroneous conclusions. Indeed, there are times when Brandt himself "slips," allowing the real reason for his support of abortion to show through the facade of his argument. At one point, for instance, he says that if allowed to develop, the fetus would "become a person." And at another place he states that it would be an "enlargement of the class 'all persons'" to include young fetuses within that group. Given these facts, then, it seems obvious that Brandt favors abortion for exactly the same reasons as do the proponents of lexical and arbitrary definition.

The reasoning of Professor Thomson, as well as the arguments of those who seek to distinguish between "human" and "human person," reflect a second way in which pro-abortionists have allowed their passions to affect their moral judgments. In both these cases, the abortion advocates expressly admit that the fetus is a human possessed of the right to life. Still, they hold, this right may be "negated" when it comes into conflict with some personal right—say, an individual's right to control her body. But we ordinarily do not think in this way (e.g., we do not believe that a human may be killed simply because his existence gives someone else great psychological pain). What, then, can be the process whereby these proponents of abortion arrive at their extreme conclusion? Surely the answer is clear: because they can identify or empathize with a suffering mother-to-be, and not with the unconscious fetus within her, these defenders of abortion feel that the former is more valuable or important than the latter. Thus, whenever the rights of the two beings conflict, the mother's rights are held to "supersede" those of her child. If added evidence is needed for the truth of this hypothesis, it may be found simply by contrasting Thomson's violinist example with my case of the shipwrecked sailor. If this is done, it readily becomes apparent that the only difference between the two examples is that in the latter case, the locus of sympathy has been shifted from the person whose body is being used to the one who is doing the using.[30]

IV

If the considerations argued for in the first three sections of this work are accepted, certain conclusions seem mandated. First, having uncovered the real reasons for the abortion advocates' belief, we must now reject that position as being without proper support. Surely no one will deny that it is essential to morality that our emotions be allowed to have some influence upon our determinations of right and wrong. But admitting this, it is equally true that in seeking to discriminate between right and wrong, one's passions should never be allowed to enter into his determinations of matters of fact. This kind of "method" for resolving ethical disputes has been used in the past, and invariably the conclusions reached were anything but moral. When African blacks were enslaved and American Indians exterminated, for example, the justifications given for these actions were twofold: either these beings were said to be not fully human (savages), or they were held to be of little worth (uncivilized beings whose rights were able to be "superseded" whenever they came into conflict with our "more enlightened and worthy" desires). If Americans found this

kind of reasoning appealing, however, it was only because they could not identify with the lifestyles of the beings in question. And when this lack of identification was coupled with the desire to exploit, the morality of slavery and Indian killing was assured. Today, the same kind of thing appears to be happening in the minds of abortion advocates. Of course, there is a difference in that those who defend abortion desire to help rather than to exploit some group. Still, the fact that these people operate from praiseworthy motives does nothing to guarantee the morality of their conclusions. And insofar as proponents of abortion allow their inability to sympathize with a prenatal human being support their desire to kill it, they are just as mistaken in their reasoning as were those who earlier argued for slavery or Indian killing.

Second, because our analysis focuses upon "conception" rather than "human," the objectivity of our determination of the facts is guaranteed. As we have seen, "human" is an "emotionally charged" term, and it may well be that its proper use will forever remain a subject of dispute. "Conception," however, does not suffer from this difficulty, and in discussing its various uses we need not worry that our subjective biases have influenced our view of the facts. Indeed, because it is true that we cannot identify with fertilized ova, the objectivity of our analysis is put beyond doubt. That is, with the possible exception of those who blindly defend catholic dogma (and as against these a modified version of my argument could easily be directed) no one can really *feel* that zygotes are human. Then, too, we all empathize with suffering mothers-to-be. If we were not bound by reason to do otherwise, then our desires would incline us to defend abortion—at least abortion performed in the first trimester of pregnancy. What better guarantee of objectivity could we have?

Third, given that we have a full and complete demonstration of the fact that human life begins at conception, there is no escaping the conclusion that abortion can be justified only when the circumstances are such that we would think it proper to take the life of a human being. Now we have allowed that there is one such case, namely, abortion must be permitted whenever the continuation of pregnancy would put in danger the lives of both the mother and her fetus. Could a case be made for the morality of abortion in any other instance? Certainly there is nothing in the abortion advocates' arguments which would incline us to believe so. Further, Professor Baruch Brody has argued convincingly that it would be morally wrong to perform an abortion, even if it were necessary to save the life of the mother.[31] And if this is true, how could any of the weaker defenses succeed? But apart from these specific claims, there are more general considerations which lead us to the same conclusion. That is, whether we like or not, the fetus is a human being of a special kind. Because he is human, he has all human rights; yet, because he can intend no action, it makes no sense to say that he has any of the duties or obligations possessed by the rest of us. He is much like a newborn baby, unconscious since birth, and kept in isolation from everyone save his mother. How could one hope to argue for the morality of killing such a being? True, there are some instances in which a mother who killed such a baby could hope to be excused (e.g., the infant had a disease which, though it caused the baby no harm, would kill the mother if she contracted it). But even here, no argument could be made for the view that the mother who killed such a child would have acted in a morally right way.

Finally, if it is true that there is no rational or factual basis upon which one can construct a sound defense of abortion, it is also true that the strength of our emotions cannot be denied. For example, what man can honestly say that he would attempt to stop his wife from having an abortion if it were clear that she would die or become psychotic given the continuation of her pregnancy? In cases such as these we are caught in a real moral dilemma: reason tells us one thing, the passions another. And even if one cannot agree with Hume that the passions *should* rule reason in deciding moral issues, he must acknowledge that (in the case of abortion at least), the emotions *do* rule. Now apparently some opponents of abortion have realized this. Attempting to combat the emotions' force, then, they ask their readers to empathize with the fetus—to "feel" its desire for life.[32] But all such injunctions fall on deaf ears, for it is simply impossible for a normal person to identify with a zygote or embryo. If this is granted, however, what possible hope is there for fostering moral conduct? Unless I am mistaken, the anti-abortionist has only one choice: he must find some way of convincing women that abortion is both undesirable and unnecessary. Can this be done? In order to support the belief that it can, I now wish to offer for consideration a general set of guidelines which, though admittedly incomplete and sketchy, do offer some hope for escape from the dilemma of abortion.

First, before any substantive changes can be effected, abortion advocates must be made to see that their moral judgment rests upon an emotively distorted view of the facts, for unless this is done there will be no impetus at all for change. After all, why should proponents of abortion not rest content with the status quo? They feel that their position is morally right, and now the law allows that it is legally right. If anything at all is to get done, then, these people (who are the majority) must be made to see that abortion presents us with a moral dilemma of sorts—one in which we cannot help but *feel* that the immoral course of action is right, and the moral course of action wrong.

Once people are educated to the point that their desire to be rational will (hopefully) cause them to want to avoid the abortion dilemma, action on several fronts is possible. If the statistics are to be believed, most women who seek abortions do so because they find themselves with unwanted pregnancies.[33] And women who have unwanted pregnancies turn to abortion for one or more of the following three reasons: (1) The woman is unmarried, the child illegitimate, and the mother wants to avoid showing her "sin" to society. (2) The woman (especially the married woman) would agree to have the child and give it up for adoption, except that there is a social stigma attached to such action. (3) The mother simply does not want to put up with pregnancy and childbirth. Given these as the primary causes for abortion, then, anti-abortion action along the following lines would seem to be indicated:

1. If it is true that we today consider illegitimacy a "sin," it need not be so. In certain Scandinavian countries, for example, illegitimacy is not frowned upon as it is here. And if our attitudes could be so modified, one of the prime motivations women now have for seeking abortions would be undercut. Indeed, if people could only be made aware of the fact that abortion is the killing of a human being, more should be able to be accomplished than a simple change in attitude concerning illegitimacy. The unwed mother who elected to carry her child to term could become a person of respect—one to whom praise was due. After all, for the sake of another human being, this woman is putting her life on the line. Why not praise her? Surely changes of this sort are not impossible. And if the Catholic Church is sincere in its opposition to abortion, it should do its utmost to see that they *do* come about.

2. If our attitudes concerning illegitimacy can be changed, so too can our feelings towards a mother who "gives away" her child. What better expression of motherly love could there be than to give up one's baby for adoption when it was apparent that such a course of action was in the best interest of the child? Is abortion a more moral course? Is it better to keep the child out of some sense of duty, and thereby condemn it to a life without love or proper care? Surely we cannot believe so. In fact, a mother who follows either of the latter two courses must be operating out of self-interest

and not love. And if people could only be made to realize this, another of the major reasons women have for seeking abortions would be nullified.

3. Some women, it is true, simply do not want to suffer through pregnancy and childbirth. And where this is the case, our hope lies, not in changing social attitudes, but in doing our best to advance scientific research. At present, the process is being developed whereby a fertilized egg can be transplanted from one woman's womb into another's. If this procedure could be perfected so that it was both successful and relatively inexpensive, women—all women—would have a viable alternative to abortion.[34] Instead of abortion clinics, we could have transplant clinics. Women who wanted children could register, just as they now register for adoption; and when the need arose, they could be called up for service. Now what could be the objections to such a procedure? Certainly the formation of transplant clinics would raise various new moral and legal problems. But could the new moral problems be as grave as those we now face in abortion? And why could we not simply look upon transplantation as early adoption, thus minimizing the need for new legislation? Of course, there are also practical matters to be considered. Before uterine transplants could be used, for example, it would have to be shown that the procedure was safe, not only for the transplanted egg, but also for both the women involved. But if we are willing to spend the money for research, such safety could be secured. There remains, then, the matter of cost. How expensive would such an operation be? Frankly, I do not know. But it need not be as inexpensive as an abortion, for the cost could be split between the donor and donee. Also, why should it not be possible to obtain a small federal subsidy for such procedures? All in all, there appears to be nothing which would make it impossible in principle for uterine transplants to serve as an alternative to abortion.

Although the above three changes seem to hold out the most hope of success for the anti-abortionist, action along other lines would also be efficacious. First, a concerted effort should be made to overcome the Catholic Church's ridiculous opposition to birth control.[35] Second, those who are sincere in their opposition to abortion should also do their utmost to make sex education mandatory in the schools. And perhaps a "refresher" course could be required for all those wishing to take out a marriage license. Further, pressure should be brought to bear for the development of more effective male contraceptives. Work is currently being done in this area—a pill is being developed—but the more procedures the better.

I harbor no illusions concerning the difficulties involved in getting something like the above program put into effect. Yet it does provide hope. Indeed, if only the process of uterine transplants could be perfected, the possibility of eradicating abortion would be much increased. If women knew that there was a viable alternative to abortion, they would find it much easier to follow the dictates of reason. And if this state of affairs ever came into being, the time *would* be right for opponents of abortion to press for legal change. Of course, whether this point will ever be reached is doubtful. But even if there are good grounds for pessimism, we must try to bring about the needed changes. After all, there are human lives at stake.

Footnotes

1. *Roe v. Wade*, 410 U.S. 113 (1973).

2. Herman Schwartz, "The Parent or the Fetus," *Humanist*, Vol. 27 (1967), p. 126.

3. The two chief proponents of this view are: Paul Ramsey, "The Morality of Abortion," in *Life or Death: Ethics and Options* (Seattle: 1968), and John T. Noonan Jr., "Abortion and the Catholic Church: A Summary History," *Natural Law Forum*, Vol. 12 (1967). For a complete discussion of the failures of these analyses, see D. Callahan, *Abortion: Law, Choice and Morality* (London: 1970), pp. 378–394.

4. For example, Herman Schwartz, op. cit., p. 126, contends that abortion is moral because the fetus is not ". . . a rational creature, with unique emotions and feelings, intellect and a personality, a being with whom we can identify." But this definition excludes (at least) newborn babies, and thus allows for infanticide.

5. Garrett Hardin, "Abortion—or Compulsory Pregnancy?" *Journal of Marriage and the Family*, Vol. 30 (May, 1968), pp. 250–251.

6. Garrett Hardin, "Semantic Aspects of Abortion," *ETC.*, (September, 1967), p. 264.

7. Glanville Williams, "The Legalization of Medical Abortion," *The Eugenics Review*, 56 (April, 1964), p. 21.

8. See Phillippe Aries, *Centuries of Childhood*, trans. Robert Baldick (New York, 1965), pp. 38–39.

9. My choice of criminals here was purely arbitrary. The argument would apply with equal force to the senile, children born with mental defects, etc.

10. Although their statements are far from clear, when members of women's liberation argue for abortion on demand, they seem to be reasoning along these lines.

11. Judith Jarvis Thomson, "A Defense of Abortion," *Philosophy and Public Affairs*, Vol. 1 (1971).

12. Ibid., p. 56.

13. This preference is evident even among those who admit that microgenetics cannot prove that human life begins at conception. See Paul Ramsey, "Abortion: A Review Article," *The Thomist*, Vol. XXXVII (1973).

14. Thomson, op. cit., p. 49.

15. Baruch Brody has challenged Professor Thomson's position by pointing out that she fails to distinguish between our duty to save someone's life, and our duty not to take it (B. Brody, "Thomson on Abortion," *Philosophy and Public Affairs*, Vol. 1 (1972), pp. 339–340. There is some doubt, however, that the distinction Brody insists upon is ever properly made in morals (see R.B. Brandt, "The Morality of Abortion," *The Monist*, Vol. 56 (1972), pp. 509–510. This being the case, I have avoided these issues entirely, attacking Thomson via an alternate route.

16. Thomas L. Hayes, "A Biological View," *Commonweal*, Vol. 85 (March, 1967); Rudolph Ehrensing, "When Is It Really Abortion?" *The National Catholic Reporter* (May, 1966).

17. Ehrensing, ibid., p. 4.

18. Brandt, op. cit.

19. Ibid., p. 506.

20. Ibid., p. 511.

21. For a more detailed version of this argument, see B. Brody, "Abortion and the Sanctity of Human Life," *American Philosophical Quarterly*, Vol. X (1973).

22. Brandt, op. cit., p. 509.

23. Ibid., p. 513.

24. Ibid., p. 523.

25. Ibid., p. 515.

26. Ibid., p. 523.

27. Ibid., p. 524.

28. Ibid., p. 525.

29. Ibid., p. 528.

30. Although there are numerous other facts supporting my identification hypothesis, most cannot be discussed in an essay of this length. One is important enough, however, that it at least bears mention. That is, accepting our thesis, one can explain why it is that certain "extremist" members of women's liberation are virtually alone in defending abortion on demand. Most abortion advocates do not favor this view because they find themselves able to identify with developed fetal organisms—e.g., seven-month-old fetuses hear sounds, move, hiccup, suck their thumbs, etc., and are thus thought to be human (they are often referred to as "unborn children," for instance). On the other hand, zealous devotion to their "cause" so biases feminists that they find it impossible to empathize even with the most developed fetal beings.

31. B. Brody, "Abortion and the Sanctity of Human Life," op. cit.

32. Germain Grisez, *Abortion: The Myths, the Realities, and the Arguments* (New York, 1970), pp. 277–287.

33. Callahan, op. cit., pp. 292–294. Alice S. Rossi, "Abortion Laws and Their Victims," *Trans-Action* (1966).

34. There is one possible exception to this statement. If a woman wanted an abortion because she knew that her child would be born deformed, it is almost certain that she would find no one willing to be a transplant recipient. This being so, the only way we can rid ourselves of abortions sought on these grounds is to find the causes of birth defects and eradicate them.

35. Obviously, I cannot use this forum to argue for the view that the Catholic position on birth control is "ridiculous." I see no escape from this conclusion, however, and except for those devices which operate as abortive mechanisms (e.g., intra-uterine devices), all contraceptive procedures ought to be condoned.

Review Questions

1. What is Hardin's position on the humanity of the fetus?
2. Why does Humber reject this position?
3. What is Williams' view?
4. Why does Humber reject it?
5. Does Humber agree that an abortion is justified to save the mother's life?
6. Humber claims that Thomson's argument about the famous violinist "rests upon a confusion." What is this alleged confusion?
7. Why is it impossible to distinguish between a human and a human person?
8. What is Brandt's principle?
9. How does Brandt use this principle to defend abortion?
10. And how does Humber reply to Brandt?
11. According to Humber, what is the source of pro-abortion views?
12. Explain Humber's conclusions.

Discussion Questions

1. Is it true that human organisms "must be seen as having a right to life?" Do human cells in the stomach have such a right?
2. Humber attacks only one of Thomson's arguments, the one about the famous violinist. How would he reply to her other examples and arguments?
3. Does genetic coding distinguish human organisms from human persons? Defend your view.
4. "What is there about being a person which, in itself, makes one better or more worthy than a being who is merely human?" Humber says that no answer can be given. Is this true?
5. Do the rights of the mother ever override the right to life of the fetus (assuming it has such a right)? Defend your view.

Problem Cases

1. Jane is a forty-four-year-old divorced mother with one child. The child has Down's syndrome and is severely retarded. Nevertheless, Jane has chosen the difficult task of caring for the child. But she wants very much to have a normal child. She gets pregnant (by artificial insemination), but she is concerned about the possibility of another defective child. Her doctor has warned her that the risk of having a Down's syndrome child increases sharply with the age of the mother, and he has advised her to undergo amniocentesis, a test of the embryonic fluid that can detect Down's syndrome. She undergoes the test and it is positive; the fetus has Down's syndrome. After careful consideration, she decides to get an abortion. She also firmly intends to get pregnant again so that she can replace the defective fetus with a normal one. Is abortion morally right or wrong in this case? Defend your answer.

2. Sara is a twenty-five-year-old lawyer who is unmarried and has no children. She has planned a vacation in Europe for some time, and she is all ready to go when she discovers that she is pregnant. She has been sexually active and she is not sure about the identity of the father. But she does not want to be pregnant or have a child, and she decides to have an abortion and go ahead with her trip. Is this decision morally correct or not? Explain your answer.

Suggested Readings

English, Jane. "Abortion and the Concept of a Person." *Canadian Journal of Philosophy* 5 (October 1975): 233–243.

Hare, R.M. "Abortion and the Golden Rule." *Philosophy and Public Affairs* 4 (Spring 1975): 201–222.

Noonan, John T., Jr. "An Almost Absolute Value in History." In John T. Noonan, Jr., *The Morality of Abortion: Legal and Historical Perspectives*. Cambridge, MA: Harvard University Press, 1970.

Tooley, Michael. "Abortion and Infanticide." *Philosophy and Public Affairs* 2 (Fall 1972): 37–65. Tooley argues that neither a fetus nor an infant has a right to life, and that both abortion and infanticide are normally acceptable.

Warren, Mary Ann. "On the Moral and Legal Status of Abortion," *The Monist* 57 (1973): 43–61.

CHAPTER 2

Euthanasia

Basic Concepts

The term euthanasia is usually used to mean "mercy killing" where this is the killing of those who are incurably ill or in great pain in order to spare them further suffering.

It is customary to distinguish between different types of euthanasia. *Voluntary euthanasia* is mercy killing with the consent of the person killed. For example, a patient suffering from very painful and terminal cancer may ask to be killed with a fatal injection of morphine. *Nonvoluntary euthanasia,* by contrast, is mercy killing without the consent of the person killed (although the consent of others such as parents or relatives can be obtained). Authors who discuss nonvoluntary euthanasia usually have in mind the killing of those who are unable to give consent, for example a comatose person such as Karen Ann Quinlan or a defective infant. There is another possibility, however, and that is the mercy killing of a person who is able to give consent but is not asked. If the person killed does not wish to die, it might be more accurate to call this involuntary euthanasia.

A further distinction is often made between active and passive euthanasia, or between killing and letting die. Just how this distinction should be drawn is a matter of some debate. Roughly speaking, we can say that *active euthanasia* is mercy killing by an action, e.g., by giving a fatal injection, while *passive euthanasia* is mercy killing by failing to act, e.g., failing to treat the infection of a defective infant.

Authors object to the distinction, but for different reasons. Gay-Williams claims that the phrase "passive euthanasia" is misleading and mistaken. On his view, what is called "passive euthanasia" is not really euthanasia at all because it is not intentional killing; rather the killing is an unintended consequence, a mere side effect, and the real aim of the action is to eliminate suffering.

The position that Gay-Williams adopts is what John Ladd calls "the absolutist position." It rests on a distinction between the intended consequence of an act and the foreseen but unintended consequence. This distinction is part of a traditional doctrine called the doctrine of double effect. According to this doctrine, as long as the intended consequence of an act is good, a bad foreseen consequence (such as death) can be morally allowed provided it is not intended and it prevents a greater evil (such as great suffering). Suppose that a doctor gives a terminal cancer patient a fatal injection of morphine. If the doctor intends only to reduce or eliminate the patient's pain, and not to kill him, and if the death of the patient is not as bad as the patient's suffering, then according to the doctrine of double effect, the doctor's action is not wrong.

Other writers maintain that the distinction between active and passive euthanasia, if there is one at all, has no moral significance. James Rachels argues that it makes no moral difference whether a person is killed or let die, the consequence is the same, and only the consequences of an action matter when it comes to judging it morally right or wrong. The intentions of the actor may be relevant to judging character, but they are irrelevant to the moral rightness or wrongness of the action itself. This view is what Ladd calls "the consequentialist position."

Ladd rejects both the absolutist and consequentialist positions; instead he adopts what he calls "contextualism." On this view, no absolute distinction between killing and letting die can be made. The distinction is always relative to the context, to the moral acts that come before and after the act in question. Some acts of "letting die" could be virtuous and others could be vicious, depending on the context, and the same can be said for acts of "killing."

Philippa Foot, in sharp contrast to both Ladd and Rachels, thinks that an absolute and morally relevant distinction between active and passive euthanasia can be drawn in terms of the right to life. This right creates a duty of noninterference, a duty that conflicts with actively killing a person, but not with letting a person die. There are, however, different sorts of interference; fatally shooting a person is obviously an interference with his life, but turning off a respirator is merely interference with treatment, and as such it should be classified as passive rather than active euthanasia.

Having made a distinction between active and passive euthanasia, and also between voluntary and nonvoluntary euthanasia, Foot discusses four distinct types: (1) active voluntary euthanasia, (2) passive voluntary euthanasia, (3) active nonvoluntary euthanasia, and (4) passive nonvoluntary euthanasia.

PHILOSOPHICAL ISSUES

As far as voluntary euthanasia is concerned, one basic issue is whether or not terminally ill persons who are rational and fully informed should be free to decide to die and then have their decisions carried out, either by themselves or by others. Philosophers such as Jonathan Glover and Tristram Engelhardt, Jr., assume that adults who satisfy the appropriate criteria should be free to make such a decision, but other writers disagree. Gay-Williams argues that a person who chooses to die, whether by suicide or by active euthanasia, is acting contrary to nature and contrary to self-interest.

Turning to nonvoluntary euthanasia, one of the issues, as we have seen, is whether or not there is a morally significant difference between killing and letting die. A related issue is whether the doctrine of double effect is acceptable or not. Critics such as John Ladd complain that the distinction between intended and merely foreseen and unintended consequences is nothing more than a "verbal trick," and that, in any event, there is no clear acceptable criterion for determining

what is and is not part of the intention of an act.

Another matter of controversy is the distinction between ordinary and extraordinary means of prolonging life. This distinction is used by the American Medical Association in a statement condemning "mercy killing," that is, the intentional killing of a person, but allowing cessation of extraordinary means of prolonging life when biological death is imminent. According to the AMA position, withdrawing a person from a respirator is allowable even if this results in death.

This distinction is defended by Thomas D. Sullivan, but Rachels finds it to be question-begging and irrelevant. It is question-begging because the definitions of "ordinary" and "extraordinary" cited by Sullivan employ terms like "excessive cost" which already assume that the life in question is not worth saving. It is irrelevant because there are cases in which even ordinary means of prolonging life should not be used. Giving insulin to a diabetic is an ordinary means of preserving life, but suppose a diabetic has terminal cancer and does not want his insulin shots. In that case, Rachels claims, failing to give the shots would not be wrong, even if they are an ordinary means of prolonging life.

What is relevant in life-or-death decisions, Rachels insists, is the quality of the person's life. Richard Brandt and Jonathan Glover also appeal to the quality of life. But how do we distinguish between good and bad lives? That is a classical problem that resists easy solution. Glover's answer is that we should ask ourselves if we would want to live the life in question. But it seems unlikely that everyone will agree about which lives are or are not worth living. Taking surveys may not be the answer. Brandt's suggestion is that we use a "happiness" criterion: A life is good or worth living if over the whole lifetime there are more moments of happiness (moments of experience that are liked) than moments of unhappiness (moments of experience that are disliked). But is happiness the only thing to be considered? What about other things like knowledge and achievement? Perhaps an unhappy life

could still be good because of achievements or knowledge.

J. GAY-WILLIAMS

The Wrongfulness of Euthanasia

From *Intervention and Reflection, Basic Issues in Medical Ethics*, 2nd ed., by Ronald Munson. ©
1983 by Wadsworth, Inc. Reprinted by permission of Wadsworth Publishing
Company, Belmont, California 94002.

J. Gay-Williams has requested that no biographical information be provided.
    Gay-Williams defines "euthanasia" as intentionally taking the life of a presumably hopeless person. Suicide can count as euthanasia, but not "passive euthanasia" because the latter does not involve intentional killing. Three main arguments are presented to show that euthanasia is wrong: the argument from nature, the argument from self-interest, and the argument from practical effects.

My impression is that euthanasia—the idea, if not the practice—is slowly gaining acceptance within our society. Cynics might attribute this to an increasing tendency to devalue human life, but I do not believe this is the major factor. The acceptance is much more likely to be the result of unthinking sympathy and benevolence. Well-publicized, tragic stories like that of Karen Quinlan elicit from us deep feelings of compassion. We think to ourselves, "She and her family would be better off if she were dead." It is an easy step from this very human response to the view that if someone (and others) would be better off dead, then it must be all right to kill that person.[1] Although I respect the compassion that leads to this conclusion, I believe the conclusion is wrong. I want to show that euthanasia is wrong. It is inherently wrong, but it is also wrong judged from the standpoints of self-interest and of practical effects.

Before presenting my arguments to support this claim, it would be well to define "euthanasia." An essential aspect of euthanasia is that it involves taking a human life, either one's own or that of another. Also, the person whose life is taken must be someone who is believed to be suffering from some disease or injury from which recovery cannot reasonably be expected. Finally, the action must be deliberate and intentional. Thus, euthanasia is intentionally taking the life of a presumably hopeless person. Whether the life is one's own or that of another, the taking of it is still euthanasia.

It is important to be clear about the deliberate and intentional aspect of the killing. If a hopeless person is given an injection of the wrong drug by mistake and this causes his death, this is wrongful killing but not euthanasia. The killing cannot be the result of accident. Furthermore, if the person is given an injection of a drug that is believed to be necessary to treat his disease or better his condition and the person dies as a result, then this is neither wrongful killing nor euthanasia. The intention was to make the patient well, not kill him. Similarly, when a patient's condition is such that it is not reasonable to hope that any medical procedures or treatments will save his life, a failure to implement the procedures or treatments is not euthanasia. If the person dies, this will be as a result of his injuries or disease and not because of his failure to receive treatment.

The failure to continue treatment after it has been realized that the patient has little chance of benefiting from it has been characterized by some as "passive euthanasia." This phrase is misleading and mistaken.[2] In such cases, the person involved is not killed (the first essential aspect of euthanasia), nor is the death of the person intended by the withholding of additional treatment (the third essential aspect of euthanasia). The aim may be to spare the person additional and unjustifiable pain, to save him from the indignities of hopeless manipulations, and to avoid increasing the financial and emotional burden on his family. When I buy a pencil it is so that I can use it to write, not to contribute to an increase in the gross national product. This may be the unintended consequence of my action, but it is not the aim of my action. So it is with failing to continue the treatment of a dying person. I intend his death no more than I intend to reduce the GNP by not using medical supplies. His is an unintended dying, and so-called "passive euthanasia" is not euthanasia at all.

THE ARGUMENT FROM NATURE

Every human being has a natural inclination to continue living. Our reflexes and responses fit us to fight attackers, flee wild animals, and dodge out of the way of trucks. In our daily lives we exercise the caution and care necessary to protect ourselves. Our bodies are similarly structured for survival right down to the molecular level. When we are cut, our capillaries seal shut, our blood clots, and fibrogen is produced to start the process of healing the wound. When we are invaded by bacteria, antibodies are produced to fight against the alien organisms, and their remains are swept out of the

body by special cells designed for clean-up work.

Euthanasia does violence to this natural goal of survival. It is literally acting against nature because all the processes of nature are bent towards the end of bodily survival. Euthanasia defeats these subtle mechanisms in a way that, in a particular case, disease and injury might not.

It is possible, but not necessary, to make an appeal to revealed religion in this connection.[3] Man as trustee of his body acts against God, its rightful possessor, when he takes his own life. He also violates the commandment to hold life sacred and never to take it without just and compelling cause. But since this appeal will persuade only those who are prepared to accept that religion has access to revealed truths, I shall not employ this line of argument.

It is enough, I believe, to recognize that the organization of the human body and our patterns of behavioral responses make the continuation of life a natural goal. By reason alone, then, we can recognize that euthanasia sets us against our own nature.[4] Furthermore, in doing so, euthanasia does violence to our dignity. Our dignity comes from seeking our ends. When one of our goals is survival, and actions are taken that eliminate that goal, then our natural dignity suffers. Unlike animals, we are conscious through reason of our nature and our ends. Euthanasia involves acting as if this dual nature—inclination towards survival and awareness of this as an end—did not exist. Thus, euthanasia denies our basic human character and requires that we regard ourselves or others as something less than fully human.

THE ARGUMENT FROM SELF-INTEREST

The above arguments are, I believe, sufficient to show that euthanasia is inherently wrong. But there are reasons for considering it wrong when judged by standards other than reason. Because death is final and irreversible, euthanasia contains within it the possibility that we will work against our own interest if we practice it or allow it to be practiced on us.

Contemporary medicine has high standards of excellence and a proven record of accomplishment, but it does not possess perfect and complete knowledge. A mistaken diagnosis is possible, and so is a mistaken prognosis. Consequently, we may believe that we are dying of a disease when, as a matter of fact, we may not be. We may think that we have no hope of recovery when, as a matter of fact, our chances are quite good. In such circumstances, if euthanasia were permitted, we would die needlessly. Death is final and the chance of error too great to approve the practice of euthanasia.

Also, there is always the possibility that an experimental procedure or a hitherto untried technique will pull us through. We should at least keep this option open, but euthanasia closes it off. Furthermore, spontaneous remission does occur in many cases. For no apparent reason, a patient simply recovers when those all around him, including his physicians, expected him to die. Euthanasia would just guarantee their expectations and leave no room for the "miraculous" recoveries that frequently occur.

Finally, knowing that we can take our life at any time (or ask another to take it) might well incline us to give up too easily. The will to live is strong in all of us, but it can be weakened by pain and suffering and feelings of hopelessness. If during a bad time we allow ourselves to be killed, we never have a chance to reconsider. Recovery from a serious illness requires that we fight for it, and anything that weakens our determination by suggesting that there is an easy way out is ultimately against our own interest. Also, we may be inclined towards euthanasia because of our concern for others. If we see our sickness and suffering as an emotional and financial burden on our family, we may feel that to leave our life is to make their lives easier.[5] The very presence of the possibility of euthanasia may keep us from surviving when we might.

THE ARGUMENT
FROM PRACTICAL EFFECTS

Doctors and nurses are, for the most part, totally committed to saving lives. A life lost is, for them, almost a personal failure, an insult to their skills and knowledge. Euthanasia as a practice might well alter this. It could have a corrupting influence so that in any case that is severe doctors and nurses might not try hard enough to save the patient. They might decide that the patient would simply be "better off dead" and take the steps necessary to make that come about. This attitude could then carry over to their dealings with patients less seriously ill. The result would be an overall decline in the quality of medical care.

Finally, euthanasia as a policy is a slippery slope. A person apparently hopelessly ill may be allowed to take his own life. Then he may be permitted to deputize others to do it for him should he no longer be able to act. The judgment of others then becomes the ruling factor. Already at this point euthanasia is not personal and voluntary, for others are acting "on behalf of" the patient as they see fit. This may well incline them to act on behalf of other patients who have not authorized them to exercise their judgment. It is only a short step, then, from voluntary euthanasia (self-inflicted or authorized), to directed euthanasia administered to a patient who has given no authorization, to involuntary euthanasia conducted as part of a social policy.[6] Recently many psychiatrists and sociologists have argued that we define as "mental illness" those forms of behavior that we disapprove of.[7] This gives us license then to lock up those who display the behavior. The category of the "hopelessly ill" provides the possibility of even worse abuse. Embedded in a social policy, it would give society or its representatives the authority to eliminate all those who might be considered too "ill" to function normally any longer. The dangers of euthanasia are too great to all to run the risk of approving it in any form. The first slippery step may well lead to a serious and harmful fall.

I hope that I have succeeded in showing why the benevolence that inclines us to give approval of euthanasia is misplaced. Euthanasia is inherently wrong because it violates the nature and dignity of human beings. But even those who are not convinced by this must be persuaded that the potential personal and social dangers inherent in euthanasia are sufficient to forbid our approv-

ing it either as a personal practice or as a public policy.

Suffering is surely a terrible thing, and we have a clear duty to comfort those in need and to ease their suffering when we can. But suffering is also a natural part of life with values for the individual and for others that we should not overlook. We may legitimately seek for others and for ourselves an easeful death, as Arthur Dyck has pointed out.[8] Euthanasia, however, is not just an easeful death. It is a wrongful death. Euthanasia is not just dying. It is killing.

Footnotes

1. For a sophisticated defense of this position see Philippa Foot, "Euthanasia," *Philosophy and Public Affairs* 6 (1977): 85–112. Foot does not endorse the radical conclusion that euthanasia, voluntary and involuntary, is always right.

2. James Rachels rejects the distinction between active and passive euthanasia as morally irrelevant in his "Active and Passive Euthanasia," *New England Journal of Medicine*, 292: 78–80. But see the criticism by Foot, pp. 100–103.

3. For a defense of this view see J.V. Sullivan, "The Immorality of Euthanasia," in *Beneficent Euthanasia*, ed.

Marvin Kohl (Buffalo, NY: Prometheus Books, 1975), pp. 34–44.

4. This point is made by Ray V. McIntyre in "Voluntary Euthanasia: The Ultimate Perversion," *Medical Counterpoint* 2: 26–29.

5. See McIntyre, p. 28.

6. See Sullivan, "Immorality of Euthanasia," pp. 34–44, for a fuller argument in support of this view.

7. See, for example, Thomas S. Szasz, *The Myth of Mental Illness*, rev. ed. (New York: Harper & Row, 1974).

8. Arthur Dyck, "Beneficent Euthanasia and Benemortasia," Kohl, op. cit., pp. 117–129.

Review Questions

1. How does Gay-Williams define "euthanasia?"

2. Why does he object to the phrase "passive euthanasia?"

3. Explain the three arguments he uses to show that euthanasia is wrong.

Discussion Questions

1. Is Gay-Williams' definition of "euthanasia" acceptable? Defend your view.

2. Are his arguments sound or not?

JOHN LADD
Positive and Negative Euthanasia

From *Ethical Issues Relating to Life and Death* by John Ladd. Copyright © 1979 by Oxford
University Press, Inc. Reprinted by permission.

*John Ladd is Professor of Philosophy at Brown University. He has
written extensively in the fields of ethics and political philosophy.*

*Ladd attacks two positions on the distinction between killing and
letting die, the absolutist view and the consequentialist view, and he
defends a third position that he calls "contextualism." He also distinguishes between an "ethics of treatment" where only the appropriateness
of further treatment is considered, and an "ethics of responsibility"
where the doctor accepts responsibility for others and treats them as
equals. The latter sort of ethics is recommended for doctors.*

It is a well-known fact that many practicing
physicians lean heavily on the distinction
between negative and positive euthanasia,
that is, between "letting a hopelessly incurable patient die" and "killing him." Polls of
physicians indicate that a large proportion of
them approve in principle and are willing to
practice negative euthanasia, whereas only a
small proportion approve or are willing to
practice positive euthanasia. Many laymen
also hold the distinction to be a helpful and
valid one.

The question I shall discuss is whether or
not there is any significant ethical difference
between these two types of euthanasia. For
example, is there any significant ethical difference between turning off a machine supporting a patient's life and not turning it on
in the first place, or between doing something positive to hasten a patient's death and
simply letting him die? I shall argue that it
is far from clear how the distinction is
drawn and how it can be defended ethically.

ABSOLUTISM AND CONSEQUENTIALISM

There are two extreme positions regarding
the distinction between negative and positive euthanasia, "letting die" and "killing."
Following Casey, I shall call them *absolutist*
and *consequentialist*.[1] The absolutist, as the
name suggests, holds that a clear-cut and
absolute distinction can be drawn between
killing and letting die. The consequentialist,
on the other hand, argues that since the

consequences of both kinds of acts are the
same, there is no significant ethical distinction between them. In the course of the
discussion, I shall try to show that neither of
these two positions is tenable and that we
ought to adopt a third position that might
tentatively be called *contextualist*.

The absolutist position, which is advocated by many Roman Catholic theologians,
holds that there is a significant difference
between doing something evil intentionally
and letting it happen as a "by-product," so
as to speak. It is never right to will evil,
even for the sake of a good end. Killing an
innocent person is always wrong, but allowing him to die may not be—under certain
circumstances. To "consent" to a person's
death when one lets him die is morally
different from "willing" his death, i.e., killing
him. Like God, who only wills what is good
but permits evil, man must also will only
what is good but may permit evil.[2] The
distinction between "consenting" and "willing" depends, in turn, on various obscure
scholastic distinctions between different
kinds of "voluntary object," "intention," etc.[3]
It is not possible in this paper to enter into a
detailed critique of the scholastic theory of
action. If that were the only ground for
accepting the distinction, its basis would be
very weak indeed.[4]

The second position with regard to the
distinction between killing and letting die is
what I have called *consequentialist*. It maintains that only the consequences of an act

are relevant for determining the nature of the act and its ethical significance. If letting an incurable patient die has the same consequence as killing him, then the actions are the same. There may, of course, be other relevant differences, e.g., in suffering, in cost, or in saving the life of another person, but for the consequentialist, the end result is the only thing that counts.[5]

This is a position that appeals to persons who are predisposed towards utilitarianism, for, in a slightly different sense of the term, utilitarianism may itself be regarded as a form of consequentialism. According to utilitarianism, only the consequences are ethically relevant to the rightness or wrongness of an act. It is unnecessary for our purposes, however, to enter into a critique of utilitarianism as an ethical theory, since it is possible to hold a consequentialist theory of action without being a utilitarian in ethics. In general, I propose to examine the distinction between killing and letting die on its own merits and without reference to any theoretical support that its defenders or critics may derive from systematic metaphysics or ethics.

THE APPEAL TO INTUITION

Apart from specialized metaphysical doctrines, the usual defense of the distinction between killing and letting die seems to rest on claims of self-evidence, i.e., intuition (in the philosophical sense). Undoubtedly, people often feel intuitively that there is a significant difference between making something happen and just letting in happen; for example, there seems to be an important moral difference between pushing someone into a river to drown and simply failing to jump in and rescue someone if he accidentally falls in. However, the question is whether feelings of this kind are sufficient to establish the philosophical claim that there is a significant ethical difference between the two.

To begin with, appeals of this kind to intuition are tricky, because examples like the one just mentioned are hardly ever unambiguous. Without being told any more about the case, one naturally assumes that there is a difference, say, in motivation, between the two cases mentioned because

there usually is. One takes for granted that anyone who deliberately pushes his victim into the water has some kind of malicious motive for doing so, whereas the bystander who refrains from acting may be motivated by fear or indifference. The acts are different because the motives are different. If this explanation in terms of motives is correct, then the relevance of this kind of example for the medical case is questionable, since as regards motives for euthanasia, we ought to assume that there is good will on all sides. Indeed, discussions of the distinction between positive and negative euthanasia, or of euthanasia in general for that matter, are pointless unless it is assumed that personal motivation (for killing or letting die) is not one of the issues.

On the other hand, if we direct our faculties of intuition to medical examples in order to establish an ethical difference between killing and letting a patient die, ambiguities arise due to the haziness of the surrounding conditions of the imagined example. Thus, we might well imagine that under some circumstances it would be better to let a patient with incurable cancer die rather than to kill him because of uncertainties about the prognosis, the amount of pain he would suffer, the possibility of remission, and so on. It is difficult if not impossible to be certain that we are not covertly or unconsciously assuming that there are other relevant differences between a case of killing and a case of letting die besides the one at issue when we try to argue from intuitions.

In sum, intuitions like those mentioned here and in the literature are inevitably subjective and unreliable, simply because it is impossible to isolate an act in imagination and to consider it apart from its context; some kind of background is always part of the perception of it. We are not always cognizant of the background and so are liable to jump to conclusions about differences by failing to take it into account. For these reasons, your perception and my perception of what is allegedly the same kind of case may not be the same at all.

In addition to the difficulties just mentioned with regard to arguments from intuition, it should also be observed that inferences from one kind of case to other kinds of cases may be unwarranted, especially the inference from nonmedical cases to medical cases; for the cases may not be analogous. Medical cases are apt to raise quite different sorts of issues from the other types of cases; at least, whether they do or not is an open question. One must not forget that the validity of an argument from analogy, which is the kind of argument involved here, depends not only on the previously established similarities between the cases being compared, but also on the denial of any relevant dissimilarities. The greater the number of dissimilarities, which the logicians call the "negative analogy," the less valid the argument tends to be.

The appeal to intuition is not limited to advocates of the distinction between killing and letting die. Consequentialists also employ this method, with opposite results, of course. Thus, we are asked to image a situation in which one person pushes a child into the water to drown and to compare it with another situation in which a bystander, who is easily able to rescue the child, just lets the child drown; and we are asked to imagine that their motivations are similar. Is there any significant ethical difference? The consequentialist's intuition says no.

They also say that there is no significant ethical difference between a doctor's turning off the oxygen when a patient is in an oxygen tent and simply letting the bottle run out of oxygen.

It is obvious that the case either for or against the distinction between killing and letting die, rests on slippery ground if it depends on intuitions alone. But in addition to the subjectivity of the appeal to intuitions, there are moral objections to the resort to intuition in ethical discussions. The recourse to intuition represents not only a breakdown in argument, a refusal to carry it forward, but also an objectionable attitude towards those with whom one disagrees. It has the effect of saying: "It is so because I say that it is so. You are stupid not to see it."

In order to determine whether or not there is a significant ethical difference between killing or letting die, it is not enough to "feel" that there is or is not a difference, or to claim to "see" the difference or not to see it. We must go further, and explain what the difference is and why it is ethically significant, or, on the other hand, why there is no difference. In order to do this, we must examine in greater detail the ethics of nonintervention, the notions of acts, nonacts and omissions, and a number of other categories that provide the context of the issue of positive and negative euthanasia . . ..

ARE OMISSIONS ACTIONS?

It is often held that there is a significant ethical difference between doing something and not doing something, between acts and omissions, or, in philosophical jargon, between positive and negative acts.[6] It is held, for instance, that not-doings—omissions—are not subject to the same kind of moral standards used to judge and critically evaluate positive doings. Thus, other things being equal, a person is not responsible for omissions (or their consequences) in the same way that he is responsible for his positive acts (and their consequences). In this sense, non-doings are not actions in the full ethical sense.

Of course, it is necessary to qualify these assertions with the phrase "other things being equal," because sometimes people are held responsible for their failing to act, that is, for their omissions. Parents who fail to take care of their children and doctors who fail to take care of their patients are held responsible for their omissions. Legally and perhaps also morally, we hold people responsible for their omissions when they have a prior duty to do what they fail to do. This is the basic notion behind the concept of negligence. We may broaden this notion by adding that roles and expectations also define actions that one can be condemned for not performing.

With these qualifications, the view in question holds that omissions per se are not the sort of thing for which a person can be held responsible. Underlying this position regarding omissions is what may be called an "interventionist" view of human actions.[7] Human action is viewed as an intervention in the normal course of nature. Not to act, then, means not to intervene, and one can be held responsible only for one's interventions. Indeed, only interventions are subject to the precepts of morality.

It is easy to see why this doctrine might appeal to a doctor who subscribes to the distinction between killing and letting die for according to it letting die (not doing anything) amounts to not intervening in the course of nature. As a nonintervention it is a nonact and therefore not something that a person can be held responsible for. Hence, except in cases of negligence, a doctor is not responsible for a person's death if he lets him die, because that is a nonact; killing him, on the other hand, would be a positive act, an intervention for which he would be responsible.

Apart from the metaphysical underpinnings of the interventionist view of action and omission, its application to the problem at hand raises new questions. What is and what is not to count as an intervention? Is the act of deliberately deciding not to intervene itself an act in the ordinary sense or an intervention? And how about the positive steps that a doctor might take to avoid doing something, for example, walking away or hanging up on the phone? It is hard to believe that leaving orders not to resuscitate is not an intervention of some kind. Can we really say that a doctor is not responsible for the act of deciding or for various measures he undertakes as part of his plan of nonintervention? It is clear that the line between intervention and nonintervention is very fuzzy, to say the least.

The other part of the interventionist doctrine is the notion of the "normal course of nature." Again, it is unclear what is and what is not to be considered "normal."

How do normal human interactions, say, of helping, fit in here? Are feeding, even intravenously; giving drugs like insulin; or massaging the heart normal or not normal?

Many versions of interventionism link the theory with a causal theory of action, that is, the theory that an action consists of a "causing something to happen," a "bringing about of something." (This theory is also sometimes called "consequentialism.")[8] According to the causal analysis, a nonaction would presumably be a not-causing something to happen and, as such, would (by definition) not be an action. In other words, the causal theory of action seems to imply that one can act only positively (in the sense of *causing* something to happen), and that the omission of an act, a nonperformance, is not an action, because it is a not-causing. If we add to this a causal theory of responsibility, namely the proposition that a person is responsible only for what he causes, then it follows that we are not responsible for our nonactions or, for that matter, for states of affairs we might have prevented. (Adherents of this view would have to say that the kind of responsibility involved in negligence is conventional or legal, rather than causal).

Two points need to be made about the causal theory I have just described. First, we might question the underlying assumption that there can only be positive causes, that is, that omissions and privations cannot be causes. It may possibly be true that this is the case in physics, but it is a strange assumption for biomedical science and even more so for clinical science, for in these latter areas, diseases are often attributed to the absence of normal or favorable conditions, e.g., the absence of oxygen (anoxia) or an insulin insufficiency (diabetes). It is therefore not illogical to attribute someone's death causally to the failure to someone else to feed him, to provide him with drugs, or to treat him.

A second and even more important point is that a presupposition of the attribution of responsibility to an agent for something he did or did not do is that he might have acted otherwise. More generally, if we want to be able to evaluate an act morally, either a past or a future act, we must be able to compare it with other possible acts. In other words, the concept of counterfactual possibility is an essential element in the ethics of action (and omission). Thus, Bennett gives a causal, consequentialist account of the difference between killing and letting die in terms of counterfactual possibilities, that is, "would . . . if's." A positive act like killing consists of "the only set of movements which *would* have produced that upshot" and an omission like letting die consists of "movements other than the only set which *would* have produced that upshot."[9] In other words, "to kill X" means that under the circumstances, there is hardly anything else that one could do that would have the effect that X dies, and "to let X die" means that almost anything that one could do would have the effect that X dies.

There are many reasons for rejecting this kind of analysis, however. As Casey points out, for example, a causal-counterfactual analysis of this type includes many things that we would not ordinarily consider "omissions," "refraining from doing," or "letting something happen." There are limits to the kind of possible nonacts that we attribute to a person. Casey writes: "The view we take of a man's character, or of his role in a certain type of situation, sets limits not only on what we can regard him as responsible for in that situation, but also, as we have seen, on what we can properly describe him as doing or refraining from doing."[10] There must be some reason to believe that the person in question is or should be *concerned* with what is happening. In his role as a doctor, a person might be expected to treat or not to treat, but not to take a thousand dollars from his private bank account to buy a drug for a patient that is needed to save her life.[11]

Consider all the things that a person might do at a certain time. Under normal circumstances, there is obviously an indefinitely large number of possibilities; he could wiggle his right middle toe, scratch his forehead, shout, jump in the air. Certainly it would be absurd to say of most of these possible actions that the person in question *failed*, refrained from, or omitted to perform them, for most of them are outside the compass of meaningful consideration; we would not blame or commend a person for not doing them, we do not deliberate about them.

These examples help make out task clear: we must find some way of distinguishing between those possible actions that are irrelevant to the assessment of conduct and those that are relevant. In our previous terminology, we need a way of determining whether an omission, a negative act, is to be regarded as an action or whether it is simply a possibility that does not fall under the rubric of action at all and to which moral categories are inapplicable. There are two ways, I believe, in which this distinction can be made. The first involves the *Why?* of an action (accountability), and the second involves the *What?* and *How?* of an action (the structure of an act).

ACCOUNTABILITY:
THE WHY OF AN ACTION

First, let us begin with the concept of an action in general. Here borrowing from Anscombe, we might say that an action is distinguished from a mere bodily movement in that it is always possible to ask for a reason for the action.[12] "Why did you do that?" This logical property of actions will be called "accountability," by which I mean that it always makes sense to ask for an account of why one does or did something. (I use the term "accountability" in order to distinguish what is involved here from other senses of the term "responsibility.")[13]

Now, it should be clear that we often can and do ask a person to account for his nonactions. "Why didn't you do that?" "Why didn't you come?" "Why didn't you treat the patient?" The request for reasons of this type also arises in connection with propositions about what one ought to do:

"Why shouldn't you refrain from treating?" "Why shouldn't you let the patient die?" In contrast, there are lots of things of which it would be absurd to ask, why didn't you do that? e.g., "Why didn't you wiggle your toe at 11:34 A.M. today?"

The point I want to emphasize is that many forms of nonaction, refrainings and omissions have the ordinary logical properties of actions, i.e., doings. This is important, because the simple not-doing of something does not mean that one is let off the hook; one still has to explain. A doctor who refrains from treating must be able to give a reason for not-treating; in most cases, I am sure that this is possible. Insofar as "letting a patient die" falls into this category of non-treatment, it represents an action for which one is as accountable as one would be for, say, killing. . . .

THE FALLACY OF
SIMPLE DESCRIPTION

The general lesson from all these theories of action is that the correctness of one description of action does not necessarily entail the falsity of other descriptions. The conception that there is only one true answer to the question: What is he doing? (or, What did he do?) may be called the *fallacy of simple description*. It is obvious that this fallacy is often employed as a sophistic device to "get oneself off the hook"—as an alibi, so to speak. Thus a person can plead: "I was just following orders" or, like Eichmann, "I was just organizing railroad schedules," or "I was just saving the baby," or "I didn't kill her, I just let her die." Such descriptions of particular acts may be perfectly correct but quite inadequate for other descriptions of the same actions (or other acts on the act-tree) might be ethically more important. It may be true that Jones pressed his finger, thereby pulled the trigger and fired the gun, but it does not follow that Jones didn't kill the man.[14] We cannot say that the bullet, not Jones, killed him. By the same token, we cannot say that a person's disease, rather than some action or nonaction of the doctor killed him.

That the fallacy of simple description is a fallacy should be clear from the fact that many of the acts on this kind of act-tree are acts for which one is accountable. It generally makes perfectly good sense to ask of each of these acts on the act-tree: Why did you do that? One can ask of Jones, for instance, Why did you press your fingers? Why did you pull the trigger? Why did you fire the gun? Why did you kill the man? With regard to genuine actions, including forbearances, such questions can be asked meaningfully all along the line—they are not odd or absurd. On the other hand, as I have already pointed out, questions like these would be patently absurd if asked with regard to other kinds of possible actions.

THE SELECTION OF
AN ACT–DESCRIPTION

There are two further points that have to be made in connection with the structure of action just discussed. The first point is that the selection of an act-description, or the construction of an act-tree, is not an arbitrary, subjective matter. It is not capricious because, excluding metaphorical uses of language, there are built-in limits as to how an act can be described or generated. In his book, Goldman examines in detail several methods of generation. According to his account, in general, an act A generates an act A′, whenever there exists a set of generating conditions (C*) such that the conjunction of A and C* entail A′.[15] What this means, in effect, is that anyone linking two particular acts by generation must be prepared to justify his doing so, that is, to give his reasons for saying that "Dr. Jones's giving orders not to resuscitate Smith" generates "Dr. Jones let Smith die," rather than "Dr. Jones killed Smith."

Although generating conditions do not need to be linked causally, they frequently do involve a causal link. When they do, the procedure of generation usually relates to specific instances rather than act-types. Hence generalizations about causal generations are apt to be deceptive. That is why "X's terminating treatment of Y" sometimes generates "X killed Y" and sometimes not.

In sum, if anyone maintains that there is a significant difference between not starting to treat a patient and stopping the treatment of a similarly situated patient, he must be able to show that the acts generated by these two acts are significantly different ethically. Thus, under certain circumstances, failing to turn on the machine may in fact generate the same type of act as turning the machine off, namely, they are both acts of "letting the patient die." I will leave it up to the reader to apply the same line of reasoning to some of the other situations discussed in this chapter. The moral point should be clear: one cannot change an act (or a nonact) into something morally neutral or avoid responsibility for it simply by using one act-description of it rather than another.

THE ETHICAL SIGNIFICANCE OF AN ACT-DESCRIPTION

The second point concerns the ethical significance of act-descriptions, act-generations and, in general, act-classifications. Some are clearly more significant ethically than others; one is tempted to say that some descriptions relate to what is ethically central and others to what is only incidental in an action. For example, whether Jones used his middle or his forefinger to press the trigger is immaterial; what is significant is that he killed the man. By the same token, whether a doctor let his patient die by giving an order to the nurse not to call him or by not giving an order to the nurse to call him may, in most cases, be immaterial. What matters ethically is that the patient died, that the doctor ended his suffering, etc.

The distinction implied here is often formulated in terms of the metaphysical concepts of essence and accident. A certain feature of an action, say, its intention, is held to be essential; other features, say, the spe-

cific bodily movements involved, are held to be accidental. The use of the essence-accident distinction represents a metaphysical doctrine known as "essentialism," which contends that there are built-in essences of things and that, as rational beings, we can identify these essences through, for example, some form of intuition. For obvious reasons, I find this doctrine quite objectionable. Instead, I adopt a pragmatic position and hold what is to be taken as essential depends on the purposes one has in mind. Thus, what is essential for legal purposes may not coincide with what is essential for ethical or clinical purposes. In this essay we are concerned with what is essential from the point of view of ethics.

In order to avoid the absolutist metaphysical and epistemological connotations of the term "essence," I shall use the term "centrality" instead. Accordingly, we may speak of certain features of actions, or certain act-descriptions, as ethically central and of others as not central. The assumption that one particular feature or type of act-description is central reflects an ethical commitment or an ethical position of one sort or another. For this reason, act-descriptions are hardly ever likely to be ethically neutral. To pretend, as certain metaphysicians and linguistic philosophers do, that those act-descriptions that are relevant to ethics (e.g., in framing moral rules and principles) are themselves logically prior to and independent of ethical presuppositions is simply a subtle way of begging the ethical question—generally in favor of the status quo morality, or at least of a particular kind of moral rule such as a rule against "killing."

It is important to recognize not only that the selection of a particular act-description of an action has ethical implications, but that the issue of what is to be taken as central in describing acts is basically an ethical issue and one that can be decided only on ethical grounds. For example, if one assumes that in the ultimate analysis an act is constituted by its consequences (e.g., changes in the world caused by the agent's intervention), then one has already chosen to side with a consequentialist ethic of some sort. On the other hand, if one focuses on the intention of an act as what is ethically central one has already committed oneself to some sort of absolutist ethics, probably one that lays undue stress on what Donagan calls "second-order rules," that is, rules for judging the culpability, blameworthiness, or sinfulness of an action or of an actor.[16]

There are obviously many other conceptions of what is ethically central in an act-description besides the two mentioned. In my opinion, the most adequate conception of ethical centrality is one that relates it to human relationships of the sort that reflect the social virtues of integrity, respect, caring, understanding, helping, healing, relieving suffering, compassion, solicitude, sympathy, and the corresponding vices. And so, I would argue, those acts on the act-tree (or act-descriptions) that come under these virtues and vices are the ones that should concern us in our medical decisions, as in our other practical decisions vis-a-vis others, if we want to view them morally.

Accordingly, the crucial difference between killing and letting die, if there is one, will depend on what kind of human relationship these acts represent in the act-tree, i.e., what moral acts they generate and from what moral acts they are generated. And to determine what this is obviously depends on the context. For example, if the act in question can be properly described as compassionate in the sense that it generates or is generated by that kind of act, then it would be virtuous; if, on the other hand, the act is best described as one of abandonment, then it might indeed be considered vicious. If this sort of analysis is followed through, then, under certain circumstances administering a lethal drug to an incurable suffering patient might be virtuous and under other circumstances not; by the same token, terminating treatment might sometimes be virtuous and at other times vicious. We must always view the question within a particular context. This is one of the tenets of the position that I call "contextualism."

THE RATIONALE FOR LETTING A PATIENT DIE

The ethical implications and consequences of adopting one particular conception of what is ethically central in an act-description rather than another will become clear if we take another look at the absolutist, intention notion of action. The absolutist believes that a distinction should be made between the intention of an act and the foreseen but unintended consequences of that act.[17] This distinction is used to explain the difference between killing and letting die; in killing, the consequence of the patient's death is what is intended, whereas in letting a patient die his death is not part of what is intended, it is merely a foreseen consequence. To some of us, this distinction seems sophistic, resting on nothing more than a verbal trick; in any event, we need a clear, acceptable criterion for determining what is and what is not part of the intention of an act.

One suggestion is that the clue to what is involved in an intention is to be found in the reasons for the action in question. Accordingly, the distinction between killing (e.g., by administering a lethal drug) and letting die (e.g., by turning off the respirator) might be reduced to a difference in rationale.[18] In the rationale for killing, humanitarian considerations are usually paramount, e.g., the pertinent reasons would be such things as the preservation of the moral integrity and the alleviation of the suffering of the patient and of his family. In the rationale for letting die (not-treating), on the other hand, the paramount consideration is the pointlessness of further treatment in view of its hopelessness and the hardship that further treatment would impose on the patient and his family, e.g., in suffering and economic burden.

It should be observed at once that when so interpreted, the rationale for killing (i.e., positive euthanasia) is, in important respects, the same as the rationale for undertaking treatment in the first place, for the aim of both is the patient's general welfare and the fulfillment of his needs. In contrast, the rationale for letting die, e.g., for ceasing or not initiating treatment, is like the rationale for not treating other sorts of incurable conditions, including many in which death is not involved at all, e.g., incurable blindness or even baldness.

When viewed in this light, the decision to "let a patient die" has the character of a purely medical decision, that is, a professional decision based on medical reasoning, rather than a decision based on more general moral considerations. It is easy to see, therefore, why physicians feel more comfortable in describing a decision that results in a patient's death as "letting him die" rather than as "killing him." By choosing this description they can subsume the decision under what might be called "the ethics of treatment," i.e., professional medical ethics, and they can thereby avoid becoming involved in wider, controversial moral issues. Of course, the professionalization of the issue in such decision ties in very neatly with the prevailing dictum that it is the doctor's business to "preserve life" rather than to "kill."

THE ETHICS OF TREATMENT

We must now consider how the ethics of treatment might be used to support the distinction between killing and letting die. Let me begin by giving a brief account of what I mean by the "ethics of treatment."

The ethics of treatment is a species of professional ethics; it is the professional ethics of physicians. Professional ethics, as intended here, lays out the special obligations and privileges that persons have as members of a profession, especially in their relation to their clients.[19] It is important to distinguish this kind of ethics from the ethics of a technician such as a plumber or a TV repairman, since the specific obligations of the latter are exhausted when they honestly and efficiently deliver the services or goods requested by their clients. Professionals, on the other hand, are expected to do more. In particular, they are required to consider not just what their clients want, but what they themselves, in their considered and informed judgment, believe to be in their client's best interest. In this regard, their professional ethics set limits to what they may do and what they must do for a client.

Consequently, one of the basic requirements of professional ethics in general is that the professional person be prepared to advise his client against a certain course of action if, in his professional opinion, it is not feasible or if it is undesirable because of the excessive cost or undue hardship that it would involve for the client. Just as it would be wrong for a lawyer to take a case to court that he knows he will not win, or for an engineer to draw up plans for a building that cannot be built, so it would be wrong, professionally, for a physician to undertake a course of treatment that he knows will be ineffective or too costly, e.g., in terms of suffering or finances.

Indeed, in cases where he thinks treatment is inadvisable for some reason or other, the physician may, in his role of professional, even be under an obligation to refuse to honor the patient's request for such treatment. Not to do so would violate his professional integrity. Thus, it would be wrong for a doctor to prescribe a drug for a patient that he knows will be ineffective or will be unnecessarily painful and costly, even though the patient asks him to do so. We should not be surprised, therefore, to find that the doctor's view of what is right for him to do is often quite at variance with the patient's view of what he ought to do.[20]

Bearing this general requirement of professional ethics in mind, we can see that a physician might, for professional reasons stemming from the ethics of treatment, decide to terminate the treatment of an incurable, dying patient on the grounds that further treatment is pointless. This decision would be made on narrow professional grounds, i.e., the ethics of treatment, where only the appropriateness of further treatment is in question. In such cases, perhaps, we would not want to say that he decided to let the patient die; rather, he decided to terminate treatment and as a result the patient died.

If this analysis is correct, then it should be clear that the real point at issue between advocates and opponents of the ethical significance of the distinction between killing and letting die in the euthanasia context is an ethical one, namely, whether a decision leading to a person's death should be made on grounds taken from an ethics of treatment or on what might be called humanitarian grounds, i.e., caring, compassion, and the desire to help the dying person die with dignity. The issue might be more simply described as the scope of a physician's moral responsibility towards his patient: Is his responsibility limited to questions concerning the appropriateness of treatment or does it extend further and include duties to his patient as a person?

TREATMENT AND
MORAL RESPONSIBILITY

Some comments on the moral aspects of an ethics of treatment are in order. To begin with, it is easy to be misled by the term "responsibility," for it means many different things to different people. Roughly speaking, ethical theories can be divided into theories of limited responsibility and theories of full responsibility.[21] Where responsibilities are tied to tasks, roles, and offices, they tend to be viewed as limited; a person is considered to have no responsibility for the wider consequences of those acts of his that are performed in carrying out his assigned tasks, roles, or offices. Thus, the ethics of treatment permits a doctor, who for professional reasons prolongs the life of a patient, to disown any responsibility for the continual hardship and suffering that his action brings to the patient or his family. Accordingly, that kind of professional ethics typically involves a theory of negative responsibility—what I have called limited responsibility.

Applied to physicians, the principle of the negative or limited responsibility of physicians implies that moral responsibility for many states of affairs involving indignity and suffering lies elsewhere or, indeed, in our society often nowhere. I have already commented on the ethical aspects of "just doing one's job" and abdicating responsibility for the consequences.

Up to this point, I have assumed that the ethics of treatment is taken as a *substitute* for the principles of common morality, for the principles of humanitarianism and of full moral responsibility for the health and welfare of others. But, of course, the ethics of treatment can be subsumed under a broader ethics, say, of humanitarianism, which recognizes everyone's positive moral responsibility for the health and welfare of others. If we do this, then the ethics of treatment will be a *supplement* to the ordinary principles of morality rather than a *substitute*. But in this case, the principle of the limited or negative responsibility of the physician for his patient has to be abandoned.

Morally speaking, then, the doctor is presented with a choice: if he accepts the ethics of treatment and an ethics of limited responsibility, he must restrict his decision-making to the purely professional sphere. In that case, however, he must abandon the role of moral entrepreneur, as Freidson calls it, and must disavow any pretense of basing his decision on moral grounds.[22] Ultimate moral decisions must be left to someone else. On the other hand, if he is willing to act on what I call an "ethics of responsibility," that is, an ethics of full and, in principle, unlimited responsibility for others, then he has to go beyond the narrow ethics of treatment as defined by his purely professional role. He must enter into decision-making as a full-fledged moral agent; as such, he must be prepared to treat others as moral equals. He must be willing to consult with patient and family as equals and to permit them to participate as fully as possible in all decision-making. Decisions themselves must be based on what is best for all concerned, particularly the welfare and moral integrity of the patient, and not simply on what is required by the physician's professional ethics, the ethics of treatment.[23]

If my analysis is correct, it follows that any doctor who chooses this course will be obliged to abandon the absolute distinction between killing an incurable, dying patient and letting him die. A further consequence, of course, is that he will have to relinquish his monopoly over decision-making and over the supervision of the care of the terminally ill. By the same token, if the time should come when the life of a dying person ought to be terminated, there is no reason why the doctor must be the one to perform the merciful act.[24]

Footnotes

1. See John Casey, "Actions and Consequences," in John Casey, ed., *Morality and Moral Reasoning* (London: Methuen, 1971). I am indebted to Casey for many insights into this problem.

2. St. Thomas Aquinas, *Summa Theologica*, IaIae, qu. 19, art. 9 ad 3.

3. The details can be found in any textbook on Roman Catholic moral theology.

4. For a careful defense of the distinction, see Joseph Boyle, "On Killing and Letting Die," *New Scholasticism* 52 (Autumn 1978). I am greatly indebted to Boyle for letting me see an advance copy of this article. I shall discuss a modified version of this theory later in the paper.

5. For a defense of the consequentialist position, see Jonathan Bennett, "Whatever the Consequences," *Analysis* 26.3 (1966): 83–97.

6. For a helpful discussion of some of the issues, see Judith Jarvis Thomson, *Acts and Other Events* (Ithaca, NY: Cornell University Press, 1977), chap. 15, "Omissions."

7. For a description of this position and bibliographical references, see Alan Donagan, *The Theory of Morality* (Chicago: University of Chicago Press, 1977), p. 46.

8. For a critique of the causal theory of action, see Ladd, "Ethical Dimensions of the Concept of Action," *Journal of Philosophy* 62 (November 1965). Also, Irving Thalberg, *Enigmas of Agency* (New York: Humanities Press, 1972), sec. 1. (References to literature on the causal theory can be found in Thalberg's book.)

9. See Jonathan Bennett, "Whatever the Consequences."

10. Casey, *Morality and Moral Reasoning*, p. 168.

11. Casey, *Morality and Moral Reasoning*, p. 167.

12. See G.E.M. Anscombe, *Intention* (Oxford: Blackwell, 1957), pp. 9, 24–28.

13. I have tried to distinguish a number of different senses of "responsibility" in "The Ethics of Participation," in J. Roland Pennock and John Chapman, eds., *Participation in Politics* (NOMOS XVI), (New York: Atherton-Lieber, 1975), pp. 98–125.

14. It is obviously quite correct to say that the shooting, the bullet, Jones, etc., etc., killed the man. One explanation does not exclude the others. Sometimes it is said that the disease killed a patient rather than a person. They are not mutually exclusive statements. Both might be true. See Alvin I. Goldman, *A Theory of Human Action* (Englewood Cliffs, NJ: Prentice-Hall, 1970), p. 80ff.

15. Goldman, *Theory of Human Action*, p. 41.

16. Donagan, *Theory of Morality*, chap. 2.

17. This distinction underlies the so-called "Principle of Double Effect." For references and a useful discussion, see Donagan, *Theory of Morality*, pp. 157–64, and the article by Boyle mentioned in note 4. Needless to say, I do not accept this principle; in fact, I regard it as an immoral principle.

18. See Donagan, *Theory of Morality*, pp. 122–27; also Boyle, "On Killing and Letting Die."

19. There is a considerable literature on professionalism. For a good discussion of professionalism in medicine, see Eliot Freidson, *Profession of Medicine* (New York: Dodd, Mead, 1973), chap. 4, "The Formal Characteristics of a Profession."

20. Here it should be noted that not only do doctors sometimes continue treatment against the wishes of patients (or of their families), but they sometimes *dis* continue treatment against their wishes. There is, thus, no reason to assume that the professional ethics of treatment will be consistent either with the wishes of patients (or their representatives) or with the general principles of morality.

21. See Ladd, "The Ethics of Participation."

22. See Freidson, *Profession of Medicine*, pp. 252–55.

23. For more on the ethics of responsibility, see Ladd, "Legalism and Medical Ethics."

24. In India, it was traditionally the oldest son who was expected to set the funeral pyre ablaze.

Review Questions

1. What is the absolutist position?

2. And the consequentialist position?

3. Explain Ladd's critique of appealing to intuition to make a distinction between killing and letting die.

4. Explain the interventionist view of human action.

5. What are the problems with this view?

6. Explain the causal theory of action.

7. Ladd makes two points about the causal theory. What are they?

8. In what ways are nonactions like actions?

9. Why is it so difficult to distinguish between "killing" and "letting die" in cases involving terminally ill patients?

10. What is the fallacy of simple description?

11. What is the ethical significance of an act-description?

12. Explain contextualism.

13. Distinguish between the "ethics of treatment" and the "ethics of responsibility."

Discussion Questions

1. Given what Ladd says, do you still think that there is a morally significant difference between killing and letting die? Defend your view.

2. Should doctors be allowed to let patients die in some cases? Why, or why not?

3. Do doctors have a moral obligation to kill their patients in some cases? Defend your position.

PHILIPPA FOOT

Euthanasia

Copyright © 1977 by Philippa Foot. From *Philosophy & Public Affairs*, vol. 6, no. 2 (Winter 1977). Reprinted by permission of Princeton University Press.

Philippa Foot is Professor of Philosophy at the University of California, Los Angeles. She has written many articles in the field of ethics.

Foot defines "euthanasia" as producing a death (by act or omission) that is good for the one who dies. She distinguishes between voluntary and nonvoluntary euthanasia, and between active and passive euthanasia. The latter distinction is based on the right to life and the correlative duty of noninterference. This duty is usually violated by active euthanasia, but not by passive euthanasia. She finds that nonvoluntary active euthanasia is never justified, but allows that the other types (nonvoluntary passive euthanasia, voluntary active euthanasia, and voluntary passive euthanasia) are compatible with both justice and charity.

The widely used *Shorter Oxford English Dictionary* gives three meanings for the word "euthanasia": the first, "a quiet and easy death"; the second, "the means of procuring this"; and the third, "the action of inducing a quiet and easy death." It is a curious fact that no one of the three gives an adequate definition of the word as it is usually understood. For "euthanasia" means much more than a quiet and easy death, or the means of procuring it, or the action of inducing it. The definition specifies only the manner of the death, and if this were all that was implied a murderer, careful to drug his victim, could claim that his act was an act of euthanasia. We find this ridiculous because we take it for granted that in euthanasia it is death itself, not just the manner of death, that must be kind to the one who dies.

To see how important it is that "euthanasia" should not be used as the dictionary definition allows it to be used, merely to signify that a death was quiet and easy, one has only to remember that Hitler's "euthanasia" program traded on this ambiguity. Under this program, planned before the War but brought into full operation by a decree of September 1, 1939, some 275,000 people were gassed in centers that were to be a model for those in which Jews were later exterminated. Anyone in a state institution could be sent to the gas chambers if it was considered that he could not be "rehabilitated" for useful work. As Dr. Leo Alexander reports, relying on the testimony of a neuropathologist who received 500 brains from one of the killing centers,

In Germany the exterminations included the mentally defective, psychotics (particularly schizophrenics), epileptics and patients suffering from infirmities of old age and from various organic neurological disorders such as infantile paralysis, Parkinsonism, multiple sclerosis and brain tumors . . . . In truth, all those unable to work and considered nonrehabilitable were killed.[1]

These people were killed because they were "useless" and "a burden on society"; only the manner of their deaths could be thought of as relatively easy and quiet.

Let us insist, then, that when we talk about euthanasia we are talking about a death understood as a good or happy event for the one who dies. This stipulation follows etymology, but is itself not exactly in line with current usage, which would be captured by the condition that the death should *not* be an evil rather than that it *should* be a good. That this is how people talk is shown by the fact that the case of Karen Ann Quinlan and others in a state of permanent coma is often discussed under the heading of "euthanasia." Perhaps it is not too late to object to the use of the word "euthanasia" in this sense. Apart from the break with the Greek origins of the word there are other unfortunate aspects of this extension of the term. For if we say that the death must be supposed to be a good to the subject we can also specify that it shall be for his sake that an act of euthanasia is performed. If we say merely that death shall not be an evil to him, we cannot stipulate that benefiting him shall be the motive where euthanasia is in question. Given the importance of the question, for whose sake are we acting? it is good to have a definition of euthanasia that brings under this heading only cases of opting for death for the sake of the one who dies. Perhaps what is most important is to say either that euthanasia is to be for the good of the subject or at least that death is to be no evil to him, thus refusing to talk Hitler's language. However, in this paper it is the first condition that will be understood, with the additional proviso that by an act of euthanasia we mean one of inducing or otherwise opting for death for the sake of the one who is to die.

A few lesser points need to be cleared up. In the first place it must be said that the word "act" is not to be taken to exclude omission; we shall speak of an act of euthanasia when someone is deliberately allowed to die, for his own good, and not only when positive measures are taken to see that he does. The very general idea we want is that of a choice of action or inaction directed at another man's death and causally effective in the sense that, in conjunction with actual circumstances, it is a sufficient condition of death. Of complications such as overdetermination, it will not be necessary to speak.

A second, and definitely minor, point about the definition of an act of euthanasia concerns the question of fact versus belief. It has already been implied that one who performs an act of euthanasia thinks that death will be merciful for the subject since we have said that it is on account of this thought that the act is done. But is it enough that he acts with this thought, or must things actually be as he thinks them to be? If one man kills another, or allows him to die, thinking that he is in the last stages of a terrible disease, though in fact he could have been cured, is this an act of euthanasia or not? Nothing much seems to hang on our decision about this. The same condition has got to enter into the definition whether as an element in reality or only as an element in the agent's belief. And however we define an act of euthanasia culpability or justifiability will be the same: if a man acts though ignorance his ignorance may be culpable or it may not.[2]

These are relatively easy problems to solve, but one that is dauntingly difficult has been passed over in this discussion of the definition, and must now be faced. It is easy to say, as if this raised no problems, that an act of euthanasia is by definition one aiming at the *good* of the one whose death is in question, and that it is *for his sake* that his death is desired. But how is this to be explained? Presumably we are thinking of some evil already with him or to come on him if he continues to live, and death is thought of as a release from this evil. But this cannot be enough. Most people's lives contain evils such as grief or pain, but we do not therefore think that death would be a blessing to them. On the contrary life is generally supposed to be a good even for someone who is unusually unhappy or frustrated. How is it that one can ever wish for

death for the sake of the one who is to die? This difficult question is central to the discussion of euthanasia, and we shall literally not know what we are talking about if we ask whether acts of euthanasia defined as we have defined them are ever morally permissible without first understanding better the reason for saying that life is a good, and the possibility that it is not always so.

If a man should save my life he would be my benefactor. In normal circumstances this is plainly true; but does one always benefit another in saving his life? It seems certain that he does not. Suppose, for instance, that a man were being tortured to death and was given a drug that lengthened his sufferings; this would not be a benefit but the reverse. Or suppose that in a ghetto in Nazi Germany a doctor saved the life of someone threatened by disease, but that the man once cured was transported to an extermination camp; the doctor might wish for the sake of the patient that he had died of the disease. Nor would a longer stretch of life always be a benefit to the person who was given it. Comparing Hitler's camps with those of Stalin, Dmitri Panin observes that in the latter the method of extermination was made worse by agonies that could stretch out over months.

Death from a bullet would have been bliss compared with what many millions had to endure while dying of hunger. The kind of death to which they were condemned has nothing to equal it in treachery and sadism.[3]

These examples show that to save or prolong a man's life is not always to do him a service; it may be better for him if he dies earlier rather than later. It must therefore be agreed that while life is normally a benefit to the one who has it, this is not always so.

What we want to know is whether acts of euthanasia, defined as we have defined them, are ever morally permissible. To be more accurate, we want to know whether it is ever sufficient justification of the choice of death for another that death can be counted a benefit rather than harm, and that this is why the choice is made.

It will be impossible to get a clear view of the area to which this topic belongs without first marking the distinct grounds on which objection may lie when one man opts for the death of another. There are two different virtues whose requirements are, in general, contrary to such actions. An unjustified act of killing, or allowing to die, is contrary to justice or to charity, or to both virtues, and the moral failings are distinct. Justice has to do with what men *owe* each other in the way of noninterference and positive service. When used in this wide sense, which has its history in the doctrine of the cardinal virtues, justice is not especially connected with, for instance, law courts but with the whole area of rights, and duties corresponding to rights. Thus murder is one form of injustice, dishonesty another, and wrongful failure to keep contracts a third; chicanery in a law court or defrauding someone of his inheritance are simply other cases of injustice. Justice as such is not directly linked to the good of another, and may require that something be rendered to him even where it will do him harm, as Hume pointed out when he remarked that a debt must be paid even to a profligate debauchee who "would rather receive harm than benefit from large possessions."[4] Charity, on the other hand, is the virtue that attaches us to the good of others. An act of charity is in question only where something is not demanded by justice, but a lack of charity and of justice can be shown where a man is denied something that he both needs and has a right to; both charity and justice demand that widows and orphans are not defrauded, and the man who cheats them is neither charitable nor just.

It is easy to see that the two grounds of objection to inducing death are distinct. A murder is an act of injustice. A culpable failure to come to the aid of someone whose life is threatened is normally contrary, not to justice, but to charity. But where one man is under contract, explicit or implicit, to come to the aid of another injustice too will

be shown. Thus injustice may be involved either in an act or an omission, and the same is true of a lack of charity; charity may demand that someone be aided, but also that an unkind word not be spoken.

The distinction between charity and justice will turn out to be of the first importance when voluntary and nonvoluntary euthanasia are distinguished later on. This is because of the connection between justice and rights, and something should now be said about this. I believe it is true to say that wherever a man acts unjustly he has infringed a right, since justice has to do with whatever a man is owed, and whatever he is owed is his as a matter of right. Something should therefore be said about the different kinds of rights. The distinction commonly made is between having a right in the sense of having a liberty, and having a "claim-right" or "right of recipience."[5] The best way to understand such a distinction seems to be as follows. To say that a man has a right in the sense of a liberty is to say that no one can demand that he not do the thing that he has a right to do. The fact that he has a right to do it consists in the fact that a certain kind of objection does not lie against his doing it. Thus a man has a right in this sense to walk down a public street or park his car in a public parking space. It does not follow that no one else may prevent him from doing so. If for some reason I want a certain man not to park in a certain place I may lawfully park there myself or get my friends to do so, thus preventing him from doing what he has a right (in the sense of a liberty) to do. It is different, however, with a claim-right. This is the kind of right that I have in addition to a liberty when, for example, I have a private parking space; now others have duties in the way of noninterference, as in this case, or of service, as in the case where my claim-right is to goods or services promised to me. Sometimes one of these rights gives other people the duty of securing to me that to which I have a right, but at other times their duty is merely to refrain from interference. If a fall of snow blocks my private parking space there is normally no obligation for anyone else to clear it away. Claim-rights generate duties; sometimes these duties are duties of noninterference; sometimes they are duties of service. If your right gives me the duty not to interfere with you I have "no right" to do it; similarly, if your right gives me the duty to provide something for you I have "no right" to refuse to do it. What *I* lack is the right that is a liberty; I am not "at liberty" to interfere with you or to refuse the service.

Where in this picture does the right to life belong? No doubt people have the right to live in the sense of a liberty, but what is important is the cluster of claim-rights brought together under the title of the right to life. The chief of these is, of course, the right to be free from interferences that threaten life. If other people aim their guns at us or try to pour poison into our drink we can, to put it mildly, demand that they desist. And then there are the services we can claim from doctors, health officers, bodyguards, and firemen, the rights that depend on contract or public arrangement. Perhaps there is no particular point in saying that the duties these people owe us belong to the right to life; we might as well say that all the services owed to anyone by tailors, dressmakers, and couturiers belong to a right called the right to be elegant. But contracts such as those understood in the patient-doctor relationship come in an important way when we are discussing the rights and wrongs of euthanasia, and are therefore mentioned here.

Do people have the right to what they need in order to survive, apart from the right conferred by special contracts into which other people have entered for the supplying of these necessities? Do people in the underdeveloped countries in which starvation is rife have the right to the food they so evidently lack? Joel Feinberg, discussing this question, suggests that they should be said to have "a claim," distinguishing this from a "valid claim," which gives a claim-right.

The manifesto writers on the other side who seem to identify needs, or at lease basic needs, with what they call "human rights," are more properly described, I think, as urging upon the world community the moral principle that all basic human needs ought to be recognized as claims (in the customary prima facie sense) worthy of sympathy and serious consideration right now, even though, in many cases, they cannot yet plausibly be treated as valid claims, that is, as grounds of any other people's duties. This way of talking avoids the anomaly of ascribing to all human beings now, even those in pre-industrial societies, such "economic and social rights" as "periodic holidays with pay." [6]

This seems reasonable, though we notice that there are some actual rights to service that are not based on anything like a contract, as for instance the right that children have to support from their parents and parents to support from their children in old age, though both sets of rights are to some extent dependent on existing social arrangements.

Let us now ask how the right to life affects the morality of acts of euthanasia. Are such acts sometimes or always ruled out by the right to life? This is certainly a possibility; for although an act of euthanasia is, by our definition, a matter of opting for death for the good of the one who is to die, there is, as we noted earlier, no direct connection between that to which a man has a right and that which is for his good. It is true that men have the right only to the kind of thing that is, in general, a good; we do not think that people have the right to garbage or polluted air. Nevertheless, a man may have the right to something that he himself would be better off without; where rights exist it is a man's will that counts, not his or anyone else's estimate of benefit or harm. So the duties complementary to the right to life— the general duty of noninterference and the duty of service incurred by certain persons— are not affected by the quality of a man's life or by his prospects. Even if it is true that he would be, as we say, "better off dead," so long as he wants to live this does not justify us in killing him and may not justify us in deliberately allowing him to die. All of us have the duty of noninterference, and some of us may have the duty to sustain his life. Suppose, for example, that a retreating army has to leave behind wounded or exhausted soldiers in the wastes of an arid or snowbound land where the only prospect is death by starvation or at the hands of an enemy notoriously cruel. It has often been the practice to accord a merciful bullet to men in such desperate straits. But suppose that one of them demands that he should be left alive? It seems clear that his comrades have no right to kill him, though it is a quite different question as to whether they should give him a life-prolonging drug. The right to life can sometimes give a duty of positive service, but does not do so here. What it does give is the right to be left alone.

Interestingly enough we have arrived by way of a consideration of the right to life as the distinction normally labeled "active" versus "passive" euthanasia, and often thought to be irrelevant to the moral issue.[7] Once it is seen that the right to life is a distinct ground of objection to certain acts of euthanasia, and that this right creates a duty of noninterference more widespread than the duties of care there can be no doubt about the relevance of the distinction between passive and active euthanasia. Where everyone may have the duty to leave someone alone, it may be that no one has the duty to maintain his life, or that only some people do.

Where then do the boundaries of the "active" and "passive" lie? In some ways the words are themselves misleading, because they suggest the difference between act and omission that is not quite what we want. Certainly the act of shooting someone is the kind of thing we were talking about under the heading of "interference," and omitting to give him a drug a case of refusing care. But the act of turning off a respirator should surely be thought of as no different from the decision not to start it; if doctors had decided that a patient should be allowed to die, either course of action might follow, and both should be counted as passive rather than active euthanasia if euthanasia were in question. The point seems to be that interference in a course of treatment is not the same as other interference in a man's life, and particularly if the same body of people are responsible for the treatment and for its discontinuance. In such a case we could speak of the disconnecting of the apparatus as killing the man, or of the hospital as allowing him to die. By and large, it is the act of killing that is ruled out under the heading of noninterference, but not in every case.

Doctors commonly recognize this distinction, and the grounds on which some philosophers have denied it seem untenable. James Rachels, for instance, believes that if the difference between active and passive is relevant anywhere, it should be relevant everywhere, and he has pointed to an example in which it seems to make no difference which is done. If someone saw a child drowning in a bath it would seem just as bad to let it drown as to push its head under water.[8] If "it makes no difference" means that one act would be as iniquitous as the other this is true. It is not that killing is *worse* than allowing to die, but that the two are contrary to distinct virtues, which gives the possibility that in some circumstances one is impermissible and the other permissible. In the circumstances invented by Rachels, both are wicked; it is contrary to justice to push the child's head under the water—something one has no right to do. To leave it to drown is not contrary to justice, but it is a particularly glaring example of lack of charity. Here it makes no practical difference because the requirements of justice and charity coincide; but in the case of the retreating army they did not: charity would have required that the wounded soldier be killed had not justice required that he be left alive.[9] In such a case it makes all the difference whether a man opts for the death of another in a positive action, or whether he allows him to die. An analogy with the right to property will make the point clear. If a man owns something he has the right to it even when its possession does him harm, and we have no right to take it from him. But if one day it should blow away, maybe nothing requires us to get it back for him; we could not deprive him of it, but we may allow it to go. This is not to deny that it will often be an unfriendly act or one based on an arrogant judgment when we refuse to do what he wants. Nevertheless, we would be within our rights, and it might be that no moral objection of any kind would lie against our refusal.

It is important to emphasize that a man's rights may stand between us and the action we would dearly like to take for his sake. They may, of course, also prevent action which we would like to take for the sake of others, as when it might be tempting to kill one man to save several. But it is interesting that the limits of allowable interference, however uncertain, seem stricter in the first case than in the second. Perhaps there are no cases in which it would be all right to kill a man against his will *for his own sake* unless they could equally well be described as cases of allowing him to die, as in the example of turning off the respirator. However, there are circumstances, even if these are very rare, in which one man's life would justifiably be sacrificed to save others, and "killing" would be the only description of what was being done. For instance, a vehicle that had gone out of control might be steered from a path on which it would kill more than one man to a path on which it would kill one.[10] But it would not be permissible to steer a vehicle towards someone in order to kill him, against his will, for his own good. An analogy with property rights illustrates the point. One may not destroy a man's property against his will on the grounds that he would be better off without it; there are however circumstances in which it could be destroyed for the sake of others. If his house is liable to fall and kill him that is his affair; it might, however, without injustice be destroyed to stop the spread of a fire.

We see then that the distinction between active and passive, important as it is elsewhere, has a special importance in the area of euthanasia. It should also be clear why James Rachels' other argument, that it is often "more humane" to kill than to allow to die, does not show that the distinction between active and passive euthanasia is morally irrelevant. It might be "more humane" in this sense to deprive a man of the property that brings evils on him, or to refuse to pay what is owed to Hume's profligate debauchee; but if we say this we must admit that an act which is "more humane" than its alternative may be morally objectionable because it infringes rights.

So far we have said very little about the right to service as opposed to the right to noninterference, though it was agreed that both might be brought under the heading of "the right to life." What about the duty to preserve life that may belong to special classes of persons such as bodyguards, firemen, or doctors? Unlike the general public they are not within their rights if they merely refrain from interfering and do not try to sustain life. The subject's claim-rights are two-fold as far as they are concerned and passive as well as active euthanasia may be ruled out here if it is against his will. This is not to say that he has the right to any and every service needed to save or prolong his life; the rights of other people set limits to what may be demanded, both because they have the right not to be interfered with and because they may have a competing right to services. Furthermore one must enquire just what the contract or implicit agreement amounts to in each case. Firemen and bodyguards presumably have a duty which is simply to preserve life, within the limits of justice to others and of reasonableness to themselves. With doctors it may however be different, since their duty relates not only to preserving life but also to the relief of suffering. It is not clear what a doctor's duties are to his patient if life can be prolonged only at the cost of suffering or suffering relieved only by measures that shorten life. George Fletcher has argued that what the doctor is under contract to do depends on what is generally done, because this is what a patient will reasonably expect.[11] This seems right. If procedures are part of normal medical practice then it seems that the patient can demand them however much it may be against his interest to do so. Once again it is not a matter of what is "most humane."

That the patient's right to life may set limits to permissible acts of euthanasia seems undeniable. If he does not want to die no one has the right to practice active euthanasia on him, and passive euthanasia may also be ruled out where he has a right to the services of doctors or others.

Perhaps few will deny what has so far been said about the impermissibility of acts of euthanasia simply because we have so far spoken about the case of one who positively wants to live, and about his rights, whereas those who advocate euthanasia are usually thinking either about those who wish to die or about those whose wishes cannot be ascertained either because they cannot properly be said to have wishes or because, for one reason or another, we are unable to form a reliable estimate of what they are. The question that must now be asked is whether the latter type of case, where euthanasia though not involuntary would again be nonvoluntary, is different from the one discussed so far. Would we have the right to kill someone for his own good so long as we had no idea that he positively wished to live? And what about the life-prolonging duties of doctors in the same circumstances? This is a very difficult problem. On the one hand, it seems ridiculous to suppose that a man's right to life is something that generates duties only where he has signaled that he wants to live; as a borrower does indeed have a duty to return something lent on indefinite loan only if the lender indicates that he wants it back. On the other hand, it might be argued that there is something illogical about the idea that a right has been infringed if someone incapable of saying

whether he wants it or not is deprived of something that is doing him harm rather than good. Yet on the analogy of property we would say that a right has been infringed. Only if someone had earlier told us that in such circumstances he would not want to keep the thing could we think that his right had been waived. Perhaps if we could make confident judgments about what anyone in such circumstances would wish, or what he would have wished beforehand had he considered the matter, we could agree to consider the right to life as "dormant," needing to be asserted if the normal duties were to remain. But as things are we cannot make any such assumption; we simply do not know what most people would want, or would have wanted, us to do unless they tell us. This is certainly the case so far as active measures to end life are concerned. Possibly it is different, or will become different, in the matter of being kept alive, so general is the feeling against using sophisticated procedures on moribund patients, and so much is this dreaded by people who are old or terminally ill. Once again the distinction between active and passive euthanasia has come on the scene, but this time because most people's attitudes to the two are so different. It is just possible that we might presume, in the absence of specific evidence, that someone would not wish, beyond a certain point, to be kept alive; it is certainly not possible to assume that he would wish to be killed.

In the last paragraph we have begun to broach the topic of voluntary euthanasia, and this we must now discuss. What is to be said about the case in which there is no doubt about someone's wish to die: either he has told us beforehand that he would wish it in circumstances such as he is now in, and has shown no sign of a change of mind, or else he tells us now, being in possession of his faculties and of a steady mind. We should surely say that the objections previously urged against acts of euthanasia, which it must be remembered were all on the ground of rights, had disappeared. It does not seem that one would infringe someone's right to life in killing him with his permission and in fact at his request. Why should someone not be able to waive his right to life, or rather, as would be more likely to happen, to cancel some of the duties of noninterference that this right entails? (He is more likely to say that he should be killed by this man at this time in this manner, than to say that anyone may kill him at any time and in any way.) Similarly someone may give permission for the destruction of his property, and request it. The important thing is that he gives a critical permission, and it seems that this is enough to cancel the duty normally associated with the right. If someone gives you permission to destroy his property it can no longer be said that you have no right to do so, and I do not see why it should not be the case with taking a man's life. An objection might be made on the ground that only God has the right to take life, but in this paper religious as opposed to moral arguments are being left aside. Religion apart, there seems to be no case to be made out for an infringement of rights if a man who wishes to die is allowed to die or even killed. But of course it does not follow that there is no moral objection to it. Even with property, which is after all a relatively small matter, one might be wrong to destroy what one had the right to destroy. For, apart from its value to other people, it might be valuable to the man who wanted it destroyed, and charity might require us to hold our hand where justice did not.

Let us review the conclusion of this part of the argument, which has been about euthanasia and the right to life. It has been argued that from this side come stringent restrictions on the acts of euthanasia that could be morally permissible. Active nonvoluntary euthanasia is ruled out by that part of the right to life that creates the duty of noninterference though passive nonvoluntary euthanasia is not ruled out, except where the right to life-preserving action has been created by some special condition such as a contract between a man and his doctor, and it is not always certain just what such a contract involves. Voluntary euthanasia is another matter; as the preceding paragraph suggested, no right is infringed if a man is allowed to die or even killed at his own request.

Turning now to the other objection that normally holds against inducing the death of another, that it is against charity, or benevolence, we must tell a very different story. Charity is the virtue that gives attachment to the good of others, and because life is normally a good, charity normally demands that it should be saved or prolonged. But as we so defined an act of euthanasia that it seeks a man's death for his own sake—for his good—charity will normally speak in favor of it. This is not, of course, to say that charity can require an act of euthanasia that justice forbids, but if an act of euthanasia is not contrary to justice—that is, it does not infringe rights—charity will rather be in its favor than against.

Once more the distinction between nonvoluntary and voluntary euthanasia must be considered. Could it ever be compatible with charity to seek a man's death although he wanted to live, or at least had not let us know that he wanted to die? It has been argued that in such circumstances active euthanasia would infringe his right to life, but passive euthanasia would not do so, unless he had some special right to life-preserving service from the one who allowed him to die. What would charity dictate? Obviously when a man wants to live there is a presumption that he will be benefited if his life is prolonged, and if it is so the question of euthanasia does not arise. But it is, on the other hand, possible that he wants to live where it would be better for him to die; perhaps he does not realize the desperate situation he is in, or perhaps he is afraid of dying. So, in spite of a very proper resistance to refusing to go along with a man's own wishes in the matter of life and death, someone might justifiably refuse to prolong the life even of someone who asked him to prolong it, as in the case of refusing to give the wounded soldier a drug that would keep him alive to meet a terrible end. And it is even more obvious that charity does not always dictate that life should be prolonged where a man's own wishes, hypothetical or actual, are not known.

So much for the relation of charity to nonvoluntary passive euthanasia, which was not, like nonvoluntary active euthanasia, ruled out by the right to life. Let us now ask what charity has to say about voluntary euthanasia both active and passive. It was suggested in the discussion of justice that if of sound mind and steady desire a man might give others the *right* to allow him to die or even to kill him, where otherwise this would be ruled out. But it was pointed out that this would not settle the question of whether the act was morally permissible, and it is this that we must now consider. Could not charity speak against what justice allowed? Indeed it might do so. For while the fact that a man wants to die suggests that his life is wretched, and while his rejection of life may itself tend to take the good out of the things he might have enjoyed, nevertheless his wish to die might here be opposed for his own sake just as it might be if suicide were in question. Perhaps there is hope that his mental condition will improve. Perhaps he is mistaken in thinking his disease incurable. Perhaps he wants to die for the sake of someone else on whom he feels he is a burden, and we are not ready to accept this sacrifice whether for ourselves or others. In such cases, and there will surely be many of them, it could not be for his own sake that we kill him or allow him to die, and therefore euthanasia as defined in this paper would not be in question. But this is not to deny that there could be acts of voluntary euthanasia both passive and active against which neither justice nor charity would speak.

We have now considered the morality of euthanasia both voluntary and nonvoluntary, and active and passive. The conclusion has been that nonvoluntary active euthanasia (roughly, killing a man against his will or without his consent) is never justified, that is

to say, that a man's being killed for his own good never justifies the act unless he himself has consented to it. A man's rights are infringed by such an action, and it is therefore contrary to justice. However, all the other combinations, nonvoluntary passive euthanasia, voluntary active euthanasia, and voluntary passive euthanasia are sometimes compatible with both justice and charity. But the strong condition carried in the definition of euthanasia adopted in this paper must not be forgotten; an act of euthanasia as here understood is one whose purpose is to benefit the one who dies.

In the light of this discussion let us look at our present practices. Are they good or are they bad? And what changes might be made, thinking now not only of the morality of particular acts of euthanasia but also of the indirect effects of instituting different practices, of the abuses to which they might be subject and of the changes that might come about if euthanasia became a recognized part of the social scene.

The first thing to notice is that it is wrong to ask whether we should introduce the practice of euthanasia as if it were not something we already had. In fact we do have it. For instance it is common, where the medical prognosis is very bad, for doctors to recommend against measures to prolong life, and particularly where a process of degeneration producing one medical emergency after another has already set in. If these doctors are not certainly within their legal rights this is something that is apt to come as a surprise to them as to the general public. It is also obvious that euthanasia is often practiced where old people are concerned. If someone very old and soon to die is attacked by a disease that makes his life wretched, doctors do not always come in with life-prolonging drugs. Perhaps poor patients are more fortunate in this respect than rich patients, being more often left to die in peace, but it is in any case a well-recognized piece of medical practice, which is a form of euthanasia.

No doubt the case of infants with mental or physical defects will be suggested as another example of the practice of euthanasia as we already have it, since such infants are sometimes deliberately allowed to die. That they are deliberately allowed to die is certain; children with severe spina bifida malformations are not always operated on even where it is thought that without the operation they will die; and even in the case of children with Down's Syndrome who have intestinal obstructions the relatively simple operation that would make it possible to feed them is sometimes not performed.[12] Whether this is euthanasia in our sense or only as the Nazis understood it is another matter. We must ask the crucial question, "Is it for the sake of the child himself that the doctors and parents choose his death?" In some cases the answer may really be yes, and what is more important it may really be true that the kind of life that is good is not possible or likely for this child, and that there is little but suffering and frustration in store for him.[13] But this must presuppose that the medical prognosis is wretchedly bad, as it may be for some spina bifida children. With children who are born with Down's Syndrome it is, however, quite different. Most of these are able to live on for quite a time in a reasonably contented way, remaining like children all their lives but capable of affectionate relationships and able to play games and perform simple tasks. The fact is, of course, that the doctors who recommend against life-saving procedures for handicapped infants are usually thinking not of them but rather of their parents and of other children in the family or of the "burden on society" if the children survive. So it is not for their sake but to avoid trouble to others that they are allowed to die. When brought out into the open this seems unacceptable; at least we do not easily accept the principle that adults who need special care should be counted too burdensome to be kept alive. It must in any case be insisted that if children with Down's Syndrome are deliberately allowed to die this is not a matter of euthanasia except in Hitler's sense. And for our children, since we scruple to gas them, not even the manner of their death is "quiet and easy"; when not treated for an intestinal obstruction a baby simply starves to death. Perhaps some will take this as an argument for allowing active euthanasia, in which case they will be in the company of an S.S. man stationed in the Warthgenau who sent Eichmann a memorandum telling him that "Jews in the coming winter could no longer be fed" and submitting for his consideration a proposal as to whether "it would not be the most humane solution to kill those Jews who were incapable of work through some quicker means."[14] If we say we are *unable* to look after children with handicaps we are no more telling the truth than was the S.S. man who said that the Jews could not be fed.

Nevertheless if it is ever right to allow deformed children to die because life will be a misery to them, or not to take measures to prolong for a little the life of a newborn baby whose life cannot extend beyond a few months of intense medical intervention, there is a genuine problem about active as opposed to passive euthanasia. There are well-known cases in which the medical staff has looked on wretchedly while an infant died slowly from starvation and dehydration because they did not feel able to give a lethal injection. According to the principles discussed in the earlier part of this paper they would indeed have had no right to give it, since an infant cannot ask that it should be done. The only possible solution—supposing that voluntary active euthanasia were to be legalized—would be to appoint guardians to act on the infant's behalf. In a different climate of opinion this might not be dangerous, but at present, when people so readily assume that the life of a handicapped baby is of no value, one would be loath to support it.

Finally, on the subject of handicapped children, another word should be said about those with severe mental defects. For them too it might sometimes be right to say that one would wish for death for their sake. But not even severe mental handicap automatically brings a child within the scope even of a possible act of euthanasia. If the level of consciousness is low enough it could not be said that life is good to them, any more than in the case of those suffering from extreme senility. Nevertheless if they do not suffer it will not be an act of euthanasia by which someone opts for their death. Perhaps charity does not demand that strenuous measures are taken to keep people in this state alive, but euthanasia does not come into the matter, any more than it does when someone is, like Karen Ann Quinlan, in a state of permanent coma. Much could be said about this last case. It might even be suggested that in the case of unconsciousness this "life" is not the life to which "the right to life" refers. But that is not our topic here.

What we must consider, even if only briefly, is the possibility that euthanasia, genuine euthanasia, and not contrary to the requirements of justice or charity, should be legalized over a wider area. Here we are up against the really serious problem of abuse. Many people want, and want very badly, to be rid of their elderly relatives and even of their ailing husbands or wives. Would any safeguards ever be able to stop them describing as euthanasia what was really for their own benefit? And would it be possible to prevent the occurrence of acts that were genuinely acts of euthanasia but morally impermissible because infringing the rights of a patient who wished to live?

Perhaps the furthest we should go is to encourage patients to make their own contracts with a doctor by making it known whether they wish him to prolong their life in case of painful terminal illness or of incapacity. A document such as the Living Will seems eminently sensible, and should surely be allowed to give a doctor following the previously expressed wishes of the patient immunity from legal proceedings by relatives.[15] Legalizing active euthanasia is, however, another matter. Apart from the special repugnance doctors feel towards the idea of a lethal injection, it may be of the very greatest importance to keep a psychological barrier up against killing. Moreover it is active euthanasia that is the most liable to abuse. Hitler would not have been able to kill 275,000 people in his "euthanasia" program if he had had to wait for them to need life-saving treatment. But there are other objections to active euthanasia, even voluntary active euthanasia. In the first place it would be hard to devise procedures that would protect people from being persuaded into giving their consent. Secondly, the possibility of active voluntary euthanasia might change the social scene in ways that would be very bad. As things are, people do, by and large, expect to be looked after if they are old or ill. This is one of the good things that we have, but we might lose it, and be much worse off without it. It might come to be expected that someone likely to need a lot of looking after should call for the doctor and demand his own death. Something comparable could be good in an extremely poverty-stricken community where the children genuinely suffered from lack of food, but in rich societies such as ours it would surely be a spiritual disaster. Such possibilities should make us very wary of supporting large measures of euthanasia, even where moral principle applied to the individual act does not rule it out.

Footnotes

1. Leo Alexander, "Medical Science under Dictatorship," *New England Journal of Medicine*, 14 (July 1949): 40.

2. For a discussion of culpable and nonculpable ignorance see Thomas Aquinas, *Summa Theologica*, First Part of the Second Part, Question 6, article 8, and Question 19, articles 5 and 6.

3. Dmitri Panin, *The Notebooks of Sologdin* (London, 1976), pp. 66–67.

4. David Hume, *Treatise*, Book III, Part II, Section I.

5. See, for example D.D. Raphael, "Human Rights Old and New," in D.D. Raphael, ed., *Political Theory and the Rights of Man* (London, 1967), and Joel Feinberg, "The Nature and Value of Rights," *The Journal of Value Inquiry* 4 (Winter 1970): 243–257. Reprinted in Samuel Gorovitz, ed., *Moral Problems in Medicine* (Englewood Cliffs, NJ, 1976).

6. Feinberg, "Human Rights," *Moral Problems in Medicine*, p. 465.

7. See, for example, James Rachels, "Active and Passive Euthanasia," *New England Journal of Medicine* 292 (9 Jan. 1975): 78–80.

8. Ibid.

9. It is not, however, that justice and charity conflict. A man does not lack charity because he refrains from an act of injustice that would have been for someone's good.

10. For a discussion of such questions, see my article "The Problem of Abortion and the Doctrine of Double Effect," *Oxford Review*, no. 5 (1967); reprinted in Rachels, *Moral Problems*, and Gorovitz, *Moral Problems in Medicine*.

11. George Fletcher, "Legal Aspects of the Decision Not to Prolong Life," *Journal of the American Medical Association* 203 (1 Jan. 1968): 119–122. Reprinted in Gorovitz.

12. I have been told this by a pediatrician in a well-known medical center in the United States. It is confirmed by Anthony M. Shaw and Iris A. Shaw, "Dilemma of Informed Consent in Children," *The New England Journal of Medicine* 289 (25 Oct. 1973): 885–890. Reprinted in Gorovitz.

13. It must be remembered, however, that many of the social miseries of spina bifida children could be avoided. Professor R.B. Zachary is surely right to insist on this. See, for example, "Ethical and Social Aspects of Spina Bifida," *The Lancet*, 3 (Aug. 1968): 274–276. Reprinted in Gorovitz.

14. Quoted by Hannah Arendt, *Eichmann in Jerusalem* (London, 1963), p. 90.

15. Details of this document are to be found in J.A. Behnke and Sissela Bok, eds., *The Dilemmas of Euthanasia* (New York, 1975), and in A.B. Downing, ed., *Euthanasia and the Right to Life: The Case for Voluntary Euthanasia* (London, 1969).

Review Questions

1. How does the dictionary define the word "euthanasia?"
2. How is the word usually understood?
3. How does Foot propose to use the word?
4. What are the "two grounds of objection to inducing death?"
5. Distinguish between rights as liberties and rights as claims.
6. Is the right to life a liberty right or a claim right?
7. How does Foot distinguish between active and passive euthanasia?
8. Why doesn't she accept Rachels' view?
9. What limits does the right to life put on permissible acts of euthanasia?
10. Explain Foot's conclusions.

Discussion Questions

1. Is Foot's distinction between active and passive euthanasia acceptable or not? Why, or why not?
2. In what cases, if any, is nonvoluntary active euthanasia justified?
3. In what cases, if any, is nonvoluntary passive euthanasia *not* justified?
4. Should active euthanasia be legalized? Defend your position.

RICHARD B. BRANDT

Defective Newborns and the Morality of Termination

From *Infanticide and the Value of Life*, ed. by Marvin Kohl (Prometheus Books, 1978). Reprinted with permission.

Richard B. Brandt is Professor of Philosophy at the University of Michigan. His most recent book on ethics is A Theory of the Good and the Right (1979).

Brandt argues that it is morally right to actively or passively terminate the life of a defective newborn if its life is bad according to a "happiness" criterion. Consent is irrelevant; the infant cannot give consent, and it will be indifferent to continued life. But the cost of caring for the infant is relevant to the decision to terminate in addition to the quality of the prospective life.

The *legal* rights of a fetus are very different from those of a newborn. The fetus may be aborted, legally, for any reason or no reason up to twenty-four or twenty-eight weeks (U.S. Supreme Court, *Roe v. Wade*). But, at least in theory, immediately after birth an infant has all the legal rights of the adult, including the right to life.

The topic of this paper, however, is to identify the moral rights of the newborn, specifically whether *defective* newborns have a right to life. But it is simpler to talk, not about "rights to life," but about when or whether it is *morally right* either actively or passively (by withdrawal of life-supportive measures) to terminate defective newborns. It is also better because the conception of a right involves the notion of a sphere of autonomy—something is to be done or omitted, but only if the subject of the rights wants or consents—and this fact is apt to be confusing or oversimplifying. Surely what we want to know is whether termination is morally right or wrong, and nothing can turn on the semantics of the concept of a "right."[1]

What does one have to do in order to support some answers to these questions? One thing we can do is ask—and I think myself that the answer to this question is definitive for our purposes—whether rational or fully informed persons would, in view of the total consequences, support a moral code for a society in which they expected to live, with one or another, provision on this matter. (I believe a fully rational person will at least normally have some degree of benevolence, or positive interest in the welfare or happiness of others; I shall not attempt to specify how much.) Since, however, I do not expect that everyone else will agree that answering this question would show what is morally right, I shall, for their benefit, also argue that certain moral principles on this matter are coherent with strong moral convictions of reflective people; or, to use Rawls's terminology, that a certain principle on the matter would belong to a system of moral principles in "reflective equilibrium."

Historically, many writers, including Pope Pius XI in *Casti Connubii* (1930), have affirmed an absolute prohibition against killing anyone who is neither guilty of a capital crime nor an unjust assailant threatening one's life (self-defense), except in case of "extreme necessity." Presumably the prohibition is intended to include withholding of food or liquid from a newborn, although strictly speaking this is only *failing* to do something, not actually *doing* something to bring about a death. (Would writers in this tradition demand, on moral grounds, that complicated and expensive surgery be undertaken to save a life? Such surgery is going beyond normal care, and in some cases beyond what earlier writers even conceived.) However the intentions of these writers may be, we should observe that historically their moral condemnation of all killing (except for the cases mentioned) derives from the Biblical injunction, "Thou shalt not kill," which, as it stands and without interpretation, may be taken to forbid suicide, killing of animals, perhaps even plants, and hence cannot be taken seriously.

Presumably a moral code that is coherent with our intuitions and that rational persons would support for their society would include some prohibition of killing, but it is another matter to identify the exact class to which such a prohibition is to apply. For one thing, I would doubt that killing one's self would be included—although one might be forbidden to kill one's self if that would work severe hardship on others, or conflict with the discharge of one's other moral obligations. And, possibly, defective newborns would *not* be included in the class. Further, a decision has to be made whether the prohibition of killing is *absolute* or only *prima facie*, meaning by "prima facie" that the duty not to kill might be outweighed by some other duty (or right) stronger in the circumstances, which could be fulfilled only by killing. In case this distinction is made, we would have to decide whether defective newborns fall within the scope of even a prima facie moral prohibition against killing. I shall, however, not attempt to make this fine distinction here, and shall simply inquire whether, everything considered, defective newborns—or some identifiable group of them—are excluded from the moral prohibition against killing.

THE PROSPECTIVE QUALITY OF LIFE OF DEFECTIVE NEWBORNS

Suppose that killing a defective newborn, or allowing it to die, would not be an *injury,*

but would rather be doing the infant a favor. In that case we should feel intuitively less opposed to termination of newborns, and presumably rational persons would be less inclined to support a moral code with a prohibition against such action. In that case we would feel rather as we do about a person's preventing a suicide attempt from being successful, in order that the person be elaborately tortured to death at a later stage. It is no favor to the prospective suicide to save his life; similarly, if the prospective life of defective newborns is bad we are doing them a favor to let them die.

It may be said that we have no way of knowing what the conscious experiences of defective children are like, and that we have no competence in any case to decide when or what kind of life is bad or not worth living. Further, it may be said that predictions about a defective newborn's prospects for the future are precarious, in view of possible further advances of medicine. It does seem, however, that here, as everywhere, the rational person will follow the evidence about the present or future facts. But there is a question how to decide whether a life is bad or not worth living.

In the case of *some* defective newborns, it seems clear that their prospective life is bad. Suppose, as sometimes happens, a child is hydrocephalic with an extremely low I.Q., is blind and deaf, has no control over its body, can only lie on its back all day and have all its needs taken care of by others, and even cries out with pain when it is touched or lifted. Infants born with spina bifida—and these number over two per one thousand births—are normally not quite so badly off, but are often nearly so.

But what criterion are we using if we say that such a life is bad? One criterion might be called a "happiness" criterion. If a person *likes* a moment of experience while he is having it, his life is so far good; if a person *dislikes* a moment of experience while he is having it, his life is so far bad. Based on such reactions, we might construct a "happiness curve" for a person, going up above the indifference axis when a moment of experience is liked—and how far above depending on how strongly it is liked—and dipping down below the line when a moment is disliked. Then this criterion would say that a life is worth living if there is a net balance of positive area under the curve over a lifetime, and that it is bad if there is a net balance of negative area. One might adopt some different criterion: for instance, one might say that a life is worth living if a person would *want* to live it over again given that, at the end, he could remember the whole of it with perfect vividness in some kind of grand intuitive awareness. Such a response to this hypothetical holistic intuition, however, would likely be affected by the state of the person's drives or moods at the time, and the conception strikes me as unconvincing, compared with the moment-by-moment reaction to what is going on. Let us, for the sake of the argument, adopt the happiness criterion.[2]

Is the prospective life of the seriously defective newborn, like the one described above, bad or good according to this criterion? One thing seems clear: that it is *less* good than is the prospective life of a normal infant. But is it bad?

We have to do some extrapolating from what we know. For instance, such a child will presumably suffer from severe sensory deprivation; he is simply not getting interesting stimuli. On the basis of laboratory data, it is plausible to think the child's experience is at best boring or uncomfortable. If the child's experience is painful, of course, its moments are, so far, on the negative side. One must suppose that such a child hardly suffers from disappointment, since it will not learn to expect anything exciting, beyond being fed and fondled, and these events will be regularly forthcoming. One might expect such a child to suffer from isolation and loneliness, but insofar as this is true, the object of dislike probably should be classified as just sensory deprivation; dislike of loneliness seems to depend on the deprivation of past pleasures of human company.

There are also some positive enjoyments: of eating, drinking, elimination, seeing the nurse coming with food, and so on. But the brief enjoyments can hardly balance the long stretches of boredom, discomfort, or even pain. On the whole, the lives of such children are bad according to the happiness criterion.

Naturally we cannot generalize about the cases of all "defective" newborns; there are all sorts of defects, and the cases I have described are about the worst. A child with spina bifida may, if he survives the numerous operations, I suppose, adjust to the frustrations of immobility; he may become accustomed to the embarrassments of no bladder or bowel control; he may have some intellectual enjoyments like playing chess; he will suffer from observing what others have but he cannot, such as sexual satisfactions, in addition to the pain of repeated surgery. How does it all balance out? Surely not as very good, but perhaps above the indifference level.

It may fairly be said, I think, that the lives of some defective newborns are destined to be bad on the whole, and it would be a favor to them if their lives were terminated. Contrariwise, the prospective lives of many defective newborns are modestly pleasant, and it would be some injury to them to be terminated, albeit the lives they will live are ones some of us would prefer not to live at all.

CONSENT

Let us now make a second suggestion, not this time that termination of a defective newborn would be doing him a favor, but this time that he *consents* to termination, in the sense of expressing a rational deliberated preference for this. In that case I suggest that intuitively we would be *more* favorably inclined to judge that it is right to let the defective die, and I suggest also that for that case rational persons would be more ready to support a moral code permitting termination. Notice that we think that if an ill person has signified what we think a rational and deliberated desire to die, we are morally better justified in withdrawing life-supporting measures than we otherwise would be.

The newborn, however, is incapable of expressing his preference (giving consent) at all, much less expressing a rational deliberated preference.   There could in theory be court-appointed guardians or proxies, presumably disinterested parties, authorized to give such consent on his behalf, but even so this would not be *his* consent.

Nevertheless, there is a fact about the mental life of the newborn (defective or not) such that, if he could understand the fact, it seems he would not object—even rationally or after deliberation, if that were possible—to his life being terminated, or to his parents substituting another child in his place.   This suggestion may seem absurd, but let us see.   The explanation runs along the lines of an argument I once used to support the morality of abortion.   I quote the paragraph in which this argument was introduced.[3]

Suppose I were seriously ill, and were told that, for a sizeable fee, an operation to save "my life" could be performed, of the following sort: my brain would be removed to another body which could provide a normal life, but the unfortunate result of the operation would be that my memory and learned abilities would be wholly erased, and that the forming of memory brain traces must begin again from scratch, as in a newborn baby. Now, how large a fee would I be willing to pay for this operation, when the alternative is my peaceful demise? My own answer would be: None at all. I would take no interest in the continued existence of "myself" in that sense, and I would rather add the sizeable fee to the inheritance of my children. . . . I cannot see the point of forfeiting my children's inheritance in order to start off a person who is brand new except that he happens to enjoy the benefit of having my present brain, without the memory traces. It appears that some continuity of memory is a necessary condition for personal identity in an important sense.

My argument was that the position of a fetus, at the end of the first trimester, is essentially the same as that of the person

contemplating this operation: he will consider that the baby born after six more months will not be *he* in any *important* and *motivating* sense (there will be no continuity of memory, and, indeed, maybe nothing to have been remembered), and the later existence of this baby, in a sense bodily continuous with his present body, would be a matter of indifference to him.   So, I argued, nothing is being done to the fetus that he would object to having done if he understood the situation.

What do I think is necessary in order for the continuation of my body with its conscious experiences to be worthwhile?   One thing is that it is able to remember the events I can now remember; another is that it takes some interest in the projects I am now planning and remembers them as my projects; another is that it recognizes my friends and has warm feelings for them, and so on.   Reflection on these states of a future continuation of my body with its experiences is what makes the idea motivating. But such motivating reflection for a newborn is impossible: he has no memories that he wants recalled later; he has no plans to execute; he has no warm feelings for other persons.   He has simply not had the length of life necessary for these to come about. Not only that: the conception of these things cannot be motivating because the concept of some state of affairs being motivating requires roughly a past experience in which similar states of affairs were satisfying, and he has not lived long enough for the requisite conditioning to have taken place.   (The most one could say is that the image of warm milk in his mouth is attractive; he might answer affirmatively if it could be put to him whether he would be aversive to the idea of no more warm milk.)   So we can say not merely that the newborn does not want the continuation of himself as a subject of experiences (he has not the conceptual framework for this), he does not want *any-thing* that his own survival would promote. It is like the case of the operation: there is nothing I want that the survival of my brain with no memory would promote. Give the newborn as much *conceptual* framework as you like; the *wants* are not there, which could give significance to the continuance of his life.

The newborn, then, is bound to be *indifferent* to the idea of a continuation of the stream of his experiences, even if he clearly has the idea of that. It seems we can *know* this about him.

The truth of all this is still not for it to be the case that the newborn, defective or not, gives *consent* to, or expresses a preference for, the termination of his life. *Consent* is a performance, normally linguistic, but always requiring some conventional *sign*. A newborn, who has not yet learned how to signalize consent, cannot give consent. And it may be thought that this difference makes all the difference.

In order to see what difference it does make in this case, we should ask what makes adult consent morally important. Why is it that we think euthanasia can be practiced on an adult only if he gives his consent, at least his implied consent (e.g., by previous statements)? There seem to be two reasons. The first is that a person is more likely to be concerned with his own welfare, and to take steps to secure it, than are others, even his good friends. Giving an individual control over his own life, and not permitting others to take control except when he consents, is normally to promote his welfare. An individual may, of course, behave stupidly or shortsightedly, but we think that on the whole a person's welfare is best secured if decisions about it are in his hands; and it is best for society in the normal case (not for criminals, etc.) if persons' own lives are well-served. The second reason is the feeling of security a person can have if he knows the major decisions about himself are in his own hands. When they are not, a person can easily, and in some cases very reasonably, suppose that other persons may well be able to do something to him that he would very much like them not to do. He does not have to worry about that

if he knows they cannot do it without his consent.

Are things different with the newborn? At least he, like the fetus, is not yet able to suffer from insecurity; he cannot worry about what others may do to him. So the second reason for requiring consent cannot have any importance in his case. His situation is thus very unlike that of the senile adult, for an adult can worry about what others may do to him if they judge him senile. And this worry can well cast a shadow over a lot of life. But how about the first reason? Here matters are more complex. In the case of children, we think their own lives are better cared for if certain decisions are in the hands of others; the child may not want to visit the dentist, but the parents know that his best interests are served by going, and they make him go. The same for compulsory school attendance. And the same for the newborn. But there is another point: that society has an interest, at certain crucial points, that may not be served by doing just exactly what is for the lifelong interest of the newborn. There are huge costs that are relevant, in the case of the defective newborn. I shall go into that problem in a moment. It seems, then, that in the case of the newborn, *consent* cannot have the moral importance that it has in the case of adults.

On the other hand, then, the newborn will not *care* whether his life is terminated, even if he understands his situation perfectly; and, on the other hand, consent does not have the moral importance in his case that it has for adults. So, while it seems true that we would feel better about permitting termination of defective newborns if only they could give rational and deliberated consent and gave it, nevertheless when we bear the foregoing two points in mind, the absence of consent does not seem morally crucial in their case. We can understand why rational persons deciding which moral code to support for their society would not make the giving of consent a necessary condition for feeling free to terminate an infant's life when such action was morally indicated by the other features of the situation.

REPLACEMENT IN ORDER
TO GET A BETTER LIFE

Let us now think of an example owing to Derek Parfit. Suppose a woman wants a child, but is told that if she conceives a child now it will be defective, whereas if she waits three months she will produce a normal child. Obviously we think it would be wrong for the mother not to delay. (If she delays, the child she will have is not the *same* child as the one she would have had if she had not delayed, but it will have a better life.) This is the sole reason why we think she should delay and have the later-born child.

Suppose, however, a woman conceives but discovers only three months later that the fetus will become a defective child, but that she can have a normal child if she has an abortion and tries again. Now this time there is still the same reason for having the abortion that there formerly was for the delay: that she will produce a child with a better life. Ought she not then to have the abortion? If the child's life is bad, he could well complain that he had been injured by deliberately being brought to term. Would he complain if he were aborted, in favor of the later normal child? Not if the argument of the preceding section is correct.

But now suppose the woman does not discover until after she gives birth, that the child is severely defective, but that she could conceive again and have a normal child. Are things really different, in the first few days? One might think that a benevolent person would want, in each of these cases, the substitution of a normal child for the defective one, of the better life for the worse one.

THE COST AND ITS RELEVANCE

It is agreed that the burden of care for a defective infant, say one born with spina bifida, is huge. The cost of surgery alone for an infant with spina bifida has been estimated to be around $275,000.[4] In many places this cost must be met by the family of the child, and there is the additional cost of care in an institution, if the child's condition does not permit care at home—and a very modest estimate of the monthly cost at present is $1,100. To meet even the surgical costs, not to mention monthly payments for continuing care, the lives of members of the family must be at a most spartan level for many years. The psychological effects of this, and equally, if not more so, of care provided at home, are far-reaching; they are apt to destroy the marriage and to cause psychological problems for the siblings. There is the on-going anxiety, the regular visits, the continuing presence of a caretaker if the child is in the home. In one way or another the continued existence of the child is apt to reduce dramatically the quality of life of the family as a whole.

It can be and has been argued that such costs, while real, are irrelevant to the moral problem of what should be done.[5] It is obvious, however, that rational persons, when deciding which moral code to support, would take these human costs into account. As indeed they should: the parents and siblings are also human beings with lives to live, and any sacrifices a given law or moral system might call on them to make must be taken into account in deciding between laws and moral codes. Everyone will feel sympathy for a helpless newborn; but everyone should also think, equally vividly, of all the others who will suffer and just how they will suffer—and, of course, as indicated above, of just what kind of life the defective newborn will have in any case. There is a choice here between allowing a newborn to die (possibly a favor to it, and in any case not a serious loss), and imposing a very heavy burden on the family for many years to come.

Philosophers who think the cost to others is irrelevant to what should be done should reflect that we do not accept the general principle that lives should be saved at no matter what cost. For instance, ships are deliberately built with only a certain margin of safety; that could be built so that they would hardly sink in any storm, but to do so would be economically unfeasible. We do not think we should require a standard of safety for automobiles that goes beyond a certain point of expense and inconvenience; we are prepared to risk a few extra deaths. And how about the lives we are willing to lose in war, in order to assure a certain kind of economic order or democracy or free speech? Surely there is a point at which the loss of a life (or the abbreviation of a life) and the cost to others become comparable. Is it obvious that the continuation of a marginal kind of life for a child takes moral precedence over providing a college education for one or more of his siblings? Some comparisons will be hard to make, but continuing even a marginally pleasant life hardly has absolute priority.

DRAWING LINES

There are two questions that must be answered in any complete account of what is the morally right thing to do about defective newborns.

The first is: If a decision to terminate is made, how soon must it be made? Obviously it could not be postponed to the age of five, or of three, or even a year and a half. At those ages, all the reasons for insisting on consent are already cogent. And at those ages, the child will already care what happens to him. But ten days is tolerable. Doubtless advances in medicine will permit detection of serious prospective defects early in pregnancy, and this issue of how many days will not arise.

Second, the argument from the quality of the prospective life of the defective newborn

requires that we decide which defects are so serious that the kind of life the defective child can have gives it no serious claim as compared with the social costs. This issue must be thought through, and some guidelines established, but I shall not attempt this here.

One might argue that, if the newborn cannot rationally care whether its life ends or not, the parents are free to dispose of a child irrespective of whether he is defective, if they simply do not want it. To this there are two replies. First, in practice there are others who want a child if the parents do not, and they can put it up for adoption. But second, the parents are *injuring* a child if they prevent it from having the good life it could have had. We do not in general accept the argument that a person is free to injure another, for no reason, even if he has that person's consent. In view of these facts, we may expect that rational, benevolent persons deciding which moral code to support would select one that required respect for the life of a normal child, but would permit the termination of the life of a seriously defective child.

ACTIVE AND PASSIVE PROCEDURES

There is a final question: that of a choice between withdrawal of life-supporting measures (such as feeding), and the active, painless taking of life. It seems obvious, however, that once the basic decision is made that an infant is not to receive the treatment necessary to sustain life beyond a few days, it is mere stupid cruelty to allow it to waste away gradually in a hospital bed—for the child to suffer, and for everyone involved also to suffer in watching the child suffer. If death is the outcome decided upon, it is far kinder for it to come quickly and painlessly.

Footnotes

1. Here I disagree with Michael Tooley, "Abortion and Infanticide," *Philosophy and Public Affairs* 2 (1972): 37–65, especially pp. 44–49.

2. Professor P. Foot has made interesting remarks on when a life is worth living. See her "Euthanasia," *Philosophy and Public Affairs*, 6 (1977): 85–112, especially pp. 95–96. She suggests that a good life must "contain a minimum of basic goods," although not necessarily a favorable balance of good over evil elements. When does she think this minimum fails? For one thing, in extreme senility or severe brain damage. She also cites as examples of conditions for minimal goods that "a man is not driven to work far beyond his capacity; that he has the support of a family or community; that he can more or less satisfy his hunger; that he has hopes for the future; that he can lie down to rest at night." Overwhelming pain or nausea, or crippling depression, she says, also can make life not worth living. All of these, of course, except for cases of senility and brain damage, are factors fixing whether stretches of living are highly unpleasant.

If a person thinks that life is not good unless it realizes certain human potentialities, he will think life can be bad even if liked—and so far sets a higher standard than the happiness criterion. But Foot and such writers may say that even when life is not pleasant on balance, it can still be good if human potentialities are being realized or these basic minimal conditions are met; and in that sense they set a lower standard.

3. Richard B. Brandt, "The Morality of Abortion," in an earlier form in *The Monist* 56 (1972): 504–526, and in revised form in R.L. Perkins, ed., *Abortion: Pro and Con* (Cambridge, MA: Schenkman Publishing Co., 1974).

4. See A.M. Shaw and I.A. Shaw, in S. Gorovitz, et al., *Moral Problems in Medicine* (Englewood Cliffs, NJ: Prentice-Hall, Inc., 1976), pp. 335–341.

5. See, for instance, Philippa Foot, "Euthanasia," especially pp. 109–111. She writes: "So it is not for their sake but to avoid trouble to others that they are allowed to die. When brought out into the open this seems unacceptable; at least we do not easily accept the principle that adults who need special care should be counted too burdensome to be kept alive." I would think that "to avoid trouble to others" is hardly the terminology to describe the havoc that is apt to be produced. I agree that adults should not be allowed to die, or actively killed, without their consent, possibly except when they cannot give consent but are in great pain; but the reasons that justify different behavior in the two situations have appeared in the section, "Consent."

Review Questions

1. Why does Brandt think it is better to *not* to talk about rights (contra Foot) when discussing the termination of defective newborns?

2. According to Brandt, how should one answer questions about moral rightness?

3. Why can't the Biblical injunction "Thou shalt not kill" be taken seriously?

4. Distinguish between absolute and prima facie duty.

5. Explain the "happiness" criterion.

6. In what cases would the life of a defective infant be bad?

7. Why would a newborn be indifferent to continued life according to Brandt?

8. Why is it better to replace a defective child with a normal one?

9. Why is active euthanasia better than passive euthanasia?

Discussion Questions

1. Is Brandt's "happiness" criterion acceptable or not? Defend your view.

2. Is the cost of caring for a defective infant morally relevant? Defend your position.

3. Do you agree that active euthanasia is better than passive euthanasia? Why, or why not?

Problem Cases

1. (This case was reported in *The New York Times*, November 6, 1973.) George Zygmaniak was injured in a motorcycle accident. At the hospital he was found to be totally paralyzed from the neck down. He could talk, but he was in considerable pain. His chances of recovery were nil. He told his doctor and his brother, Lester, that he did not want to live, and begged them to kill him. Later Lester smuggled a gun into the hospital, went to his brother's room, and asked him if he was sure that he wanted to be killed. After his brother nodded affirmatively (he could not talk because of an operation to help his breathing), Lester shot him through the temple, killing him instantly. Did Lester do the morally correct thing or not? Defend your answer.

2. Sally is a surrogate mother, that is, she is being paid $5,000 to have a child. One of the conditions of her contract with the father who is paying her is that the child be normal. Other-

wise, the father pays the medical expenses only. Unfortunately at birth the child turns out to have spina bifida, a defect in the spine causing paralysis in the lower limbs. The child also has hydrocephaly, a condition where excess fluid accumulates in the skull causing brain damage. Sally does not want the child, and neither does the father. No one is likely to adopt it. The doctor agrees to not perform the operation required to drain the fluid from the skull. This means that the child will die in a matter of days. The doctor's failure to perform the operation (the installation of a tube to drain the fluid from the skull) is perfectly legal, and is allowed by the AMA. Is this "passive euthanasia" morally right or not? Defend your answer. Would it make any difference from the moral point of view if the doctor killed the child with a fatal injection? Explain your answer.

Suggested Readings

Englehardt, H. Tristram, Jr. "Ethical Issues in Aiding the Death of Young Children." In Marvin Kohl, ed., *Beneficent Euthanasia.* Buffalo, NY: Prometheus Books, 1975, pp. 180–192.

Glover, Jonathan. *Causing Death and Saving Lives.* Harmondsworth, Middlesex, England: Penguin Books, Ltd., 1977, pp. 182–189.

Rachels, James. "Active and Passive Euthanasia," *The New England Journal of Medicine* 292 (January 9, 1975): 78–80.

———. "More Impertinent Distinctions." In T.A. Mappes and J.S. Zembaty, eds., *Biomedical Ethics.* New York: McGraw-Hill, Inc., 1981, pp. 355–359.

Sullivan, Thomas D. "Active and Passive Euthanasia: An Impertinent Distinction?" *Human Life Review* III (Summer 1977): 40–46.

CHAPTER 3

Hunger and Starvation

Basic Concepts

The World Health Organization conservatively estimates that there are ten million children under five in the world who are chronically malnourished. If these children survive at all, they will suffer lasting effects—stunted growth and brain damage from lack of protein. In addition, if we calculate from the ratio of children to adults in the world, we get a total of about seventy million chronically malnourished people in the world. Most of these people are not in the U.S., but in the subcontinent (India, Pakistan, and Bangladesh), and in poor nations of the Caribbean, Latin America, Southeast Asia, and Africa.

It is theoretically possible for the U.S. and other rich nations to feed the world's hungry people. But to determine the amount of aid actually required to do this, we need to know how many people need food, their nutritional requirements, how distribution can be made, what population growth will be, and other facts relevant to the problem. According to Nick Eberstadt, there are no accurate figures in these areas. If there are more than a billion people to be fed, as the Overseas Development Council claims, then perhaps the task is hopeless. But if there are only seventy million people to feed (this is Eberstadt's estimate), which is less than two percent of the world's population, then food relief and development projects are a manageable undertaking, given some international cooperation. According to Eberstadt, enough food is produced each year to feed everyone comfortably: If 1.3 billion tons of grain are produced each year, and one person needs 500 pounds, then 5.2 billion people could be fed, and this is more than the highest estimates for the world's population.

On Eberstadt's view, the reason that people starve is not because there is not enough food, but because rich nations (e.g., the U.S., Russia, European countries, and Japan) con-

sume seventy percent more protein than the rest of the world. They do this by consuming grain indirectly via feedstocks converted into animal protein rather than directly in the form of bread, noodles, rice, and so on. In other words, the problem is the result of unequal food distribution rather than inadequate food production.

MORAL ISSUES

But do rich nations have any moral obligation to help poor ones? A common view, expressed by Foot and others who distinguish between killing and letting die, is that we have a negative duty to not kill people, but not a positive duty to prevent people from dying of starvation. As we have seen in the last chapter, however, the distinction between killing and letting die is problematic. Rachels denies that this distinction has any moral relevance to euthanasia, and he takes the same line on starvation. His view is that letting people die from starvation is just as bad as killing them. He tries to convince us of this with an example: Suppose there is a starving child in the room right now, and you have a sandwich you don't need. Wouldn't you be a "moral monster" if you allowed her to die? But is there any morally relevant difference between this case and the case of the millions of people who are starving right now? Rachels discusses some possible differences such as spatial location, the number of people, "dischargeability," the action/inaction distinction, and "optionality" and he finds that none of these differences have any moral significance. He concludes that we have no good reason for not giving money to support famine relief efforts.

At this point it will be objected that starving people do not have any right to be fed—they do not have any claim against us such that we must help them. Our duty to help them is merely optional; helping others is an act of charity that is morally praiseworthy, but not morally required. Against this, Henry Shue and others contend that the millions of malnourished children and adults in the world who cannot provide for themselves have a welfare right to subsistence. This right includes not just a right to adequate food, but also to air, water, clothing, shelter, and minimum health care. This right, along with the right to security, is basic in that it must be fulfilled before any other rights can be enjoyed.

Shue thinks that rich nations (those with a gross domestic product per capita of U.S. $400 or more) should transfer food or money to the poor nations. They could do this, he claims, without impoverishing themselves or even causing a decline in their growth rate. Garrett Hardin raises objections to such welfare-style transfers from rich nations to poor ones. In his view, nations are lifeboats with limited carrying capacity; they cannot afford to feed poor nations. Besides, aid to poor nations just makes matters worse—the result is a vicious cycle of more overpopulation, more starvation, more aid, and so on until there is ecological disaster. The implication is that we should let people in poor nations die.

Onora O'Neill does not agree. She assumes that people have a right not to be killed and a corresponding duty not to kill. This duty not to kill, she argues, implies that we have a moral obligation to try to prevent and postpone death from malnutrition and starvation. To persuade us of this, she uses a hypothetical lifeboat example: If five persons on a well-equipped lifeboat withhold food from a sixth person, who consequently dies, they would be violating the sixth person's right not to be killed unjustifiably. Similarly, if rich people on the well-equipped lifeboat Earth withhold food from poor people so that they die, then the rich people are violating the rights of the poor people, and particularly their right not to be killed unjustifiably. O'Neill concludes that if we take the right not to be killed seriously, we ought to support famine relief policies, and also population policies that reduce overpopulation and appropriate resource policies.

NICK EBERSTADT

Myths of the Food Crisis

Nick Eberstadt teaches at the Center for Population Studies at Harvard University.

Eberstadt argues that the cause of starvation today is not overpopulation, but inequality. But this inequality cannot be eliminated by welfare-style transfers of income. Instead the productivity of the world's poor must be improved.

How little we know about the world food problem is frightening. There are really no accurate figures on food production for any poor country; the margin of error in the estimate for India alone could feed or starve twelve million people. Nutritionists' estimates of the "average" daily adult protein requirement have ranged from 20 grams a day to over 120. Perhaps most astonishing, we do not know the world's population within 400 million people. In short, we do not know how much food there is, how much food people need, or even how many people there are.

If we wish to help the world's poor, a question that naturally arises is: whom should we listen to for our information and advice? The sad answer seems to be that almost all our sources are inaccurate and unreliable. Because of the death of information and the high stakes involved (literally, control over millions of lives), this field has produced a litter of instant experts, who demonstrate an aggressive, arrogance in situations requiring humility and caution. Their "facts" are often half true, sometimes entirely false; their judgments tend to be sweeping, majestic, and impossible to stand by for more than a year.

Thus Lester Brown, a popular food guru who is frequently quoted in *Give Us This Day* . . ., writes in 1971 that the Green Revolution of high-yielding seeds and increased agricultural inputs (pesticides, fertilizer, irrigation) is "likely to be a greater force for change than any technology or ideology ever introduced into the poor countries." [1] By 1973 Brown finds that the Green Revolution is an "opportunity lost," [2] too heavily dependent on high-priced items, enriching rich farmers while impoverishing poor ones. Similarly, other experts pronounce either that we have vanquished hunger or are doomed to live in an age of scarcity, depending on how the next six months of crops look.

Almost invariably, the flashiest, most arrogant, and most inaccurate of our various food informants teach and advise the public. There is a reason for this, and it has to do with the realities of big business and the nature of journalism. Like steel or computers, news is an industry, and it must subordinate the quality of its product to its promotion. A million people starving is better business for the press than a thousand people starving, but a billion people starving is best of all! Here the interests of the instant experts and the press dovetail: the expert

gives an outrageous quote (last year one man predicted fifty million Indians might starve in 1975) and gets his name promoted, the press publishes a horror story and sells news. This is the Catch-22 of food reporting: if you read prognostications, they are probably not worth taking seriously for the very reasons that got them into the papers.

The misinformation network promoting the food crisis is more than intellectually unpleasant. Because the network "informs" the rich world, and the rich world so often makes crucial decisions over lives in the poor world, news about food can be an outright threat to many of the world's poorest people. Bangladesh is a case in point. The cameramen who photograph those living corpses for your evening consumption work hard to evoke a nation of unrecognizable monsters starving by the roadside. Unless you have been there, you would find it hard to imagine that the people of Bangladesh are friendly and energetic, and perhaps ninety-five percent of them eat enough to get by. Or that Bangladesh has the richest cropland in the world, and that a well-guided aid program could help turn it from a famine center into one of the world's great breadbaskets. To most people in America the situation must look hopeless and our involvement, therefore, pointless. If the situation is so bad, why shouldn't we cut off our food and foreign aid to Bangladesh, and use it to save people who aren't going to die anyhow? So *The New York Times* literally holds lives in its hands.

And how does it treat them? If *Give Us This Day* . . . is any indication, clumsily. This series of *Times* articles on famine, food production, and the 1974 Rome Food Conference, which has been slapped together into a book, is not even one of the more objectionable books on the food problem; nevertheless its analysis is shallow and its statements frequently inaccurate. By comparing it with one of the most sensitive and accurate publications on food in recent years, an issue of *Science* magazine that has just been turned into a book, we can perhaps see how serious are the fallacies behind some of the food myths we accept daily as fact.

MYTHS FROM 1972

Give Us This Day . . . has two spectacular conclusions about the food crisis of June 1972—June 1973. First, a cooling trend in weather is causing crop failures. Besides making much of our northern cropland unusable, this meteorological aberration might destroy future crops in more temperate zones by playing havoc with the winds and rains. Second, the explosive price increases for food are proof that we have entered an age of permanent food shortage, in which demand will be inexorably driven ahead of supply by affluence in the rich world and population in the poor. Luckily for all of us who must eat, this analysis is superficial and inaccurate.

It is true that we have been blessed by unusually mild weather in the last twenty years, and that a well-known meteorologist, Reid Bryson, has guessed the odds against its continuing another twenty to be about 10,-000 to one. But as Louis Thompson points out in the *Science* collection, "weather variability is a much more important consideration in grain production than a cooling trend." Crop yields could actually be higher with slightly cooler weather; "it is when weather variability [is highest] that yields are lowest. Even if the weather does trend toward the coolness of a century ago, yields will not be significantly reduced unless weather becomes more variable."

There are, moreover, few signs that we are entering an age of permanent food scarcity. Quite the opposite: as food prices rose, so did investment and production, and prices then fell. All things considered, the world market exhibited surprisingly flexible and rapid response to a sudden stimulus.

There was a time, not so long ago, when the poor perished en masse if grain prices went wild. The world is different today: social conditions in the poor world and grain prices in the international marketplace seldom correlate, for the grain market is dominated by the rich world, which has the money to buy. During 1972 and 1973, corn, wheat, rice, and soybeans all more than doubled their 1971 prices; four new famines struck in 1972 (Philippines, Burundi, Nicaragua, Sudan), while fifteen had occurred in 1971.

Americans may have assumed famine was striking down the rest of the world during the "food shortage" because for the first time in twenty years *their* food prices were rising faster than their cost of living. But the immediate cause of the rise was a huge grain purchase not by the starving but by Russia, which had committed itself to raising meat consumption, and had fallen short of feedstocks. India never could have made this kind of purchase: it would have cost three percent of its gross national product, almost twenty-five percent of its annual government revenue. As Jean Mayer notes sadly in "Management of Famine Relief" in the *Science* collection, "There has been a serious famine somewhere practically every year since the end of World War II," and these tragedies are likely to recur in the future. But they are also likely to have little bearing on the price we pay for bread and steak.

What did the "food shortage" of 1972–1973 prove? It showed how heartless administrators can become when humanitarianism is no longer to their advantage. Three years ago fifty percent of the American food shipped to the poor world was aid; last year the proportion was fifteen percent.[3] During the 1960s we had been trying quite literally, to *give* our surpluses away; for years America had been producing more food than it could get rid of. It saw its stockpiles as a liability that cost half a billion dollars a year to maintain.

What to America was a liability, however, was for the grain-buying nations (practically the rest of the world) protection against widespread hunger in the event of a disaster. In 1961 world grain reserves could feed the entire earth for ninety-five days. As America happily depleted its stockpiles, the figure fell steadily; in 1974 it was twenty-seven days. The grain market is volatile, poorly supervised, and thin (only about twenty percent of the world's wheat and three percent of its rice is sold internationally), and the thinner it gets, the more pronounced the dislocations when they hit. Unless concern for humanity, the profit motive, or some combination of the two moves America to build up its stockpiles, dislocations are likely to recur. It must be stressed, however, that these dislocations are caused by bureaucratic shortcomings and market imperfections, not by inexorable trends.

MALNUTRITION MYTHS

Every bureaucracy exaggerates to its advantage the size of the problems it must tackle, and the hunger relief organizations are no exception. In a field where not only basic information, such as caloric intake requirements, but also basic definitions, such as "undernutrition" or "chronic malnutrition," are highly conjectural, these organizations can bully their facts. Conceptually, malnutrition is a deviation from an ideal, and few things in this world are perfect. Remember that ad about fifty percent of all American housewives suffering from iron-poor blood; if you wish to assume that anyone who does not receive daily a sufficient and proper balance of proteins, carbohydrates, fats, minerals, and vitamins is malnourished, you can say that almost everyone in the poor world and most in the rich world suffer from malnutrition.

This is roughly what the United Nation's Food and Agricultural Organization (FAO) did with its first World Food Survey in 1945, in which it "proved" that sixty percent of the planet, then estimated to be about 1.5 billion people, were inadequately nourished. To prove this, as Thomas Poleman points out in the *Science* collection, all they had to do was leave the typical ten percent understatement of food supplies in the poor world uncorrected, and posit that the average human being needed 2,500 kilocalories of energy a

day.[4] This is only 100 less than required for the U.S. Food and Nutrition Board's "reference man," a moderately active adult male weighing 70 kilograms (154 pounds).

More recently FAO has altered caloric intake requirement and food supply estimates to "prove" that a more conservative ten percent of the world's population, about 400 million people (ninety-four percent of them living in poor countries), are malnourished, although they add that "a less conservative definition of malnutrition might double this figure." Thus 400 million people has become the magical answer to any question about how many hungry people live in the world. Again and again in this latter-day numerology that figure is faithfully recorded in the pages of *Give Us This Day*. . . . Occasionally, it is even improved upon: the Overseas Development Council, for example, places the number of people who "go hungry" for some part of the year at over one billion.

When these numbers are used to describe the extent of serious hunger, they overstate the problem by a whole order of magnitude. Malnutrition is a misleading term; it is like sickness. Its shades of severity range from vitamin deficiencies to chronic protein calorie malnutrition to the Gomez-3 variety, just as respiratory ailments range from sore throats to terminal tuberculosis. Few of us can say our health or diet is biologically optimal; many, on the other hand, can say it is biologically acceptable. Malnutrition is usefully defined in functional rather than aesthetic terms—as a state, say, in which a one percent increase in food consumption leads to more than a one percent increase in activity and energy. A body that is truly hungry devotes its energy to maintaining itself; it can "afford" practically no other activity. If it is given extra calories, it will resume normal physical activities at a rate higher than that of the increase in nutrition. But such a definition eliminates a great deal of what is defined as malnutrition in the world.

Whom does this leave? Most importantly, it leaves the chronically malnourished—those who are physically threatened by malnutrition. A World Health Organization estimate puts the number of severely malnourished children under five in the world of ten million. While all figures in the food field may be regarded with skepticism, WHO is a health organization, and need not inflate its hunger figures for its own good. If ten million infants are chronically malnourished, this would imply, in view of the ratio of children to adults in the poor world, a total population of about seventy million chronically malnourished people. This figure, however, would tend to be on the high side, for children under five need more protein and calories for their body weight than adults do—pound for pound, often up to sixty percent more. For seventy million people to be threatened with death through starvation in a world as rich as ours is so shocking and outrageous that it may tend to obscure the fact that this is less than two percent of the world's population—a lower proportion, in all likelihood, than ever before.

It is, moreover, a proportion that is small enough to be eliminated altogether. Here, however, is where the hunger relief lobby's rhetoric and inflated figures hurt its clients. Food relief and development projects for seventy million people, spread across perhaps ninety countries, are a manageable undertaking, and with some international cooperation could be attempted fairly easily. If on the other hand the number of starving were believed to be a billion the task might seem unmanageable or hopeless, and for the governments involved, politically dangerous to boot. Fear of social change among the ruling elites is no small consideration in attempts to eliminate hunger. During much of the Sahelian drought Chad's president actually *refused* food aid. A large proportion of his people were hungry, and hungry people, he knew, were inactive people, in no condition to rebel against a well-fed army.

Where do the desperately hungry live? The answer may seem surprising. Although millions do live in India, Pakistan, and Bangladesh, since a quarter of the poor world's population inhabit the subcontinent, many more proportionately live in some of the poor nations of the Caribbean, Latin America, Southeast Asia, and especially Africa. India may be the workhorse for famine metaphors, but the fact is that at least twenty-six nations—including Haiti, Colombia, North Vietnam, and Algeria—are estimated to have lower per capita protein consumption, and it is Zaire, not Bangladesh, whose inhabitants receive less protein than any other nation.

India, we often forget, is one of the world's great civilizations and great powers; for a state of 600 million simply to function at all it must have reached an impressive stage of political and economic development. Poor as it is, India has a highly sophisticated system of social services. As one Indian official quoted in *Give Us This Day* . . . explains it, "For a person to starve in Calcutta, he would have to be in social isolation—either a crazy person, or an old and sick person who literally couldn't cry out for help." There are many nations, especially in Africa, that virtually lack social services altogether—where to live is to live in social isolation. It is here, far from newsmen's hotels and photographer's cameras, that people literally *do* die of hunger.

This is reflected in the death rates. Although India's states of health and nutrition horrify Westerners, and rightly, life expectancy there is about fifty-three years, higher than that of nineteenth-century European nobility. Life expectancy in Sahelian Africa, on the other hand, is under forty, and in some areas under thirty. Death rates for the Sahelian region as a whole are fifty percent higher than India's. In the last three years up to half a million people may have died quietly in remote corners of Ethiopia from such diseases as cholera that were exacerbated by famine. Yet we never heard from those places. They had no public health officers, reporters, or diplomats to represent them. India as the world's third largest population of scientists and college graduates, as well as the ninth largest industrial sector, fourth largest army, and sixth largest atomic force; the corruption, waste, and red tape of relief efforts notwithstanding, the Indian poor are immeasurably better off because the rest of the world hears about it when India is hit by famine, and sends food, at least part of which is not funneled away from those who most need it.

With all the talk about starvation, it is seldom if ever mentioned how extremely difficult it is to die from it. People are not docile about dying; they fight to live, and man is an exceptionally rugged animal. He has always been able to survive conditions that quickly killed off other mammals. Conditions must be fantastically adverse for people to succumb to death from hunger. During the recent Sahelian famines tribes lived on practically nothing for seasons, and sometimes even years, before the death rates started going up. And when they went up, as Michael Latham explains in the *Science* collection, very few of the deaths were ostensibly caused by "starvation or malnutrition, but deaths from measles, respiratory infections, and other infectious diseases were . . . very much above pre-famine levels." [5]

To say that one dies from starvation is to say that the body wards off tuberculosis, diphtheria, smallpox, dysentery, and whatever else while its defenses progressively break down; it is a very unlikely situation. This is why so few poor governments see death by starvation as a serious problem, and concentrate on medical relief rather than food. It may seem carping or even inhumane to point out that death by starvation is more of an emotional codeword than an actual condition, but one must realize that the casual mass exploitation of the concept by the *Times* and others has made us take starvation for granted. When someone is in danger of starving to death, he or she is facing conditions none of us in the rich world can understand or even imagine.

THE CAUSES OF HUNGER

Do people starve because they must starve?

The plausible and widely accepted answer is, yes. A popular Malthusian syllogism explains why: people starve when there is too little food to go around; because of constant population expansion there is already too little food to go around, and there will be even less in the future; therefore, people must starve, and starve in ever greater numbers. What is most puzzling about this syllogism is that it stands undisputed when so many facts could upset it.

There is no logical justification for hunger of any kind anywhere; enough food is produced each year to feed everyone on earth comfortably. The Japanese get by with less than 600 pounds of grain per person annually [6] (they are, in fact, among the best nourished people on earth), yet there is less food available per person in Japan than in the world as a whole. For 1974 somewhere between 590 and 720 pounds of foodgrain, depending on whose figures one believes (a reasonable middle estimate might be 650 pounds), were available for each person in the world, not including reserves. Put another way, if 1.3 billion tons of grain are produced and one person could get by on 500 pounds, the world could feed—and feed well—5.2 billion people, 800 million more than the highest estimates for today's population.

The availability of food per person, moreover, is increasing, not declining. In 1972–1973, the year that supposedly signaled the beginning of a chronic world food shortage, the most reasonable estimate for grain production per person on earth was 632 pounds; yet in 1960, a year of supposed plenty, the comparable figure was under 600. At 500 pounds of grain per person the world in 1960 could have supported 300 million more people than the highest population estimates claimed existed; by 1973, despite the fact that world population had grown by almost a billion in the meantime, the new "margin of safety" was 600 million.

Why, then *do* people starve?

Re-examine the Malthusian syllogism: it blames today's hunger not on the wealth of the rich, but on the sexual habits of the poor. It neatly avoids the issue of inequality, when it is inequality and inequality alone that can be blamed for hunger today.

People in the rich world (Europe and Russia, countries settled by descendants of the English, Israel, Japan) consume forty percent more calories and seventy percent more protein than the rest of the world, and use almost three times as much grain.[7] Inequality in consumption, moreover, is rising: food production per capita for the world as a whole has risen about nine percent since 1960. But during those same fifteen years inequality in calorie consumption has risen four percent, in protein consumption eighteen percent, and in grain use about twenty percent.[8]

Although grain use in the poor world averages about 430 pounds per capita, inequality here is marked: Argentina, one of the rich of the poor world nations, uses about 900 pounds per person (more than West Germany) while Bangladesh must make do with about 300. Even the poorest nations in the world, however, probably produce enough food to provide adequately for all their people. The data on age, sex, weight, and activity levels in the poor world suggest that any poor nation with thirty-nine grams of protein a day and 285 pounds of grain a year per capita has enough so that its inhabitants need not suffer from malnutrition of any sort. Only two nations in the world (Liberia and Zaire) might fall below these minimums, although the margins of error in their food-production estimates are sufficiently large that they may not.

As James Gavan and John Dixon point out in their essay "India: A Perspective on the Food Situation" in the *Science* collection, it is unequal food distribution—not lack of production—that causes hunger in India. Even in the famine years of 1965 and 1966 the nation had thirteen percent more food than it needed to feed everyone adequately. Similarly, Bangladesh today probably produces enough food to prevent malnutrition altogether, but the rich consume thirty percent more calories than the poor (as well as twice as much protein and several times as much grain). A flourishing black market—approved by the government—ships perhaps as much as a third of all marketed grain into India, for in Bangladesh the rupee is a prized currency.

The FAO, in its *State of Food and Agriculture 1974*, repeats its claim that "malnutrition . . . is strongly correlated with poverty." It is perhaps more significant that marked social inequality, which is also "strongly correlated" with extreme poverty, in fact probably causes malnutrition. Brazil has vast numbers of the underfed (its northeast region is said to be one of the grimmest in the world) while China has very few; yet China's per capita GNP is only a third as high as Brazil's.

PRODUCTION MYTHS

With holocaust through atomic warfare at least temporarily less likely and the threat of environmental self-destruction apparently overrated, the *Times* collection is not the only publication that has now picked up the baton of Malthusianism. Malthusians believe they have two unanswerable propositions: first, that the poor world is procreating away all its advances in crop production; second, that the world's population is doubling every thirty-five years, and it is impossible for food production to keep pace with this. Fortunately for the poor of the world, neither proposition stands up.

It is true that per capita increases in food production since World War II have been about five times as rapid in the rich countries as in the poor (1.5 versus 0.3 percent per year), that total food production has risen just slightly faster in the poor world than in the rich, and that the poor world's population has been growing twice as rapidly. But does this mean the poor are converting grain into babies and saving none to improve their lives?

Not necessarily. The economies of rich nations and poor nations work very differently: in the former, economic growth is practically divorced from population growth. In the latter, labor rather than technology is the primary factor stimulating growth, so that growth of the economy hinges on growth of the labor force. One could argue that a poor nation with 3.3 and 3.0 percent rates of growth per annum for food production and population could quadruple its annual per capita food increase by lowering population growth to two percent. But poor nations are characterized by low productivity per worker. Under existing conditions it is more likely that lowering the growth of the labor force by a third would cut the growth of output by a third, and hence slash the already pitifully low rate of increase in food consumption by a third.[9]

It is the poorest of the poor who depend most on population growth for their economic welfare, and for them it is not irrational to produce more children. People will be better fed in poor countries not simply by making them lower their birth rates (if accomplished through coercion, as now seems likely will be tried in India's Punjab, this could lead to economic as well as political tragedy). What is needed instead are the institutional changes that would make it in the interest of the poor to lower their own birth rates. To be ninety-five percent sure that one will see a son reach adulthood, one must have a least six children in India today; with better health care, more of the children born would grow up, and parents would be less inclined to produce "spare" children. Education raises one's aspirations and decreases the desire for children. Jobs for women open up opportunities for self-fulfillment outside the nursery.

In every nation where equality of income has increased, fertility has decreased, perhaps because parents no longer need to depend on their children as a source of income and old-age security. Similarly, improving workers' productivity eliminates their main reason for having large families: it is no longer necessary to have an array of sons in the fields for a family to scratch out a living.

In agriculture, raising worker productivity means increasing crop yields per acre. Few people realize the potential that lies here. We think Bangladesh a basket case because it uses every inch of its land, sends eighty-five percent of its workforce to the fields, and still seems to grow too little food to get by. But how many of us know that rice yields per hectare in Bangladesh are only fifty-three percent as great as the world average, twenty-four percent as great as America's, and only fifteen percent as great as can be obtained on experimental stations in *Bangladesh*? Were Bangladesh merely to raise its rice yields to the world average, its per capita production would be over 530 pounds, higher than Japan's at the beginning of the 1960s. There is no technical reason why this could not be done.

Moreover, the world yields for most crops are only a fraction of the maximums that have actually been obtained: for wheat the fraction is one-third; for maize and sorghum, one-fourth; for rice, one-fifth. In agricultural colleges, research stations, and crop improvement centers today there is already enough know-how literally to flood the world with food. Roger Revelle has estimated that the earth could feed between thirty-eight and forty-eight billion people on a European diet, were we to plow all unused but cultivable land around the world and farm it with the methods and technology practiced in Iowa today.[10]

If this estimate's range seems too precise, its order of magnitude is certainly correct. And this order of magnitude understates the world's feeding potential. As various articles in the *Science* collection's sections on research and basic biology show,[11] tropical soils may hold more agricultural promise than we thought, pest control may save a larger portion of the crop, and genetic improvements not yet undertaken may lead to substantial increments in yields. The best wheat field on earth, for example, yields only half its genetic potential; the best banana grove, only a tenth. Demographers now say we should expect about seven billion people by the year 2000; it would be highly unrealistic to say that we could feed *seventy* billion by then, but it would not be inaccurate to say we could have the technology to do so.

I have argued that the present food situation is not as desperate as reported, and the future not as hopeless as predicted; that our misunderstanding of food realities demonstrates how little we actually know about the problem. If, as I assumed at the beginning of this article, we wish to help the poor, where do we go from here? We could start by examining why we know least about the world's poor themselves. Why do we know so little about their lives and their problems? It is certainly not because of a shortage of research funds and fact-finding commissions. Why, moreover, do the myriad fact-findings groups always seem to require high budgets, limousines, interpreters, and the best hotel suites in town? The answer is symptomatic of the problem: it is beneath our dignity to learn about the poor by working with them or living with them. We are ignorant about the poor of the earth because we are separated from them by a social and economic gap that they are unable to cross, and that we are unwilling to.

In the recent past we have seen the birth of a world economy and the development of an international division of labor. Although many complex factors have produced this division, and there are variations within it, it is still true that on one side have been those whose economic surplus was being expropriated, on the other those who were expropriating it. This international division of labor allowed the countries that are now rich to develop and multiply their productive resources, while growth was stifled and perverted in many of the countries that are now poor. As perhaps a quarter of the world's population was propelled up to a level of material comfort enjoyed a few generations before only by the aristocracy, fully half the world saw its standard of living

stagnate and in some cases (Indonesia, perhaps Bangladesh) even decline.[12] It is impossible to separate the issue of unequal food distribution (which is the question behind the food crisis, not some absolute lack of food) from the acceleration of inequality that the development of the world economy has encouraged. Historically, the food crisis is merely the most recent in a long series of manifestations of inequality between the rich and the poor worlds.

This inequality, however, cannot be separated from productivity, for it is differing rates of growth in productivity that have caused it. An American may use five times as much grain as an Indian, but this is so because he can buy five times as much, and he can buy five times as much because, farmer to farmer, he produces *seventy-five* times as much. The plaintive calls for Americans to keep their standard of living high but to go without hamburger, or for nations to redistribute their food supplies without altering the balance of productive resources, have gone unheeded because inequality cannot be eliminated by welfare-style transfers of income. Inequality is inextricably linked with production; the only way the nations of the world can become more equal is through making their productivities more equal.

How, then, can the poor world's productivity be raised? As Pierre Crosson explains in the *Science* collection, three conditions must be satisfied to expand food production: (1) technology must exist; (2) farmers must know how to use it efficiently; (3) they must have incentives to use it. The first condition is already satisfied. You don't need tractors, spray planes, and other trappings of the Green Revolution to raise yields. With know-how and little else (a few simple hand tools, some good seeds, a little pesticide, manure or fertilizer) a diligent but poor farmer can produce at least one crop a year with yields higher than those now harvested in rich countries.

This is not easy, but it can be done, and men such as the Reverend Carl Reither, a missionary in the town of Feni, Bangladesh, and Dr. Dale Haws, an agronomist in the Philippines, have shown farmers how to do it. (To my knowledge, nothing has yet been written about the extraordinary Rev. Reither. On Haws's low-investment harvest, see *Research Highlights* for 1974.[13]) Poor countries, moreover, are tropical countries. With an investment in irrigation and drainage, which in most cases pays for itself in less than two years, the poor farmer can be harvesting three crops a year to our one.

Fulfilling the second condition depends on reaching the smallest, poorest farmer. There are no general rules for doing this. Voluntary farmer associations, which flourished in Japan, have failed in the Philippines. The brutal *kolkhoz* system of rounding up peasants, dropping them on a farm, and making them work for the state, which is still holding back Russian agriculture, is said to have had some limited success in Tanzania. Information does not seek out its audience; word of mouth, open-air meetings, even color TV will not bring a message across to peasant farmers unless a number of other factors encourage them to be receptive, including their culture, their degree of political development, the position of farmers in the social system, and the inclinations of their leaders. South Korea and Taiwan are currently touted as models for poor world agricultural development, their experience supposedly proving that income redistribution is a precondition for progress and that political development is an important form of economic development. An educated, disciplined mass party or voting public, so the argument runs, is only a step away from an educated, disciplined labor force.

There is truth in these claims, but a crucial—and almost totally ignored—reason that agriculture has been so successful in those countries since World War II is that they were Japanese colonies before the war. Where the other imperial powers wanted export earnings from their colonies, Japan needed food, and built the roads, market system, and the rest of the "infrastructure"

to deliver it. Small farmers in South Korea and Taiwan were reached not through social justice but foreign fiat; yields began to rise sharply long before land reform programs even existed.

The farmer's life is not only strenuous, boring, and poorly paid, but brutal. Throughout most of the world (India's Punjab experience perhaps being a significant exception) successful efforts to reach him and raise his productivity have been accompanied by some tort of coercion. The lower his level of political culture (his ability, if you will, to be moved to act by the existing political channels), the greater has been the use of force in changing his situation, for better or worse.

The third condition implies that if national needs are to be fulfilled it must be in the interest of the small farmer to fulfill them, since he produces the lion's share of crops in every poor nation. This means regulating the power and the privileges of the classes that exploit him. Class privilege in the Philippines, for example, causes yields to stagnate and population to explode. Most of the labor is tenant or landless, and the tenure system puts the burden of risk on the *campesino;* if the crop fails, he pays, and if it thrives it is the landlord who prospers. Thus, the only really safe investment a peasant can make is children: they don't eat much, or need clothes or schooling, and they start earning their living at about age five. Because unemployment rates are high, it is good to have many children so that one or two are always employed; because infant mortality is high, it is good to have many children so that a few might grow up to support you when you are too weak to work. On the other hand, in Japan, a former poor nation, the conflict between national needs and individual aspirations was largely eliminated regarding agricultural production. Land is more equally distributed, irrigation, pesticides, fertilizers, good seeds, credit, guaranteed markets, high support prices are easily available. It is in the farmer's interest to raise a good crop.

On millions of small farms throughout the world, optimum production and social justice are closely linked; you probably can't have one for any length of time without the other.[14] This is because, in the world economy, it is the structure rather than the fact of poverty that perpetuates poverty. As Mao Tse-tung, the great economic-development genius of our age, has proven, within at least one poor nation vast reserves of unused productive power can be liberated by altering the social system. A little bit of justice goes a long way in production. Land reform, for example, has been credited with raising production in many countries where it is enacted; although the claim is no doubt exaggerated, we can see why it should be conducive to higher yields. With effective land redistribution, many more farmers get a homestead. Thus, rural unemployment (commonly thirty percent) tends to disappear. With land (and thus money) of their own, the former poor buy more food and become stronger; hence the quantity and the quality of the labor force simultaneously increase.

Moreover, the labor force now has reason to work hard and seek out new ways to improve yields. Output improves, and because it is more evenly distributed, so do health and education, which in turn further improve output. Farm demand leads now to appropriate industrialization—shoes, hammocks, roofs (not El Dorados)—which in turn leads to greater demand for farm goods, and so on. It has been estimated that Brazil could raise its crop output immediately by twenty percent simply by rearranging factors of production (i.e., land reform).[15] Such an estimate, however, takes into account neither the current political and social obstacles to rearranging those factors nor the present and future social dividends that would be reaped. Clearly both are very great.

When we put the proportion of poor and hungry around the world in historical perspective we can prove that things have never been better. But if we choose to compare the number of people who could be well fed with the number who are well fed, we can also prove that things have never been worse. Little as we know about the food crisis, we know that it is a social, not a technical, problem; the know-how, and even the food, to eliminate hunger are already here.

If we wish to help the poor of the earth, what should we be doing? Our usual, self-indulgent response is to shed crocodile tears over the starving or to accept as inevitable the prospect of emaciated bodies by dirt roadsides. As I have already explained, this does not merely leave the poor unaffected; it can hurt them. If man is a rational animal with a drive for self-improvement we would be better advised to think whether our governments in the rich world are, deliberately or inadvertently, helping to erect further social barriers to the progress of the poor; for literally hundreds of millions of people today are living in poverty that is, technologically speaking, totally unnecessary. The first step toward helping the poor is to stop hurting them, and we have a long way to go before we get that far.

Footnotes

1. Lester R. Brown. "The Social Impact of the Green Revolution," *International Conciliation*, 1971, quoted in Keith Griffin, *The Political Economy of Agrarian Change* (Harvard University Press, 1974).

2. Lester R. Brown, *In the Human Interest* (Norton, 1974).

3. Emma Rothschild, "Food Politics," *Foreign Affairs*, January 1976.

4. Poleman demonstrates how difficult it is to interpret what scanty evidence does exist on malnutrition by using food figures from Sri Lanka. Between the lowest class (representing forty-three percent of the survey population) and the next lowest (thirty-seven percent) a ten gram protein and 200 kilocalorie energy gap existed, but diet compositions were identical.

"What does this mean? Because the FAO now (quite reasonably) reckons energy needs in South Asia average 1,900 kilocalories daily and protein adequacy to be a function of energy adequacy, it could mean either of two things. If the standard factor of fifteen percent is applied to account for wastage between purchase and ingestion, the 200 kilocalorie gap could be interpreted as implying enforced reduced activity among the poor or actual physical deterioration (or both).

Alternatively, one might postulate caloric adequacy among the element of society that is too poor to waste anything, and that because of the high rate of unemployment in Sri Lanka leads a less active life and thus has lower energy needs. Thus you can have it either way: depending on your assumptions you can prove beyond a statistical doubt that forty-three percent of the Ceylonese population suffer protein calorie malnutrition or none do."

5. It should be noted that hunger usually picks off children, not adults. Children need both more food and more special kinds of food, pound for pound, than adults, and when things get tough they are likely, pound for pound, to get less. They are often not strong enough or old enough to go out and feed themselves, and so instead they die: almost half the deaths in Central Africa are among children under five, and in Indonesia, a one-year-old has worse odds of surviving another year than a sixty-one-year-old. With food, as with so many other things in life, those most desperately in need of your help cannot assault you for it; at best they can wheedle and beg.

6. FAO, *Food Balance Sheets.*

7. The rich consume their grain primarily indirectly (feedstocks converted into animal protein). The poor's consumption is mainly direct (gruels, breads, noodles, rice dishes).

8. Like death, food consumption is a biological process and hence an equalizer of men: one can spend 100 times as much money as someone else, or use 500 times as much energy, but one cannot, over any length of time, eat three times as much food. In a world of inequality, however, levelers cut both ways: I can survive on one-hundredth of your income and one-five-hundredth of your energy use, but I shall die if my calorie consumption is only thirty percent of yours consistently.

9. Simon Kuznets is one of the few American economists who have worked on this problem. See his *Modern Economic Growth* (Yale University Press, 1966), *Economic Growth of Nations* (Harvard University Press, 1971), and *Population, Capital, and Growth* (Norton, 1974).

10. *Scientific American*, September 1974.

11. S.H. Wittwer, "Food Production: Technology and the Resource Base"; W.B. Ennis, Jr., W. Dowler, W. Klassen, "Crop Protection to Increase Food Supplies"; P.A. Sanchez and S.W. Buol, "Soils of the Tropics and the World Food Crisis"; I. Zeitlich, "Improving the Efficiency of Photosynthesis."

12. See Immanuel Wallerstein, *The Modern World System* (Academic Press, 1975); Samir Amin, *Accumulation on a World Scale* (Monthly Review Press, 1972); A. Emmanuel, *Unequal Exchange* (Monthly Review Press, 1973). For the effect of the world economy on particular areas, see the work of Clifford Geertz (Indonesia), Andre Gunder Frank (Latin America), and Giovanni Arrighi (Africa).

13. International Rice Research Institute, Los Baños, Philippines; see also my forthcoming "Los Baños Diary," *R.F. Illustrated*, published by the Rockefeller Foundation, New York.

14. There are of course exceptions: Costa Rica exports more meat every year while growing numbers at home go hungry; South Vietnam in the last six months may have seen its crop production and its numbers of malnourished fall simultaneously. We may suspect, however, that the exceptions are temporary exceptions: in the first case, the contradiction between justice and production may eventually damage production; in the second, where the contradiction between justice and production reportedly is being solved, we might expect production to be enhanced.

15. W.R. Cline, *Economic Consequences of Land Reform in Brazil*, quoted in Keith Griffin, *The Political Economy of Agrarian Change* (Harvard University Press, 1974).

Review Questions

1. Why is there so much misinformation about the food crisis?

2. Why do people starve when there is enough food produced each year to feed everyone on earth?

3. What is the Malthusian explanation of hunger?

4. What three conditions must be satisfied to expand food production?

Discussion Questions

1. Is the Malthusian explanation acceptable? Why, or why not?

2. Could inequalities in standard of living be eliminated by welfare-style transfers of income? Why, or why not?

3. Eberstadt says that it is "totally unnecessary" for hundreds of millions of people to live in poverty. Is this true or not? Defend your view.

JAMES RACHELS
Killing and Starving to Death
"Killing and Starving to Death," by James Rachels in *Philosophy* 54, no. 208 (April 1979): 159–171.
Reprinted with the permission of Cambridge University Press.

James Rachels is Professor of Philosophy at the University of Alabama in Birmingham. He is the author of several articles on ethics, and he is the editor of Moral Problems: A Collection of Philosophical Essays (1971, 3rd ed., 1979).

Rachels argues that our duty not to let people die of starvation is as strong as our duty not to kill them. He defends this Equivalence Thesis against various attempts to show that there is a moral difference between killing and letting die.

Although we do not know exactly how many people die each year of malnutrition or related health problems, the number is very high, in the millions.[1] By giving money to support famine relief efforts, each of us could save at least some of them. By not giving, we let them die.

Some philosophers have argued that letting people die is not as bad as killing them, because in general our "positive duty" to give aid is weaker than our "negative duty" not to do harm.[2] I maintain the opposite: letting die is just as bad as killing.[3] At first this may seem wildly implausible. When reminded that people are dying of starvation while we spend money on trivial things, we may feel a bit guilty, but certainly we do not feel like murderers. Philippa Foot writes:

Most of us allow people to die of starvation in India and Africa, and there is surely something wrong with us that we do; it would be nonsense, however, to pretend that it is only in law that we make a distinction between allowing people in the underdeveloped countries to die of starvation and sending them poisoned food. There is worked into our moral system a distinction between what we owe people in the form of aid and what we owe them in the way of non-interference.[4]

No doubt this would be correct if it were intended only as a description of what most people believe. Whether this feature of "our moral system" is rationally defensible is, however, another matter. I shall argue that we are wrong to take comfort in the fact that we "only" let these people die, because our duty not to let them die is equally as strong as our duty not to kill them, which, of course, is very strong indeed.

Obviously, this Equivalence Thesis is not morally neutral, as philosophical claims about ethics often are. It is a radical idea that, if true, would mean that some of our "intuitions" (our prereflective beliefs about what is right and wrong in particular cases) are mistaken and must be rejected. Neither is the view I oppose morally neutral. The idea that killing is worse than letting die is a relatively conservative thesis that would allow those same intuitions to be preserved. However, the Equivalence Thesis should not be dismissed merely because it does not conform to all our prereflective intuitions. Rather than being perceptions of the truth, our "intuitions" might sometimes signify nothing more than our prejudices or selfishness or cultural conditioning. Philosophers often admit that, in theory at least, some intuitions might be unreliable—but usually this possibility is not taken seriously, and conformity to prereflective intuition is used uncritically as a test of the acceptability of moral theory. In what follows I shall argue that many of our intuitions concerning killing and letting die *are* mistaken, and should not be trusted.

I

We think that killing is worse than letting die, not because we overestimate how bad it is to kill, but because we underestimate how bad it is to let die. The following chain of reasoning is intended to show that letting people in foreign countries die of starvation is very much worse than we commonly assume.

Suppose there were a starving child in the room where you are now—hollow-eyed, belly bloated, and so on—and you have a sandwich at your elbow that you don't need. Of course you would be horrified; you would stop reading and give her the sandwich or, better, take her to a hospital. And you would not think this an act of supererogation; you would not expect any special praise for it, and you would expect criticism if you did not do it. Imagine what you would think of someone who simply ignored the child and continued reading, allowing her to die of starvation. Let us call the person who would do this Jack Palance, after the very nice man who plays such vile characters in the movies. Jack Palance indifferently watches the starving child die; he cannot be bothered even to hand her the sandwich. There is ample reason for judging him very harshly; without putting too fine a point on it, he shows himself to be a moral monster.

When we allow people in faraway countries to die of starvation, we may think, as Mrs. Foot puts it, that "there is surely something wrong with us". But we most emphatically do not consider ourselves moral monsters. We think this, in spite of the striking similarity between Jack Palance's behavior and our own. He could easily save the child; he does not, and the child dies. We could easily save some of those starving people; we do not, and they die. If we are not monsters, there must be some important

difference between him and us. But what is it?

One obvious difference between Jack Palance's position and ours is that the person he lets die is in the same room with him, while the people we let die are mostly far away. Yet the spatial location of the dying people hardly seems a relevant consideration.[5] It is absurd to suppose that being located at a certain map coordinate entitles one to treatment that one would not merit if situated at a different longitude or latitude. Of course, if a dying person's location meant that we *could not* help, that would excuse us. But, since there are efficient famine relief agencies willing to carry our aid to the faraway countries, this excuse is not available. It would be almost as easy for us to send these agencies the price of the sandwich as for Palance to hand the sandwich to the child.

The location of the starving people does make a difference, psychologically, in how we feel. If there were a starving child in the same room with us, we could not avoid realizing, in a vivid and disturbing way, how it is suffering and that it is about to die. Faced with this realization our consciences probably would not allow us to ignore the child. But if the dying are far away, it is easy to think of them only abstractly, or to put them out of our thoughts altogether. This might explain why our conduct would be different if we were in Jack Palance's position, even though, from a moral point of view, the location of the dying is not relevant.

There are other differences between Jack Palance and us, which may seem important, having to do with the sheer numbers of people, both affluent and starving, that surround us. In our fictitious example Jack Palance is one person, confronted by the need of one other person. This makes his position relatively simple. In the real world our position is more complicated, in two ways: first, in that there are millions of people who need feeding, and none of us has the resources to care for all of them; and second, in that for any starving person we *could* help there are millions of other affluent people who could help as easily as we.

On the first point, not much needs to be said. We may feel, in a vague sort of way, that we are not monsters because no one of us could possibly save *all* the starving people—there are just too many of them, and none of us has the resources. This is fair enough, but all that follows is that, individually, none of us is responsible for saving everyone. We may still be responsible for saving someone, or as many as we can. This is so obvious that it hardly bears mentioning, yet it is easy to lose sight of, and philosophers have actually lost sight of it. In his article "Saving Life and Taking Life," [6] Richard Trammell says that one morally important difference between killing and letting die is "dischargeability." By this he means that, while each of us can discharge completely a duty not to kill anyone, no one among us can discharge completely a duty to save everyone who needs it. Again, fair enough; but all that follows is that since we are only bound to save those we can, the class of people we have an obligation to save is much smaller than the class of people we have an obligation not to kill. It does *not* follow that our duty with respect to those we can save is any less stringent. Suppose Jack Palance were to say: "I needn't give this starving child the sandwich because, after all, I can't save everyone in the world who needs it." If this excuse will not work for him, neither will it work for us with respect to the children we could save in India or Africa.

The second point about numbers was that, for any starving person we *could* help, there are millions of other affluent people who could help as easily as we. Some are in an even better position to help since they are richer. But by and large these people are doing nothing. This also helps explain why we do not feel especially guilty for letting people starve. How guilty we feel about something depends, to some extent, on how we compare with those around us. If we

were surrounded by people who regularly sacrificed to feed the starving and we did not, we would probably feel ashamed. But because our neighbors do not do any better than we, we are not so ashamed.

But again, this does not imply that we should not feel more guilty or ashamed than we do. A psychological explanation of our feelings is not a moral justification of our conduct. Suppose Jack Palance were only one of twenty people who watched the child die; would that decrease his guilt? Curiously, I think many people assume it would. Many people seem to feel that if twenty people do nothing to prevent a tragedy, each of them is only one-twentieth as guilty as he would have been if he had watched the tragedy alone. It is as though there is only a fixed amount of guilt, which divides. I suggest, rather, that guilt multiplies, so that each passive viewer is fully guilty, if he could have prevented the tragedy but did not. Jack Palance watching the girl die alone would be a moral monster; but if he calls in a group of his friends to watch with him, he does not diminish his guilt by dividing it among them. Instead, they are all moral monsters. Once the point is made explicit, it seems obvious.

The fact that most other affluent people do nothing to relieve hunger may very well have implications for one's own obligations. But the implication may be that one's own obligations *increase* rather than decrease. Suppose Palance and a friend were faced with two starving children, so that, if each did his "fair share," Palance would only have to feed one of them. But the friend will do nothing. Because he is well-off, Palance could feed both of them. Should he not? What if he fed one and then watched the other die, announcing that he has done *his* duty and that the one who died was his friend's responsibility? This shows the fallacy of supposing that one's duty is only to do one's fair share, where this is determined by what would be sufficient *if* everyone else did likewise.

To summarize: Jack Palance, who refuses to hand a sandwich to a starving child, is a moral monster. But we feel intuitively that we are not so monstrous, even though we also let starving children die when we could feed them almost as easily. If this intuition is correct, there must be some important difference between him and us. But when we examine the most obvious differences between his conduct and ours—the location of the dying, the differences in numbers—we find no real basis for judging ourselves less harshly than we judge him. Perhaps there are some other grounds on which we might distinguish our moral position, with respect to actual starving people, from Jack Palance's position with respect to the child in my story. But I cannot think of what they might be. Therefore, I conclude that if he is a monster, then so are we—or at least, so are we after our rationalizations and thoughtlessness have been exposed.

This last qualification is important. We judge people, at least in part, according to whether they can be expected to realize how well or how badly they behave. We judge Palance harshly because the consequences of his indifference are so immediately apparent. By contrast, it requires an unusual effort for us to realize the consequences of our indifference. It is normal behavior for people in the affluent countries not to give to famine relief, or if they do give, to give very little. Decent people may go along with this normal behavior pattern unthinkingly, without realizing, or without comprehending in a clear way just what this means for the starving. Thus, even though those decent people may act monstrously, we do not judge them monsters. There is a curious sense, then, in which moral reflection can transform decent people into indecent ones; for if a person thinks things through, and realizes that he is, morally speaking, in Jack Palance's position, his continued indifference is more blameworthy than before.

The preceding is not intended to prove that letting people die of starvation is as bad as killing them. But it does provide strong evidence that letting die is much worse than we normally assume, and so that letting die is much *closer* to killing than we normally assume. These reflections also go some way towards showing just how fragile and unreliable our intuitions are in this area. They suggest that, if we want to discover the truth, we are better off looking at arguments that do not rely on unexamined intuitions.

II

Before arguing that the Equivalence Thesis is true, let me explain more precisely what I mean by it. I take it to be a claim about what does, or does not, count as a morally good reason in support of a value judgment: the bare fact that one act is an act of killing, while another act is an act of "merely" letting someone die, is not a morally good reason in support of the judgment that the former is worse than the latter. Of course there may be *other* differences between such acts that are morally significant. For example, the family of an irreversibly comatose hospital patient may want their loved one to be allowed to die, but not killed. Perhaps the reason for their preference is religious. So we have at least one reason to let the patient die rather than to kill him—the reason is that the family prefers it that way. This does not mean, however, that the distinction between killing and letting die *itself* is important. What is important is respecting the family's wishes. (It is often right to respect people's wishes even if we think those wishes are based on false beliefs.) In another sort of case, a patient with a painful terminal illness may want to be killed rather than allowed to die because a slow, lingering death would be agonizing. Here we have a reason to kill and not let die, but once again the reason is not that one course is intrinsically preferable to the other. The reason is, rather, that the latter course would lead to no more suffering.

It should be clear then, that I will *not* be arguing that every act of letting die is equally as bad as every act of killing. There are lots of reasons why a particular act of killing may be morally worse than a particular act of letting die, or vice versa. If a healthy person is murdered, from a malicious motive, while a person in irreversible coma is allowed to die upon a calm judgment that maintaining him alive is pointless, certainly this killing is very much worse than this letting die. Similarly, if an ill person who could be saved is maliciously allowed to die, while a terminal patient is killed, upon his request, as an act of kindness, we have good reason to judge the letting die worse than the killing. All that I want to argue is that, whatever reasons there may be for judging one act worse than another, the simple fact that one is killing, whereas the other is only letting die, is not among them.

The first stage of the argument is concerned with some formal relations between moral judgments and the reasons that support them. I take it to be a point of logic that moral judgments are true only if good reasons support them; for example, if there is no good reason why you ought to do some action, it cannot be true that you ought to do it. Moreover, when there is a choice to be made from among several possible actions, the preferable alternative is the one that is backed by the strongest reasons.

But when are the reasons for or against one act stronger than those for or against another act? A complete answer would have to include some normative theory explaining why some reasons are intrinsically weightier than others. Suppose you are in a situation in which you can save someone's life only by lying: the normative theory would explain why "Doing A would save someone's life" is a stronger reason in favor of doing A than "Doing B would be telling the truth" is in favor of doing B.

However, there are also some purely formal principles that operate here. The simplest and least controversial such principle is this:

(i) If there are the *same* reasons for or against A as for or against B, then the reasons in favor of A are neither stronger nor weaker than the reasons in favor of B; and so A and B are morally equivalent—neither is preferable to the other.

Now, suppose we ask why killing is morally objectionable. When someone is killed, there may of course be harmful effects for people other than the victim himself. Those who loved him may grieve, and those who were depending on him in one way or another may be caused hardship because, being dead, he will be unable to perform as expected. However, we cannot explain the wrongness of killing purely, or even mainly, in terms of the bad effects for the survivors. The primary reason why killing is wrong is that something very bad is done to the victim himself: he ends up dead; he no longer has a good—his life—that he possessed before. But notice that exactly the same can be said about letting someone die. The primary reason why it is morally objectionable to let someone die, when we could save him, is that he ends up dead; he no longer has a good—his life—that he possessed before. Secondary reasons again have to do with harmful effects on those who survive. Thus, the explanation of why killing is bad mentions features of killing that are also features of letting die, and vice versa. Since there are no comparably general reasons in favor of either, this suggests that:

(ii) There are the same reasons for and against letting die as for and against killing.

And if this is true, we get the conclusion:

(iii) Therefore, killing and letting die are morally equivalent—neither is preferable to the other.

The central idea of this argument is that there is no morally relevant difference between killing and letting die, that is, no difference that may be cited to show that one is worse than the other. The argument therefore contains a premise—(ii)—that is supported only inductively. The fact that the explanation of why killing is wrong applies equally well to letting die, and vice versa, provides strong evidence that the inductive generalization is true. Nevertheless, no matter how carefully we analyze the matter, it will always be possible that there is some subtle, morally relevant difference between the two that we have overlooked. In fact, philosophers who believe that killing is worse than letting die have sometimes tried to identify such differences. I believe that these attempts have failed; here are three examples.

1. The first is one that I have already mentioned. Trammell urges that there is an important difference in the "dischargeability" of duties not to kill and not to let die. We can completely discharge a duty not to kill anyone; but we cannot completely discharge a duty to save everyone who needs aid. This is obviously correct, but it does not show that the Equivalence Thesis is false, for two reasons. In the first place, the difference in dischargeability only shows that the class of people we have a duty to save is smaller than the class of people we have a duty not to kill. It does not show that our duty with respect to those we *can* save is any less stringent. In the second place, if we *cannot* save someone, and that person dies, then we do not let him die. It is not right to say that I let Josef Stalin die, for example, since there is no way I could have saved him. So if I cannot save everyone, then neither can I let everyone die.

2. It has also been urged that, in killing someone, we are *doing* something—namely, killing him—whereas, in letting someone die, we are not doing anything. In letting people die of starvation, for example, we only *fail* to do certain things, such as sending food. The difference is between action and inaction; somehow, this is supposed to make a moral difference.[7]

There are also two difficulties with this suggestion. First, it is misleading to say, without further ado, that in letting someone die we do nothing. For there is one very important thing that we do: we let someone die. "Letting someone die" is different, in some ways, from other sorts of actions, mainly in that it is an action we perform *by way of* not performing other actions. We

may let someone die by way of not feeding him, just as we may insult someone by way of not shaking his hand. (If it is said, "I didn't do anything; I simply refrained from taking his hand when he offered it," it may be replied "You did do one thing—you insulted him.") The distinction between action and inaction is relative to a specification of *what* actions are or are not done. In insulting someone, we may *not* smile, speak, shake hands, and so on—but we *do* insult or snub the person. And in letting someone die, the following may be among the things that are not done: we do not feed the person, we do not give medication, and so on. But the following is among the things that are done: we let him die.

Second, even if letting die were only a case of inaction, why should any moral conclusion follow from *that* fact? It may seem that a significant conclusion follows if we assume that we are not responsible for inactions. However, there is no general correlation between the action-inaction distinction and any sort of moral assessment. We ought to do some things, and we ought not do others, and we can certainly be morally blameworthy for not doing things as well as for doing them—Jack Palance was blameworthy for not feeding the child. (In many circumstances we are even legally liable for not doing things: tax fraud may involve only "inaction"—failing to report certain things to the Department of Internal Revenue—but what of it?) Moreover, failing to act can be subject to all the other kinds of moral assessment. Not doing something may, depending on the circumstances, be right, wrong, obligatory, wise, foolish, compassionate, sadistic, and so on. Since there is no general correlation between the action-inaction distinction and *any* of these matters, it is hard to see how anything could be made out of this distinction in the present context.

3. My final example is from Trammell again. He argues that "optionality" is a morally relevant difference between killing and letting die. The point here is that if we fail to save someone, we leave open the option

for someone else to save him; whereas if we kill, the victim is dead and that is that. This point, I think, has little significance. For one thing, while "optionality" may mark a difference between killing and *failing to save,* it does not mark a comparable difference between killing and *letting die.* If X fails to save Y, it does not follow that Y dies; someone else may come along and save him. But if X lets Y die, it does follow that Y dies; Y is dead and that is that.[8] When Palance watches the child die, he does not merely fail to save the child; he lets her die. And when we fail to send food to the starving, and they die, we let them die—we do not merely fail to save them.

The importance of "optionality" in any particular case depends on the actual chances of someone else's saving the person we do not save. Perhaps it is not so bad not to save someone if we know that someone else *will* save him. (Although even here, we do not behave as we ought; for we ought not simply to leave what needs doing to others.) And perhaps it even gets us off the hook a little if there is the *strong chance* that someone else will step in. But in the case of the world's starving, we know very well that no person or group of persons is going to come along tomorrow and save all of them. We know that there are at least some people who will *not* be saved, if we do not save them. So, as an excuse for not giving aid to the starving, the "optionality" argument is clearly in bad faith. To say those people, after they are dead, that someone else *might* have saved them, in the very weak sense in which that will be true, does not excuse us at all. The others who might have saved them, but did not, are as guilty as we, but that does not diminish our guilt—as I have already remarked, guilt in these cases multiplies, not divides.

III

I need now to say a few more things about the counter-intuitive nature of the Equivalence Thesis.

The fact that this view has radical implications for conduct has been cited as a reason for rejecting it. Trammell complains that "Denial of the distinction between negative and positive duties leads straight to an ethic so strenuous that it might give pause even to a philosophical John the Baptist."[9] Suppose John is about to buy a phonograph record, purely for his enjoyment, when he is reminded that with this five dollars a starving person could be fed. On the view I am defending, he ought to give the money to feed the hungry person. This may not seem exceptional until we notice that the reasoning is reiterable. Having given the first five dollars, John is not free to use another five to buy the record. For the poor are always with him; there is always *another* starving person to be fed, and then another, and then another. "The problem," Trammell says, "is that, even though fulfillment of one particular act of aid involves only minimal effort, it sets a precedent for millions of such efforts."[10] So we reach the bizarre conclusion that it is almost always immoral to buy phonograph records! And the same goes for fancy clothes, cars, toys, and so on.

This sort of *reductio* argument is of course familiar in philosophy. Such arguments may be divided into three categories. The strongest sort shows that a theory entails a contradiction, and, since contradictions cannot be tolerated, the theory must be modified or rejected. Such arguments, when valid, are of course devastating. Second, an argument may show that a theory has a consequence that, while not inconsistent, is nevertheless demonstrably false—that is, an independent proof can be given that the offensive consequence is unacceptable. Arguments of this second type, while not quite so impressive as the first, can still be irresistible. The third type of *reductio* is markedly weaker than the others. Here, it is merely urged that some consequence of a theory is counter-intuitive. The supposedly embarrassing consequence is perfectly consistent, and there is no proof that it is false; the complaint is only that it goes against our unreflective, pretheoretical beliefs. Now sometimes even this weak sort of argument can be effective, especially when we have not much confidence in the theory, or when our confidence in the pretheoretical belief is unaffected by the reasoning that supports the theory. However, it may happen that *the same reasoning that leads one to accept a theory also persuades one that the pretheoretical beliefs were wrong.* (If this did not happen, philosophy would always be in the service of what we already think; it could never challenge and change our beliefs, and would be, in an important sense, useless.) The present case, it seems to me, is an instance of this type. The same reasoning that leads to the view that we are as wicked as Jack Palance, and that killing is no worse than letting die, also persuades (me, at least) that the prereflective belief in the rightness of our affluent lifestyle is mistaken.[11]

So, I want to say about all this what H.P. Grice once said at a conference when someone objected that his theory of meaning had an unacceptable implication. Referring to the supposedly embarrassing consequence, Grice said, "See here, that's not an *objection* to my theory—*that's* my theory!"[12] Grice not only accepted the implication, he claimed it as an integral part of what he wanted to say. Similarly, the realization that we are morally wrong to spend money on inessentials, when that money could go to feed the starving, is an integral part of the view I am defending. It is not an embarrassing consequence of the view; it is (part of) the view itself.

There is another way in which the counter-intuitive nature of the Equivalence Thesis may be brought out. It follows from that thesis that if the *only* difference between a pair of acts is that one is killing, while the other is letting die, those actions are equally good or bad—neither is preferable to the other. Defenders of the distinction between positive and negative duties have pointed out that in such cases our intuitions often tell us just the opposite: killing seems obvi-

ously worse. Here is an example produced by Daniel Dinello:

Jones and Smith are in a hospital. Jones cannot live longer than two hours unless he gets a heart transplant. Smith, who has had one kidney removed, is dying of an infection in the other kidney. If he does not get a kidney transplant, he will die in about four hours. When Jones dies, his one good kidney can be transplanted to Smith, or Smith could be killed and his heart transplanted to Jones . . . it seems clear that it would, in fact, be wrong to kill Smith and save Jones, rather than letting Jones die and saving Smith.[13]

And another from Trammell:

If someone threatened to steal $1000 from a person if he did not take a gun and shoot a stranger between the eyes, it would be very wrong for him to kill the stranger to save his $1000. But if someone asked from that person $1000 to save a stranger, it would seem that his obligation to grant this request would not be as great as his obligation to refuse the first demand—even if he has good reason for believing that without his $1000 the stranger would certainly die. . . . In this particular example, it seems plausible to say that a person has a greater obligation to refrain from killing someone, even though the effort required of him ($1000) and his motivation toward the stranger be assumed identical in both cases.[14]

The conclusion we are invited to draw from these examples is that, contrary to what I have been arguing, the bare difference between killing and letting die *must be* morally significant.

Now Dinello's example is badly flawed, since the choice before the doctor is not a choice between killing and letting die at all. If the doctor kills Smith in order to transplant his heart to Jones, he will have killed Smith. But if he waits until Jones dies, and then transfers the kidney to Smith, he will *not* have "let Jones die." The reason is connected with the fact that not every case of not saving someone is a case of letting him die. (Josef Stalin died, and I did not save him, but I did not let Stalin die.) Dinello himself points out that, in order for it to be true that X lets Y die, X must be "in a position" to save Y, but not do so.[15] (I was never in a position to save Stalin.) Now the doctor is in a position to save Jones only if there is a heart available for transplantation. But no such heart is available—Smith's heart, for example, is not available since Smith is still using it. Therefore, since the doctor is not in a position to save Jones, he does not let Jones die.[16]

Trammell's example is not quite so easy to dismiss. Initially, I share the intuition that it would be worse to kill someone to prevent $1000 from being stolen than to refuse to pay $1000 to save someone. Yet on reflection I have not much confidence in this feeling. What is at stake in the situation described is the person's $1000 and the stranger's life. But we end up with the *same* combination of lives and money, no matter which option the person chooses: if he shoots the stranger, the stranger dies and he keeps his $1000; and if he refuses to pay to save the stranger, the stranger dies and he keeps his $1000. It makes no difference, either to the person's interests or to the stranger's interests, which option is chosen; why, then, do we have the curious intuition that there is a big difference here?

I conceded at the outset that most of us believe that in letting people die we are not behaving as badly as if we were to kill them. I think I have given good reasons for concluding that this belief is false. Yet giving reasons is often not enough, even in philosophy. For if an intuition is strong enough, we may continue to rely on it and assume that *something* is wrong with the arguments opposing it, even though we are not sure exactly what is wrong. It is a familiar remark: "X is more certain than any argument that might be given against it." So in addition to the arguments, we need some ac-count of why people have the allegedly mistaken intuition and why it is so persistent. Why do people believe so firmly that killing is so much worse than letting die, both in fictitious cases such as Trammell's, and in the famine relief cases in the real world? In some ways the explanation of this is best left to the psychologists; the distinctly philosophical job is accomplished when the intuition is shown to be false. However, I shall hazard a hypothesis, since it shows how our intuitions can be explained without assuming that they are perceptions of the truth.

Human beings are to some degree altruistic, but they are also to a great degree selfish, and their attitudes on matters of conduct are largely determined by what is in their own interests, and what is in the interests of the few other people they especially care about. In terms of both the costs and the benefits, it is to their own advantage for people in the affluent countries to regard killing as worse than letting die. First, the *costs* of never killing anyone are not great; we can live very well without ever killing. But the cost of not allowing people to die, when we could save them, would be very great. For any one of us to take seriously a duty to save the starving would require that we give up our affluent lifestyles; money could no longer be spent on luxuries while others starve. On the other side, we have much more to *gain* from a strict prohibition on killing than from a like prohibition on letting die. Since we are not in danger of starving, we will not suffer if people do not regard feeding the hungry as so important; but we would be threatened if people did not regard killing as very, very bad. So, both the costs and the benefits encourage us, selfishly, to view killing as worse than letting die. It is to our own advantage to believe this, and so we do.

Footnotes

1. For an account of the difficulties of getting reliable information in this area, see Nick Eberstadt, "Myths of the Food Crisis," *New York Review of Books* (19 February 1976); 32–37.

2. Richard L. Trammell, "Saving Life and Taking Life," *Journal of Philosophy* 72 (1975): 131–137, is the best defense of this view of which I am aware.

3. This article is a companion to an earlier one, "Active and Passive Euthanasia," *New England Journal of Medicine* 292 (9 January 1975): 78–80, in which I discuss the (mis)use of the killing/letting die distinction in medical contexts. But nothing in this article depends on the earlier one.

4. Philippa Foot, "The Problem of Abortion and the Doctrine of the Double Effect," *Oxford Review* No. 5 (1967); reprinted in J. Rachels (ed.), *Moral Problems*, 2nd ed. (New York: Harper and Row, 1975), p. 66.

5. On this point, and more generally on the whole subject of our duty to contribute for famine relief, see Peter Singer, "Famine, Affluence, and Morality," *Philosophy and Public Affairs* 1 (Spring 1972): 232.

6. Trammell, p. 133.

7. This argument is suggested by Paul Ramsey in *The Patient as Person* (New Haven, CN: Yale University Press, 1970), p. 151.

8. This difference between failing to save and letting die was pointed out by David Sanford in a very helpful paper, "On Killing and Letting Die," read at the Western Division meeting of the American Philosophical Association, New Orleans, 30 April 1976.

9. Trammell, p. 133.

10. Trammell, p. 134.

11. There is also some independent evidence that this prereflective belief is mistaken; see Singer, "Famine, Affluence, and Morality."

12. Grice made this remark several years ago at Oberlin. I do not remember the surrounding details of the discussion, but the remark seems to me an important one that applies to lots of "objections" to various theories. The most famous objections to act-utilitarianism, for example, are little more than descriptions of the theory, with the question-begging addendum, "Because it says *that*, it can't be right."

13. Daniel Dinello, "On Killing and Letting Die," *Analysis* 31 (January 1971): 85–86.

14. Trammell, p. 131.

15. Dinello, p. 85.

16. There is another way to meet Dinello's counter-example. A surprisingly strong case can be made that it would *not* be any worse to kill Smith than to "let Jones die." I have in mind adapting John Harris's argument in "The Survival Lottery," *Philosophy* 50 (1975): 81–87.

Review Questions

1. What is the Equivalence Thesis?
2. Why isn't spatial location a morally relevant consideration?
3. What is "dischargeability?" Why isn't it relevant?
4. According to Rachels, why isn't there a difference between action and inaction?
5. What is "optionality?" Why isn't it morally relevant?
6. Rachels distinguishes between three sorts of *reductio* arguments. What are they?
7. Why doesn't Rachels accept the objection that the Equivalence Thesis is counter-intuitive?

Discussion Questions

1. Does Rachels refute Foot's view of the duty to give aid? Defend your answer.
2. Rachels says that many of our moral intuitions are mistaken. Is this true? If you agree, give some examples.
3. Does Rachels himself appeal to intuition in his examples? Why, or why not?

GARRETT HARDIN

Living on a Lifeboat

Garrett Hardin is Professor of Biology at the University of California at Santa Barbara. He is the author of many books, including The Limits of Altruism: An Ecologist's View of Survival (1977).

Hardin uses the metaphor of a lifeboat to argue that rich nations such as the United States do not have a moral obligation to help poor nations. In fact, he claims, aid in the form of food makes matters worse; it results in more population growth, and eventually the ruin of natural resources such as oceans.

Susanne Langer (1942) has shown that it is probably impossible to approach an unsolved problem save through the door of metaphor. Later, attempting to meet the demands of rigor, we may achieve some success in cleansing theory of metaphor, though our success is limited if we are unable to avoid using common language, which is shot through and through with fossil metaphors. (I count no less than five in the preceding two sentences.)

Since metaphorical thinking is inescapable it is pointless merely to weep about our human limitations. We must learn to live with them, to understand them, and to control them. "All of us," said George Eliot in Middlemarch, "get our thoughts entangled in metaphors, and act fatally on the strength of them." To avoid unconscious suicide we are well advised to pit one metaphor against another. From the interplay of competitive metaphors, thoroughly developed, we may come closer to metaphor-free solutions to our problems.

No generation has viewed the problem of the survival of the human species as seriously as we have. Inevitably, we have entered this world of concern through the door of metaphor. Environmentalists have emphasized the image of the earth as a spaceship— Spaceship Earth. Kenneth Boulding (1966) is the principal architect of this metaphor. It is time, he says, that we replace the wasteful "cowboy economy" of the past with the frugal "spaceship economy" required for continued survival in the limited world we now see ours to be. The metaphor is notably useful in justifying pollution-control measures.

Unfortunately, the image of a spaceship is also used to promote measures that are suicidal. One of these is a generous immigration policy, which is only a particular instance of a class of policies that are in error because they lead to the tragedy of the commons (Hardin 1968). These suicidal policies are attractive because they mesh with what we unthinkingly take to be the ideals of "the best people." What is missing in the idealistic view is an insistence that rights and responsibilities must go together. The "generous" attitude of all too many people results in asserting inalienable rights while ignoring or denying matching responsibilities.

For the metaphor of a spaceship to be correct the aggregate of people on board would have to be under unitary sovereign control (Ophuls 1974). A true ship always has a captain. It is conceivable that a ship could be run by a committee. But it could not possibly survive if its course were determined by bickering tribes that claimed rights without responsibilities.

What about Spaceship Earth? It certainly has no captain, and no executive committee. The United Nations is a toothless tiger, because the signatories of its charter wanted it that way. The spaceship metaphor is used only to justify spaceship demands on common resources without acknowledging corresponding spaceship responsibilities.

An understandable fear of decisive action leads people to embrace "incrementalism"—moving toward reform by tiny stages. As we shall see, this strategy is counterproductive in the area discussed here if it means accepting rights before responsibilities. Where human survival is at stake, the acceptance of responsibilities is a precondition to the acceptance of rights, if the two cannot be introduced simultaneously.

LIFEBOAT ETHICS

Before taking up certain substantive issues let us look at an alternative metaphor, that of a lifeboat. In developing some relevant examples the following numerical values are assumed. Approximately two-thirds of the world is desperately poor, and only one-third is comparatively rich. The people in poor countries have an average per capita GNP (Gross National Product) of about $200 per year; the rich, of about $3,000. (For the United States it is nearly $5,000 per year.) Metaphorically, each rich nation amounts to a lifeboat full of comparatively rich people. The poor of the world are in other, much more crowded lifeboats. Continuously, so to speak, the poor fall out of their lifeboats and swim for a while in the water outside, hoping to be admitted to a rich lifeboat, or in some other way to benefit from the "goodies" on board. What should the passengers on a rich lifeboat do? This is the central problem of "the ethics of a lifeboat."

First we must acknowledge that each lifeboat is effectively limited in capacity. The land of every nation has a limited carrying capacity. The exact limit is a matter for argument, but the energy crunch is convincing more people every day that we have already exceeded the carrying capacity of the land. We have been living on "capital"—stored petroleum and coal—and soon we must live on income alone.

Let us look at only one lifeboat—ours. The ethical problem is the same for all, and is as follows. Here we sit, say fifty people in a lifeboat. To be generous, let us assume our boat has a capacity of ten more, making sixty. (This, however, is to violate the engineering principle of the "safety factor." A new plant disease or a bad change in the weather may decimate our population if we don't preserve some excess capacity as a safety factor.)

The fifty of us in the lifeboat see 100 others swimming in the water outside, asking for admission to the boat, or for handouts. How shall we respond to their calls? There are several possibilities.

One. We may be tempted to try to live by the Christian ideal of being "our brother's keeper," or by the Marxian ideal (Marx 1875) of "from each according to his abilities, to each according to his needs." Since the needs of all are the same, we take all the needy into our boat, making a total of 150 in a boat with a capacity of sixty. The boat is swamped, and everyone drowns. Complete justice, complete catastrophe.

Two. Since the boat has an unused excess capacity of ten, we admit just ten more to it. This has the disadvantage of getting rid of the safety factor, for which action we will sooner or later pay dearly. Moreover, *which* ten do we let in? "First come, first served?" The best ten? The neediest ten? How do we *discriminate?* And what do we say to the ninety who are excluded?

Three. Admit no more to the boat and preserve the small safety factor. Survival of the people in the lifeboat is then possible (though we shall have to be on our guard against boarding parties).

The last solution is abhorrent to many people. It is unjust, they say. Let us grant that it is.

"I feel guilty about my good luck," say some. The reply to this is simple: *Get out and yield your place to others.* Such a selfless action might satisfy the conscience of those who are addicted to guilt but it would not change the ethics of the lifeboat. The needy person to whom a guilt-addict yields his place will not himself feel guilty about his sudden good luck. (If he did he would not climb aboard.) The net result of conscience-stricken people relinquishing their unjustly held positions is the elimination of their kind of conscience from the lifeboat. The lifeboat, as it were, purifies itself of guilt. The ethics of the lifeboat persist, unchanged by such momentary aberrations.

This then is the basic metaphor within which we must work out our solutions. Let us enrich the image step by step with substantive additions from the real world.

REPRODUCTION

The harsh characteristics of lifeboat ethics are heightened by reproduction, particularly by reproductive differences. The people inside the lifeboats of the wealthy nations are doubling in numbers every eighty-seven years; those outside are doubling every thirty-five years, on the average. And the relative difference in prosperity is becoming greater.

Let us, for a while, think primarily of the U.S. lifeboat. As of 1973 the United States had a population of 210 million people, who were increasing by 0.8% per year, that is, doubling in number every eighty-seven years.

Although the citizens of rich nations are outnumbered two to one by the poor, let us imagine an equal number of poor people outside our lifeboat—a mere 210 million poor people reproducing at a quite different rate. If we imagine these to be the combined populations of Columbia, Venezuela, Ecuador, Morocco, Thailand, Pakistan, and the Philippines, the average rate of increase of the people "outside" is 3.3% per year. The doubling time of this population is twenty-one years.

Suppose that all these countries, and the United States, agreed to live by the Marxian ideal, "to each according to his needs," the

ideal of most Christians as well. Needs, of course, are determined by population size, which is affected by reproduction. Every nation regards its rate of reproduction as a sovereign right. If our lifeboat were big enough in the beginning it might be possible to live *for a while* by Christian-Marxian ideals. *Might.*

Initially, in the model given, the ratio of non-Americans to Americans would be one to one. But consider what the ratio would be eighty-seven years later. By this time Americans would have doubled to a population of 420 million. The other group (doubling every twenty-one years) would now have swollen to 3,540 million. Each American would have more than eight people to share with. How could the lifeboat possibly keep afloat?

All this involves extrapolation of current trends into the future, and is consequently suspect. Trends may change. Granted: but the change will not necessarily be favorable. If—as seems likely—the rate of population increase falls faster in the ethnic group presently inside the lifeboat than it does among those now outside, the future will turn out to be even worse than mathematics predicts, and sharing will be even more suicidal.

RUIN IN THE COMMONS

The fundamental error of the sharing ethics is that it leads to the tragedy of the commons. Under a system of private property the man (or group of men) who own property recognize their responsibility to care for it, for if they don't they will eventually suffer. A farmer, for instance, if he is intelligent, will allow no more cattle in a pasture than its carrying capacity justifies. If he overloads the pasture, weeds take over, erosion sets in, and the owner loses in the long run.

But if a pasture is run as a commons open to all, the right of each to use it is not matched by an operational responsibility to take care of it. It is no use asking independent herdsmen in a commons to act responsibly, for they dare not. The considerate herdsman who refrains from overloading the commons suffers more than a selfish one who says his needs are greater. (As Leo Durocher says, "Nice guys finish last.") Christian-Marxian idealism is counterproductive. That it *sounds* nice is no excuse. With distribution systems, as with individual morality, good intentions are no substitute for good performance.

A social system is stable only if it is insensitive to errors. To the Christian-Marxian idealist a selfish person is a sort of "error." Prosperity in the system of the commons cannot survive errors. If *everyone* would only restrain himself, all would be well; but it takes *only one less than everyone* to ruin a system of voluntary restraint. In a crowded world of less than perfect human beings—and we will never know any other—mutual ruin is inevitable in the commons. This is the core of the tragedy of the commons.

One of the major tasks of education today is to create such an awareness of the dangers of the commons that people will be able to recognize its many varieties, however disguised. There is pollution of the air and water because these media are treated as commons. Further growth of population and growth in the per capita conversion of natural resources into pollutants require that the system of the commons be modified or abandoned in the disposal of "externalities."

The fish populations of the oceans are exploited as commons, and ruin lies ahead. No technological invention can prevent this fate; in fact, all improvements in the art of fishing merely hasten the day of complete ruin. Only the replacement of the system of the commons with a responsible system can save oceanic fisheries.

The management of western range lands, though nominally rational, is in fact (under the steady pressure of cattle ranchers) often merely a government-sanctioned system of the commons, drifting toward ultimate ruin for both the rangelands and the residual enterprisers.

WORLD FOOD BANKS

In the international arena we have recently heard a proposal to create a new commons, namely an international depository of food reserves to which nations will contribute according to their abilities, and from which nations may draw according to their needs. Nobel laureate Norman Borlaug has lent the prestige of his name to this proposal.

A world food bank appeals powerfully to our humanitarian impulses. We remember John Donne's celebrated line, "Any man's death diminishes me." But before we rush out to see for whom the bell tolls let us recognize where the greatest political push for international granaries comes from, lest we be disillusioned later. Our experience with Public Law 480 clearly reveals the answer. This was the law that moved billions of dollars worth of U.S. grain to food-short, population-long countries during the past two decades. When P.L. 480 first came into being, a headline in the business magazine *Forbes* (Paddock and Paddock 1970) revealed the power behind it: "Feeding the World's Hungry Millions: How it will mean billions for U.S. business."

And indeed it did. In the years 1960 to 1970 a total of $7.9 billion was spent on the "Food for Peace" program, as P.L. 480 was called. During the years 1948 to 1970 an additional $49.9 billion were extracted from American taxpayers to pay for other economic aid programs, some of which went for food and food-producing machinery. (This figure does *not* include military aid.) That P.L. 480 was a giveaway program was concealed. Recipient countries went through the motions of paying for P.L. 480 food—with IOUs. In December 1973 the charade was brought to an end as far as India was concerned when the United States "forgave" India's $3.2 billion debt (Anonymous 1974). Public announcement of the cancellation of the debt was delayed for two months; one wonders why.

"Famine—1974!" (Paddock and Paddock 1970) is one of the few publications that points out the commercial roots of this humanitarian attempt. Though all U.S. taxpayers lost by P.L. 480, special interest groups gained handsomely. Farmers benefited because they were not asked to contribute the grain—it was bought from them by the taxpayers. Besides the direct benefit there was the indirect effect of increasing demand and thus raising prices of farm products generally. The manufacturers of farm machinery, fertilizers, and pesticides benefited by the farmers' extra efforts to grow more food. Grain elevators profited from storing the grain for varying lengths of time. Railroads made money hauling it to port, and shipping lines by carrying it overseas. Moreover, once the machinery for P.L. 480 was established an immense bureaucracy had a vested interest in its continuance regardless of its merits.

Very little was ever heard of these selfish interests when P.L. 480 was defended in public. The emphasis was always on its humanitarian effects. The combination of multiple and relatively silent selfish interests with highly vocal humanitarian apologists constitutes a powerful lobby for extracting money from taxpayers. Foreign aid has become a habit that can apparently survive in the absence of any known justification. A news commentator in a weekly magazine (Lansner 1974), after exhaustively going over all the conventional arguments for foreign aid—self-interest, social justice, political advantage, and charity—and concluding that none of the known arguments really held water, concluded: "So the search continues for some logically compelling reasons for giving aid . . .." In other words, *Act now, justify later*—if ever. (Apparently a quarter of a century is too short a time to find the justification for expending several billion dollars yearly).

The search for a rational justification can be short-circuited by interjecting the word "emergency." Borlaug uses this word. We need to look sharply at it. What is an "emergency?" It is surely something like an accident, which is correctly defined as *an event that is certain to happen, though with a*

low frequency (Hardin 1972a). A well-run organization prepares for everything that is certain, including accidents and emergencies. It budgets for them. It saves for them. It expects them—and mature decision-makers do not waste time complaining about accidents when they occur.

What happens if some organizations budget for emergencies and others do not? If each organization is solely responsible for its own well-being, poorly managed ones will suffer. But they should be able to learn from experience. They have a chance to mend their ways and learn to budget for infrequent but certain emergencies. The weather, for instance, always varies and periodic crop failures are certain. A wise and competent government saves out of the production of the good years in anticipation of bad years that are sure to come. This is not a new idea. The Bible tells us that Joseph taught this policy to Pharaoh in Egypt more than 2,000 years ago. Yet it is literally true that the vast majority of the governments of the world today have no such policy. They lack either the wisdom or the competence, or both. Far more difficult than the transfer of wealth from one country to another is the transfer of wisdom between sovereign powers or between generations.

"But it isn't their fault! How can we blame the poor people who are caught in an emergency? Why must we punish them?" The concepts of blame and punishment are irrelevant. The question is, what are the operational consequences of establishing a world food bank? If it is open to every country every time a need develops, slovenly rulers will not be motivated to take Joseph's advice. Why should they? Others will bail them out whenever they are in trouble.

Some countries will make deposits in the world food bank and others will withdraw from it; there will be almost no overlap. Calling such a depository-transfer unit a "bank" is stretching the metaphor of *bank* beyond its elastic limits. The proposers, of course, never call attention to the metaphorical nature of the word they use.

THE RATCHET EFFECT

An "international food bank" is really, then, not a true bank but a disguised one-way transfer device for moving wealth from rich countries to poor. In the absence of such a bank, in a world inhabited by individually responsible sovereign nations, the population of each nation would repeatedly go through a cycle of the sort shown in Exhibit A. P_2 is greater than P_1, either in absolute numbers or because a deterioration of the food supply has removed the safety factor and produced a dangerously low ratio of resources to population. P_2 may be said to represent a state of overpopulation, which becomes obvious upon the appearance of an "accident," e.g., a crop failure. If the "emergency" is not met by outside help, the population drops back to the "normal" level—the "carrying capacity" of the environment—or even below. In the absence of population control by a sovereign, sooner or later the population grows to P_2 again and the cycle repeats. The long-term population curve (Hardin 1966) is an irregularly fluctuating one, equilibrating more or less about the carrying capacity.

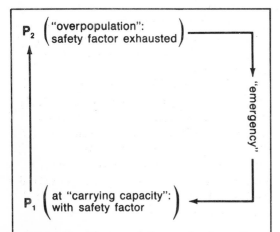

Exhibit A. The population cycle of a nation that has no effective, conscious population control, and which receives no aid from the outside. P_2 is greater than P_1.

A demographic cycle of this sort obviously involves great suffering in the restrictive phase, but such a cycle is normal to any independent country with inadequate population control. The third century theologian Tertullian (Hardin 1969a) expressed what must have been the recognition of many wise men when he wrote: "The scourges of pestilence, famine, wars, and earthquakes have come to be regarded as a blessing to overcrowded nations, since they serve to prune away the luxuriant growth of the human race."

Only under a strong and farsighted sovereign—which theoretically could be the people themselves, democratically organized—can a population equilibrate at some set point below the carrying capacity, thus avoiding the pains normally caused by periodic and unavoidable disasters. For this happy state to be achieved it is necessary those in power be able to contemplate with equanimity the "waste" of surplus food in times of bountiful harvests. It is essential that those in power resist the temptation to convert extra food into extra babies. On the public relations level it is necessary that the phrase "surplus food" be replaced by "safety factor."

But wise sovereigns seem not to exist in the poor world today. The most anguishing problems are created by poor countries that are governed by rulers insufficiently wise and powerful. If such countries can draw on a world food bank in times of "emergency," the population *cycle* of Exhibit A will be replaced by the population *escalator* of Exhibit B. The input of food from a food bank acts as the pawl of a ratchet, preventing the population from retracting its steps to a lower level. Reproduction pushes the population upward, inputs from the world bank prevent its moving downward. Population size escalates, as does the absolute magnitude of "accidents" and "emergencies." The process is brought to an end only by the total collapse of the whole system, producing a catastrophe of scarcely imaginable proportions.

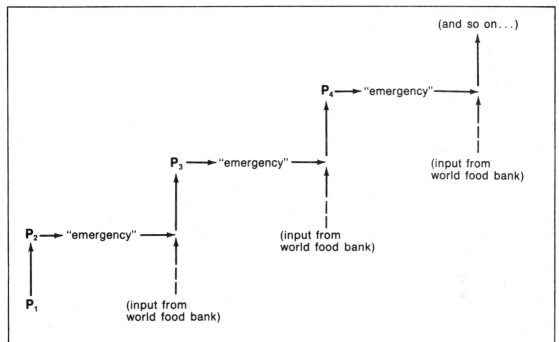

Exhibit B. The population escalator. Note that input from a world food bank acts like the pawl of a ratchet, preventing the normal population cycle shown in Exhibit A from being completed. P_{n+1} is greater than P_n, and the absolute magnitude of the "emergencies" escalates. Ultimately the entire system crashes. The crash is not shown, and few can imagine it.

Such are the implications of the well-meant sharing of food in a world of irresponsible reproduction.

I think we need a new word for systems like this. The adjective "melioristic" is applied to systems that produce continual improvement; the English word is derived from the Latin *meliorare,* to become or make better. Parallel with this it would be useful to bring in the word *pejoristic* (from the Latin *pejorare,* to become or make worse). This word can be applied to those systems that by their very nature, can be relied upon to make matters worse. A world food bank coupled with sovereign state irresponsibility in reproduction is an example of a pejoristic system.

This pejoristic system creates an unacknowledged commons. People have more motivation to draw from than to add to the common store. The license to make such withdrawals diminishes whatever motiva-tion poor countries might otherwise have to control their populations. Under the guidance of this ratchet, wealth can be steadily moved in one direction only, from the slowly-breeding rich to the rapidly-breeding poor, the process finally coming to a halt only when all countries are equally and miserably poor.

All this is terribly obvious once we are acutely aware of the pervasiveness and danger of the commons. But many people still lack this awareness and the euphoria of the "benign demographic transition" (Hardin 1973) interferes with the realistic appraisal of pejoristic mechanisms. As concerns public policy, the deductions drawn from the benign demographic transition are these:

1. If the per capita GNP rises the birth rate will fall; hence, the rate of population increase will fall, ultimately producing ZPG (Zero Population Growth).

2. The long-term trend all over the world (including the poor countries) is of a rising per capita GNP (for which no limit is seen).
3. Therefore, all political interference in population matters is unnecessary; all we need to do is foster economic "development"—*note the metaphor*—and population problems will solve themselves.

Those who believe in the benign demographic transition dismiss the pejoristic mechanism of Exhibit B in the belief that each input of food from the world outside fosters development within a poor country thus resulting in a drop in the rate of population increase. Foreign aid has proceeded on this assumption for more than two decades. Unfortunately it has produced no indubitable instance of the asserted effect. It has, however, produced a library of excuses. The air is filled with plaintive calls for more massive foreign aid appropriations so that the hypothetical melioristic process can get started.

The doctrine of demographic laissez-faire implicit in the hypothesis of the benign demographic transition is immensely attractive. Unfortunately there is more evidence against the melioristic system than there is for it (Davis 1963). On the historical side there are many counter-examples. The rise in per capita GNP in France and Ireland during the past century has been accompanied by a rise in population growth. In the twenty years following the Second World War the same positive correlation was noted almost everywhere in the world. Never in world history before 1950 did the worldwide population growth reach one percent per annum. Now the average population growth is over two percent and shows no signs of slackening.

On the theoretical side, the denial of the pejoristic scheme of Exhibit B probably springs from the hidden acceptance of the "cowboy economy" that Boulding castigated. Those who recognize the limitations of a spaceship, if they are unable to achieve population control at a safe and comfortable level, accept the necessity of the corrective feedback of the population cycle shown in Exhibit A. No one who knew in his bones that he was living on a true spaceship would countenance political support of the population escalator shown in Exhibit B.

ECO–DESTRUCTION VIA THE GREEN REVOLUTION

The demoralizing effect of charity on the recipient has long been known. "Give a man a fish and he will eat for a day; teach him how to fish and he will eat for the rest of his days." So runs an ancient Chinese proverb. Acting on this advice the Rockefeller and Ford Foundations have financed a multipronged program for improving agriculture in the hungry nations. The result, known as the "Green Revolution," has been quite remarkable. "Miracle wheat" and "miracle rice" are splendid technological achievements in the realm of plant genetics.

Whether or not the Green Revolution can increase food production is doubtful (Harris 1972, Paddock 1970, Wilkes 1972), but in any event not particularly important. What is missing in this great and well-meaning humanitarian effort is a firm grasp of fundamentals. Considering the importance of the Rockefeller Foundation in this effort it is ironic that the late Alan Gregg, a much-respected vice-president of the Foundation, strongly expressed his doubts of the wisdom of all attempts to increase food production some two decades ago. (This was before Borlaug's work—supported by Rockefeller—had resulted in the development of "miracle wheat.") Gregg (1955) likened the growth and spreading of humanity over the surface of the earth to the metastasis of cancer in the human body, wryly remarking that "Cancerous growths demand food; but, as far as I know, they have never been cured by getting it."

"Man does not live by bread alone"—the scriptural statement has a rich meaning even in the material realm. Every human being born constitutes a draft on all aspects of the environment—food, air, water, unspoiled scenery, occasional and optional solitude, beaches, contact with wild animals, fishing, hunting—the list is long and incompletely known. Food can, perhaps, be significantly increased, but what about clean beaches, unspoiled forests, and solitude? If we satisfy the need for food in a growing population we necessarily decrease the supply of other goods, and thereby increase the difficulty of equitably allocating scarce goods (Hardin 1969b, 1972b).

The present population of India is 600 million, and it is increasing by fifteen million per year. The environmental load of this population is already great. The forests of India are only a small fraction of what they were three centuries ago. Soil erosion, floods, and the psychological costs of crowding are serious. Every one of the net fifteen million lives added each year stresses the Indian environment more severely. *Every life saved this year in a poor country diminishes the quality of life for subsequent generations.*

Observant critics have shown how much harm we wealthy nations have already done to poor nations through our well-intentioned but misguided attempts to help them (Paddock and Paddock 1973). Particularly reprehensible is our failure to carry out post-audits of these attempts (Farvar and Milton 1972). Thus have we shielded our tender consciences from knowledge of the harm we have done. Must we Americans continue to fail to monitor the consequences of our external "do-gooding?" If, for instance, we thoughtlessly make it possible for the present 600 million Indians to swell to 1,200 million by the year 2001—as their present growth rate promises—will posterity in India thank *us* for facilitating an even greater destruction of *their* environment? Are good intentions ever a sufficient excuse for bad consequences?

IMMIGRATION CREATES A COMMONS

I come now to the final example of a commons in action, one for which the public is least prepared for rational discussion. The topic is at present enveloped by a great silence that reminds me of a comment made by Sherlock Holmes in A. Conan Doyle's story, "Silver Blaze." Inspector Gregory had asked, "Is there any point to which you wish to draw my attention?" To this Holmes responded:

"To the curious incident of the dog in the night-time."
"The dog did nothing in the night-time," said the Inspector.
"That was the curious incident," remarked Sherlock Holmes.

By asking himself what would repress the normal barking instinct of a watch dog Holmes realized that it must be the dog's recognition of his master as the criminal trespasser. In a similar way we should ask ourselves what repression keeps us from discussing something as important as immigration?

It cannot be that immigration is numerically of no consequence. Our government acknowledges a *net* inflow of 400,000 a year. Hard data are understandably lacking on the extent of illegal entries, but a not implausible figure is 600,000 per year. (Buchanan 1973). The natural increase of the resident population is now about 1.7 million per year. This means that the yearly gain from immigration is at least nineteen percent and may be thirty-seven percent, of the total increase. It is quite conceivable that educational campaigns like that of Zero Population Growth, Inc., coupled with adverse social and economic factors—inflation, housing shortage, depression, and loss of confidence in national leaders—may lower the fertility of American women to a point at which all of the yearly increase in population would be accounted for by immigration. Should we not at least ask if that is what we want? How curious it is that we so seldom discuss immigration these days!

Curious, but understandable—as one finds out the moment he publicly questions the wisdom of the status quo in immigration.

He who does so is promptly charged with *isolationism, bigotry, prejudice, ethnocentrism, chauvinism,* and *selfishness.* These are hard accusations to bear. It is pleasanter to talk about other matters, leaving immigration policy to wallow in the crosscurrents of special interests that take no account of the good of the whole—*or of the interests of posterity.*

We Americans have a bad conscience because of things we said in the past about immigrants. Two generations ago the popular press was rife with references to *Dagos, Wops, Pollacks, Japs, Chinks,* and *Krauts*—all pejorative terms that failed to acknowledge our indebtedness to Goya, Leonardo, Copernicus, Hiroshige, Confucius, and Bach. Because the implied inferiority of foreigners was *then* the justification for keeping them out, it is *now* thoughtlessly assumed that restrictive policies can only be based on the assumption of immigrant inferiority. *This is not so.*

Existing immigration laws exclude idiots and known criminals; future laws will almost certainly continue this policy. But should we also consider the quality of the average immigrant, as compared with the quality of the average resident? Perhaps we should, perhaps we shouldn't. (What is "quality" anyway?) But the quality issue is not our concern here.

From this point on, *it will be assumed that immigrants and native-born citizens are of exactly equal quality,* however quality may be defined. The focus is only on quantity. The conclusions reached depend on nothing else, so all charges of ethnocentrism are irrelevant.

World food banks move food to the people, thus facilitating the exhaustion of the environment of the poor. By contrast, unrestricted immigration moves people to the food, thus speeding up the destruction of the environment in rich countries. Why poor people should want to make this transfer is no mystery, but why should rich hosts encourage it? This transfer, like the reverse one, is supported by both selfish interests and humanitarian impulses.

The principal selfish interest in unimpeded immigration is easy to identify: it is the interest of the employers of cheap labor, particularly that needed for degrading jobs. We have been deceived about the forces of history by the lines of Emma Lazarus inscribed on the Statue of Liberty:

Give me your tired, your poor,
Your huddled masses yearning to breathe free,
The wretched refuse of your teeming shore,
Send these, the homeless, tempest-tossed to me:
I lift my lamp beside the golden door.

The image is one of an infinitely generous earth-mother, passively opening her arms to hordes of immigrants who come here on their own initiative. Such an image may have been adequate for the early days of colonization, but by the time these lines were written (1886) the force for immigration was largely manufactured inside our own borders by factory and mine owners who sought cheap labor not to be found among laborers already here. One group of foreigners after another was thus enticed into the United States to work at wretched jobs for wretched wages.

At present, it is largely the Mexicans who are being so exploited. It is particularly to the advantage of certain employers that there be many illegal immigrants. Illegal immigrant workers dare not complain about their working conditions for fear of being repatriated. Their presence reduces the bargaining power of all Mexican-American laborers. Cesar Chavez has repeatedly pleaded with congressional committees to close the doors to more Mexicans so that those here can negotiate effectively for higher wages and decent working conditions. Chavez understands the ethics of a lifeboat.

The interests of the employers of cheap labor are well served by the silence of the intelligentsia of the country. WASPS—White Anglo-Saxon Protestants—are particularly reluctant to call for a closing of the doors to immigration for fear of being called ethnocentric bigots. It was, therefore, an occasion of pure delight for this particular WASP to be present at a meeting when the points he would like to have made were made better by a non-WASP speaking to other non-WASPS. It was in Hawaii, and most of the people in the room were second-level Hawaiian officials of Japanese ancestry. All Hawaiians are keenly aware of the limits of their environment, and the speaker had asked how it might be practically and constitutionally possible to close the doors to more immigrants to the islands. (To Hawaiians, immigrants from the other forty-nine states are as much of a threat as those from other nations. There is only so much room in the islands, and the islanders know it. Sophistical arguments that imply otherwise do not impress them.)

Yet the Japanese-Americans of Hawaii have active ties with the land of their origin. This point was raised by a Japanese-American member of the audience who asked the Japanese-American speaker: "But how can we shut the doors now? We have many friends and relations in Japan that we'd like to bring to Hawaii some day so that they can enjoy this beautiful land."

The speaker smiled sympathetically and responded slowly, "Yes, but we have children now and someday we'll have grandchildren. We can bring more people here from Japan only by giving away some of the land that we hope to pass on to our grandchildren some day. What right do we have to do that?"

To be generous with one's own possessions is one thing; to be generous with posterity's is quite another. This, I think, is the point that must be gotten across to those who would, from a commendable love of distributive justice, institute a ruinous system of the commons, either in the form of a world food bank or that of unrestricted immigration. Since every speaker is a member of some ethnic group it is always possible to charge him with ethnocentrism. But even after purging an argument of ethnocentrism the rejection of the commons is still valid

and necessary if we are to save at least some parts of the world from environmental ruin. Is it not desirable that at least some of the grandchildren of people now living should have a decent place in which to live?

THE ASYMMETRY OF DOOR–SHUTTING

We must now answer this telling point: "How can you justify slamming the door once you're inside? You say that immigrants should be kept out. But aren't we all immigrants, or the descendants of immigrants? Since we refuse to leave, must we not, as a matter of justice and symmetry, admit all others?"

It is literally true that we Americans of non-Indian ancestry are the descendants of thieves. Should we not, then, "give back" the land to the Indians, that is, give it to the now-living Americans of Indian ancestry? As an exercise in pure logic I see no way to reject this proposal. Yet I am unwilling to live by it, and I know no one who is. Our reluctance to embrace pure justice may spring from pure selfishness. On the other hand, it may arise from an unspoken recognition of consequences that have not yet been clearly spelled out.

Suppose, becoming intoxicated with pure justice, we "Anglos" should decide to turn our land over to the Indians. Since all our other wealth has also been derived from the land, we would have to give that to the Indians, too. Then what would we non-Indians do? Where would we go? There is no open land in the world on which men without capital can make their living (and not much unoccupied land on which men with capital can either). Where would 209 million putatively justice-loving, non-Indian Americans go? Most of them—in the persons of their ancestors—came from Europe, but they wouldn't be welcomed back there. Anyway, Europeans have no better title to their land than we to ours. They also would have to give up their homes. (But to whom? And where would *they* go?)

Clearly, the concept of pure justice produces an infinite regress. The law long ago invented statutes of limitations to justify the rejection of pure justice, in the interest of preventing massive disorder. The law zealously defends property rights—but only *recent* property rights. It is as though the physical principle of exponential decay applies to property rights. Drawing a line in time may be unjust, but any other action is practically worse.

We are all the descendants of thieves, and the world's resources are inequitably distributed, but we must begin the journey to tomorrow from the point where we are today. We cannot remake the past. We cannot, without violent disorder and suffering, give land and resources back to the "original" owners—who are dead anyway.

We cannot safely divide the wealth equitably among all present peoples, so long as people reproduce at different rates, because to do so would guarantee that our grandchildren—everyone's grandchildren—would have only a ruined world to inhabit.

MUST EXCLUSION BE ABSOLUTE?

To show the logical structure of the immigration problem I have ignored many factors that would enter into real decisions made in a real world. No matter how convincing the logic may be it is probable that we would want, from time to time, to admit a few people from the outside to our lifeboat. Political refugees in particular are likely to cause us to make exceptions: We remember the Jewish refugees from Germany after 1933, and the Hungarian refugees after 1956. Moreover, the interests of national defense, broadly conceived, could justify admitting many men and women of unusual talents, whether refugees or not. (This raises the quality issue, which is not the subject of this essay.)

Such exceptions threaten to create runaway population growth inside the lifeboat, i.e., the receiving country. However, the threat can be neutralized by a population policy that includes immigration. An effective policy is one of flexible control.

Suppose, for example, that the nation has achieved a stable condition of ZPG, which (say) permits 1.5 million births yearly. We must suppose that an acceptable system of allocating birth-rights to potential parents is in effect. Now suppose that an inhumane regime in some other part of the world creates a horde of refugees, and that there is a widespread desire to admit some to our country. At the same time, we do not want to sabotage our population control system. Clearly, the rational path to pursue is the following. If we decide to admit 100,000 refugees this year we should compensate for this by reducing the allocation of birth-rights in the following year by a similar amount, that is, downward to a total of 1.4 million. In that way we could achieve both humanitarian and population control goals. (And the refugees would have to accept the population controls of the society that admits them. It is not inconceivable that they might be given proportionately fewer rights than the native population.)

In a democracy, the admission of immigrants should properly be voted on. But by whom? It is not obvious. The usual rule of a democracy is votes for all. But it can be questioned whether a universal franchise is the most just one in a case of this sort. Whatever benefits there are in the admission of immigrants presumably accrue to everyone. But the costs would be seen as falling most heavily on potential parents, some of whom would have to postpone or forego having their (next) child because of the influx of immigrants. The double question *Who benefits? Who pays?* suggests that a restriction of the usual democratic franchise would be appropriate and just in this case. Would our particular quasi-democratic form of government be flexible enough to institute such a novelty? If not, the majority might, out of humanitarian motives, impose an unacceptable burden (the foregoing of parenthood) on a minority, thus producing political instability.

Plainly many new problems will arise when we consciously face the immigration question and seek rational answers. No workable answers can be found if we ignore population problems. And—if the argument of this essay is correct—so long as there is no true world government to control repro-duction everywhere it is impossible to sur-vive in dignity if we are to be guided by Spaceship ethics. Without a world govern-ment that is sovereign in reproductive mat-ters mankind lives, in fact, on a number of sovereign lifeboats. For the foreseeable fu-ture survival demands that we govern our actions by the ethics of a lifeboat. Posterity will be ill served if we do not.

References

Anonymous. 1974. *Wall Street Journal* 19 Feb.

Borlaug, N. 1973. Civilization's future: a call for inter-national granaries. *Bull. At. Sci.* 29: 7–15.

Boulding, K. 1966. The economics of the coming Spaceship Earth. *In* H. Jarrett, ed. Environmental Quality in a Growing Economy. Baltimore: John Hopkins Press.

Buchanan, W. 1973. Immigration statistics. *Equilib-rium* 1(3): 16–19.

Davis, K. 1963. Population. *Sci. Amer.* 209(3): 62–71.

Farvar, M.T., and J.P. Milton. 1972. The Careless Tech-nology. Garden City, NY: Natural History Press.

Gregg, A. 1955. A medical aspect of the population problem. *Science* 121:681–682.

Hardin, G. 1966. Chap. 9 *in* Biology: Its Principles and Implications, 2nd ed. San Francisco: Freeman.

———. 1968. The tragedy of the commons. *Science* 162: 1243–1248.

———. 1969a Page 18 *in* Population, Evolution, and Birth Control, 2nd ed. San Francisco: Freeman.

———. 1969b. The economics of wilderness. *Nat. Hist.* 78(6): 20–27.

———. 1972a. Pages 81–82 *in* Exploring New Ethics for Survival: The Voyage of the Spaceship *Beagle*. New York: Viking.

———. 1972b. Preserving quality on Spaceship Earth. *In* J.B. Trefethen, ed. Transactions of the Thirty-Sev-enth North American Wildlife and Natural Resources Conference. Wildlife Management Institute, Wash-ington, D.C.

———. 1973. Chap. 23 *in* Stalking the Wild Taboo. Los Altos, CA: Kaufmann.

Harris, M. 1972. How green the revolution. *Nat. Hist.* 81(3): 28–30.

Langer, S.K. 1942. Philosophy in a New Key. Cam-bridge, MA: Harvard University Press.

Lansner, K. 1974. Should foreign aid begin at home? *Newsweek,* 11 Feb., p. 32.

Marx, K. 1875. Critique of the Gotha program. Page 388 *in* R.C. Tucker, ed. The Marx-Engels Reader. New York: Norton, 1972.

Ophuls, W. 1974. The scarcity society. *Harpers* 248(1487): 47–52.

Paddock, W.C. 1970. How green is the green revolu-tion? *BioScience* 20: 897–902.

Paddock, W., and E. Paddock. 1973. We Don't Know How. Ames, IA: Iowa State University Press.

Paddock, W., and P. Paddock. 1967. Famine—1975! Boston: Little, Brown.

Wilkes, H.G. 1972. The green revolution. *Environment* 14(8): 32–39.

Review Questions

1. Distinguish between a "cowboy economy" and a "spaceship economy."
2. What is wrong with the spaceship metaphor?
3. Explain Hardin's lifeboat metaphor.
4. Why can't we live by the Christian or the Marxian ideal?
5. What are the reproductive differences between rich and poor nations?
6. Explain the "tragedy of the commons."
7. What is wrong with Public Law 480?
8. Explain the "ratchet effect."
9. What is a "pejoristic system?"
10. What is a "benign demographic transition?" Why isn't such a transition possible according to Hardin?
11. Explain the "Green Revolution." Why won't it solve the problem?

Discussion Questions

1. Are there any respects in which the U.S. is *not* a lifeboat?

2. Is there any solution to the problem of overpopulation in poor countries that does not involve letting people die? What is it?

3. Is there any way to avoid the "tragedy of the commons" that does not involve private ownership? Explain.

4. Is there any way to avoid the "ratchet effect?" Explain.

ONORA O'NEILL

Lifeboat Earth

Copyright © 1975 by Princeton University Press. *Philosophy & Public Affairs*, vol. 4, no. 3 (Spring 1975). Reprinted by permission of Princeton University Press.

Onora O'Neill teaches philosophy at the University of Essex in England. She is the author of Acting on Principle *(1975).*

O'Neill assumes that people on the lifeboat Earth have a right not to be killed (except in cases of unavoidable killing and self-defense), and that there is a corollary duty not to kill others. It follows from this, she argues, that we ought to adopt policies that will prevent others from dying from starvation, particularly prefamine, population, and resources policies.

If in the fairly near future millions of people die of starvation, will those who survive be in any way to blame for those deaths? Is there anything that people ought to do now, and from now on, if they are to be able to avoid responsibility for unjustifiable deaths in famine years? I shall argue from the assumption that persons have a right not to be killed unjustifiably to the claim that we have a duty to try to prevent and postpone famine deaths. A corollary of this claim is that if we do nothing we shall bear some blame for some deaths.

JUSTIFIABLE KILLING

I shall assume that persons have a right not to be killed and a corresponding duty not to kill. I shall make no assumptions about the other rights persons may have. In particular, I shall not assume that persons have a right not to be allowed to die by those who could prevent it or a duty to prevent others'

deaths whenever they could do so. Nor will I assume that persons lack this right.

Even if persons have no rights other than a right not to be killed, this right can justifiably be overridden in certain circumstances. Not all killings are unjustifiable. I shall be particularly concerned with two sorts of circumstances in which the right not to be killed is justifiably overridden. The first of these is the case of unavoidable killings; the second is the case of self-defense.

Unavoidable killings occur in situations in which a person doing some act causes some death or deaths that he could not avoid. Often such deaths will be unavoidable because of the killer's ignorance of some relevant circumstance at the time of his decision to act. If B is driving a train, and A blunders onto the track and is either unnoticed by B or noticed too late for B to stop the train, and B kills A, then B could not have avoided killing A, given his decision to drive the train. Another sort of case of unavoidable killing occurs when B could avoid killing A or could avoid killing C, but cannot avoid killing one of the two. For example, if B is the carrier of a highly contagious and invariably fatal illness, he might find himself so placed that he cannot avoid meeting and so killing either A or C, though he can choose which of them to meet. In this case the unavoidability of B's killing someone is not relative to some prior decision B made. The cases of unavoidable killings with which I want to deal here are of the latter sort, and I shall argue that in such cases B kills justifiably if certain further conditions are met.

A killing may also be justifiable if it is undertaken in self-defense. I shall not argue here that persons have a right of self-defense that is independent of their right not to be killed, but rather that a minimal right of self-defense is a corollary of a right not to be killed. Hence the notion of self-defense on which I shall rely is in some ways different from, and narrower than, other interpretations of the right of self-defense. I shall also assume that if A has a right to defend himself against B, then third parties ought to defend A's right. If we take seriously the right not to be killed and its corollaries, then we ought to enforce others' rights not to be killed.

The right of self-defense that is a corollary of the right not to be killed is a right to take action to prevent killings. If I have a right not to be killed then I have a right to prevent others from endangering my life, though I may endanger their lives in so doing only if that is the only available way to prevent the danger to my own life. Similarly if another has the right not to be killed then I should, if possible, do something to prevent others from endangering his life, but I may endanger their lives in so doing only if that is the only available way to prevent the danger to his life. This duty to defend others is *not* a general duty of beneficence but a very restricted duty to enforce others' rights not to be killed.

The right to self-defense so construed is quite narrow. It includes no right of action against those who, though they cause or are likely to cause us harm, clearly do not endanger our lives. (However, specific cases are often unclear. The shopkeeper who shoots a person who holds him up with a toy gun was not endangered, but it may have been very reasonable of him to suppose that he was endangered.) And it includes no right to greater than minimal preventive action against a person who endangers one's life. If B is chasing A with a gun, and A could save his life either by closing a bullet-proof door or by shooting B, then if people have only a right not to be killed and a minimal corollary right of self-defense, A would have no right to shoot B. (Again, such cases are often unclear—A may not know that the door is bullet-proof or not think of it or may simply reason that shooting B is a better guarantee of prevention.) A right of proportionate self-defense that might justify A in shooting B, even were it clear that closing the door would have been enough to prevent B, is not a corollary of the right not to be killed. Perhaps a right of proportionate retaliation might be justified by some claim such as that aggressors lose certain rights, but I shall take no position on this issue.

In one respect the narrow right of self-defense, which is the corollary of a right not to be killed, is more extensive than some other interpretations of the right of self-defense. For it is a right to take action against others who endanger our lives whether or not they do so intentionally. A's right not to be killed entitles him to take action not only against aggressors but also against those "innocent threats"[1] who endanger lives without being aggressors. If B is likely to cause A's death inadvertently or involuntarily, then A has, if he has a right not to be killed, a right to take whatever steps are necessary to prevent B from doing so, provided that these do not infringe B's right not to be killed unnecessarily. If B approaches A with a highly contagious and invariably lethal illness, then A may try to prevent B from getting near him even if B knows nothing about the danger he brings. If other means fail, A may kill B in self-defense, even though B was no aggressor.

This construal of the right of self-defense severs the link between aggression and self-defense. When we defend ourselves against innocent threats there is no aggressor, only somebody who endangers life. But it would be misleading to call this right a right of self-preservation. For self-preservation is commonly construed (as by Locke) as including a right to subsistence, and so a right to engage in a large variety of activities whether or not anybody endangers us. But the right that is the corollary of the right not to be killed is a right only to prevent others from endangering our lives, whether or not they intend to do so, and to do so with minimal danger to their lives. Only if one takes a Hobbesian view of human nature and sees others' acts as always completely threatening will the rights of self-defense and self-preservation tend to merge and everything done to maintain life be done to prevent its destruction. Without Hobbesian assumptions, the contexts where the minimal right of self-defense can be invoked are fairly special, yet not, I shall argue, rare.

There may be various other circumstances in which persons' rights not to be killed may be overridden. Perhaps, for example, we may justifiably kill those who consent to us doing so. I shall take no position on whether persons can waive their rights not to be killed or on any further situations in which killings might be justifiable.

JUSTIFIABLE
KILLINGS ON LIFEBOATS

The time has come to start imagining lurid situations, which is the standard operating procedure for this type of discussion. I shall begin by looking at some sorts of killings that might occur on a lifeboat and shall consider the sorts of justifications that they might be given.

Let us imagine six survivors on a lifeboat. There are two possible levels of provisions:

(**1**) Provisions are on all reasonable calculations sufficient to last until rescue. Either the boat is near land, or it is amply provisioned or it has gear for distilling water, catching fish, etc.

(**2**) Provisions are on all reasonable calculations unlikely to be sufficient for all six to survive until rescue.

We can call situation (1) *the well-equipped lifeboat situation;* situation (2) *the under-equipped lifeboat situation.* There may, of course, be cases in which the six survivors are unsure which situation they are in, but for simplicity I shall disregard those here.

On a well-equipped lifeboat it is possible for all to survive until rescue. No killing could be justified as unavoidable, and if someone is killed, then the justification could only be self-defense in special situations. Consider the following examples:

(**1A**) On a well-equipped lifeboat with six persons, A threatens to jettison the fresh water, without which some or all would not survive till rescue. A may be either hostile or deranged. B reasons with A, but when this fails, shoots him. B can appeal to his own and the others' right of self-defense to justify the killing. "It was him or us," he may reasonably say, "for he would have placed us in an under-equipped lifeboat situation." He may say this both when A acts to harm the others and when A acts as an innocent threat.

(**1B**) On a well-equipped lifeboat with six persons, B, C, D, E, and F decide to withhold food from A, who consequently dies. In this case they cannot appeal to self-defense—for all could have survived. Nor can they claim that they merely let A die—"We didn't *do* anything"—for A would not otherwise have died. This was not a case of violating the problematic right not to be allowed to die but of violating the right not to be killed, and the violation is without justification of self-defense or of unavoidability.

On an under-equipped lifeboat it is not possible for all to survive until rescue. Some deaths are unavoidable, but sometimes there is no particular person whose death is unavoidable. Consider the following examples:

(2A) On an under-equipped lifeboat with six persons, A is very ill and needs extra water, which is already scarce. The others decide not to let him have any water, and A dies of thirst. If A drinks, then not all will survive. On the other hand it is clear that A was killed rather than allowed to die. If he had received water he might have survived. Though some death was unavoidable, A's was not and selecting him as the victim requires justification.

(2B) On an under-equipped lifeboat with six persons, water is so scarce that only four can survive (perhaps the distillation unit is designed for supplying four people). But who should go without? Suppose two are chosen to go without, either by lot or by some other method, and consequently die. The others cannot claim that all they did was to allow the two who were deprived of water to die—for these two might otherwise have been among the survivors. Nobody had a greater right to be a survivor, but given that not all could survive, those who did not survive were killed justifiably if the method by which they were chosen was fair. (Of course, a lot needs to be said about what would make a selection procedure fair.)

(2C) The same situation as in (2B) holds, but the two who are not to drink ask to be shot to ease their deaths. Again the survivors cannot claim that they did not kill but at most that they killed justifiably. Whether they did so is not affected by their shooting rather than dehydrating the victims, but only by the unavoidability of some deaths and the fairness of procedures for selecting victims.

(2D) Again the basic situation is as in (2B). But the two who are not to drink rebel. The others shoot them and so keep control of the water. Here it is all too clear that those who died were killed, but they too may have been justifiably killed. Whether the survivors kill justifiably depends neither on the method of killing nor on the victims' cooperation, except insofar as cooperation is relevant to the fairness of selection procedures.

Lifeboat situations do not occur very frequently. We are not often confronted starkly with the choice between killing or being killed by the application of a decision to distribute scarce rations in a certain way. Yet this is becoming the situation of the human species on this globe. The current metaphor "spaceship Earth" suggests more drama and less danger; if we are feeling sober about the situation, "lifeboat Earth" may be more suggestive.

Some may object to the metaphor "lifeboat Earth." A lifeboat is small; all aboard have equal claims to be there and to share equally in the provisions. Whereas the earth is vast and, while all may have equal rights to be there, some also have property rights that give them special rights to consume, while others do not. The starving millions are far away and have no right to what is owned by affluent individuals or nations, even if it could prevent their deaths. If they die, it will be said, this is a violation at most of their right not to be allowed to die. And this I have not established or assumed.

I think that this could reasonably have been said in times past. The poverty and consequent deaths of far-off persons was something that the affluent might perhaps have done something to prevent, but that they had (often) done nothing to bring about. Hence they had not violated the right not to be killed of those living far off. But the economic and technological interdependence of today alters this situation.[2] Sometimes deaths are produced by some persons or groups of persons in distant, usually affluent, nations. Sometimes such persons and groups of persons violate not only some persons' alleged right not to be allowed to die but also their more fundamental right not to be killed.

We tend to imagine violations of the right not to be killed in terms of the killings so frequently discussed in the United States today: confrontations between individuals where one directly, violently, and intentionally brings about the other's death. As the lifeboat situations have shown, there are other ways in which we can kill one another. In any case, we do not restrict our vision to the typical mugger or murderer context. B may violate A's right not to be killed even when

(a) B does not act alone.

(b) A's death is not immediate.

(c) It is not certain whether A or another will die in consequence of B's action.

(d) B does not intend A's death.

The following set of examples illustrates these points about killings:

(aa) A is beaten by a gang consisting of B, C, D, etc. No one assailant single-handedly killed him, yet his right not to be killed was violated by all who took part.

(bb) A is poisoned slowly by daily doses. The final dose, like earlier ones, was not, by itself, lethal. But the poisoner still violated A's right not to be killed.

(cc) B plays Russian roulette with A, C, D, E, F, and G, firing a revolver at each once, when he knows that one firing in six will be lethal. If A is shot and dies, then B has violated his right not to be killed.

(dd) Henry II asks who will rid him of the turbulent priest, and his supporters kill Becket. It is reasonably clear that Henry did not intend Becket's death, even though he in part brought it about, as he later admitted.

These explications of the right not to be killed are not too controversial taken individually, and I would suggest that their conjunction is also uncontroversial. Even when A's death is the result of the acts of many persons and is not an immediate consequence of their deeds, nor even a certain consequence, and is not intended by them, A's right not to be killed may be violated.

FIRST CLASS VERSUS STEERAGE ON LIFEBOAT EARTH

If we imagine a lifeboat in which special quarters are provided for the (recently) first-class passengers, and on which the food and water for all passengers are stowed in those

quarters, then we have a fair, if crude, model of the present human situation on lifeboat Earth. For even on the assumption that there is at present sufficient for all to survive, some have control over the means of survival and so, indirectly, over others' survival. Sometimes the exercise of control can lead, even on a well-equipped lifeboat, to the starvation and death of some of those who lack control. On an ill-equipped lifeboat some must die in any case and, as we have already seen, though some of these deaths may be killings, some of them may be justifiable killings. Corresponding situations can, do, and will arise on lifeboat Earth, and it is to these that we should turn our attention, covering both the presumed present situation of global sufficiency of the means of survival and the expected future situation of global insufficiency.

Sufficiency Situations

Aboard a well-equipped lifeboat any distribution of food and water that leads to a death is a killing and not just a case of permitting a death. For the acts of those who distribute the food and water are the causes of a death that would not have occurred had those agents either had no causal influence or done other acts. By contrast, a person whom they leave in the water to drown is merely allowed to die, for his death would have taken place (other things being equal) had those agents had no causal influence, though it could have been prevented had they rescued him.[3] The distinction between killing and allowing to die, as here construed, does not depend on any claims about the other rights of persons who are killed. The death of the shortchanged passenger of example (1B) violated his property rights as well as his right not to be killed, but the reason the death was classifiable as a killing depended on the part that the acts of the other passengers had in causing it. If we suppose that a stowaway on a lifeboat has no right to food and water and is denied them, then clearly his property rights have not been violated. Even so, by the above definitions he is killed rather than allowed to die. For if the other passengers had either had no causal influence or done otherwise, his death would not have occurred. Their actions—in this case distributing food only to those entitled to it—caused the stowaway's death. Their acts would be justifiable only if property rights can sometimes override the right not to be killed.

Many would claim that the situation on lifeboat Earth is not analogous to that on ordinary lifeboats, since it is not evident that we all have a claim, let alone an equal claim, on the earth's resources. Perhaps some of us are stowaways. I shall not here assume that we do all have some claim on the earth's resources, even though I think it plausible to suppose that we do. I shall assume that even if persons have unequal property rights and some people own nothing, it does not follow that B's exercise of his property rights can override A's right not to be killed.[4] Where our activities lead to others' deaths, which would not have occurred had we either done something else or had no causal influence, no claim that the activities were within our economic rights would suffice to show that we did not kill.

It is not far-fetched to think that at present the economic activity of some groups of persons leads to others' deaths. I shall choose a couple of examples of the sort of activity that can do so, but I do not think that these examples do more than begin a list of cases of killing by economic activities. Neither of these examples depends on questioning the existence of unequal property rights; they assume only that such rights do not override a right not to be killed. Neither example is one for which it is plausible to think that the killing could be justified as undertaken in self-defense.

Case one might be called the *foreign investment* situation. A group of investors may form a company that invests broad—perhaps in a plantation or in a mine—and so manage their affairs that a high level of profits is repatriated, while the wages for the laborers are so minimal that their survival

rate is lowered, that is, their expectation of life is lower than it might have been had the company not invested there. In such a case the investors and company management do not act alone, do not cause immediate deaths, and do not know in advance who will die; it is also likely that they intend no deaths. But by their involvement in the economy of an underdeveloped area they cannot claim, as can another company that has no investments there, that they are "doing nothing." On the contrary, they are setting the policies that determine the living standards that determine the survival rate. When persons die because of the lowered standard of living established by a firm or a number of firms that dominate a local economy and either limit persons to employment on their terms or lower the other prospects for employment by damaging traditional economic structures, and these firms could either pay higher wages or stay out of the area altogether, then those who establish these policies are violating some persons' rights not to be killed. Foreign investment that *raises* living standards, even to a still abysmal level, could not be held to kill, for it causes no additional deaths, unless there are special circumstances, as in the following example.

Even when a company investing in an underdeveloped country establishes high wages and benefits and raises the expectation of life for its workers, it often manages to combine these payments with high profitability only by having achieved a tax-exempt status. In such cases the company is being subsidized by the general tax revenue of the underdeveloped economy. It makes no contribution to the infrastructure—e.g., roads and harbors and airports—from which it benefits. In this way many underdeveloped economies have come to include developed enclaves whose development is achieved in part at the expense of the poorer majority.[5] In such cases, government and company policy combine to produce a high wage sector at the expense of a low wage sector. In consequence, some of the persons in the low wage sector, who would not otherwise have died, may die; these persons, whoever they may be, are killed and not merely allowed to die. Such killings may sometimes be justifiable—perhaps, if they are outnumbered by lives saved through having a developed sector—but they are killings nonetheless, since the victims might have survived if not burdened by transfer payments to the developed sector.

But, one may say, the management of such a corporation and its investors should be distinguished more sharply. Even if the management may choose a level of wages, and consequently of survival, the investors usually know nothing of this. But the investors, even if ignorant, are responsible for company policy. They may often fail to exercise control, but by law they have control. They choose to invest in a company with certain foreign investments, they profit from it; they can, and others cannot, affect company policy in fundamental ways. To be sure the investors are not murderers—they do not intend to bring about the deaths of any persons; nor do the company managers usually intend any of the deaths company policies cause. Even so, investors and management acting together with the sorts of results just described do violate some persons' rights not to be killed and usually cannot justify such killings either as required for self-defense or as unavoidable.

Case two, in which even under sufficiency conditions some persons' economic activities result in the deaths of other persons, might be called the *commodity pricing* case. Underdeveloped countries often depend heavily on the price level of a few commodities. So a sharp drop in the world price of coffee or sugar or cocoa may spell ruin and lowered survival rates for whole regions. Yet such drops in price levels are not in all cases due to factors beyond human control. Where they are the result of action by investors, brokers, or government agencies, these persons and bodies are choosing policies that will kill some people. Once again, to be sure, the killing is not single handed, it is not

instantaneous, the killers cannot foresee exactly who will die, and they may not intend anybody to die.

Because of the economic interdependence of different countries, deaths can also be caused by rises in the prices of various commodities. For example, the present near-famine in the Sahelian region of Africa and in the Indian subcontinent is attributed by agronomists partly to climatic shifts and partly to the increased prices of oil and hence of fertilizer, wheat, and other grains.

The recent doubling in international prices of essential foodstuffs will, of necessity, be reflected in higher death rates among the world's lowest income groups, who lack the income to increase their food expenditures proportionately, but live on diets near the subsistence level to begin with.[6]

Of course, not all of those who die will be killed. Those who die of drought will merely be allowed to die, and some of those who die because less has been grown with less fertilizer will also die because of forces beyond the control of any human agency. But to the extent that the raising of oil prices is an achievement of Arab diplomacy and oil company management rather than a windfall, the consequent deaths are killings. Some of them may perhaps be justifiable killings (perhaps if outnumbered by lives saved within the Arab world by industrialization), but killings nonetheless.

Even on a sufficiently equipped earth some persons are killed by others' distribution decisions. The causal chains leading to death-producing distributions are often extremely complex. Where they can be perceived with reasonable clarity we ought, if we take seriously the right not to be killed and seek not merely to avoid killing others but to prevent third parties from doing so, to support policies that reduce deaths. For example—and these are only examples—we should support certain sorts of aid policies rather than others; we should oppose certain sorts of foreign investment; we should oppose certain sorts of commodity speculation, and perhaps support certain sorts of price support agreements for some commodities (e.g., those that try to maintain high prices for products on whose sale poverty-stricken economies depend).

If we take the view that we have no duty to enforce the rights of others, then we cannot draw so general a conclusion about our duty to support various economic policies that might avoid some unjustifiable killings. But we might still find that we should take action of certain sorts either because our own lives are threatened by certain economic activities of others or because our own economic activities threaten others' lives. Only if we knew that we were not part of any system of activities causing unjustifiable deaths could we have no duties to support policies that seek to avoid such deaths. Modern economic causal chains are so complex that it is likely that only those who are economically isolated and self-sufficient could know that they are part of no such systems of activities. Persons who believe that they are involved in some death-producing activities will have some of the same duties as those who think they have a duty to enforce others' rights not to be killed.

Scarcity Situations

The last section showed that sometimes, even in sufficiency situations, some might be killed by the way in which others arranged the distribution of the means of subsistence. Of far more importance in the long run is the true lifeboat situation—the situation of scarcity. We face a situation in which not everyone who is born can live out the normal span of human life and, further, in which we must expect today's normal lifespan to be shortened. The date at which serious scarcity will begin is not generally agreed upon, but even the more optimistic prophets place it no more than decades away.[7] Its arrival will depend on factors such as the rate of technological invention and innovation, especially in agriculture and pollution control, and the success of programs to limit human fertility.

Such predictions may be viewed as exonerating us from complicity in famine deaths. If famine is inevitable, then—while we may have to choose whom to save—the deaths of those whom we do not or cannot save cannot be seen as killings for which we bear any responsibility. For these deaths would have occurred even if we had no causal influence. The decisions to be made may be excruciatingly difficult, but at least we can comfort ourselves that we did not produce or contribute to the famine.

However, this comforting view of famine predictions neglects the fact that these predictions are contingent upon certain assumptions about what people will do in the prefamine period. Famine is said to be inevitable *if* people do not curb their fertility, alter their consumption patterns, and avoid pollution and consequent ecological catastrophes. It is the policies of the present that will produce, defer, or avoid famine. Hence if famine comes, the deaths that occur will be results of decisions made earlier. Only if we take no part in systems of activities that lead to famine situations can we view ourselves as choosing whom to save rather than whom to kill when famine comes. In an economically interdependent world there are few people who can look on the approach of famine as a natural disaster from which they may kindly rescue some, but for whose arrival they bear no responsibility. We cannot stoically regard particular famine deaths as unavoidable if we have contributed to the emergence and extent of famine.

If we bear some responsibility for the advent of famine, then any decision on distributing the risk of famine is a decision whom to kill. Even a decision to rely on natural selection as a famine policy is choosing a policy for killing—for under a different famine policy different persons might have survived, and under different prefamine policies there might have been no famine or a less severe famine. The choice of a particular famine policy may be justifiable on the grounds that once we have let it get to that point there is not enough to go around, and somebody must go, as on an ill-equipped lifeboat. Even so, the famine policy chosen will not be a policy of saving some but not all persons from an unavoidable predicament.

Persons cannot, of course, make famine policies individually. Famine and prefamine policies are and will be made by governments individually and collectively and perhaps also by some voluntary organizations. It may even prove politically impossible to have a coherent famine or prefamine policy for the whole world; if so, we shall have to settle for partial and piecemeal policies. But each person who is in a position to support or oppose such policies, whether global or local, has to decide which to support and which to oppose. Even for individual persons, inaction and inattention are often a decision—a decision to support the famine and prefamine policies, which are the status quo whether or not they are "hands off" policies. There are large numbers of ways in which private citizens may affect such policies. They do so in supporting or opposing legislation affecting aid and foreign investment, in supporting or opposing certain sorts of charities or groups such as Zero Population Growth, in promoting or opposing ecologically conservative technology and lifestyles. Hence we have individually the onus of avoiding killing. For even though we

(a) do not kill single-handedly those who die of famine

(b) do not kill instantaneously those who die of famine

(c) do not know which individuals will die as the result of the prefamine and famine policies we support (unless we support something like a genocidal famine policy)

(d) do not intend any famine deaths

we nonetheless kill and do not merely allow to die. For as the result of our actions in concert with others, some will die who might have survived had we either acted otherwise or had no causal influence.

FAMINE POLICIES
AND PREFAMINE POLICIES

Various principles can be suggested on which famine and prefamine policies might reasonably be based. I shall list some of these, more with the aim of setting out the range of possible decisions than with the aim of stating a justification for selecting some people for survival. One very general policy might be that of adopting whichever more specific policies will lead to the fewest deaths. An example would be going along with the consequences of natural selection in the way in which the allocation of medical care in situations of great shortage does, that is, the criteria for relief would be a high chance of survival if relief is given and a low chance otherwise—the worst risks would be abandoned. (This decision is analogous to picking the ill man as the victim on the lifeboat in 2A.) However, the policy of minimizing deaths is indeterminate, unless a certain time horizon is specified. For the policies that maximize survival in the short run —e.g., preventive medicine and minimal living standards—may also maximize population increase and lead to greater ultimate catastrophe.[8]

Another general policy would be to try to find further grounds that can justify overriding a person's right not to be killed. Famine policies adopted on these grounds might permit others to kill those who will forgo their right not to be killed (voluntary euthanasia, including healthy would-be suicides) or to kill those whom others find dependent and exceptionally burdensome, e.g., the unwanted sick or aged or unborn or newborn (involuntary euthanasia, abortion, and infanticide). Such policies might be justified by claims that the right not to be killed may be overridden in famine situations if the owner of the right consents or if securing the right is exceptionally burdensome.

Any combination of such policies is a policy of killing some and protecting others. Those who are killed may not have their right not to be killed violated without reason; those who set and support famine policies and prefamine policies will not be able to claim that they do not kill, but if they reason carefully they may be able to claim that they do not do so without justification.

From this vantage point it can be seen why it is not relevant to restrict the right of self-defense to a right to defend oneself against those who threaten one's life but do not do so innocently. Such a restriction may make a great difference to one's view of abortion in cases in which the mother's life is threatened, but it does not make much difference when famine is the issue. Those who might be chosen as likely victims of any famine policy will probably be innocent of contributing to the famine, or at least no more guilty than others; hence the innocence of the victims is an insufficient ground for rejecting a policy. Indeed it is hard to point a finger at the guilty in famine situations. Are they the hoarders of grain? The parents of large families? Inefficient farmers? Our own generation?

In a sense we are all innocent threats to one another's safety in scarcity situations, for the bread one person eats might save another's life. If there were fewer people competing for resources, commodity prices would fall and starvation deaths be reduced. Hence famine deaths in scarcity situations might be justified on grounds of the minimal right of self-defense as well as on grounds of the unavoidability of some deaths and the reasonableness of the policies for selecting victims. For each famine death leaves fewer survivors competing for whatever resources there are, and the most endangered among the survivors might have died—had not others done so. So a policy that kills some may be justified on the grounds that the most endangered survivors could have been defended in no other way.

Global scarcity is not here yet. But its imminence has certain implications for today. If all persons have a right not to be killed and a corollary duty not to kill others, then we are bound to adopt prefamine policies that ensure that famine is postponed as long as possible and is minimized. And a

duty to try to postpone the advent and minimize the severity of famine is a duty on the one hand to minimize the number of persons there will be and on the other to maximize the means of subsistence.[9] For if we do not adopt prefamine policies with these aims we shall have to adopt more drastic famine policies sooner.

So if we take the right not to be killed seriously, we should consider and support not only some famine policy for future use but also a population and resources policy for present use. There has been a certain amount of philosophical discussion of population policies.[10] From the point of view of the present argument it has two defects. First, it is for the most part conducted within a utilitarian framework and focuses on problems such as the different population policies required by maximizing the total and the average utility of a population. Second, this literature tends to look at a scarcity of resources as affecting the quality of lives but not their very possibility. It is more concerned with the question, How many people should we add? than with the question, How few people could we lose? There are, of course, many interesting questions about population policies that are not relevant to famine. But here I shall consider only population and resource policies determined on the principle of postponing and minimizing famine, for these are policies that might be based on the claim that persons have a right not to be killed, so that we have a duty to avoid or postpone situations in which we shall have to override this right.

Such population policies might, depending upon judgments about the likely degree of scarcity, range from the mild to the draconian. I list some examples. A mild population policy might emphasize family planning, perhaps moving in the direction of fiscal incentives or measures that stress not people's rights but their duties to control their bodies. Even a mild policy would require a lot both in terms of invention (e.g., the development of contraceptives suitable for use in poverty-stricken conditions) and innovation (e.g., social policies that reduce the incentives and pressures to have a large family).[11] More draconian policies would enforce population limitation—for example, by mandatory sterilization after a certain number of children were born or by reducing public health expenditures in places with high net reproduction rates to prevent death rates from declining until birth rates do so. A policy of completely eliminating all further births (e.g., by universal sterilization) is also one that would meet the requirement of postponing famine, since extinct species do not suffer famine. I have not in this argument used any premises that show that a complete elimination of births would be wrong, but other premises might give reasons for thinking that it is wrong to enforce sterilization or better to have some persons rather than no persons. In any case the political aspects of introducing famine policies make it likely that this most austere of population policies would not be considered.

There is a corresponding range of resource policies. At the milder end are the various conservation and pollution-control measures now being practiced or discussed. At the tougher end of the spectrum are complete rationing of energy and materials consumption. If the aim of a resources policy is to avoid killing those who are born, an adequate policy may require both invention (e.g., solar energy technology and better waste-retrieval techniques) and innovation (e.g., introducing new technology in such a way that its benefits are not quickly absorbed by increasing population, as has happened with the green revolution in some places).

At all events, if we think that people have a right not to be killed, we cannot fail to face up to its long-range implications. This one right by itself provides ground for activism on many fronts. In scarcity situations that we help produce, the defeasibility of the right not to be killed is important, for there cannot be any absolute duty not to kill persons in such situations but only a commitment to kill only for reasons. Such a commitment requires consideration of the condition or quality of life that is to qualify for survival. Moral philosophers are reluctant to face up to this problem; soon it will be staring us in the face.

Footnotes

1. Cf. Robert Nozick, *Anarchy State and Utopia* (New York, 1974), p. 34. Nozick defines an innocent threat as "someone who is innocently a causal agent in a process such that he would be an aggressor had he chosen to become such an agent."

2. Cf. Peter Singer, "Famine, Affluence, and Morality," *Philosophy & Public Affairs* (Spring 1972): 229–243, 232. I am in agreement with many of the points that Singer makes, but am interested in arguing that we must have some famine policy from a much weaker set of premises. Singer uses some consequentialist premises: starvation is bad; we ought to prevent bad things when we can do so without worse consequences; hence we ought to prevent starvation whether it is nearby or far off and whether others are doing so or not. The argument of this article does not depend on a particular theory about the grounds of obligation, but should be a corollary of any nonbizarre ethical theory that has any room for a notion of rights.

3. This way of distinguishing killing from allowing to die does not rely on distinguishing "negative" from "positive" acts. Such attempts seem unpromising since any act has multiple descriptions of which some will be negative and others positive. If a clear distinction is to be made between killing and letting die, it must hinge on the *difference* that an act makes for a person's survival, rather than on the description under which the agent acts.

4. The point may appear rather arbitrary, given that I have not rested my case on one theory of the grounds of obligation. But I believe that almost any such theory will show a right not to be killed to override a property right. Perhaps this is why Locke's theory can seem so odd—in moving from a right of self-preservation to a justification of unequal property rights, he finds himself gradually having to reinterpret all rights as property rights, thus coming to see us as the owners of our persons.

5. Cf. P.A. Baron, *The Political Economy of Growth* (New York, 1957), especially chap. 5, "On the Roots of Backwardness"; or A.G. Frank, *Capitalism and Underdevelopment in Latin America* (New York, 1967). Both works argue that underdeveloped economies are among the products of developed ones.

6. Lester R. Brown and Erik P. Eckholm "The Empty Breadbasket," *Ceres* (F.A.O. Review on Development), March-April 1974, p. 59. See also N. Borlaug and R. Ewell, "The Shrinking Margin," in the same issue.

7. For discussions of the time and extent of famine see, for example, P.R. Ehrlich, *The Population Bomb*, rev. ed. (New York, 1971); R.L. Heilbroner, *An Inquiry into the Human Prospect* (New York, 1974); *Scientific American* September 1974, especially R. Freedman and B. Berelson, "The Human Population"; P. Demeny, "The Populations of the Underdeveloped Countries"; R. Revelle, "Food and Population."

8. See *Scientific American*, September 1974, especially A.J. Coale, "The History of the Human Population."

9. The failure of "right to life" groups to pursue these goals seriously casts doubt upon their commitment to the preservation of human lives. Why are they active in so few of the contexts where human lives are endangered?

10. For example, J.C.C. Smart, *An Outline of a System of Utilitarian Ethics* (Melbourne, 1961), pp. 18, 44ff.; Jan Narveson, "Moral Problems of Population," *Monist* 57 (1973): 62–86; "Utilitarianism and New Generations," *Mind* 76 (1967): 62–72.

11. Cf. Mahmood Mamdani, *The Myth of Population Control* (New York, 1972), for evidence that high fertility can be based on rational choice rather than on ignorance or incompetence.

Review Questions

1. In what two cases can the right not to be killed be justifiably overridden?

2. What is the point of the lifeboat examples?

3. Why does economic activity lead to death?

4. What duty do we have with respect to famines?

5. What sorts of population policies are possible?

Discussion Questions

1. Are there any other rights that override the right not to be killed? For example, do property rights override this right?

2. What sort of prefamine policy is best? Explain your answer.

3. How about population and resource policies? Which policies should be adopted? Explain your views.

Problem Cases

1. Currently there is a severe drought in central Africa affecting an area about one-half the size of the United States. Thousands of people have already died despite attempts to give aid. The area is rapidly turning into a barren desert. Even though the people can no longer grow food in the area, they refuse to leave, even if this means death. Should these people be forced to leave the area or not? Why, or why not? Should massive aid be provided to save these people from death? Explain your answer.

2. The population of Brazil is growing rapidly. If its present rate of growth of 2.8 percent continues, it will soon become the most populous country in the Western hemisphere. Although Brazil is rich in natural resources, and has significant economic growth, the benefits have mostly gone to the rich. Forty percent of the population is under fifteen years of age, and unemployment is high. Population growth in the cities has made it difficult for the government to provide education, health care, water, sanitation, food, and housing for the poor. What steps, if any, should be taken to provide for the poor and needy people in this country? Explain your proposals.

Suggested Readings

Shue, Henry. *Basic Rights*. Princeton, NJ: Princeton University Press, 1980, Chapters 1 and 5.

Shuman, Charles B. "Food aid and the free market." In Peter G. Brown and Henry Shue, eds., *Food Policy*. New York: The Free Press, 1977, pp. 145–163. In opposition to Shue, Shuman advocates a free-market approach to the problem of hunger and starvation.

Singer, Peter. *Practical Ethics*. Cambridge, MA: Cambridge University Press, 1979, pp. 158–181. Singer argues that rich nations have a moral obligation to help poor nations.

CHAPTER 4

The Death Penalty

Basic Concepts

The Eighth Amendment to the Constitution of the United States prohibits "cruel and unusual" punishment. Is the death penalty an example of cruel and unusual punishment, and thus unconstitutional? This is a matter of debate. In the case of *Furman* v. *Georgia* (1972), the Supreme Court ruled (by a five-to-four majority) that the death penalty was unconstitutional because it was being administered in an arbitrary and capricious manner. Juries were allowed to inflict the death sentence without any explicit guidelines or standards, and the result was that blacks were much more likely to receive the sentence than whites.

After the *Furman* decision, states wishing to retain the death sentence reacted in two ways. One way was to meet the objection about standardless discretion of juries by making the death penalty mandatory for certain crimes. But in *Woodson* v. *North Carolina* (1976), the Court ruled (again by a mere five-to-four majority) that mandatory death sentences are unconstitutional.

The second approach to the objection raised in *Furman* was to provide standards for juries. Georgia specified in its law ten statutory aggravating circumstances, one of which had to be found by the jury to exist beyond reasonable doubt before a death sentence could be imposed. This second approach proved to be successful. For in *Gregg* v. *Georgia* (1976), the majority ruled, with only Justice Marshall and Justice Brennan dissenting, that the death penalty is not unconstitutional for the crime of murder, provided there are safeguards against any arbitrary or capricious imposition by juries.

But why isn't the death penalty cruel and unusual? In their majority opinion, Justices Stewart, Powell, and Stevens answered this important question. First, they gave an explanation of "cruel and unusual." In their view, a punishment is "cruel and unusual" if it either fails to accord with "evolving standards of decency" or fails to accord with the "dignity of man" that is the "basic concept underlying the Eighth Amendment." This second stipulation rules out "excessive" punishment that involves unnecessary pain or is disproportionate to the crime. Second, they argued that the death penalty does not satisfy either of these stipulations. It is acceptable to the majority of the people, since thirty-five states have statutes providing for the death penalty, and it is not excessive because it achieves two important social purposes, retribution and deterrence.

RETRIBUTIVISM

To fully understand the appeal to retribution, it is necessary to examine the theory on which it is based, namely retributivism. On this theory of punishment, a person guilty of a crime ought to pay a penalty, and the penalty must fit the crime, or be proportionate to the crime. Most people will agree that those guilty of a crime ought to pay some penalty unless they have a good excuse, e.g., the crime was accidental. But how do we tell which penalty fits which crime, and in particular how do we know that death is the only punishment that fits the crime of murder? Why not agree with Justice Marshall that life imprisonment is a more appropriate punishment?

The traditional view is that the punishment must exactly match the crime, and that life imprisonment does not match the crime of murder. This view is often formulated as *lex talionis*, the principle of retaliation that says, "life for life, eye for eye, tooth for tooth." But is this principle acceptable? Hugo Adam Bedau does not think so. He points out that even the Biblical world allowed the death penalty for nonhomicidal crimes such as kidnapping, and that persons in our time have been executed for sabotage and espionage. Besides, not all murderers deserve death. Our laws recognize a large class of murders that do not deserve the death penalty, namely those that are unintentional, accidental, unpremeditated, and so on. Finally, Bedau claims that there may be some horrible and vicious crimes that deserve some punishment worse than death, such as torture. It seems that retributivism can be used to justify punishment that is indeed cruel.

But retributivism can be defended against the charge that it justifies cruel and unusual punishment. Perhaps it does not even justify the death sentence. According to Robert S. Gerstein, retributivism requires us to punish a member of the community who has acted unjustly, but there are limits to the severity of the punishment. We must treat the criminal with the respect due to a member of the community, and because of this requirement, it may be that we cannot deliberately kill a person because such a punishment might show a lack of respect for the moral worth and dignity of the person.

UTILITARIANISM

The appeal to deterrence is founded on a quite different theory of punishment, the utilitarian theory. An important difference between this theory and retributivism is that retributivism does not consider the consequences of punishment (it is a nonconsequentialist theory), while utilitarianism considers only the consequences (making it a consequentialist theory).

The fundamental principle of utilitarianism is the Principle of Utility. This principle is formulated in different ways, but a standard version is this:

Everyone ought to act so as to bring about the greatest possible balance of good over evil.

Utilitarians do not agree about what is good or bad. Some of them, called *hedonists,* think that only pleasure is intrinsically good (that is, good in itself), and that only pain is intrinsically bad. For example, the classical utilitarians Jeremy Bentham (1748–1832) and John Stuart Mill (1806–1873), were *hedonistic utilitarians.* Other utilitarians believe that satisfaction of one's desires is what is good and not having them satisfied is bad. They are called *preference utilitarians.*

What utilitarian justification can be given for capital punishment? It can be maintained that the social benefits of this punishment, the good consequences it produces for society, outweigh the suffering of the person killed and the bad side effects. The particular social benefits claimed for the death penalty by its defenders are deterrence and prevention. It deters other potential criminals from killing, and it prevents the criminal who is executed from committing further crimes.

But does the death penalty actually have these consequences? This is a factual question that is much debated.

Glover argues that capital punishment has not been shown to be a substantial deterrent and that there is a strong presumption against it because of its special evils and bad side effects.

Bedau claims that the verdict of scientists who have studied the issue is that the deterrence achieved by the death penalty is not measurably greater than the deterrence achieved by life imprisonment. As for preventing convicted murderers from killing again, Bedau asserts that there is little evidence that the death sentence does this. In fact, less than one convicted murderer in a hundred commits another murder.

Bedau adds that there are other bad consequences of the death penalty to be considered. It may incite criminals to murder and thus act as a counterdeterrent. Also, innocent people may be unjustly executed. Bedau concludes that, everything considered, the case for the abolition of the death penalty is stronger than the case for its retention.

Sidney Hook does not agree that the death penalty should never be applied. He thinks that there are two cases in which the death sentence is justified. One is the case in which a defendant convicted of murder chooses the death sentence rather than life imprisonment. Hook is assuming, of course, that the satisfaction of the criminal's desire is good, and that we ought to do what is good. The second case is one in which a criminal who has been sentenced to prison for premeditated murder commits another murder. Such a second offender ought to get the death sentence because it is likely that this criminal will kill again and again, and this should be prevented.

THE SUPREME COURT
Gregg v. *Georgia*

Potter Stewart, Lewis F. Powell, Jr., and John Paul Stevens are associate justices of the United States Supreme Court. Justice Stewart, a graduate of Yale Law School, was appointed to the Court in 1958. Justice Powell, LL.M. (Harvard), was appointed in 1971. Justice Stevens graduated from Northwestern University School of Law, and was appointed to the Court in 1975.

Thurgood Marshall, associate justice of the United States Supreme Court, was appointed to the Court in 1967. He was the first black ever to be appointed.

William Brennan, associate justice of the United States Supreme Court, graduated from Harvard Law School. He was appointed to the Court in 1956.

The main issue before the Court in the case of Gregg v. Georgia was whether the death penalty violates the Eighth Amendment prohibition of cruel and unusual punishment. The majority of the Court, with Justice Marshall and Justice Brennan dissenting, held that the death penalty does not violate the Eighth Amendment because it is in accord with contemporary standards of decency, it serves both a deterrent and retributive purpose, and in the case of the Georgia law being reviewed, it is no longer arbitrarily applied.

In his dissenting opinion, Justice Brennan claims that the reasons given do not suffice to prove that the death penalty is constitutional. To do that, it would have to be shown that capital punishment is not degrading to human dignity.

Justice Marshall objects that the death sentence is not necessary for deterrence, that the purely retributive justification for the death penalty is not consistent with human dignity, and that contemporary standards of decency are not based on informed opinion.

The issue in this case is whether the imposition of the sentence of death for the crime of murder under the law of Georgia violates the Eighth and Fourteenth Amendments.

I

The petitioner, Troy Gregg, was charged with committing armed robbery and murder. In accordance with Georgia procedure in capital cases, the trial was in two stages, a guilt stage and a sentencing stage. . . .

. . . The jury found the petitioner guilty of two counts of armed robbery and two counts of murder.

At the penalty stage, which took place before the same jury, . . . the trial judge instructed the jury that it could recommend either a death sentence or a life prison sentence on each count. . . . The jury returned verdicts of death on each count.

The Supreme Court of Georgia affirmed the convictions and the imposition of the death sentences for murder. . . . The death sentences imposed for armed robbery, however, were vacated on the grounds that the death penalty had rarely been imposed in Georgia for that offense. . . .

II

. . . The Georgia statute, as amended after our decision in *Furman* v. *Georgia* (1972), retains the death penalty for six categories of crime: murder, kidnaping for ransom or where the victim is harmed, armed robbery, rape, treason, and aircraft hijacking. . . .

III

We address initially the basic contention that the punishment of death for the crime of murder is, under all circumstances, "cruel and unusual" in violation of the Eighth and Fourteenth Amendments of the Constitution. In Part IV of this opinion, we will consider the sentence of death imposed under the Georgia statutes at issue in this case.

The Court on a number of occasions has both assumed and asserted the constitutionality of capital punishment. In several cases that assumption provided a necessary foundation for the decision, as the Court was asked to decide whether a particular method of carrying out a capital sentence would be allowed to stand under the Eighth Amendment. But until *Furman* v. *Georgia* (1972), the Court never confronted squarely the fundamental claim that the punishment of death always, regardless of the enormity of

the offense or the procedure followed in imposing the sentence, is cruel and unusual punishment in violation of the Constitution. Although this issue was presented and addressed in *Furman*, it was not resolved by the Court. Four Justices would have held that capital punishment is not unconstitutional *per se;* two Justices would have reached the opposite conclusion; and three Justices, while agreeing that the statutes then before the Court were invalid as applied, left open the question whether such punishment may ever be imposed. We now hold that the punishment of death does not invariably violate the Constitution.

A

The history of the prohibition of "cruel and unusual" punishment already has been reviewed at length. The phrase first appeared in the English Bill of Rights of 1689, which was drafted by Parliament at the accession of William and Mary. The English version appears to have been directed against punishments unauthorized by statute and beyond the jurisdiction of the sentencing court, as well as those disproportionate to the offense involved. The American draftsmen, who adopted the English phrasing in drafting the Eighth Amendment, were primarily concerned, however, with proscribing "tortures" and other "barbarous" methods of punishment.

In the earliest cases raising Eighth Amendment claims, the Court focused on particular methods of execution to determine whether they were too cruel to pass constitutional muster. The constitutionality of the sentence of death itself was not at issue, and the criterion used to evaluate the mode of execution was its similarity to "torture" and other "barbarous" methods. . . .

But the Court has not confined the prohibition embodied in the Eighth Amendment to "barbarous" methods that were generally outlawed in the 18th century. Instead, the Amendment has been interpreted in a flexible and dynamic manner. The Court early recognized that "a principle to be vital must

be capable of wider application than the mischief which gave it birth." Thus the Clause forbidding "cruel and unusual" punishments "is not fastened to the obsolete but may acquire meaning as public opinion becomes enlightened by a humane justice."
. . .

It is clear from the foregoing precedents that the Eighth Amendment has not been regarded as a static concept. As Mr. Chief Justice Warren said, in an oftquoted phrase, "[t]he Amendment must draw its meaning from the evolving standards of decency that mark the progress of a maturing society." Thus, an assessment of contemporary values concerning the infliction of a challenged sanction is relevant to the application of the Eighth Amendment. As we develop below more fully, this assessment does not call for a subjective judgment. It requires, rather, that we look to objective indicia that reflect the public attitude toward a given sanction.

But our cases also make clear that public perceptions of standards of decency with respect to criminal sanctions are not conclusive. A penalty also must accord with "the dignity of man," which is the "basic concept underlying the Eighth Amendment." This means, at least, that the punishment not be "excessive." When a form of punishment in the abstract (in this case, whether capital punishment may ever be imposed as a sanction for murder) rather than in the particular (the propriety of death as a penalty to be applied to a specific defendant for a specific crime) is under consideration, the inquiry into "excessiveness" has two aspects. First, the punishment must not involve the unnecessary and wanton infliction of pain. Second, the punishment must not be grossly out of proportion to the severity of the crime.

B

Of course, the requirements of the Eighth Amendment must be applied with an awareness of the limited role to be played by the courts. This does not mean that judges have no role to play, for the Eighth Amendment is a restraint upon the exercise of legislative power. . . .

But, while we have an obligation to ensure that constitutional bounds are not over-reached, we may not act as judges as we might as legislators. . . .

Therefore, in assessing a punishment selected by a democratically elected legislature against the constitutional measure, we presume its validity. We may not require the legislature to select the least severe penalty possible so long as the penalty selected is not cruelly inhumane or disproportionate to the crime involved. And a heavy burden rests on those who would attack the judgment of the representatives of the people.

This is true in part because the constitutional test is intertwined with an assessment of contemporary standards and the legislative judgment weighs heavily in ascertaining such standards. "[I]n a democratic society legislatures, not courts, are constituted to respond to the will and consequently the moral values of the people."

The deference we owe to the decisions of the state legislatures under our federal system is enhanced where the specification of punishments is concerned, for "these are peculiarly questions of legislative policy." Caution is necessary lest this Court become, "under the aegis of the Cruel and Unusual Punishment Clause, the ultimate arbiter of the standards of criminal responsibility . . . throughout the country." A decision that a given punishment is impermissible under the Eighth Amendment cannot be reversed short of a constitutional amendment. The ability of the people to express their preference through the normal democratic processes, as well as through ballot referenda, is shut off. Revisions cannot be made in the light of further experience.

C

In the discussion to this point we have sought to identify the principles and considerations that guide a court in addressing an Eighth Amendment claim. We now consider specifically whether the sentence of death for the crime of murder is a *per se* violation of the Eighth and Fourteenth Amendments to the Constitution. We note first that history and precedent strongly support a negative answer to this question.

The imposition of the death penalty for the crime of murder has a long history of acceptance both in the United States and in England. . . .

It is apparent from the text of the Constitution itself that the existence of capital punishment was accepted by the Framers. At the time the Eighth Amendment was ratified, capital punishment was a common sanction in every State. Indeed, the First Congress of the United States enacted legislation providing death as the penalty for specified crimes.
. . .

For nearly two centuries, this Court, repeatedly and often expressly, has recognized that capital punishment is not invalid *per se*.
. . .

Four years ago, the petitioners in *Furman* and its companion cases predicated their argument primarily upon the asserted proposition that standards of decency had evolved to the point where capital punishment no longer could be tolerated. The petitioners in those cases said, in effect, that the evolutionary process had come to an end, and that standards of decency required that the Eighth Amendment be construed finally as prohibiting capital punishment for any crime regardless of its depravity and impact on society. This view was accepted by two Justices. Three other Justices were unwilling to go so far; focusing on the procedures by which convicted defendants were selected for the death penalty rather than on the actual punishment inflicted, they joined in the conclusion that the statutes before the Court were constitutionally invalid.

The petitioners in the capital cases before the Court today renew the "standards of decency" argument, but developments during the four years since *Furman* have undercut substantially the assumptions upon which their argument rested. Despite the continuing debate, dating back to the nineteenth century, over the morality and utility of capital punishment, it is now evident that a large proportion of American society continues to regard it as an appropriate and necessary criminal sanction.

The most marked indication of society's endorsement of the death penalty for murder is the legislative response to *Furman*. The legislatures of at least thirty-five States have enacted new statutes that provide for the death penalty for at least some crimes that result in the death of another person. And the Congress of the United States, in 1974, enacted a statute providing the death penalty for aircraft piracy that results in death. These recently adopted statutes have attempted to address the concerns expressed by the Court in *Furman* primarily (i) by specifying the factors to be weighed and the procedures to be followed in deciding when to impose a capital sentence, or (ii) by making the death penalty mandatory for specified crimes. But all of the post-*Furman* statutes make clear that capital punishment itself has not been rejected by the elected representatives of the people. . . .

The jury also is a significant and reliable objective index of contemporary values because it is so directly involved. The Court has said that "one of the most important functions any jury can perform in making . . . a selection [between life imprisonment and death for a defendant convicted in a capital case] is to maintain a link between contemporary community values and the penal system." It may be true that evolving standards have influenced juries in recent decades to be more discriminating in imposing the sentence of death. But the relative infrequency of jury verdicts imposing the death sentence does not indicate rejection of capital punishment *per se*. Rather, the reluctance of juries in many cases to impose the sentence may well reflect the humane feeling that this most irrevocable of sanctions should be reserved for a small number of extreme cases. Indeed, the actions of juries in many States since *Furman* are fully compatible with the legislative judgments, reflected in the new statutes, as to the continued utility and necessity of capital punishment in appropriate cases. At the close of 1974 at least 254 persons had been sentenced to death since *Furman*, and by the end of March 1976, more than 460 persons were subject to death sentences.

As we have seen, however, the Eighth Amendment demands more than that a challenged punishment be acceptable to contemporary society. The Court also must ask whether it comports with the basic concept of human dignity at the core of the Amendment. Although we cannot "invalidate a category of penalties because we deem less severe penalties adequate to serve the ends of penology," the sanction imposed cannot be so totally without penological justification that it results in the gratuitous infliction of suffering.

The death penalty is said to serve two principal social purposes: retribution and deterrence of capital crimes by prospective offenders.[1]

In part, capital punishment is an expression of society's moral outrage at particularly offensive conduct. This function may be unappealing to many, but it is essential in an ordered society that asks its citizens to rely on legal processes rather than self-help to vindicate their wrongs.

The instinct for retribution is part of the nature of man, and channeling that instinct in the administration of criminal justice serves an important purpose in promoting the stability of a society governed by law. When people begin to believe that organized society is unwilling or unable to impose upon criminal offenders the punishment they "deserve," then there are sown the seeds of anarchy—if self-help, vigilante justice, and lynch law. Furman v. Georgia (Stewart, J., concurring).

"Retribution is no longer the dominant objective of the criminal law," but neither is it a forbidden objective nor one inconsistent with our respect for the dignity of men. Indeed, the decision that capital punishment may be the appropriate sanction in extreme cases is an expression of the community's belief that certain crimes are themselves so grievous an affront to humanity that the only adequate response may be the penalty of death.

Statistical attempts to evaluate the worth of the death penalty as a deterrent to crimes by potential offenders have occasioned a great deal of debate. The results simply have been inconclusive. . . .

Although some of the studies suggest that the death penalty may not function as a significantly greater deterrent than lesser penalties, there is no convincing empirical evidence either supporting or refuting this view. We may nevertheless assume safely that there are murderers, such as those who act in passion, for whom the threat of death has little or no deterrent effect. But for many others, the death penalty undoubtedly is a significant deterrent. There are carefully contemplated murders, such as murder for hire, where the possible penalty of death may well enter into the cold calculus that precedes the decision to act. And there are some categories of murder, such as murder by a life prisoner, where other sanctions may not be adequate.

The value of capital punishment as a deterrent of crime is a complex factual issue the resolution of which properly rests with the legislatures, which can evaluate the results of statistical studies in terms of their own local conditions and with a flexibility of approach that is not available to the courts. Indeed, many of the post-*Furman* statutes reflect just such a responsible effort to define those crimes and those criminals for which capital punishment is most probably an effective deterrent.

In sum, we cannot say that the judgment of the Georgia Legislature that capital punishment may be necessary in some cases is clearly wrong. Considerations of federalism, as well as respect for the ability of a legislature to evaluate, in terms of its particular State, the moral consensus concerning the death penalty and its social utility as a sanction, require us to conclude, in the absence of more convincing evidence, that the infliction of death as a punishment for murder is not without justification and thus is not unconstitutionally severe.

Finally, we must consider whether the punishment of death is disproportionate in relation to the crime for which it is imposed. There is no question that death as a punishment is unique in its severity and irrevocability. When a defendant's life is at stake, the Court has been particularly sensitive to insure that every safeguard is observed. But we are concerned here only with the imposition of capital punishment for the crime of murder, and when a life has been taken deliberately by the offender,[2] we cannot say that the punishment is invariably disproportionate to the crime. It is an extreme sanction, suitable to the most extreme of crimes.

We hold that the death penalty is not a form of punishment that may never be imposed, regardless of the circumstances of the offense, regardless of the character of the offender, and regardless of the procedure followed in reaching the decision to impose it.

IV

We now consider whether Georgia may impose the death penalty on the petitioner in this case.

A

While *Furman* did not hold that the infliction of the death penalty *per se* violates the Constitution's ban on cruel and unusual punishments, it did recognize that the penalty of death is different in kind from any other punishment imposed under our system of criminal justice. Because of the uniqueness of the death penalty, *Furman* held that it could not be imposed under sentencing procedures that created a substantial risk that it would be inflicted in an arbitrary and capricious manner. . . .

Furman mandates that where discretion is afforded a sentencing body on a matter so grave as the determination of whether a human life should be taken or spared, that discretion must be suitably directed and limited so as to minimize the risk of wholly arbitrary and capricious action.

It is certainly not a novel proposition that discretion in the area of sentencing be exercised in an informed manner. We have long recognized that "[f]or the determination of sentences, justice generally requires . . . that there be taken into account the circumstances of the offense together with the character and propensities of the offender." . . .

Jury sentencing has been considered desirable in capital cases in order "to maintain a link between contemporary community values and the penal system—a link without which the determination of punishment could hardly reflect 'the evolving standards of decency that mark the progress of a maturing society.'" But it creates special problems. Much of the information that is relevant to the sentencing decision may have no relevance to the question of guilt, or may even be extremely prejudicial to a fair determination of that question. This problem, however, is scarcely insurmountable. Those who have studied the question suggest that a bifurcated procedure—one in which the question of sentence is not considered until the determination of guilt has been made—is the best answer. . . . When a human life is at stake and when the jury must have information prejudicial to the question of guilt but relevant to the question of penalty in order to impose a rational sentence, a bifurcated system is more likely to ensure elimination of the constitutional deficiencies identified in *Furman*.

But the provision of relevant information under fair procedural rules is not alone sufficient to guarantee that the information will be properly used in the imposition of punishment, especially if sentencing is performed by a jury. Since the members of a jury will have had little, if any, previous experience in sentencing, they are unlikely to be skilled in dealing with the information they are given. To the extent that this problem is inherent in jury sentencing, it may not be totally correctable. It seems clear, however, that the problem will be alleviated if the jury is given guidance regarding the factors about the crime and the defendant that the State, representing organized society, deems particularly relevant to the sentencing decision. . . .

While some have suggested that standards to guide a capital jury's sentencing deliberations are impossible to formulate, the fact is that such standards have been developed. When the drafters of the Model Penal Code faced this problem, they concluded "that it is within the realm of possibility to point to the main circumstances of aggravation and of mitigation that should be weighed *and weighed against each other* when they are presented in a concrete case."[3] While such standards are by necessity somewhat general, they do provide guidance to the sentencing authority and thereby reduce the likelihood that it will impose a sentence that fairly can be called capricious or arbitrary. Where the sentencing authority is required to specify the factors it relied upon in reaching its decision, the further safeguard of meaningful appellate review is available to ensure that death sentences are not imposed capriciously or in a freakish manner.

In summary, the concerns expressed in *Furman* that the penalty of death not be imposed in an arbitrary or capricious manner can be met by a carefully drafted statute that ensures that the sentencing authority is given adequate information and guidance. As a general proposition these concerns are best met by a system that provides for a bifurcated proceeding at which the sentencing authority is apprised of the information relevant to the imposition of sentence and provided with standards to guide its use of the information.

We do not intend to suggest that only the above-described procedures would be permissible under *Furman* or that any sentencing system constructed along these general lines would inevitably satisfy the concerns of *Furman*, for each distinct system must be examined on an individual basis. Rather,

we have embarked upon this general exposition to make clear that it is possible to construct capital-sentencing systems capable of meeting *Furman*'s constitutional concerns.

B

We now turn to consideration of the constitutionality of Georgia's capital-sentencing procedures. In the wake of *Furman*, Georgia amended its capital punishment statute, but chose not to narrow the scope of its murder provisions. Thus, now as before *Furman*, in Georgia "[a] person commits murder when he unlawfully and with malice aforethought, either express or implied, causes the death of another human being." All persons convicted of murder "shall be punished by death or by imprisonment for life."

Georgia did act, however, to narrow the class of murderers subject to capital punishment by specifying ten statutory aggravating circumstances, one of which must be found by the jury to exist beyond a reasonable doubt before a death sentence can ever be imposed. In addition, the jury is authorized to consider any other appropriate aggravating or mitigating circumstances. The jury is not required to find any mitigating circumstance in order to make a recommendation of mercy that is binding on the trial court, but it must find a *statutory* aggravating circumstance before recommending a sentence of death.

These procedures require the jury to consider the circumstances of the crime and the criminal before it recommends sentence. No longer can a Georgia jury do as Furman's jury did: reach a finding of the defendant's guilt and then, without guidance or direction, decide whether he should live or die. Instead, the jury's attention is directed to the specific circumstances of the crime: Was it committed in the course of another capital felony? Was it committed for money? Was it committed upon a peace officer or judicial officer? Was it committed in a particularly heinous way or in a manner that endangered the lives of many persons? In addition, the jury's attention is focused on the characteristics of the person who committed the crime: Does he have a record of prior convictions for capital offenses? Are there any special facts about this defendant that mitigate against imposing capital punishment (*e.g.*, his youth, the extent of his cooperation with the police, his emotional state at the time of the crime)? As a result, while some jury discretion still exists, "the discretion to be exercised is controlled by clear and objective standards so as to produce nondiscriminatory application."

As an important additional safeguard against arbitrariness and caprice, the Georgia statutory scheme provides for automatic appeal of all death sentences to the State's Supreme Court. That court is required by statute to review each sentence of death and determine whether it was imposed under the influence of passion or prejudice, whether the evidence supports the jury's finding of a statutory aggravating circumstance, and whether the sentence is disproportionate compared to those sentences imposed in similar cases.

In short, Georgia's new sentencing procedures require as a prerequisite to the imposition of the death penalty, specific jury findings as to the circumstances of the crime or the character of the defendant. Moreover, to guard further against a situation comparable to that presented in *Furman*, the Supreme Court of Georgia compares each death sentence with the sentences imposed on similarly situated defendants to ensure that the sentence of death in a particular case is not disproportionate. On their face these procedures seem to satisfy the concerns of *Furman*. No longer should there be "no meaningful basis for distinguishing the few cases in which [the death penalty] is imposed from the many cases in which it is not."
. . .

V

The basic concern of *Furman* centered on those defendants who were being condemned to death capriciously and arbitrarily. Under the procedures before the Court

in that case, sentencing authorities were not directed to give attention to the nature or circumstances of the crime committed or to the character or record of the defendant. Left unguided, juries imposed the death sentence in a way that could only be called freakish. The new Georgia sentencing procedures, by contrast, focus the jury's attention on the particularized nature of the crime and the particularized characteristics of the individual defendant. While the jury is permitted to consider any aggravating or mitigating circumstances, it must find and identify at least one statutory aggravating factor before it may impose a penalty of death. In this way the jury's discretion is channeled. No longer can a jury wantonly and freakishly impose the death sentence; it is always circumscribed by the legislative guidelines. In addition, the review function of the Supreme Court of Georgia affords additional assurance that the concerns that prompted our decision in *Furman* are not present to any significant degree in the Georgia procedure applied here.

For the reasons expressed in this opinion, we hold that the statutory system under which Gregg was sentenced to death does not violate the Constitution. Accordingly, the judgment of the Georgia Supreme Court is affirmed.

DISSENTING OPINION

In *Furman* v. *Georgia* (1972) (concurring opinion), I set forth at some length my views on the basic issue presented to the Court in [this case]. The death penalty, I concluded, is a cruel and unusual punishment prohibited by the Eighth and Fourteenth Amendments. That continues to be my view.

I have no intention of retracing the "long and tedious journey" that led to my conclusion in *Furman*. My sole purposes here are to consider the suggestion that my conclusion in *Furman* has been undercut by developments since then, and briefly to evaluate the basis for my Brethren's holding that the extinction of life is a permissible form of punishment under the Cruel and Unusual Punishments Clause.

In *Furman* I concluded that the death penalty is constitutionally invalid for two reasons. First, the death penalty is excessive. And second, the American people, fully informed as to the purposes of the death penalty and its liabilities, would in my view reject it as morally unacceptable.

Since the decision in *Furman,* the legislatures of thirty-five States have enacted new statutes authorizing the imposition of the death sentence for certain crimes, and Congress has enacted a law providing the death penalty for air piracy resulting in death. I would be less than candid if I did not acknowledge that these developments have a significant bearing on a realistic assessment of the moral acceptability of the death penalty to the American people. But if the constitutionality of the death penalty turns, as I have urged, on the opinion of an *informed* citizenry, then even the enactment of new death statutes cannot be viewed as conclusive. In *Furman,* I observed that the American people are largely unaware of the information critical to a judgment on the morality of the death penalty, and concluded that if they were better informed they would consider it shocking, unjust, and unacceptable. A recent study, conducted after the enactment of the post-*Furman* statutes, has confirmed that the American people know little about the death penalty, and that the opinions of an informed public would differ significantly from those of a public unaware of the consequences and effects of the death penalty.

Even assuming, however, that the post-*Furman* enactment of statutes authorizing the death penalty renders the prediction of the views of an informed citizenry an uncertain basis for a constitutional decision, the enactment of those statutes has no bearing whatsoever on the conclusion that the death penalty is unconstitutional because it is excessive. An excessive penalty is invalid under the Cruel and Unusual Punishments Clause "even though popular sentiment may

favor" it. The inquiry here, then, is simply whether the death penalty is necessary to accomplish the legitimate legislative purposes in punishment, or whether a less severe penalty—life imprisonment—would do as well.

The two purposes that sustain the death penalty as nonexcessive in the Court's view are general deterrence and retribution. In *Furman,* I canvassed the relevant data on the deterrent effect of capital punishment. The state of knowledge at that point, after literally centuries of debate, was summarized as follows by a United Nations Committee:

It is generally agreed between the retentionists and abolitionists, whatever their opinions about the validity of comparative studies of deterrence, that the data which now exist show no correlation between the existence of capital punishment and lower rates of capital crime.

The available evidence, I concluded in *Furman,* was convincing that "capital punishment is not necessary as a deterrent to crime in our society." . . .

The evidence I reviewed in *Furman* remains convincing, in my view, that "capital punishment is not necessary as a deterrent to crime in our society." The justification for the death penalty must be found elsewhere.

The other principal purpose said to be served by the death penalty is retribution. The notion that retribution can serve as a moral justification for the sanction of death finds credence in the opinion of my Brothers Stewart, Powell, and Stevens. . . . It is this notion that I find to be the most disturbing aspect of today's unfortunate [decision].

The concept of retribution is a multifaceted one, and any discussion of its role in the criminal law must be undertaken with caution. On one level, it can be said that the notion of retribution or reprobation is the basis of our insistence that only those who have broken the law be punished, and in this sense the notion is quite obviously central to a just system of criminal sanctions. But our recognition that retribution plays a crucial role in determining who may be punished by no means requires approval of retribution as a general justification for punishment. It is the question whether retribution can provide a moral justification for punishment—in particular, capital punishment—that we must consider.

My Brothers Stewart, Powell, and Stevens offer the following explanation of the retributive justification for capital punishment:

The instinct for retribution is part of the nature of man, and channeling that instinct in the administration of criminal justice serves an important purpose in promoting the stability of a society governed by law. When people begin to believe that organized society is unwilling or unable to impose upon criminal offenders the punishment they "deserve," then there are sown the seeds of anarchy—of self-help, vigilante justice, and lynch law.

This statement is wholly inadequate to justify the death penalty. As my Brother Brennan stated in *Furman,* "[t]here is no evidence whatever that utilization of imprisonment rather than death encourages private blood feuds and other disorders." It simply defies belief to suggest that the death penalty is necessary to prevent the American people from taking the law into their own hands.

In a related vein, it may be suggested that the expression of moral outrage through the imposition of the death penalty serves to reinforce basic moral values—that it marks some crimes as particularly offensive and therefore to be avoided. The argument is akin to a deterrence argument, but differs in that it contemplates the individual's shrinking from antisocial conduct, not because he fears punishment, but because he has been told in the strongest possible way that the conduct is wrong. This contention, like the previous one, provides no support for the death penalty. It is inconceivable that any individual concerned about conforming his conduct to what society says is "right" would fail to realize that murder is "wrong" if the penalty were simply life imprisonment.

The foregoing contentions—that society's expression of moral outrage through the imposition of the death penalty preempts the citizenry from taking the law into its own hands and reinforces moral values—are not retributive in the purest sense. They are essentially utilitarian in that they portray the death penalty as valuable because of its beneficial results. These justifications for the death penalty are inadequate because the penalty is, quite clearly I think, not necessary to the accomplishment of those results.

There remains for consideration, however, what might be termed the purely retributive justification for the death penalty—that the death penalty is appropriate, not because of its beneficial effect on society, but because the taking of the murderer's life is itself morally good. Some of the language of the opinion of my Brothers Stewart, Powell, and Stevens . . . appears positively to embrace this notion of retribution for its own sake as a justification for capital punishment. They state:

[T]he decision that capital punishment may be the appropriate sanction in extreme cases is an expression of the community's belief that certain crimes are themselves so grievous an affront to humanity that the only adequate response may be the penalty of death.

They then quote with approval from Lord Justice Denning's remarks before the British Royal Commission on Capital Punishment:

The truth is that some crimes are so outrageous that society insists on adequate punishment, because the wrong-doer deserves it, irrespective of whether it is a deterrent or not.

Of course, it may be that these statements are intended as no more than observations as to the popular demands that it is thought must be responded to in order to prevent anarchy. But the implication of the statements appears to me to be quite different—namely, that society's judgment that the murderer "deserves" death must be respected not simply because the preservation of order requires it, but because it is appropriate that society make the judgment and carry it out. It is this latter notion, in particular, that I consider to be fundamentally at odds with the Eighth Amendment. The mere fact that the community demands the murderer's life in return for the evil he has done cannot sustain the death penalty, for as Justices Stewart, Powell, and Stevens remind us, "the Eighth Amendment demands more than that a challenged punishment be acceptable to contemporary society." To be sustained under the Eighth Amendment, the death penalty must "compor[t] with the basic concept of human dignity at the core of the Amend-

ment;" the objective in imposing it must be "[consistent] with our respect for the dignity of [other] men." Under these standards, the taking of life "because the wrongdoer deserves it" surely must fail, for such a punishment has as its very basis the total denial of the wrongdoer's dignity and worth.

The death penalty, unnecessary to promote the goal of deterrence or to further any legitimate notion of retribution, is an excessive penalty forbidden by the Eighth and Fourteenth Amendments. I respectfully dissent from the Court's judgment upholding the [sentence] of death imposed upon the [petitioner in this case].

Footnotes

1. Another purpose that has been discussed is the incapacitation of dangerous criminals and the consequent prevention of crimes that they may otherwise commit in the future.

2. We do not address here the question whether the taking of the criminal's life is a proportionate sanction where no victim has been deprived of life—for example, when capital punishment is imposed for rape, kidnapping, or armed robbery that does not result in the death of any human being.

3. The Model Penal Code proposes the following standards:

"**(3)** Aggravating Circumstances.

"**(a)** The murder was committed by a convict under sentence of imprisonment.

"**(b)** The defendant was previously convicted of another murder or of a felony involving the use or threat of violence to the person.

"**(c)** At the time the murder was committed the defendant also committed another murder.

"**(d)** The defendant knowingly created a great risk of death to many persons.

"**(e)** The murder was committed while the defendant was engaged or was an accomplice in the commission of, or an attempt to commit, or flight after committing or attempting to commit robbery, rape or deviate sexual intercourse by force or threat of force, arson, burglary or kidnapping.

"**(f)** The murder was committed for the purpose of avoiding or preventing a lawful arrest or effecting an escape from lawful custody.

"**(g)** The murder was committed for pecuniary gain.

"**(h)** The murder was especially heinous, atrocious or cruel, manifesting exceptional depravity.

"**(4)** Mitigating Circumstances.

"**(a)** The defendant has no significant history of prior criminal activity.

"**(b)** The murder was committed while the defendant was under the influence of extreme mental or emotional disturbance.

"**(c)** The victim was a participant in the defendant's homicidal conduct or consented to the homicidal act.

"**(d)** The murder was committed under circumstances which the defendant believed to provide a moral justification or extenuation for his conduct.

"**(e)** The defendant was an accomplice in a murder committed by another person and his participation in the homicidal act was relatively minor.

"**(f)** The defendant acted under duress or under the domination of another person.

"**(g)** At the time of the murder, the capacity of the defendant to appreciate the criminality [wrongfulness] of his conduct or to conform his conduct to the requirements of law was impaired as a result of mental disease or defect or intoxication.

"**(h)** The youth of the defendant at the time of the crime." ALI Model Penal Code § 210.6 (Proposed Official Draft 1962).

Review Questions

1. What is the basic concept underlying the Eighth Amendment?
2. When is a punishment excessive?
3. Does the death penalty violate contemporary standards of decency?
4. What "two principal social purposes" does the death penalty serve?
5. Do statistics prove that the death penalty is a deterrent?
6. Who is supposed to be deterred by the death penalty?

7. Why don't the Georgia sentencing procedures allow arbitrary application of the death sentence?

8. What are Justice Brennan's objections?

9. Explain Justice Marshall's objections.

Discussion Questions

1. Try to define the phrase "cruel and unusual."

2. How could it be proven that the death penalty really deters potential murderers? Explain.

3. Should the "instinct for retribution" be satisfied? Defend your answer.

ROBERT S. GERSTEIN

Capital Punishment—"Cruel and Unusual"?: A Retributivist Response

From Robert S. Gerstein, "Capital Punishment—'Cruel and Unusual'?: A Retributivist Response" ETHICS vol. 85, #1, pp. 75–79. Published by the University of Chicago Press.

Robert S. Gerstein teaches philosophy at the University of California, Los Angeles.

Gerstein offers a defense of retributivism. It should not be equated with vengeance. Rather it is the view that punishment restores the balance of advantages to a just community. The punishment must be proportionate to the offense, but also it must treat the offender with the respect due a member of a community founded on principles of justice.

Thomas Long, in his article "Capital Punishment—'Cruel and Unusual'?"[1] canvasses the various arguments made for the view that capital punishment is cruel and unusual punishment and comes to the conclusion that the only argument with substantial merit is that which holds that capital punishment is unconstitutional because the pain and suffering it involves cannot be shown to be justified by its effectiveness as a deterrent. It must therefore be regarded as an irrational imposition of pain and suffering until such time as it can be shown that it is a more effective deterrent than less severe punishments would be. He then goes on to admit that this argument has its "sinister" aspects: it is probably true that no punishment could meet the burden of proof required by this standard of rationality. The force of the argument then is to undermine the justification for punishment generally.

I would suggest that Long arrives at this surprising result largely because he has chosen to restrict his consideration of the legitimacy of capital punishment to utilitarian considerations. The key to understanding this restriction is to be found, I believe in his decision to disregard the retributivist view because "nonretributive views are today predominant among theoreticians of crime and punishment."[2] Having rejected retributivism, and any consideration of whether people "deserve" certain sorts of punishments or not, he is left with a classic utilitarian calculus in which the pain caused to the criminal is to be balanced against the benefits society would gain from the example his punishment sets to others. The dilemma in which he finds himself at the end of his indecisive calculations serves to underline Kant's warning to the penologist who stops being concerned with giving people what they deserve and instead "rummages around in the winding paths of a theory of happiness"[3] for guidance.

It is true that many judges and scholars simply reject retributivism out of hand.[4] It is also true, however, that there has in recent years been a revival of interest in retributive theory.[5] I would like to suggest that the rejection of retributivism is largely a product of misunderstanding and that, properly understood, the retributive view offers a more plausible basis for the solution of the problems surrounding cruel and unusual punishment generally, and capital punishment in particular, than do utilitarian views such as Long's.

The most common way of misunderstanding retributivism is to take it to be a fancy word for revenge. Those who assume that it is simply a rationalization for the venting of our passion for vengeance[6] quite rightly conclude that retributivism can offer us little help in deciding what is cruel and unusual punishment. Obviously this passion is not subject to any inherent limits on cruelty: it has been known to lead people to kill not only wrongdoers, but their whole families as well; it has led to boilings in oil and burnings at the stake. Others who connect retributivism with revenge construe it as a kind of utilitarian argument. In this view the retributivist is not one who justifies the urge to vengeance, but one who thinks that punishment is useful because it allows people to vent this emotion in a (relatively) harmless and orderly way.[7] People who see retributivism in this way also quite rightly come to the conclusion that it offers us no help in deciding what kinds of punishments should be ruled out as cruel and unusual.

These misunderstandings have at their heart the equation of vengeance with retribution. The equation is made understandable by the fact that there are connections, historical and conceptual, between these two ideas. It is mistaken because it misses the enormous and crucial differences between them.

Vengefulness is an emotional response to injuries done to us by others: we feel a desire to injure those who have injured us. Retributivism is not the idea that it is good to have and satisfy this emotion. It is rather the view that there are good arguments for including that kernel of rationality to be found in the passion for vengeance as a part of any just system of laws. Assuming the existence of a generally just legal system, the argument for making retributive punishment a part of it has been succinctly stated in this way:

In order to enjoy the benefits that a legal system makes possible, each man must be prepared to make an important sacrifice—namely, the sacrifice of obeying the law even when he does not desire to do so. Each man calls on others to do this, and it is only just or fair that he bear a comparable burden when his turn comes. Now if the system is to remain just, it is important to guarantee that those who disobey will not thereby gain an unfair advantage over those who obey voluntarily. Criminal punishment thus attempts to maintain the proper balance between benefit and obedience by insuring that there is no profit in criminal wrongdoing.[8]

It has been seen that some critics of retributivism regard it as a theory that would lead us to use criminals as objects upon which to vent our emotions, as scapegoats to be dealt with without regard to their value as people. In fact, nothing could be further from the truth. It is a major tenet of the standard form of retributivism that "a human being can never be manipulated merely as a means to the purposes of someone else."[9] Punishment is not, in this view, a matter of injuring people because it is useful to us but of dealing with them in the way they deserve to be dealt with. The question for the retributivist is not: what will be the most advantageous way of disposing of this criminal? Rather it is: what is the just way to treat one of our fellow citizens who has willfully taken unjust advantage of the rest of us?

It is especially surprising that critics suggest that retributivism leads to the destruction of all limits on the severity of punishment. Retributivism in its classic form has within it a standard that measures out the severity of the punishment with great care: *lex talionis.*[10] Indeed, if the purpose of punishment is to restore the balance of advantages necessary to a just community, then punishment must be proportioned to the offense; any unduly severe punishment would unbalance things in the other direction.

In fact, one of the great advantages of retributivism over other views is that it serves not only as a justification for punishment but also as a guide to the appropriate kind of punishment and a limit on the severity of punishment. Most other views require us to balance various utilitarian considerations against each other to come to our conclusions. So, for example, a very harsh punishment might be warranted for a particular crime from the point of view of the needs of deterrence, but we might decide to mitigate it because it would simply be too painful to those that would undergo it. Understood from this perspective, the problem of deciding whether some particular punishment was cruel and unusual would, of course, be a matter of weighing the social advantages to be derived from it against the pain it would cause the criminal. A variety of policies, including deterrence, security, and rehabilitation, must all be taken into account.

In retributivism, on the other hand, we have a single coherent perspective from which to make a principled judgment as to the punishment appropriate for this offense and this person. Because punishment is justified as the deserved response of the community to a member who has acted unjustly, it is essential that the punishment meted out to him be consistent with his position as a member of the community. He is not to be treated as an object or even as an enemy. Our duty to treat him justly is no less stringent than that which we have toward any other member of the community. The purpose of punishment is to restore the balance of justice within the community, not further to derange it.

What then would retributivism regard as cruel and unusual punishment? Clearly, any punishment the severity of which was out of proportion with the offense. But further, any punishment that would be inconsistent with the criminal's status as a member of the community whose capacity for a sense of justice (a capacity of which he did not make use when he committed his crime)[11] is worthy of our respect. This is not to say that we may not cause him pain, and even very great pain. To say that punishment is justified is to say that a man with the capacity for a sense of justice ought to feel guilty and recognize that he should suffer for what he has done. The line is not to be drawn in terms of the degree, but in terms of the kind of suffering that is inflicted. As Plato pointed out, it can never be the business of a just man to make another man less just than he was.[12] An affliction that undermines a man's self-respect rather than awakening his conscience, that impairs his capacity for justice rather than stimulating it, could not serve as just punishment.

In fact, one of the most widely accepted views of the meaning of "cruel and unusual punishment," that developed by Justice Brennan,[13] fits very well into the retributivist perspective. Brennan argues that cruel and unusual punishments are those that "treat members of the human race as nonhumans, as objects to be toyed with and discarded."[14] He sums up his view in terms of the "primary principle . . . that a punishment must not in its severity be degrading to human dignity."[15] Brennan's position gains both force and clarity when it is seen in the context of retributivism. In this context the distinction between punishments that destroy human dignity and those that do not becomes more plausible because the theory shows us how we can justify the imposition of some afflictive punishments on a person while giving full respect to his human dignity. The idea of human dignity is also given content when it is explicated in terms of the capacity for a sense of justice. Just as we justify punishment as a response to those who abuse this capacity, so we shape and limit punishment out of the desire to preserve and stimulate it.

How does capital punishment fit into this scheme? The retributivist view, to the extent it is dealt with at all, is dealt with only as providing arguments in favor of capital punishment.[16] This is, first, because it does offer a justification for punishment in general, and, second, because the *lex talionis* can be seen as a justification for capital punishment in particular: "life for life, eye for eye, tooth for tooth." Of course, this should make it clear that retributivism would almost certainly rule out as cruel and unusual the use of capital punishment for rape, or for any other crime but murder. But is the retributivist committed to the support of capital punishment for murder? Kant argued that because there is "no sameness of kind between death and remaining alive even under the most miserable conditions" only capital punishment can restore the balance of justice where murder has been committed.[17]

The retributive theory contains the foundation of a very different sort of argument, however.[18] It can lead us to ask how it is possible for us to continue to respect the moral capacity of another while we prepare for and carry out his execution. The answer to this question might depend on attitudes that do change over time. Perhaps the people involved in the ceremony surrounding

the public beheading of a nobleman in the eighteenth century could continue to have profound respect for him as a moral being.[19] But ceremonial public executions would not be tolerated among us today. Given our surreptitious and mechanical approach to execution, it is hard to see that the condemned are treated as anything more than "objects to be . . . discarded." The condemned man's physical suffering may be minimized, but that is no more than we would do for a domestic animal to be disposed of. It is not the degree of suffering that might lead the retributivist to regard capital punishment as cruel and unusual, but its dehumanizing character, its total negation of the moral worth of the person to be executed.

I have not attempted here to give a justification of retributivism but only to establish that it would be a serious mistake not to include it among the alternative positions to be considered in gaining a full understanding of the issues involved in declaring the death penalty unconstitutional. Retributivism does offer a coherent and intuitively sound approach to understanding what the phrase "cruel and unusual punishment" can be taken to mean. It is not subject to the difficulties that beset positions like that developed by Long. And if it does not give us an easy answer to the question whether the death penalty is cruel and unusual, it does present the question to us in a form that presses us to make a principled judgment of the most serious sort: when, if ever, can we say that a person whom we continue to respect as a fellow member of a community founded on the principles of justice is deserving of death at our hands?

Footnotes

1. *Ethics* 83 (April 1973): 214–23.

2. Ibid., p. 220, n. 21.

3. Kant, *The Metaphysical Elements of Justice*, trans. John Ladd (Indianapolis: Bobbs-Merrill Co., 1965), p. 100.

4. See Furman v. Georgia, 92 S.Ct. 2726, 2779–80 (Marshall, J., concurring 1972), and the authorities cited at 2780, no. 86.

5. See Moberly, *The Ethics of Punishment* (London: Faber & Faber, 1968); Herbert Morris, "Persons and Punishment," *Monist* 52 (October 1968): 475; Jeffrey

Murphy, "Three Mistakes about Retributivism," *Analysis* 31 (April 1971): 166.

6. See Furman v. Georgia, 92 S.Ct. 2726, 2779 (Marshall, J. concurring 1972).

7. Ibid., at 2761 (Stewart, J., concurring), 2836 (Powell, J., dissenting); Goldberg and Dershowitz, "Declaring the Death Penalty Unconstitutional," *Harvard Law Review* 83 (June 1970): 1773, 1796.

8. Murphy, p. 166.

9. Kant, p. 100.

10. Ibid., p. 101.

11. The concept of the capacity for a sense of justice is developed in Rawls, "The Sense of Justice," *Philisophical Review* 72 (1963): 281.

12. *Republic*, trans. Cornford (Oxford: Oxford University Press, 1941), p. 13.

13. Concurring in Trop v. Dulles, 356 U.S. 86, 102 (1958), and Furman v. Georgia, 92 S.Ct. 2726, 2742–48 (1972).

14. Furman v. Georgia, at 2743.

15. Ibid., at 2748.

16. See ibid., 92 S.Ct. 2726, 2779 (Marshall, J., concurring), 2761 (Stewart, J., concurring), 2836 (Powell, J., dissenting).

17. Kant, p. 102.

18. Moberly, on whose view I have drawn extensively here, is one leading retributivist who opposes capital punishment (see *The Ethics of Punishment*, pp. 296–99).

19. See Kant, p. 103, where such an execution is used as an example.

Review Questions

1. Explain Long's argument for saying that capital punishment is cruel and unusual.

2. What is the "classic utilitarian calculus?"

3. What are the differences between vengefulness and retribution?

4. What would retributivism regard as cruel and unusual punishment?

5. What does *lex talionis* mean?

Discussion Questions

1. Can we deliberately kill a person and still treat her with the respect due to a fellow member of the community? Defend your answer.

2. Is the principle of *lex talionis* acceptable or not? Why, or why not?

JONATHAN GLOVER

Execution and Assassination

From Jonathan Glover: CAUSING DEATH & SAVING LIVES (Pelican Books 1977) pp. 228–245.
Copyright © Jonathan Glover, 1977. Reprinted by permission of Penguin Books Ltd.

Jonathan Glover is a Fellow and tutor in philosophy at New College, Oxford, and has written Responsibility (1970).

Glover begins with a discussion of Kant's retributive view and the absolutist rejection of capital punishment. He finds both of these to be unacceptable from a utilitarian point of view. The utilitarian approach is that the death penalty is justified if the number of lives saved exceeds the number of executions. But due to the bad side effects of execution on the person executed and on others, as well as other undesirable features, the death penalty is not justified unless it has a substantial deterrent effect. After considering arguments for this deterrent effect, Glover concludes that the case for capital punishment as a substantial deterrent fails.

The Penal Law is a Categorical Imperative; and woe to him who creeps through the serpent-windings of Utilitarianism to discover some advantage that may discharge him from the Justice of Punishment, or even from the due measure of it . . . For if Justice and Righteousness perish, human life would no longer have any value in the world . . . Whoever has committed murder must die.
                    Immanuel Kant, The Philosophy of Law

It is curious, but till that moment I had never realized what it means to destroy a healthy, conscious man. When I saw the prisoner step aside to avoid the puddle I saw the mystery, the unspeakable wrongness, of cutting a life short when it is in full tide. This man was not dying, he was alive just as we are alive. All the organs of his body were working—bowels digesting food, skin renewing itself, nails growing, tissues forming—all toiling away in solemn foolery. His nails would still be growing when he stood on the drop, when he was falling through the air with a tenth of a second to live. His eyes saw the yellow gravel and the grey walls, and his brain still remembered, foresaw, reasoned, even about puddles. He and we were a party of men walking together, seeing, hearing, feeling, understanding the same world; and in two minutes, with a sudden snap, one of us would be gone—one mind less, one world less.
           George Orwell, "A Hanging," Adelphi, 1931

The debate about capital punishment for murder is, emotionally at lest, dominated by two absolutist views. On the retributive view, the murderer must be given the punishment he deserves, which is death. On the other view, analogous to pacifism about war, there is in principle no possibility of justifying capital punishment; in execution there is only "the unspeakable wrongness of cutting a life short when it is in full tide." Supporters of these two approaches agree only in rejecting the serpent-windings of utilitarianism.

Let us look first at the retributive view. According to retributivism in its purest form, the aim of punishment is quite independent of any beneficial social consequences it may have. To quote Kant again:

Even if a Civil Society resolved to dissolve itself with the consent of all its members—as might be supposed in the case of a people inhabiting an

island resolving to separate and scatter themselves throughout the whole world—the last Murderer lying in the prison ought to be executed before the resolution was carried out. This ought to be done in order that everyone may realize the desert of his deeds, and that blood-guiltiness may not remain upon the people; for otherwise they might all be regarded as participators in the murder as a public violation of justice.

This view of punishment, according to which it has a value independent of its contribution to reducing the crime rate, is open to the objection that acting on it leads to what many consider to be pointless suffering. To impose suffering or deprivation on someone, or to take his life, is something that those of us who are not retributivists think needs very strong justification in terms of benefits, either to the person concerned or to other people. The retributivist has to say either that the claims of justice can make it right to harm someone where no one benefits, or else to cite the curiously metaphysical "benefits" of justice being done, such as Kant's concern that we should have "blood-guiltiness" removed. I have no way of refuting these positions, as they seem to involve no clear intellectual mistake. I do not expect to win the agreement of those who hold them, and I am simply presupposing the other view, that there is already enough misery in the world, and that adding to it requires a justification in terms of nonmetaphysical benefits to people.

This is not to rule out retributive moral principles perhaps playing a limiting role in a general theory of punishment. There is a lot to be said for the retributive restrictions that *only* those who deserve punishment should receive it and that they should never get more punishment than they deserve. (The case for this, which at least partly rests on utilitarian considerations, has been powerfully argued by H.L.A. Hart.[1]) But the approach to be adopted here rules out using retributive considerations to justify any punishment not already justifiable in terms of social benefits. In particular it rules out the argument that capital punishment can be justified, whether or not it reduces the crime rate, because the criminal deserves it.

This approach also has the effect of casting doubt on another way of defending capital punishment, which was forthrightly expressed by Lord Denning: "The ultimate justification of any punishment is not that it is a deterrent, but that it is the emphatic denunciation by the community of a crime: and from this point of view, there are some murders which, in the present state of public opinion, demand the most emphatic denunciation of all, namely the death penalty."[2] The question here is whether the point of the denunciation is to reduce the murder rate, in which case this turns out after all to be a utilitarian justification, or whether denunciation is an end in itself. If it is an end in itself, it starts to look like the retributive view in disguise, and should be rejected for the same reasons.

If we reject retribution for its own sake as a justification for capital punishment we are left with two alternative general approaches to the question. One is an absolute rejection in principle of any possibility of capital punishment being justified, in the spirit of Orwell's remarks. The other is the rather more messy approach, broadly utilitarian in character, of weighing up likely social costs and benefits.

THE ABSOLUTIST REJECTION OF CAPITAL PUNISHMENT

To some people, it is impossible to justify the act of killing a fellow human being. They are absolute pacifists about war and are likely to think of capital punishment as "judicial murder." They will sympathize with Beccaria's question: "Is it not absurd that the laws which detest and punish homicide, in order to prevent murder, publicly commit murder themselves?"

The test of whether an opponent of capital punishment adopts this absolutist position is whether he would still oppose it if it could be shown to save many more lives than it cost, if, say, every execution deterred a dozen potential murderers. The absolutist, unlike the utilitarian opponent of the death penalty, would be unmoved by any such evidence. This question brings out the links between the absolutist position and the acts and omissions doctrine. For those of us who reject the acts and omissions doctrine, the deaths we fail to prevent have to be given weight, as well as the deaths we cause by execution. So those of us who do not accept the acts and omissions doctrine cannot be absolutist opponents of capital punishment.

There is a variant on the absolutist position that at first sight seems not to presuppose the acts and omissions doctrine. On this view, while saving a potential murder victim is in itself as important as not killing a murderer, there is something so cruel about the kind of death involved in capital punishment that this rules out the possibility of its being justified. Those of us who reject the acts and omissions doctrine have to allow that sometimes there can be side effects associated with an act of killing, but not with failure to save a life, which can be sufficiently bad to make a substantial moral difference between the two. When this view is taken of the cruelty of the death penalty, it is not usually the actual method of execution that is objected to, though this can seem important, as in the case where international pressure on General Franco led him to substitute shooting for the garrote. What seems peculiarly cruel and horrible about capital punishment is that the condemned man has the period of waiting, knowing how and when he is to be killed. Many of us would rather die suddenly than linger for weeks or months knowing we were fatally ill, and the condemned man's position is several degrees worse than that of the person given a few months to live by doctors. He has the additional horror of knowing exactly when he will die, and of knowing that his death will be in a ritualized killing by other people, symbolizing his ultimate rejection by the members of his community. The whole of his life may seem to have a different and horrible meaning when he sees it leading up to this end.

For reasons of this kind, capital punishment can plausibly be claimed to fall under the United States Constitution's ban on "cruel and unusual punishments," so long as the word unusual is not interpreted too strictly. The same reasons make the death penalty a plausible candidate for falling under a rather similar ethical ban, which has been expressed by H.L.A. Hart: "There are many different ways in which we think it morally incumbent on us to *qualify* or *limit* the pursuit of the utilitarian goal by methods of punishment. Some punishments are ruled out as too barbarous to use *whatever their social utility*"[3] (final italics mine). Because of the extreme cruelty of capital punishment, many of us would, if forced to make a choice between two horrors, prefer to be suddenly murdered than be sentenced to death and executed. This is what makes it seem reasonable to say that the absolutist rejection of the death penalty need not rest on the acts and omissions doctrine.

But this appearance is illusory. The special awfulness of capital punishment may make an execution even more undesirable than a murder (though many would disagree on the grounds that this is outweighed by the desirability that the guilty rather than the innocent should die). Even if we accept that an execution is worse than an average murder, it does not follow from this that capital punishment is too barbarous to use *whatever its social utility*. For supposing a single execution deterred many murders? Or suppose that some of the murders deterred would themselves have been as cruel as an execution? When we think of the suffering imposed in a famous kidnapping case, where the mother received her son's ear through the post, we may feel uncertain even that capital punishment is more cruel than some "lesser" crimes than murder. The view that some kinds of suffering are too great to impose, whatever their social utility, rules out the possibility of justifying them, however much more suffering they would prevent. And this does presuppose the acts and omissions doctrine, and so excludes some of us even from this version of absolutism.

A UTILITARIAN APPROACH

It is often supposed that the utilitarian alternative to absolutism is simply one of adopting an unqualified maximizing policy. On such a view, the death penalty would be justified if, and only if, it was reasonable to think the number of lives saved exceeded the number of executions. (The question of what to do where the numbers exactly balance presupposes a fineness of measurement that is unattainable in these matters.) On any utilitarian view, numbers of lives saved must be a very important consideration. But there are various special features that justify the substantial qualification of a maximizing policy.

The special horror of the period of waiting for execution may not justify the absolutist rejection of the death penalty, but it is a powerful reason for thinking that an execution may normally cause more misery than a murder, and so for thinking that, if capital punishment is to be justified, it must do better than break even when lives saved through deterrence are compared with lives taken by the executioner.

This view is reinforced when we think of some of the other side effects of the death penalty. It must be appalling to be told that your husband, wife, or child has been murdered, but this is surely less bad than the experience of waiting a month or two for your husband, wife, or child to be executed. And those who think that the suffering of the murderer himself matters less than that of an innocent victim will perhaps not be prepared to extend this view to the suffering of the murderer's parents, wife, and children.

There is also the possibility of mistakenly executing an innocent man, something which it is very probable happened in the case of Timothy Evans. The German Federal

Ministry of Justice is quoted in the Council of Europe's report on *The Death Penalty in European Countries* as saying that in the hundred years to 1953, there were twenty-seven death sentences "now established or presumed" to be miscarriages of justice. This point is often used as an argument against capital punishment, but what is often not noticed is that its force must depend on the special horrors of execution as compared with other forms of death, including being murdered. For the victim of murder is innocent too, and he also has no form of redress. It is only the (surely correct) assumption that an innocent man faces something much worse in execution than in murder that gives this argument its claim to prominence in this debate. For, otherwise, the rare cases of innocent men being executed would be completely overshadowed by the numbers of innocent men being murdered. (Unless, of course, the acts and omissions doctrine is again at work here, for execution is something that we, as a community, *do* while a higher murder rate is something, we at most *allow.*)

The death penalty also has harmful effects on people other than the condemned man and his family. For most normal people, to be professionally involved with executions, whether as judge, prison warden, chaplain, or executioner, must be highly disturbing. Arthur Koestler quotes the case of the executioner Ellis, who attempted suicide a few weeks after he executed a sick woman "whose insides fell out before she vanished through the trap."[4] (Though the chances must be very small of the experience of Mr. Pierrepoint, who describes in his autobiography how he had to execute a friend with whom he often sang duets in a pub.[5]) And there are wider effects on society at large. When there is capital punishment, we are all involved in the horrible business of a long-premeditated killing, and most of us will to some degree share in the emotional response George Orwell had so strongly when he had to be present. It cannot be good for children at school to know that there is an execution at the prison down the road. And there is another bad effect, drily stated in the *Report of the Royal Commission on Capital Punishment:* "No doubt the ambition that prompts an average of five applications a week for the post of hangman, and the craving that draws a crowd to the prison where a notorious murderer is being executed, reveal psychological qualities that no state would wish to foster in its citizens."

Capital punishment is also likely to operate erratically. Some murderers are likely to go free because the death penalty makes juries less likely to convict. (Charles Dickens, in a newspaper article quoted in the 1868 Commons debate, gave the example of a forgery case, where a jury found a £ 10 note to be worth thirty-nine shillings, in order to save the forger's life.) There are also great problems in operating a reprieve system without arbitrariness, say, in deciding whether being pregnant or having a young baby should qualify a woman for a reprieve.

Finally, there is the drawback that the retention or reintroduction of capital punishment contributes to a tradition of cruel and horrible punishment that we might hope would wither away. Nowadays we never think of disemboweling people or chopping off their hands as a punishment. Even if these punishments would be especially effective in deterring some very serious crimes, they are not regarded as a real possibility. To many of us, it seems that the utilitarian benefits from this situation outweigh the loss of any deterrent power they might have if reintroduced for some repulsive crime like kidnapping. And the longer we leave capital punishment in abeyance, the more its use will seem as out of the question as the no more cruel punishment of mutilation. (At this point, I come near to Hart's view that some punishments are too barbarous to use whatever their social utility. The difference is that I think that arguments for and against a punishment should be based on social utility, but that a widespread view that some things are unthinkable is itself of great social utility.)

For these reasons, a properly thought-out utilitarianism does not enjoin an unqualified policy of seeking the minimum loss of life, as the no trade-off view does. Capital punishment has its own special cruelties and horrors, which change the whole position. In order to be justified, it must be shown, with good evidence, that it has a deterrent effect not obtainable by less awful means, and one that is quite substantial rather than marginal.

DETERRENCE AND MURDER

The arguments over whether capital punishment deters murder more effectively than less drastic methods are of two kinds: statistical and intuitive. The statistical arguments are based on various kinds of comparisons of murder rates. Rates are compared before and after abolition in a country, and, where possible, further comparisons are made with rates after reintroduction of capital punishment. Rates are compared in neighboring countries, or neighboring states of the U.S. C.A., with and without the death penalty. I am not a statistician and have no special competence to discuss the issue, but will merely purvey the received opinion of those who have looked into the matter. Those who have studied the figures are agreed that there is no striking correlation between the absence of capital punishment and any alteration in the curve of the murder rate. Having agreed on this point, they then fall into two schools. On one view, we can conclude that capital punishment is not a greater deterrent to murder than the prison sentences that are substituted for it. On the other, more cautious, view, we can only conclude that we do not know that capital punishment is a deterrent. I shall not attempt to choose between these interpretations. For, given that capital punishment is justified only where there is good evidence that it is a substantial deterrent, either interpretation fails to support the case for it.

If the statistical evidence were conclusive that capital punishment did not deter more

than milder punishments, this would leave no room for any further discussion. But, since the statistical evidence may be inconclusive, many people feel there is room left for intuitive arguments. Some of these deserve examination. The intuitive case was forcefully stated in 1864 by Sir James Fitzjames Stephen: [6]

No other punishment deters men so effectually from committing crimes as the punishment of death. This is one of those propositions which it is difficult to prove, simply because they are in themselves more obvious than any proof can make them. It is possible to display ingenuity in arguing against it, but that is all. The whole experience of mankind is in the other direction. The threat of instant death is the one to which resort has always been made when there was an absolute necessity for producing some result. . . . No one goes to certain inevitable death except by compulsion. Put the matter the other way. Was there ever yet a criminal who, when sentenced to death and brought out to die, would refuse the offer of a commutation of his sentence for the severest secondary punishment? Surely not. Why is this? It can only be because "All that a man has will he give for his life." In any secondary punishment, however terrible, there is hope; but death is death; its terrors cannot be described more forcibly.

These claims turn out when scrutinized to be much more speculative and doubtful than they at first sight appear.

The first doubt arises when Stephen talks of "certain inevitable death." The Royal Commission, in their *Report*, after quoting the passage from Stephen above, quote figures to show that, in the fifty years from 1900 to 1949, there was in England and Wales one execution for every twelve murders known to the police. In Scotland in the same period there was less than one execution for every twenty-five murders known to the police. Supporters of Stephen's view could supplement their case by advocating more death sentences and fewer reprieves, or by optimistic speculations about better police detection or greater willingness of juries to convict. But the reality of capital punishment as it was in these countries, unmodified by such recommendations and speculations, was not one where the potential murderer faced certain, inevitable death. This may incline us to modify Stephen's estimate of its deterrent effect, unless we buttress his view with the further speculation that a fair number of potential murderers falsely believed that what they would face was certain, inevitable death.

The second doubt concerns Stephen's talk of "the threat of instant death." The reality again does not quite fit this. By the time the police conclude their investigation, the case is brought to trial, and verdict and sentence are followed by appeal, petition for reprieve, and then execution, many months have probably elapsed, and when this time factor is added to the low probability of the murderers being executed, the picture looks very different. For we often have a time bias, being less affected by threats of future catastrophes than by threats of instant ones. The certainty of immediate death is one thing; it is another thing merely to increase one's chances of death in the future. Unless this were so, no one would smoke or take on such high-risk jobs as diving in the North Sea.

There is another doubt when Stephen very plausibly says that virtually all criminals would prefer life imprisonment to execution. The difficulty is over whether this entitles us to conclude that it is therefore a more effective deterrent. For there is the possibility that, compared with the long term of imprisonment that is the alternative, capital punishment is what may appropriately be called an "overkill." It may be that, for those who will be deterred by threat of punishment, a long prison sentence is sufficient deterrent. I am not suggesting that this is so, but simply that it is an open question whether a worse alternative here generates any additional deterrent effect. The answer is *not* intuitively obvious.

Stephen's case rests on the speculative psychological assumptions that capital punishment is not an overkill compared with a prison sentence, and that its additional deterrent effect is not obliterated by time bias, nor by the low probability of execution, nor by a combination of these factors. Or else it must be assumed that, where the additional deterrent effect would be obliterated by the low probability of death, either on its own or in combination with time bias, the potential murderer thinks the probability is higher than it is. Some of these assumptions may be true, but, when they are brought out into the open, it is by no means obvious that the required combination of them can be relied upon.

Supporters of the death penalty also sometimes use what David A. Conway, in his valuable discussion of this issue, calls "the best-bet argument."[7] On this view, since there is no certainty whether or not capital punishment reduces the number of murders, either decision about it involves gambling with lives. It is suggested that it is better to gamble with the lives of murderers than with the lives of their innocent potential victims. This presupposes the attitude, rejected here, that a murder is a greater evil than the execution of a murderer. But, since this attitude probably has overwhelmingly widespread support, it is worth noting that, even if it is accepted, the best-bet argument is unconvincing. This is because, as Conway has pointed out, it overlooks the fact that we are not choosing between the chance of a murderer dying and the chance of a victim dying. In leaving the death penalty, we are opting for the certainty of the murderer dying that we hope will give us a chance of a potential victim being saved. This would look like a good bet only if we thought an execution substantially preferable to a murder and either the statistical evidence or the intuitive arguments made the effectiveness of the death penalty as a deterrent look reasonably likely.

Since the statistical studies do not give any clear indication that capital punishment makes any difference to the number of murders committed, the only chance of its supporters discharging the heavy burden of justification would be if the intuitive arguments were extremely powerful. We might then feel justified in supposing that other factors distorted the murder rate, masking the substantial deterrent effect of capital punishment. The intuitive arguments, presented as the merest platitudes, turn out to be speculative and unobvious. I conclude that the case for capital punishment as a substantial deterrent fails.

DETERRENCE AND POLITICAL CRIMES BY OPPOSITION GROUPS

It is sometimes suggested that the death penalty may be an effective deterrent in the case of a special class of "political" crimes. The "ordinary" murder (killing one's wife in a moment of rage, shooting a policeman in panic after a robbery, killing someone in a brawl) may not be particularly sensitive to different degrees of punishment. But some killings for political purposes have a degree of preparation and thought that may allow the severity of the penalty to affect the calculation. Two different kinds of killing come to mind here. There are killings as part of a political campaign, ranging from assassination through terrorist activities up to full-scale guerrilla war. And then there are policies carried out by repressive governments, varying from "liquidation" of individual opponents with or without "trial" to policies of wholesale extermination, sometimes, but not always, in wartime.

Let us look first at killings by groups opposed to governments. Would the various sectarian terrorist groups in Ireland stop their killings if those involved were executed? Would independence movements in countries like Algeria or Kenya have confined themselves to nonviolent means if more executions had taken place? Could the Nazis have deterred the French resistance by more executions? Could the Americans have deterred guerrillas war in Vietnam by more executions?

To ask these questions is to realize both the variety of different political situations in

which the question of deterrent killing arises, and also to be reminded, if it is necessary, that moral right is not always on the side of the authorities trying to do the deterring. But let us, for the sake of argument, assume a decent government is trying to deal with terrorists or guerrillas whose cause has nothing to be said for it. People have always gone to war knowing they risk their lives, and those prepared to fight in a guerrilla war seem scarcely likely to change their mind because of the marginal extra risk of capital punishment if they are arrested. If the case is to be made, it must apply to lower levels of violence than full-scale guerrilla war.

Given the death penalty's drawbacks, is there any reason to think it would be sufficiently effective in deterring a campaign of terrorist violence to be justified? The evidence is again inconclusive. In many countries there have been terrorist campaigns where the authorities have responded with executions without stopping the campaign. It is always open to someone to say that the level of terrorist activity might have been even higher but for the executions, but it is hard to see why this should be likely. Those who do the shooting or the planting of bombs are not usually the leaders and can be easily replaced by others willing to risk their lives. Danger to life does not deter people from fighting in wars, and a terrorist gunman may be just as committed to his cause as a soldier. And executions create martyrs, which helps the terrorist cause. They may even raise the level of violence by leading to reprisals.

But it may be that a sufficiently ruthless policy of executions would be effective enough to overcome these drawbacks. It has been claimed that the policy of the Irish government in 1922–3 is an instance of this. David R. Bates describes it as follows: [8]

In the turbulent period following the establishment of the Irish Free State, military courts with power to inflict the death penalty were set up to enable the Irregulars (opposing the Treaty) to be crushed. These powers were first used on 17

November 1922, when four young men were arrested in Dublin and, on being found to be armed, were executed. Shortly afterwards the Englishman, Erskine Childers, captured while carrying a revolver, was also executed. On 7 December two Deputies were shot (one fatally) by the Irregulars. The Minister for Defense, with the agreement of the Cabinet, selected four Irregular leaders who had been in prison since the fall of the Four Courts on 29 June. They were wakened, told to prepare themselves, and were executed by firing squad at dawn. During a six-month period, almost twice as many Irregular prisoners were executed as had been executed by the British from 1916 to 1921. At the end of April 1923, the Irregulars sought a ceasefire to discuss terms. The Free State Government refused. In May 1924, the Irregulars conceded military defeat.

This is an impressive case, and it may be that this degree of ruthlessness by the government involved fewer deaths than would have taken place during a prolonged terrorist campaign. But against this must be set some doubts. What would have happened if the terrorists had been as ruthless in reprisal as the government, perhaps announcing that for every man executed there would be two murders? Is it clear that after a period of such counter-retaliation it would have been the Irregulars rather than the government who climbed down? Does not any net saving of lives by the government's ruthless policy depend on the terrorists refraining from counter-retaliation, and can this be relied on in other cases? And is there not something dangerous in the precedent set when a government has prisoners executed without their having been convicted and sentenced for a capital offence? And, in this case, is it even clear that the defeat of the Irregulars ended once and for all the violence associated with the issues they were campaigning about? I raise these questions, not to claim that the government policy was clearly wrong, but to show how even a case like this is ambiguous in the weight it lends to the argument for using the death penalty against terrorism.

I do not think that the chance of a net saving of lives will in general outweigh the combination of the general drawbacks of capital punishment combined with the danger of its merely leading to a higher level of violence in a terrorist situation. But this is a matter of judgment rather than proof, and I admit that it *may* be that the opposite view had better results than mine would have had in 1922.

DETERRENCE AND POLITICAL CRIMES BY THE AUTHORITIES

The other category of political crimes that sometimes seems so special as to justify the death penalty is atrocities committed by governments or their agents. The executions of leading Nazis after the Nuremberg trials and the execution of Eichmann after his trial in Jerusalem come to mind. The justification usually advanced for these executions is retributive, and it is hard to imagine any more deserving candidates for the death penalty. But, for those of us who do not consider retribution an acceptable aim of punishment, the question must be whether executing them made their kind of activity less likely to happen again in the future. For, if not, we have no answer to the question asked by Victor Gollancz at the time of the Eichmann trial: why should we think we improve the world by turning six million deaths into six million and one?

The chances of people who design or carry out governmental policies of murder being tried and sentenced must often be very small. Sometimes this happens as the result of revolution or defeat in war, but those in power stand a fairly good chance of being killed under these circumstances anyway, and the additional hazard of capital punishment may not have much deterrent effect. As with "ordinary" murderers, the hope of not being caught reduces the punishment's terrors. Some of those who murdered for Hitler were executed; their opposite numbers under Stalin paid no penalty. The torturers who worked for the Greek colonels were brought to trial, but those now at work in Chile, Brazil, and South Africa have every expectation of not being punished.

When considering isolated cases of governmental murder (perhaps the assassination of a troublesome foreign leader by a country's intelligence agency, or the single killing of a political opponent) there seems no reason to think capital punishment more of a deterrent than it is of "ordinary" nonpolitical murder. If anything, it is likely to be less of a deterrent because of the reduced chance of a murder charge ever being brought. So there seems no case for treating these crimes as other than ordinary murders. But when considering large-scale atrocities, on the scale of those of Hitler or Stalin, or even on the scale of Lyndon Johnson in Vietnam or General Gowon in Nigeria, a version of the best-bet argument comes into play. There are two possible advantages to the death penalty here. One is simply that of totally eliminating the chance of the same mass murderer occupying a position of leadership again. Suppose Hitler had been captured at the end of the Second World War and the question of executing him had arisen. If he had not been executed, it is overwhelmingly probable that he would have spent the rest of his life in Spandau prison, writing his memoirs and giving increasingly senile lectures on world history to visiting journalists. But there would always be the very slight risk of an escape and return to power in the style of Napoleon. This slight risk is removed by execution. The other advantage of the death penalty is the chance, which we have seen to be probably very slight, of deterring repetition of such policies by other leaders.

The best-bet argument in these cases can be used by someone who accepts that the dangers of a defeated leader returning to power are very small and that the chances of execution deterring future leaders from similar policies are also very small. The argument is simply that, where the prevention of such enormous atrocities is in question, even an extremely small probability of prevention is valuable. Consider a case in which num-

bers and probabilities are parallel, but in which act and omission are reversed. Suppose someone in the hospital can have his life saved only by the making of some organism that has previously been banned. The reason for the ban is that there is a danger, but only a very faint one, of the organism getting out of control. If it does this, the death rate will run into millions. Let us suppose that our intuitive estimate of the unquantifiable risk here is the same as our intuitive estimate of the unquantifiable reduction of risk caused by executing the murdering leader. Those who would rather let the hospital patient die than breach the ban on the dangerous organism must either rely on the acts and omissions doctrine, or else rely on some difference of side effects, if they are not prepared to support executing the murdering politician or official.

Part of the difficulty in interpreting comparisons of this sort arises from the fact that we are dealing with probabilities that cannot be measured. And, even if they could be measured, most of us are unclear what sacrifices are worth making for the reduction of some risk that is already very small. But if we make the highly artificial assumption that the alterations in probability of risk are the same in the medical case as in the execution case, the dilemma remains. Let us suppose that the risk is one that we would not take in the medical case to save a single life. Those of us who do not accept the acts and omissions doctrine must then either find some difference of side effects or else support the execution.

Side effects do go some way towards separating the two cases. For, to breach the ban on producing the organism, even if it does no harm itself, contributes by example to a less strict observance of that ban (and possibly others) in cases in which the risk may be much greater. In the case of the Nazi leaders, such bad side effects as exist follow from execution rather than from saving their lives. These side effects include the contribution made to a climate of opinion where the death penalty seems more acceptable in other contexts, and the precedent that may encourage politicians to have their overthrown rivals, at home or abroad, executed. This last effect could be mitigated by more effort than was made at Nuremberg to remove the impression of the defeated being tried by the victors. It would be possible to set up a court of a genuinely international kind, independent of governmental pressure, to which prosecutions for a large-scale murder could be brought. But the general effect on the public consciousness of having capital punishment as a serious possibility would remain. I am uncertain how to weigh this against the small chance of helping to avert a great evil. For this reason my own views on this question are undecided.

Footnotes

1. H.L.A. Hart, "Prolegomenon to the Principles of Punishment," *Proceedings of the Aristotelian Society*, 1959–60.

2. Quoted in the *Report of the Royal Commission on Capital Punishment*, 1953.

3. H.L.A. Hart, "Murder and the Principles of Punishment," *Northwestern Law Review*, 1958.

4. Arthur Koestler, *Reflections on Hanging*, London, 1956.

5. Albert Pierrepoint, *Executioner: Pierrepoint*, London, 1974.

6. James Fitzjames Stephen, "Capital Punishments," *Fraser's Magazine*, 1864.

7. David A. Conway, "Capital Punishment and Deterrence," *Philosophy and Public Affairs*, 1974.

8. Professor David R. Bates, Letter to *The Times*, 14 October 1975.

Review Questions

1. Explain Kant's retributive view of capital punishment.
2. What objection can be made to this view?
3. What is the "other view" that Glover is presupposing?
4. What is Lord Denning's justification of capital punishment?
5. State the absolutist rejection of capital punishment and give the reasons used to defend it.
6. Why doesn't Glover accept this view?
7. Why can capital punishment plausibly be claimed to be a "cruel and unusual punishment?"
8. According to Glover, in what cases can capital punishment be justified even if it is cruel?
9. State the maximizing policy.
10. Glover introduces several considerations that justify the qualification of the maximizing policy. What are they?
11. According to Glover, how can capital punishment be justified?
12. What do the statistical arguments show, if anything, about capital punishment?
13. State the intuitive argument given by Fitzjames Stephen.
14. What doubts are raised about this argument?
15. What is "the best-bet argument?"
16. Why is this argument unconvincing?
17. What is Glover's position on capital punishment for political crimes?

Discussion Questions

1. "Whoever has committed murder must *die*." Do you agree, or not? Explain your view.

2. Is the death penalty a "cruel and unusual punishment," or not? Explain your answer.

3. Glover concludes that the case for capital punishment as a substantial deterrent fails. Do you agree, or not? Defend your position.

4. Can you think of any cases in which capital punishment would be justified? What are they?

SIDNEY HOOK

The Death Sentence

Sidney Hook, "The Death Sentence," in Hugo Adam Bedau, ed., *The Death Penalty in America* (Garden City, NY: Doubleday, 1967). Since the original essay was published Professor Hook advises that he is now prepared to extend the scope of discretionary death sentences in cases of multiple and aggravated capital crimes.

Sidney Hook is Professor Emeritus of Philosophy at New York University. He is the author of The Paradoxes of Freedom (1962) and The Place of Religion in a Free Society (1968).

Hook supports the retention of the death penalty in two cases: (1) defendants convicted of murder who choose the death sentence rather than life imprisonment, and (2) those who have been sentenced to prison for premeditated murder, and then murder again.

Since I am not a fanatic or absolutist, I do not wish to go on record as being categorically opposed to the death sentence in all circumstances. I should like to recognize two exceptions. A defendant convicted of murder and sentenced to life should be permitted to choose the death sentence instead. Not so long ago a defendant sentenced to life imprisonment made this request and was rebuked by the judge for his impertinence. I can see no valid grounds for denying such a request out of hand. It may sometimes be denied, particularly if a way can be found to make the defendant labor for the benefit of the dependents of his victim as is done in some European countries. Unless such considerations are present, I do not see on what reasonable ground the request can been denied, particularly by those who believe in capital punishment. Once they argue that life imprisonment is either a more effective deterrent or more justly punitive, they have abandoned their position.

In passing, I should state that I am in favor of permitting *any* criminal defendant, sentenced to life imprisonment, the right to choose death. I can understand why certain jurists, who believe that the defendant wants thereby to cheat the state out of its mode of punishment, should be indignant at the idea. They are usually the ones who believe that even the attempt at suicide should be deemed a crime—in effect saying to the unfortunate person that if he doesn't succeed in his act of suicide, the state will punish him for it. But I am baffled to understand why the absolute abolitionist, dripping with treacly humanitarinism, should oppose this proposal. I have heard some people actually oppose capital punishment in certain cases on the ground that: "Death is too good for the vile wretch! Let him live and suffer to the end of his days." But the absolute abolitionist should be the last person in the world to oppose the wish of the lifer, who regards this form of punishment as torture worse than death, to leave our world.

My second class of exceptions consists of those who having been sentenced once to prison for premeditated murder, murder again. In these particular cases we have evidence that imprisonment is not a sufficient deterrent for the individual in question. If the evidence shows that the prisoner is so psychologically constituted that, without being insane, the fact that he can kill again with impunity may lead to further murderous behavior, the court should have the discretionary power to pass the death sentence if the criminal is found guilty of a second murder.

In saying that the death sentence should be *discretionary* in cases in which a man has killed more than once, I am *not* saying that a murderer who murders again is more deserving of death than the murderer who murders once. Bluebeard was not twelve times more deserving of death when he was finally caught. I am saying simply this: that in a subclass of murderers, i.e., those who murder several times, there may be a special group of sane murderers who, knowing that they will not be executed, will not hesitate to kill again and again. For *them* the argument from deterrence is obviously valid. Those who say that there must be no exceptions to the abolition of capital punishment cannot rule out the existence of such cases on *a priori* grounds. If they admit that there is a reasonable probability that such murderers will murder again or attempt to murder again, a probability that usually grows with the number of repeated murders, and still insist they would *never* approve of capital punishment, I would conclude that they are indifferent to the lives of the human beings doomed, on their position, to be victims. What fancies itself as a humanitarian attitude is sometimes an expression of sentimentalism. The reverse coin of sentimentalism is often cruelty.

Our charity for all human beings must not deprive us of our common sense. Nor should our charity be less for the future of potential victims of the murderer than for the murderer himself. There are crimes in this world that are, like acts of nature, beyond the power of men to anticipate or control. But not all or most crimes are of this character. So long as human beings are responsible and educable, they will respond to praise and blame and punishment. It is hard to imagine it but even Hitler and Stalin were once infants. Once you *can* imagine them as infants, however, it is hard to believe that they were already monsters in their cradles. Every confirmed criminal was once an amateur. The existence of confirmed criminals testifies to the defects of our education—where they can be reformed—and of our penology—where they cannot. That is why we are under the moral obligation to be intelligent about crime and punishment. Intelligence should teach us that the best educational and penological system is the one that prevents crimes rather than punishes them; the next best is one that punishes crime in such a way as to prevent it from happening again.

Review Questions

1. In what two cases is the death penalty justified according to Hook?
2. In what case is the "argument from deterrence" (as Hook calls it) obviously valid?

Discussion Questions

1. Should a defendant convicted of murder be allowed to choose death rather than life imprisonment? Defend your answer.
2. Which is worse—death or life imprisonment? Explain your view.
3. Is there any way besides the death penalty to prevent murderers from killing again? What is it?

Problem Cases

1. (Gregg v. Georgia, 428 U.S. 153, 1976). Troy Gregg and Floyd Allen were hitchhiking when they were picked up by Fred Simmons and Bob Moore. Simmons and Moore left the car at a rest stop. According to the testimony of Allen, Gregg said that they were going to rob Simmons and Moore, and Gregg fired at them when they came back to the car. Gregg then went up and shot each of them in the head, robbed them, and then drove away with Allen. Gregg first admitted that Allen's account was accurate, but later denied it. Gregg's story was that Simmons had attacked him and that he had killed the two men in self-defense. The jury found Gregg guilty of two counts of murder, and determined that the murders were committed for the purpose of robbery. Should Gregg be given the death sentence or not? Defend your answer.

2. In New York City there are a series of unsolved murders. In each case an elderly man or woman is found dead from arsenic poisoning. Fingerprints are found at the scene of one of the crimes, and they are identified as belonging to George Smith, a twenty-year-old man with a record of drug offenses. He is picked up and he admits he is the killer. It also turns out that he is a heavy user of drugs, particularly LSD. At the trial, he testifies that he was an "angel of death" commanded by God to help old people go to heaven. Three psychiatrists testify that Smith is legally sane, but that while on drugs he suffers from psychotic episodes in which he hears voices that he believes are from God. The jury determines that Smith is legally sane, and that he is guilty of five counts of murder. Should Smith be given the death sentence or not? Explain your position.

Suggested Readings

Bedau, Hugo Adam. "Capital Punishment." In Tom Regan, ed., *Matters of Life and Death.* New York: Random House, 1980, pp. 148–182.

Goldberg, Steven. "On Capital Punishment," *Ethics* 85 (October 1974): 67–74. Goldberg examines the factual issue of whether or not the death penalty is a uniquely effective deterrent. A revised version entitled "Does Capital Punishment Deter?" appears in Richard A. Wasserstrom, ed., *Today's Moral Problems,* 2nd ed., New York: Macmillan, 1979, pp. 538–551.

Long, Thomas. "Capital Punishment—'Cruel and Unusual'?" *Ethics* 83 (April 1973): 214–223. Long discusses various arguments for the view that capital punishment is cruel and unusual.

CHAPTER 5

Sexual Morality

Basic Concepts

THE TRADITIONAL VIEW

The traditional view of sex is that nonmarital sex is morally wrong. Nonmarital sex includes activities such as adultery, premarital sex, fornication, adultery, prostitution, masturbation, and homosexuality. Those who accept the traditional view have different opinions about the use of contraceptives. The official teaching of the Roman Catholic Church, stated in the 1969 papal encyclical *Humane Vitae,* is that artificial birth control is immoral. But there are plenty of Catholics and non-Catholics who think that there is nothing wrong with using artificial means of birth control.

NATURAL LAW THEORY

To understand the traditional view of sex, it is useful to know something about the natural law theory that is the foundation of this view. The term "natural law" is used to mean a set of prescriptive rules of conduct that are binding on all human beings simply because of human nature. On natural law theory, human action is naturally directed towards certain goals and purposes such as life and procreation. These natural goals and purposes are good, and the pursuit of them is morally right, while interfering with them is morally wrong. The natural goal or purpose of sexual activity is reproduction within the context of marriage. Interfering with this natural goal or purpose of sex is morally wrong.

This natural law theory is espoused in the Vatican Declaration on Sexual Ethics. According to this Declaration, masturbation is a "seriously disordered act" because it "contradicts its finality," that is, it opposes the natural end of sex, which is procreation. Homosexuality is also a serious disorder for the same reason. Premarital sexual relations are condemned because they often exclude the prospect of children, and even if chil-

dren are produced, they will be deprived of a proper and stable environment.

Russell Vannoy attacks the natural law view. He finds nothing particularly wrong with so-called perversions such as homosexuality, necrophilia, and masturbation. He makes a number of points in reply to the view that such acts are perverse and wrong because they are "unnatural" in the sense of being nonprocreative: sex for pleasure is just as natural as reproductive sex, perhaps even more so; we cannot assume that whatever is natural is good, for nature can inflict evil on us; sex as an expression of love is natural even if it is not procreative; and how do we know that God or nature intends sex only for procreation, given the fact that sex seems to have other purposes?

SEXUAL PERVERSION

There are problems, then, with defining a sexual perversion as an unnatural (in the sense of nonprocreative) sex act. But how is the concept of sexual perversion to be explained then? Donald Levy attacks this problem in his article "Perversion and the Unnatural as Moral Categories." His account of the unnatural and the perverse is that an unnatural act is one that deprives a person unnecessarily of a basic human good, and a perverted sex act is an unnatural act that is done to get sexual pleasure. This account is in agreement with the natural law view of sex, for an implication is that sexually perverse acts are wrong. At the end of his paper, however, Levy admits that his view has some defects. One is that he is not clear about whether homosexuality is perverse or not; another is that rape, on Levy's analysis, turns out to be a sexual perversion, and this is contrary to the usual view that rape can be nonperverse even though it is morally wrong.

RAPE

But if rape is not wrong because it is perverse, then what exactly is wrong with it? The standard view of rape (of women) is that it is wrong because it treats women as objects, as entities inferior to men, and also because it is using a person without her consent.

Pamela Foa objects that this view does not uncover the special wrongness of rape. Rape is wrong even if it is not an act between equals; thus rape of children is just as bad as rape of adults even though children do not have the same status as adults. Moreover, Foa does not agree with Levy's view that rape is wrong because it is in some sense "unnatural." Unnatural acts are not wrong in the first place and, besides, rape can be the fulfillment of a "natural" sexual impulse. Nor is rape just a kind of wrongful assault on a person; being raped is not being wronged in the same way as being assaulted. What makes rape specially wrong, according to Foa, is the societal attitude that victims of rape enjoy themselves in a nonprivate and nonintimate environment, and that this is particularly shameful and humiliating. In fact, she says, rape in our society is only different in degree from marriage: both involve sex without real intimacy. The alternative to our society's rape model of sexuality, she suggests, is sex between friends who are willing to be intimate with each other.

THE VATICAN
Declaration on Sexual Ethics

The Declaration on Sexual Ethics was issued in Rome by the Sacred Congregation for the Doctrine of the Faith on December 29, 1975.
The authors defend the Christian doctrine that "every genital act must be within the framework of marriage." Premarital sex, masturbation, and homosexuality are specifically condemned, and chastity is recommended as a virtue.

1. According to contemporary scientific research, the human person is so profoundly affected by sexuality that it must be considered as one of the factors which give to each individual's life the principal traits that distinguish it. In fact it is from sex that the human person receives the characteristics which, on the biological, psychological and spiritual levels, make that person a man or a woman, and thereby largely condition his or her progress towards maturity and insertion into society. Hence sexual matters, as is obvious to everyone, today constitute a theme frequently and openly dealt with in books, reviews, magazines, and other means of social communication.

In the present period, the corruption of morals has increased, and one of the most serious indications of this corruption is the unbridled exaltation of sex. Moreover, through the means of social communication and through public entertainment this corruption has reached the point of invading the field of education and of infecting the general mentality.

In this context certain educators, teachers, and moralists have been able to contribute to a better understanding and integration into life of the values proper to each of the sexes; on the other hand there are those who have put forward concepts and modes of behavior which are contrary to the true moral exigencies of the human person. Some members of the latter group have even gone so far as to favor a licentious hedonism.

As a result, in the course of a few years, teachings, moral criteria, and modes of living hitherto faithfully preserved have been very much unsettled, even among Christians. There are many people today who, being confronted with so many widespread opinions opposed to the teaching which they received from the Church, have come to wonder what they must still hold as true.

2. The Church cannot remain indifferent to this confusion of minds and relaxation of morals. It is a question, in fact, of a matter which is of the utmost importance both for the personal lives of Christians and for the social life of our time.[1]

The Bishops are daily led to note the growing difficulties experienced by the faithful in obtaining knowledge of wholesome moral teaching, especially in sexual matters, and of the growing difficulties experienced by pastors in expounding this teaching effectively. The Bishops know that by their pastoral charge they are called upon to meet the needs of their faithful in this very serious matter, and important documents dealing with it have already been published by some of them or by Episcopal Conferences. Nevertheless, since the erroneous opinions and resulting deviations are continuing to spread everywhere, the Sacred Congregation for the Doctrine of the Faith, by virtue of its function in the universal Church[2] and by a mandate of the Supreme Pontiff, has judged it necessary to publish the present Declaration.

3. The people of our time are more and more convinced that the human person's dignity and vocation demand that they should discover, by the light of their own intelligence, the values innate in their nature, that they should ceaselessly develop these values and realize them in their lives, in order to achieve an ever greater development.

In moral matters man cannot make value judgments according to his personal whim: "In the depths of his conscience, man detects a law which he does not impose on himself, but which holds him to obedience. . . . For man has in his heart a law written by God. To obey it is the every dignity of man; according to it he will be judged."[3]

Moreover, through his revelation God has made known to us Christians his plan of salvation, and he has held up to us Christ, the Saviour and Sanctifier, in his teaching and example, as the supreme and immutable Law of life: "I am the light of the world; anyone who follows me will not be walking in the dark, he will have the light of life."[4]

Therefore there can be no true promotion of man's dignity unless the essential order of his nature is respected. Of course, in the history of civilization many of the concrete conditions and needs of human life have changed and will continue to change. But all evolution of morals and every type of life must be kept within the limits imposed by the immutable principles based upon every human person's constitutive elements and essential relations—elements and relations which transcend historical contingency.

These fundamental principles, which can be grasped by reason, are contained in "the divine law—eternal, objective, and universal—whereby God orders, directs, and governs the entire universe and all the ways of the human community, by a plan conceived in wisdom and love. Man has been made by God to participate in this law, with the result that, under the gentle disposition of divine Providence, he can come to perceive ever increasingly the unchanging truth."[5] This divine law is accessible to our minds.

4. Hence, those many people are in error who today assert that one can find neither in human nature nor in the revealed law any absolute and immutable norm to serve for particular actions other than the one which expresses itself in the general law of charity and respect for human dignity. As a proof of their assertion they put forward the view that so-called norms of the natural law or precepts of Sacred Scripture are to be regarded only as given expressions of a form of particular culture at a certain moment of history.

But in fact, divine Revelation and, in its own proper order, philosophical wisdom, emphasize the authentic exigencies of human nature. They thereby necessarily manifest the existence of immutable laws inscribed in the constitutive elements of human nature and which are revealed to be identical in all beings endowed with reason.

Furthermore, Christ instituted his Church as "the pillar and bulwark of truth." [6] With the Holy Spirit's assistance, she ceaselessly preserves and transmits without error the truths of the moral order, and she authentically interprets not only the revealed positive law but "also . . . those principles of the moral order which have their origin in human nature itself" [7] and which concern man's full development and sanctification. Now in fact the Church throughout her history has always considered a certain number of precepts of the natural law as having an absolute and immutable value, and in their transgression she has seen a contradiction of the teaching and spirit of the Gospel.

5. Since sexual ethics concern certain fundamental values of human and Christian life, this general teaching equally applies to sexual ethics. In this domain there exist principles and norms which the Church has always unhesitatingly transmitted as part of her teaching, however much the opinions and morals of the world may have been opposed to them. These principles and norms in no way owe their origin to a certain type of culture, but rather to knowledge of the divine law and of human nature. They therefore cannot be considered as having become out of date or doubtful under the pretext that a new cultural situation has arisen.

It is these principles which inspired the exhortations and directives given by the Second Vatican Council for an education and an organization of social life taking account of the equal dignity of man and woman while respecting their difference. [8]

Speaking of "the sexual nature of man and the human faculty of procreation," the Council noted that they "wonderfully exceed the dispositions of lower forms of life." [9] It then took particular care to expound the principles and criteria which concern human sexuality in marriage, and which are based upon the finality of the specific function of sexuality.

In this regard the Council declares that the moral goodness of the acts proper to conjugal life, acts which are ordered according to true human dignity, "does not depend solely on sincere intentions or on an evaluation of motives. It must be determined by objective standards. These, based on the nature of the human person and his acts, preserve the full sense of mutual self-giving and human procreation in the context of true love." [10]

These final words briefly sum up the Council's teaching—more fully expounded in an earlier part of the same Constitution [11]—on the finality of the sexual act and on the principal criterion of its morality: it is respect for its finality that ensures the moral goodness of this act.

This same principle, which the Church holds from divine Revelation and from her authentic interpretation of the natural law, is also the basis of her traditional doctrine, which states that the use of the sexual function has its true meaning and moral rectitude only in true marriage. [12]

6. It is not the purpose of the present Declaration to deal with all the abuses of the sexual faculty, nor with all the elements involved in the practice of chastity. Its object is rather to repeat the Church's doctrine on certain particular points, in view of the urgent need to oppose serious errors and widespread aberrant modes of behavior.

7. Today there are many who vindicate the right to sexual union before marriage, at least in those cases where a firm intention to marry and an affection which is already in some way conjugal in the psychology of the subjects require this completion, which they judge to be connatural. This is especially the case when the celebration of the marriage is impeded by circumstances or when this intimate relationship seems necessary in order for love to be preserved.

This opinion is contrary to Christian doctrine, which states that every genital act must be within the framework of marriage. However firm the intention of those who practice such premature sexual relations may be, the fact remains that these relations cannot ensure, in sincerity and fidelity, the interpersonal relationship between a man and a woman, nor especially can they protect this relationship from whims and caprices. Now it is a stable union that Jesus willed, and he restored its original requirement, beginning with the sexual difference. "Have you not read that the creator from the beginning made them male and female and that he said: This is why a man must leave father and mother, and cling to his wife, and the two become one body? They are no longer two, therefore, but one body. So then, what God has united, man must not divide." [13] Saint Paul will be even more explicit when he shows that if unmarried people or widows cannot live chastely they have no other alternative than the stable union of marriage: ". . . it is better to marry than to be aflame with passion." [14] Through marriage, in fact, the love of married people is taken up into that love which Christ irrevocably has for the Church,[15] while dissolute sexual union [16] defiles the temple of the Holy Spirit which the Christian has become. Sexual union therefore is only legitimate if a definitive community of life has been established between the man and the woman.

This is what the Church has always understood and taught,[17] and she finds a profound agreement with her doctrine in men's reflection and in the lessons of history.

Experience teaches us that love must find its safeguard in the stability of marriage, if sexual intercourse is truly to respond to the requirements of its own finality and to those of human dignity. These requirements call for a conjugal contract sanctioned and guaranteed by society—a contract which establishes a state of life of capital importance both for the exclusive union of the man and the woman and for the good of their family and of the human community. Most often, in fact, premarital relations exclude the possibility of children. What is represented to be conjugal love is not able, as it absolutely should be, to develop into paternal and maternal love. Or, if it does happen to do so, this will be to the detriment of the children, who will be deprived of the stable environment in which they ought to develop in order to find in it the way and the means of their insertion into society as a whole.

The consent given by people who wish to be united in marriage must therefore be manifested externally and in a manner which makes it valid in the eyes of society. As far as the faithful are concerned, their consent to the setting up of a community of conjugal life must be expressed according to the laws of the Church. It is a consent which makes their marriage a Sacrament of Christ.

8. At the present time there are those who, basing themselves on observations in the psychological order, have begun to judge indulgently, and even to excuse completely, homosexual relations between certain people. This they do in opposition to the constant teaching of the Magisterium and to the moral sense of the Christian people.

A distinction is drawn, and it seems with some reason, between homosexuals whose tendency comes from a false education, from a lack of normal sexual development, from habit, from bad example, or from other similar causes, and is transitory or at least not incurable; and homosexuals who are definitively such because of some kind of innate instinct or a pathological constitution judged to be incurable.

In regard to this second category of subjects, some people conclude that their tendency is so natural that it justifies in their case homosexual relations within a sincere communion of life and love analogous to marriage insofar as such homosexuals feel incapable of enduring a solitary life.

In the pastoral field, these homosexuals must certainly be treated with understanding and sustained in the hope of overcoming their personal difficulties and their inability to fit into society. Their culpability will be judged with prudence. But no pastoral method can be employed which would give moral justification to these acts on the grounds that they would be consonant with the condition of such people. For according to the objective moral order, homosexual relations are acts which lack an essential and indispensable finality. In Sacred Scripture they are condemned as a serious depravity and even presented as the sad consequence of rejecting God.[18] This judgment of Scripture does not of course permit us to conclude that all those who suffer from this anomaly are personally responsible for it, but it does attest to the fact that homosexual acts are intrinsically disordered and can in no case be approved.

9. The traditional Catholic doctrine that masturbation constitutes a grave moral disorder is often called into doubt or expressly denied today. It is said that psychology and sociology show that it is a normal phenomenon of sexual development, especially among the young. It is stated that there is real and serious fault only in the measure that the subject deliberately indulges in solitary pleasure closed in on self ("ipsation"), because in this case the act would indeed be radically opposed to the loving communion between persons of different sex which some hold is what is principally sought in the use of the sexual faculty.

This opinion is contradictory to the teaching and pastoral practice of the Catholic Church. Whatever the force of certain arguments of a biological and philosophical nature, which have sometimes been used by theologians, in fact both the Magisterium of the Church—in the course of a constant tradition—and the moral sense of the faithful have declared without hesitation that masturbation is an intrinsically and seriously disordered act.[19] The main reason is that, whatever the motive for acting in this way, the deliberate use of the sexual faculty outside normal conjugal relations essentially contradicts the finality of the faculty. For it lacks the sexual relationship called for by the moral order, namely the relationship which realizes "the full sense of mutual self-giving and human procreation in the context of true love."[20] All deliberate exercise of sexuality must be reserved to this regular relationship. Even if it cannot be proved that Scripture condemns this sin by name, the tradition of the Church has rightly understood it to be condemned in the New Testament when the latter speaks of "impurity," "unchasteness," and other vices contrary to chastity and continence.

Sociological surveys are able to show the frequency of this disorder according to the places, populations, or circumstances studied. In this way facts are discovered, but facts do not constitute a criterion for judging the moral value of human acts.[21] The frequency of the phenomenon in question is certainly to be linked with man's innate weakness following original sin; but it is also to be linked with the loss of a sense of God, with the corruption of morals engendered by the commercialization of vice, with the unrestrained licentiousness of so many public entertainments and publications, as well as with the neglect of modesty, which is the guardian of chastity.

On the subject of masturbation modern psychology provides much valid and useful information for formulating a more equitable judgment on moral responsibility and for orienting pastoral action. Psychology helps one to see how the immaturity of adolescence (which can sometimes persist after that age), psychological imbalance, or habit can influence behavior, diminishing the deliberate character of the act and bringing about a situation whereby subjectively there may not always be serious fault. But in general, the absence of serious responsibility must not be presumed; this would be to misunderstand people's moral capacity.

In the pastoral ministry, in order to form an adequate judgment in concrete cases, the habitual behavior of people will be considered in its totality, not only with regard to the individual's practice of charity and of justice but also with regard to the individual's care in observing the particular precepts of chastity. In particular, one will have to examine whether the individual is using the necessary means, both natural and supernatural, which Christian asceticism from its long experience recommends for overcoming the passions and progressing in virtue. . . .

Footnotes

1. See Vatican II, *Pastoral Constitution on the Church in the World of Today*, no. 47: *Acta Apostolicae Sedis* 58 (1966) 1067 [*The Pope Speaks* XI, 289–290].

2. See the Apostolic Constitution *Regimini Ecclesiae universae* (August 15, 1967), no. 29: *AAS* 59 (1967) 897 [*TPS* XII, 401–402].

3. *Pastoral Constitution on the Church in the World of Today*, no.16: *AAS* 58 (1966) 1037 [*TPS* XI, 268].

4. *Jn* 8, 12.

5. *Declaration on Religions Freedom*, no. 3: *AAS* 58 (1966) 931 [*TPS* XI, 86].

6. 1 *Tm* 3, 15.

7. *Declaration on Religious Freedom*, no. 14: *AAS* 58 (1966) 940 [*TPS* XI, 93]. See also Pius XI, Encyclical *Casti Connubii* (December 31, 1930): *AAS* 22 (1930) 579–580; Pius XII, Address of November 2, 1954 *AAS* 46 (1954) 671–672 [*TPS* I 380–381]; John XXIII, Encyclical *Mater et Magistra* (May 25, 1961), no. 239: *AAS* 53 (1961) 457 [*TPS* VII, 388]; Paul VI, Encyclical *Humanae Vitae* (July 25, 1968), no. 4: *AAS* 60 (1968) 483 [*TPS* XIII, 331–332].

8. See Vatican II, *Declaration on Christian Education*, nos. 1 and 8: *AAS* 58 (1966) 729–730, 734–736 [*TPS* XI, 201–202, 206–207]; *Pastoral Constitution on the Church in the World of Today*, nos. 29, 60, 67: *AAS* 58 (1966) 1048–1049, 1080–1081, 1088–1089 [*TPS* XI, 276–277, 299–300, 304–305].

9. *Pastoral Constitution on the Church in the World of Today*, no. 51: *AAS* 58 (1966) 1072 [*TPS* XI, 293].

10. *Loc. cit.;* see also no. 49: *AAS* 58 (1966) 1069–1070 [*TPS* XI, 291–292].

11. See *Pastoral Constitution on the Church in the World of Today*, nos. 49–50: *AAS* 58 (1966) 1069–1072 [*TPS* XI, 291–293].

12. The present Declaration does not review all the moral norms for the use of sex, since they have already been set forth in the encyclicals *Casti Connubii* and *Humanae Vitae*.

13. *Mt* 19, 4–6.

14. 1 *Cor* 7, 9.

15. See *Eph* 5, 25–32.

16. Extramarital intercourse is expressly condemned in *1 Cor* 5, 1; 6, 9; 7, 2; 10, 8; *Eph* 5, 5–7; *1 Tm* 1, 10; *Heb* 13, 4; there are explicit arguments given in *1 Cor* 6, 12–20.

17. See Innocent IV, Letter *Sub Catholicae professione* (March 6, 1254) (*DS* 835); Pius II, Letter *Cum sicut accepimus* (November 14, 1459) (*DS* 1367); Decrees of the Holy Office on September 24, 1665 (*DS* 2045) and March 2, 1679 (*DS* 2148); Pius XI, Encyclical *Casti Conubii* (December 31, 1930): *AAS* 22 (1930) 538–539.

18. *Rom* 1:24–27: "In consequence, God delivered them up in their lusts to unclean practices; they engaged in the mutual degradation of their bodies, these men who exchanged the truth of God for a lie and worshiped and served the creature rather than the Creator—blessed be he forever, amen! God therefore delivered them to disgraceful passions. Their women exchanged natural intercourse for unnatural, and the men gave up natural intercourse with women and burned with lust for one another. Men did shameful things with men, and thus received in their own persons the penalty for their perversity." See also what St. Paul says of sodomy in *1 Cor* 6, 9; *1 Tm* 1, 10.

19. See Leo IX, Letter *Ad splendidum nitentes* (1054) (*DS* 687–688); Decree of the Holy Office on March 2, 1679 (*DS* 2149); Pius XII, Addresses of October 8, 1953: *AAS* 45 (1953) 677–678, and May 19, 1956: *AAS* 48 (1956) 472–473.

20. *Pastoral Constitution on the Church in the World of Today*, no. 51: *AAS* 58 (1966) 1072 [*TPS* XI, 293].

21. See Paul VI, Apostolic Exhortation *Quinque iam anni* (December 8, 1970): *AAS* 63 (1971) 102 [*TPS* XV, 329]: "If sociological surveys are useful for better discovering the thought patterns of the people of a particular place, the anxieties and needs of those to whom we proclaim the word of God, and also the oppositions made to it by modern reasoning through the widespread notion that outside science there exists no legitimate form of knowledge, still the conclusions drawn from such surveys could not of themselves constitute a determining criterion of truth."

Review Questions

1. What is the Christian doctrine about sex?

2. Why are premarital sexual relations immoral?

3. What is the objection of homosexuality?

4. What is wrong with masturbation?

Discussion Questions

1. Is celibacy a violation of natural law or not? Explain your view.

2. Is contraception wrong too? Defend your answer.

3. Is procreation the only natural purpose of sex? Defend your position.

RUSSELL VANNOY

Sexual Perversion: Is There Such a Thing?

From *Sex Without Love* by Russell Vannoy (Prometheus Books, Buffalo, NY, 1980). Copyright © 1980 by Russell Vannoy.

Russell Vannoy teaches philosophy at the State University College of New York at Buffalo.

Vannoy attacks the natural law view of sex. He claims that sex for pleasure is just as natural as reproductive sex, that we cannot assume that whatever is natural is good, and that sex can be a natural expression of love even if it is not procreative.

INTRODUCTORY CONSIDERATIONS

One of my students once insisted that he could conclusively prove that homosexuality was immoral. "What," he asked, "if everyone were a homosexual? The human race would perish." My own response was to ask,"Since you are a deeply religious person, what if everyone became a priest? The human race would also perish." It seems that the very sort of argument that proves that homosexuals are immoral also proves that priests are immoral as well—an odd conclusion indeed. (Of course, not everyone is going to become a priest, but not everyone is going to become a homosexual, either.) Arguments of the purely hypothetical "what if everybody did it" sort are very common in accusations against sexual deviancy, yet in this instance it goes nowhere. Just how does one prove that perversions are immoral or "sick?" Can one even prove that there *are* such things as perversions—some of society's and some psychiatrists' convictions notwithstanding?

Another example of perversion given by a student was that of necrophilia or sex with a dead body, an example that immediately sent a shock wave of disgust through the lecture room. But if one uses the criterion that an act is immoral if it causes pain to the victim, such a criterion would hardly be applicable to a corpse! Of course such sex suffers from a distinct lack of responsiveness from the object of one's affections, but this is hardly a *moral* objection to such sex. One seems to be left only with one's shock, horror, and disgust with such a phenomenon, but this is hardly a criterion either; for conservative people are shocked by the sight of innocent lovemaking in a public park. Disgust seems to reveal more about the nature and conditioning of the one who is disgusted than it does about the object of one's disgust.

Even certain enlightened writers about sexual morality who avoid superficial moral arguments nevertheless insist on finding strained arguments to attack homosexuality. The Whiteleys, for example, do a brilliant job of exposing the manifold fallacies in condemnation of homosexuality as "unnatural," yet they persist in labeling such sex "unfruitful":

In family life, two parents are biologically necessary to produce children and, it would seem, psychologically desirable to bring them up. The homosexual is usually a persons who opts out of family life and parenthood, provides no children, and deprives whoever might have been his wife (or her husband) of the opportunity for family life. A community of such people stands apart from and at odds with the rest of society. A selfish, pleasure-seeking pattern of living is common among them, not because they are constitutionally like this, but because their manner of life leaves them less incentive for the taking of responsibility. They rarely achieve the full personal relationship between partners marriage makes possible. Love affairs are common amongst them, but they are usually short-lived; they lack the support of law and custom. . . . They can hardly avoid some degree of estrangement from their normal associates. . . .[1] *(Emphasis mine.)*

But the Whiteleys never stop to think where the real blame for the estrangement of homosexuals lies. For is it not the heterosexual majority who formulate the laws and customs that force homosexuals into a group alienated from the rest of society? Does this rejection not breed the self-hate that prevents long-lasting love attachments between homosexuals? (One must love oneself before one can love another.) And if the homosexual feels his creative accomplishments will be rejected by society because he is homosexual, will he not be driven to "selfish pleasure-seeking" as a form of compensation and to find some degree of happiness?

If homosexuals can be accused of being perverts because they are isolated from the rest of society, we can imagine an even more extreme case of lonely sex. Joe, for example, is a loner, who finds that reality is no match for the beautiful fantasies and orgasms he can have while his Accu-Jac machine masturbates him. What could be more in tune with this world of labor-saving devices, he asks, than to sit back and to avoid the hassle and expense of putting up with the demands and unpredictable whims of other people? Can we say that Joe is a pervert if he prefers this form of sex to the exclusion of penile-vaginal intercourse? Or must we say that if Joe is satisfied with his Accu-Jac, then that, for him, is the best sex? Nor should we call it perverted or even "bad sex" if it harms no one and brings him the gratification he seeks.

It might, however, be argued that even if we do not wish to label Joe a pervert, his is nevertheless "bad sex," for bringing relief from sexual tension is surely not the same as full sexual gratification. We can imagine someone who likes steak more than anything else but then discovers that he can eat a certain kind of pill that gives him identical nourishment and a sense of a full stomach. But although his hunger has been relieved, he has not been truly satisfied in the way he would have been had he eaten steak. Is his case like Joe's?

But this reply would not hold for someone who prefers sex of a very simple sort to one who wants a "full course" treatment. In aesthetics we sometimes contrast a "thin" sense of aesthetic perception with a "thick" sense of perception; the former perceiver prefers to focus on the pure form of the work of art itself, while the latter prefers to enrich his perception by bringing to it all the associations the work calls to his mind, such as memories of his childhood, the tragedy of the human condition, and so forth. Yet each experience can be as intense and rich in its own way as the other. The advocates of "thin" aesthetic experiences feel that the intensity of such experiences is diluted by having one's total absorption in the work for its own sake distracted by irrelevant associations. Someone who prefers masturbation to other forms of sex could then be said to prefer a "thin" sexual experience for reasons similar to those who prefer thin aesthetic experiences of works of art.[2] Nor need masturbation always be viewed as a "thin" form of sex concerned solely with an orgasmic release of sexual tension. For when it is accompanied by fantasies or by one's sensuous caresses of one's own body or by the enjoyment of sexual arousal for its own sake, it may be as rich or "thick" an experience as any other form of sex.

One's response to Joe's preference for masturbation does, I think, tend to reveal more about the lifestyle and value system of Joe's critic then it does about Joe himself. Can Joe be refuted in any objective way by saying that his sex life is lonely, nonproductive, impersonal, self-centered, or mechanistic if Joe himself has tried both types of sex and has decided on the type he thinks is best for him? Does this sort of example reveal that the concept of a nonperverted act has built into it a concept of what "good" sex is, what the good life is, what is presumably necessary to hold society together into a community of procreative, interacting individuals? If so, it is far from the clinically objective term it is often presented as being, and it is riddled with value systems that are subject to dissent and disagreement without one's necessarily being sick or perverted if he does dissent from what society considers to be healthy or normal sex.

Let us now look at some of the things that have been called sexual perversions, a phrase that has been used to cover such diverse phenomena as sadism and masochism, sex with corpses, homosexuality, voyeurism, exhibitionism, erotic attachments to certain types of clothing, or any sex that departs from the usual penile-vaginal sort, such as oral or anal sex. From time to time we receive mysterious pronouncements from psychiatrists that certain of these acts have been "declassified" as sicknesses; for example, psychiatrists (by a majority vote!) no longer classify homosexuals as sick, provided they have successfully adapted to and accepted their condition; oral and anal sex between heterosexuals has similarly been declassified, on grounds that they are commonly practiced by humans and animals. But many psychiatrists will still condemn such practices if they are allowed to take predominance over "normal" penile-vaginal intercourse, rather than being occasional supplements to the "normal" routine.

A philosopher who is looking for some clear principle to distinguish the perverted from the normal will obviously find this to be a chaotic situation, indeed. He may well wonder how many more such acts will be similarly freed from the stigma of being labeled as perverted. Is the concept of perversion, after all, perhaps an all-too-human interpretation or value judgment placed on certain sexual phenomena rather than an objective or descriptive term? Can we, for example, see the perverted quality of a sex act in the way that there can be a consensus in seeing the awkward quality of an inept dancer? Can we see the disorder in perverted sex in the same way we can see the disorder of someone undergoing an epileptic seizure? Surely there is no consensus that this could be the case, except among those who have already been conditioned to believe there must be something disordered in perverted sex.

THE "HARMONY OF OPPOSITES" PRINCIPLE

One of the most commonly offered criteria for perversion is that it is somehow a violation of the natural order of things. It has been argued, for example, that nature is governed by a "harmony of opposites" between the male and female principles. The male is active, the female passive; the active male penis is a shaft, which by nature "fits" its opposite, the passive vaginal emptiness. The male is the aggressive provider who goes forth into the world to provide for the family; the female's role is stay home, raise the children, and with her feminine tenderness help her husband relax after a long day. Each gives what the other presumably lacks, and this is supposed to be a beautiful phenomenon indeed.

It is clear, however, that the entire principle as traditionally expressed rests on sexist stereotypes of "active" males and "passive" females that have been vigorously challenged for several years now. Furthermore, the defenders of the principle overlook the obvious fact that there can be a harmony of opposites that need not involve differences of gender at all. Opposites can take many forms; between a passive and an active male, for example, an opposite exists on the psychological as well as on the physiological level. The possibility of sodomy between two males, with one male preferring the active or masculine role of penetrating the anus and the other preferring the passive feminine role of being penetrated, is but one illustration of how there could also be a harmony of opposites between homosexuals. The fact that traditional defenders of the principle speak of "male and female genders" rather than "masculine and feminine temperaments," two sets of concepts that need have no connection, shows clearly that the defenders of the principle have interpreted it to rationalize their heterosexual preferences that antedated the formulation of the principle itself. Indeed, if defenders of such a principle could be brought to see the validity of forms of sex other than the traditional penile-vaginal sort, they would discover many sexual practices that do not require the two partners to take "harmoniously opposite" active-passive roles at all. For exam-

ple, certain forms of mutual oral stimulation of the sexual organs can be performed in the lateral position by partners of the same or opposite sex. Both are active; neither dominate the other.

Indeed, as I have noted before, my own research from student term papers reveals a decided difference in sexual philosophy between males and females, with the former preferring the more aggressive, quick sexual act and the latter preferring the more prolonged, relaxed, "loving" sensuous eroticism. If there is any "harmony" here, it is apparent that one of the two sexes is subordinating its wishes to the other, and in a sexist society it is no mystery which gender is doing the surrendering.

Furthermore, there is the curious phenomenon of males wooing females in the most devoted fashion, yet also condoning or fostering a sexist society where women are not treated as equals. It is as if men down through history said, "I love you, but stay in the kitchen where you belong and take care of the children." If true love is love between equals, each complementing the other in a harmonious attitude of mutual respect for each other's dignity, then one wonders how much true heterosexual love has existed in history.

IS PERVERSION "UNNATURAL"?

Perhaps the most familiar use of the term *natural* in a sexual context is the claim that the sexual organs have a certain natural purpose: that nature or God intended them for procreation. It is, however, apparent that nature also gives sexual desires and sexual pleasures to those who cannot procreate, either temporarily or permanently, such as those who are too young or too old, or those who are sterile or who are in a temporarily nonreproductive cycle.

The reply might be that nonreproductive intercourse could still be "natural," provided it is the sort of intercourse that could lead to procreation *were conditions normal*. But this reply would mean that a female who is in a temporarily nonreproductive cycle is somehow abnormal. Yet the period of the month when she is fertile and the years of her life when she can bear children are quite brief compared to the times she cannot reproduce. Her fertile period could then just as easily be characterized as an abnormal phenomenon. Furthermore, the number of times people have sex for pleasure so vastly outnumbers the times when sex is meant for procreation that one could argue that sex for procreation is kind of statistical abnormality. And if our sexual desires come from nature, the abnormality is not merely statistical.

Indeed, the ability to have sexual pleasure rather than the ability to or the desire to reproduce would seem to be what defines us as sexual beings. For if we could only reproduce but not have sexual feelings, we would not speak of sexual acts or sexual organs at all; rather we would speak only of reproductive acts or reproductive organs.

But the main difficulty is that there seems to be a contradiction in nature, in giving us desires for nonprocreative sex when procreation is said to be its *sole* sexual purpose. What then becomes of the claim that an act that violates nature is a sexual disorder if nature is confused about its purposes? And what becomes of the theory that nature is created by a deity or presided over by a biology that arranges all things in an orderly means-end relationship directed toward procreation if nature is contradicting herself in also allowing—indeed making us desire—nonprocreative sex?

The deeper question, however, is whether and how anything unnatural can happen in the world of nature at all. Is there some point in the universe where nature ceases and the unnatural begins? We might, for example, compare the universe to a solid bowl of pure Jello; wherever we bite into the gelatin, we will find that its creator has included in it nothing other than Jello. There would thus be no basis for saying that one should eat only the Jello and avoid anything that deviates from what its creator intended the bowl to contain. Thus, just as

one would be puzzled as to how anything that is Jello could be non-gelatinous, one might equally well wonder how anything in the world of nature could be unnatural. For if something were unnatural it couldn't be part of our universe at all; the universe *is* nature, and thus everything in it is natural.

If, then, one feels an urge to commit sodomy, has one discovered some mysterious gap in the world of nature where nature does not exist? Or cannot one say that the prompting is as much a part of nature as any other? Such an urge may be unusual and widely deplored, but so is a hurricane, which is a perfectly natural phenomenon. Perhaps what we should say is that the only thing that is sexually unnatural is whatever nature does not allow us to do. A man might, for example, have the desire to ejaculate by penetrating someone's ear canal and engage in thrusting motions of the penis much as he would in a vagina. But nature clearly makes this mode of ejaculation out of the question; thus it would be unnatural. One could, of course, masturbate and shoot his semen into someone's ear (or onto any part of someone's body, for that matter). Such an act would be natural, since nature does not forbid it by making it impossible to do so.

It might, however, be argued that such an argument about the naturalness of all things that are possible destroys a perfectly familiar distinction: that between the natural and antinatural (or artificial or synthetic). Self-preservation is a natural phenomenon, yet why is it that so many people kill themselves? Isn't suicide "unnatural"? Germs are a part of nature, yet we develop man-made (that is, unnatural) drugs to destroy germs.

Indeed, if all these things were natural, wouldn't nature be contradicting herself if both disease and the drugs to conquer disease were natural, or if nature gave both the desire for self-preservation and, to some, a desire for self-destruction?

None of these considerations, however, necessarily disprove the principle that whatever exists and whatever we desire and can do is natural. Nietzsche, for example, argued that nature is a battleground of conflicting wills to power, with each one trying to expand its influence and strength and destroying whatever stands in its way. A virus or cancer, for example, is a phenomenon of nature that tries to conquer the body, and we try to conquer the virus and cancer in turn because of another phenomenon of nature—our instinct for self-preservation. The materials we use to conquer disease may be manmade, but their ingredients can be traced back to nature, as well as the natural ingenuity we use to create these materials. Furthermore, there may not be only an instinct for self-preservation; as Freud once noted, there may also exist a natural death wish, of which suicide would be the most extreme example.

It is clear, therefore, that the term *natural* can be defined to refer to many things, even if one still wanted to insist that some things are unnatural. Those who claim that only one kind of sex, procreative sex, is natural are simply selecting one aspect of our sexual nature to suit their own moral presuppositions about what the purpose of sex ought to be. Furthermore, those who attempt to give a religious or moralistic backing to such sexual doctrines make the following questionable assumptions.

• They assume that they know exactly what God's will is in sexual matters, that He intended sex only for the purpose of procreation, despite the fact that the deity has clearly created us with many other sexual needs and desires.

• They assume that whatever is natural is good, despite the fact that nature daily, through no fault of man's, inflicts on us catastrophes of all sorts. Furthermore, many would hold that aggression is a perfectly natural instinct: witness infants' screams and kicking of feet and pounding of fists when they are frustrated. Babies didn't learn to be aggressive; and if one holds that one learns aggression from society, how did society come to be aggressive in the first

place and require endless laws to keep the social order? But if aggression is natural and if whatever is natural is held to be good, then under the "obey nature" philosophy, one would be driven to the highly unwelcome conclusion that rape is natural and therefore good.

• Defenders of the philosophy that nature intends sex only for procreation assume that all men have the same basic nature, even though some men (they say) willfully violate nature. This overlooks the fact that nature has clearly made us all different in some respects; could it not therefore be true that nature has created some persons with a unique sexual nature of their own that has nothing to do with procreation? But if this is true, then under the "obey nature" philosophy one should allow such persons to fulfill their own individual natures (so long as they do not harm others) rather than accuse them of having committed so-called crimes against nature.

One can therefore say that if someone who differs from what is usually considered natural and who commits acts most persons would find perverted, then the fact that such a person was endowed by nature with (1) the imagination to conceive the act, (2) the desire to perform the act, (3) the ability to carry it out, and (4) the ability to enjoy it, makes that act perfectly natural for him or her. If nature had not intended a person to perform such acts, it would have been impossible to acquire these four abilities. (If some persons claim they do not desire or cannot enjoy something that deviates from the norm, this may only mean that their unique nature has been buried under layers of repressive social conditioning.)

• It should be noted further that to reduce human sex to procreation is, in effect, to reduce sex to the purely animal level where sex is performed in only one way for one purpose—the reproduction of the species. But men and women are also beings with free will and powers of reason and imagination, and these are completely overlooked when one reduces sex to a purely animalistic function. If nature gives man freedom and imagination, doesn't nature want him to use these talents to conceive of and freely choose forms of sex other than the purely animal one? Some defenders of procreation try to meet this charge that they are reducing sex to an animal level by allowing sex to have a secondary function: sex as an expression of love. Then they condemn sex with a non-lover that is for pleasure alone, even though nature clearly gives pleasure to non-lovers, as well. Nor can one call sex for sex's sake animalistic, for it seems to be uniquely human. This is particularly true if such sex is performed with imagination, thereby utilizing a distinctively human ability.

• If sex for procreation were a law of nature implanted in all living creatures by, say, an all-powerful God, it is difficult to see why defenders of procreation have to write elaborate treatises and deliver endless sermons telling us we ought to obey the dictates of nature. For if there is a natural law regarding procreation, it would seem plausible to assume that we would all have to obey it automatically as a matter of course, just as we must all obey the natural dictates to breathe, defecate, and eventually die. But the fact that defenders of nature have to struggle to convince us to procreate (or else face eternal damnation), and the fact that so many heterosexuals do not procreate (nor do any homosexuals), indicate that there are no natural laws compelling us to procreate or even to be heterosexual.

• Defenders of procreation make the mistaken assumption that if X results from Y, X was the purpose of Y. Babies, of course, do result from sex quite frequently (although not, oddly enough, during a female's infertile period, despite the fact that nature gave her sexual desires during this period, a fact the procreation theorist cannot explain). But, once again, because X results from Y, it does not follow that X was the exclusive or main goal or purpose of Y. All sorts of things result from sex, everything from ecstatic pleasure to venereal disease. (Certainly one would not say that gonorrhea is a purpose of sex, even though it is an all too common result of sex.)

Turning from this brief critique of traditional moral and religious views on the one true purpose of sex, we also find that there are those who have questioned the idea that sex is a natural instinct at all—whatever its purpose. Ti-Grace Atkinson, for example, argues that the desire for sex is really a function of the male's desire to dominate the female in the bedroom. When this need to dominate—and the correlative culturally conditioned desire in the female to surrender—is obliterated in some future era when the sexes are equal and feel no need for the dominance-submission syndrome, sexual desire will reveal itself for the culturally conditioned phenomenon it is and, according to Ms. Atkinson, will simply disappear.[3] The difficulty with Ms. Atkinson's theory is that she, like the conservative defenders of the natural-instinct philosophy, has assumed there is only one motive for sex: the culturally conditioned desire for dominance and submission. The fact that sex can have many purposes escapes both Ms. Atkinson and the defender of a natural instinct for procreation alone. In response to Ms. Atkinson's argument that sex will disappear when the dominance-submission syndrome is ended by overcoming sexist social conditioning, one could hold that since there are many other purposes sex might have (be they natural or socially conditioned), desires for sex will continue even after sexism is eliminated.

Finally, it might be noted that those who give up any attempt to define perversion as something that violates nature often turn to another criterion: A pervert is someone who disobeys social norms. But adultery violates a social norm, and it is not considered a perversion. Furthermore, such things as kissing in public and oral sex once violated social norms, though they are now widespread social phenomena that only a few conservatives would condemn. Basing a concept of perversion on disobedience to what is often a narrow-minded society, therefore, commits a person to basing his

philosophy on the shifting sands of obedience to current fashions in sex. Anyone
who prides himself on thinking for himself
and on being able to transcend social condi-

tioning would be revolted (and justifiably so)
by such a socially defined concept of perversion. . . .

Footnotes

1. C.H. and Winifred Whiteley, *Sex and Morals* (New
York: Basic Books, 1967), p. 91.

2. This "thin" versus "thick" example of sexual experience is also aptly illustrated by the dark-room orgy
example that we might use to prove that "an orgasm is
an orgasm," that is, that one orgasm is as good as
another no matter how obtained and that there is no
such thing as a perversion or bad sex. Suppose, for
example, that a heterosexual male were placed in a dark
room which, without his knowing it, contained a man,
a woman, and perhaps even a sheep. Suppose further
that he had sexual intercourse with each person or
animal and that he could not tell which was which.
Wouldn't he be equally satisfied with each? Of course,
for those who want just an orgasm, the example is

perfectly apt; but for those who want to know precisely
whom they are having intercourse with, with all the
psychological associations that entails, the example
would not work. Whether they *should* be concerned
about whom they have sex with, and whether they
should not rather learn that any object is a potential
object of sexual enjoyment if one only tries to learn to
enjoy it is another question. De Sade would regard our
selectivity as merely the product of our own socially
conditioned hangups.

3. Ms. Atkinson's views are summarized in Elizabeth
Rapaport, "On the Future of Love: Rousseau and the
Radical Feminists," *The Philosophical Forum* 5 (Fall-Win-
ter, 1973–74): 188.

Review Questions

1. What is the most common account of sexual perversion?
2. Why doesn't Vannoy accept this account?
3. What are Vannoy's main criticisms of the view that the natural purpose of sex
   is procreation?

Discussion Questions

1. Does sex have other purposes besides procreation? What are they?
2. How do we tell when an activity is "natural" or not? Explain your view.

DONALD LEVY

Perversion and the Unnatural
as Moral Categories

Donald Levy, "Perversion and the Unnatural as Moral Categories," from Alan Soble, ed., *The Philosophy of Sex*, Littlefield, Adams and Co., 1980, pp. 169–189. Reprinted with permission.

*Donald Levy teaches philosophy at Brooklyn College, the City University
of New York.*
    *Levy begins with a survey of the definitions of the concept of sexual
perversion given by Freud, Balint, Nagel, Ruddick, Solomon, Fried, Goldman, and Gray. None of these is found to be acceptable. His own
account is that an unnatural act is one that deprives a person unnecessarily of a basic human good, and a perverted sex act is an unnatural act
that is done to get sexual pleasure.*

For whatever reasons, the recent revival of philosophical interest in problems relating to love and sexuality began with attempts to analyze the concept of sexual perversion. Is it essentially an incoherent idea, one we moderns ought to seek to do without in thinking about sex? Is a revival of one or another of the traditional theologically based accounts of sexual perversion to be undertaken, perhaps updated, by the addition of the latest psychiatric findings? Or does the concept conceal hitherto unsuspected patterns of meaning that philosophical analysis might uncover for the first time? If sexual perversion is to be taken seriously, problems of definition demand solution at the start; what makes a sexual practice perverted? What differentiates sexual perversions from nonsexual perversions, if there are any such things? What makes a human activity perverted at all?

The range of human sexual activities commonly called "sexual perversions" is very wide, and vague in outline. Its vagueness will be clear from the following list, which I have adapted from Michael Balint.[1]

1. First of all, there are the various kinds of homosexuality.

2. Next, the several forms of sadism and masochism.

3. Exhibitionism, voyeurism, use of other parts of the body (i.e., other than the genitals).

4. Fetishism, transvestism, possibly kleptomania.

5. Bestiality.

6. Necrophilia, pedophilia.

I should add that this list can be misleading by its abstractness; fetishism, for example, may cover a great variety of behaviors.

One can get some sense of the confusion in this field from the fact that Balint does not regard bestiality as a "proper" perversion—it never reaches the height of a proper perversion, he says, since it always comes about for want of something better. In addition, practices classified under necrophilia and pedo-

philia belong to the psychoses, he thinks. Even if we grant these unintuitive reasons for separating bestiality, necrophilia, and pedophilia from the main group, it is not at all easy to see what the first four categories have in common that nothing else in the way of sexual behavior shares.

Given the vague outlines of the classification, it is not surprising that the definitions proposed for this concept have not been very satisfactory. Ideas about various of the perversions can be found in Freud's writings, though it is fairly clear that he does not regard the term as a specially psychoanalytic one, for whose definition he bears responsibility. In that sense it is incorrect to speak of Freud as having a theory of the perversions at all. (Freud sometimes uses the word in quotes, and once even refers to narcissism, which is of course not even a sexual activity, as sometimes having "the significance of a perversion.")[2] If this is understood, we can say that Freud does tend to think of perversion as the undisguised expression of an infantile sexual wish.[3] Normal sex differs from the perverted variety in integrating the infantile sexual wish with other sexual wishes, not isolating it, and in gratifying it in disguised form. The difference between normal and perverted is one of degree, however.[4]

The most acute criticism of the account I am attributing to Freud comes from within psychoanalysis itself. Balint points out that many forms of homosexuality on the one hand, and of the sadomasochistic group on the other, are definitely not survivals of infantile forms of sexuality but rather are later developments. Balint's own attempt at definition focuses on perversions as

attempts to escape from the two main demands of mature genitality: (1) accepting as real the intense need in ourselves for periodic regressions in the form of heterosexual coitus, and (2) accepting the necessity of the work of conquest, i.e., changing an indifferent object into a cooperative genital partner.[5]

There are several reasons for doubting the adequacy of this approach. In the first place, Balint has made it clear that homosexuality is to be included among the perversions, yet he also maintains that in homosexual love "there is also the same bliss" [6] as in heterosexual love, from which it is reasonable to infer that the need for regression is felt and fulfilled in both alike. As for the second feature, Balint also asserts that "all the altruistically loving . . . features of heterosexual love can be found in homosexual love as well." [7] Besides, the first condition of Balint's definition would appear to make all celibates perverts; and the second condition would classify as perverted all selfish, crude, negligent—but heterosexual—lovers.

Recent philosophical attempts to define sexual perversion have not achieved any greater success than have the efforts of the psychoanalysts. Thomas Nagel conceives of sexual perversion in psychological terms, he says,[8] but it is nothing psychoanalytic he has in mind. Sexual perversions, according to Nagel, are incomplete versions of the "multi-level interpersonal awareness," which is "the basic psychological content of sexual interaction."[9] Perversions are incomplete versions of the complete configuration. Nagel's view seems close to the one usually ascribed to Freud—fixation on an infantile level being a kind of incompleteness. Nagel's view seems even closer to the idea contained in Catholic canon law, which defines as immoral any sex act which is "designed to be preparatory to the complete act" but which is "entirely divorced from the complete act." [10] Nagel does not indicate why it is important or noteworthy that some people seem to want only incomplete versions of sex instead of the complete ones, or why we need the classification "perversion" at all. (After all, we have no special designation for those who select their meals from the à la carte menu instead of ordering the complete dinner.) Another trouble with Nagel's view is that the prostitute, for example, who hardly participates at all in the interpersonal awareness Nagel refers to, would be

perverted—yet neither ordinary usage nor any traditional classification of the perversions has such a result. (Nagel seems to be aware of this problem, but does not regard it as crucial.) Besides, the sadomasochistic pair do complete the psychological process Nagel refers to, that is, there is interpersonal awareness between them on many levels, yet they would commonly be classified as perverted. It is surprising and puzzling that Nagel claims that sexual perversions

will have to be sexual desires or practices that can be plausibly described as in some sense unnatural, though the explanation of this natural/unnatural distinction is of course the main problem. [11]

Yet he does not attempt to explain the distinction, or relate the concept of perversion to it.

Sara Ruddick defines "perverse" sex acts as deviations from the natural—the natural being defined as "of the type that can lead to reproduction." [12] Thus far, her view resembles Aquinas' account of sex that is contrary to nature.[13] However, unlike Aquinas, she sees no moral significance to an act's being perverted.[14] Nevertheless, it seems odd to lump together masturbation, the use of birth control, and (heterosexual) sex between sterile partners as perverted or unnatural, while remaining unclear whether the (heterosexual) child-molester is perverted or not. (A twelve-year-old girl may be capable of reproducing, yet sex with her by an adult male counts as pedophilia, regardless of that biological fact.[15]) Against Ruddick's view, an alternative account would be preferable if it explained why the perverted and the unnatural are not coextensive.

Robert C. Solomon faults Nagel's definition of perversion for emphasizing the form of the interpersonal awareness in sex rather than its content.[16] According to Solomon, sadism, for example, is not so much a breakdown in communication as

an excessive expression of a particular content, namely the attitude of domination, perhaps mixed with hatred, fear, and other negative attitudes. [17]

Solomon offers no account explaining at what point the expression of attitudes of domination becomes excessive enough to warrant being labeled perversion; more important, it is hard to see why being excessive in the expression of domination should count as perversion at all, and not merely as rudeness, perhaps.

According to Charles Fried, a case of perversion exists when an actor uses another person to attain his end, and when it is a necessary constitutive element of that end that another person be used, but it is also a necessary element of the actor's "rational principle" that the other person thereby not attain an end of his own.[18] One objection to this is that it is too broad—the nonsexual joker, swindler, or con man fits the definition, yet they are hardly perverted, certainly not sexually perverted. A sexual trickster also not excluded by Fried's definition would be the sterile man seeking sex with a woman who merely wishes to conceive by him. If he keeps his sterility a secret from her, his pursuit of her fits Fried's definition of perversion, though he would normally be called neither perverted nor sexually perverted— just malicious.[19] Secondly, the exclusive fetishist, transvestite, bestialist, is clearly beyond Fried's definition, yet Fried would probably accept them as being as genuine cases of perversion as any. Fried's view of perversion is unusual in providing an account of the concept apparently conceived in moral terms. (This seems to be his intent—though it is not clear that it would always be morally wrong for one person to use another in the way described in Fried's definition.) In this respect, Fried's account appears to be unique among recent philosophical discussions of perversion.

The opposite extreme is Alan H. Goldman's purely statistical interpretation, according to which those sexual desires are perverted that are statistically abnormal in form.[20] Identifying the form of a desire is problematic, however. Goldman gives the following examples of desires whose abnormality in form makes them perverted desires:

desire, not for contact with another, but for merely looking, for harming or being harmed, for contact with items of clothing.[21]

Desiring to engage in sex continuously for three hours is not, it seems, abnormal in form in the requite sense.[22] Nevertheless, plausible counterexamples seem to be available; the male officeworker whose lustful desires are restricted exclusively to his female superiors would seem to be one, since his sexual desires are abnormal (statistically), yet hardly perverted. It might at first appear that this example involves only an abnormality in the content of the desire, not in its form. But if the officeworker case is dismissed as a case of perversion on account of the form/content distinction, there is the danger that the heterosexual transvestite, necrophiliac, child-molester will also lie outside the definition of perversion. This problem with the form/content distinction arises again when Goldman writes

Raping a sheep may be more perverted than raping a woman, but certainly not more condemnable morally.[23]

It is hard to see how raping a woman could be perverted at all on Goldman's account, since the form of the act would appear to be normal.[24] (Incidentally, I doubt that it even makes sense to speak of raping a sheep, whose consent or lack of it cannot exist.[25])

Evolutionary theory is the basis of Robert Gray's definition of perversion and the unnatural, which, following Ruddick, he equates.[26] Like Ruddick, he too regards these terms as descriptive and nonevaluative, carrying no moral connotations.[27]

If, then, we are able to show that there is some adaptive function or end that sexual activity evolved to fulfill, we may speak of sexual activity that departs from that function and, more clearly, of sexual activity that, by departing from that function, is maladaptive, as counterproductive and, in that sense, contrary to nature or unnatural. . . . Put more simply, those forms of sexual activity would be perverted which, in evolutionary terms are dysfunctional.[28]

For Gray, the advantage of this definition is that it alone enables us to avoid cultural relativism in defining perversion.[29] This claim is puzzling, given his later remark that

It may turn out, too, that the natural adaptive functions of human sexual activity are not culturally independent. In this case, a behavior that is maladaptive in one society may not be so in another.[30]

However, a more serious problem with Gray's definition arises when he comes to consider what "the natural adaptive function" of sex in humans is. To the suggestion (perhaps Ruddick's) that reproduction is the sole function of sexual activity, Gray's reply is unclear. On the one hand, he seems to deny it:

if reproduction were, as some think, the sole function of sexual activity, the scientist would have no further questions to ask about the matter, and all nonreproductive sexual activity might correctly be described as perverted. However, it would seem that this is not the case.[31]

But on the other hand, the reasons he gives for denying it point in the opposite direction—instead of considering other functions sex might fulfill, or the possibility that sex need not serve any function at all, his denial seems to rest on interpreting reproductive activity to include

all those activities minimally necessary to bring those new individuals themselves to reproductive maturity. Among other things, this would seem to include the formation and maintenance of well organized, stable societies and the establishment and maintenance of fairly stable male-female reproductive pairs.[32]

From this it follows that

maintenance of that degree (and kind) of social organization and stability requisite to the mainte- *nance of human society is a function that normal sexual behavior has evolved to fulfill, and if this is so, it is clear that the range of nonperverted sexual activity will be much broader than it has traditionally been taken to be.*[33]

Therefore, it would not be strained to ascribe to Gray the view that reproduction is "the natural adaptive function" of sex, but that reproduction includes very much more than usually supposed.

The trouble with this account is not, however, in its determination of what the natural adaptive function of sex is—anyway, Gray claims no special authority or expertise in the question, which he regards as answerable only by the scientist.[34] More problematic is the essentially utilitaran nature of Gray's use of evolutionary theory in defining perversion. This comes out in his appeals to "the maintenance of human society,"[35] "the maintenance of the over-all social order,"[36] and "the long-term viability of society"[37] as the crucial considerations in deciding which sexual activities are perverted. As with any utilitarian theory, paradoxical implications can be expected, and one does seem to be implicit in Gray's view. Consider, for example, a society in which artificial insemination has become the form of reproduction most conducive to "the long-term viability of society." (Given certain global conditions, we might imagine this to be true of the whole species, i.e., of all human societies.) Then, heterosexual sex (between loving spouses in the missionary position) would turn out to be perverted by the functional criteria Gray suggests. This paradoxical result will be derivable even if some function (or functions) other than reproduction is decided upon by the experts to be "the natural adaptive function" of sex. Whatever the function or functions might be, nothing guarantees that normal, heterosexual sex performs this function more effectively than any other sexual practice (or combination of sexual and nonsexual practices). In some conditions, heterosexual sex may perform the function or functions of sex far less effectively than other practices and will then have to be categorized as a sexual perversion, according to Gray's definition.

Perhaps in despair at the problems such efforts at definition as these confront, the temptation arises to declare the concepts of perversion and the unnatural to be empty, idle, or meaningless. Such a trend (with regard to the unnatural) can be traced as far back as Mill's essay *On Nature,* Diderot's *D'Alembert's Dream,* Descartes' *Sixth Meditation,* and perhaps the ancient sophists. The most recent expression of this position is Michael Slote's "Inapplicable Concepts and Sexual Perversion."[38] The best response to this temptation would be a theory of perversion and the unnatural—one that succeeds in overcoming the difficulties to be found in Nagel, Ruddick, Solomon, Fried, Goldman, Gray, and Slote.

In offering the following theory, I have started by trying to do something different from what has been previously attempted. In the first place, I have tried to separate analysis of the concepts of perversion and the unnatural from the discussion of the criteria to be employed in applying these terms to particular cases. (The separation of concept analysis from consideration of criteria is at least as old as the philosophy of love and sexuality itself; in the *Symposium* Socrates proposes "first to treat of the nature of Eros and then to treat of his acts." (199C5–6; 201E1–2).) Also, I believe the account to be sketched here makes better sense of the differences between calling something unnatural and calling it perverted than have the accounts of the seven philosophers I have reviewed. (For the most part, they do not concern themselves with this at all.) Secondly, I have set out to provide a moral theory of perversion and the unnatural. Regardless of whether or not commonly held, unreflective applications of the terms "perversion" and "unnatural" are agreed to, there seems to be little point in providing a definition emptying them of their most obvious feature—that is, that their normal use is as terms of serious moral condemnation. I have accordingly tried to provide an account

that preserves and explains this aspect of their use. To seek a theory of sexual perversion that accounts for our having such a concept at all in purely psychological, aesthetic, biological, or statistical terms seems a futile endeavor. Thirdly, a theory of sexual perversion ought to make it possible to revise some of our moral judgments in applying the concept. It ought to enable us to make more reasoned judgments, recognizing that some of what has been labelled "perversion" in the past may have been mistakenly so labelled, as well as enabling us to add to the class of perversions acts that may not have been traditionally included there.

A good way to begin is to return to the historical origin of the idea of the unnatural, which is philosophical. It apparently first occurs in Plato's *Phaedrus,* where Socrates refers to "unnatural pleasure" (251A), but Plato's *Laws* (Book VIII, 836ff) contains the earliest occurrence of an argument for the unnaturalness of a human action (here, a sexual practice, homosexuality). Plato is thinking of male homosexuality, but male masturbation is perhaps also forbidden as unnatural, too. Two sorts of reasons are given; one (at 838E) is that since the natural purpose of the sex act is procreation, an unnatural sex act is one in which the purpose is other than procreation. A quite different sort of consideration is offered earlier, however (at 836D):

Will the spirit of courage spring to life in the soul of the seduced person? Will the soul of the seducer learn habits of self-control?

the Athenian asks. Speaking of homosexuality he says

such practices are incompatible with what in our view should be the constant aim of the legislator—that is, we're always asking "which of our regulations encourages virtue, and which does not?" . . . Everyone will censure the weakling who yields to temptation, and condemn his all-too-effeminate partner who plays the role of the woman.[39]

I believe this passage (at 836D) provides the basis for a defensible view of the unnatural even if its application by Plato is questioned. Certainly the other definition of Plato's, the one that depends upon identifying the natural purpose of sex, is more familiar, having marked one dominant trend in traditional sexual morality. But in this passage, Plato speaks of an unnatural sex act as involving the denial to someone (whether oneself or another) of a vital capacity—courage or self-control—by seduction.

First of all, the traditional treatments (in Plato, Aquinas, and Kant, for example) discuss perversion under the heading of the unnatural, and this is where I shall begin, too. Modern philosophers tend to ignore the concept of the natural—and so, too, of the unnatural—perhaps out of verificationist concern about the apparent impossibility of giving nonemotive sense to talk about the unnatural in moral matters, and perhaps also out of considerations of the sort Sartre offers in *Existentialism Is a Humanism*. To talk of human nature, he argues, is possible only on the assumption that man is an artifact, a product of divine handicraft, made for a purpose. Apart from that framework, that view of the universe, no sense can be given to talk of human nature. I intend to take issue with that view; indeed, my argument will have the implication that, whatever may be the case with other things in the universe, man is one thing we can know has a nature—we can know man's nature regardless of whether man is seen as created for a purpose, or created at all.

To define the unnatural, of which the perverted is a subcategory, I shall need first to make a distinction between a limited set of basic human goods on the one hand, and the indefinitely large set of nonbasic, nonessential goods on the other. Among the latter I include such things as enjoying one's dinner, getting to be famous in one's profession, winning at the next drawing of the state lottery, having children of whom one can be proud. It should be clear from these examples that classifying something as a nonbasic human good is not at all to claim that it is unimportant. By contrast, what I count as the basic human goods can be rather completely listed—life, health, control of one's bodily and psychic functions, the capacity for knowledge and love. These goods seem to be basic in the (Rawlsian) sense that these will be desired whatever else will, insofar as they are necessary for the getting of any other human goods; but two other ways occur to me to identify the basic human goods and to distinguish them from the others.

One mark of a basic human good is that it is hard to make literal sense of the claim that a person has too much of it—what is commonly called being loved too much, i.e., being spoiled, is really a case of having been loved badly.[40]. Hence, too, I exclude wealth from the list. I doubt that much disagreement about what belongs on the list is possible, though different cultures may order them differently in importance. My reasons for claiming much disagreement is not possible may be connected with the other, major, way of picking out the basic human goods, which is this—a basic human good is a feature of human life one can actively seek to reduce to a minimum among humans only at the expense of one's own status as a human being. For example, a creature (perhaps human in appearance) who acts out of a "moral" obligation to reduce health among humans as much as possible (in much the same way we normally feel obliged, on principle, to avoid causing disease as much as possible) would be a creature whom we would not perceive as human. (Imagine a creature who sincerely offered excuses for having failed to spread disease in a particular situation in which he had the opportunity.) It is at that point that simple people begin to speak of creatures as being possessed by evil demons, that is, the point at which a creature manifests negative concern for the basic human goods. (The zombie and Frankenstein's monster are variants of demon-possession; in them, absence of awareness or care about the basic human goods is manifested.) People around the world intuitively avoid dealing with human wickedness as if it consisted of an infinite continuum with no lower end; instead, they cut off at a certain point and call whatever lies on the other side alien, nonhuman, demonic, possessed. I offer this general (though not universal) fact as evidence of a deep distinction between basic and nonbasic human goods; it also seems to me to pick out as basic those goods I listed as such. Any creature, however rational or articulate, who does not value the basic human goods is not human. The basic human goods may be defined as those aspects of human existence such that principled lack of concern for them by a creature is a sufficient condition of the creature's nonhumanity.[41]

As a first approximation, I suggest that an unnatural act is one that denies a person (oneself or another) one or more of these basic human goods without necessity, that is, without having to do so in order to prevent losing some other basic human good. A person might intelligibly deny himself or another one or more of these basic human goods for the sake of another basic human good; a priest might adopt celibacy, admitting that it is against nature to seek to live without human love. An artist might sacrifice his health for his art. (A sacrifice is the giving up of something valued; we cannot sacrifice our garbage to the city dump.) But denying oneself or another a basic human good without some other basic human good being expected or intended to be made possible thereby is always wrong; it is also, as I shall show, a necessary condition of perversion. Sports-car racers enjoy risking their lives, partly at least for the gain in skill achieved thereby. Although the likelihood may be great that they will die in a racing accident, it is not probable that they will die in any particular race. If this were likely, their participation in that race might well seem unnatural. Similar arguments apply in the case of the smoker, the drinker, and the drug user.[42]

The perverted is a sub-class of the unnatural. When a person denies himself or another one of the basic human goods (or the capacity for it) and no other basic human good is seen as resulting thereby, and when pleasure is the motive of the denial, the act is perverted. When the pleasure is sexual, the perversion is sexual. It should be clear from this definition of perversion that pleasure is assumed not to be a basic human good. First, because one can have too much of it—to see this, consider the case of a person hooked up to a machine stimulating the pleasure center of the brain. Suppose he were unwilling to disconnect himself even long enough to obtain food to sustain life. He would have died for a bit of extra pleasure. Besides, a person can seek to minimize human pleasure quite generally (perhaps as an obstacle to the maximization of knowledge or other basic human goods) without casting his humanity into doubt—a rather extreme puritan might illustrate this.

This account distinguished sexual from nonsexual perversions. An example of the latter would be the man who takes pleasure in frightening small children by holding them close up to speeding trains. His pleasure would be perverted, since the effects on his victims can be expected to be traumatic. Killing for pleasure, or maiming for the fun of it, would of course also be perverted, but not a sexual perversion. A surgeon who performs operations for the excitement, when not required for the health of the patient, is perverted. In individual cases it may be difficult to determine just what motivated someone to do what he did—rationalizations may be common. But this uncertainty of verification is distinguishable from the blurring of the line *defining* perverted and nonperverted acts. I shall assume that the child-molester is a case of sexual perversion, even though it is not the sort of case central to (or even mentioned in) several familiar accounts of the concept. It has the requisite completeness for natural sex in the canon law sense, its form is normal, and it can lead to reproduction; thus Aquinas does not consider it in his treatment of the unnatural in sex. Nevertheless, the young girl, for example, who is sexually initiated by an older person can easily be traumatized; that there is no way of undoing the harmful effects with the ease and certainty with which they were induced establishes the correctness of classifying the case as one of sexual perversion. (The mere intensity of an adult's sexual feeling can be traumatic to a child, even if the adult is not strange or threatening.[43])

The sort of damage I refer to is properly called degradation, corruption. *Perversion degrades* is a necessary truth (perhaps a trivial one) as I have defined perversion.[44] To categorize some activity as perverted is to say something important about what is wrong with it.[45] One advantage of this account of sexual perversion is that accepting it does not commit us to accepting any of the common views of particular sex acts, although it does in fact capture many of our intuitions about what is perverted. How the concept of perversion as defined here would apply, for instance, to homosexuality is not obvious, if only because homosexuality is a complex phenomenon—it can be viewed merely as an activity, one among many engaged in by those whose lives at the same time include other sexual activities such as heterosexual ones. But homosexuality can also occur as an institution, which it is in many societies other than our own; there, it is often typical of one stage of normal development, leading to, and compatible with, heterosexual functioning in marriage. Lastly, homosexuality can also be considered as a form of life, when it practically excludes heterosexuality. It is this meaning that modern gay liberation intends, and about which little can be learned from other societies. However, consideration of homosexuality as a form of life would take us far from the question of perversion and the unnatural.

Although the definition of the concept does not, by itself, produce criteria strong enough to allow us to be decisive in the important case of homosexuality,[46] the definition might seem to require rape to be included among the sexual perversions, contrary to the traditional accounts.[47] Rape does degrade—this would seem to be a necessary truth—but whether in the way the definition of perversion requires is unclear. (All perversions degrade, but not all degrading acts or experiences are cases of perversion.) What more must be added to the definition of perversion in order to generate criteria applicable to homosexuality deserves a paper of its own, as does the question of why rape has not traditionally been perceived as perversion at all.

Footnotes

1. Michael Balint, "Perversions and Genitality" in *Primary Love and Psycho-analytic Technique* (New York: Liveright, 1965), pp. 136–144.

2. Sigmund Freud, "On Narcissism: An Introduction" *Standard Edition XIV* (London: Hogarth Press 1957), p. 73.

3. Sigmund Freud, *Three Essays on the Theory of Sexuality, Standard Edition VII* (London: Hogarth Press 1953), p. 231.

4. Valuable accounts of the perversion concept in psychoanalysis can be found in J. Laplanche and J.B. Pontalis, *The Language of Psycho-Analysis* (New York: W.W. Norton, 1973), pp. 306–309; H. Nagera, ed., *Basic Psychoanalytic Concepts on the Libido Theory*, vol. I of The Hempstead Clinic Psychoanalytic Library (New York: Basic Books, 1969), chapter 23, pp. 158–170; post-Freudian as well as Freudian developments are discussed in J.R. Bemporad, "Sexual Deviation: A Critical Review of Psychoanalytic Theory" in E.T. Adelson, ed., *Sexuality and Psychoanalysis* (New York: Brunner/Mazel, 1975), pp. 267–290.

5. Balint, op.cit., p. 144.

6. Ibid., p. 137.

7. Ibid., p. 137.

8. Thomas Nagel, "Sexual Perversion," *Journal of Philosophy* 66 (1969): 5–17, at p. 6.

9. Nagel, op.cit.

10. H.C. Gardiner, S.J., "Moral Principles Toward a Definition of the Obscene," *Law and Contemporary Problems* 20 (Autumn, 1955): 560–620, at p. 564.

11. Nagel, op.cit.

12. Sara Ruddick, "Better Sex," in Robert Baker and Frederick Elliston, eds., *Philosophy and Sex* (Buffalo: Premetheus, 1975), p. 91.

13. St. Thomas Aquinas, "The Reasons Why Simple Fornication Is a Sin According to Divine Law, and That Matrimony Is Natural," in V.J. Bourke, trans., *On The Truth of the Catholic Faith (Summa Contra Gentiles)*, Book III, Part 2, *Providence* (Garden City, NY: Doubleday, 1956), ch. 22, pp. 142–147 at p. 144.

14. Ruddick, op.cit., p. 95.

15. Ruddick's later complete formulation is apparently designed to avoid these odd consequences, at least in the sterile couple case (perhaps the use of birth control, too, is meant to be exempt). She writes—

> The perversity of sex acts does not depend upon whether they are intended to achieve reproduction. "Natural" sexual desire is for heterosexual genital activity, not for reproduction. The ground for classifying that desire as natural is that it is so organized that it *could* lead to reproduction in normal physiological circumstances. (Ibid., p. 92.)

I shall assume that Ruddick means to refer to sex *acts*, not desires, whose organization makes them capable of leading to reproduction, in the last quoted sentence; then Ruddick's argument can be represented as follows—

1. All sex acts that could lead to reproduction in normal physiological circumstances are natural.
2. All heterosexual genital activities are sex acts so organized that they could lead to reproduction in normal physiological circumstances.
3. Therefore, all heterosexual genital activities are natural.

There is a problem, however, in interpreting (2). For how might "in normal physiological circumstances" be specified in it? After all, on a sufficiently wide interpretation of that expression, it might be said of masturbation and even of homosexual acts that they could lead to reproduction if they took place in normal physiological circumstances. More to the point—heterosexual sex between elderly partners cannot lead to reproduction in normal physiological circumstances. Unless we are merely to mean by that expression "circumstances in which reproduction could result," in which case (2) is redundant and false, since the sterile couple is excluded as before—it must be possible to specify the meaning of "in normal physiological circumstances" without simply defining it to be true that reproduction is possible whenever physiological circumstances are normal. However, if we succeed in providing a specification of the meaning "in normal physiological circumstances" that leaves it open whether or not reproduction could result from heterosexual genital activities engaged in in normal physiological circumstances, then (2) seems to be self-contradictory, since it will then state that

2*. All heterosexual genital activities are so organized that they could lead to reproduction whether or not physiological circumstances are such that reproduction could result (i.e., even if physiological circumstances are such that reproduction could not result).

If we reject (2), and so the revised formulation of Ruddick's definition, we are left with her first account, which classifies masturbation, birth control, and heterosexual sex between sterile partners as perverted.

Is the heterosexual child-molester perverted? Ruddick writes—

> "Natural" sexual desire has as its "object" living persons of the opposite sex, and in particular their post-pubertal genitals. (Ibid., p. 91.)

"Post-pubertal genitals" probably means here "genitals able to reproduce"—but then many cases of sex between adult males and twelve-year-old girls, e.g., will count as natural, hence not perverted, sex. "Post-pubertal genitals" might mean merely "genitals of one past a certain age (say, twelve or over)"; but then Ruddick's remark would entail that some cases of natural sex exist in which reproduction is not (yet) possible, contrary to her earlier formulation. Aquinas' difficulties with the sterile couple case are discussed in J.T. Noonan, Jr., *Contraception* (Cambridge, MA: Harvard University Press, 1965), pp. 238–246 and pp. 289–292. See especially page 242—"In the acts of nonprocreative intercourse accepted as natural, semen can be deposited in the vagina. In the acts stamped as unnatural, insemination has been made impossible. What is taken as sacral is the act of coitus resulting in insemination." Noonan does not comment here on the implications of this distinction for determining the naturalness of artificial insemination, nor is it clear how to apply the distinction to forms of birth control that do not interfere with the deposition of semen in the vagina.

16. Robert C. Solomon, "Sexual Paradigms," *Journal of Philosophy* 71 (1974): 336–345, at p. 344.

17. Solomon, op.cit.

18. Charles Fried, *An Anatomy of Values* (Cambridge, MA: Harvard University Press, 1970), p. 50.

19. I owe this example to Paul Shupack.

20. Alan H. Goldman, "Plain Sex," *Philosophy and Public Affairs* 6 (Spring, 1977): 267–287, at p. 284.

21. Ibid.

22. Ibid.

23. Ibid.

24. Alan Soble pointed this out to me.

25. Goldman ascribes to Nagel and Solomon evaluative accounts of perversion—but the value, if it is there at all, seems not to be moral, only perhaps aesthetic. Compare Nagel and Solomon: "perverse sex is not necessarily bad or immoral sex."

26. Robert Gray, "Sex and Sexual Perversion," *Journal of Philosophy* 75 (1978): 189–199, at p. 189.

27. Ibid., p. 198.

28. Ibid., p. 190.

29. Ibid., p. 190.

30. Ibid., pp. 197–198.

31. Ibid., p. 197.

32. Ibid., p. 197.

33. Ibid.

34. Ibid., p. 199.

35. Ibid., p. 197.

36. Ibid., p. 198.

37. Ibid.

38. Michael Slote, "Inapplicable Concepts and Sexual Perversion" in Robert Baker and Frederick Elliston, eds., in *Philosophy and Sex* (Buffalo: Prometheus, 1975), pp. 261–267.

39. Plato, *Laws*, trans. by T.J. Saunders (Harmondsworth: Penguin, 1970), 836D.

40. Descartes seems to mean something like this when he says that in certain conditions love "can never be too great," *The Passions of the Soul*, Part II, article CXXXIX, in E.S. Haldane and G.R.T. Ross, trans. *Philosophical Works of Descartes I* (New York: Dover, 1955), p. 383.

41. There is something essentially incomprehensible about principled lack of concern for the basic human goods; in this respect, there appears to be a categorical contrast with the way we think about the insane. However serious their disturbance, the mentally ill seem to us to be distorted versions of creatures like ourselves, with original instincts (if there are such things) like ours. This way of regarding the insane as comprehensible remains intact even when we do not know what motivates them, or might be motivating them. Making the distinction between the demonic and the insane in this way conflicts with Joel Feinberg's discussion in "What Is So Special About Mental Illness?" [in *Doing and Deserving* (Princeton, NJ: Princeton University Press, 1970), pp. 272–292], since he appears to regard the motivations of the mentally ill, and certainly of the criminally insane, as unintelligible, senseless, and incoherent. I believe he would not think this if he did not also implicitly accept a somewhat Olympian conception of the noninsane, noncriminal individual, whose motives Feinberg seems to think fit together and make a coherent whole (Ibid., p. 287). Such a person, he suggests, has an overriding interest in personal integration and internal harmony and is thus comparable to a machine in proper working order (Ibid., p. 288). I doubt that there are many noncriminals of the sane category who fit this description; no one, however sane, whose view of life is tragic, does. Besides, the demonic creatures I hypothesize may have motives that fit together in coherent wholes, etc. What makes us perceive them as demonic is our inability to understand why anyone would have the motives they have, not the lack of fit of these motives with each other. (Fairness to Feinberg requires that I note that his position is more complex than indicated here; but it is not different.)

42. Defining the unnatural in this way, as a certain definite kind of exchange of basic for nonbasic human goods presupposes that the basic human goods I have specified are not "culturally relative." This has been questioned, however; writing in response to Rawls's list

of *primary goods* that my list of basic human goods closely resembles, Michael Teitelman writes:

> some things may be primary goods only relative to the social institutions in which persons who have these preferences find themselves, but we might be inclined to regard these as primary goods *simpliciter* because of a failure to appreciate the role of social circumstances. I think this holds of some of the things that Rawls regards as primary. Wealth and power, for instance, may be essential for the attainment of a person's ends in some kinds of societies but not in others. Indeed, there are possible life plans in which possession of wealth and power are genuine nuisances. ["The Limits of Individualism," *Journal of Philosophy* 69 (5 October, 1972): 545–556, at pp. 550–551.]

Since the list of basic human goods does not, on principle, include wealth or power, the only one of the basic human goods about which the problem of social relativity might be raised is the capacity for love, I believe. Those thinkers to whom love has appeared not to be a basic human good can be divided into two groups: (1) those, like Plato, for whom love is neither good nor bad in itself (Socrates and Diotima agree about this in the *Symposium*, 201B–202B); and (2) those who appear to hold that we ought to minimize love on principle. They appear to regard love as evil. Concerning the first group, I would point out merely that the refusal to treat love as a basic human good does not seem to be the result of social relativity, but of genuine difference in philosophical viewpoint, i.e., of different conceptions about what love really consists in, about the definition of love. They do not pose the sort of problem the second group appears to present. (If the difference in viewpoint between Plato and us were attributable to social relativity, one would expect all other Athenians of his time to agree with him. That this was not so is evident from the earlier speeches in the *Symposium*.)

It is only the second group that seems to maintain that we ought to minimize love on principle, a claim that I have characterized as an unintelligible proposal for a human being to make. Two apparent examples of the second group would be the Buddha, who is sometimes thought to have explained all suffering as derived from desire, and the Gnostics, e.g., Marcion and Mani, who abstained from sex and marriage as inherently evil. In the case of Buddha, however, it is not desire, but craving, grasping desire, in which suffering originates, according to him; and the Gnostics rejected sex and marriage not because they placed negative value on love itself, but because of hopes to obstruct what they took to be the evil of the creation and its maker, which reproduction would prolong. Man's "native realm of light" and the transmundane god were worthy of love, however. [See articles on "Buddhism," "Gnosticism," "Mani and Manichaeism," and "Marcion" in *The Encyclopedia of Philosophy*, P. Edwards, ed. (New York: Macmillan and the Free Press, 1967).] This pattern will be repeated in other likely cases, I believe. It is not love itself that is held to be evil; on the contrary, the value placed on one sort of love or object of love leads to rejection of all others.

43. The dominant view of the effects of pedophilia, opposed to this one, is well represented in L. Bender and A.E. Grugett, Jr., "A Follow-up Report on Children Who Had Atypical Sexual Experience," *American Journal of Orthopsychiatry* 22 (1952): 825–837.

Whether coprophilia or necrophilia are covered by the definition of perversion proposed here has been questioned. What basic human good is a person deprived of in engaging in either of these practices? Briefly, each involves the use of a fetish, which Charles Rycroft defines as "an object which a *fetishist* endows with sexual significance and in the absence of which he is incapable of sexual excitement. A sexual fetish is either an inanimate object or nonsexual part of a person . . .," *A Critical Dictionary of Psycho-analysis* (Totowa, NJ: Littlefield, Adams, 1973), p. 51. So, the coprophiliac or necrophiliac has lost the ability to love another human being sexually in pursuing pleasure with some inanimate object.

44. It would not make sense, I think, to substitute "perversity" for "perversion" in the italicized sentence; this suggests that those dictionaries are wrong that define the terms as synonyms in any of their senses. Perverse acts might be thought of as defective cases of the perverted, since the harm enjoyed in a perverse act is the denial of a good, but not the denial of a basic human good. Such acts are not necessarily degrading; a person who enjoys (temporarily) depriving someone of comfort, information, pleasure does not degrade himself or anyone else necessarily, though he may ruin their evening.

45. Sexual perversion, as interpreted here, is not the perversion *of* sex, of the sexual function or of the sex organs—anymore than se*xual* relations are relations *of* the sex organs. The genitals of two people may have all sorts of relations (e.g., spatial relations, relations of resemblance) without there being any sexual relations between them. The expression "sexual perversion" signifies perversion (as defined) *by way of sex*. The harm in sexual perversion is not to the organs, but to the person or persons whose organs they are. Sexual perversion is perversion, sexual in form. There is no such thing as perversion of sex or of the sex organs, since such entities are not human beings, and therefore cannot be deprived of basic human goods. For the same reason, there is no such thing as perversion of the teeth or of mastication, of the eyes or of sight. A person who enjoys biting off the caps from soda-pop bottles is not perverting his teeth, even if they fall out as a result. In denying there can be a perversion of a human bodily organ or function apart from the harm to the person (or persons) whose organ's function it is, I am in conflict with Aquinas, it seems, and certainly with Nagel. Aquinas writes—

> Now, it is good for each person to attain his end, whereas it is bad for him to swerve away from his proper end. Now, this should be considered applica-

ble to the parts, just as it is to the whole being; for instance, each and every part of man, and every one of his acts, should attain the proper end . . . every emission of semen, in such a way that generation cannot follow, is contrary to the good for man. And if this be done deliberately, it must be a sin. Now, I am speaking of a way from which, *in itself,* generation could not result: such would be any emission of semen apart from the natural union of male and female. For which reason, sins of this type are called *contrary to nature.* (Op.cit., pp. 143–144.)

If "the parts" in the second sentence quoted refers to the parts of an individual human being's body, then Aquinas appears to be saying that an act contrary to nature could consist merely in some organ not attaining its proper end, even if no harm occurs to the individual whose organ it is. However, Aquinas seems to be thinking of the harm done in such an act as harm to the human race as a whole. But it is hard to see that it is true in all cases that "every emission of semen, in such a way that generation cannot follow, is contrary to the good for man," if "man" here means the human race; for the statement now means what Gray meant when he appealed to "the maintenance of human society" to define natural sex, and which I have criticized above as an essentially utilitarian claim. Nagel writes of a perversion of hunger, but his examples are rather fantastic (Op.cit., p. 78); a preference for eating cookbooks over ordinary food, seeking satisfaction of hunger by fondling a napkin or ashtray from a favorite restaurant. This last, he says, it would be natural to describe as a case of gastronomical fetishism. (One wonders if a person on a diet might not reasonably adopt such a habit, if it worked, to lose weight.) He writes—

> there is little temptation to describe as perverted an appetite for substances that are not nourishing. We should probably not consider someone's appetite as *perverted* if he liked to eat paper, sand, wood, or cotton. Those are merely rather odd and very unhealthy tastes; they lack the psychological complexity that we expect of perversions. (Op.cit., p. 78.)

This psychological complexity he explains as follows—

> Displacements or serious restrictions of the desire to eat could then be described as perversions, if they undermined that direct relation between man and food which is the natural expression of hunger. This explains why it is easy to imagine gastronomical fetishism, voyeurism, exhibitionism, or even gastronomical sadism and masochism. Indeed some of these perversions are fairly common. (Ibid., p. 79.)

This claim appears to treat Freud's interpretive ideas abut perversions (mechanisms of displacement, isolation) as constitutive of them, even though these same mechanisms are employed by Freud in interpreting many other phenomena besides perversions, e.g., dreams. Presumably, liking to eat paper, sand, wood, or cotton would be explainable by reference to these same mechanisms. By contrast, there is a real disturbance of appetite, called pica, which the *Oxford English Dictionary* defines as "a perverted craving for substances unfit for food. %y(3)2" I take it to be confirmatory of my claim that there can be no perversion of a natural function as such, that is, apart from harm to the person (or persons) whose organ's function it is, that the earliest explanatory occurrence recorded for the term pica in the *OED* is "1584 Fenner *Def. Ministers* (1587) 49. When one is oppressed with the disease Pica, so that hee can not eate anie thing but pitche." If there are any perversions of hunger, they must consist in more than the mere craving for nonfood substances. At least they must also be cravings whose satisfaction is dangerously unhealthy to the person, as eating nothing but pitch would be. (A perversion of appetite would also have to have pleasure as the goal of the craving, which is not clearly so in cases of pica.) Nagel does not regard danger to the health (or other basic human good) of the person as necessary to perversion of appetite, whereas my account does; Nagel regards explainability by Freudian mechanisms "psychological complexity" as sufficient for perversion, whereas my account does not—only a certain kind of moral complexity would be sufficient on my view.

The confusion concerning the analysis of the concept of perversion sketched here is not confined to philosophers reflecting on sex and hunger. The neurologist Walter Freeman and his associate in neurosurgery J. W. Watts claim, in their work on prefrontal lobotomy, *Psychosurgery* (Springfield, IL., Baltimore, Md: Charles C. Thomas, 1942), p. vii, Preface, that

certain individuals may suffer from perverted activity of these areas [the frontal lobes] and may become capable of better adaptation when these lobes are partially inactivated. Theories are developed [by Freeman and Watts] concerning the mechanism by which the perverted activity of the frontal lobes produces deviation in behavior . . ..

Referring to the pioneering surgery of G. Burckhardt on a schizophrenic patient, they write

Thinking that the hallucinations were at the base of the disturbed behavior, Burckhardt argued further that perverted speech mechanisms prevented potentially normal associations. This patient was particularly active in response to outside noises, so that attention was paid to the hearing center. "If one could remove these exciting impulses from the brain mechanism, the patient might be transformed from a disturbed to a quiet dement." (p. 7.)

I believe it would be fair to say that a whole medical ideology is contained in this confusion of meanings.

46. This point has been pursued in David A.J. Richards' *The Moral Criticism of Law* (Encino, CA.: Dickenson, 1977), ch. 3. A fuller expansion of these ideas can be found in the same author's "Unnatural Acts and the Constitutional Right to Privacy: A Moral Theory," *Fordham Law Review* XLV (May, 1977): 1281–1348.

47. Sara Ruddick says rape "can constitute perversion if rape, rather than genital intercourse, is the aim of desire" (op.cit., p. 99).

Review Questions

1. How does Freud distinguish between perverted and normal sex?
2. How does Balint define sexual perversion?
3. Explain Nagel's view of sexual perversion.
4. How does Ruddick define "perverse sex acts?"
5. What is Fried's account of perversion?
6. And Goldman's account?
7. What is Gray's definition?
8. Explain Levy's own theory of perversion and the unnatural.

Discussion Questions

1. Is homosexuality a sexual perversion or not? Defend your view.
2. Is rape a sexual perversion or not? Defend your answer.

PAMELA FOA

What's Wrong with Rape

Pamela Foa, "What's Wrong with Rape" from Mary Vetterling-Braggin, Frederick A. Elliston, and Jane English, eds., *Feminism and Philosophy*, Littlefield, Adams and Co., 1981, pp. 347–359.
Reprinted with permission.

Pamela Foa teaches philosophy at the University of Pittsburgh.
Foa wants to discover what is specially wrong about rape. It is wrong even if it is not an act between equals, but it is not wrong because it is in some sense "unnatural." What makes rape specially wrong, in Foa's view, is our society's rape model of sexuality.

It is clear that rape is wrong. It is equally clear that the wrongness of rape is not completely explained by its status as a criminal assault. Dispute begins, however, when we attempt to account for the special features of rape, the ways in which its wrongness goes beyond its criminal character. I shall argue against those who maintain that the special wrongness of rape arises from and is completely explained by a societal refusal to recognize women as *people*. I shall offer a different explanation: The special wrongness of rape is due to, and is only an exaggeration of, the wrongness of our sexual interactions in general. Thus, a clear analysis of the special wrongness of rape will help indicate some of the essential features of healthy, nonrapine sexual interactions.

THE WRONGNESS OF RAPE GOES BEYOND ITS CRIMINALITY

It is to be expected during this period of resurgent feminism that rape will be seen primarily as a manifestation of how women are mistreated in our society. For example, consider these remarks of Simone de Beauvoir:

All men are drawn to B[rigitte] B[ardot]'s seductiveness, but that does not mean that they are kindly disposed towards her. . . . They are unwilling to give up their role of lord and master. . . . Freedom and full consciousness remain their [the men's] right and privilege. . . . In the game of love BB is as much a hunter as she is a prey. The male is an object to her, just as she is to him. And that is precisely what wounds the masculine pride. In the Latin countries where men cling to the myth of "the woman as object," BB's naturalness seems to them more perverse

than any possible sophistication. It is to assert that one is man's fellow and equal, to recognize that between the woman and him there is a mutual desire and pleasure. . . .

But the male feels uncomfortable, if, instead of a doll of flesh and blood, he holds in his arms a conscious being who is sizing him up. "You realize," an average Frenchman once said to me, "that when a man finds a woman attractive, he wants to be able to pinch her behind." A ribald gesture reduces a woman to a thing that a man can do with as he pleases without worrying about what goes on in her mind and heart and body.[1]

And rape is apparently the quintessential instance of women being viewed as objects, of women being treated as entities other than, and morally inferior to, men. It is implicit in this object-view that if men, and therefore society, viewed women as full moral equals, rape would be an assault no different in kind than any other. Thus, it is a consequence of this view that the special wrongness of rape is to be found in the nonsexual aspects of the act.

To this end, Marilyn Frye and Carolyn Shafer suggest in their paper "Rape and Respect" that the wrongness of rape is twofold: first, it is the use of a person without her consent in the performance of an act or event that is against her own best interests; and second, it is a social means of reinforcing the status of women as kinds of entities who lack and ought to lack the full privileges of personhood—importantly, the freedom to move as they will through what is rightfully their domain.[2] What is good about this account is that it provides one way of understanding the sense of essential violation of one's *person* (and not mere sexual abuse), which seems to be the natural concomitant of rape.

This account, further, gives one explanation for the continuous social denial of the common fact of criminal rape. On this view, to recognize rape as a criminal act, one must recognize the domains of women. But if domains are inextricably connected with personhood—if personhood, in fact, is to be analyzed in terms of domains—then it ought to be obvious that where there is no domain there can be no criminal trespass of domain; there can only be misperceptions or misunderstandings. To recognize domains of consent is to recognize the existence of people at their centers. Without such centers, there can be no rape.

Unfortunately, I do not believe that this kind of account can serve as an adequate explanation of what's wrong with rape. I find irrelevant its emphasis on the ontological status of women as persons of the first rank. It is granted that in any act of rape a person is used without proper regard to her personhood, but this is true of every kind of assault. If there is an additional wrongness to rape, it must be that more is wrong than the mere treatment of a person by another person without proper regard for her personhood. Later in this paper, I shall show that there is no need to differentiate ontologically between victim and assailant in order to explain the special wrongness of rape. However, it is important to recognize that rape is profoundly wrong even if it is not an act between ontological equals.

The special wrongness of rape cannot be traced to the fact that in this act men are not recognizing the full array of moral and legal rights and privileges that accrue to someone of equal status. Rape of children is at least as heinous as rape of adults, though few actually believe that children have or ought to have the same large domain of consent adults (male and female) ought to have. In part, this is what is so disturbing about a recent English decision I shall discuss in a moment: it seems to confuse the ontological with the moral. Men's wishes, intentions, and beliefs are given a different (and more important) weight, just because they are

(wrongly in this case, perhaps rightly in the case of children) viewed as different kinds of entities than women.

But even if one thinks that women are not people, or that all people (for example, children) do not have the same rights or, prima facie, the same domains of consent, it seems that rape is still especially horrible, awful in a way that other assaults are not. There is for example, something deeply distressing, though not necessarily criminal, about raping one's pet dog. It is disturbing in ways no ordinary assault, even upon a person, seems to be disturbing. It may here be objected that what accounts for the moral outrage in these two cases is that the first is an instance of pedophilia, and the second of bestiality. That is, the special wrongness of these acts is due to the "unnatural" direction of the sexual impulse, rather than to the abusive circumstances of the fulfillment of a "natural" sexual impulse.

I would argue in response that outrage at "unnatural" acts is misdirected and inappropriate. The notion that acting "against" nature is immoral stems from the false belief that how things are in the majority of cases is, morally speaking, how things always ought to be. Acting unnaturally is not acting immorally unless there is a moral design to the natural order—and there is no such structure to it. This means, then, that if it is reasonable to feel that something very wrong has occurred in the above two cases, then it must be because they are rapes and not because they are "unnatural acts." However, even if this argument is not conclusive, it must be agreed that the random raping of a mentally retarded adult is clearly wrong even though such an individual does not, in our society, have all the legal and moral rights of normal people.[3]

Of course, another very reasonable point to make here may well be that it is not just people who have domains, and that what's wrong with rape is the invasion by one being into another's domain without consent or right. But if something like this is true, then rape would be wrong because it was an "incursion" into a domain. This would make it wrong in the same way that other assaults are wrong. The closer the incursion comes to the center of a person's identity, the worse the act.

The problem here is that such an argument suggests that rape is wrong the same way, and only the same way, that other assaults are wrong. And yet the evidence contradicts this. There is an emotional concomitant to this assault, one that is lacking in nonsexual criminal assaults. What must be realized is that when it comes to sexual matters, people—in full recognition of the equal ontological status of their partners—treat each other abominably. Contrary to the Frye/Shafer theory, I believe that liberated men and women—people who have no doubts about the moral or ontological equality of the sexes—can and do have essentially rape-like sexual lives.

The following case is sufficient to establish that it is not just the assault upon one's person, or the intrusion into one's domain, that makes for the special features of rape. In New York twenty or so years ago, there was a man who went around Manhattan slashing people with a very sharp knife. He did not do this as part of any robbery or other further bodily assault. His end was simply to stab people. Although he was using people against their own best interests, and without their consent—that is, although he was broadly violating domains—to be the victim of the Mad Slasher was not to have been demeaned or dirtied as a person in the way that the victim of rape was demeaned or dirtied. It was not to be wronged or devalued in the same way that to be raped is to be wronged or devalued. No one ever accused any of the victims of provoking, initiating, or enjoying the attack.

Yet the public morality about rape suggests that unless one is somehow mutilated, broken, or killed in addition to being raped, one is suspected of having provoked, initiated, complied in, consented to, or even enjoyed the act. It is this public response, the fear of such a response, and the belief (often) in the rationality of such a response (even from those who do unequivocally view you

as a person) that seems to make rape especially horrible.

Thus, what is especially bad about rape is a function of its place in our society's sexual views, not in our ontological views. There is, of course, nothing necessary about these views, but until they change, no matter what progress is made in the fight for equality between the sexes, rape will remain an especially awful act.

SEX, INTIMACY, AND PLEASURE

Our response to rape brings into focus our inner feelings about the nature, purpose, and morality of all sexual encounters and of ourselves as sexual beings. Two areas that seem immediately problematic are the relation between sex and intimacy and the relation between sex and pleasure.

Our Victorian ancestors believed that sex in the absence of (at least marital) intimacy was morally wrong and that the only women who experienced sexual pleasure were nymphomaniacs.[4] Freud's work was revolutionary in part just because he challenged the view of "good" women and children as asexual creatures.[5] Only with Masters and Johnson's work, however, has there been a full scientific recognition of the capacity of ordinary women for sexual pleasure.[6] But though it is now recognized that sexual pleasure exists for all people at all stages of life and is, in its own right, a morally permissible goal, this contemporary attitude is still dominated by a Victorian atmosphere. It remains the common feeling that it is a kind of pleasure that should be experienced only in private and only between people who are and intend to be otherwise intimate. Genital pleasure is private not only in our description of its physical location, but also in our conception of its occurrence or occasion.

For the rape victim, the special problem created by the discovery of pleasure in sex is that now some people believe that *every* sex act must be pleasurable to some extent, including rape.[7] Thus, it is believed by some that the victim in a rape must at some level be enjoying herself—and that this enjoyment in a nonintimate, nonprivate environment is shameful. What is especially wrong about rape, therefore, is that it makes evident the essentially sexual nature of women, and this has been viewed, from the time of Eve through the time of Victoria, as cause for their humiliation. Note that on this view the special evil of rape is due to the feminine character and not to that of her attacker.[8]

The additional societal attitude that sex is moral only between intimates creates a further dilemma in assessing the situation of the rape victim. On the one hand, if it is believed that the sex act itself creates an intimate relationship between two people, then, by necessity, the rape victim experiences intimacy with her assailant. This may incline one to deny the fact of the rape by pointing to the fact of the intimacy. If one does not believe that sex itself creates intimacy between the actors, but nonetheless believes that sex is immoral in the absence of intimacy, then the event of sex in the absence of an intimate relationship, even though involuntary, is cause for public scorn and humiliation. For the rape victim, to acknowledge the rape is to acknowledge one's immorality. Either way, the victim has violated the social sexual taboos and she must therefore be ostracized.

What is important is no longer that one is the victim of an assault, but rather that one is the survivor of a social transgression. This is the special burden that the victim carries.

There is support for my view in Gary Wills' review of Tom Wicker's book about the Attica prisoners' revolt.[9] What needs to be explained is the apparently peculiar way in which the safety of the prisoners' hostages was ignored in the preparations for the assault on the prison and in the assault itself. What strikes me as especially important in this event is that those outside the prison walls treated the *guards* exactly like the *prisoners.* The critical similarity is the alleged participation in taboo sexual activity, where such activity is seen as the paradigm of

humiliating behavior. In his review Wills says,

Sexual fantasy played around Attica's walls like invisible lightning. Guards told their families that all the inmates were animals.# . . .

When the assault finally came, and officers mowed down the hostages along with the inmates, an almost religious faith kept faked stories alive against all the evidence—that the hostages were found castrated; that those still living had been raped. . . . None of it was true, but the guards knew what degradation the prisoners had been submitted to, and the kind of response that might call for. . . .

One has to go very far down into the human psyche to understand what went on in that placid town. . . . The bloodthirsty hate of the local community was so obvious by the time of the assault that even Rockefeller . . . ordered that no correction personnel join the attack. . . . [Nonetheless] eleven men managed to go in. . . . Did they come to save the hostages, showing more care for them than outsiders could? Far from it. They fired as early and indiscriminately as the rest. Why? I am afraid Mr. Wicker is a bit too decent to understand what was happening, though his own cultural background gives us a clue. Whenever a white girl was caught with a black in the old South, myth demanded that a charge of rape be brought and the "boy" be lynched. But a shadowy ostracism was inflicted on the girl. Did she fight back? Might she undermine the myth with a blurted tale or a repeated episode? At any rate, she was tainted. She had, willed she or nilled she, touched the untouchable and acquired her own evil halo of contamination. Taboos take little account of "intention." In the same way, guards caught in that yard were tainted goods. . . . They were an embarrassment. The white girl may sincerely have struggled with her black assailant; but even to imagine that resistance was defiling—and her presence made people imagine it. She was a public pollution—to be purged. Is this [comparison] fanciful? Even Wicker . . . cannot understand the attitude of those in charge who brought no special medical units to Attica before the attack began. . . . The lynch mob may kill the girl in its urgency to get at the boy—and it will regret this less than it admits.[10]

Accounts like the one offered by Frye and Shafer might explain why the *prisoners* were treated so callously by the assaulting troops, but they cannot explain the brutal treatment of the hostages. Surely they cannot say that the guards who were hostages were not and had never been viewed as people, as ontological equals, by the general society. And yet there was the same special horror in being a hostage at Attica as there is for a woman who has been raped. In both cases the *victim* has acquired a "halo of contamination" that permanently taints. And this cannot be explained by claiming that in both cases society is denying personhood or domains of consent to the victim.

The victim in sexual assault cases is as much a victim of our confused beliefs about sex as of the assault itself. The tremendous strains we put on such victims are a cruel result of our deep confusion about the place of, and need for, sexual relationships and the role of pleasure and intimacy in those relationships.

In spite of the fact, I believe, that as a society we share the *belief* that sex is only justified in intimate relationships, we act to avoid real intimacy at almost any cost. We seem to be as baffled as our predecessors were about the place of intimacy in our sexual and social lives. And this is, I think, because we are afraid that real intimacy creates or unleashes sexually wanton relationships, licentious lives—and this we view as morally repugnant. At the same time, we believe that sex in the absence of an intimate relationship is whoring and is therefore also morally repugnant. It is this impossible conflict that I think shows us that we will be able to make sense of our response to rape only if we look at rape as the model of all our sexual interactions, not as its antithesis.

THE MODEL OF SEX: RAPE

Though we may sometimes speak as though sexual activity is most pleasurable between friends, we do not teach each other to treat our sexual partners as friends. Middle-class children, whom I take to be our cultural models, are instructed from the earliest possible time to ignore their sexual feelings.

Long before intercourse can be a central issue, when children are prepubescent, boys are instructed to lunge for a kiss and girls are instructed to permit nothing more than a peck on the cheek. This encouragement of miniature adult sexual behavior is instructive on several levels.

It teaches the child that courting behavior is rarely spontaneous and rarely something that gives pleasure to the people involved— that is, it is not like typical playing with friends. It gives the child a glimpse of how adults do behave, or are expected to behave, and therefore of what is expected in future life and social interactions. Importantly, boys are instructed *not* to be attentive to the claims of girls with respect to their desires and needs. And girls are instructed *not* to consult their feelings as a means of or at least a check on what behavior they should engage in.

Every American girl, be she philosopher-to-be or not, is well acquainted with the slippery-slope argument by the time she is ten. She is told that if she permits herself to become involved in anything more than a peck on the cheek, anything but the most innocent type of sexual behavior, she will inevitably become involved in behavior that will result in intercourse and pregnancy. And such behavior is wrong. That is, she is told that if she acquiesces to any degree to her feelings, then she will be doing something immoral.

Meanwhile, every American boy is instructed, whether explicitly or not, that the girls have been given this argument (as a weapon) and that therefore, since everything that a girl says will be a reflection of this argument (and not of her feelings), they are to ignore everything that she says.

Girls are told never to consult their feelings (they can only induce them to the edge of the slippery slope); they are always to say "no." Boys are told that it is a sign of their growing manhood to be able to get a girl way beyond the edge of the slope, and that it is standard procedure for girls to say "no" independently of their feelings. Thus, reasonably enough, boys act as far as one can tell independently of the explicit information they are currently receiving from the girl.

For women, it is very disconcerting to find that from the age of eight or nine or ten, one's reports of one's feelings are no longer viewed as accurate, truthful, important, or interesting. R.D. Laing, the English psychiatrist and theorist, claims that it is this type of adult behavior that creates the environment in which insanity best finds its roots.[11] It is clear, at least, that such behavior is not a model of rationality or health. In any event, rape is a case in which only the pretense of listening has been stripped away. It is the essence of what we have all been trained to expect.

In a sexually healthier society, men and women might be told to engage in that behavior that gives them pleasure as long as that pleasure is not (does not involve actions) against anyone's will (including coerced actions) and does not involve them with responsibilities they cannot or will not meet (emotional, physical, or financial).

But as things are now, boys and girls have no way to tell each other what gives them pleasure and what not, what frightens them and what not; there are only violence, threats of violence, and appeals to informing on one or the other to some dreaded peer or parental group. This is a very high-risk, high-stake game, which women and girls, at least, often feel may easily become rape (even though it is usually played for little more than a quick feel in the back seat of the car or corner of the family sofa). But the ultimate consequences of this type of instruction are not so petty. Consider, for example, the effects of a recent English high-court decision:

Now, according to the new interpretation, no matter how much a woman screams and fights, the accused rapist can be cleared by claiming he believed the victim consented, even though his belief may be considered unreasonable or irrational.

On a rainy night seven months ago, a London housewife and mother of three claims she was dragged into this dilapidated shed. Annie Baker says she screamed for help and she fought but she was raped. Mrs. Baker lost her case in court

because the man claimed he thought when she said no, she meant yes.

One member of Parliament [predicts juries will] "now have the rapist saying that the woman asked for what she got and she wanted what they [sic] gave her."

However, the Head of the British Law Society maintains, "Today juries are prepared to accept that the relationship between the sexes has become much more promiscuous, and they have to look much more carefully to see whether the woman has consented under modern conditions. . . . One mustn't readily assume that a woman did not consent, because all indications are that there is a greater willingness to consent today than there was thirty years ago." [12]

"The question to be answered in this case," said Lord Cross of Chelsea, "as I see it, is whether, according to the ordinary use of the English language, a man can be said to have committed rape if he believed that the woman was consenting to the intercourse. I do not think he can." [13]

This is the most macabre extension imaginable of our early instruction. It is one that makes initially implausible and bizarre any suggestion that the recent philosophical analyses of sexuality as the product of a mutual desire for communication—or even for orgasm or sexual satisfaction—bear any but the most tangential relation to reality.[14]

As we are taught, sexual desires are desires woman ought not to have and men must have. This is the model that makes necessary an eternal battle of the sexes. It is the model that explains why rape is the prevalent model of sexuality. It has the further virtue of explaining the otherwise puzzling attitude of many that women will cry "rape" falsely at the slightest provocation. It explains, too, why men believe that no woman can be raped. It is as though what was mildly unsatisfactory at first (a girl's saying "no") becomes, over time, increasingly erotic, until the ultimate turn-on becomes a woman's cry of "rape!"

AN ALTERNATIVE: SEX BETWEEN FRIENDS

Understanding what's wrong with rape is difficult just because it is a member of the most common species of social encounter. To establish how rape is wrong is to establish that we have *all* been stepping to the wrong beat. Rape is only different in degree from the quintessential sexual relationship: marriage.

As Janice Moulton has noted, recent philosophical attention to theories of sexuality seem primarily concerned with sex between strangers.[15] On my view, we can explain this primary interest by noticing that our courting procedures are structured so that the couple must remain essentially estranged from each other. They do not ever talk or listen to each other with the respect and charity of friends. Instead, what is taken as the height of the erotic is sex without intimacy.

As long as we remain uncertain of the legitimacy of sexual pleasure, it will be impossible to give up our rape model of sexuality. For it can only be given up when we are willing to talk openly to each other without shame, embarrassment, or coyness about sex. Because only then will we not be too afraid to listen to each other.

Fortunately, to give this up requires us to make friends of our lovers.[16] Once we understand that intimacy enlarges the field of friendship, we can use some of the essential features of friendship as part of the model for sexual interaction, and we can present the pleasures of friendship as a real alternative to predatory pleasures.

I am not here committing myself to the view that the correct model for lovers is that of friends. Though I believe lovers involved in a healthy relationship have a fairly complex friendship, and though I am at a loss to find any important feature of a relationship between lovers that is not also one between

friends, it may well be that the two relationships are merely closely related and not, in the end, explainable with the identical model.

It remains an enormously difficult task to throw over our anachronistic beliefs, and to resolve the conflict we feel about the sexual aspects of ourselves. But once this is done, not only will there be the obvious benefits of being able to exchange ignorance and denial of ourselves and others for knowledge, and fear for friendship, but we will also be able to remove the taboo from sex—even from rape. There will be no revelation, no reminder in the act of rape that we will need so badly to repress or deny that we must transform the victim into a guilt-bearing survivor. An act of rape will no longer remind us of the "true" nature of sex or our sexual desires.

Where there is nothing essentially forbidden about the fact of our sexual desires, the victim of rape will no longer be subject to a taboo or be regarded as dirty and in need of societal estrangement. The victim can then be regarded as having been grievously insulted, without simultaneously and necessarily having been permanently injured.

Further, if the model of sexual encounters is altered, there will no longer be any motivation for blaming the victim of rape. Since sex and rape will no longer be equated, there will be no motive for covering our own guilt or shame about the rapine nature of sex in general by transferring our guilt to the victim and ostracizing her. Rape will become an unfortunate aberration, the act of a criminal individual, rather than a symbol of our systematic ill-treatment and denial of each other.

Footnotes

1. Simone de Beauvoir, *Brigitte Bardot and the Lolita Syndrome* (London: New English Library, 1962), pp. 28, 30, 32.

2. Frye and Shafer characterize a domain as "where . . . a person . . . lives. . . . Since biological life and health are prerequisites for the pursuit of any other

interests and goals, . . . everything necessary for their maintenance and sustenance evidently will fall very close to the center of the domain. Anything which exerts an influence on . . . a person's will or dulls its intelligence or affects its own sense of its identity . . . also comes very near the center of the domain. Whatever has a relatively permanent effect on the person, whatever effects its relatively constant surroundings, whatever causes it discomfort or distress—in short, whatever a person has to live with—is likely to fall squarely within its domain."

3. This societal attitude, however, that the mentally retarded are not the equals of normal people is not one with which I associate myself.

4. Francoise Basch, *Relative Creatures: Victorian Women in Society and the Novel* (New York: Schocken Books, 1974), pp. 8–9, 270–71.

5. See *The Basic Writings of Sigmund Freud*, ed. A.A. Brill (New York: Random House, 1948), pp. 553–633.

6. William H. Masters and Virginia E. Johnson, *Human Sexual Response* (Boston: Little, Brown, 1966).

7. It may well be that Freud's theory of human sexuality is mistakenly taken to support this view. See Sigmund Freud, *A General Introduction to Psychoanalysis* (New York: Washington Square Press, 1962), pp. 329–47.

8. What is a complete non sequitur, of course, is that the presence of such pleasure is sufficient to establish that no criminal assault has occurred. The two events are completely independent.

9. Tom Wicker, *A Time to Die* (New York: Quadrangle Books, 1975).

10. Gary Wills, "The Human Sewer," *New York Review of Books*, 3 April 1975, p. 4.

11. See, for example, R.D. Laing and A. Esterson, *Sanity, Madness and the Family* (Baltimore: Penguin, Pelican Books, 1970).

12. CBS Evening News with Walter Cronkite, 22 May 1975.

13. *New American Movement Newspaper,* May 1975, p. 8.

14. See R.C. Solomon, "Sex and Perversion," Tom Nagel, "Sexual Perversion," and Janice Moulton, "Sex and Reference," in *Philosophy and Sex,* ed. Robert Baker and Frederick Elliston (Buffalo, NY: Prometheus Books, 1975).

15. Janice Moulton, "Sex and Sex," unpublished manuscript.

16. See Lyla O'Driscoll, "On the Nature and Value of Marriage," in Mary Vettereing-Braggin, Frederick A. Elliston, and Jane English, eds., *Feminism and Philosophy* (Littlefield, Adams and Co., 1981). She argues that marriage and the sexual relations it entails should be based on friendship rather than romantic love.

Review Questions

1. How do Frye and Shafer explain the wrongness of rape?

2. What are Foa's criticisms of this account?

3. How is rape different from other sorts of assault?

4. What was the Victorian view of sex?

5. How does this influence contemporary thinking about rape?

6. Explain the "halo of contamination" that permanently taints rape victims.

7. Explain the rape model of sex.

8. Explain the friendship model of sex.

Discussion Questions

1. Is it true that "rape is only different in degree from the quintessential sexual relationship: marriage?"

2. Is Foa's friendship model of sex acceptable or not? Defend your answer.

Problem Cases

1. (*Pettit* v. *State Board of Education,* 1973) Mrs. Pettit was a teacher of retarded, elementary-school children in the public-school system. She and her husband joined a private club in Los Angeles called The Swingers. An undercover policeman attended a private party during which Mrs. Pettit was observed in several acts of oral copulation. She was arrested, charged with oral copulation under the California Penal Code, and pleaded guilty to the lesser charge of outraging public decency. After disciplinary proceedings, her teaching credential was revoked on the grounds that her conduct involved moral turpitude. Although Mrs. Pettit petitioned the courts to order the State Board of Education to restore her teaching credential, the courts denied her request. Was Mrs. Pettit's conduct at the party morally wrong or not? Defend your view. Should there be a law against private sex acts performed by consenting adults? Why, or why not?

2. (*Doe* v. *Commonwealth's Attorney for City of Richmond*, 1975) In this case, two anonymous homosexuals sought to have the Virginia sodomy statute making homosexual activity a crime declared unconstitutional. In a two-to-one decision, the District Court in Richmond, Virginia, upheld the constitutionality of the statute. The case was subsequently appealed to the United States Supreme Court, but in 1976, by a vote of six to three, the Court refused to hear arguments and affirmed the lower-court ruling. Should there be a law making sodomy a crime? Defend your position.

Suggested Readings

Cameron, Paul. "A Case Against Homosexuality," *Human Life Review* 4 (Summer 1978): 17–49. Cameron is a psychologist who provides facts about homosexuality. He maintains that it is an undesirable lifestyle.

Vannoy, Russell. *Sex Without Love: A Philosophical Exploration.* Buffalo, NY: Prometheus Books, 1980, Part Two, Chapter 2. This chapter has a useful discussion of the concept of love.

Wasserstrom, Richard. "Is Adultery Immoral?" In Richard Wasserstrom, ed., *Today's Moral Problems*, 2nd ed. New York: Macmillan, 1979, pp. 288–299. Wasserstrom discusses various arguments used to show that adultery is immoral.

CHAPTER 6

Sexual Equality

BASIC CONCEPTS

Basic Concepts

In the last century women were denied many of the legal rights they have today. They could not vote, own property, enter into contracts, serve on juries, or enter certain male-dominated professions. After a long and bitter struggle, women received the right to vote in England in 1918, and in the United States in 1920. They also demanded and won many other rights previously denied them.

In the late 1960s and early 1970s, the feminist movement for sexual equality won more important victories. There was the Equal Pay Act of 1963, which asserted that men and women had to be given equal pay for equal work. Also noteworthy was Title VII of the Civil Rights Act of 1964, which prohibited any discrimination on the basis of race, color, religion, sex, or national origin.

But the fight for sexual equality continues. Women are still paid less than men. For example, a recent study of college teachers shows that the average salary for women is still about $5,000 less than the average yearly salary for men. Despite improvements there are still very few women in the male-dominated professions of professor, lawyer, physician, and engineer. There continues to be controversy about the ERA or Equal Rights Amendment. What this Amendment says is simple: "Equality of rights under the law shall not be denied or abridged by the United States or by any state on account of sex." This Amendment was proposed by Alice Paul in 1923, but it was not approved by Congress until 1971. It was not ratified by three fourths of the state legislatures and is now dead unless Congress revives it.

SEXISM

Opponents of sexual equality are often called "sexists." In general sexism is the view that women should not be treated in the same way as men because they are inferior to men in certain important respects. Specifically, sexists claim that there are important physiological and psychological differences between women and men that justify unequal treatment. The most common objection to the ERA, for example, is that it would make women subject to the draft, but women should not be drafted for combat. Why not? The common sexist belief is that only men have the strength and aggressiveness necessary for combat; women are too weak, emotional, and nonaggressive.

According to Marilyn Frye, there are three kinds of sexists: doctrinaire sexists who have a theoretical justification for their sexist beliefs; primitive sexists who have no such theory, but believe male superiority to be a matter of metaphysical truth; and operational sexists who have neither a theory of male superiority nor a metaphysical justification for their sexist beliefs.

An influential doctrinaire sexist is Steven Goldberg. He argues that the male hormone testosterone causes aggressive behavior, and that this gives men an aggression advantage over women. The result is inevitable male dominance in all known societies. Furthermore, since women are at a disadvantage in competing against men for high-status positions, positions that they have little chance of winning so that they will be frustrated, women are better off being socialized to accept male dominance and play feminine roles involving helping and nurturing; they should be wives, mothers, secretaries, and nurses.

FEMINISM

Those who do not accept sexism often call themselves "feminists." Roughly, feminism is the view that sexism is unacceptable, and that women should no longer accept unjust treatment or oppression (as they call it). Although feminists agree that justice requires equality for women, they disagree about the causes of women's oppression and what should be done about it. Alison Jaggar distinguishes between five types of feminist theory. Liberal feminists believe that changing discriminatory laws and practices can be accomplished without changing either capitalism or the technology of reproduction. They emphasize equal opportunity for individuals within the existing system. Radical feminists think that the source of women's oppression is fundamentally biological. In order to achieve equality with men, women must be relieved of the burden of childbearing; this could be done by technological means. They also endorse the end of exclusively heterosexual relationships. Classical Marxist feminists see capitalism as the primary cause of women's oppression, and hold that women's liberation requires the dissolution of the capitalist society. Lesbian separatists believe that women should refrain from heterosexual relationships. Some see this as a temporary necessity, while others want permanent lesbianism. Socialist feminism is a combination of classical Marxism and radical feminism. It agrees with the Marxist contention that socialism is the main precondition for women's liberation. But socialism is not enough. Other changes in the production of goods, reproduction, sexuality, and socialization are required too.

Joyce Trebilcot is an example of a liberal feminist who emphasizes equal opportunity and freedom. She rejects the argument of Goldberg that women will be happier if they do not challenge male dominance, and play only feminine roles. This will produce unhappiness in women who want to succeed in male-dominated roles, say as surgeons, and are not allowed to do so. Furthermore, women will lose their freedom, and this in itself is undesirable.

Trebilcot also attacks the argument that male dominance is inevitable. She points out, to begin with, that natural psychological characteristics such as aggression are merely correlated with sex and are not exclusively associated with sex. Even though men are typically taller than women, some women are taller than some men. The same statistical distribution point applies to psychological traits such as aggression. Even though it is true that men are typically more aggressive than women, still some women are more aggressive than most men. So even if it is true that the male hormone causes aggression, as Goldberg claims, it does not follow that women cannot be aggressive or that male dominance is inevitable. Besides it is a fact that social roles are produced by socialization, not hormones. But if this is so, then sex roles could not be inevitable—for why would society need to teach them and enforce them if they were really inevitable?

SEX ROLES

As we have seen, part of the sexist view defended by Goldberg is that men and women ought to play roles according to their sex, that is, they should play sex roles. The traditional male role is that of provider and protector, while the traditional female role is that of wife and mother. The view of Goldberg and others is that playing these sex roles makes people happy. But Herb Goldberg maintains that just the opposite is true. The traditional masculine ideal requires a man to be a machine driven by an unending need to succeed, while the feminine ideal makes the woman a dependent child who is helpless, weak, emotional, and compliant. The result is serious problems for both men and women. The traditional man cannot express his real needs and feelings; instead he is compulsively active and competitive and represses his emotions. This produces a variety of problems for the male including insensitivity, workaholism, alcoholism, heart attacks, hypertension, anxiety, self-hatred, and failure. The traditional woman tries to be nonassertive and nonaggressive and this has bad effects on her such as rage, depression, illness, low self-esteem, helplessness, and a feeling of being a victim.

But if men and women do not play traditional sex roles, then what roles should they play? An answer given by many feminists is that both men and women should be androgynous. As Ann Ferguson explains it, the ideal androgynous person is not both masculine and feminine, but rather transcends these old categories. The ideal androgynous person would be active and independent with a desire to be autonomous but also with a desire to do socially meaningful work. He or she would want to have loving relations with other human beings, but the ideal love would be a love between equals, and not involve an unequal balance of power. The androgynous woman would be just as assertive as men and just as active and competitive. The androgynous man would be more sensitive and emotional than the traditional man.

But how is this androgynous ideal to be achieved? According to Ferguson, it cannot be achieved in a society that is racist or sexist or in a society that fosters the patriarchal nuclear family and sex-role stereotypes. The alternative suggested by Ferguson is communal living that de-emphasizes biological parenthood and allows homosexuals and bisexuals the opportunity to raise children.

MARILYN FRYE

Male Chauvinism: A Conceptual Analysis

Reprinted from *Philosophy and Sex,* ed. by Robert Baker and Frederick Elliston (Buffalo, N.Y.: Prometheus Books, 1975, 1984) by permission of the publisher.

Marilyn Frye, formerly Assistant Professor at the University of Pittsburgh, has held various appointments at several universities.

Frye distinguishes between three types of sexists: doctrinaire, primitive, and operational sexists. She also discusses the term "male chauvinism." She finds that the common male attitude towards females is not really chauvinism, but what is more properly called "phallism." This is the self-deceptive denial that females are full persons.

Some years ago the new feminist rhetoric brought into common use the term "male chauvinist."[1] The term found ready acceptance among feminists, and it seems to wear its meaning on its sleeve. But many males to whom it has been applied have found it rather puzzling. This puzzlement cannot properly be dismissed as a mere expression of defensiveness. In the first place, the term is frequently used as though it were interchangeable with the term "sexist," with the consequence that it can be difficult to see clearly that there may be different kinds of sin here. In the second place, a bit of analysis of the phenomenon called male chauvinism shows that it is not likely to work in male psychology quite as a chauvinism should work, though it may bear considerable resemblance to a chauvinism when viewed from the position of the female. As if this were not enough to cloud the picture, male chauvinism involves self-deception, and thus it is bound to escape notice on the first round of self-examination. So for this reason also it is difficult for a male chauvinist, even one eager to repent, clearly to discern the nature of his offense and the extent of his guilt.

One of my tasks here is to disentangle the notions of a male chauvinist and a sexist.

The other is to provide the outlines of an analysis of male chauvinism itself. I shall to some extent be describing feminist usage and theory as I understand it and to some extent be developing and improving upon it. There is no sharp line here between description and improvisation.

SEXISM

The term "sexist" in its core and perhaps most fundamental meaning is a term that characterizes anything whatever that creates, constitutes, promotes, or exploits any irrelevant or impertinent marking of the distinctions between the sexes. I borrow the term "mark" here from a use in linguistics. Different distinctions may be "marked" in different languages. For example, the distinction between continuous and instantaneous present action is marked in some languages and not in others, that is, some do and some do not have different syntactic or semantic forms corresponding to this distinction. Behavior patterns very frequently mark the distinction between the sexes. For instance, behavior required in polite introductions differs according to the sexes of the participants. This means, curiously enough, that one must know a person's genital configuration before one has made that person's acquaintance, in order to know *how* to make her or his acquaintance. In general, "correct" or "appropriate" behavior, both non-linguistic and linguistic, so frequently varies with (that is, marks) the sexes of the persons involved that it is of the utmost importance that a person's sex be immediately obvious upon the briefest encounter, even in conditions relatively unfavorable to observation. Hence our general need for abundant redundancy in sex marking.

The term "sexist" can be, and sometimes is, used in such a way that it is neutral with respect to what, if any, advantage or favor is associated with the marking of the distinction between the sexes and whether such advantage is enjoyed by the female or the male. But it is not standardly used in this neutral sense. As it is standardly used, the unqualified term denotes only those impertinent markings of the sexes that are in some way or sense associated with advantage to the male. To refer to such markings when they are associated with advantage to the female, one standardly must qualify the noun, using some such phrase as "reverse sexism." There is a kind of irony here with which one is now depressingly familiar. The word "sexist" is itself male-centered—one may perhaps say sexist. Nonetheless, for present purposes, I shall use and refer to the term "sexist" in its male-centered sense.

Although the term "sexist" is commonly applied to specific acts or behavior or to certain institutional processes, laws, customs, and so forth when they irrelevantly mark the distinction between the sexes, these uses seem to me to be relatively unproblematic, and I shall not directly discuss them. I shall focus instead on the characterization of persons as sexists—the notion of *a sexist*.

THREE KINDS OF SEXISTS AND AN IMPOSTER

One would standardly characterize a person as a sexist in virtue of his sexist beliefs, opinions, convictions, and principles.[2] A person might also be called a sexist in virtue of his acts and practices, but in general only if they are seen as associated with sexist beliefs. There may be people whose sexist behavior is nothing but an unthinking adoption of the habits of those around them, for instance, a door-opening habit whose genesis is like that of peculiarities of dishwashing or driving techniques picked up from one's parents. If a person's sexist behavior consisted solely of such habits, perhaps he would be found innocent of sexist belief. In that case I think that though his behavior might be labeled sexist (and he might reasonably be expected to change it), one should probably refrain from labeling *him* sexist.[3] Actually, it is a bit difficult to imagine someone having many such habits and not developing sexist beliefs to link the habits to each other and to various aspects of social life. Perhaps much of our sexist training takes this route, from unthinking habit to conviction.

Speaking quite generally, sexists are those who hold certain sorts of general beliefs about sexual differences and their consequences. They hold beliefs that would, for instance, support the view that physical differences between the sexes must always make for significant social and economic differences between them in any human society, such that males and females will in general occupy roles at least roughly isomorphic to those they now occupy in most extent human societies. In many cases, of course, these general beliefs might more accurately be represented by the simple proposition: Males are innately superior to females.

It is central to most feminist views that these general beliefs (assuming they are beliefs and not mere sentiments) are to be viewed as theories subject to the test of evidence and in principle falsifiable. And one kind of sexist is one who shares this attitude with respect to the epistemological status of such beliefs and differs from the feminist primarily in taking one version or another of them to be true, while the feminist holds that all such theories are false.[4] I call this person a *doctrinaire sexist.* When the feminist and the doctrinaire sexist are both fairly sophisticated, their debates tend to focus on preferred modes of empirical testing and the weights of various kinds of evidence.

There is another kind of sexist who would cheerfully assent to the same sorts of sexist propositions as those accepted by the doctrinaire sexist but who does not view them as mere theories. Such people, whom I call *primitive sexists,* are committed to these propositions as a priori truths, or ultimate metaphysical principles. A value-laden male/female dualism is embedded in their conceptual schemes more or less as a value-laden mind/body dualism is embedded in

the conceptual schemes of may people of our culture. Looking at things from the point of view of the primitive sexist, these beliefs or principles cannot simply be refuted by empirical evidence, for they are among the principles of interpretation involved in *taking in* evidence. Even so, there is a point in challenging and haranguing the primitive sexist, for the turmoil of attack and defense may generate a reorganization of his conceptual scheme, changing the role of his sexist beliefs. One may be able to convert the primitive sexist to doctrinaire sexism, which is vulnerable to evidence and argument. (I am inclined to think that much of what feminists think of as unconscious sexism may really be primitive sexism.)

Borrowing a Quinean analogy, we might say that the sexist beliefs of the doctrinaire sexist are relatively near the periphery of his conceptual net, and that those of the primitive sexist have a central position. Sexist beliefs may indeed be anywhere between the center and the periphery of a conceptual net, and accordingly, sexists come in all shades, from empirical to metaphysical.

The stances of the doctrinaire and primitive sexists mark ends of a spectrum. Another spectrum of cases differs from the doctrinaire position in the degree to which a person's sexist beliefs are internally coherent and distinct from sundry other beliefs. Certainly, many people would assent (unless the new social pressure inhibited them) to quite a variety of statements the doctrinaire sexist would make; yet they could not in conscience be said to be adherents of a theory. There are those in whom such beliefs are scattered helter-skelter among religious persuasions, racist notions, beliefs and uncertainties about their own excellences and flaws, and so on. These sexist beliefs, though perhaps empirical enough, are not sufficiently organized or distinct from other networks of beliefs to constitute something so dignified as a theory. Sexists such as these I call *operational sexists.* They live pretty much as though they were doctrinaire sexists, but they are not so academic about it. Like the primitive sexist, the operational sexist may be more receptive to persuasion if first educated to the doctrinaire position.

There are other sorts of sexists that would have to be mentioned if we were striving for a complete catalog of members of the species according to the status of their sexist beliefs, but enough has been said to indicate the gist of the list. One other creature, however, should not go unmentioned—the *Opportunist*. The Opportunist is an impostor: he either has no particular beliefs about sexual differences and their consequences or in one degree or another accepts feminist claims about them, but he pretends to sexist convictions in order to gain the privileges and advantages associated with their acceptance by others. Regularly carrying on as though it is one's natural destiny to have some woman tend to one's laundry has, in the context of our present lives, a tendency to bring about the regular appearance of clean and mended clothes without effort on one's own part. Such opportunities abound in our society and are not missed by many persons of normal intelligence and normal distaste for distasteful tasks. (Many of us should recall here that in our youth we took advantage of such opportunities with respect to the rich variety of services our mothers were expected to perform but which we could well have performed for ourselves.) The Opportunist, furthermore, can share not only the advantages but also the excuses of the genuine sexists. The privilege attendant upon the opportunistic pretense of sexism can often be protected by availing oneself of the excuses and sympathy available to the genuine sexist—sexism is, after all, deeply ingrained in our society and in our individual lives, and who can blame the poor soul if he cannot rid himself of it overnight? One may well wonder how many of the people we identify as sexists are really cynical impostors; and while one's speculation on this question may place one on an optimist-pessimist spectrum, it is unfortunately not obvious which end of the spectrum is which.[5]

To accuse a person of being a sexist is to accuse him of having certain false beliefs and, in some cases, of having tendencies to certain reprehensible behavior presumed to be related in one way or another to such beliefs. Those justly accused of being sexists may or may not be blameworthy in this matter; personal responsibility for holding false beliefs varies greatly with persons and circumstances.

MALE CHAUVINISM

The accusation of male chauvinism is a deeper matter than the accusation of sexism. "Male chauvinism" is one of the strongest terms in feminist rhetoric; "male chauvinism pig," which to some ears sounds pleonastic, belongs to a vocabulary of stern personal criticism. In the more extreme instances, persons called male chauvinists are not seen as ignorant or stupid, nor as hapless victims of socialization, but as wicked—one might almost say, perverted. They are accused of something whose relation to belief and action is like that of a defect of character, or a moral defect—a defect that might partially account for an otherwise reasonable and reasonably virtuous and self-critical person holding beliefs that are quite obviously false and behaving in ways that are obviously reprehensible. I believe the defect in question is a particularly nasty product of closely related moral failure and conceptual perversity.

Prior to its new association with the term "male," the concept of chauvinism was connected primarily, perhaps exclusively, with excessive and blind patriotism and closely similar phenomena. Patriotism seems at a glance to be an identification of some kind with one's country. One is personally affronted if one's country is criticized, and one takes personal pride in the country's real or imagined strengths and virtues. A national chauvinism is an exaggerated version of this identification, in which the righteousness and intolerance are extreme. Other chauvinisms will presumably be similar identifications with other sorts of groups, such as religious sects. In any of these cases the chauvinist will be convinced of the goodness, strength, and virtue—in general, the superiority—of his nation, sect, or so on, and will have some sort of psychological mechanisms linking this virtue with his own goodness, strength, and virtue—his own superiority.

Given roughly this view of chauvinisms, it might seem that if we could analyze and understand the mechanisms linking the supposed virtue and superiority of the nation or sect to the supposed personal virtue and superiority of the chauvinist, we could then transfer that understanding to the case of the male chauvinist to see how he is accused of ticking.

But there is a serious obstacle to pursuing this course. An analogy between national and male chauvinisms will not hold up because the objects of the identifications are not relevantly similar. Whatever the mechanisms of national and religious chauvinism might turn out to be, they are mechanisms that associate a person with an entity that is pseudo-personal. Nations and sects act and are responsible for their actions; they are therefore pseudo-persons. Identification with such an entity is identification with a pseudo-person, and its mechanisms therefore will presumably be similar in some fairly important and enlightening ways to those of identifications with persons. Now, if we take the label "male chauvinism" at face value, male chauvinism should be an identification with the group consisting of all male human beings from which the chauvinist derives heightened self-esteem. But the group of all male human beings is not a pseudo-person: it does not have an internal structure that would give it an appropriate sort of unity; it does not act as a unit; it does not relate pseudo-personally to any other pseudo-persons; it is not virtuous or vicious. There cannot be a self-elevating identification with the group of all males the mechanisms of which would be like those of a national or sectarian chauvinism. The

group with which the person supposedly identifies is the wrong sort of entity; in fact, one might say it is not an entity at all.

These reflections point to the conclusion that the phenomenon called male chauvinism is not in fact a chauvinism—a conclusion that should not be surprising. There clearly is some kind of mental set in which a male's knowledge that he is male [6] is closely connected with his self-esteem and with the perception and treatment of females as "other," or "alien." But to picture this as a chauvinism is quite obviously odd. So diverse, varied, and amorphous a group as that consisting of all male members of the species homo sapiens is an implausible peg on which to hang self-esteem. I do think however, that this phenomenon, like a chauvinism, critically involves an identification through which one gains support of one's self-esteem. Drawing on a prevalent current in feminist thought, I suggest it is at bottom a version of a self-elevating identification with Humanity or Mankind—a twisted version in which mankind is confused with malekind. Superficially it looks somewhat like a chauvinism, and a female's experience in confronting it is all too much like that of an Algerian in France; but actually the feminist is accusing the so-called male chauvinist not of improperly identifying with some *group* but of acting as though what really is *only* a group of human beings were all there is to the human race. Since that is not a chauvinism and calling it such can only be misleading, I shall hereafter refer to it as *phallism*.

PHALLISM

Feminists have always been sensitive to the tendency to conflate and confuse the concepts of Man and male. We tend (we are explicitly taught) to think of distinctively human characteristics as distinctively masculine and to credit distinctively human achievements like culture, technology, and science, to men, that is, to males. This is one element of phallism: a picture of humanity as consisting of males. Blended with this, there is a (distinctively human?) tendency to romanticize and aggrandize the human species and to derive from one's rosy picture of it a sense of one's individual specialness and superiority.

Identifying with the human race, with the species, seems to involve a certain consciousness of the traits or properties one has qua member of the species. In this, we generally focus on those specific differences that we can easily construe as marking our elevation above the rest of the animal kingdom, among which the powers of speech and reason and moral sentiment are prime. Being the highest animals, the crowning achievement of evolution, we feel it morally acceptable to treat members of other species with contempt, condescension, and patronage. We supervise their safety, we decide what is best for them, we cultivate and train them to serve our needs and please us, we arrange that they shall be fed and sheltered as we please and shall breed and have offspring at our convenience (and often our concern for their welfare is sincere and our affection genuine). Every single human being, simply qua human being and regardless of personal virtues, abilities, or accomplishments, has these rights and, in some cases, duties with respect to members of any other species. All human beings can be absolutely confident of their unquestionable superiority over every creature of other species, however clever, willful, intelligent, or independently capable of survival.

We are all familiar enough with this self-serving arrogance. It might suitably be called *humanism.* It is just this sort of arrogance and assumption of superiority that is characteristic of the phallist. It is an assumption of superiority, with accompanying rights and duties, that is not seen as needing to be justified by personal virtue or individual merit, and is seen as justifying a contemptuous or patronizing attitude toward certain others. What the phallist does, generally, is to behave toward women with humanist contempt and patronage. The confusion of

"man" with lowercase "m" and "Man" with uppercase "m" is revealed when the attitudes with which a man meets a lower animal are engaged in the male man's encounter with the female man.

It will be noted by the alert liberal that women are not the only human creatures that are not, or not generally, treated with the respect apparently due members of so elevated a species as ours. This is, of course, quite true. An arrogation of rights and duties fully analogous to humanism is carried out also in relation to infants, the aged, the insane, the criminal, the retarded, and other sorts of outcasts. It turns out that only certain of the creatures that are human (as opposed to equine, canine, and so on) are taken to be blessed with the superiority natural to the species; others are defective or underdeveloped and are not to be counted among the superior "us." The point here is that phallists place females of the species in just this latter category. The words "defective" and "underdeveloped" and similar terms actually are used, with deadly seriousness, in descriptions of female psychology and anatomy broadcast by some of those assumed to have professional competence in such things.

With this degree of acquaintance with the phallist, I think one can see quite clearly why women complain of not being treated as persons by those who have been called male chauvinists. Those human creatures that we approach and treat with not the slightest trace of humanistic contempt are those we recognize unqualifiedly as fully actualized, fully normal, morally evaluable *persons.* The phallist approaches females with a superiority and condescension that we all take to be more or less appropriate to encounters with members of other species and with defective or underdeveloped members of our own. In other words, phallists do not treat women as persons.

I speak here of "the slightest trace of humanist contempt" and "fully actualized, fully normal, morally evaluable persons." These heavy qualifications are appropriate because much of our behavior suggests that there are degrees of personhood. But for now I wish to avoid this matter of degrees. I propose to simplify things by concentrating on unqualified fully actualized personhood. When in the rest of this essay I speak of persons or of the treatment or recognition of someone as a person, it is "full" personhood that I have in mind. Anything less than that, in any dimension, is covered by phrases like "not a person" or "not as a person." I shall also confine my attention to females and males who are not very young nor generally recognized as criminal or insane.

THE PHALLIST FANTASY—I

The phallist does not treat women as persons. The obvious question is, Does he withhold this treatment in full awareness that women are persons? Are we dealing with simple malice? I have no doubt that there are cases of this transparent wickedness, but it may be more common for a person to shrink from such blatant immorality, guarding his conscience with a protective membrane of self-deception. The phallist can arrange things so that he does not experience females as persons in the first place, and thus will not have to justify to himself his failure to treat them as persons. In this and the succeeding section, I shall sketch out the phallist's characteristic strategies.

What makes a human creature a person is its possession of a range of abilities and traits whose presence is manifest in certain behavior under certain circumstances. Sacrificing elegance to brevity, I shall refer to these traits and abilities as person-abilities and to the behavior in which they are manifest as person-behavior. As with abilities in general, and their manifestations in behavior, certain circumstances are, and others are not, suitable for the manifestation of person-abilities in person-behavior.

Given this general picture one can easily see that the possibilities for self-deceptive avoidances of attributing personhood are plentiful. (1) One can observe a creature that is in fact person-behaving and deceive oneself straight out about the facts before one; one can come away simply denying that the behavior took place. (2) One can observe certain behavior and self-deceptively take it as a manifestation of a lower degree or smaller range of abilities than it in fact manifests. (3) One may self-deceptively judge circumstances that are adverse to the manifestation of the abilities to have been optimal and then conclude from the fact that the abilities were not manifest that they are not present. I have no doubt that persons anxious to avoid perceiving females as persons use all of these devices, singly and in combination. But another, more vicious device is at hand. It is not a matter of simple misinterpretation of presented data but a matter of rigging the data and then self-deceptively taking them at face value.

Person-abilities are manifest only in certain suitable circumstances; so one can ensure that an individual will seem not to have these abilities by arranging for the false appearance that the individual has been in suitable circumstances for their manifestation. The individual will not in fact have been in suitable circumstances, which guarantees that the abilities will not be manifest; but it will seem that the individual was in suitable circumstances and the deceived observer will sensibly perceive the individual to lack the abilities in question. Then to wrap it up, one can deceive oneself about having manipulated the data, take the position of the naive observer, and conclude for oneself that the individual lacks the abilities. Parents are often in a position to do this. Presenting their daughters with unsuitable learning situations self-deceptively arranged to appear suitable, they convince themselves that they have discovered the children's inability to learn those things. A simple but illuminating example is frequently acted out in a father's attempt to teach his daughter to throw a baseball. He goes through various superficial maneuvers and declares failure—her failure—without having engaged anything like the perseverence and ingenuity that he would have engaged in the training of his son.

But even this does not exhaust the tricks available to the phallist. A critical central range of the traits and abilities that go into a creature's being a person are traits and abilities that can be manifest only in circumstances of interpersonal interaction wherein another person maintains a certain level of communicativeness and cooperativeness. One cannot, for instance, manifest certain kinds of intelligence in interactions with a person who has a prior conviction of one's stupidity, lack of insight, absence of wit; one cannot manifest sensitivity or loyalty in interactions with someone who is distrustful and will not share relevant information. It is this sort of thing that opens up the possibility for the most elegant of the self-deceptive moves of the phallist, one that very nicely combines simplicity and effectiveness. He can avoid seeing the critical central range of a woman's person-abilities simply by being uncooperative and uncommunicative and can, at the same time, do it without knowing he has done it by self-deceptively believing he has been cooperative and communicative. The ease with which one can be uncooperative and uncommunicative while believing oneself to the opposite is apparent from the most casual acquaintance with common interpersonal problems. The manipulation of the circumstances is easy, the deception is easy, and the effects are broad and conclusive.

The power and rigidity of the phallist's refusal to experience women as persons is exposed in a curious perceptual flip he performs when he is forced or tricked into experiencing as a person someone who is in fact female. Those of her female characteristics that in another woman would irresistibly draw his attention go virtually unnoticed, and she becomes "one of the boys." Confronted with the dissonant appearance of a female person in a situation in which he is unable to deny that she is a person, he denies that she is female.

The frustration of trying to function as a person in interaction with someone who is self-deceptively exercising this kind of control over others and over his own perceptions is one of the primary sources of feminist rage.

THE PHALLIST FANTASY—II

It has been assumed in the preceding section that it is obvious that women are persons. Otherwise, failure to perceive women as persons would not have to involve self-deception. Some women, however, clearly think there is some point in asserting that they are persons, and some women's experience is such that they are inclined to say that they are denied personhood.

To some, there seems to be a certain silliness about the assertion that women are persons, which derives from the fact that almost everybody, female and male alike, seems to *agree* that women are people. But in many instances this constitutes no more than an acceptance of the fact that females are biologically human creatures with certain linguistic capacities and emotional needs; in accepting this, one is committed to no more than the belief that women should be treated humanely, as we are enjoined to treat the retarded and elderly. But the personhood of which I am speaking here is "full" personhood. I am speaking of unqualified participation in the radical superiority of the species, without justification by individual virtue or achievement—unqualified membership of that group of beings that may approach all other creatures with humanist arrogance. Members of this group are to be treated not humanely but with respect. It is plain that not everybody, not even almost everybody, agrees that women belong to this group. The assertion that they do is hardly the assertion of something so generally deemed obvious as to be unworthy of assertion.

The other claim—that women are denied personhood—also seems strange to some people. But it by no means emerges parthenogenetically from feminine fantasy. To some, the concept of a person seems somewhat like the concepts that are sometimes called "institutional," such as the concepts of a lawyer or a knight. To some it seems that "person" denotes a social or institutional role and that one may be allowed or forbidden to adopt that role. It seems that we (persons) have some sort of power to admit creatures to personhood. I do not find this view plausible, but it surely recommends itself to some, and it must be attractive to the phallist, who would fancy the power to create persons. His refusal to perceive women as persons could then be taken by him as an exercise of this power. Some phallists give every sign of accepting this or a similar view, and some women seem to be taken in by it too. Hence, some women are worked into the position of asking to be granted personhood. It is a peculiar position for a person to be in, but such are the almost inevitable effects of phallist magic on those not forewarned. Of course, one cannot make what is a person not a person by wishing it so. And yet some vague impression lingers that phallists do just that—and it is not without encouragement that it lingers.

Even apart from the cases of institutional concepts, there is in the employment of concepts, as in the employment of words, a certain collective subjectivity. Every concept has some standard use or uses in some community—the "conceptual community" whose usage fixes its correct application. While admitting that various hedges and qualifications should be made here, one may say that, generally, if everyone in the community where the concept Y is in general use declares Xs to be Ys, then Xs are Ys. For concepts employed only by specialists or, say, used only within certain neighborhoods, the relevant conceptual communities consist of those specialists or the residents of those neighborhoods. In general, the conceptual community whose use of a concept fixes its correct application simply consists of all the people who use it. To determine its correct application, one identifies the people who

use it and then describes or characterizes their use of it.

The concept of a person is a special case here. To discover the range of application of the concept of a person, one might identify the conceptual community in which that concept is used. It consists, of course, of all the persons who use the concept. To identify that conceptual community, one must decide which human creatures are persons, for one will not want to take into account the usages of simply any and every human creature which shows the slightest sign of using concepts. The upshot is that the phallist who self-deceptively adjusts the range of application of the concept of a person is also manipulating appearances with respect to the constitution of the conceptual community. Males who live their lives under the impression that only males are persons (and in the belief that this impression is shared by other males) will see *themselves* (the persons) as completely constituting the conceptual community and thence take *their* agreement in the (overt) application of the concept of a person as fixing its correct application, much as we all take our agreement in the application of the concept of a tree as fixing its correct application. We do not have the power to make what is a tree not a tree, but the collective subjectivity of conceptual correctness can be mistaken to mean that we do. Nor could the phallists, if they did constitute the conceptual community, thereby have the power to make what is a person not a person. But it is here, I think, that one finds the deepest source of the impression that women are *denied* personhood.

The self-deceptive denial that women are (full) persons adds up to an attempt to usurp the community's control over concepts in general by denying females membership in the conceptual community, or rather, by failing to see that they are members of the conceptual community. The effect is not simply the exclusion of females from the rights and duties of full persons but is a conceptual banishment that ensures that their complaints about this exclusion simply do not fit into the resulting conceptual scheme. Hence the phallist's almost incredible capacity for failure to understand what on earth feminists are talking about. His self-deception is locked into his conceptual framework, not simply as his analytic or a priori principles are, but in the underlying determinants of its entire structure and content. The self-deception fixes his conception of the constitution of the conceptual community whose existence makes conceptualization possible and whose collective perceptions determine in outline its progress.

The rejection of females by phallists is both morally and conceptually profound. The refusal to perceive females as persons is conceptually profound because it excludes females from that community whose conceptions of things one allows to influence one's own concepts—it serves as a police-lock on a closed mind. Furthermore, the refusal to treat women with the respect due to persons is in itself a violation of a moral principle that seems to many to be *the* founding principle of all morality. This violation of moral principle is sustained by an active manipulation of circumstances that is systematic and habitual and self-deceptively unacknowledged. The exclusion of women from the conceptual community simultaneously excludes them from the moral community. So the self-deception here is designed not just to dodge particular applications of moral principles but to narrow the moral community itself, and is therefore particularly insidious. It is the sort of thing that leavens the moral schizophrenia of the gentle, honest, god-fearing racist monster, the self-anointed *übermensch*, and other moral deviates. The phallist is confined with the worst of moral company in a self-designed conceptual closet—and he has taken great pains to ensure that this escape will not be abetted by any woman.

Postscript: It may seem that I have assumed here that all sexists and phallists are males. I do assume that in the paradigm cases phallists are male, but the suggestion that all sexists and all phallists are male arises innocently from the standard English usage of personal pronouns. "He," "him," and "his" are of course to be understood in their generic sense.

Footnotes

1. I am heavily indebted to Carolyn Shafer, with whom I thoroughly and profitably discussed all parts of this essay at all stages of its development; her contribution is substantial. I also profited from discussion with an audience of philosophers and others at Michigan State University, and an audience at a meeting of the Eastern Division of the Society of Women in Philosophy, in April 1974, at Wellesley College.

2. I will refer to beliefs, opinions, convictions, and principles all indifferently as "beliefs." Not that it does not make any difference; a fuller analysis of sexism would take these distinctions into account.

3. This might be seen as an instance when we condemn the sin but not the sinner.

4. It should be noted that such theories are sexist only if they are false; for if true, they would not count as marking the sexes irrelevantly or impertinently. Consequently my own use of the terms "sexist" and "sexism" in connection with such theories constitutes a certain commitment in this regard.

5. Women are warmly encouraged to view belief in the ubiquity of Opportunists as paranoia. In this connection I refer the reader to a speech by William Lloyd Garrison, included under the title "Intelligent Wickedness" in *Feminism: The Essential Historical Writings*, edited by Miriam Schneir (New York: Vintage Books, 1972). He points out that men "manifest their guilt to a demonstration, in the manner in which they receive this movement [feminism] . . . they who are only ignorant, will never rage, and rave, and threaten, and foam, when the light comes. . . ." One cannot but believe that there are also some who, well aware of the point Garrison makes, prudently refrain from foaming in public.

6. I am not attending to pathological cases in this essay, so I here ignore cases of females who fancy they are males.

Review Questions

1. What is the fundamental meaning of the term "sexist?"
2. Who is a doctrinaire sexist?
3. And who is a primitive sexist?
4. Who is an operational sexist?
5. Describe the Opportunist.
6. What is humanism?
7. Explain phallism including the phallist fantasies.

Discussion Questions

1. Frye implies that humanism is objectionable. Do you agree? Why or why not?
2. Is the biologist who teaches that there are biological differences between males and females a sexist? Explain your answer.
3. What does Frye mean by "full" personhood? Who has this status and who doesn't?
4. Can a woman be a sexist and a phallist? Why or why not?

STEVEN GOLDBERG

The Inevitability of Patriarchy

Abridged from pp. 49, 51, 63, 81, 93, 105–109, 166–168 in THE INEVITABILITY OF PATRIARCHY by Steven Goldberg. Copyright © 1973, 1974 by Steven Goldberg. By permission of William Morrow & Company.

Steven Goldberg teaches sociology at City College of the City University of New York.

Goldberg defends the sexist view that there are important psychological differences between men and women. In particular, he argues that the male hormone testosterone gives men an aggression advantage over women, making it impossible for women to successfully compete against men for high-status positions. Consequently women are better off if they accept male dominance and play traditional female roles involving helping and nurturing.

THE UNIVERSALITY OF PATRIARCHY

The definitions of patriarchy and male dominance used in this book while they are similar to the orthodox anthropological definitions, will be meant to connote no more than is stated here. Patriarchy is any system of organization (political, economic, religious, or social) that associates authority and leadership primarily with males and in which males fill the vast majority of authority and leadership positions. Patriarchy refers only to suprafamilial levels of organization; authority in familial and dyadic relationships is described by the term *male dominance*. Patriarchy is universal. For all the variety different societies have demonstrated in developing different types of political, economic, religious, and social systems, there has never been a society that has failed to associate authority and leadership in these areas with men. No anthropologist contests the fact that patriarchy is universal. Indeed, of all social institutions there is probably none whose universality is so totally agreed upon. . . .

MALE DOMINANCE
DEFINED AND DISCOVERED

Male dominance refers to the *feeling* acknowledged by the emotions of both men and women that the woman's will is somehow subordinate to the male's and that general authority in dyadic and familial relationships, in whatever terms a particular society defines authority, ultimately resides in the male. I realize that this is not the most graceful way of defining male dominance, but it is the most accurate. As was the case with patriarchy, male dominance is universal; no society has ever failed to conform its expectations of men and women, and the social roles relevant to these expectations, to the feeling of men and women that it is the male who "takes the lead" I will attempt to demonstrate that every society accepts the existence of these feelings, and conforms to their existence by socializing children accordingly, because every society must.

For all but a very few societies the presence of male dominance is apparent from the customs of deference so well documented by the anthropologists. It is important to bear in mind, however, that dominance and deference refer to the *feelings* that come into play in male-female and familial relationships. Anthropologists tend to discuss such feelings in terms of their manifestations in customs of deference because, among other reasons, the inconcreteness of feelings makes it difficult to deal with them in any other way. . . .

The voluminous writings of the feminists attest to the fact that, despite the virtual absence of customs of deference in American society, the feelings and emotional expectations that underpin the customs of every other society affect our behavior as surely as these feelings affect the behavior of the men and women of every other society. . . .

Thus the feminist novelist objects to the fact that it is somehow the male who "takes the lead" in endless numbers of situations as varied as crossing streets and choosing friends. The husband tends to "tell" ("my husband told me to take the TV to the repair shop") while the wife tends to "ask" ("my wife asked me to take the TV to the repair shop"). To be sure, women do, as these novelists acknowledge, have a great deal of power in that they make decisions in many areas, but it is the *feeling* that the husband *lets* them make such decisions (that he delegates authority, that he "allows") that annoys the feminist and that is the evidence of the presence of male dominance. . . .

MALE ATTAINMENT
OF HIGH–STATUS
ROLES AND POSITIONS

Occasionally one who attempts to deny the universality of male dominance will mimic those who claim the existence of a matriarchy: he will not actually name a society whose institutions do not acknowledge male dominance but will merely make vague reference to unnamed societies. He knows that, if he were to be specific, reference to the ethnographic materials on the society he named would show that, while it was perhaps matrilineal or matrilocal, the society's institutions conformed to patriarchy and male dominance as much as, or more than, do ours.

More often, however, he invokes societies such as the Bamendas, the Hopi, the Iroquois, the Mbuti Pygmies, the Nayar, certain Philippine groups, the people of the Kibbutz, or even the fictitious Amazons. These alleged exceptions are merely societies that associate with women *tasks* or *functions* that *we* associate with men. These are not exceptions to the universality of male dominance, for—in addition to the fact that dominance-deference refers to the *feelings* of men and women in every society that authority resides in the male, feelings that are reflected in the expectations of male and female behavior in every society—male dominance in no way precludes the possibility that any task or function that we (as uninvolved outsiders) may choose to emphasize can be seen to be served by women in one society or another. As was the case with customs of deference, what is important here is the attitudes of the members of the society in question. In every society, whatever the particular tasks performed by women, the members feel that women do "women's tasks" (as defined by the particular society) either because only women are biologically capable of the tasks or because men serve functions that are more crucial to the society's survival. *Every society gives higher status to male roles than to the nonmaternal roles of females.* To put it another, and I believe more illuminating, way: *in every society males attain the high-status (nonmaternal) roles and positions and perform the high-status tasks, whatever those tasks are.*

Margaret Mead has written:

In every known human society, the male's need for achievement can be recognized. Men may cook, or weave or dress dolls or hunt hummingbirds, but if such activities are appropriate occupations of men, then the whole society, men and women alike, votes them as important. When the same occupations are performed by women, they are regarded as less important.[1]

A woman who is older, wealthier, from a higher class or "better" family, more intelligent, or more educated than a particular male may be given authority over that male and perhaps she may even feel dominance over him, but she will have less status and authority than an equivalent male and she will feel deference toward him. Thus in some societies the older woman whose husband has died rules the family, and the presence of an educated, wealthy woman will make the less wealthy and educated male experience feelings of insecurity. *But whatever variable one chooses, authority, status, and dominance within each stratum rest with the male in contacts with equivalent females.*

Men do not merely fill most of the roles in high-status areas, they also fill the high-status roles in low-status areas. The higher the level of power, authority, status, prestige, or position—whether the area be economic, occupational, political, or religious—the higher the percentage of males. Thus the percentage of women in the work force in the United States has risen by seventy-five percent since 1900, but the percentage of women in the high-status area of medicine has declined during this period. In the Soviet Union, where medicine has a far lower status than it does in the United States, the majority of all doctors are women, but as one ascends from the level of practical medicine to the levels of authority the percentage of males rises until, at the top, males constitute the overwhelming majority.[2]

Of all the *tasks* one might think of or choose to emphasize, virtually every one, with the exception of those related to protection, fighting, and political authority, is associated with women in one society or another,[3] but in every society it is the roles filled by men that are given high status. None of this, of course, denies that in every society it is women who are responsible for the care and rearing of the young, the single most important function served in any society or in nature itself. Just as patriarchy, male dominance, and male attainment of high-status roles and positions are universal, so is the association of nurturance and emotional socialization with the woman universal, and these female roles are, in some societies, given the highest of status. . . .

TESTOSTERONE AND AGGRESSION

The hormonal etiology of aggression is exceedingly complex. It is a gross oversimplification, at best, to speak merely in terms of hormone levels. The male hormone is not, in itself, "aggressive." The biological aggression of which we shall speak is a function of an interaction between the fetally prepared central nervous system and the later presence of endogenous testosterone. This explains the possibility of the rare exceptional species in which the effect of testosterone in the male is the reverse of that in humans and in which the female is more aggressive than the male. It is by no means clear that there are any such exceptions at all among mammals. Certainly there are none in the species closely related to man. It has been suggested that the golden hamster is the single experimental exception to the development of sexual differences in aggression outlined here,[4] but this has recently been brought into question.[5] Even if the female hamster is more aggressive than the male, this does not indicate an unwarranted selectivity on our part when we consider the mouse, the rat, and all the other animals for which aggression is associated primarily with the male, as analogues of the human male and exclude the hamster. For, unlike the mouse, rat, and other experimental animals, the female hamster is also larger than the male. This would seem a good indication that the entire CNS (Central Nervous System)—hormonal development of the hamster is the reverse of that in the other experimental animals so that, if one wants to consider the hamster, rather than the other animals, as analogous in its development to humans, he must indicate not only that the human female is more aggressive than the human male but also that she is larger.

With all this in mind, I refer the reader to a number of experiments that indicate beyond a shadow of a doubt that, at least among rats, mice, and many other mammals, testosterone is related not only to sexual differentiation but to aggression itself. In paired tests, females treated with exogenous testosterone during the crucial neonatal period will develop an aggression as adults, if appropriately hormonally treated as adults, equal to that of the male who receives neonatal testosterone stimulation of the CNS endogenously from his own testis. Females treated with androgen on the tenth day following birth will, as adults, demonstrate an aggression, dominance, propensity for fighting, and willingness to fight greater than that of the normal female, but less than that of neonatally treated females or normal males. . . .

HUMAN AGGRESSION

Aggression in human beings is not, of course, as easily described as it is in rats, but for our purposes this fact offers no difficulty. I do not purport to describe the specific nature of human social aggression, but merely to demonstrate that the hormonal differences between men and women will inevitably manifest themselves in certain societal institutions. I use *aggression* only as a convenient hypothetical term, a nexus that flows from hormones and to which certain societal institutions conform. The reader is free to substitute *the X factor, male behavior,* or any other term that represents an element that flows from specifiable hormonal factors and that determines the limits of specifiable social institutions (patriarchy, male dominance, and male attainment of high-status roles and positions). Likewise, the reader is free to perceive the reality I refer to as a "male-female difference in the capacity for aggression" as a difference in the level of the threshold at which "aggressive" and "dominance" behavior is released. (In one respect the paradigm that envisions a sexual difference in threshold is superior to the paradigm that sees a difference in capacity; one might suggest that the ferocity with which a mother defends her endangered infant demonstrates that the female has a capacity for aggression equal to that of the male. I do not think that such behavior is "aggression" in any meaningful sense, but even if it is the same thing as aggression such female behavior demonstrates only that the environmental threat to her child is sufficient to reach the high threshold at which a female's aggression is released. We would then ask why, if there is no physiological difference between males and females that is relevant to aggression, male aggression is released at a much lower level, i.e., why does a much less threatening stimulus release male aggression so much more easily?) In any case, all that is necessary for the theory presented here is that there is a physiologically generated difference between males and females that engenders in males, to a greater degree or more easily than in females, the behavior to which the social institutions we discuss conform.

This is not, as it might seem at quick glance, tautological, because each of the two elements (the biological and the social) is specified, defined, and described without reference to the other. Thus I use *aggression* as one might use *strength* in an explanation of why young boys are socialized toward boxing prowess and young girls away from it. Greater adult male muscularity engenders greater male "strength," which makes the male a better boxer than the female, so that it is inevitable that boxing champions will be men, boxing will be associated with men, and small children will be socialized accordingly. Similarly, it will be argued, the male hormonal system engenders a greater male "aggression" that results in a male superiority at attaining roles and positions given high status (except when men are biologically incapable of playing a role) so that it is inevitable that positions and roles of leadership and status will be attained by men, and small children will be socialized accordingly.

. . . *The thesis put forth here is that the hormonal renders the social inevitable.* . . .

THE IRRELEVANCE OF EXCEPTIONS

Whenever a biologist speaks of men and women he is speaking in virtually absolute terms. For all intents and purposes every human being begins life as either a genetic male or a genetic female. When a biologist speaks of masculine and feminine characteristics he is almost always speaking in the statistical terms of probability. When one deals with probability of any sort he expects exceptions. The biological nature of height is not brought into question by the fact that some women are taller than some men or by

the fact that within-sex differences in height are much greater than the between-sex differences in height. Few genetic females have testosterone levels approaching that which would be normal for a male; a woman whose testosterone level is even half that of a normal male displays undeniable signs of hirsuteness and general virilization. But even if ten percent of all women had higher testosterone levels than ten percent of all men one would not be led to the conclusion that the parameters of hormone distribution by sex are irrelevant any more than he would say that the fact that there are some six-foot women and five-foot men disproves the biological nature of human height. . . .

SOCIALIZATION'S CONFORMATION TO BIOLOGICAL REALITY

Socialization is the process by which society prepares children for adulthood. The way in which its goals conform to the reality of biology is seen quite clearly when we consider the method in which testosterone generates male aggression (testosterone's serially developing nature). Preadolescent boys and girls have roughly equal testosterone levels, yet young boys are far more aggressive than young girls. Eva Figes has used this observation to dismiss incorrectly the possibility of a hormone-aggression association.[6] Now it is quite probable that the boy is more aggressive than the girl for a purely biological reason. We have seen that it is simplistic to speak simply in terms of hormone levels and that there is evidence of male-female differences in the behavior of infants shortly after birth (when differential socialization is not a plausible explanation of such differences). The fetal alteration of the boy's brain by the testosterone that was generated by his testes has probably left him far more sensitive to the aggression-related properties of the testosterone that is present during boyhood than the girl, who did not receive such alteration. But let us for the moment assume that this is not the case. This does not at all reduce the importance of the hormonal factor. For even if the boy is more aggressive than the girl only because the society allows him to be, the boy's socialization still flows from society's acknowledging biological reality. Let us consider what would happen if girls had the same innate aggression as boys and if a society did not socialize girls away from aggressive competitions. Perhaps half of the third-grade baseball team would be female. As many girls as boys would frame their expectations in masculine values and girls would develop not their feminine abilities but their masculine ones. During adolescence, however, the same assertion of the male chromosomal program that causes the boys to grow beards raises their testosterone level, and their potential for aggression, to a level far above that of the adolescent woman. If society did not teach young girls that beating boys at competitions was unfeminine (behavior inappropriate for a woman), if it did not socialize them away from the political and economic areas in which aggression leads to attainment, these girls would grow into adulthood with self-images based not on suc-

ceeding in areas for which biology has left them better prepared than men, but on competitions that most women could not win. If women did not develop feminine qualities as girls (assuming that such qualities do not spring automatically from female biology) they then would be forced to deal with the world in the aggressive terms of men. They would lose every source of power their feminine abilities now give them and they would gain nothing. . . .

DISCRIMINATION OF A SORT

If one is convinced that sexual biology gives the male an advantage in aggression, competitiveness, and dominance, but he does not believe that it engenders in men and women different propensities, cognitive aptitudes, and modes of perception, and if he considers it discrimination when male aggression leads to attainment of position even when aggression is not relevant to the task to be performed, then the unavoidable conclusion is that discrimination so defined is unavoidable. . . .

Footnotes

1. Margaret Mead, *Male and Female* (New York: William Morrow, 1949), p. 168. Emphasis added. As we shall see, one need not postulate a male "need to achieve" any greater than that of the female to explain why men attain the high-status roles in every society; the male aggression advantage is enough to explain why high-status roles and positions are always attained primarily by men and why every society associates its (nonmaternal) high-status roles with men.

2. See William J. Goode, *World Revolution and Family Patterns* (New York: Free Press of Glencoe, 1963), pp. 57–66.

3. While there are no exceptions in these three spheres (every society's military and leadership functions are served primarily by men), it should be noted for the record that in the mid-nineteenth century the army of Dahomey included a corps of female warriors (different authors estimate their percentage of the total number of

warriors as being between five and fifteen percent) and that at one time Iroquoian women served a vital political function in selecting male leaders (though women were not permitted to lead).

4. C.H. Phoenix, et al., "Sexual Differentiation as a Function of Androgenic Stimulation," in *Perspectives in Reproduction and Sexual Behavior*, M. Diamond, ed. (Bloomington: Indiana University Press, 1969), pp. 33–49.

5. Leonore Tiefer, "Gonadal Hormones and Mating Behavior in the Adult Golden Hamster," *Hormones and Behavior*, 1 (1970). If Dr. Tiefer's suggestion is correct and the hamster differs only in mating behavior but not in fighting, then our discussion of hamsters is irrelevant and there are no genuine exceptions at all.

6. Eva Figes, *Patriarchal Attitudes* (Greenwich, CN: Fawcett World, 1971), p. 8.

Review Questions

1. What is patriarchy?
2. What is male dominance?
3. Does every society give higher status to male roles than to nonmaternal female roles?
4. What causes biological aggression in mammals?
5. How does Goldberg use the term "aggression?"
6. What causes the difference in aggression between human males and females?
7. Why does the hormonal render the social inevitable?
8. What is socialization?
9. Why should socialization conform to biological reality?

Discussion Questions

1. Goldberg admits that there are exceptions to his thesis that the hormonal renders the social inevitable. Does this disprove his thesis? Why or why not?
2. Should women be socialized to be competitive or not? Explain your view.

JOYCE TREBILCOT

Sex Roles: The Argument from Nature

Joyce Trebilcot, "Sex Roles: The Argument from Nature," *Ethics*, vol. 85, no. 3 (April 1975), pp. 249–255. Copyright © 1975 by The University of Chicago Press. Reprinted with permission.

Joyce Trebilcot teaches philosophy at Washington University in St. Louis. Trebilcot critically examines three arguments used to support sexism. First, there is the argument that alleged psychological differences between the sexes make sex roles and male dominance inevitable. Second, there is the argument that each sex is happier playing traditional sex roles. Third, there is the argument from efficiency, that sex roles are justified by their efficiency.

I am concerned here with the normative question of whether, in an ideal society, certain roles should be assigned to females and others to males. In discussions of this issue, a great deal of attention is given to the claim that there are natural psychological differences between the sexes. Those who hold that at least some roles should be sex roles generally base their view primarily on an appeal to such natural differences, while many of those advocating a society without sex roles argue either that the sexes do not differ in innate psychological traits or that

there is no evidence that they do.[1] In this paper I argue that whether there are natural psychological differences between females and males has little bearing on the issue of whether society should reserve certain roles for females and others for males.

Let me begin by saying something about the claim that there are natural psychological differences between the sexes. The issue we are dealing with arises, of course, because there are biological differences among human beings that are bases for designating some as females and others as males. Now it is held by some that, in addition to biological differences between the sexes, there are also natural differences in temperament, interests, abilities, and the like. In this paper I am concerned only with arguments that appeal to these psychological differences as bases of sex roles. Thus I exclude, for example, arguments that the role of jockey should be female because women are smaller than men or that boxers should be male because men are more muscular than women. Nor do I discuss arguments that appeal directly to the reproductive functions peculiar to each sex. If the physiological processes of gestation or of depositing sperm in a vagina are, apart from any psychological correlates they may have, bases for sex roles, these roles are outside the scope of the present discussion.

It should be noted, however, that virtually all those who hold that there are natural psychological differences between the sexes assume that these differences are determined primarily by differences in biology. According to one hypothesis, natural psychological differences between the sexes are due at least in part to differences between female and male nervous systems. As the male fetus develops in the womb, the testes secrete a hormone that is held to influence the growth of the central nervous system. The female fetus does not produce this hormone, nor is there an analogous female hormone that is significant at this stage. Hence it is suggested that female and male brains differ in structure, that this difference is due to the prenatal influence of testicular hormone, and that the difference in brains is the basis of some later differences in behavior.[2]

A second view about the origin of allegedly natural psychological differences between the sexes, a view not incompatible with the first, is psychoanalytical. It conceives of feminine or masculine behavior as, in part, the individual's response to bodily structure. On this view, one's more or less unconscious experience of one's own body (and in some versions, of the bodies of others) is a major factor in producing sex-specific personality traits. The classic theories of this kind are, of course, Freud's; penis envy and the castration complex are supposed to arise largely from perceptions of differences between female and male bodies. Other writers make much of the analogies between genitals and genders: the uterus is passive and receptive, and so are females; penises are active and penetrating, and so are males.[3] But here we are concerned not with the etiology of allegedly natural differences between the sexes but rather with the question of whether such differences, if they exist, are grounds for holding that there should be sex roles.

That a certain psychological disposition is natural only to one sex is generally taken to mean in part that members of that sex are more likely to have the disposition, or to have it to a greater degree, than persons of the other sex. The situation is thought to be similar to that of height. In a given population, females are on the average shorter than males, but some females are taller than some males, as suggested by Exhibit A. The shortest members of the population are all females, and the tallest are all males, but there is an area of overlap. For psychological traits, it is usually assumed that there is some degree of overlap and that the degree of overlap is different for different characteristics. Because of the difficulty of identifying natural psychological characteristics, we have of course little or no data as to the actual distribution of such traits.

I shall not undertake here to define the concept of role, but examples include voter,

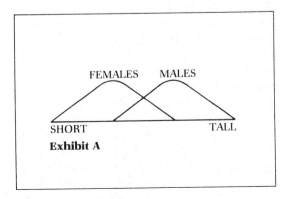

FEMALES   MALES

SHORT   TALL

Exhibit A

librarian, wife, president. A broad concept of role might also comprise, for example, being a joker, a person who walks gracefully, a compassionate person. The genders femininity and masculinity, may also be conceived as roles. On this view each of the gender roles includes a number of more specific sex roles, some of which may be essential to it. For example, the concept of femininity may be construed in such a way that it is necessary to raise a child in order to be fully feminine, while other feminine roles—teacher, nurse, charity worker—are not essential to gender. In the arguments discussed below, the focus is on sex roles rather than genders, but, on the assumption that the genders are roles, much of what is said applies, *mutatis mutandis*, to them.

A sex role is a role performed only or primarily by persons of a particular sex. Now if this is all we mean by "sex role," the problem of whether there should be sex roles must be dealt with as two separate issues: "Are sex roles a good thing?" and "Should society enforce sex roles?" One might argue, for example, that sex roles have value but that, even so, the demands of individual autonomy and freedom are such that societal institutions and practices should not enforce correlations between roles and sex. But the debate over sex roles is of course mainly a discussion about the second question, whether society should enforce these correlations. The judgment that there should be sex roles is generally taken to mean not just that sex-exclusive roles are a good thing, but that society should promote such exclusivity.

In view of this, I use the term "sex role" in such a way that to ask whether there should be sex roles is to ask whether society should direct women into certain roles and away from others, and similarly for men. A role is a sex role then (or perhaps an "institutionalized sex role") only if it is performed exclusively or primarily by persons of a particular sex *and* societal factors tend to encourage this correlation. These factors may be of various kinds. Parents guide children into

what are taken to be sex-appropriate roles. Schools direct students into occupations according to sex. Marriage customs prescribe different roles for females and males. Employers and unions may refuse to consider applications from persons of the "wrong" sex. The media carry tales of the happiness of those who conform and the suffering of the others. The law sometimes penalizes deviators. Individuals may ridicule and condemn role crossing and smile on conformity. Societal sanctions such as these are essential to the notion of sex role employed here.

I turn now to a discussion of the three major ways the claim that there are natural psychological differences between the sexes is held to be relevant to the issue of whether there should be sex roles.

INEVITABILITY

It is sometimes held that if there are innate psychological differences between females and males, sex roles are inevitable. The point of this argument is not, of course, to urge that there should be sex roles, but rather to show that the normative question is out of place, that there will be sex roles, whatever we decide. The argument assumes first that the alleged natural differences between the sexes are inevitable; but if such differences are inevitable, differences in behavior are inevitable; and if differences in behavior are inevitable, society will inevitably be structured so as to enforce role differences according to sex. Thus, sex roles are inevitable.

For the purpose of this discussion, let us accept the claim that natural psychological differences are inevitable. We assume that there are such differences and ignore the possibility of their being altered, for example, by evolutionary change or direct biological intervention. Let us also accept the second claim, that behavior differences are inevitable. Behavioral differences could perhaps be eliminated even given the assumption of natural differences in disposition (for example, those with no natural inclination to a certain kind of behavioral might neverthe-less learn it), but let us waive this point. We assume then that behavioral differences, and hence also role differences, between the sex-es are inevitable. Does it follow that there must be sex roles, that is, that the institu-tions and practices of society must enforce correlations between roles and sex?

Surely not. Indeed, such sanctions would be pointless. Why bother to direct women into some roles and men into others if the pattern occurs regardless of the nature of society? Mill makes the point elegantly in *The Subjection of Women:* "The anxiety of mankind to interfere in behalf of nature, for fear lest nature should not succeed in effect-ing its purpose, is an altogether unnecessary solicitude."[4]

It may be objected that if correlations be-tween sex and roles are inevitable, societal sanctions enforcing these correlations will develop because people will expect the sexes to perform different roles and these expecta-tions will lead to behavior that encourages their fulfillment. This can happen of course, but it is surely not inevitable. One need not act so as to bring about what one expects.

Indeed, there could be a society in which it is held that there are inevitable correla-tions between roles and sex but institutional-ization of these correlations is deliberately avoided. What is inevitable is presumably not, for example, that every woman will perform a certain role and no man will perform it, but rather that most women will perform the role and most men will not. For any individual, then, a particular role may not be inevitable. Now suppose it is a value in the society in question that people should be free to choose roles according to their individual needs and interests. But then there should not be sanctions enforcing correlations between roles and sex, for such sanctions tend to force some individuals into roles for which they have no natural inclina-tion and that they might otherwise choose against.

I conclude then that, even granting the assumptions that natural psychological dif-ferences, and therefore role differences, be-tween the sexes are inevitable, it does not follow that there must be sanctions enforc-ing correlations between roles and sex. In-deed, if individual freedom is valued, those who vary from the statistical norm should not be required to conform to it.

WELL–BEING

The argument from well-being begins with the claim that, because of natural psycholog-ical differences between the sexes, members of each sex are happier in certain roles than in others, and the roles that tend to promote happiness are different for each sex. It is also held that if all roles are equally available to everyone regardless of sex, some individu-als will choose against their own well-being. Hence, the argument concludes, for the sake of maximizing well-being there should be sex roles: society should encourage individuals to make "correct" role choices.

Suppose that women, on the average, are more compassionate than men. Suppose also that there are two sets of roles, "female" and "male," and that because of the natural compassion of women, women are happier in female than in male roles. Now if females and males overlap with respect to compas-sion, some men have as much natural com-passion as some women, so they too will be happier in female than in male roles. Thus, the first premise of the argument from well-being should read: Suppose that because of natural psychological differences between the sexes *most* women are happier in female roles and *most* men in male roles. The argument continues: If all roles are equally available to everyone, some of the women who would be happier in female roles will choose against their own well-being, and similarly for men.

Now if the conclusion that there should be sex roles is to be based on these premises, another assumption must be added—that the loss of potential well-being resulting from societally produced adoption of unsui-table roles by individuals in the overlapping areas of the distribution is *less* than the loss that would result from "mistaken" free choices if there were no sex roles. With sex roles, some individuals who would be happier in roles assigned to the other sex perform roles assigned to their own sex, and so there is a loss of potential happiness. Without sex roles, some individuals, we assume, choose against their own well-being. But surely we are not now in a position to compare the two systems with respect to the number of mismatches produced. Hence, the additional premise required for the argument, that overall well-being is greater with sex roles than without them, is entirely unsupported.

Even if we grant, then, that because of innate psychological differences between the sexes members of each sex achieve greater well-being in some roles than in others, the argument from well-being does not support the conclusion that there should be sex roles. In our present state of knowledge, there is no reason to suppose that a sex role system that makes no discriminations within a sex would produce fewer mismatches between individuals and roles than a system in which all roles are open equally to both sexes.

EFFICIENCY

If there are natural differences between the sexes in the capacity to perform socially valuable tasks, then, it is sometimes argued, efficiency is served if these tasks are assigned to the sex with the greatest innate ability for them. Suppose, for example, that females are naturally better than males at learning foreign languages. This means that, if everything else is equal and females and males are given the same training in a foreign language, females, on the average, will achieve a higher level of skill than males. Now suppose that society needs interpreters and translators and that in order to have such a job one must complete a special training program whose only purpose is to provide persons for these roles. Clearly, efficiency is served if only individuals with a good deal of natural ability are selected for training, for

the time and effort required to bring them to a given level of proficiency is less than that required for the less talented. But suppose that the innate ability in question is normally distributed within each sex and that the sexes overlap (see Exhibit B). If we assume that a sufficient number of candidates can be recruited by considering only persons in the shaded area, they are the only ones who should be eligible. There are no men in this group. Hence, although screening is necessary in order to exclude nontalented women, it would be inefficient even to consider men, for it is known that no man is as talented as the talented women. In the interest of efficiency, then, the occupational roles of interpreter and translator should be sex roles; men should be denied access to these roles but women who are interested in them, especially talented women, should be encouraged to pursue them.

This argument is sound. That is, if we grant the factual assumptions and suppose also that efficiency for the society we are concerned with has some value, the argument from efficiency provides one reason for holding that some roles should be sex roles. This conclusion of course is only prima facie. In order to determine whether there should be sex roles, one would have to weigh efficiency, together with other reasons for such roles, against reasons for holding that there should not be sex roles. The reasons against sex roles are very strong. They are couched in terms of individual rights—in terms of liberty, justice, equality

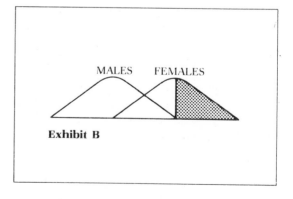

Exhibit B

of opportunity. Efficiency by itself does not outweigh these moral values. Nevertheless, the appeal to nature, if true, combined with an appeal to the value of efficiency, does provide one reason for the view that there should be sex roles.

The arguments I have discussed here are not the only ones that appeal to natural psychological differences between the sexes in defense of sex roles, but these three arguments—from inevitability, well-being, and efficiency—are, I believe the most common and the most plausible ones. The argument from efficiency alone, among them, provides a reason—albeit a rather weak reason—for thinking that there should be sex roles. I suggest, therefore, that the issue of natural psychological differences between women and men does not deserve the central place it is given, both traditionally and currently, in the literature on this topic.

It is frequently pointed out that the argument from nature functions as a cover, as a myth to make patriarchy palatable to both women and men. Insofar as this is so, it is surely worthwhile exploring and exposing the myth. But of course most of those who use the argument from nature take it seriously and literally, and this is the spirit in which I have dealt with it. Considering the argument in this way, I conclude that whether there should be sex roles does not depend primarily on whether there are innate psychological differences between the sexes. The question is, after all, not what women and men naturally are, but what kind of society is morally justifiable. In order to answer this question, we must appeal to the notions of justice, equality, and liberty. It is these moral concepts, not the empirical issue of sex differences, that should have pride of place in the philosophical discussion of sex roles.

Footnotes

1. For support of sex roles, see, for example, Aristotle, *Politics*, book 1; and Erik Erikson, "Womanhood and the Inner Space," *Identity: Youth and Crisis* (New York: W.W. Norton & Co., 1968). Arguments against sex roles may be found, for example, in J.S. Mill, "The Subjection of Women," in *Essays on Sex Equality: John Stuart Mill and Harriet Taylor Mill*, ed. Alice S. Rossi (Chicago: University of Chicago Press, 1970); and Naomi Weisstein, "Psychology Constructs the Female," in *Women in Sexist Society*, ed. Vivian Gornick and Barbara K. Moran (New York: Basic Books, 1971).

2. See John Money and Anke A. Ehrhardt, *Man and Woman, Boy and Girl* (Baltimore: Johns Hopkins Press, 1972).

3. For Freud, see, for example, "Some Psychological Consequences of the Anatomical Distinctions between the Sexes," in *Sigmund Freud: Collected Papers*, ed. James Strachey (New York: Basic Books, 1959), 5:186–97. See also Karl Stern, *The Flight from Woman* (New York: Farrar, Straus & Giroux, 1965), chap. 2; and Erikson.

4. Mill, p. 154.

Review Questions

1. What are the two views about the natural psychological differences between the sexes?
2. What is a sex role?
3. Explain the argument from inevitability.
4. How does Trebilcot criticize this argument?
5. Explain the argument from well-being.
6. How does Trebilcot attack this argument?
7. What is the argument from efficiency?
8. What is Trebilcot's conclusion?

Discussion Questions

1. Should women and men be free to choose what roles they play? Defend your position.

2. Trebilcot grants that the argument from efficiency is sound. Do you agree? Why, or why not?

HERB GOLDBERG

The Machine and the Child

"The Machine and the Child" from *The New Male Female Relationship* by Herb Goldberg, Ph.D. Copyright © 1983 by Herb Goldberg, Ph.D. By permission of William Morrow &. Company.

Herb Goldberg is Professor of Psychology at the California State University. In addition he has had a private practice with individuals, couples, and families for over ten years. He is the author of The Hazards of Being Male and The New Male.

Goldberg describes and evaluates traditional sex roles. The traditional male role requires the man to be a machine driven by an unending need to succeed, while the feminine role makes the woman a dependent child who is helpless, weak, emotional, and compliant. According to Goldberg, these roles produce serious problems for both men and women.

The traditional male-female relationship is a relationship between a machine and a child. The more closely she resembles the feminine ideal, the more childlike the woman is psychologically. The more accurately he approximates the masculine ideal, the more machinelike the man is in his behavior and consciousness of himself and his life. The relationship between the two produces guilt and hopelessness in the male, and feelings of rage, helplessness, and victimization in the female.

Both have expectations, of themselves and each other, that are psychologically impossible to meet, and that therefore give rise to a sense of failure and personal inadequacy. Because of the perpetuation of relationship myths, men and women alike are haunted by the feeling that something is wrong with them, when actually failure is built into the basis and structure of these relationships. Those that survive it or, seemingly, succeed in it do so largely by denying and submerging their inner experience in obedience to their roles. A rare few find genuine and mutual satisfaction, because they have managed to free themselves from the defensive strictures of masculine and feminine role defensiveness.

We have paid the price for this impossible dream with the growing breakdown of the male-female relationship. Traditional masculinity and femininity produce people who have a distorted awareness of the world and of their emotions, impulses, and bodies. This leads naturally to the destruction of the relationship.

He is a machine, driven by the unending need to prove himself. Therefore, he lives by acquiring symbols that validate him, rather than by experiencing the process of his life. He is motivated by how things make him look as a man, not how they actually feel. As a result, he loses his capacity for human connection and intimacy.

The male's strength is an illusion, built on the defensive belief that he can transcend humanness to become a well-oiled, perfectly functioning machine. A self-made business tycoon and athletic champion described his life thus: "I'm running so fast, I'm gonna burn myself out." He then reflected on his own father: "He decided when he was about seventeen, that he was going to be a millionaire when he was thirty. He didn't accomplish it until he was fifty. When he achieved his dream, he was dead by his own hand two years later. He told me, when I was twenty-four, 'Don't ever set your goal. Don't let your dream be something you can accomplish in your lifetime.'"[1]

Not all male machines can even justify their dehumanization with the rewards of wealth, power, or fame. Most are machines because that's all they really know how to be, even if it is destroying them in the process.

Asbestos workers, for example, are in a high-risk occupation, and often their payoff is disease and death. Said one union leader, "There was one day I woke thinking, 'Gee, we work with this stuff and it's killing us.' I could never believe it. . . . Even when my friends started dying, it was hard to accept." He added, "I can't admit that I could die from it. I've seen the terrified looks when they got ill. One fellow had cancer. When he found out, he wouldn't go back to the doctor. He died a few months ago. All he ever said was, 'The only thing I can do is cover pipes.'"[2]

The writer of a book on living without working in a "nine-to-five world" described his experience with his father this way: "One night, ten years ago, my father was complaining about his job. After forty years of selling women's hats on the same street in Manhattan, the pay was still lousy, his boss didn't give a damn about him, and nobody bought hats anymore. . . . That night, I wanted to say something because I knew time was running out, that every morning he had to put a nitroglycerin tablet under his tongue to make it up the subway steps with

his sample case. So I offered him some money and suggested he take time off to relax. . . . 'I can't quit,' he said. About a year later, he died."[3]

While the male is transformed into a machine, the female remains in a childlike state. Feminine conditioning stunts her so that she will not, perhaps cannot, use her potential power and strength directly to function autonomously, decisively, and by taking direct responsibility for the shape of her life and her experiences. For decades, American films have made the love goddess a child-woman. From Clara Bow to Lillian Gish, Mary Pickford, Shirley Temple, Jean Harlow, Marilyn Monroe, and Brigitte Bardot, the message is clear: baby talk, a pouty manner, and cooing helplessness are the techniques that make a sex goddess. Forever children, these love queens are worshipped for being infantile, helpless, emotional, weak, clinging, and compliant. Rescuing and protecting them allows the male to "feel like a man."

Author Una Stannard summed it up: "The woman [is] forced to remain a charming, dependent child. . . . Woman's mask of beauty if the face of the child, a revelation of the tragic sexual immaturity of both sexes in our culture."[4]

Clare Boothe Luce, former congresswoman, also described the state of femininity well:

Now consider how the average little girl is brought up in middle- and upper-class America. She is generally led to believe that she can remain a child (a sheltered dependent) her whole life long, on one condition: that she find a "good man," i.e., a substitute for Daddy, to marry her. This husband-daddy, she is told, will give her a real doll's house to "play house" in, with real furniture in it, and a real range to cook on, and best of all, he will give her real live dolls—babies—to play with. Early in life she is taught to think of herself as a housewife and to expect that as a housewife she will "belong" to her husband, just the way she "belongs" to Mom and Daddy. She will let him decide what is best for her in all important questions. And if is she is a good little Big Girl, who gives him his way in all the big things, she can *have her way like Mom in all the little things. And Mom will show her how to tease, pout, cry, and coax him in such a way that only little things ever come up. As for love, well, if she just stays pretty and sweetsmelling, soft, yielding, and submissive (feminine), she will be loved by her daddy-husband in that special way in which grown boys are permitted to love grown-up little girls. All this, and sex too! Marriage—wow! Childhood plus if you can get it.*

. . . The Venus image, the Love Goddess, "Oh-you-beautiful-doll" erotic image of woman has been similarly reinforced by the media. Endless commercials and T.V. programs show the lovable woman as a cuddly, soft, yielding girl-child sex object, with hair that bounces, teeth that invite deep kisses, a body that smells like Heavenly Spring. The message is that woman is a creature intended by nature itself to be endlessly made happy by being showered with goodies and gifts from her husband or lover (clothes, jewels, cars, etc.).[5]

WOMAN: WHAT FEMININE SOCIALIZATION DOES TO HER

Her Assertion Complex

The author of a self-assertion guide for women wrote, "The woman in our society who conforms to the traditional feminine role is basically a nonassertive person. In social situations, she finds it difficult to express negative opinions or to set limits against the intrusion of others on her time and energy. She expresses emotions but not strong opinions. She is intuitive, not analytical. She underemphasizes her accomplishments. She maintains 'an attitude of frail dependence on men.' "[6]

That frail dependence leaves her feeling unsure of herself, uncomfortable making decisions, and with the deeply frightening sense of having no identity of her own. She comes to feel that she is not a person and that she is not taken seriously. She is a boring companion because she has difficulty defining personal preferences and passions, and she comes to blame the man in her life for having deprived her of identity. The blaming has a hollow ring, however, because even when encouraged and supported by

him in her desire to be assertive, she continues to react passively, being unable to clearly define herself and her preferences, and even becomes angered by the pressure on her to *act* rather than *react*.

Painful symptoms of her repression of assertion include a sense of being exploited and controlled, a strong desire to fuse her identity with a man's, feeling lost without him, and psychosomatic complaints such as chronic fatigue, headaches, and other pains that express her resentment at being controlled.

Her Aggression Complex

To be feminine is to be "sweet," "nice," "cheerful," "friendly," "compassionate," "kind," and without "an angry bone in her body." In short, it is to deny aggression.

The more feminine a woman is in this way, the more hopeless the prospect of true intimacy with a man becomes, because conflict between the two, when it occurs, can never be negotiated and resolved successfully. The repression of her aggression causes her to view herself as a victim. In any argument or fight, therefore, she tends to see herself as blameless and cannot own up to her part of the problem.

Generally, her response to an argument is fourfold. She cries, blames, withdraws, and then punishes by withholding affection. This usually incites guilt in her affection-hungry husband, who apologizes in order to make up, only to face another, similar, but even more agonizing round of arguments soon after. The rhythm of the relationship is endless and frustrating: painful fights followed by sentimental, short-lived reconciliations.

Her underlying aggression emerges in unmanageable, passive, indirect ways. Forgetfulness, procrastination, misunderstanding, saying the wrong thing at the wrong time, lateness, nagging, withholding affection, depression, moodiness, listlessness, compulsive mothering and homemaking, sexual manipulation, blaming and inciting guilt, acting helpless, being unpredictable, religious fanaticism, mysticism, self-righteousness, and even a nervous breakdown all may be expressions of it. Once she decides to get a divorce, the full force of her rage often emerges directly. Then she can be remorseless in her desire for retribution for all her years of being a "victim."

Her smothered aggression also causes her to be excessively fearful in social situations. She exaggerates the threat of such situations, overestimating the strength of others and underestimating her own. She is damaging to the man she is involved with in needlessly encouraging him to fight for her and over her. In that sense, the more feminine she is, the more dangerous she potentially is to men. The weaker the man perceives her to be, the more he will feel compelled to be aggressive, to "defend" her, and to prove himself in order to keep her love. Often this translates into senseless, violent, and self-destructive confrontations with other men over minor incidents, and taking on excessive burdens and challenges.

On an abstract level, however, she sees the world in an unrealistically optimistic, naïve way ("People are nice," "The world is a loving place"). Her femininity requires her to be seen as "sweet," "nice," and well liked. She unconsciously avoids perceiving and immersing herself in "harsh" realities and expects protection from the male.

In addition, she displays an endless array of physical ailments because her passivity makes it difficult for her to maintain her physical health, and because her repressed aggression can use this as a substitute way of gaining control. At the same time, these ailments silently express her resistance and anger.

The myth of the nonaggressive woman, the "sweet angel," is surely one of the most lethal for men. Relationships with her are stagnant, frustrating, unpredictable, and ultimately violent.

Her Autonomy Complex

Just as ideal masculinity translates into militant independence, ideal femininity involves clinging dependency, helplessness, and the search for a "strong" man to "take care of me."

The more helpless a woman feels, the more will she be attracted to a man based on his power symbols. Falling in love will be accompanied by baby talk, childlike admiration of his strength, an infantile desire to be held and "snuggled," and the use of affectionate names such as "baby." She will find it increasingly difficult to know who she is and what she wants. Particularly when she's in a relationship, she will tend only to react, and to fuse her own identity with the man's. She will engulf her male partner because of her need to compensate for her underlying feelings of helplessness. Inevitably, rage will build within her over feeling controlled and being treated like a child, with no awareness on her part of how she helped set it up that way. When she suddenly demands autonomy and freedom, it will have an adolescent flavor. That is, her motivation will be to rebel against her husband, the authority figure.

The degree of her feelings of dependency and lack of personal power directly determine the amount of anger that will build within her over being controlled, even though her anxieties about being independent cause her to be attracted to dominant, powerful men and to play a childlike role. *These feelings develop regardless of how well or badly she is actually treated.*

In extreme cases, depression, suicide, and the tragedy of spouse violence can result from this deeply rooted feminine dependency. Severe spouse violence rarely occurs without an extended prior history of lesser incidents of physical abuse. The woman often fails to leave the relationship because of her feeling of helplessness and fear of being on her own. The rage that builds up behind her dependency is manifested in indirect provocations, blaming, and emotional volatility. Her relationship with her husband will alternate between childlike clinging and periodic eruptions of hatred. A pattern of relationship brinkmanship will develop, as dependency and rage become equally and precariously balanced.

Her Sexuality Complex

The feminine woman is sensual, not sexual. She wants to be held more than to have sex. One married woman spoke of her disgust and feeling of being cheapened when her husband would ask her during intercourse, "Isn't this a wonderful fuck feeling?" A woman learns as a little girl that sex is nasty—something men manipulate women to get, and something women grant as a gift and use as a source of power to control men.

The fact that she is not truly sexual is seen by the fact that she can do without sex for long periods of time if the man or the situation does not please her. Sex is not *her* driving need. Her dominant need is to be "loved."

Because she does not take direct responsibility for her sexuality, she comes to feel used by her man, and to see men in general as sexual exploiters. She is "at his service" because sex occurs at his initiation and she does it to please him.

In some cases, she comes to hate men for their "animal impulses," to view them as rapists, and to develop psychosomatic illnesses in order to avoid sexual contact. She may also develop physical oversensitivity and experience pain during sex. Naturally, the more femininely passive she is in bed, the more likely she will find sex painful and feel she is being handled too roughly.

Her Rationality Complex

The counterpart to masculine repression of emotion is feminine repression of the rational side. A traditionally feminine woman tends, therefore, to be credulous and mystical in her way of perceiving things. The more feminine she is, the more she is drawn to superstition, gurus, astrology, religion, and development of a personal sense of moral superiority. She is also vulnerable to manipulation by charismatic leaders, "healers," and doctors.

In relationships, she resists logical exploration of issues and tends instead to overemotionalize in the face of a conflict. "I don't care whether it makes logical sense or not. It's just how I feel," she will say. The rational resolution of problems therefore becomes impossible.

In moments of crisis, she tends to fall apart, crying and screaming. She resists developing competence with finance, business, machinery, politics, and systematic long-range life planning. Tending to avoid responsibility in these matters, she then finds herself resenting her vulnerability and the feelings she has of being treated like a child and being "kept powerless."

MAN: WHAT HIS MASCULINE DEFENSES DO TO HIM

His Dependency Complex

In masculine consciousness, dependency and need are equivalent to weakness. The underlying fear of being dependent walls in the traditional man and isolates him. He has difficulty articulating his real needs and fears, and asking for help. He comes to feel uncared for, unknown, and cynical about relationships because he can't be real and be himself in them; he can't feel safe even with his supposedly closest intimate, his wife.

His resentment over feeling uncared about and having his unspoken needs unfulfilled emerges in countless indirect forms, including withdrawal and nonresponsiveness, criticism and sarcastic humor, passive indifference, insensitivity, workaholism, and even self-destructive behavior like alcoholism, reckless driving, and gambling, which damages his family as well as himself. At the same time, he comes to see his rewards in life as opposite to what he anticipated. In spite of doing all the "right" things, he feels unloved, dissatisfied, like a failure.

He relies totally on his relationship with his wife because she is his sole intimate involvement, and although he becomes deeply dependent on her, he rarely recognizes it. He likes to feel that he doesn't really need anybody. When his wife does suddenly leave, however, often he collapses. His independence then is seen for what it is: a pose that is both brittle and superficial.

His Fear Complex

Fear equals femininity. To be fearful is to be a sissy. Masculinity means transcending fear. The less fear this kind of man experiences, the more manly he sees himself as being. The need to overcome fear often leads to self-destructive actions. He throws himself into situations and accepts challenges that endanger him and that he is frightened of, in order to prove to himself that he is not afraid, or that he can defy fear.

His defensiveness against fear muddies his ability to perceive his real feelings. When he experiences inner resistance, his major motivation is to prove to himself and others that he is courageous and unafraid, and therefore he ignores fearful feelings.

The potential destructiveness of this need can be seen metaphorically in famous daredevil circus performer Karl Wallenda, who died of a fall during his act. One magazine reader commented, "Would the Wallendas' seven person pyramid have been any less magnificent with a net? Would crossing a wind-swept street on a high wire require any less skill with a net?"[7]

His Passivity Complex

To the traditional male, passivity equals femininity, while activity means masculinity. Therefore, the more active he is, the more masculine he feels. He may in fact become compulsively active. Sleeping is seen as an unmanly waste of time. He has difficulty recognizing and giving in to tiredness. Transcending fatigue validates him. Therefore, the more closely he approximates the masculine ideal, the more likely he is to physically burn out prematurely. He lacks pacing, and a recuperation cycle to balance the intense activity.

His is a driven personality. The high rate of heart attacks and hypertension among men may reflect, in part, the overstress of constant activity without due recognition of fatigue. A man can be deeply tired without knowing it, or giving in to it. To overcome it, and to make up for the human stimula-tion he's not getting, he doses himself with cigarettes, coffee, liquor, a high-protein diet, and excitement.

His Emotions Complex

A man-machine conducts his life in a defensively cerebral way. Emotions are seen as weaknesses, and are therefore repressed. This makes him extraordinarily competent with the mechanical aspects of life, but stupid, vulnerable, and often a victim of his own blindness in intimate relationships. He fails at his attempts to conduct his relationships by means of rules and intellectualization. He often cannot differentiate a genuine response from a manipulative one. His relationships break down without his understanding why.

His woman leaves and he didn't know she was unhappy. His children feel alienated from him though he gave them his "best." He has no close, intimate friends of either sex. He is successful in the world, but humanly isolated.

He is the victim of psychosomatic disorders such as ulcers and back problems, stemming from the repression of feelings of dependency, fear, resistance, and so on. His moods swing constantly and uncontrollably. He is a numbing, unsatisfying friend because he is insensitive to the emotional and interpersonal aspects of a relationship and his conversation is therefore impersonal, boring, indeed deadening.

His Sensuality Complex

He is sexual but not sensual. He wants sexual relief, but is uncomfortable with non-goal-directed holding and caressing. Consequently, he approaches sex mechanically and eventually turns off his partner. Sex in a relationship becomes work, rather than play. Sexual pleasure is severely limited because he experiences sex as an act, not as a part of being close.

Extensive touching makes him uncomfortable. Being touched by a man is intolerable, and by a woman it is not meaningful, comfortable, or satisfying if it does not relate to sex. Even then, he cannot handle very much of it.

The more masculine he is, the worse he is as a lover, despite his sexual illusions about himself and his quest to be a superperformer, because he is uncomfortable with playful, sustained sensuality and is insensitive to emotional cues. Therefore, his sexual relationships inevitably deteriorate and begin to irritate and repel his woman, thus becoming a source of anxiety to him.

His Femininity Complex

Anything that suggests the feminine threatens him and makes him uncomfortable—women's activities, interests, jobs, attitudes, and even clothes, colors, drinks, food. That is, he won't wear certain colors because they are feminine, nor will he drink or eat certain beverages or food that he considers to be for women only.

Closeness to other men on a warm, affectionate basis is a threat because it implies homosexuality. His relationships with other men are therefore competitive, distant, unsatisfying; they only intensify his loneliness and dependency on the woman in his life.

The more he fears being feminine, the more fixated he is on masculine symbols, e.g., guns, cars, motorcycles, football games, and liquor. As a result, there is almost no basis for any real sharing and connection with his woman; and the more feminine the woman—his romantic ideal—the more this is true.

Researcher Evelyn P. Stevens writes cogently of the defensive masculine style: "Because the fear of losing his potency is ever present, the macho lives in a nightmare world; like a writer between books, or an actor between plays, he is desperately unsure about whether he can produce another hit. . . ."[8]

His Submission Complex

His equation of submission with weakness and unmanliness means he can only relate and connect comfortably when he is in control. He will risk life and health when only his masterful self-image is at stake. His need for control in his close relationships—with his woman, his children, and others—causes him to be resented and even hated. Even in his "benevolent" moments, when he believes he is giving to others generously, anger builds toward him because others feel patronized, condescended to, and controlled.

The fear of submission also translates into a competitive compulsion to win. It creates a grim seriousness, even when he's "playing," that infects every interactive experience. Therefore, there is no relief for him in games. Everything becomes a variation on war. He is resentful when he loses and resented when he wins. Eventually, it becomes more draining and unpleasant for him to engage himself socially than to isolate himself.

He hates losers and he hates himself when he loses. Since losing becomes more likely as he gets older, feelings of self-hate and failure are built in to his life experience.

His Proving Complex

Masculinity is a draining, lethal, and insatiable defensive process. Everything a man strives to prove he is not, actually he is. He basically identifies with women because his earliest imprinting and socialization as a child was largely through his mother, grandmother, and other female relatives, teachers, and nurturers. Therefore, his masculinity is, in many ways, a hollow defensive posture.

The internal experience of one highly successful businessman, age forty-nine, thrice divorced, vice-president of a major corporation at the time he wrote this, illustrates the consuming, constricting, and frustrating results of this proving complex:

I have to keep proving that I'm better than other men. It's never good enough to be just as good as other men. I must get rid of competition and must prove that I'm better every day, all the time. I can't stand to compete with other men. I must keep aloof and above them.

I only function sexually with a woman when I'm the only one. But then I get possessive and fearful that I can't fulfill all of her needs and that I'm not perfect.

Even amongst my competitors in business, I'm very aloof and snotty. I don't want them to get close. I don't want to come down to their level for fear I'll be just one of the boys and get swallowed up, consumed, laughed at, or beaten.

I don't want to get close. I'm actually embarrassed about myself and all of these feelings. Therefore, I try to be better and appear superior. But inside I'm lying to myself.

I want the confidence of being no better and no worse than the next guy. I'm tired of being angry all the time, defending myself against my feelings of being no good. The slightest thing that goes wrong evokes anger, because the going wrong means that I'm no good!

Being alone is confirmation that I'm NO GOOD!

Not having someone to love is a feeling of being NO GOOD!

Being poor and unsuccessful is being NO GOOD!

Being late, held up in traffic, delayed, encumbered, not having the answer, not being as I think I'm supposed to be is NO GOOD!

As long as I think I have to be super special, better, superior, I'm going to lose. Every moment of every day I'm trying to prove this. How do I lose my desire to fulfill the fantasy of being superior so that I can come down to earth and enjoy myself? The desire to fulfill the fantasies of being better makes me run and search, twenty-four hours a day. I can't stop long enough to love myself and appreciate myself and my accomplishments and my own humanness.

BREAKING DOWN

Countless studies by psychological researchers have demonstrated a direct relationship between traditional masculinity and femininity, and the presence of anxiety and low self-esteem and acceptance.[9]

The consequences of this gender socialization process, in which boys are conditioned to be masculine and girls to be feminine, are already manifested early in life. The prevalent behavior of young boys and young girls is a compelling variation on the typical characteristics of masculine men and feminine women.

Male children have a four- to eight-times-greater incidence than females of infantile autism, hyperactivity, and contact disorders.[10] These disorders can be seen as extreme developments of normal or even lauded masculine traits. That is, autism is a pathological resistance to human attachment and emotional connection, often accompanied by a fixation on mechanical objects. It resembles the obsession of grown men with their automobiles, television sets, and gadgets, men who are uncomfortable in person-to-person involvement.

The hyperactivity syndrome involves an uncontrollable tendency to be in motion and unable to slow down. Again, this can be seen as a variation on the behavior of the adult male who has to always be doing something and who prides himself on his "endless" energy and ability to go on little sleep.

Females beyond puberty have a two- to four-times-greater incidence than males of depression and social phobia.[11] Depression has been shown to be related, at least in part, to an inability to express aggression directly and fully. It is also known to be the result of learned helplessness and feelings of being powerless to control one's life. The female's significantly higher rate of social phobia is an outgrowth of her difficulty with assertion, aggression, sexuality, and independent strength. The more feminine she is, the more will people and life in general become a source of fear and intimidation.

When the machine and the child begin to unravel as adults and have breakdowns, their experiences will be predictable as direct outgrowths of their separate defense systems.

According to psychiatrist Peter A. Martin, this is a common pattern for women at the time of a marital breakdown:

The wife comes for treatment first because she has been experiencing severe anxiety, depressions, or incapacitating physical symptoms. . . . She claims that her sickness is due entirely to the coldness and cruelty of her husband. She insists that he does not care about what she wants or what she feels. She states emphatically that she has a deep capacity to love, but that her husband is cold, unsympathetic, cruel or psychotic. . . . She complains that her husband is either sexually inadequate or oversexed. She blames her sexual unresponsiveness on her husband. . . . To her, the only solution is a change in her husband.

Their relation to their husbands is of a symbiotic, parasitic type. They suffer from the narcissistic problem of low self-esteem. They do not experience a fixed, firm, stable personality of their own as distinct from the need-satisfying object. . . .[12]

In her novel *The Bell Jar,* based on her own life, Sylvia Plath, a renowned writer and herself later a suicide, describes the breakdown of the heroine, Esther. It is a tragic variation on the pathology emerging from the traditional feminine consciousness.

Esther hears from her boyfriend's mother that "what a man is, is an arrow into the future and what a woman is, is the place the arrow shoots off from." [13] The cause of her problems is the feminine conditioning that denied and degraded her total personhood. She is obsessed with the feeling that others will notice how stupid she is, and will be repulsed by her hairy legs and general ugliness.

In the process of trying to find the ideal man, who will love and rescue her, the same thing continually happens. "I would catch sight of some flawless man off in the distance, but as soon as he moved closer I immediately saw he wouldn't do at all." [14] Her endless struggle to find her identity is expressed through her constant self-assuring inner refrain "I am, I am, I am."

When the breakdown of a woman is accompanied by the direct acting out of rage toward her husband in the form of murder, it is with a guiltless sense of righteous anger. In *A Staff Report to the National Commission on the Causes and Prevention of Violence,* sociologist William Goode wrote, "Wives rarely commit suicide after committing homicide; the combination most often carried out by males. . . . The husband is more likely to feel guilt and remorse than wives do." [15]

The symptoms of a woman's emotional breakdown are but a logical extension of her femininity: a sense of having no identity ("I don't know who I am or what I want"), blaming rage toward the man in her life,

depression and feelings of helplessness, a host of psychosomatic symptoms, feelings of sexual repulsion and/or extreme frigidity, and a sense of confusion that makes her almost immobile.

When the male breaks down, his symptoms too are the inevitable outcome of his conditioning. The details are, however, more difficult to see and explore because he is embarrassed by weakness and so resists asking for help, is unable to readily perceive and articulate his deeper feelings, and tends to self-destruct through alcohol or direct suicide rather than express his conflict, rage, and pain openly. Nevertheless, the portrait of a traditional man in the process of breaking down would probably include:

• Feelings of extreme isolation and loneliness; a sense that nobody gives a damn about him.

• Fear of opening up lest he be seen as cowardly, weak, or a burden on others.

• Intense guilt about a multitude of things, in addition to feelings of being a failure.

• Great anxiety about his sexual capacities, adequacy, and performance.

• An attitude of extreme cynicism and despair.

• Physical debilitation, alcoholism, chain smoking, and so on. His physical condition, because of his distorted macho health consciousness, is badly damaged. He has stomach problems, hypertension, back problems, or overall enervation, and can't sleep or go to the bathroom properly.

• Hopelessness about ever getting help or effecting any change. He is resigned and feels defeated.

• Self-condemning inner ruminations, such as:

"My life is going nowhere."

"I haven't got enough money to do the things I really want."

"Other men are passing me by."

"If I had only tried harder when I had the chance."

"I am inferior."

"I am unlovable."

"I've destroyed everything that I've touched."

• Finally, bitterness because the promised rewards of being successful and living up to masculine expectations did not materialize. Indeed, he feels further away than ever from leading the life he envisions for himself. If his wife has left him, he may see no reason to continue. He feels his children hate him and condemn him for all the family problems. "They'd all be better off without me," he tells himself.

HIS "FEAR" OF AND HER "DESIRE" FOR INTIMACY

In the traditional depiction of the male-female relationship, the man is seen as fearing intimacy and loss of control, while the woman is seen as having a great capacity to commit herself, to love, and to be intimate.

Viewed, however, from the perspective of their conditioning, it becomes clear that neither the man nor the woman has the capacity for genuine intimacy. His "fear" of it and her "desire" for it are both distortions based on their gender conditioning and expectations. He fears losing control by getting close because he is subconsciously aware that he will be engulfed by her needs and the pressure to perform and take care of her, and will feel guilty if he fails.

In the process, he will lose the edge of excitement he originally had in the relationship, which was provided by distance and a sense of challenge. His resistance to intimacy and marriage is, therefore, healthy self-protection.

Likewise, her desire to be intimate cloaks her deeper sense of helplessness, repressed aggression, dependency, and anxiety about experiencing untrammeled sexuality. *What she really wants is not intimacy, but the fulfillment of her need to define her identity through him, to be taken care of and protected, and to have her sexuality legitimized by a "committed" relationship.*

Her capacity for real intimacy, therefore, is no greater than his; it simply has the appearance of being greater. The result of all this, however, is that the male is left with guilt, self-doubt, and self-hatred as he accuses himself and is accused by others of an inability to be loving; while the woman is left feeling frustrated, deprived, and resentful over her inability to find the deep, meaningful relationship that she imagines she wants and believes is available to her somewhere.

THE REAL DIFFERENCES BETWEEN MALE AND FEMALE

We are born male and female. We are socialized to become masculine and feminine. The common contention that the differences between men and women are deeply rooted in genetics and biology derails us from an awareness of how we prevent little boys and little girls from expressing their humanness to the fullest. If indeed we are programmed genetically to be masculine and feminine, then the programming is enormously damaging psychologically to men and women, and we need to question and work toward altering the destructive course we are on. Indeed, *a "healthy" relationship of genuine intimacy and growth becomes impossible in direct proportion to the degree a couple fits the ideal models of masculinity and femininity.*

The artifacts of conditioning known as masculinity and femininity can be seen as defensive reactions against oneself, because they often produce a sudden, dramatic reaction to the other extreme.

Mr. Autonomous emerges as a clinging, desperate baby.

Miss Helpless announces that no one will ever again control her.

Mr. Decisive is paralyzed with indecision.

Mrs. Sweetness becomes a raging fury with a guiltless capacity for homicide against her husband.

Mr. Animal Sex becomes unable to get an erection and is terrified by intercourse.

Ms. Passive, once divorced and on her own, works fulltime, goes to school, raises her children, and juggles several lovers.

Mr. Autonomy won't let his wife out of his sight and doesn't want to go on when she leaves.

Mrs. Dependent says, "I just need to be alone."

The defensiveness of masculinity and femininity produces a rigid balance between men and women, making change frightening and painful. It is, therefore, less threatening to rationalize that we are products of biological inevitability than to experience the anxiety and chaos involved in the process of growth.

A world of "machos" (masculine males) and "earth mothers" (feminine females),

however, is a world that keeps both sexes at a low level of human potential, causing men to be overtly self-destructive and women indirectly so. It distorts body (health) consciousness, makes the sexual experience stressful and threatening, and produces feelings of rage and helplessness in women and guilt, failure, and self-hatred in men. It blocks change in relationships and distorts the capacity to be aware of reality. It encourages parenting by unprepared, infantile men and women ("babies having babies"), turns men into machines, stunts women at the child level, and vastly accelerates the death process.

Footnotes

1. Ted Turner in Studs Terkel, *American Dreams* (New York: Pantheon Books, 1980), pp. 67–68.

2. Lee Hotz, "Asbestos Workers Find Payoff Is Disease, Death," *The Pittsburgh Press*, March 30, 1980, Section C, p. 1.

3. Bernard Lefkowitz, "Life Without Work," *Newsweek*, May 14, 1979, p. 31.

4. Una Stannard, "The Mask of Beauty," in *Woman in Sexist Society*, ed. by Vivian Gornick and Barbara K. Moran (New York: New American Library, 1971), p. 203.

5. Libby Severinghaus Warner, "Clare Boothe Luce Talks About Women and Success," *Bulletin of the Baldwin School*, Vol. 40, No. 5 (Sept. 1974), p. 1.

6. Pamela Butler, *Self-Assertion for Women: A Guide to Becoming Androgynous* (San Francisco: Canfield Press, 1976), p. 5.

7. Joseph J. Jaffa, letter to the editor, *Newsweek*, April 17, 1978, p. 8.

8. Evelyn P. Stevens, "Machismo and Marianismo," *Society*, Vol. 10 (Sept.-Oct. 1973), p. 58.

9. Sandra Lipsitz Bem, "Androgeny vs. the Tight Little Lives of Fluffy Women and Chesty Men," *Psychology Today*, Sept. 1975, p. 9.

10. J. Conrad Schwarz, "Childhood Origins of Psychopathology," *American Psychologist*, Vol. 34, No. 10 (Oct. 1979), p. 880.

11. Ibid.

12. Peter A. Martin, *A Marital Therapy Manual* (New York: Brunner/Mazel, 1976), pp. 16–17.

13. Sylvia Plath, *The Bell Jar* (New York: Bantam Books, 1975), p. 58.

14. Ibid., p. 67.

15. William Goode, *A Staff Report to the National Commission on the Causes and Prevention of Violence*, ed. by Donald J. Mulvihill and Melvin M. Tumin (Washington, D.C.: U.S. Government Printing Office, 1969), Vol. 13, Appendix 19.

Review Questions

1. Describe the traditional masculine role.
2. What problems do men have who try to play this role?
3. Describe the traditional feminine role.
4. What problems do women have who try to play this role?

Discussion Questions

1. Can men or women be happy playing traditional sex roles? Explain your answer.
2. Is there anything wrong with "role switching," that is, men playing a feminine role, and women playing a masculine role? Defend your answer.
3. How can men and women have a "healthy" relationship?

ANN FERGUSON

Androgyny As an Ideal
for Human Development

Ann Ferguson, "Androgyny As an Ideal for Human Development," from Mary Vetterling-Braggin, Frederick A. Elliston, and Jane English, eds., *Feminism and Philosophy*, Littlefield, Adams and Co., 1981, pp. 45–69.

Ann Ferguson teaches philosophy at the University of Massachusetts in Amherst.

Ferguson recommends androgyny as an ideal for human development rather than traditional sex roles. As she explains it, the ideal androgynous person would not be both masculine and feminine, but would transcend these categories, would be active and independent, with a desire to do autonomous and socially meaningful work, and would also want equal and loving relationships with others.

In this paper I shall defend androgyny as an ideal for human development. To do this I shall argue that male/female sex roles are neither inevitable results of "natural" biological differences between the sexes, nor socially desirable ways of socializing children in contemporary societies. In fact, the elimination of sex roles and the development of androgynous human beings is the most rational way to allow for the possibility of, on the one hand, love relations among equals, and on the other, development of the widest possible range of intense and satisfying social relationships between men and women.

ANDROGYNY: THE IDEAL DEFINED

The term "androgyny" has Greek roots: *andros* means man and *gyne*, woman. An androgynous person would combine some of each of the characteristic traits, skills, and interests that we now associate with the stereotypes of masculinity and femininity. It is not accurate to say that the ideal androgynous person would be both masculine and feminine, for there are negative and distorted personality characteristics associated in our minds with these ideas.[1] Furthermore, as we presently understand these stereotypes, they exclude each other. A masculine person is active, independent, aggressive (demanding), more self-interested than altruistic, competent and interested in physical activities, rational, emotionally controlled, and self-disciplined. A feminine person, on the other hand, is passive, dependent, nonassertive, more altruistic than self-interested (supportive of others), neither physically competent nor interested in becoming so, intuitive but not rational, emotionally open, and impulsive rather than self-disciplined. Since our present conceptions of masculinity and femininity thus defined exclude each other, we must think of an ideal androgynous person as one to whom these categories do not apply—one who is neither masculine nor feminine, but human: who transcends those old categories in such a way as to be able to develop positive human potentialities denied or only realized in an alienated fashion in the current stereotypes.

The ideal androgynous being, because of his or her combination of general traits, skills, and interests, would have no internal blocks to attaining self-esteem. He or she would have the desire and ability to do socially meaningful productive activity (work), as well as the desire and ability to be autonomous and to relate lovingly to other human beings. Of course, whether or not such an individual would be able to *achieve* a sense of autonomy, self-worth, and group contribution will depend importantly on the way the society in which he/she lives is structured. For example, in a classist society characterized by commodity production, none of these goals is attainable by anyone, no matter how androgynous, who comes from a class lacking the material resources to acquire (relatively) nonalienating work. In a racist and sexist society there are social roles and expectations placed upon the individual that present him/her with a conflict situation: either express this trait (skill, interest) and be considered a social deviant or outcast, or repress the trait and be socially accepted. The point, however, is that the androgynous person has the requisite skills and interests to be able to achieve these goals if only the society is organized appropriately.

LIMITS TO HUMAN DEVELOPMENT: THE NATURAL COMPLEMENT THEORY

There are two lines of objection that can be raised against the view that androgyny is an ideal for human development: first, that it is not possible, given the facts we know about human nature; and second, that even if it is possible, there is no reason to think it particularly desirable that people be socialized to develop the potential for androgyny. In this section I shall present and discuss Natural Complement theories of male/female human nature and the normative conclusions about sex roles.

There are two general facts about men and women and their roles in human societies that must be taken into account by any theory of what is possible in social organization of sex roles: first, the biological differences between men and women—in the bio-

logical reproduction of children, in relative physical strength, and in biological potential for aggressive (dominant, demanding) behavior; and second, the fact that all known human societies have had a sexual division of labor.

According to the Natural Complement theory, there are traits, capacities, and interests that inhere in men and women simply because of their biological differences, and that thus define what is normal "masculine" and normal "feminine" behavior. Since men are stronger than women, have bodies better adapted for running and throwing, and have higher amounts of the male hormone androgen, which is linked to aggressive behavior,[2] men have a greater capacity for heavy physical labor and for aggressive behavior (such as war). Thus it is natural that men are the breadwinners and play the active role in the production of commodities in society and in defending what the society sees as its interests in war. Since women bear children, it is natural that they have a maternal, nurturing instinct that enables them to be supportive of the needs of children, perceptive and sensitive to their needs, and intuitive in general in their understanding of the needs of people.

The Natural Complement theory about what men and women should do (their moral and spiritual duties, ideal love relations, etc.) is based on this conception of what are the fundamental biologically based differences between men and women. The universal human sexual division of labor is not only natural, but also desirable: men should work, provide for their families, and when necessary, make war; women should stay home, raise their children, and, with their greater emotionality and sensitivity, administer to the emotional needs of their men and children.

The ideal love relationship in the Natural Complement view is a heterosexual relationship in which man and woman complement each other. On this theory, woman needs man, and man, woman; they need each other essentially because together they form a whole being. Each of them is incomplete without the other; neither could meet all their survival and emotional needs alone. The woman needs the man as the active agent, rationally and bravely confronting nature and competitive social life, while the man needs the woman as his emotional guide, ministering to the needs he doesn't know he has himself, performing the same function for the children, and being the emotional nucleus of the family to harmonize all relationships. Love between man and woman is the attraction of complements, each being equally powerful and competent in his or her own sphere—man in the world, woman in the home—but each incompetent in the sphere of the other and therefore incomplete without the other.

The validity of the Natural Complement theory rests on the claim that there are some natural instincts (drives and abilities) inherent in men and women that are so powerful that they will determine the norm of masculine and feminine behavior for men and women under any conceivable cultural and economic conditions. That is, these natural instincts will determine not only what men and women can do well, but also what will be the most desirable (individually satisfying and socially productive) for them.

Even strong proponents of the Natural Complement theory have been uneasy with the evidence that in spite of "natural" differences between men and women, male and female sex roles are not inevitable. Not only are there always individual men and women whose abilities and inclinations make them exceptions to the sexual stereotypes in any particular society, but there is also a wide cross-cultural variation in just what work is considered masculine or feminine. Thus, although all known societies indeed do have a sexual division of labor, the evidence is that what behavior is considered masculine and what feminine is *learned* through socialization rather than mandated through biological instincts. So, for example, child care is said by the proponents of the Natural Complement theory to be women's work,

supposedly on the grounds that women have a natural maternal instinct that men lack, due to women's biological role in reproduction. And it is true that in the vast majority of societies in the sexual division of labor women do bear a prime responsibility for child care. However, there are some societies where that is not so. The Arapesh have both mother and father play an equally strong nurturant role.[3] A case of sex-role reversal in child care would be the fabled Amazons, in whose society those few men allowed to survive past infancy reared the children. In the case of the Amazons, whose historical existence may never be conclusively proved, what is important for the purposes of our argument is not the question of whether such a culture actually existed. Rather, insofar as it indicated that an alternative sexual division of labor was possible, the existence of the myth of the Amazon culture in early Western civilizations was an ongoing challenge to the Natural Complement theory.

It is not only the sexual division of labor in child care that varies from society to society, but also other social tasks. Natural Complement theorists are fond of arguing that because men are physically stronger than women and more aggressive, it is a natural division of labor for men to do the heavy physical work of society as well as that of defense and war. However, in practice, societies have varied immensely in the ways in which heavy physical work is parceled out. In some African societies, women do all the heavy work of carrying wood and water, and in most South American countries Indian men and women share these physical chores. In Russia, women do the heavy manual labor involved in construction jobs, while men do the comparatively light (but higher-status) jobs of running the machinery.[4] In predominantly agricultural societies, women's work overlaps men's. From early American colonial times, farm women had to be prepared to fight native American Indians and work the land in cooperation with men. Israeli women make as aggressive and dedicated soldiers as Israeli men. Furthermore, if we pick any *one* of the traits supposed to be primarily masculine (e.g., competitiveness, aggressiveness, egotism), we will find not only whole societies of both men *and* women who seem to lack these traits, but also whole societies that exhibit them.[5]

Further evidence that general sex-linked personality traits are learned social roles rather than inevitable biological developments is found in studies done on hermaphrodites.[6] When children who are biological girls, but because of vestigial penises are mistaken for boys, are trained into male sex roles, they develop the cultural traits associated with males in their society and seem to be well adjusted to their roles.

Faced with the variability of the sexual division of labor and the evidence that human beings as social animals develop their self-concept and their sense of values from imitating models in their community rather than from innate biological urges, the Natural Complement theorists fall back on the thesis that complementary roles for men and women, while not inevitable, are desirable. Two examples of this approach are found in the writings of Jean-Jacques Rousseau (in *Émile*) and in the contemporary writer George Gilder (in *Sexual Suicide*).[7] Both of these men are clearly male supremacists in that they feel women ought to be taught to serve, nurture, and support men.[8] What is ironic about their arguments is their belief in the biological inferiority of men, stated explicitly in Gilder and implicitly in Rousseau. Rousseau's train of reasoning suggests that men can't be nurturant and emotionally sensitive the way women can, so if we train women to be capable of abstract reasoning, to be self-interested and assertive, women will be able to do both male and female roles, and what will be left, then, for men to excel at? Gilder feels that men need to be socialized to be the breadwinners for children and a nurturant wife, because otherwise men's aggressive and competitive tendencies would make it impossible for them to cooperate in productive social work.

The desirability of complementary sex roles is maintained from a somewhat different set of premises in Lionel Tiger's book *Men in Groups*.[9] Tiger argues that the earliest sexual division of labor in hunting and gathering societies required men to develop a cooperative division of tasks in order to achieve success in hunting. Therefore, men evolved a biological predisposition toward "male bonding" (banding together into all-male cohort groups) that women lack (presumably because activities like gathering and child care didn't require a cooperative division of tasks that would develop female bonding). Because of this lack of bonding, women are doomed to subjection by men, for this biological asset of men is a trait necessary for achieving political and social power.

It is hard to take these arguments seriously. Obviously, they are biased toward what would promote male interests, and give little consideration to female interests. Also, they reject an androgynous ideal for human development, male and female, merely on the presumption that biological lacks in either men or women make it an unattainable ideal. It simply flies in the face of counter-evidence (for example, single fathers in our society) to argue as Gilder does that men will not be providers and relate to family duties of socializing children unless women center their life around the nurturing of men. And to argue as Tiger does that women cannot bond ignores not only the present example of the autonomous women's movement, but also ethnographic examples of women acting as a solidarity group in opposing men. The women of the Ba-Ila in southern Africa may collectively refuse to work if one has a grievance against a man.[10] A more likely theory of bonding seems to be that it is not biologically based, but learned through the organization of productive and reproductive work.

HISTORICAL MATERIALIST EXPLANATIONS OF SEX ROLES

Even if we reject the Natural Complement theory's claims that sex roles are either inevitable or desirable, we still have to explain the persistence, through most known societies, of a sexual division of labor and related sexual stereotypes of masculine and feminine behavior. This is due, I shall maintain, to patriarchal power relations between men and women based initially on men's biological advantages in two areas: that women are the biological reproducers of children, and that men as a biological caste are, by and large, physically stronger than women.[11] As Shulamith Firestone argues in *The Dialectic of Sex* and Simone de Beauvoir suggests in *The Second Sex*, the fact that women bear children from their bodies subjects them to the physical weaknesses and constraints that pregnancy and childbirth involve. Being incapacitated for periods of time makes them dependent on men (or at least the community) for physical survival in a way not reciprocated by men. Breastfeeding children, which in early societies continued until the children were five or six years old, meant that women could not hunt or engage in war. Men have both physical and social advantages over women because of their biological reproductive role and the fact that allocating childrearing to women is the most socially efficient division of reproductive labor in societies with scarce material resources. Thus, in social situations in which men come to perceive their interests to lie in making women subservient to them, men have the edge in a power struggle based on sexual caste.

It is important to note at this point, however, that these biological differences between men and women are only *conditions* that may be *used* against women by men in certain economic and political organizations of society and in social roles. They are like *tools* rather than mandates. A tool is only justified if you agree with both the tool's efficiency and the worth of the task that it is being used for, given other available options in achieving the task. In a society with few material resources and no available means of birth control, the most efficient way of ensuring the reproduction of the next genera-

tion may be the sexual division of labor in which women, constantly subject to pregnancies, do the reproductive work of breast-feeding and raising the children, while the men engage in hunting, trading and defense. In a society like ours, on the other hand, where we have the technology and means to control births, feed babies on formula food, and combat physical strength with weapons, the continuation of the sexual division of labor can no longer be justified as the most efficient mode for organizing reproductive work.

It seems that we should look for a social explanation for the continued underdevelopment and unavailability of the material resources for easing women's reproductive burden. This lack is due, I maintain, to a social organization of the forces of reproduction that perpetuates the sexual division of labor at home and in the job market, and thus benefits the perceived interests of men, not women.

The two biological disadvantages of women, relative male strength and the female role in biological reproduction, explain the persistence of the sexual division of labor and the sexual stereotypes based on this. Variations in the stereotypes seem to relate fairly directly to the power women have relative to men in the particular society. This, in turn, depends on the mode of production of the society and whether or not women's reproductive work of raising children is in conflict with their gaining any power in the social relations of production.

There are disagreements between anthropological theorists as to whether early human history contained matriarchal societies, in which bloodlines and property were traced through the maternal side and in which women had the edge over men in political and economic power. Early theorists like Engels and Morgan [12] argue that the social organization of the family and women's power in society is directly related to women's role in production. In primitive hunting-and-gathering and agricultural societies, organization of production is communal and tribal. Women have a central role in production and reproduction, there is no separation of productive work from home and reproductive work, and bloodlines are matrilineal. Moreover, Engels uses examples like the Iroquois Indians, and Bachofen, myths of powerful goddesses, to argue that these societies were not just matrilineal but also matriarchal. According to Engels' theory, the "world-historical defeat of the female sex" came when the mode of production changed to an animal-herding economy, and the sexual division of labor gave men control over production and over any surplus. Men thus gained political and economic power over women, whose productive and reproductive work was concentrated on production for use in the home rather than for exchange.

Engels' theory is somewhat too simple. It doesn't sufficiently account for the fact that in *any* noncommunal mode of production, the ability to control biological reproduction (progeny, future labor power) is a material power to be struggled for, and that there will be a dialectical struggle to control both production and reproduction in all but the most simple tribal societies.[13] It also doesn't take into account the possibility that even in communal modes of production there may be patriarchal power relations between men and women caused by male fear of women's biological ability to reproduce. This may result in "womb-envy," and in male attempts to compensate for women's reproductive power by setting up male-dominated areas in economic, political, and religious relations.[14]

Whatever the origin of the power struggle between men and women to control reproduction, the fact seems to be that the degree of a woman's oppression in a society is related to the amount of power she has at any particular historical period in the relations of reproduction in the family as well as the relations of production in society. Her oppression is thus relative to her class position as well as to her power in relation to men in her family.

There is no easy formula by which to determine the amount of power women have by simply looking at how much productive work and child care they do relative to men in a certain historical period. What is important is not the *amount* of work done, but the control a woman has over her work and the kind of independence this control offers her in the case of actual or potential conflicts with men over how the work should be done. Thus, although American slave women did as much productive work as slave men, and were almost totally responsible for the child care not only for their own children but for those of the plantation owner as well, slave women had no control over this work. Their children could be sold away from them, and they could be brutally punished if they refused to do the work assigned them by their masters. The lady of the plantation, on the other hand, did little productive work. She was more in a managerial position, usually responsible for managing the health care, clothing, and food of the slaves. She usually had little say in economic decisions about the plantation, since she was not considered a joint owner. On the other hand, the Victorian sexual division of labor and the Cult of True Womanhood gave the wealthy white woman almost total control over her children in decisions about childrearing. Relative to her husband, all in all, she had less power; relative to her female slave she had more; and her female slave in turn had more power than the male slave because of her central role in childrearing and the greater likelihood that fathers rather than mothers would be sold away from children.

THE SOCIAL ARTICULATION OF THE NATURAL COMPLEMENT THEORY

If we look at the beliefs of different societies about the proper roles for men and women, we note that these beliefs vary widely. We also see that societies always tend to appeal to the Natural Complement theory to back up their socially relative allocations of sex roles. The question arises, then: why, in the light of this obvious social variation, do people *persist* in clinging to the belief that there are inherent natural roles for men and women?

It would be simplistic to maintain that the ideology of sex roles directly reflects the degree of women's power in relation to men at a given historical period in a society. The Medieval religious view of women was extremely low,[15] yet there is evidence that women had more power than the simple reflective view of ideology would lead us to believe. In fact, there were women who were sheriffs, innkeepers, and managers of large households. The elevation of the Virgin Mary as the ideal woman on a pedestal seems to contradict the other elements in the Medieval religious view of women, and, indeed, it should make us wary of assuming a one-to-one correlation between ideology and reality. So, for example, nineteenth century Americans placed women on a pedestal where they were considered morally superior to men, but this, ironically, was in an economic, legal, and political context where they had less power than their Puritan ancestors.[16] Middle-class women had no role in commodity production, which had become the dominant mode of production in the nineteenth century. Women could not own property if they were married, nor receive an education, nor hold political office, nor vote. Their husbands had complete legal control over children in case of divorce.

There is a more plausible way to understand how the ideology of sex roles is connected to the actual social and historical roles of men and women. Sex-role ideologies mystify the existing power relations between men and women and economic classes. This mystification justifies the social and economic roles of two dominant groups: men as a caste, on the one hand, and the dominant economic class on the other.

If we look at nineteenth century America, we see the prevailing ideology, which held that women are too frail, "moral," and emotional to take part in commodity production (the amoral, competitive world of business). This ideology ignored the reality of black slave women, treated the same as male slaves and forced to do field work under brutal conditions. It ignored immigrant women, who worked long hours in crowded factories under conditions that caused many sicknesses and deaths. And it ignored farm women, who continued production for use on the farm. These working women made up the majority of the female population, yet the reality of their productive role was overlooked.

Why? A number of factors seem to be at work here. All end by supporting the interests and maintaining the status-quo power relations of the white male bourgeoisie. The first factor was the need to pacify bourgeois wives, whose role in production had evaporated but who were crucial to maintaining the system by lending emotional support and being subservient to their husbands, and by training their children, the future owners and controllers of capital. There was also a need for the bourgeois male to justify his position of dominance over his wife in legal, political, and financial matters. Second, the hierarchical control that the bourgeois male enjoyed over men of the lower classes was seen as inevitable (after all, it is masculine nature to be competitive and avaricious, and may the best man win!). Third, lower-class working women were thought to be fallen women, degraded and unnatural because of their role in production, and this conveniently made them free targets for bourgeois men (with their "natural" sexual appetites) to lure into prostitution. Finally, as production became more alienating, hierarchical, and competitive, working-class men as well needed the haven of women's emotional support and also the male dominance that being the breadwinner allowed them. As a result, both the men and the women of the working class struggled to achieve the ideal complementary sex-role relationships of woman-at-home/man-as-breadwinner that the Cult of True Womanhood assumed.

CONCLUSIONS ABOUT THE
NATURAL COMPLEMENT THEORY

We have discussed several different views of the "natural" sex differences between men and women prevalent in different historical periods. When we observe the shift in ideology as to what constitutes "true" female and male nature, we note that the shift has nothing to do with the further scientific discovery of biological differences between men and women. It seems rather to correlate to changes in the relation between men's and women's roles in production and reproduction, and to what serves the interests of the dominant male economic class. Given this fact of its ideological role, the Natural Complement theory, and any other static universal theory of what the "natural relationship" of man to woman should be, loses credibility.

Instead, it seems more plausible to assume that human nature is plastic and moldable, and that women and men develop their sexual identities, their sense of self, and their motivations through responding to the social expectations placed upon them. They develop the skills and personality traits necessary to carry out the productive and reproductive roles available to them in their sociohistorical context, given their sex, race, ethnic identity, and class background.

If we wish to develop a realistic ideal for human development, then, we cannot take the existing traits that differentiate men from women in this society as norms for behavior. Neither can we expect to find an ideal in some biological male and female substratum, after we strip away all the socialization processes we go through to develop our egos. Rather, with the present-day women's movement, we should ask: what traits are desirable and possible to teach people in order for them to reach their full individual human potential? And how would our society have to restructure its productive and reproductive relations in order to allow people to develop in this way?

AN IDEAL LOVE RELATIONSHIP

One argument for the development of androgynous personalities (and the accompanying destruction of the sexual division of labor in production and reproduction) is that without such a radical change in male and female roles an ideal love relationship between the sexes is not possible. The argument goes like this. An ideal love between two mature people would be love between equals. I assume that such an ideal is the only concept of love that is historically compatible with our other developed ideals of political and social equality. But, as Shulamith Firestone argues,[17] an equal love relationship requires the vulnerability of each partner to the other. There is today, however, an unequal balance of power in male-female relationships. Contrary to the claims of the Natural Complement theory, it is not possible for men and women to be equal while playing the complementary sex roles taught in our society. The feminine role makes a woman less equal, less powerful, and less free than the masculine role makes men. In fact, it is the emotional understanding of this lack of equality in love relations between men and women that increasingly influences feminists to choose lesbian love relationships.

Let us consider the vulnerabilities of women in a heterosexual love relationship under the four classifications Juliet Mitchell gives for women's roles:[18] production, reproduction, socialization of children, and sexuality.

1. *Women's role in production.* In the United States today, forty-two percent of women work, and about thirty-three percent of married women work in the wage-labor force. This is much higher than the six percent of women in the wage-labor force around the turn of the century, and higher than in other industrialized countries. Nonetheless, sex-role socialization affects women's power in two important ways. First, because of job segregation by sex into part-time and low-paying jobs, women, whether single or married, are at an economic disadvantage in comparison with men

when it comes to supporting themselves. If they leave their husbands or lovers, they drop to a lower economic class, and many have to go on welfare. Second, women who have children and who also work in the wage-labor force have two jobs, not one: the responsibility for the major part of childraising and housework, as well as the outside job. This keeps many housewives from seeking outside jobs, and makes them economically dependent on their husbands. Those who do work outside the home expend twice as much energy as the man and are less secure. Many women who try to combine career and motherhood find that the demands of both undermine their egos because they don't feel that they can do both jobs adequately.[19]

2. *Women's role in reproduction.* Although women currently monopolize the means of biological reproduction, they are at a disadvantage because of the absence of free contraceptives, adequate health care, and free legal abortions. A man can enjoy sex without having to worry about the consequences the way a woman does if a mistake occurs and she becomes pregnant. Women have some compensation in the fact that in the United States today they are favored legally over the father in their right to control of the children in case of separation or divorce. But this legal advantage (a victory won by women in the early twentieth century in the ongoing power struggle between the sexes for control of children, i.e., control over social reproduction) does not adequately compensate for the disadvantages to which motherhood subjects one in this society.

3. *Women's role in socialization: as wife and mother.* The social status of women, and hence their self-esteem, is measured primarily in terms of how successful they are in their relationships as lovers, wives, and mothers. Unlike men, who learn that their major social definition is success in work, women are taught from childhood that their ultimate goal is love and marriage. Women thus have more invested in a love relation-

ship than men, and more to lose if it fails. The "old maid" or the "divorcee" is still an inferior status to be pitied, while the "swinging bachelor" is rather envied.

The fact that men achieve self- and social definition from their work means that they can feel a lesser commitment to working out problems in a relationship. Furthermore, men have more options for new relationships than do women. The double standard in sexuality allows a man to have affairs more readily than his wife. Ageism is a further limitation on women: an older man is considered a possible lover by both younger and older women, but an older woman, because she is no longer the "ideal" sex object, is not usually considered a desirable lover by either male peers or by younger men.

A woman's role as mother places her in a more vulnerable position than the man. Taking care of children and being attentive to their emotional needs is very demanding work. Many times it involves conflicts between the woman's own needs and the needs of the child. Often it involves conflict and jealousy between husband and children for her attention and emotional energy. It is the woman's role to harmonize this conflict, which she often does at the expense of herself, sacrificing her private time and interests in order to provide support for the projects of her husband and children.

No matter how devoted a parent a father is, he tends to see his time with the children as play time, not as work time. His job interests and hobbies take precedence over directing his energy to children. Thus he is more independent than the woman, who sees her job as making husband and children happy. This is the sort of job that is never completed, for there are always more ways to make people happy. Because a woman sees her job to be supporting her husband and mothering her children, the woman sees the family as her main "product." This makes her dependent on their activities, lives, and successes for her own success, and she lives vicariously through their activities.

But as her "product" is human beings, when the children leave, as they must, to live independent lives, middle age brings an end to her main social function. The woman who has a career has other problems, for she has had to support her husband's career over hers wherever there was a conflict, because she knows male egos are tied up with success and "making it" in this competitive society. Women's egos, on the other hand, are primed for failure. Successful women, especially successful women with unsuccessful husbands, are considered not "true" women, but rather as deviants, "castrating bitches," "ballbusters," and "masculine women." For all these reasons, a woman in a love relationship with a man is geared by the Natural Complement view of herself as a woman to put her interests last, to define herself in terms of husband and children, and therefore to be more dependent on them than they are on her.

A woman is also vulnerable in her role as mother because there are limited alternatives if, for example, she wishes to break of her relationship with the father of her children. As a mother, her social role in bringing up children is defined as more important, more essential for the well-being of the children than the man's. Therefore, she is expected to take the children to live with her, or else she is considered a failure as a mother. But the life of a divorced or single mother with children in a nuclear-family-oriented society is lonely and hard; she must now either do two jobs without the companionship of another adult, in a society where jobs for women are inadequate, or she must survive on welfare or alimony with a reduced standard of living. When this is the alternative, is it any wonder that mothers are more dependent on maintaining a relationship—even when it is not satisfying—than the man is?

4. *Women's role in sexuality.* A woman's sexual role is one in which she is both elevated by erotic romanticism and deflated to being a mere "cunt"—good for release of male sexual passions but interchangeable with other women. Because women play a subordinate role in society and are not seen as equal agents or as equally productive, men must justify a relationship with a particular woman by making her something special, mystifying her, making her better than other women. In fact, this idealization doesn't deal with her as a real *individual;* it treats her as either a beautiful object or as a mothering, supportive figure.

This idealization of women, which occurs in the first stages of infatuation, wears off as the couple settles into a relationship of some duration. What is left is the idea of woman as passive sex object whom one possesses and whose job as wife is to give the husband pleasure in bed. Since the woman is not seen as (and doesn't usually see herself as) active in sex, she tends to see sex as a duty rather than as a pleasure. She is not socially expected to take the active kind of initiative (even to the extent of asking for a certain kind of sex play) that would give her a sense of control over her sex life. The idea of herself as a body to be dressed and clothed in the latest media-advertised fashions "to please men" keeps her a slave to fashion and forces her to change her ego-ideal with every change in fashion. She can't see herself as an individual.

ANDROGYNY AS A PROGRESSIVE IDEAL

It is the sexual division of labor in the home and at work that perpetuates complementary sex roles for men and women. In underdeveloped societies with scarce material resources such an arrangement may indeed be the most rational way to allow for the most efficient raising of children and production of goods. But this is no longer true for developed societies. In this age of advanced technology, men's relative strength compared to women's is no longer important, either in war or in the production of goods. The gun and the spinning jenny have equalized the potential role of men and women in both repression and production. And the diaphragm, the pill, and other advances in the technology of reproduction have equalized the potential power of women and men to control their bodies and to reproduce themselves.[20] (The development of cloning would mean that men and women could reproduce without the participation of the opposite sex.)

We have seen how complementary sex roles and their extension to job segregation in wage labor make an ideal love relationship between equals impossible for men and women in our society. The questions that remain are: would the development of androgynous human beings through androgynous sex-role training be possible? If possible, would it allow for the development of equal love relationships? What other human potentials would androgyny allow to develop? And how would society have to be restructured in order to allow for androgynous human beings and equal love relationships?

There is good evidence that human babies are bisexual, and only *learn* a specific male or female identity by imitating and identifying with adult models. This evidence comes from the discovery that all human beings possess both male and female hormones (androgen and estrogen respectively), and also from concepts first developed at length by Freud. Freud argued that heterosexual identity is not achieved until the third stage of the child's sexual development. Sex identity is developed through the resolution of the Oedipus complex, in which the child has to give up a primary attachment to the mother and learn either to identify with, or love, the father. But Shulamith Firestone suggests that this process is not an inevitable one, as Freud presents it to be. Rather, it is due to the power dynamics of the patriarchal nuclear family.[21] Note that, on this analysis, if the sexual division of labor were destroyed, the mechanism that trains boys and girls to develop heterosexual sexual identities would also be destroyed. If fathers and mothers played equal nurturant roles in childrearing and had equal social, economic, and political power outside the home, there would be no

reason for the boy to have to reject his emotional side in order to gain the power associated with the male role. Neither would the girl have to assume a female role in rejecting her assertive, independent side in order to attain power indirectly through manipulation of males. As a sexual identity, bisexuality would then be the norm rather than the exception.

If bisexuality were the norm rather than the exception for the sexual identities that children develop,[22] androgynous sex roles would certainly be a consequence. For, as discussed above, the primary mechanism whereby complementary rather than androgynous sex roles are maintained is through heterosexual training, and through the socialization of needs for love and sexual gratification to the search for a love partner of the opposite sex. Such a partner is sought to complement one in the traits that one has repressed or not developed because in one's own sex such traits were not socially accepted.

THE ANDROGYNOUS MODEL

I believe that only androgynous people can attain the full human potential possible given our present level of material and social resources (and this only if society is radically restructured). Only such people can have ideal love relationships; and without such relationships, I maintain that none can develop to the fullest potential. Since human beings are social animals and develop through interaction and productive activity with others, such relationships are necessary.

Furthermore, recent studies have shown that the human brain has two distinct functions: one associated with analytic, logical, sequential thinking (the left brain), and the other associated with holistic, metaphorical, intuitive thought (the right brain). Only a person capable of tapping both these sides of him/herself will have developed to full potential. We might call this characteristic of the human brain "psychic bisexuality,"[23] since it has been shown that women in fact have developed skills that allow them to tap the abilities of the right side of the brain more than men, who on the contrary excel in the analytic, logical thought characteristic of the left side. The point is that men and women have the potential for using both these functions, and yet our socialization at present tends to cut off from one or the other of these parts of ourselves.[24]

What would an androgynous personality be like? My model for the ideal androgynous person comes from the concept of human potential developed by Marx in *Economic and Philosophical Manuscripts*. Marx's idea is that human beings have a need (or a potential) for free, creative, productive activity that allows them to control their lives in a situation of cooperation with others. Both men and women need to be equally active and independent; with an equal sense of control over their lives; equal opportunity for creative, productive activity; and a sense of meaningful involvement in the community.

Androgynous women would be just as assertive as men about their own needs in a love relationship: productive activity outside the home, the right to private time, and the freedom to form other intimate personal and sexual relationships. I maintain that being active and assertive—traits now associated with being "masculine"—are positive traits that all people need to develop. Many feminists are suspicious of the idea of self-assertion because it is associated with the traits of aggression and competitiveness. However, there is no inevitability to this connection: it results from the structural features of competitive, hierarchical economic systems, of which our own (monopoly capitalism) is one example. In principle, given the appropriate social structure, there is no reason why a self-assertive person cannot also be nurturant and cooperative.

Androgynous men would be more sensitive and aware of emotions than sex-role stereotyped "masculine" men are today. They would be more concerned with the feelings of all people, including women and children, and aware of conflicts of interests. Being sensitive to human emotions is necessary to an effective care and concern for others. Such sensitivity is now thought of as a "motherly," "feminine," or "maternal" instinct, but in fact it is a role and skill learned by women, and it can equally well be learned by men. Men need to get in touch with their own feelings in order to empathize with others, and, indeed, to understand themselves better so as to be more in control of their actions.

We have already discussed the fact that women are more vulnerable in a love relationship than men because many men consider a concern with feelings and emotions to be part of the woman's role. Women, then, are required to be more aware of everyone's feelings (if children and third parties are involved) than men, and they are under more pressure to harmonize the conflicts by sacrificing their own interests.

Another important problem with a nonandrogynous love relationship is that it limits the development of mutual understanding. In general, it seems true that the more levels people can relate on, the deeper and more intimate their relationship is. The more experiences and activities they share, the greater their companionship and meaning to each other. And this is true for emotional experiences. Without mutual understanding of the complex of emotions involved in an ongoing love relationship, communication and growth on that level are blocked for both people. This means that, for both people, self-development of the sort that could come from the shared activity of understanding and struggling to deal with conflicts will not be possible.

In our society as presently structured, there are few possibilities for men and women to develop themselves through shared activities. Men and women share more activities with members of their own sex than with each other. Most women can't get jobs in our sexist, job-segregated society that allow them to share productive work with men. Most men just don't have the skills (or the time, given the demands of their wage-labor jobs) to understand the emotional needs of children and to share the activity of childrearing equally with their wives.

How must our society be restructured to allow for the development of androgynous personalities? How can it be made to provide for self-development through the shared activities of productive and reproductive work? I maintain that this will not be possible (except for a small privileged elite) without the development of a democratic socialist society. In such a society no one would benefit from cheap labor (presently provided to the capitalist class by a part-time reserve army of women). Nor would anyone benefit from hierarchical power relationships (which encourage competition among the working class and reinforce male sex-role stereotypes as necessary to "making it" in society).

As society is presently constituted, the patriarchal nuclear family and women's reproductive work therein serve several crucial roles in maintaining the capitalist system. In the family women do the unpaid work of social reproduction of the labor force (childrearing). They also pacify and support the male breadwinner in an alienating society where men who are not in the capitalist class have little control of their product or work conditions. Men even come to envy their wives' relatively nonalienated labor in childrearing rather than dealing with those with the real privilege, the capitalist class. Since those in power relations never give them up without a struggle, it is utopian to think that the capitalist class will allow for the elimination of the sexual division of labor without a socialist revolution with feminist priorities. Furthermore, men in the professional and working classes must be challenged by women with both a class and feminist consciousness to begin the process of change.

In order to eliminate the subordination of women in the patriarchal nuclear family and the perpetuation of sex-role stereotypes therein, there will need to be a radical reorganization of childrearing. Father and mother must have an equal commitment to raising children. More of the reproductive work must be socialized—for example, by community child care, perhaps with parent cooperatives. Communal living is one obvious alternative that would de-emphasize biological parenthood and allow homosexuals and bisexuals the opportunity to have an equal part in relating to children. The increased socialization of child care would allow parents who are incompatible the freedom to dissolve their relationships without denying their children the secure, permanent loving relationships they need with both men and women. A community responsibility for childrearing would provide children with male and female models other than their biological parent—models that they would be able to see and relate to emotionally.

Not only would men and women feel an equal responsibility to do reproductive work, they would also expect to do rewarding, productive work in a situation where they had equal opportunity. Such a situation would of course require reduced workweeks for parents, maternity and paternity leaves, and the development of a technology of reproduction that would allow women complete control over their bodies.

As for love relationships, with the elimination of sex roles and the disappearance, in an overpopulated world, of any biological need for sex to be associated with procreation, there would be no reason why such a society could not transcend sexual gender. It would no longer matter what biological sex individuals had. Love relationships, and the sexual relationships developing out of them, would be based on the individual meshing-together of androgynous human beings.

Footnotes

1. I owe these thoughts to Jean Elshtain and members of the Valley Women's Union in Northampton, Massachusetts, from discussions on androgyny.

2. See Roger Brown, *Social Psychology* (New York: Free Press, 1965).

3. For information on the Arapesh and variations in male/female roles in primitive societies, see Margaret Mead, *Sex and Temperament* (New York: William Morrow, 1963).

4. See "The Political Economy of Women," *Review of Radical Political Economics*, Summer 1973.

5. Contrast the Stone Age tribe recently discovered in the Philippines, where competition is unknown, with the competitive male and female Dobus from Melanesia. See Ruth Benedict, *Patterns of Culture* (Boston: Houghton Mifflin, 1934).

6. See Eleanor E. Maccoby, ed., *The Development of Sex Differences* (Stanford, CA: Stanford University Press, 1966).

7. George Gilder, *Sexual Suicide* (New York: Bantam Books, 1973).

8. Rousseau says, in a typical passage from *Émile*, "When once it is proved that men and women are and ought to be unlike in constitution and in temperament, it follows that their education should be different." And on a succeeding page he concludes, "A woman's education must therefore be planned in relation to man. To be pleasing in his sight, to win his respect and love, to train him in childhood, to tend him in manhood, to counsel and console, to make his life pleasant and happy, these are the duties of woman for all time, and this is what she should be taught while she is young. The further we depart from this principle, the further we shall be from our own good, and all our precepts will fail to secure her happiness or our own" (trans. Barbara Foxley [New York: E.P. Dutton, 1911] pp. 326, 328).

Gilder's conclusion is as follows: "But at a profounder level the women are tragically wrong. For they fail to understand their own sexual power; and they fail to perceive the sexual constitution of our society, or if they see it, they underestimate its importance to our civilization and to their own interest in order and stability. In general across the whole range of the society, marriage and careers—and thus social order—will be best served if most men have a position of economic superiority over the relevant women in his [*sic*] community and if in most jobs in which colleagues must work together, the sexes tend to be segregated either by level or function." *Sexual Suicide*, p. 108.

9. Lionel Tiger, *Men in Groups* (New York: Random House, 1969).

10. Edwin W. Smith and Andrew M. Dale, *The Ila-Speaking Peoples of Northern Rhodesia* (London: Macmillan, 1920).

11. It is not simply the fact that men are physically stronger than women which gives them the edge in sexual power relations. It is also women's lesser psychological capacity for violence and aggressiveness. However, this has as much to do with socialization into passive roles from early childhood as it does with any inequality in the amount of the male hormone androgen, which is correlated to aggressive behavior in higher primates. As Simone de Beauvoir points out in *The Second Sex* (New York: Knopf, 1953), male children develop training in aggressive behavior from an early age, while female children are kept from the psychological hardening process involved in physical fights. Feeling that one is by nature submissive will cause one to be submissive; so even women who are equal in strength to men will appear to themselves and to men not to be so.

12. See Friedrich Engels, *The Origin of the Family, Private Property and the State* (New York: International Publishers, 1942); also Lewis Morgan, *Ancient Society*, ed. Eleanor Leacock (New York: World Publishing Co., 1963).

13. Perhaps part of the reason for the solidarity in these societies is due to the meager resources to be struggled for.

14. Karen Horney develops this theory in her book *Feminine Psychology* (New York: W.W. Norton, 1967); as does Eva Figes in *Patriarchal Attitudes* (New York: Stein & Day, 1970). Note the striking difference between Horney's and Tiger's (op. cit.) explanations of the phenomenon of male bonding.

15. Catholic Church doctrine maintains a dualism between soul and body. The soul is thought to be rational and spiritual, the valuable part of the self that loves God; while the body is sinful, animal, given to sexual lusts and passions. Women are identified with the body because of their childbearing function, hence with sexuality, evil, and the devil. (The story of Eve in Genesis was used to support this view.) It is women who lead men away from the pure spiritual life and into the evils of sexuality; they are thus inferior beings whose only positive function is the reproduction of children. Even in this role they are merely receptacles, for the theory of reproduction is that woman is the lowly, unclean vessel into which man puts the seed of life.

16. In the Cult of True Womanhood prevalent in America and England in the nineteenth century, women are thought to be passive and emotional but *not* sexual or tied to the body. Rather, the woman is the moral and spiritual guardian of the male, who is thought to be more naturally sinful than she—avaricious, competitive, self-interested, and imbued with sexual passions. The one sphere, then, in which woman is thought to be naturally skilled is the home and the spiritual education of children and husband.

17. Shulamith Firestone, *The Dialectic of Sex* (New York: William Morrow, 1970), chap. 6.

18. Juliet Mitchell, *Woman's Estate* (New York: Random House, 1971).

19. Socialization into complementary sex roles is responsible not only for job segregation practices' keeping women in low-paid service jobs that are extensions of the supportive work women do in the home as mothers, but also for making it difficult for women to feel confident in their ability to excel at competitive "male-defined" jobs.

20. Thanks to Sam Bowles for this point.

21. Firestone, op. cit. The boy and girl both realize that the father has power in the relationship between him and the mother, and that his role, and not the mother's, represents the possibility of achieving economic and social power in the world and over one's life. The mother, in contrast, represents nurturing and emotionality. Both boy and girl, then, in order to get power for themselves, have to reject the mother as a love object—the boy, because he is afraid of the father as rival and potential castrator, and the girl, because the only way as a girl she can attain power is through manipulating the father. So she becomes a rival to her mother for her father's love. The girl comes to identify with her mother and to choose her father and, later, other men for love objects; while the boy identifies with his father, sublimates his sexual attraction to his mother into super-ego (will power), and chooses mother substitutes, other women, for his love objects.

22. It should be understood here that no claim is being made that bisexuality is more desirable than homo- or heterosexuality. The point is that with the removal of the social mechanisms in the family that channel children into heterosexuality, there is no reason to suppose that most of them will develop in that direction. It would be more likely that humans with androgynous personalities would be bisexual, the assumption here being that there are no innate biological preferences in people for sexual objects of the same or opposite sex. Rather, this comes to be developed because of emotional connections of certain sorts of personality characteristics with the male and female body, characteristics that develop because of complementary sex-role training, and that would not be present without it.

The other mechanism that influences people to develop a heterosexual identity is the desire to reproduce. As long as the social institution for raising children is the heterosexual nuclear family, and as long as society continues to place social value on biological parenthood, most children will develop a heterosexual identity. Not, perhaps, in early childhood, but certainly after puberty, when the question of reproduction becomes viable. Radical socialization and collectivization of childrearing would thus have to characterize a society before bisexuality would be the norm not only in early childhood, but in adulthood as well. For the purposes of developing androgynous individuals, however, full social bisexuality of this sort is not necessary. All that is needed is the restructuring of the sex roles of father and mother in the nuclear family so as to eliminate the sexual division of labor there.

23. Charlotte Painter, Afterword to C. Painter and M.J. Moffet, eds., *Relevations: Diaries of Women* (New York: Random House, 1975).

24. It is notable that writers, painters, and other intellectuals, who presumably would need skills of both sorts, have often been misfits in the prevalent complementary sex stereotyping. In fact, thinkers as diverse as Plato (in the *Syposium*) and Virginia Woolf (in *A Room of One's Own*) have suggested that writers and thinkers need to be androgynous to tap all the skills necessary for successful insight.

Review Questions

1. Describe the androgynous person.

2. Explain the Natural Complement theory.

3. Why aren't sex roles inevitable?

4. Why aren't sex roles desirable?

5. Why are sex roles found in most known societies?

6. Why do people persist in believing that there are natural roles for men and women?

7. What is wrong with the traditional male-female relationship?

8. Is it possible for human beings to attain the ideal of being androgynous? How?

Discussion Questions

1. Is the androgynous ideal preferable to traditional sex roles? Defend your position.

2. Is the communal living that Ferguson suggests really desirable or not? Explain your answer.

Problem Cases

1. The Equal Rights Amendment states that equality of rights under the law shall not be denied or abridged by the United States or by any state on account of sex. Should this amendment be passed or not? Defend your position.

2. At the 1984 summer Olympic Games held in Los Angeles, there was a ten-kilometer race for men but not for women. Thousands of women have run this distance and it is perhaps the most popular distance for long-distance running races. Is not having a ten-kilometer race for women at the Olympic Games justified or not? Explain your answer.

3. The current policy of the Air Force is that women are not allowed to fly combat jets. Is this policy justified or not? Why, or why not?

Suggested Readings

Jaggar, Alison. "Political Philosophies of Women's Liberation." In Mary Vetterling-Braggin, Frederick A. Elliston, and Jane English, eds., *Feminism and Philosophy*. Totowa, NJ: Littlefield, Adams and Co., 1977, pp. 5–21.

Trebilcot, Joyce. "Two Forms of Androgynism," *Journal of Social Philosophy* VIII (January 1977): 4–8. Trebilcot distinguishes between two forms of androgynism, monoandrogynism and polyandrogyism, and recommends the latter.

CHAPTER 7

Animals and the Environment

Basic Concepts

ANIMAL SUFFERING

Humans cause a great deal of animal suffering. Consider this example of animal experimentation taken from Peter Singer's book *Animal Liberation*. At the Lovelace Foundation in New Mexico experimenters forced sixty-four beagles to inhale radioactive strontium 90. Twenty-five of the dogs died, most of them after being feverish and anemic, and having hemorrhages and bloody diarrhea. One of the deaths occurred during an epileptic seizure, and another resulted from a brain hemorrhage. In a similar experiment, beagles were injected with enough strontium 90 to produce "early death" in fifty percent of the group. Are experiments such as these really necessary? It was already known that strontium 90 was unhealthy, and that the dogs would suffer and die. Furthermore, these experiments did not save any human lives or have any important benefits for humans. So why were they done?

Another common human practice that produces considerable animal suffering is factory farming. Take the treatment of veal calves for example. In order to make their flesh pale and tender, these calves are given special treatment. They are put in narrow stalls and tethered with a chain so that they cannot turn around, lie down comfortably, or groom themselves. They are fed a totally liquid diet to promote rapid weight gain. This diet is deficient in iron and, as a result, the calves lick the sides of the stall, which are impregnated with urine containing iron. They are given no water because thirsty animals eat more than those who drink water. Is this cruel treatment morally justified? Should we do this to animals just because we enjoy eating their flesh?

SPECIESISM

In his book *Animal Liberation*, Singer introduces the term "speciesism." As he defines it, speciesism is "a prejudice or attitude of bias toward the interests of members of one's own species and against those of members of other species." Singer goes on to argue that speciesism is analogous to racism and sexism. It is unjust to discriminate against blacks because of their color, or against women because of their sex. Their interests, e.g., their interest in voting, have to be considered equally to those of whites and men. Similarly, it is unjust to discriminate against nonhuman animals because of their species. Their interests, and particularly their interest in not suffering, have to be considered too.

But how do we go about reducing animal suffering? Does this mean that we should become vegetarians and eat no meat? Singer thinks so, but of course this is very controversial in our meat-eating society. In Singer's view we should stop eating meat in order to eliminate factory farming or at least to protest against it, and also because we should not treat animals as "means to our end." These arguments for vegetarianism are attacked by Leslie Pickering Francis and Richard Norman. Even though they agree that it is wrong to cause animal suffering, other things being equal, Francis and Norman do not agree that this principle requires us to embrace vegetarianism or abandon animal experimentation that serves human needs. They maintain that human beings can justifiably give more weight to their own interests than to animal interests because human beings have important relations to other human beings that they do not have to animals. Thus speciesism is justified to some extent, and it is not analogous to racism or sexism.

Tom Regan has a different view of the matter. He contends that the duty to become a vegetarian cannot be based on utilitarianism as Singer thinks. Utilitarianism is not an acceptable moral theory because it incorrectly makes the morality of individual acts depend on how others behave. Nevertheless, Regan does think that we ought to be vegetarians and oppose commercial animal agriculture. The reason for doing this is not that there will be good consequences, but because some animals are persons who have moral rights, and commercial animal agriculture violates these rights.

RIGHTS THEORY

In his defense of vegetarianism, Regan relies heavily on the concept of a moral right, but there is controversy about the meaning of the concept of a right and how it should be applied.

According to Joel Feinberg, "to have a right is to have a claim *to* something and *against* someone." On Feinberg's view, only beings who are capable of having interests are capable of having these claim-rights. But animals do have interests, and so they can have rights.

H.J. McCloskey has a different theory of rights. On McCloskey's analysis, a right is an entitlement to something and not a claim against someone. A person could have a right and not have a claim against someone else, for example, if he or she were the last person on earth. Furthermore, McCloskey holds that being able to make a claim, either directly or through a representative, is essential to the possession of rights. But since animals cannot do this, they cannot be possessors of rights.

Regan agrees with Feinberg that in order for an individual to have a right, there must be other people; it would not make sense to say that the last person on earth has any rights. On Regan's account, if an individual has a moral right, then there must be other moral agents who have a duty to respect it. But who possesses rights? Regan's answer is different from that of Feinberg and McCloskey. Regan's position is that only individuals who have "inherent value" have rights, where "inherent value" is a value that does not depend on utility. Those who have this

"inherent value" are persons, and according to Regan, some animals are persons who have rights.

SENTIENTISM

Both Singer and Regan assume that only beings with mental states are a subject of moral concern. But isn't this another kind of prejudice (which might be called "sentientism")? They have escaped one prejudice (speciesism) only to embrace another, namely sentientism. Why not say that nonsentient things such as forests are of moral concern too? After all, human beings are rapidly destroying and polluting the natural environment. Isn't this morally wrong?

HOLISM

One way of defending environmental conservation and preservation is to argue that the environment has instrumental value for humans and animals. But William Godfrey-Smith argues that instrumental justifications for environmental conservation—saving the wilderness because it is a cathedral, a laboratory, a silo, or a gymnasium—all fail to provide a satisfactory rationale. Not only are there conflicts between the activities justified, there is also the feeling that the wilderness has more than instrumental value, that it has an intrinsic value. Instead of sentientism or an anthropocentric view, Godfrey-Smith suggests that we adopt a "holistic conception" of nature where we think of humans and nature together forming a moral community, and where we must engage in cooperative behavior (and not exploitive behavior) for the sake of the health of the whole community. This means that we should have empathy for nature, and not think of ourselves as separate from it or superior to it.

Regan thinks that this holism amounts to "environmental fascism." It implies that we are morally obligated to save wild grasses at the expense of the life and welfare of people. But it is morally obvious that the interests of people are more important than the health or existence of wild grasses.

Frankena also rejects holism. He distinguishes between eight different types of ethics about the environment, and one of these is a type 5 ethics that takes everything to be morally relevant, even things like rocks, which are not conscious. This type of theory can be given a nonholistic or a holistic interpretation. But after examining both of these versions of type 5 ethics, Frankena concludes that they are unacceptable. Either they require the incredible belief that we should give moral consideration to things like rocks, which are not even conscious, or else they involve problematic beliefs about the Whole. Frankena ends up favoring a type 3 ethics where we morally consider only all consciously sentient beings (and so he accepts sentientism). He believes that this type of ethics, unlike the others, provides an adequate basis for an ethics about the environment.

PETER SINGER

All Animals Are Equal

Peter Singer is Professor of Philosophy at Monash University in Australia. His publications include Animal Liberation (1975) and Practical Ethics (1979).

Singer defines speciesism as a prejudice towards the interests of members of one's own species and against those of members of other species. He argues that speciesism is analogous to racism and sexism. If it is unjust to discriminate against women and blacks by not considering their interests, it is also unfair to ignore the interests of animals, particularly their interest in not suffering.

"Animal Liberation" may sound more like a parody of other liberation movements than a serious objective. The idea of "The Rights of Animals" actually was once used to parody the case for women's rights. When Mary Wollstonecraft, a forerunner of today's feminists, published her *Vindication of the Rights of Women* in 1792, her views were widely regarded as absurd, and before long an anonymous publication appeared entitled *A Vindication of the Rights of Brutes.* The author of this satirical work (now known to have been Thomas Taylor, a distinguished Cambridge philosopher) tried to refute Mary Wollstonecraft's arguments by showing that they could be carried one stage further. If the argument for equality was sound when applied to women, why should it not be applied to dogs, cats, and horses? The reasoning seemed to hold for these "brutes" too, yet to hold that brutes had rights was manifestly absurd; therefore the reasoning by which this conclusion had been reached must be unsound, and if unsound when applied to brutes, it must also be unsound when applied to women, since the very same arguments had been used in each case.

In order to explain the basis of the case for the equality of animals, it will be helpful to start with an examination of the case for the equality of women. Let us assume that we wish to defend the case for women's rights against the attack by Thomas Taylor. How should we reply?

One way in which we might reply is by saying that the case for equality between men and women cannot validly be extended to nonhuman animals. Women have a right to vote, for instance, because they are just as capable of making rational decisions about the future as men are; dogs, on the other hand, are incapable of understanding the significance of voting, so they cannot have the right to vote. There are many other obvious ways in which men and women resemble each other closely, while humans and animals differ greatly. So, it might be said, men and women are similar beings and should have similar rights, while humans and nonhumans are different and should not have equal rights.

The reasoning behind this reply to Taylor's analogy is correct up to a point, but it does not go far enough. There *are* important differences between humans and other animals, and these differences must give rise to *some* differences in the rights that each have. Recognizing this obvious fact, however, is no barrier to the case for extending the basic principle of equality to nonhuman animals. The differences that exist between men and women are equally undeniable, and the supporters of Women's Liberation are aware that these differences may give rise to different rights. Many feminists hold that women have the right to an abortion on request. It does not follow that since these same feminists are campaigning for equality between men and women they must support the right of men to have abortions too. Since a man cannot have an abortion, it is meaningless to talk of his right to have one. Since a dog can't vote, it is meaningless to talk of its right to vote. There is no reason why either Women's Liberation or Animal Liberation should get involved in such nonsense. The extension of the basic principle of equality from one group to another does not imply that we must treat both groups in exactly the same way, or grant exactly the same rights to both groups. Whether we should do so will depend on the nature of the members of the two groups. The basic principle of equality does not require equal or identical *treatment;* it requires equal con-

sideration. Equal consideration for different beings may lead to different treatment and different rights.

So there is a different way of replying to Taylor's attempt to parody the case for women's rights, a way that does not deny the obvious differences between humans and nonhumans but goes more deeply into the question of equality and concludes by finding nothing absurd in the idea that the basic principle of equality applies to so-called brutes. At this point such a conclusion may appear odd; but if we examine more deeply the basis on which our opposition to discrimination on grounds of race or sex ultimately rests, we will see that we would be on shaky ground if we were to demand equality for blacks, women, and other groups of oppressed humans while denying equal consideration to nonhumans. To make this clear we need to see, first exactly why racism and sexism are wrong.

When we say that all human beings, whatever their race, creed, or sex, are equal, what is it that we are asserting? Those who wish to defend hierarchical, inegalitarian societies have often pointed out that by whatever test we choose it simply is not true that all humans are equal. Like it or not we must face the fact that humans come in different shapes and sizes; they come with different moral capacities, different intellectual abilities, different amounts of benevolent feeling and sensitivity to the needs of others, different abilities to communicate effectively, and different capacities to experience pleasure and pain. In short, if the demand for equality were based on the actual equality of all human beings, we would have to stop demanding equality.

Still, one might cling to the view that the demand for equality among human beings is based on the actual equality of the different races and sexes. Although, it may be said, humans differ as individuals there are no differences between the races and sexes *as such.* From the mere fact that a person is black or a woman we cannot infer anything about that person's intellectual or moral capacities. This, it may be said, is why racism and sexism are wrong. The white racist claims that whites are superior to blacks, but this is false—although there are differences among individuals, some blacks are superior to some whites in all of the capacities and abilities that could conceivably be relevant. The opponent of sexism would say the same: a person's sex is no guide to his or her abilities, and this is why it is unjustifiable to discriminate on the basis of sex.

The existence of individual variations that cut across the lines of race or sex, however, provides us with no defense at all against a more sophisticated opponent of equality, one who proposes that, say, the interests of all those with IQ scores below 100 be given less consideration than the interests of those with ratings over 100. Perhaps those scoring below the mark, would, in this society, be made the slaves of those scoring higher. Would a hierarchical society of this sort really be so much better than one based on race or sex? I think not. But if we tie the moral principle of equality to the factual equality of the different races or sexes, taken as a whole, our opposition to racism and sexism does not provide us with any basis for objecting to this kind of inegalitarianism.

There is a second important reason why we ought not to base our opposition to racism and sexism on any kind of actual equality, even the limited kind that asserts that variations in capacities and abilities are spread evenly between the different races and sexes: we can have no absolute guarantee that these capacities and abilities really are distributed evenly, without regard to race or sex, among human beings. So far as actual abilities are concerned there do seem to be certain measurable differences between both races and sexes. These differences do not, of course, appear in each case, but only when averages are taken. More important still, we do not yet know how much of these differences is really due to the different genetic endowments of the different races and sexes, and how much is due to poor schools, poor housing, and other factors that are the result of past and continuing discrimination. Perhaps all the important differences will eventually prove to be environmental rather than genetic. Anyone opposed to racism and sexism will certainly hope that this will be so, for it will make the task of ending discrimination a lot easier; nevertheless it would be dangerous to rest the case against racism and sexism on the belief that all significant differences are environmental in origin. The opponent of, say, racism who takes this line will be unable to avoid conceding that *if* differences in ability do after all prove to have some genetic connection with race, racism would in some way be defensible.

Fortunately there is no need to pin the case for equality to one particular outcome of a scientific investigation. The appropriate response to those who claim to have found evidence of genetically based differences in ability between the races or sexes is not to stick to the belief that the genetic explanation must be wrong, whatever evidence to the contrary may turn up: instead we should make it quite clear that the claim to equality does not depend on intelligence, moral capacity, physical strength, or similar matters of fact. Equality is a moral idea, not an assertion of fact. There is no logically compelling reason for assuming that a factual difference in ability between two people justifies any difference in the amount of consideration we give to their needs and interests. *The principle of the equality of human beings is not a description of an alleged actual equality among humans; it is a prescription of how we should treat humans.*

Jeremy Bentham, the founder of the reforming utilitarian school of moral philosophy, incorporated the essential basis of moral equality into his system of ethics by means of the formula: "Each to count for one and none for more than one." In other words, the interests of every being affected by an action are to be taken into account and given the same weight as the like interests of any other being. A later utilitarian, Henry Sidgwick, put the point in this way:

"The good of any one individual is of no more importance, from the point of view (if I may say so) of the Universe, than the good of any other." More recently the leading figures in contemporary moral philosophy have shown a great deal of agreement in specifying as a fundamental presupposition of their moral theories some similar requirement that operates so as to give everyone's interests equal consideration—although these writers generally cannot agree on how this requirement is best formulated.[1]

It is an implication of this principle of equality that our concern for others and our readiness to consider their interests ought not to depend on what they are like or on what abilities they may possess. Precisely what this concern or consideration requires us to do may vary according to the characteristics of those affected by what we do: concern for the well-being of a child growing up in America would require that we teach him to read; concern for the well-being of a pig may require no more than that we leave him alone with other pigs in a place where there is adequate food and room to run freely. But the basic element—the taking into account of the interests of the being, whatever those interests may be—must, according to the principle of equality, be extended to all beings, black or white, masculine or feminine, human or nonhuman.

Thomas Jefferson, who was responsible for writing the principle of the equality of men into the American Declaration of Independence, saw this point. It led him to oppose slavery even though he was unable to free himself fully from his slaveholding background. He wrote in a letter to the author of a book that emphasized the notable intellectual achievements of Negroes in order to refute the then common view that they had limited intellectual capacities:

Be assured that no person living wishes more sincerely than I do, to see a complete refutation of the doubts I have myself entertained and expressed on the grade of understanding allotted to them by nature, and to find that they are on a par with ourselves . . . but whatever be their degree of talent it is no measure of their rights. Because Sir Isaac Newton was superior to others in understanding, he was not therefore lord of the property or person of others.[2]

Similarly when in the 1850s the call for women's rights was raised in the United States a remarkable black feminist named Sojourner Truth made the same point in more robust terms at a feminist convention:

. . . they talk about this thing in the head; what do they call it? ["Intellect," whispered someone near by.] That's it. What's that got to do with women's rights or Negroes' rights? If my cup won't hold but a pint and yours holds a quart, wouldn't you be mean not to let me have my little half-measure full?[3]

It is on this basis that the case against racism and the case against sexism must both ultimately rest; and it is in accordance with this principle that the attitude that we may call "speciesism," by analogy with racism, must also be condemned. Speciesism—the word is not an attractive one, but I can think of no better term—is a prejudice or attitude of bias toward the interests of members of one's own species and against those of members of other species. It should be obvious that the fundamental objections to racism and sexism made by Thomas Jefferson and Sojourner Truth apply equally to speciesism. If possessing a higher degree of intelligence does not entitle one human to use another for his own ends, how can it entitle humans to exploit nonhumans for the same purpose?[4]

Many philosophers and other writers have proposed the principle of equal consideration of interests, in some form or other, as a basic moral principle, but not many of them have recognized that this principle applies to members of other species as well as to our own. Jeremy Bentham was one of the few who did realize this. In a forward-looking passage written at a time when black slaves had been freed by the French but the British dominions were still being treated in the way we now treat animals, Bentham wrote:

The day may come when the rest of the animal creation may acquire those rights which never could have been withholden from them but by the hand of tyranny. The French have already discovered that the blackness of the skin is no reason why a human being should be abandoned without redress to the caprice of a tormentor. It may one day come to be recognized that the number of the legs, the villosity of the skin, or the termination of the os sacrum are reasons equally insufficient for abandoning a sensitive being to the same fate. What else is it that should trace the insuperable line? Is it the faculty of reason, or perhaps the faculty of discourse? But a full-grown horse or dog is beyond comparison a more rational, as well as a more conversable animal, than an infant of a day or a week or even a month old. But suppose they were otherwise, what would it avail? The question is not, Can they reason? nor Can they talk? but, Can they suffer? [5]

In this passage Bentham points to the capacity for suffering as the vital characteristic that gives a being the right to equal consideration. The capacity for suffering—or more strictly, for suffering and/or enjoyment or happiness—is not just another characteristic like the capacity for language or higher mathematics. Bentham is not saying that those who try to mark "the insuperable line" that determines whether the interests of a being should be considered happen to have chosen the wrong characteristic. By saying that we must consider the interests of all beings with the capacity for suffering or enjoyment Bentham does not arbitrarily exclude from consideration any interests at all—as those who draw the line with reference to the possession of reason or language do. The capacity for suffering and enjoyment is *a prerequisite for having interests at all*, a condition that must be satisfied before we can speak of interests in a meaningful way. It would be nonsense to say that it was not in the interests of a stone to be kicked along the road by a schoolboy. A stone does not have interests because it cannot suffer. Nothing that we can do to it could possibly make any difference to its welfare. A mouse, on the other hand, does

have an interest in not being kicked along the road, because it will suffer if it is.

If a being suffers there can be no moral justification for refusing to take that suffering into consideration. No matter what the nature of the being, the principle of equality requires that its suffering be counted equally with the like suffering—insofar as rough comparisons can be made—of any other being. If a being is not capable of suffering, or of experiencing enjoyment or happiness, there is nothing to be taken into account. So the limit of sentience (using the term as a convenient if not strictly accurate shorthand for the capacity to suffer and/or experience enjoyment) is the only defensible boundary of concern for the interests of others. To mark this boundary by some other characteristic like intelligence or rationality would be to mark it in an arbitrary manner. Why not choose some other characteristic, like skin color?

The racist violates the principle of equality by giving greater weight to the interests of members of his own race when there is a clash between their interests and the interests of those of another race. The sexist violates the principle of equality by favoring the interests of his own sex. Similarly the speciesist allows the interests of his own species to override the greater interests of members of other species. The pattern is identical in each case.

Most human beings are speciesists. Ordinary human beings—not a few exceptionally cruel or heartless humans, but the overwhelming majority of humans—take an active part in, acquiesce in, and allow their taxes to pay for practices that require the sacrifice of the most important interests of members of other species in order to promote the most trivial interests of our own species.

There is, however, one general defense of certain practices that needs to be disposed of before we discuss the practices themselves. It is a defense that, if true, would allow us to do anything at all to nonhumans for the slightest reason, or for no reason at all, without incurring any justifiable reproach. This defense claims that we are never guilty of neglecting the interests of other animals for one breathtakingly simple reason: they have no interests. Nonhuman animals have no interests, according to this view, because they are not capable of suffering. By this is not meant merely that they are not capable of suffering in all the ways that humans are—for instance, that a calf is not capable of suffering from the knowledge that it will be killed in six months' time. That modest claim is, no doubt, true, but it does not clear humans of the charge of speciesism, since it allows that animals may suffer in other ways—for instance, by being given electric shocks, or being kept in small, cramped cages. The defense I am about to discuss is the much more sweeping, although correspondingly less plausible, claim that animals are incapable of suffering in any way at all, that they are, in fact, unconscious automata, possessing neither thoughts nor feelings nor a mental life of any kind.

Although the view that animals are automata was proposed by the seventeenth-century French philosopher René Descartes, to most people, then and now, it is obvious that if, for example, we stick a sharp knife into the stomach of an unanesthetized dog, the dog will feel pain. That this is so is assumed by the laws in most civilized countries that prohibit wanton cruelty to animals. Readers whose common sense tells them that animals do suffer may prefer to skip ahead since the pages in between do nothing but refute a position that they do not hold. Implausible as it is, though, for the sake of completeness this skeptical position must be discussed.

Do animals other than humans feel pain? How do we know? Well, how do we know if anyone, human or nonhuman, feels pain? We know that we ourselves can feel pain. We know this from the direct experiences of pain that we have when, for instance, somebody presses a lighted cigarette against the back of our hand. But how do we know that anyone else feels pain? We cannot di-

rectly experience anyone else's pain, whether that "anyone" is our best friend or a stray dog. Pain is a state of consciousness, a "mental event," and as such it can never be observed. Behavior like writhing, screaming, or drawing one's hand away from the lighted cigarette is not pain itself; nor are the recordings a neurologist might make of activity within the brain observations of pain itself. Pain is something that we feel, and we can only infer that others are feeling it from various external indications.

In theory, we *could* always be mistaken when we assume that other human beings feel pain. It is conceivable that our best friend is really a very cleverly constructed robot, controlled by a brilliant scientist so as to give all the signs of feeling pain, but really no more sensitive than any other machine. We can never know, with absolute certainty, that this is not the case. But while this might present a puzzle for philosophers, none of us has the slightest real doubt that our best friends feel pain just as we do. This is an inference, but a perfectly reasonable one, based on observations of their behavior in situations in which we would feel pain, and on the fact that we have every reason to assume that our friends are beings like us, with nervous systems like ours that can be assumed to function as ours do, and to produce similar feelings in similar circumstances.

If it is justifiable to assume that other humans feel pain as we do, is there any reason why a similar inference should be unjustifiable in the case of other animals?

Nearly all the external signs that lead us to infer pain in other humans can be seen in other species, especially the species most closely related to us—other species of mammals, and birds. Behavioral signs—writhing, facial contortions, moaning, yelping or other forms of calling, attempts to avoid the source of pain, appearance of fear at the prospect of its repetition, and so on—are present. In addition, we know that these animals have nervous systems very like ours, which respond physiologically as ours do when the animal is in circumstances in which we would feel pain: an initial rise of blood pressure, dilated pupils, perspiration, an increased pulse rate, and, if the stimulus continues, a fall in blood pressure. Although humans have a more developed cerebral cortex than other animals, this part of the brain is concerned with thinking functions rather than with basic impulses, emotions, and feelings. These impulses, emotions, and feelings are located in the diencephalon, which is well developed in many other species of animals, especially mammals and birds.[6]

We also know that the nervous systems of other animals were not artificially constructed to mimic the pain behavior of humans, as a robot might be artificially constructed. The nervous systems of animals evolved as our own did, and in fact the evolutionary history of humans and other animals, especially mammals, did not diverge until the central features of our nervous systems were already in existence. A capacity to feel pain obviously enhances a species' prospects of survival, since it causes members of the species to avoid sources of injury. It is surely unreasonable to suppose that nervous systems that are virtually identical physiologically, have a common origin and a common evolutionary function, and result in similar forms of behavior in similar circumstances should actually operate in an entirely different manner on the level of subjective feelings.

It has long been accepted as sound policy in science to search for the simplest possible explanation of whatever it is we are trying to explain. Occasionally it has been claimed that it is for this reason "unscientific" to explain the behavior of animals by theories that refer to the animal's conscious feelings, desires, and so on—the idea being that if the behavior in question can be explained without invoking consciousness or feelings, that will be the simpler theory. Yet we can now see that such explanations, when placed in the overall context of the behavior of both human and nonhuman animals, are actually far more complex than their rivals. For we know from our own experience that explanations of our own behavior that did not refer to consciousness and the feeling of pain would be incomplete; and it is simpler to assume that the similar behavior of animals with similar nervous systems is to be explained in the same way than to try to invent some other explanation for the behavior of nonhuman animals as well as an explanation for the divergence between humans and nonhumans in this respect.

The overwhelming majority of scientists who have addressed themselves to this question agree. Lord Brain, one of the most eminent neurologists of our time, has said:

I personally can see no reason for conceding mind to my fellow men and denying it to animals. . . . I at least cannot doubt that the interests and activities of animals are correlated with awareness and feeling in the same way as my own, and which may be, for aught I know, just as vivid.[7]

While the author of a recent book on pain writes:

Every particle of factual evidence supports the contention that the higher mammalian vertebrates experience pain sensations at least as acute as our own. To say that they feel less because they are lower animals is an absurdity; it can easily be shown that many of their senses are far more acute than ours—visual acuity in certain birds, hearing in most wild animals, and touch in others; these animals depend more than we do today on the sharpest possible awareness of a hostile environment. Apart from the complexity of the cerebral cortex (which does not directly perceive pain) their nervous systems are almost identical to ours and their reactions to pain remarkably similar, though lacking (so far as we know) the philosophical and moral overtones. The emotional element is all too evident, mainly in the form of fear and anger.[8]

In Britain, three separate expert government committees on matters relating to animals have accepted the conclusion that animals feel pain. After noting the obvious behavioral evidence for this view, the Committee on Cruelty to Wild Animals said:

. . . we believe that the physiological, and more particularly the anatomical, evidence fully justifies and reinforces the commonsense belief that animals feel pain.

And after discussing the evolutionary value of pain they concluded that pain is "of clear-cut biological usefulness" and this is "a third type of evidence that animals feel pain." They then went on to consider forms of suffering other than mere physical pain, and added that they were "satisfied that animals do suffer from acute fear and terror." In 1965, reports by British government committees on experiments on animals, and on the welfare of animals under intensive farming methods, agreed with this view, concluding that animals are capable of suffering both from straightforward physical injuries and from fear, anxiety, stress, and so on.[9]

That might well be thought enough to settle the matter; but there is one more objection that needs to be considered. There is, after all, one behavioral sign that humans have when in pain which nonhumans do not have. This is a developed language. Other animals may communicate with each other, but not, it seems, in the complicated way we do. Some philosophers, including Descartes, have thought it important that while humans can tell each other about their experience of pain in great detail, other animals cannot. (Interestingly, this once neat dividing line between humans and other species has now been threatened by the discovery that chimpanzees can be taught a language.)[10] But as Bentham pointed out long ago, the ability to use language is not relevant to the question of how a being ought to be treated—unless that ability can be linked to the capacity to suffer, so that the absence of a language casts doubt on the existence of this capacity.

This link may be attempted in two ways. First, there is a hazy line of philosophical thought, stemming perhaps from some doctrines associated with the influential philosopher Ludwig Wittgenstein, that maintains that we cannot meaningfully attribute states of consciousness to beings without language.

This position seems to me very implausible. Language may be necessary for abstract thought, at some level anyway, but states like pain are more primitive, and have nothing to do with language.

The second and more easily understood way of linking language and the existence of pain is to say that the best evidence that we can have that another creature is in pain is when he tells us that he is. This is a distinct line of argument, for it is not being denied that a non-language-user conceivably *could* suffer, but only that we could ever have sufficient reason to *believe* that he is suffering. Still, this line of argument fails too. As Jane Goodall has pointed out in her study of chimpanzees, *In the Shadow of Man*, when it comes to the expressions of feelings and emotions language is less important than in other areas. We tend to fall back on nonlinguistic modes of communication such as a cheering pat on the back, an exuberant embrace, a clasp of the hands, and so on. The basic signals we use to convey pain, fear, anger, love, joy, surprise, sexual arousal, and many other emotional states are not specific to our own species.[11]

Charles Darwin made an extensive study of this subject, and the book he wrote about it, *The Expression of the Emotions in Man and Animals*, notes countless nonlinguistic modes of expression. The statement "I am in pain" may be one piece of evidence for the conclusion that the speaker is in pain, but it is not the only possible evidence, and since people sometimes tell lies, not even the best possible evidence.

Even if there were stronger grounds for refusing to attribute pain to those who do not have a language, the consequences of this refusal might lead us to reject the conclusion. Human infants and young children are unable to use language. Are we to deny that a year-old child can suffer? If not, language cannot be crucial. Of course, most parents understand the responses of their children better than they understand the responses of other animals, but this is just a fact about the relatively greater knowledge that we have of our own species, and the greater contact we have with infants, as compared to animals. Those who have studied the behavior of other animals, and those who have pet animals, soon learn to understand their responses as well as we understand those of an infant, and sometimes better. Jane Goodall's account of the chimpanzees she watched is one instance of this, but the same can be said of those who have observed species less closely related to our own. Two among many possible examples are Konrad Lorenz's observations of geese and jackdaws, and N. Tinbergen's extensive studies of herring gulls.[12] Just as we can understand infant human behavior in the light of adult human behavior, so we can understand the behavior of other species in the light of our own behavior—and sometimes we can understand our own behavior better in the light of the behavior of other species.

So to conclude: there are no good reasons, scientific or philosophical, for denying that animals feel pain. If we do not doubt that other humans feel pain we should not doubt that other animals do so too.

Animals can feel pain. As we saw earlier, there can be no moral justification for regarding the pain (or pleasure) that animals feel as less important than the same amount of pain (or pleasure) felt by humans. But what exactly does this mean, in practical terms? To prevent misunderstanding I shall spell out what I mean a little more fully.

If I give a horse a hard slap across its rump with my open hand, the horse may start, but it presumably feels little pain. Its skin is thick enough to protect it against a mere slap. If I slap a baby in the same way, however, the baby will cry and presumably does feel pain, for its skin is more sensitive. So it is worse to slap a baby than a horse, if both slaps are administered with equal force. But there must be some kind of blow—I don't know exactly what it would be, but perhaps a blow with a heavy stick—that would cause the horse as much pain as we cause a baby by slapping it with our hand.

That is what I mean by "the same amount of pain" and if we consider it wrong to inflict that much pain on a baby for no good reason then we must, unless we are speciesists, consider it equally wrong to inflict the same amount of pain on a horse for no good reason.

There are other differences between humans and animals that cause other complications. Normal adult human beings have mental capacities that will, in certain circumstances, lead them to suffer more than animals would in the same circumstances. If, for instance, we decided to perform extremely painful or lethal scientific experiments on normal adult humans, kidnapped at random from public parks for this purpose, every adult who entered a park would become fearful that he would be kidnapped. The resultant terror would be a form of suffering additional to the pain of the experiment. The same experiments performed on nonhuman animals would cause less suffering since the animals would not have the anticipatory dread of being kidnapped and experimented upon. This does not mean, of course, that it would be right to perform the experiment on animals, but only that there is a reason, which is *not* speciesist, for preferring to use animals rather than normal adult humans, if the experiment is to be done at all. It should be noted, however, that this same argument gives us a reason for preferring to use human infants—orphans perhaps—or retarded humans for experiments, rather than adults, since infants and retarded humans would also have no idea of what was going to happen to them. So far as this argument is concerned nonhuman animals and infants and retarded humans are in the same category; and if we use this argument to justify experiments on nonhuman animals we have to ask ourselves whether we are also prepared to allow experiments on human infants and retarded adults; and if we make a distinction between animals and these humans, on what basis can we do it, other than a barefaced—and morally indefensible—preference for members of our own species?

There are many areas in which the superior mental powers of normal adult humans make a difference: anticipation, more detailed memory, greater knowledge of what is happening, and so on. Yet these differences do not all point to greater suffering on the part of the normal human being. Sometimes an animal may suffer more because of his more limited understanding. If, for instance, we are taking prisoners in wartime we can explain to them that while they must submit to capture, search, and confinement they will not otherwise be harmed and will be set free at the conclusion of hostilities. If we capture a wild animal, however, we cannot explain that we are not threatening its life. A wild animal cannot distinguish an attempt to overpower and confine from an attempt to kill; the one causes as much terror as the other.

It may be objected that comparisons of the sufferings of different species are impossible to make, and that for this reason when the interests of animals and humans clash the principle of equality gives no guidance. It is probably true that comparisons of suffering between members of different species cannot be made precisely, but precision is not essential. Even if we were to prevent the infliction of suffering on animals only when it is quite certain that the interests of humans will not be affected to anything like the extent that animals are affected, we would be forced to make radical changes in our treatment of animals that would involve our diet, the farming methods we use, experimental procedures in many fields of science, our approach to wildlife and to hunting, trapping and the wearing of furs, and areas of entertainment like circuses, rodeos, and zoos. As a result, a vast amount of suffering would be avoided.

So far I have said a lot about the infliction of suffering on animals, but nothing about killing them. This omission has been deliberate. The application of the principle of equality to the infliction of suffering is, in theory at least, fairly straightforward. Pain and suffering are bad and should be prevented or minimized, irrespective of the race, sex, or species of the being that suffers. How bad a pain is depends on how intense it is and how long it lasts, but pains of the same intensity and duration are equally bad, whether felt by humans or animals.

The wrongness of killing a being is more complicated. I have kept, and shall continue to keep, the question of killing in the background because in the present state of human tyranny over other species the more simple, straightforward principle of equal consideration of pain or pleasure is a sufficient basis for identifying and protesting against all the major abuses of animals that humans practice. Nevertheless, it is necessary to say something about killing.

Just as most humans are speciesists in their readiness to cause pain to animals when they would not cause a similar pain to humans for the same reason, so most humans are speciesists in their readiness to kill other animals when they would not kill humans. We need to proceed more cautiously here, however, because people hold widely differing views about when it is legitimate to kill humans, as the continuing debates over abortion and euthanasia attest. Nor have moral philosophers been able to agree on exactly what it is that makes it wrong to kill humans, and under what circumstances killing a human being may be justifiable.

Let us consider first the view that it is always wrong to take an innocent human life. We may call this the "sanctity of life" view. People who take this view oppose abortion and euthanasia. They do not usually, however, oppose the killing of nonhumans—so perhaps it would be more accurate to describe this view as the "sanctity of *human* life" view.

The belief that human life, and only human life, is sacrosanct is a form of speciesism. To see this, consider the following example.

Assume that, as sometimes happens, an infant has been born with massive and irreparable brain damage. The damage is so severe that the infant can never be any more than a "human vegetable," unable to talk, recognize other people, act independently of others, or develop a sense of self-awareness. The parents of the infant, realizing that they cannot hope for any improvement in their child's condition and being in any case unwilling to spend, or ask the state to spend, the thousands of dollars that would be needed annually for proper care of the infant, ask the doctor to kill the infant painlessly.

Should the doctor do what the parents ask? Legally, he should not, and in this respect the law reflects the sanctity of life view. The life of every human being is sacred. Yet people who would say this about the infant do not object to the killing of nonhuman animals. How can they justify their different judgments? Adult chimpanzees, dogs, pigs, and may other species far surpass the brain-damaged infant in their ability to relate to others, act independently, be self-aware, and any other capacity that could reasonably be said to give value to life. With the most intensive care possible, there are retarded infants who can never achieve the intelligence level of a dog. Nor can we appeal to the concern of the infant's parents, since they themselves, in this imaginary example (and in some actual cases), do not want the infant kept alive.

The only thing that distinguishes the infant from the animal, in the eyes of those who claim it has a "right to life," is that it is, biologically, a member of the species Homo sapiens, whereas chimpanzees, dogs, and pigs are not. But to use *this* difference as the basis for granting a right to life to the infant and not to the other animals is, of course, pure speciesism.[13] It is exactly the kind of arbitrary difference that the most crude and overt kind of racist uses in attempting to justify racial discrimination.

This does not mean that to avoid speciesism we must hold that it is as wrong to kill a dog as it is to kill a normal human being. The only position that is irredeemably speciesist is the one that tries to make the boundary of the right to life run exactly parallel to the boundary of our own species. Those who hold the sanctity of life view do this because while distinguishing sharply between humans and other animals they allow no distinctions to be made within our own species, objecting to the killing of the severely retarded and the hopelessly senile as strongly as they object to the killing of normal adults.

To avoid speciesism we must allow that beings that are similar in all relevant respects have a similar right to life—and mere membership in our own biological species cannot be a morally relevant criterion for this right. Within these limits we could still hold that, for instance, it is worse to kill a normal adult human, with a capacity for self-awareness, and the ability to plan for the future and have meaningful relations with others, than it is to kill a mouse, which presumably does not share all of these characteristics; or we might appeal to the close family and other personal ties that humans have but mice do not have to the same degree; or we might think that it is the consequences for other humans, who will be put in fear of their own lives, that makes the crucial difference; or we might think it is some combination of these factors, or other factors altogether.

Whatever criteria we choose, however, we will have to admit that they do not follow precisely the boundary of our own species. We may legitimately hold that there are some features of certain beings which make their lives more valuable than those of other beings; but there will surely be some nonhuman animals whose lives, by any standards, are more valuable than the lives of some humans. A chimpanzee, dog, or pig, for instance, will have a higher degree of self-awareness and a greater capacity for meaningful relations with others than a severely retarded infant or someone in a state of advanced senility. So if we base the right to life on these characteristics we must grant these animals a right to life as good as, or better than, such retarded or senile humans.

Now this argument cuts both ways. It could be taken as showing that chimpanzees, dogs, and pigs, along with some other species, have a right to life and we commit a grave moral offense whenever we kill them, even when they are old and suffering and our intention is to put them out of their misery. Alternatively one could take the argument as showing that the severely retarded and hopelessly senile have no right to life and may be killed for quite trivial reasons, as we now kill animals.

Since the focus here is on ethical questions concerning animals and not on the morality of euthanasia I shall not attempt to settle this issue finally. I think it is reasonably clear, though, that while both of the positions just described avoid speciesism, neither is entirely satisfactory. What we need is some middle position that would avoid speciesism but would not make the lives of the retarded and senile as cheap as the lives of pigs and dogs now are, nor make the lives of pigs and dogs so sacrosanct that we think it wrong to put them out of hopeless misery. What we must do is bring nonhuman animals within our sphere of moral concern and cease to treat their lives as expendable for whatever trivial purposes we may have. At the same time, once we realize that the fact that a being is a member of our own species is not in itself enough to make it always wrong to kill that being, we may come to reconsider our policy of preserving human lives at all costs, even when there is no prospect of a meaningful life or of existence without terrible pain.

I conclude, then, that a rejection of speciesism does not imply that all lives are of equal worth. While self-awareness, intelligence, the capacity for meaningful relations with others, and so on are not relevant to the question of inflicting pain—since pain is pain, whatever other capacities, beyond the capacity to feel pain, the being may have—these capacities may be relevant to the question of taking life. It is not arbitrary to hold that the life of a self-aware being, capable of abstract thought, of planning for the future, of complex acts of communication, and so on, is more valuable than the life of a being without these capacities. To see the difference between the issues of inflicting pain and taking life, consider how we would choose within our own species. If we had to choose to save the life of a normal human or a mentally defective human, we would probably choose to save the life of the normal human; but if we had to choose between preventing pain in the normal human or the mental defective—imagine that both have received painful but superficial injuries, and we only have enough painkiller for one of them—it is not nearly so clear how we ought to choose. The same is true when we consider other species. The evil of pain is, in itself, unaffected by the other characteristics of the being that feels the pain; the value of life is affected by these other characteristics.

Normally this will mean that if we have to choose between the life of a human being and the life of another animal we should choose to save the life of the human, but there may be special cases in which the reverse holds true, because the human being in question does not have the capacities of a normal human being. So this view is not speciesist, although it may appear to be at first glance. The preference, in normal cases, for saving a human life over the life of an animal when a choice *has* to be made is a preference based on the characteristics that normal humans have, and not on the mere fact that they are members of our own species. This is why when we consider members of our own species who lack the characteristics of normal humans we can no longer say that their lives are always to be preferred to those of other animals. In general, the question of when it is wrong to kill (painlessly) an animal is one to which we need give no precise answer. As long as we remember that we should give the same respect to the lives of animals as we give to the lives of those humans at a similar mental level, we shall not go far wrong.

In any case, the conclusions that are argued for here flow from the principle of minimizing suffering alone. The idea that it is also wrong to kill animals painlessly gives some of these conclusions additional support that is welcome, but strictly unnecessary.

Interestingly enough, this is true even of the conclusion that we ought to become vegetarians, a conclusion that in the popular mind is generally based on some kind of absolute prohibition on killing.

Footnotes

1. For Bentham's moral philosophy, see his *Introduction to the Principles of Morals and Legislation,* and for Sidgwick's see *The Methods of Ethics* (the passage quoted is from the seventh edition, p. 382). As examples of leading contemporary moral philosophers who incorporate a requirement of equal consideration of interests, see R.M. Hare, *Freedom and Reason* (New York, Oxford University Press, 1963) and John Rawls, *A Theory of Justice* (Cambridge: Harvard University Press, Belknap Press, 1972). For a brief account of the essential agreement on this issue between these and other positions, see R.M. Hare, "Rules of War and Moral Reasoning," *Philosophy and Public Affairs* 1 (1972).

2. Letter to Henri Gregoire, February 25, 1809.

3. Reminiscences by Francis D. Gage, from Susan B. Anthony, *The History of Woman Suffrage,* vol. 1; the passage is to be found in the extract in Leslie Tanner, ed., *Voices from Women's Liberation* (New York: Signet, 1970).

4. I owe the term "speciesism" to Richard Ryder.

5. *Introduction to the Principles of Morals and Legislation,* chapter 17.

6. Lord Brain, "Presidential Address" in C.A. Keele and R. Smith, eds., *The Assessment of Pain in Men and Animals* (London: Universities Federation for Animal Welfare, 1962).

7. Ibid., p. 11.

8. Richard Serjeant, *The Spectrum of Pain* (London: Hart-Davis, 1969), p. 72.

9. See the reports of the Committee on Cruelty to Wild Animals (Command Paper 8266, 1951), paragraphs 36–42; the Departmental Committee on Experiments on Animals (Command Paper 2641, 1965), paragraphs 179–182: and the Technical Committee to Enquire into the Welfare of Animals Kept under Intensive Livestock Husbandry Systems (Command Paper 2836, 1965), paragraphs 26–28 (London: Her Majesty's Stationery Office).

10. One chimpanzee, Washoe, has been taught the sign language used by deaf people, and acquired a vocabulary of 350 signs. Another, Lana, communicates in structured sentences by pushing buttons on a special machine. For a brief account of Washoe's abilities, see Jane van Lawick-Goodall, *In the Shadow of Man* (Boston: Houghton Mifflin, 1971), pp. 252–254; and for Lana, see *Newsweek,* 7 January 1974, and *New York Times,* 4 December 1974.

11. *In the Shadow of Man,* p. 225; Michael Peters makes a similar point in "Nature and Culture," in Stanley and Roslind Godlovitch and John Harris, eds., *Animals, Men and Morals* (New York: Taplinger Publishing Co., 1972).

12. Konrad Lorenz, *King Solomon's Ring* (New York: T.Y. Crowell, 1952); N. Tinbergen, *The Herring Gull's World,* rev. ed. (New York: Basic Books, 1974).

13. I am here putting aside religious views, for example the doctrine that all and only humans have immortal souls, or are made in the image of God. Historically these views have been very important, and no doubt are partly responsible for the idea that human life has a special sanctity. Logically, however, these religious views are unsatisfactory, since a reasoned explanation of why it should be that all humans and no nonhumans have immortal souls is not offered. This belief too, therefore, comes under suspicion as a form of speciesism. In any case, defenders of the "sanctity of life" view are generally reluctant to base their position on purely religious doctrines, since these doctrines are no longer as widely accepted as they once were.

Review Questions

1. Explain the principle of equality that Singer adopts.

2. How does Singer define speciesism?

3. How do we know that animals suffer?

4. What is the "sanctity of life" view? Why does Singer reject this view?

Discussion Questions

1. Is speciesism analogous to racism and sexism? Why, or why not?
2. Is there anything wrong with killing animals painlessly? Defend your view.
3. Do human interests outweigh animal interests? Explain your position.

TOM REGAN

Ethical Vegetarianism and Commercial Animal Farming

From R. Haynes and R. Lanier, eds., *Agriculture, Change, and Human Values: Proceedings of a Multi-Disciplinary Conference*, October 1982. Humanities and Agriculture Program, Gainesville, Florida, 1984. Copyright © 1984 Tom Regan. Reprinted by permission.

Tom Regan teaches philosophy at North Carolina State University. He has written numerous books and articles, and he has edited many textbooks. His most recent books on the subject of animal rights are All That Dwell Therein: Essays on Animal Rights and Environmental Ethics (1982) and The Case for Animal Rights (1983).

Regan begins with a discussion of moral anthropocentrism, the view of Kant and others that only human interest should be morally considered. This view is rejected by utilitarianism and by some proponents of moral rights including Regan. Regan does not find the utilitarianism of Bentham and Singer to be morally acceptable. Instead he defends a rights theory. On this theory, moral rights imply a duty to respect the rights. Persons with "inherent value" possess rights, and some animals are persons. So we have a duty to respect animal rights by abolishing commercial animal farming and becoming vegetarians.

INTRODUCTION

Time was when a few words in passing usually were enough to exhaust the philosophical interest in the moral status of animals other than human beings. "Lawless beasts," writes Plato. "Of the order of sticks and stones," opines the nineteenth-century Jesuit W.D. Ritchie. True, there are notable exceptions, at least as far back as Pythagoras, who advocated vegetarianism on ethical grounds—Cicero, Epicurus, Herodotus, Horace, Ovid, Plutarch, Seneca, Virgil: hardly a group of "animal crazies"! By and large, however, a few words would do nicely, thank you, or, when one's corpus took on grave proportions, a few paragraphs or pages. Thus we find Kant, for example, by all accounts one of the most influential philosophers in the history of ideas, devoting almost two full pages to the question of our duties to animals, while St. Thomas Aquinas, easily the most important philosopher-theologian in the Catholic tradition, bequeaths perhaps ten pages to the topic at hand.

Times change. Today an even modest bibliography listing titles of the past decade's work on the moral status of animals would easily equal the length of Kant's and Aquinas' treatments combined, a quantitative symbol of the changes that have taken place, and continue to take place, in philosophy's attempts to rouse slumbering prejudices lodged in the anthropocentrism of western thought.

With relatively few speaking to the contrary (St. Francis always comes to mind in this context), theists and humanists, rowdy bedfellows in most quarters, have gotten along amicably when questions were raised about the moral center of the terrestrial universe: *Human* interests form the center of that universe. Let the theist look hopefully beyond the harsh edge of bodily death, let the humanist denounce, in Freud's terms, this "infantile view of the world," at least the two could agree that the moral universe revolves around us humans—our desires, our needs, our goals, our preferences, our love for one another. The intense dialectic now characterizing philosophy's assaults on the traditions of humanism and theism, assaults aimed not only at the traditional account of the moral status of animals but at the foundation of our moral dealings with the natural environment, with Nature generally—these assaults should not be viewed as local skirmishes between obscure academicians each bent on occupying a deserted fortress. At issue are the validity of alternative visions of the scheme of things and our place in it. The growing philosophical debate over our treatment of animals and the environment is both a symptom and a cause of a culture's attempt to come to critical terms with its past as it attempts to shape its future.

At present there are three major challenges being raised against moral anthropocentrism. The first is the one issued by *utilitarians;* the second, by proponents of *moral rights;* and the third emanates from the camp of those who advocate what we shall term a *holistic ethic.* This essay offers brief summaries of each position with special reference to how their advocates answer two questions: (a) Is vegetarianism required on ethical grounds? and (b) Judged ethically, what should we say, and what should we do, about commercial animal agriculture? To ask whether vegetarianism is required on ethical grounds is to ask whether there are reasons other than those that relate to one's own welfare (for example, other than those that relate to one's own health or financial well-being) that call for leading a vegetarian

way of life. As for the expression "commercial animal agriculture," that should be taken to apply to the practice of raising animals to be sold for food. The ethics of other practices that involve killing animals (for example, hunting, the use of animals in science, "the family farm" where the animals raised are killed and eaten by the people who raise them, etc.) will not be considered, except in passing, not because the ethics of these practices should not demand our close attention but because space and time preclude our giving them this attention here. Time and space also preclude anything approaching "complete" assessments of the three views to be discussed. None can be proven right or wrong in a few swift strokes. Even so, it will be clear where my own sympathies lie.

TRADITIONAL MORAL ANTHROPOCENTRISM

Aquinas and Kant speak for the anthropocentric tradition. That tradition does not issue a blank check when it comes to the treatment of animals. Morally, we are enjoined to be kind to animals and, on the other side of the coin, not to be cruel to them. But we are not enjoined to be the one and prohibited from being the other because we owe such treatment to *animals themselves*—not, that is, because we have any duties *directly* to nonhumans; rather, it is because of *human* interests that we have these duties regarding animals. "So far as animals are concerned," writes Kant, "we have no direct duties. . . . Our duties to animals are merely indirect duties to mankind." In the case of cruelty, we are not to be cruel to animals because treating them cruelly will develop a habit of cruelty, and a habit of cruelty, once it has taken up lodging in our breast, will in time include human beings among its victims. "(H)e who is cruel to animals becomes hard also in his dealings with men." And *that* is why cruelty to animals is wrong. As for kindness, "(t)ender feelings towards dumb animals develop humane feelings toward mankind."[1] And *that* is why we have a duty to be kind to animals.

So reasons Kant. Aquinas, predictably, adds theistic considerations, but the main storyline is the same, as witness the following passage from his *Summa Contra Gentiles.*

Hereby is refuted the error of those who said it is sinful for a man to kill dumb animals: for by divine providence they are intended for man's use in the natural order. Hence it is no wrong for man to make use of them, either by killing, or in any other way whatever. . . . And if any passages of Holy Writ seem to forbid us to be cruel to dumb animals, for instance to kill a bird with its young: this is either to remove men's thoughts from being cruel to other men, and lest through being cruel to animals one becomes cruel to human beings: or because injury to an animal leads to the temporal hurt of man, either of the doer of the deed, or of another: or on account of some (religious) signification: thus the Apostle expounds the prohibition against muzzling the ox that treadeth the corn.[2]

To borrow a phrase from the twentieth-century English philosopher Sir W.D. Ross, our treatment of animals, both for Kant and Aquinas, is "a practice ground for moral virtue." The *moral game* is played between human players or, on the theistic view, human players plus God. The way we treat animals is a sort of moral warmup, character calisthentics, as it were, for the moral game in which animals themselves play no part.

THE UTILITARIAN CHALLENGE

The first fairly recent spark of revolt against moral anthropocentrism comes, as do other recent protests against institutionalized prejudice, from the pens of the nineteenth-century utilitarians, most notably Jeremy Bentham and John Stuart Mill. These utilitarians—who count the balance of pleasure over pain for all sentient creatures as the yardstick of moral right and wrong, and who reject out of hand Descartes' famous teaching that animals are "nature's machines," lacking any trace of conscious awareness— recognize the direct moral significance of the pleasures and pains of animals. In an oft-quoted passage, Bentham enfranchises animals within the utilitarian moral community by declaring that "(t)he question is not, Can they talk?, or Can they reason?, but, Can they suffer?"[3] And Mill stakes the credibility of utilitarianism itself on its implications for the moral status and treatment of animals, writing that "(w)e (that is, those who subscribe to utilitarianism) are perfectly willing to stake the whole question on this one issue. Granted that any practice causes more pain to animals than it gives pleasure to man: is that practice moral or immoral? And if, exactly in proportion as human beings raise their heads out of the slough of selfishness, they do not with one voice answer 'immoral' let the morality of the principle of utility be forever condemned."[4] The duties we have regarding animals, then, are duties we have *directly to them,* not indirect duties to humanity. For utilitarians, animals are themselves involved in the moral game.

Viewed against this historical backdrop, the position of the contemporary Australian moral philosopher Peter Singer can be seen to be an extension of the attack on the tradition of moral anthropocentrism initiated by his utilitarian forebears. For though this sometimes goes unnoticed by friend and foe alike, Singer, whose book *Animal Liberation* is unquestionably the most influential work published in the 1970s on the topic of the ethics of our treatment of animals, *is* a utilitarian.[5] That view requires, he believes, observance of the equality of interests principle. This principle requires that, before we decide what to do, we consider the interests (that is, the preferences) of all those who are likely to be affected by what we do *and* weigh equal interests equally. We must not, that is, refuse to consider the interests of some of those who will be affected by what we do because, say, they are Catholic, or female, or black. *Everyone's* interests must be considered. And we must not discount the importance of comparable interests because they are the interests of, say, a Catholic, woman, or black. Everyone's interests must be weighed *equitably.* Of course, to ignore or discount the importance of a woman's interests *because she is a woman* is the very paradigm of the moral prejudice we call sexism, just as to ignore or discount the importance of the interests of blacks (or Native Americans, Chicanos, etc.) are paradigmatic forms of racism. It remained for Singer to argue, which he does with great vigor, passion, and skill, that a similar moral prejudice lies at the heart of moral anthropocentrism, a prejudice that Singer, borrowing a term first coined by the English author and animal activist Richard Ryder, denominates *speciesism.*[6] Like Bentham and Mill before him, Singer, the utilitarian, *denies* that we are to treat animals well in the name of the betterment of humanity, *denies* that we are to do this because this will help us discharge our duties to our fellow humans, *denies* that acting dutifully toward animals is a moral warmup for the real moral game played between humans, or, as theists would add, between humans-and-humans-and-God. *We owe it to those animals who have interests to take their interests into account, just as we also owe it to them to count their interests equitably.* Our duties regarding animals are, in these respects, *direct* duties we have to them, not indirect duties to humanity. To think otherwise is to give sorry testimony to the prejudice of speciesism Singer is intent upon unmasking.

FARMING TODAY

Singer believes that the utilitarian case for ethical vegetarianism is strengthened when we inform ourselves of the changes taking place in commercial animal farming today. In increasing numbers, animals are being brought in off the land and raised indoors, in unnatural, crowded conditions—raised "intensively," to use the jargon of the animal industry, in structures that look for all the world like factories. Indeed, it is now common practice to refer to such commercial ventures as *factory farms.* The inhabitants of these "farms" are kept in cages, or stalls,

or pens, or closely-confined in other ways, living out their abbreviated lives in a technologically created and sustained environment: automated feeding, automated watering, automated light cycles, automated waste removal, automated what-not. And the crowding: as many as nine hens in cages that measure eighteen by twenty-four inches; veal calves confined to twenty-two inch wide stalls; hogs similarly confined, sometimes in tiers of cages—two, three, four rows high. Could any impartial, morally sensitive person view what goes on in a factory farm with benign approval? Certainly many of the basic interests of the animals are simply ignored or undervalued, Singer claims, because they do not compute economically. Their interest in physical freedom or in associating with members of their own species, these interests routinely go by the board. And for what? So that we humans can dine on steaks and chops, drumsticks and roasts, food that is simply inessential for our own physical well-being. Add to this sorry tale of speciesism on today's farm the enormous waste that characterizes animal industry, waste to the tune of six or seven pounds of vegetable protein to produce a pound of animal protein in the case of beef cattle, for example, and add to the accumulated waste of nutritious food the chronic need for just such food throughout the countries of the Third World, whose populations characteristically are malnourished at best and literally starving to death at worst—add all these factors together and we have, Singer believes, the basis for the utilitarian's answers to our two questions. In response to the question, "Is vegetarianism required on ethical grounds?" the Singer-type utilitarian replies affirmatively. For it is not for self-interested reasons that Singer calls us to vegetarianism (though such reasons, including a concern for one's health, are not irrelevant). It is for ethical reasons that we are to take up a vegetarian way of life. And as for our second question, the one that asks what we should think and do about commercial animal farming, Singer's utilitarian argument prescribes, he thinks, that we should think ill of today's factory farms and act to bring about significant humane improvements by refusing to purchase their products. Ethically considered, we ought to become vegetarians.

THE CHALLENGE
TO UTILITARIANISM

Singer, then, is the leading contemporary representative of the utilitarian critique of the anthropocentric heritage bequeathed to us by humanism and theism. How should we assess his critique? Our answer requires answering two related questions. First, How adequate is the general utilitarian position Singer advocates? Second, How adequate is Singer's application of this general position to the particular case of commercial animal agriculture and, allied with this, the case for ethical vegetarianism? A brief response to each question, beginning with the second, will have to suffice. Consider Singer's claim that each of us has a duty to become a vegetarian. How can this alleged duty be defended on *utilitarian* grounds? Well, on this view, we know, the act I *ought* to perform, the act I have a *duty* to do, is the one that will bring about the best consequences for all those affected by the outcome, which, for Singer, means the act that will bring about the optimal balance of preference satisfaction over preference frustration. But it is naive in the extreme to suppose that, were *I* individually henceforth to abstain from eating meat and assiduously lead a vegetarian existence, this will improve the lot of a single animal. Commercial animal farming simply does not work in this way. It does not, that is, fine-tune its production to such a high degree that it responds to the decisions of each individual consumer. So, no, the individual's abstention from meat will not make the slightest dent, will not effect the smallest change, in commercial animal agriculture. No one, therefore, Singer included, can ground *the individual's* ethical obligation to be vegetarian on the effects *the individual's* acts will have on the welfare of animals.

Similar remarks apply to the other presumed beneficiaries of the individual's conversion to vegetarianism. The starving, malnourished masses of the Third World will not receive the food they need if I would but stop eating animals. For it is, again, naive in the extreme to suppose that the dietary decisions and acts of any given *individual* will make the slightest difference to the quality of life for any inhabitant in the Third World. Even were it true, which it is not (and it is not true because commercial animal agriculture is not so fine-tuned in this respect either), that a given amount of protein-rich grain *would not be fed to animals* if I abstained from eating meat, it simply would not follow that this grain *would find its way to any needy human being*. To suppose otherwise is to credit one's individual acts and decisions with a kind of godlike omnipotence a robust sense of reality cannot tolerate. Thus, since the type of utilitarianism Singer advocates prescribes that we decide what our ethical duties are by asking what will be the consequences of our acts, and since there is no realistic reason to believe that the consequences of my abstaining from meat will make any difference whatever to the quality of life of commercially raised farm animals or the needy people of the Third World, the alleged duties to become a vegetarian and to oppose commercial animal agriculture lack the kind of backing a utilitarian like Singer requires.

Here one might attempt to defend Singer by arguing that it is the total or sum of the consequences of *many* people becoming vegetarians, not just the results of each individual's decisions, that will spare some animals the rigors of factory farms and save some humans from malnutrition or starvation. Two replies to this attempted defense may be briefly noted. First, this defense at most gives *a sketch of a possible* reply; it does not give a finished one. As a utilitarian, Singer must show that the consequences for everyone involved would be better if a number of people became vegetarians than if they did not. But to show this, Singer must provide a

thorough rundown of what the consequences would be, or would be in all probability, if we abstained from eating meat, *or*
ate less of it, *or* ate none at all. And this is
no easy task. Would the grains not fed to
animals even be grown if the animal industry's requirements for them were reduced or
eliminated? Would there be an economically viable market for corn, oats, and other
grains if we became vegetarians? Would
farmers have the necessary economic incentive to produce enough grain to feed the
world's hungry human beings? Who
knows? In particular, does Singer know?
One looks in vain to find the necessary empirical backing for an answer here. Or consider: Suppose the grain is available. From
a utilitarian point of view, would it be best
(that is, would we be acting to produce the
best consequences) if we made this grain
available to the present generation of the
world's malnourished? Or would it be better in the long run to refuse to aid these
people at this point in time? After all, if we
assist them now, will they not simply reproduce? And won't their additional numbers
make the problem of famine for the next
generation even more tragic? Who knows
what the correct answers to these questions
are? Who knows what is even "most likely"
to be true? It is not unfair to a utilitarian
such as Singer to mark the depths of our
ignorance in these matters. And neither is it
unfair to emphasize how our ignorance
stands in the way of his attempt to ground
the obligatoriness of vegetarianism on utilitarian considerations. If we simply do not
know what the consequences of our becoming vegetarians would be, or are most likely
to be, and if we simply do not know whether the consequences that would result would
be, or are most likely to be, better than those
that would obtain if we did not become
vegetarians, then we simply lack any sem-
blance of a utilitarian justification for the
obligation to become vegetarians or for
amounting a frontal assault on commercial
animal agriculture. The decision to lead a
vegetarian way of life and, by doing so, to

lodge a moral complaint against commercial
animal agriculture, viewed from the perspective of Singer's utilitarianism, must be diag-
nosed as at best symbolic gestures.

Aside from these matters, what can be said
about the adequacy of utilitarianism in general? That is a question raised earlier to
which we must now direct our attention.
There is a vast literature critical of utilitarian
theory, and it will obviously not be possible
to survey it here. Here let us note just one
difficulty. Utilitarianism, at least as understood by Singer, implies that whether *I* am
doing what I ought to do is crucially dependent on what *other* people do. For example,
although the consequences of *my* abstaining
from eating meat are too modest to make
any difference to how animals are raised or
whether grains are made available to needy
people, if enough *other* people join me in a
vegetarian way of life we could collectively
bring about changes in the number of animals raised, how they are raised, what use is
made of grain, etc. The situation, in other
words, is as follows: If enough people join
me so that the consequences of what we do
collectively makes some impact, then what I
do might be right, whereas if too few people
join me, with the result that the consequences of what we do fails to make any
difference to how animals are raised, etc.,
then I am *not* doing what is right.

To make the morality of an individual's
acts depend on how others behave is a highly unsatisfactory consequence for any moral
theory. When people refuse to support racist or sexist practices (for example, in employment or education), they do what is
right, but their doing what is right does not
depend on how many *other* people join
them. The number of people who join them
determines how many people do or support
what is right, *not* what is right in the first
place. Utilitarianism, because it makes *what
is right* dependent in many cases on how
many people act in a certain way, puts the
moral cart before the horse. What we want
is a theory that illuminates moral right and
wrong independently of how many people

act in this or that way. And that is precisely what utilitarianism, at least in the form advocated by Singer, fails to give us. For all its promise as an attack on the anthropocentric traditions of humanism and theism, for all its insistence on the direct relevance of the interests of animals, and despite the radical sounding claims made by utilitarians in criticism of current practices on the farm and in the laboratory, utilitarianism proves to be more ethical shadow than substance. If we look beyond the rhetoric and examine the arguments, utilitarianism might not change these practices as much as it would fortify them.[7]

THE RIGHTS VIEW

An alternative to the utilitarian attack on anthropocentrism is what we shall call "the rights view."[8] Those who accept this view hold that (1) certain individuals have certain moral rights, (2) these individuals have these rights independently of considerations about the value of the consequences of treating them in one way or another, and (3) the duty the individual has to respect the rights of others does not depend on how many other people act in ways that respect these rights. The first point distinguishes proponents of the rights view from, among others, those utilitarians like Bentham and Singer who deny that individuals have moral rights; the second distinguishes advocates of the rights view from, among others, those utilitarians such as Mill who hold that individuals have moral rights if, and only if, the general welfare would be promoted by saying and acting as if they do; and the third point distinguishes those who champion the rights view from, among others, any advocate of utilitarianism who holds that my duty to act in certain ways depends on how many other people act in these ways. According to the rights view, certain individuals have moral rights, and my duty to act in ways that respect such an individual's (A's) rights is a duty I have directly to A, a duty I have to A that is not grounded in considerations about

the value of consequences for all those affected by the outcome, and a duty I have to A whatever else others might do to A. *Those who advocate animal rights, understanding this idea after the fashion of the rights view, believe that some of those individuals who have moral rights, and thus some of those to whom we have duties of the type just described, are animals.*

GROUNDS FOR THE RIGHTS VIEW

To proclaim "the moral rights of Man" sounds good but is notoriously difficult to defend. Bentham, who writes more forcefully to support what he rejects than to establish what he accepts, dismisses rights other than legal rights as "nonsense upon stilts." So we will not settle the thorny question about human rights of an essay's reading or writing. And, it goes without saying, the moral rights of animals must remain even less established. Were Bentham in his grave (in fact he remains above ground, encased in glass in an anteroom in University College, London, where he is dutifully brought to dinner each year on the occasion of his birthday) he would most certainly roll over at the mere mention of *animal* rights! Still, something needs to be said about the rational grounds for the rights view.

An important (but not the only possible) argument in this regard takes the following form: Unless we recognize that certain individuals have moral rights, we will be left holding moral principles that sanction morally reprehensible conduct. Thus, in order to avoid holding principles that allow such conduct, we must recognize that certain individuals have moral rights. The following discussion of utilitarianism is an example of this general line of argument.

Utilitarians cut from the same cloth as Bentham would have us judge moral right and wrong by appeal to the consequences of what we do. Well, suppose aged Aunt Bertha's heirs could have a lot more pleasure than she is likely to have in her declining years if she were to die. But suppose that neither nature nor Aunt Bertha will cooperate: She simply refuses to die as expeditiously as, gauged by the interest of her heirs, is desirable. Why not speed up the tempo of her demise? The reply given by Bentham-type utilitarians shows how far they are willing to twist our moral intuitions to save their theory. If we were to kill Aunt Bertha, especially if we took care to do so painlessly, then, these utilitarians submit, we would do no wrong to Aunt Bertha. However, if *other* people found out about what we did, they would quite naturally grow more anxious, more insecure about their own safety and mortality, and these mental states (anxiety, insecurity, and the like) are painful. Thus, so we are told, killing Aunt Bertha is wrong (if it is) because of the painful consequences for others!

Except for those already committed to a Bentham-style utilitarianism, few are likely to find this account satisfactory. Its shortcomings are all the more evident when we note that *if* others did not find out about our dastardly deed (and so were not made more anxious and insecure by their knowledge of what we did), and *if* we have a sufficiently undeveloped conscience not to be terribly troubled by what we did, and *if* we do not get caught, and *if* we have a jolly good time with Aunt Bertha's inheritance, a much better time, in fact, than we would have had if we had waited for nature to run its course, then Bentham-style utilitarianism implies that we did nothing wrong in killing Aunt Bertha and, indeed, acted as we morally ought to have acted. People who, in the face of this kind of objection, remain Bentham-type utilitarians, may hold a consistent position. But one pays a price for a "foolish consistency." The spectacle of people "defending their theory to the last" in spite of its grave implications must, to put it mildly, take one's moral breath away.

There are, of course, many ethical theories in addition to utilitarianism, and many versions of utilitarianism in addition to the one associated with Bentham. So even if the sketch of an argument against Bentham's

utilitarianism proves successful, the rights view would not thereby "win" in its competition with other theories. But the foregoing does succeed in giving a representative sample of one argument deployed by those who accept the rights view: If you deny moral rights, as Bentham does, then the principles you put in their place, which, in Bentham's case, is the principle of utility, will sanction morally reprehensible conduct (for example, the murder of Aunt Bertha). If those who affirm and defend the rights view could show this given *any* initially plausible theory that denies moral rights, and if they could crystalize and defend the methodology on which this argument depends, then they would have a powerful reason for their position.

THE VALUE OF THE INDIVIDUAL

The rights view aspires to satisfy our intellect, not merely our appetite for rhetoric, and so it is obliged to provide a theoretical home for moral rights. Part, but by no means not the whole, of this home is furnished by the rights views' theory of value. Unlike utilitarian theories (for example, value hedonism), the rights view recognizes *the value of individuals*, not just the value of their mental states (for example, their pleasures). Following custom, let us call these latter sorts of value "intrinsic values" and let us introduce the term "inherent value" for the type of value attributed to individuals. Then the notion of inherent value can be explained as follows. First, the inherent value of an individual who has such value is not the same as, is not reducible to, and is incommensurate with the intrinsic value of that individual's, or of any combination of individuals', mental states. The inherent value of an individual, in other words, is not equal to any sum of intrinsic values (for example, any sum of pleasures). Second, all individuals who have inherent value have it equally. Inherent value, that is, does not come in degrees; some who have it do not have it more or less than others. One either has it or one does not, and all who have it have it to the same extent. It is, one might say, a categorical concept. Third, the possession of inherent value by individuals does not depend on their utility relative to the interests of others, which, if it were true, would imply that some individuals have such value to a greater degree than do others, because some (for example, surgeons) have greater utility than do others (for example, bank thieves). Fourth, and relatedly, individuals cannot acquire or lose such value by anything they do. And fifth, and finally, the inherent value of individuals does not depend on what or how others think or feel about them. The loved and admired are neither more nor less inherently valuable than the despised and forsaken.

Now, the rights view claims that any individual who has inherent value is due treatment that respects this value (has, that is, a *moral right* to such treatment), and though not everything can be said here about what such respect comes to, at least this much should be clear: We fail to treat individuals with the respect they are due whenever we assume that how we treat them can be defended *merely* by asking about the value of the mental states such treatment produces for those affected by the outcome. This must fail to show appropriate respect since it is tantamount to treating these individuals as if they lacked inherent value—as if, that is, we treat them as we ought whenever we can justify our treatment of them *merely* on the grounds that it promotes the interests other individuals have in obtaining preferred mental states (for example, pleasure). Since individuals who have inherent value have a kind of value that is not reducible to their utility relative to the interests of others, we are not to treat them merely as a means to bringing about the best consequences. We ought not, then, kill Aunt Bertha, given the rights view, even if doing so brought about "the best" consequences. That would be to treat her with a lack of appropriate respect, something she has a moral right to. To kill her for these reasons would be to violate her rights.

WHICH INDIVIDUALS HAVE INHERENT VALUE?

Even assuming the rights view could succeed in providing a coherent, rationally persuasive theoretical framework for "the rights of Man," further argument would be necessary to illuminate and justify the rights of animals. That argument, not surprisingly, will be long and torturous. At least we can be certain of two things, however. First, it must include considerations about the criteria of right possession; and, second, it will have to include an explanation and defense of how animals meet these criteria. A few remarks about each of these two points will have to suffice.

Persons [9] are the possessors of moral rights, and though most human beings are persons, not all are. And some persons are not human beings. Persons are individuals who have a cluster of actual (not merely potential or former) abilities. These include awareness of their environment, desires and preferences, goals and purposes, feelings and emotions, beliefs and memories, a sense of the future and of their own identity. Most adult humans have these abilities and so are persons. But some (the irreversibly comatose, for example) lack them and so are not persons. Human fetuses and infants also are not persons, given this analysis, and so have no moral rights (which is not to say that we may therefore do anything to them that we have a mind to; there are moral constraints on what we may do in addition to those constraints that involve respect for the moral rights of others—but this is a long story . . .!).

As for nonhumans who are persons, the most famous candidate is God as conceived, for example, by Christians. When believers speak of "the blessed Trinity, three persons in one," they don't mean "three human beings in one." Extraterrestrials are another obvious candidate, at least as they crop up in standard science fiction. The extraterrestrials in Ray Bradbury's *Martian Chronicals,* for example, are persons, in the sense explained, but they assuredly are not human beings. But, of course, the most important candidates for our purposes are animals. And they are successful candidates if they perceive and remember, believe and desire, have feelings and emotions, and, in general, actually possess the other abilities mentioned earlier.

Those who affirm and defend the rights of animals believe that some animals actually possess these abilities. Of course, there are some who will deny this. All animals, they will say, lack all, or most, or at least some of the abilities that make an individual a person. In a fuller discussion of the rights view, these worries would receive the respectful airing they deserve. It must suffice here to say that the case for animal rights involves the two matters mentioned and explained—first, considerations about the criteria of right possession (or, alternatively, personhood), and, second, considerations that show that some animals satisfy these criteria. Those who would squelch the undertaking before it gets started by claiming that "it's *obvious* that animals cannot be persons!" offer no serious objection; instead, they give sorry expression to the very speciesist prejudice those who affirm and defend the rights of animals seek to overcome.

LINE DRAWING

To concede that some animals are persons and so have moral rights is not to settle the question, *Which* animals are persons? "Where do we draw the line?" it will be asked; indeed, it must be asked. The correct answer seems to be: We do not know with certainty. Perhaps there is no exact line to be drawn in this case, any more than there is an exact line to be drawn in other cases (for example, "Exactly how tall do you have to be to be tall?" "Exactly how old must you be before you are old?"). What we must ask is where in the animal kingdom we

find individuals who are *most like* paradigmatic persons—that is, most like us, both behaviorally and physiologically. The greater the similarity in these respects, the stronger the case for believing that these animals have *a mental life similar to our own* (including memory and emotion, for example), a case that is strengthened given the major thrust of evolutionary theory. So, while it remains a matter of uncertainty *exactly* where we are to draw this line, it is implausible to deny that adult mammalian animals have the abilities in question (just as, analogously, it would be implausible to deny that eighty-eight-year-old Aunt Bertha is old because we don't know exactly how old someone must be before they are old). To get this far in the argument for animal rights is not to finish the story, but it is to give a rough outline of a major chapter in it.

THE INHERENT VALUE OF ANIMALS

Moral rights, as explained earlier, need a theoretical home, and the rights view provides this by its use of the notion of inherent value. Not surprisingly, therefore, the rights view affirms this value in the case of those animals who are persons; not to do so would be to slide back into the prejudice of speciesism. Moreover, because all who possess this value possess it equally, the rights view makes no distinction between the inherent value human persons possess as distinct from that possessed by those persons who are animals. And just as *our* inherent value, as persons, does not depend on our utility relative to the interests of others, or on how much we are liked or admired, or on anything we do or fail to do, the same must be true in the case of animals who, as persons, have the same inherent value we do.

To regard animals in the way advocated by the rights view makes a truly profound difference to our understanding of what, morally speaking, we may do to them, as well as how, morally speaking, we can defend what we do. Those animals who have inherent value have a moral right to respectful treatment, a right we fail to respect whenever we attempt to justify what we do to them by appeal to "the best consequences." What these animals are due, in other words, is the same respectful treatment we are. We must never treat them in this or that way merely because, we claim, doing so is necessary to bring about "the best consequences" for all affected by the outcome.

The rights view therefore calls for the total dissolution of commercial animal agriculture as we know it. Not merely "modern" intensive rearing methods must cease. For though the harm visited upon animals raised in these circumstances is real enough and is morally to be condemned, its removal would not eliminate the basic wrong its presence compounds. The *basic* wrong is that animals raised for commercial profit are viewed and treated in ways that fail to show respect for their moral right to respectful treatment. *They* are not (though of course they may be treated as if they are) "commodities," "economic units," "investments," "a renewable resource," etc. They are, like us, persons and so, like us, are owed treatment that accords with their right to be treated with respect, a respect we fail to show when we end their life before doing so can be defended on the grounds of mercy. Since animals are routinely killed on grounds other than mercy in the course of commercial animal agriculture, that human enterprise violates the rights of animals.

Unlike the utilitarian approach to ethical vegetarianism, the rights view basis does not require that we know what the consequences of our individual or collective abstention from meat will be. The moral imperatives to treat farm animals with respect and to refuse to support those who fail to do so do not rest on calculations about consequences. And unlike a Singer-type utilitarianism, the rights view does not imply that the individual's duty to become a vegetarian depends on how many other people join the ranks. *Each individual* has the duty to treat others with the respect they are due independently of how many others do so, and each has a similar duty to refrain in principle from supporting practices that fail to show proper respect. Of course, anyone who accepts the rights view must profoundly wish that others *will* act similarly, with the result that commercial animal agriculture, from vast agribusiness operations to the traditional family farm, will go the way of the slave trade—will, that is, cease to exist. But the *individual's* duty to cease to support those who violate the rights of animals does not depend on humanity in general doing so as well.

The rights view is, one might say, a "radical" position, calling, as it does, for the total abolition of a culturally accepted institution to wit, commercial animal farming. The way to "clean up" this institution is not by giving animals bigger cages, cleaner stalls, a place to roost, thus and so much hay, etc. When an institution is grounded in injustice, because it fails to respect the rights of those involved, there is no room for internal house cleaning. Morality will not be satisfied with anything less than its total abolition. And that, for the reasons given, is the rights view's verdict regarding commercial animal agriculture.

HOLISM

The "radical" implications of the rights view suggest how far some philosophers have moved from the anthropocentric traditions of theism and humanism. But, like the utilitarian attacks on this tradition, one should note that the rights view seeks to make its case by working within the major ethical categories of this tradition. For example, hedonistic utilitarians do not deny the moral relevance of human pleasures and pain, so important to our humanist forebears; rather, they accept this and seek to extend our moral horizons to include the moral relevance of the pleasures and pains of animals. And the rights view does not deny the distinctive moral importance of the individual, a central article of belief in theistic thought;

rather, it accepts this moral datum and seeks to widen the class of individuals who are to be thought of in this way to include many animals.

Because both the positions discussed in the preceding work with major ethical categories handed down to us by our predecessors, some influential thinkers argue that these positions are, despite all appearances, in the hip pocket, so to speak, of the *Weltanschauung* they aspire to overturn. What is needed, these thinkers contend or imply, is not a broader interpretation of traditional categories (for example, the category of "the rights of the individual"); rather, what is required is the overthrow of these categories. Only then will we have a new vision, one that liberates us from the last vestiges of anthropocentrism.

"THE LAND ETHIC"

Among those whose thought moves in this direction, none is more influential than Aldo Leopold.[10] *Very* roughly, Leopold can be seen as rejecting the "atomism" dear to the hearts of those who build their moral thinking on "the value (or rights) of the individual." What has ultimate value is not the individual but the collective, not the "part" but the "whole," whereby "the whole" is meant the entire biosphere: the *totality* of the things and systems in the natural order. Acts are right, Leopold claims, if they tend to promote the integrity, beauty, diversity, and harmony of the biosphere; they are wrong if they tend contrariwise. As for individuals, be they humans or animals, they are merely "members of the biotic team," having neither more nor less value in themselves than any other member—having, that is, *no* value "in themselves." What good individuals have, so far as this is computable at all, is instrumental only: They are good to the extent that they promote the "welfare," so to speak, of the biosphere. For a Leopoldian, the rights view rests on the fictional view that individuals have a kind of value they in fact lack.

Traditional utilitarianism, not just the rights view, goes by the board, given Leopold's vision. To extend our moral concern to the experiences of animals (for example, their pleasures and pains) is not to overcome the prejudices indigenous to anthropocentrism. One who does this is still in the grip of these prejudices, supposing that mental states that matter to humans must be the yardstick of what matters morally. Utilitarians are people who escape from one prejudice (speciesism) only to embrace another (what we might call "sentientism," the view that mental states allied with or reducible to pleasure and pain are what matter morally). "Animal liberation" is not "nature liberation." In order to forge an ethic that liberates us from our anthropocentric tradition, we must develop a holistic understanding of things, a molecular, rather than an atomistic, vision of the scheme of things and our place in it. "The land" must be viewed as meriting or moral concern. Water, soil, plants, rocks—inanimate, not just animate, existence must be seen to be morally considerable. All are "members" of the same team—the "biotic team."

HOLISM AND ETHICAL VEGETARIANISM

The holism Leopold advocates has interesting implications regarding how we should approach the issue of ethical vegetarianism. Appeals to the rights of animals, of course, are ruled out from the start. Based, as they are, on ideas about the independent value of the individual, such appeals are the voice of anthropocentrism past. That ghost can be exorcised once and for all only if we see the illusoriness of the atomistic view of the individual, *any* individual, as having an independent value, dignity, sanctity, etc. Standard versions of utilitarianism, restricted, as they are, to sentient creation, are similarly out of place. The "moral community" is comprised of all that inhabits the biosphere, not just some select portion of it, and there is no guarantee that what optimizes the balance of, say, pleasure over pain for sentient creation would be the right thing to do, when gauged by what promotes the "welfare" of the biosphere as a whole. If we are to approach the question of ethical vegetarianism with a clear head, therefore, we should refuse the guidance of both the rights view and utilitarianism.

Holism implies that the case for or against ethical vegetarianism must be decided by asking how certain practices involving animals promote or diminish the integrity, diversity, beauty, and harmony of the biosphere. This will be no easy task. Utilitarianism, as was noted earlier, encounters a very serious problem, when it faces the difficulty of saying what the consequences will be, or are most likely to be, if we do one thing rather than another. And this problem arises for utilitarians despite the fact that they restrict their calculations just to the effects on sentient creation. How much more difficult it must be, then, to calculate the consequences for *the biosphere*! There is some danger that "the Land Ethic" will not be able to get off the ground.

Let us assume, however, that this challenge could be met. Then it seems quite likely that the land ethic might judge some practices involving animals morally right, others wrong. For example, raising cattle on nonarable pastures might promote the biosphere's "welfare," whereas destroying a delicately balanced ecosystem in order to construct a factory farm, or allowing chemicals used in animal agriculture to pollute a stream or pond, might be roundly condemned as "unhealthy" for the biosphere. Holism, in short, presumably would decide the ethics of animal agriculture on a case by case basis. When a given commercial undertaking meets the principles of the land ethic, it is right, and we are free to support it by purchasing its wares. When a given commercial undertaking fails to meet the appropriate principles, it is wrong, and we ought not to help it along by buying its products. So far as the matter of the pain, stress, and deprivations that might be caused

farm animals in a commercial endeavor that promotes the "welfare" of the biosphere, these "mental states" simply do not compute, and to be morally troubled by such concerns is unwittingly to slip back into the misplaced atomistic concern for the individual holism aspires to redirect.

HOLISM AS ENVIRONMENTAL FASCISM

Few will be easily won over to this "new vision" of things. Like political fascism, where "the good of the State" supercedes "the good of the individual," what holism gives us is a fascist understanding of the environment. Rare species of wild grasses doubtless contribute more to the diversity of the biosphere than do the citizens of Cleveland. But are we therefore morally obliged to "save the wild grasses" at the expense of the life or welfare of these people? If holism is to hold its ground, it must acknowledge that it has this implication, and, in acknowledging this it must acknowledge further that its theoretical boat will come to grief on the shoals of our considered moral beliefs. Of course, those who are determined to awaken us to holism's virtues may be expected to reply that they are out to *reform* our moral vision, to *change* it, and so should not be expected to provide us with a theory that conforms with our "moral intuitions"—intuitions that, they are likely to add, are but another layer of our uncritical acceptance of our anthropocentric traditions and the ethnocentrism with which they are so intimately allied.

Well, perhaps this is so. Everything depends on the arguments given to support these bold pronouncements. What those arguments come to, or even if they come, must be considered elsewhere.[11] Here it must suffice to note that people who remain sympathetic to notions like "the rights of Man" and "the value of the individual" will not find environmental fascism congenial. And that is a crucial point, given the debate over ethical vegetarianism and commercial animal agriculture. For one cannot consistently defend meat-eating or commercial animal agriculture by appeal to the principles of "the Land Ethic," on the one hand, and, on the other, appeal to principles involving human rights and the value of the individual to defend one's convictions about how human beings should be treated. Environmental fascism and *any* form of a rights theory are like oil and water; they don't mix.

SUMMARY

Two related questions have occupied our attention throughout: (1) Is vegetarianism required on moral grounds? and (2) Judged ethically, what should we say, and what should we do, about commercial animal agriculture? Three different ways to approach these questions have been characterized: utilitarianism, the rights view, and holism. Of the three, the rights view is the most "radical"; it calls for the total abolition of commercial animal agriculture and argues that, as individuals, we have an obligation to cease eating meat, including the meat produced by the animal industry, independently of how many other people do so and independently of the actual consequences our individual abstention have on this industry. Since this industry routinely violates the rights of farm animals, those who support it, not just those who run and profit from it, have "dirty hands."

Some utilitarians evidently seek the same answers offered by the rights view, but their arguments are radically different. Since what we ought to do depends on the consequences, and since our individual abstention from meat eating would not make a whit of difference to any individual animal, it seems we cannot have an obligation to be vegetarians, judged on utilitarian grounds. If, in reply, we are told that it is the consequences of *many* people becoming vegetarians, not just those that flow from the individual's abstention, that grounds the obligation to be vegetarian, utilitarians are, so to speak, out of the frying pan but into the fire. First, we

do not know what the consequences will be (for example, for the economy, the starving masses of the Third World, or even farm animals) if many people became vegetarians, and, second, it distorts our very notion of the duties of the individual to suppose that these duties depend on how many other people act in similar ways. So, no, these utilitarians do not succeed in showing *either* that we have an obligation to be vegetarians *or* that commercial animal agriculture is morally to be condemned. These utilitarians may want the conclusions the rights view reaches, but, paradoxically, their utilitarianism stands in the way of getting them.

Holism (the kind of theory we find in Aldo Leopold's work, for example) was the third view considered. So long as we have reason to believe that this or that commercial endeavor in farm animals is not contrary to the beauty, harmony, diversity, and integrity of the biosphere, we have no reason to condemn its operation nor any reason to refuse to consume its products. If, however, particular commercial ventures are destructive of these qualities of the biosphere, we ought to bring them to a halt, and one way of helping to do this is to cease to buy their products. Holism, in short, answers our two questions, one might say, with an unequivocal "Yes and no." Very serious questions remain, however, concerning how we can know what, according to holism, we must know, before we can say that a given act or practice is right or wrong. Can we really presume to know the consequences of our acts "for the biosphere?" Moreover, holism implies that individuals are of no consequence apart from their role as "members of the biotic team," a fascist view of the individual that would in principle allow mass destruction of the members of a plentiful species (for example, Homo sapiens) in order to preserve the last remaining members of another (for example, a rare wild flower), all in the name of preserving "the diversity" of the biosphere. Few will find holism intuitively congenial, and none can rely on it to answer our two questions and, in mid-stride, invoke "the rights of man" to defend a privileged moral status for human beings. At least none can consistently do this.

Despite their noteworthy differences, the three views we have examined speak with one voice on the matter of the tradition of anthropocentrism bequeathed to us by humanism and theism. That tradition is morally bankrupt. On that the three are agreed. And on this, it seems, we may all agree as well. That being so, and while conceding that the foregoing does not "prove" its merits, it can be no objection to the rights view's answers to our two questions to protest that they are at odds with our moral traditions. To be at odds with these traditions is devoutly to be wished.

Nor is it an objection to the rights view to claim that because it proclaims the rights of animals, it must be unmindful of "the rights of Man" or insensitive to the beauty or integrity of the environment. The rights view does not deny "the rights of Man"; it only refuses to be species-bound in its vision of inherent value and moral rights. No principle it upholds opposes making grains not fed to animals available to needy humans, as commercial animal agriculture winds down. It simply insists that *these* (real or imaginary) consequences of the dissolution of commercial animal agriculture are not the reason why we ought to seek to dissolve it. As for the natural environment, one can only wonder what more one could do to ensure that its integrity and beauty are promoted or retained, than to act in ways that show respect to animals, including wild animals. In respecting the rights of this "part" of the biosphere, will not the "welfare of the whole" be promoted?

CONCLUSION

Theories are one thing; our practice quite another. And so it may seem that all this talk about rights and duties, utility and preferences, the biosphere and anthropocentrism comes to naught. People are people, and they will do what they are used to doing, what they like to do. History gives the lie to this lazy acquiescence in the face of custom and convenience. Were it true, whites would still own blacks, women would still lack the vote, and people could still be put to death for sodomy. Times and customs change, and one (but by no means not the only) force for change are the ideas that trickle down over time into the language and thought of a culture. The language of "animal rights" is in the air, and the thought behind those words is taking root. What not too long ago could be laughed out of court now elicits serious concern. Mill says it well: "All great movements go through three stages: ridicule, discussion, adoption." The movement for animal rights is beyond the stage of ridicule. For those persuaded of its truth, it is an irresistible force. Commercial animal agriculture is the movable object.

Footnotes

1. Immanuel Kant, "Duties to Animals and Spirits," *Lectures on Ethics*, trans. Louis Infield (New York: Harper and Row, 1963), pp. 239–41. Collected in *Animal Rights and Human Obligations*, Tom Regan and Peter Singer, eds. (Englewood Cliffs, NJ: Prentice-Hall Inc., 1976), pp. 122–23.

2. St. Thomas Aquinas, *Summa Contra Gentiles*, literally translated by the English Dominican Fathers (Benzinger Books, 1928), Third Book, Part II, Chap. C XII. Collected in *Animal Rights and Human Obligations*, op. cit., pp. 58–59.

3. Jeremy Bentham, *The Principles of Morals and Legislation* (1789: many editions), Chapter XVII, Section 1. Collected in *Animal Rights and Human Obligations*, op. cit., pp. 129–30.

4. John Stuart Mill, "Whewell on Moral Philosophy," *Collected Works*, Vol. X, pp. 185–87. Collected in *Animal Rights and Human Obligations*, op. cit., pp. 131–32.

5. Peter Singer, *Animal Liberation* (New York: Avon Books, 1975). By far the best factual account of factory farming is J. Mason and Peter Singer, *Animal Factories* (New York: Collier Books, 1982).

6. Richard Ryder, "Experiments on Animals," in *Animals, Men and Morals*, ed. S. and R. Godlovitch and J. Harris (New York: Taplinger, 1972). Collected in *Animal Rights and Human Obligations*, op. cit., pp. 33–47.

7. These criticisms of utilitarianism are developed at greater length in my *The Case For Animal Rights* (Berkeley: University of California Press. London: Routledge and Kegan Paul, 1983).

8. The rights view is developed at length in *The Case For Animal Rights*, ibid.

9. I use the familiar idea of "person" here because it is helpful. I do not use it in *The Case For Animal Rights*.

I do not believe anything of substance turns on its use or nonuse.

10. Aldo Leopold, *A Sand County Almanac* (New York: Oxford University Press, 1949). For additional criticism and suggested readings, see William Aiken, "Ethical Issues in Agriculture," in Tom Regan, ed., *Earthbound: New Introductory Essays in Environmental Ethics* (New York: Random House (paper); Philadelphia: Temple University Press (cloth), 1983), pp. 268–70.

11. See *The Case For Animal Rights*, op. cit., ch. 5.

Review Questions

1. Explain traditional moral anthropocentrism.

2. What is the utilitarian objection to this view?

3. What objections does Regan make to Singer's position?

4. Explain the rights view.

5. What is "inherent value?"

6. Who has rights?

7. Why does commercial animal agriculture violate the rights of animals, assuming they have rights?

8. Explain the holism advocated by Leopold.

9. Why doesn't Regan accept this view?

Discussion Questions

1. Does Regan refute utilitarianism or not? Explain your answer.

2. Is Regan's notion of "inherent value" coherent?

3. Do you agree that some animals are persons? Defend your answer.

4. Do you eat meat? If so, do you think that there is anything morally wrong with this practice? Defend your position.

WILLIAM GODFREY–SMITH

The Value of Wilderness

Reprinted with permission of *Environmental Ethics* and the author.

William Godfrey-Smith teaches philosophy at Australian National University (Canberra, Australia).

Godfrey-Smith explores two kinds of justification for wilderness preservation, an instrumental justification and a holistic one based on the intrinsic value of the wilderness. He finds that the instrumental justifications for conservation—saving the wilderness because it is a cathedral, a laboratory, a silo, or a gymnasium—all fail to provide a satisfactory rationale. Instead he suggests a holistic conception of nature where we think of humans and nature together forming a moral community, and where we must engage in cooperative behavior for the sake of the whole community.

Wilderness is the raw material out of which man has hammered the artifact called civilization.[1]
                                                                       Aldo Leopold

The framework that I examine is the framework of *Western* attitudes toward our natural environment, and wilderness in particular. The philosophical task to which I shall address myself is an exploration of attitudes toward wilderness, especially the sorts of justification to which we might legitimately appeal for the preservation of wilderness: what grounds can we advance in support of the claim that wilderness is something that we should *value?*

There are two different ways of appraising something as valuable. It may be that the thing in question is good or valuable *for the sake* of something that we hold to be valuable. In this case the thing is not considered to be good in itself; value in this sense is ascribed in virtue of the thing's being a *means* to some valued end, and not as an *end in itself.* Such values are standardly designated *instrumental* values. Not everything that we hold to be good or valuable can be good for the sake of something else; our values must ultimately be *grounded* in something that is held to be good or valuable in itself. Such things are said to be *intrinsically* valuable. As a matter of historical fact, those things that have been held to be intrinsically valuable, within our Western traditions of thought, have nearly always been taken to be states or conditions of *persons*, e.g., happiness, pleasure, knowledge, or self-realization, to name but a few.

It follows from this that a very central assumption of Western moral thought is that value can be ascribed to the nonhuman world only insofar as it is good for the sake of the well-being of human beings.[2] Our entire attitude toward the natural environment, therefore, has a decidedly anthropocentric bias, and this fact is reflected in the sorts of justification that are standardly provided for the preservation of the natural environment.

A number of thinkers, however, are becoming increasingly persuaded that our anthropocentric morality is in fact inadequate to provide a satisfactory basis for a moral philosophy of ecological obligation. It is for this reason that we hear not infrequently the claim that we need a "new morality." A new moral framework—that is, a network of recognized obligations and duties—is not, however, something that can be casually conjured up in order to satisfy some vaguely felt need. The task of developing a sound biologically based moral philosophy, a philosophy that is not anthropocentrically based, and that provides a satisfactory justification for ecological obligation and concern, is, I think, one of the most urgent tasks confronting moral philosophers at the present. It will entail a radical reworking of accepted attitudes—attitudes that we currently accept as "self-evident"—and this is not something that can emerge suddenly. Indeed, I think the seminal work remains largely to be done, though I suggest below the broad outline that an environmentally sound moral philosophy is likely to take.

In the absence of a comprehensive and convincing ecologically based morality we naturally fall back on *instrumental* justifications for concern for our natural surroundings, and for preserving wilderness areas and animal species. We can, I think, detect at least four main lines of instrumental justification for the preservation of wilderness. By *wilderness* I understand any reasonably large tract of the earth, together with its plant and animal communities, which is substantially unmodified by humans and in particular by human technology. The natural contrast to *wilderness* and *nature* is an *artificial* or *domesticated* environment. The fact that there are borderline cases that are difficult to classify does not, of course, vitiate this distinction.

The first attitude toward wilderness espoused by conservationists to which I wish to draw attention is what I shall call the "cathedral" view. This is the view that wilderness areas provide a vital opportunity for spiritual revival, moral regeneration, and aesthetic delight. The enjoyment of wilderness is often compared in this respect with religious or mystical experience. Preservation of magnificent wilderness areas for those who subscribe to this view is essential for human well-being, and its destruction is conceived as something akin to an act of vandalism, perhaps comparable to—some may regard it as more serious than [3]—the destruction of a magnificent and moving human edifice, such as the Parthenon, the Taj Mahal, or the Palace of Versailles.

Insofar as the "cathedral" view holds that value derives solely from human satisfactions gained from its contemplation it is clearly an instrumentalist attitude. It does, however, frequently approach an *intrinsic value* attitude, insofar as the feeling arises that there is importance in the fact that it is there to be contemplated, whether or not anyone actually takes advantage of this fact. Suppose for example, that some wilderness was so precariously balanced that *any* human intervention or contact would inevitably bring about its destruction. Those who maintained that the area should, nevertheless, be preserved, unexperienced and unenjoyed, would certainly be ascribing to it an intrinsic value.

The "cathedral" view with respect to wilderness in fact is a fairly recent innovation in Western thought. The predominant Greco-Christian attitude, which generally speaking was the predominant Western attitude prior to eighteenth- and nineteenth-century romanticism, had been to view wilderness as threatening or alarming, an attitude still reflected in the figurative uses of the expression *wilderness,* clearly connoting a degenerate state to be avoided. Christianity, in general, has enjoined "the transformation of wilderness, those dreaded haunts of demons, the ancient nature-gods, into farm and pasture," [4] that is, to a domesticated environment.

The second instrumental justification of the value of wilderness is what we might call the "laboratory" argument. This is the argument that wilderness areas provide vital subject matter for scientific inquiry that provides us with an understanding of the intricate interdependencies of biological systems, their modes of change and development, their energy cycles, and the source of their stabilities. If we are to understand our own biological dependencies, we require natural systems as a norm, to inform us of the biological laws that we transgress at our peril.

The third instrumentalist justification is the "silo" argument, which points out that one excellent reason for preserving reasonable areas of the natural environment intact is that we thereby preserve a stockpile of genetic diversity, which it is certainly prudent to maintain as a backup in case something should suddenly go wrong with the simplified biological systems that, in general, constitute agriculture. Further, there is the related point that there is no way of anticipating our future needs, or the undiscovered applications of apparently useless plants, which might turn out to be, for example, the source of some pharmacologically valuable drug—a cure, say, for leukemia. This might be called, perhaps, the "rare herb" argument, and it provides another persuasive instrumental justification for the preservation of wilderness.

The final instrumental justification that I think should be mentioned is the "gymnasium" argument, which regards the preservation of wilderness as important for athletic or recreational activities.

An obvious problem that arises from these instrumental arguments is that the various activities that they seek to justify are not always possible to reconcile with one another. The interests of the wilderness lover who subscribes to the "cathedral" view are not always reconcilable with those of the ordinary vacationist. Still more obvious is the conflict between the recreational use of wilderness and the interests of the miner, the farmer, and the timber merchant.

The conflict of interest that we encounter here is one that it is natural to try and settle through the economic calculus of cost-benefit considerations. So long as the worth of natural systems is believed to depend entirely on instrumental values, it is natural to suppose that we can sort out the conflict of interests within an objective frame of reference, by estimating the human satisfactions to be gained from the preservation of wilderness, and by weighing these against the satisfactions that are to be gained from those activities that may lead to its substantial modification, domestication, and possibly even destruction.

Many thinkers are liable to encounter here a feeling of resistance to the suggestion that we can apply purely economic considerations to settle such conflicts of interest. The assumption behind economic patterns of thought, which underline policy formulation and planning, is that the values that we attach to natural systems and to productive activities are commensurable; this is an assumption that may be called into question. It is not simply a question of the difficulty of quantifying what value should be attached to the preservation of the natural environment. The feeling is more that economic considerations are simply out of place. This feeling is one that is often too lightly dismissed by tough-minded economists as being obscurely mystical or superstitious; but it is a view worth examining. What it amounts to, I suggest, is the belief that there is something *morally* objectionable in the destruction of natural systems, or at least in their wholesale elimination, and this is precisely the belief that natural systems, or economically "useless" species do possess an *intrinsic* value. That is, it is an attempt to articulate the rejection of the anthropocentric view that all value, ultimately, resides in *human* interests and concerns. But it is a difficult matter to try to provide justification for such attitudes, and this is, for reasons that are deeply bound up with the problems of resolving basic value conflict, a problem that I have discussed elsewhere.[5]

The belief that all values are commensurable, so that there is no problem *in principle* in providing a satisfactory resolution of value conflict, involves the assumption that the quantitative social sciences, in particular economics, can provide an *objective* frame of reference within which all conflicts of interest can be satisfactorily resolved. We should, however, note that in the application of cost-benefit analyses there is an inevitable bias in the sorts of values that figure in the calculation, to wit, a bias toward those considerations that are readily quantifiable, and toward those interests that will be staunchly defended. This is a fairly trivial point, but it is one that has substantial consequences, for there are at least three categories of values and interests that are liable to be inadequately considered, or discounted altogether.[6] First, there are the interests of those who are too widely distributed spatially, or too incrementally affected over time, to be strongly supported by any single advocate. Second, there are the interests of persons not yet existing, to wit, future generations, who are clearly liable to be affected by present policy, but who are clearly not in a position to press any claims. Third, there are interests not associated with humans at all, such as the "rights" of wild animals.[7]

This last consideration, in particular, is apt to impress many as ludicrous, as quite simply "unthinkable." It is an unquestioned axiom of our present code of ethics that the class of individuals to which we have obligations is the class of humans. The whole apparatus of rights and duties is in fact based on an ideal of reciprocal contractual obligations, and in terms of this model the class of individuals to whom we may stand in moral relations—i.e., those with whom we recognize a network of rights, duties, and obligations—is the class of humans. A major aspect of a satisfactory ethic of ecological obligation and concern will be to challenge this central anthropocentric assumption. I return to this point below.

Even restricting our attention to the class of human preference havers, however, we should be wary of dismissing as simply inadmissible the interests of future generations. The claims of posterity tend to be excluded from our policy deliberations not, I suspect, because we believe that future generations will be unaffected by our policies, but because we lack any clear idea as to how to set about attaching weight to their interests. This is an instance of the familiar problem of "the dwarfing of soft variables." In settling conflicts of interest, any consideration that cannot be precisely quantified tends to be given little weight or, more likely, left out of the equation altogether: "If you can't measure it, it doesn't exist."[8] The result of ignoring soft variables is a spurious appearance of completeness and precision, but in eliminating all soft variables from our cost-benefit calculations, the conclusion is decidedly biased. If, as seems plausible, it is *in principle* impossible to do justice to soft variables, such as the interests of posterity, it may be that we have to abandon the idea that the economic models employed in cost-benefit calculations are universally applicable for sorting out all conflicts of interest. It may be necessary to abandon the economic calculus as the universal model for rational deliberation.[9]

Another category of soft variable that tends to be discounted from policy deliberations is that which concerns economically unimportant species of animals or plants. A familiar subterfuge that we frequently encounter is the attempt to invest such species with spurious economic value, as illustrated in the rare herb argument. A typical example of this, cited by Leopold, is the reaction of ornithologists to the threatened disappearance of certain species of songbirds: they at once came forward with some distinctly shaky evidence that they played an essential role in the control of insects.[10] The dominance of economic modes of thinking is again obvious: the evidence has to be economic in order to be acceptable. This exemplifies the way in which we turn to instrumentalist justifications for the maintenance of biotic diversity.

The alternative to such instrumentalist justifications, the alternative that Leopold advocated with great insight and eloquence, is to widen the boundary of the moral community to include animals, plants, the soil, or collectively *the land.*[11] This involves a radical shift in our conception of nature, so that land is recognized not simply as property, to be dealt with or disposed of as a matter of expediency; land in Leopold's view is not a commodity that belongs to us, but a community to which we belong. This change in conception is far-reaching and profound. It involves a shift in our metaphysical conception of nature—that is, a change in what sort of thing we take our natural surroundings to *be.* This is a point that I would like to elaborate, albeit sketchily.

The predominant Western conception of nature is exemplified in—and to no small extent is a consequence of—the philosophy of Descartes, in which nature is viewed as something separate and apart, to be transformed and controlled at will. Descartes divided the world into conscious thinking substances—minds—and extended, mechanically arranged substances—the rest of nature. It is true that we find in Western thought alternatives to the Cartesian metaphysical conception of nature—the views of Spinoza and Hegel might be mentioned in particular[12]—but the predominant spirit, especially among scientists, has been Cartesian. These metaphysical views have become deeply embedded in Western thought, which has induced us to view the world through Cartesian spectacles. One of the triumphs of Descartes' mechanistic view of nature has been the elimination of occult qualities and forces from the explanation of natural events. The natural world is to be understood, in the Cartesian model, in purely mechanistic terms. An unfortunate consequence of the triumph, nevertheless, has been a persistent fear among some thinkers that the rejection of Cartesian metaphysics may lead to the reinstatement of occult and mystical views of nature.

An important result of Descartes' sharp ontological division of the world into active mental substances and inert material substances, has been the alienation of man from the natural world. Although protests have been raised against Cartesian metaphysics ever since its inception, it has exercised a deep influence on our attitudes toward nature. Descartes' mechanistic conception of nature naturally leads to the view that it is possible in principle to obtain complete mastery and technical control over the natural world. It is significant to recall that for Descartes the paradigm instance of a natural object was a lump of wax, the perfect exemplification of malleability. This conception of natural objects as wholly pliable and passive is clearly one that leaves no room for anything like a network of obligations.

A natural corollary of the mechanistic conception of nature, and integral to the Cartesian method of inquiry, is the role played by reductive thinking. In order to understand a complex system one should, on this view, break it into its component parts and examine them. The Cartesian method of inquiry is a natural correlate of Cartesian metaphysics, and is a leitmotif of our science-based technology.

It should be stressed that a rejection of the Cartesian attitude and its method of inquiry need *not* involve a regression to occult and mystical views about the "sacredness" of the natural world, and the abandoning of systematic rational inquiry. It must be conceded, however, that the rejection of the view that nature is an exploitable commodity has, unfortunately, frequently taken this form. This sort of romantic nature mysticism *does* provide a powerful exhortation for exercising restraint in our behavior to the natural world, but it carries with it a very clear danger. This is that while prohibiting destructive acts toward the natural world, it equally prohibits constructive acts; we surely cannot rationally adopt a complete "hands off" policy with respect to nature, on the basis of what looks like the extremely implausible—and highly cynical—a priori assumption that *any* attempt to modify our surroundings is bound to be for the worse.

It may, however, be that advocates of the "sacredness" of nature are attempting to do no more than articulate the idea that natural

systems have their own intrinsic value, and adopt this manner of speaking as a convenient way of rejecting the dominant anthropocentric morality. If *this* is all that is being claimed, then I have no quarrel with it. And it may be inevitable that this mode of expression is adopted in the absence of a developed ecologically sound alternative morality. But I think we should be wary of this style of justification; what is needed, as Passmore has nicely expressed it, is not the spiritualizing of nature, but the naturalizing of man.[13] This involves a shift from the piecemeal reductive conception of natural items to a *holistic* or systemic view in which we come to appreciate the symbiotic interdependencies of the natural world. On the holistic or total-field view, organisms—including man—are conceived as nodes in a biotic web of intrinsically related parts.[14] That is, our understanding of biological organisms requires more than just an understanding of their structure and properties; we also have to attend seriously to their interrelations. Holistic or systemic thinking does not deny that organisms are complex physicochemical systems, but it affirms that the methods employed in establishing the high-level functional relationships expressed by physical laws are often of very limited importance in understanding the nature of biological systems. We may now be facing, in the terminology of Thomas Kuhn,[15] a shift from a physical to a biological paradigm in our understanding of nature. This seems to me to be an important aspect of the rejection of Cartesian metaphysics.

The limitations of the physical paradigm have long been accepted in the study of human society, but the tendency has been to treat social behavior and human action as quite distinct from the operations of our natural surroundings. The inappropriateness of the physical paradigm for understanding *human* society seems to me to be quite correct; what is comparatively new is the post-Cartesian realization that the physical paradigm is of more limited application for our understanding of *nature* than was previously supposed.

The holistic conception of the natural world contains, in my view, the possibility of extending the idea of community beyond human society. And in this way biological wisdom does, I think, carry implications for ethics. Just as Copernicus showed us that man does not occupy the physical center of the universe, Darwin and his successors have shown us that man occupies no *biologically* privileged position. We still have to assimilate the implications that this biological knowledge has for morality.

Can we regard man and the natural environment as constituting a community in any morally significant sense? Passmore, in particular, has claimed that this extended sense of community is entirely spurious.[16] Leopold, on the other hand, found the biological extension of community entirely natural.[17] If we regard a community as a collection of individuals who engage in cooperative behavior, Leopold's extension seems to me entirely legitimate. An ethic is no more than a code of conduct designed to ensure cooperative behavior among the members of a community. Such cooperative behavior is required to underpin the health of the community, in this biologically extended sense, *health* being understood as the biological capacity for self-renewal,[18] and *ill-health* as the degeneration or loss of this capacity.

Man, of course, cannot be placed on "all fours" with his biologically fellow creatures in all respects. In particular, man is the only creature who can act as a full-fledged moral agent, i.e., an individual capable of exercising reflective rational choice on the basis of principles. What distinguishes man from his fellow creatures is not the capacity to *act,* but the fact that his actions are, to a great extent, free from programming. This capacity to modify our own behavior is closely bound up with the capacity to acquire knowledge of the natural world, a capacity that has enabled us, to an unprecedented extent, to manipulate the environment, and—especially in the recent past—to

alter it rapidly, violently, and globally. Our hope must be that the capacity for knowledge, which has made ecologically hazardous activities possible, will lead to a more profound understanding of the delicate biological interdependencies that some of these actions now threaten, and thereby generate the wisdom for restraint.

To those who are skeptical of the possibility of extending moral principles in the manner of Leopold, to include items treated heretofore as matters of expediency, it can be pointed out that extensions have, to a limited extent, already taken place. One clear—if partial—instance, is in the treatment of animals. It is now generally accepted, and this is a comparatively recent innovation,[19] that we have at least a prima facie obligation not to treat animals cruelly or sadistically. And this certainly constitutes a shift in moral attitudes. If—as seems to be the case—cruelty to animals is accepted as intrinsically wrong, then there *is* at least one instance in which it is *not* a matter of moral indifference how we behave toward the nonhuman world.

More familiar perhaps are the moral revolutions that have occurred within the specific domain of human society—witness the progressive elimination of the "right" to racial, class, and sex exploitation. Each of these shifts involves the acceptance, on the part of some individuals, of new obligations, rights, and values that, to a previous generation, would have been considered unthinkable.[20] The essential step in recognizing an enlarged community involves coming to see, feel, and understand what was previously perceived as alien and apart: it is the evolution of the capacity of *empathy*.

I have digressed a little into the history of ideas, stressing in particular the importance of the influence of Descartes.[21] My justification for this excursion is that our present attitudes toward nature, and toward wilderness, are very largely the result of Descartes' metaphysical conception of what nature is, and the concomitant conception that man has of himself. Our metaphysical assumptions are frequently extremely influential invisible persuaders; they determine the boundaries of what is thinkable. In rejecting the Cartesian conception the following related shifts in attitudes can, I think, be discerned.

1. A change from reductive convergent patterns of thought to divergent holistic patterns.

2. A shift from man's conception of himself as the center of the biological world, to one in which he is conceived of as a component in a network of biological relations, a shift comparable to the Copernican discovery that man does not occupy the *physical* center of the universe.

3. An appreciation of the fact that in modifying biological systems we do not simply modify the properties of a substance, but alter a network of relations. This rejection of the Cartesian conception of nature as a collection of independent physical parts is summed up in the popular ecological maxim "it is impossible to do only one thing."

4. A recognition that the processes of nature are independent and indifferent to human interests and concerns.

5. A recognition that biological systems are items that possess intrinsic value, in Kant's terminology, that they are "ends in themselves."

We can, however, provide—and it is important that we can provide—an answer to the question: "What is the *use* of wilderness?" We certainly ought to preserve and protect wilderness areas as gymnasiums, as laboratories, as stockpiles of genetic diversity, and as cathedrals. Each of these reasons provides a powerful and sufficient instrumental justification for their preservation.

But note how the very posing of this question about the *utility* of wilderness reflects an anthropocentric system of values. From a genuinely ecocentric point of view the question "What is the *use* of wilderness?" would be as absurd as the question "What is the *use* of happiness?"

The philosophical task is to try to provide adequate justification, or at least clear the way for a scheme of values according to which concern and sympathy for our environment is immediate and natural, and the desirability of protecting and preserving wilderness self-evident. When once controversial propositions become platitudes, the philosophical task will have been successful.

I will conclude, nevertheless, on a deflationary note. It seems to me (at least much of the time) that the shift in attitudes that I think is required for promoting genuinely harmonious relations with nature is too drastic, too "unthinkable," to be very persuasive for most people. If this is so, then it will be more expedient to justify the preservation of wilderness in terms of instrumentalist considerations, and I have argued that there *are* powerful arguments for preservation that can be derived from the purely anthropocentric considerations of human self-interest. I hope, however, that there will be some who feel that such anthropocentric considerations are not wholly satisfying, i.e., that they do not really do justice to our intuitions. But at a time when *human* rights are being treated in some quarters with a great deal of skepticism it is perhaps unrealistic to expect the rights of nonhumans to receive sympathetic attention. Perhaps, though, we should not be too abashed by this; extensions in ethics have seldom followed the path of political expediency.

Footnotes

1. Aldo Leopold, *A Sand County Almanac* (New York: Oxford University Press, 1949), p. 188.

2. Other cultures have certainly included the idea that nature should be valued for its own sake in their moral codes, e.g., the American Indians (cf. Chief Seattle's letter to President Franklin Pierce of 1854, reprinted in *The Canberra Times*, 5 July 1966, p. 9), the Chinese (cf. Joseph Needham, "History and Human Values," in H.

and S. Rose, eds. *The Radicalisation of Science* [London: Macmillan, 1976], pp. 90–117), and the Australian Aborigines (cf. W.E.H. Stanner, *Aboriginal Man in Australia* [Sydney: Angus and Robertson, 1965], pp. 207–237).

3. We can after all *replace* human artifacts such as buildings with something closely similar, but the destruction of a wilderness or a biological species is irreversible.

4. John Passmore, *Man's Responsibility for Nature* (London: Duckworth, 1974; New York: Charles Scribner's Sons, 1974), p. 17; cf. ch. 5.

5. In "The Rights of Non-humans and Intrinsic Values," in M.A. McRobbie, D. Mannison, and R. Routley, eds. *Environmental Philosophy* (Canberra: Australian National University Research School of Social Sciences, forthcoming).

6. Cf. Laurence H. Tribe, "Policy Science: Analysis or Ideology?" *Philosophy and Public Affairs* 2 (1972–3): 66–110.

7. I should mention that I am a skeptic about "rights"; it seems to me that talk about rights is always eliminable in favor of talk about legitimate claims for considerations, and obligations to respect those claims. Rights-talk does, however, have useful rhetorical effect in exhorting people to recognize claims. The reason for this is that claims pressed in these terms perform the crucial trick of shifting the onus of proof. This is accomplished by the fact that a *denial* of a right appears to be a more positive and deliberate act than merely refusing to acknowledge an obligation.

8. Laurence H. Tribe, "Trial by Mathematics: Precision and Ritual in Legal Process," *Harvard Law Review* 84 (1971): 1361.

9. Of course, in practice cost-benefit considerations *do* operate within deontic constraints, and we do *not* accept economics unrestrictedly as providing the model for rational deliberation. We would not accept exploitative child labor, for example, as a legitimate mode of production, no matter how favorable the economics. This is not just because we attach too high a cost to this form of labor; it is just unthinkable.

10. Aldo Leopold, "The Land Ethic," in *A Sand County Almanac*, p. 210.

11. Cf. Aldo Leopold, "The Conservation Ethic," *Journal of Forestry* 31 (1933): 634–43, and "The Land Ethic," *Sand County Almanac*.

12. Cf. John Passmore, "Attitudes to Nature," in R.S. Peters, ed., *Nature and Conduct* (London: Macmillan, 1975), pp. 251–64.

13. Ibid., p. 260.

14. Cf. Arne Naess, "The Shallow and the Deep, Long-Range Ecology Movement," *Inquiry* 16 (1973): 95–100.

15. T.S. Kuhn, *The Structure of Scientific Revolutions* (Chicago: University of Chicago Press, 1962).

16. Passmore, *Man's Responsibility for Nature*, ch. 6; "Attitudes to Nature," p. 262.

17. Leopold, "The Land Ethic."

18. Ibid., p. 221.

19. Cf. Passmore, "The Treatment of Animals," *Journal of the History of Ideas* 36 (1975): 195–218.

20. Cf. Christopher D. Stone, "Should Trees Have Standing? Toward Legal Rights for Natural Objects," *Southern California Law Review* 45 (1972): 450–501.

21. Here I differ from the well-known claim of Lynn White ("The Historical Roots of Our Ecological Crisis," *Science* 155 [1967]: 1203–7) that the Judeo-Christian tradition is predominantly responsible for the development of Western attitudes toward nature.

Review Questions

1. Distinguish between instrumental value and intrinsic value.
2. How does Godfrey-Smith define "wilderness?"
3. What is the "cathedral view?"
4. Explain the "laboratory argument."
5. What is the "silo" argument?
6. And the "gymnasium argument?"
7. What problems arise for these instrumental justifications for preserving wilderness areas?
8. What is the dominant Western conception of nature?
9. Explain the "holistic conception" of the natural world.

Discussion Questions

1. Is the "holistic conception" of the natural world acceptable or not? Defend your position.
2. Should human beings frustrate important interests in order to preserve the natural environment? Defend your answer.

WILLIAM K. FRANKENA

Ethics and the Environment

Reprinted with the permission of the author. From *Ethics and Problems of the 21st Century*, ed. by Goodpaster and Sayre (1979), pp. 3–19.

William K. Frankena is Emeritus Professor of Philosophy at the University of Michigan. He is the author of Ethics (1963, 1973), and many articles on ethics.

Frankena distinguishes between eight types of ethics: (1) ethical egoism, (2) humanism or personalism, (3) sentientism or the view that the class of moral patients includes only sentient beings, (4) the ethics of "reverence for life," (5) the view that everything should be morally considered, (6) theistic ethics, (7) combination ethics where different types of ethics are combined, and (8) naturalistic ethics. He finds ethical egoism, humanism, and personalism to be morally inadequate, and he has doubts about theistic ethics and combination ethics. He concludes that ethics of type 3 or sentientism provides an adequate basis for environmental ethics.

As has often been pointed out by environmentalists, we humans have for the most part, at least in the West and until recently, thought of our ethics in terms of what we are or do or are disposed to be or do in relation to other people, ourselves, or God—or, in other words, to persons; we have thought of it very little in terms of our relations to other animals and still less, if at all, in terms of what we do or how we "relate" to plants, air, earth, water, or minerals. Thus, for example, Samuel Clarke wrote in the eighteenth century that "the eternal law of righteousness" has "three great and principal branches, from which all the other and smaller instances of duty do naturally flow, or may without difficulty be derived," namely, a rule of righteousness in respect of God, another in respect of our fellow-creatures, and a third with respect to ourselves; and, although in spelling out the second he says that "every rational creature *ought* . . . to do all the good it can to all its fellow-creatures," he actually equates our duties under this head with those of love and justice for other human beings or "men."[1] Lately, however, many people have become envi-

ronment watchers, looking at what we have done, are doing, or seem about to do to the nonhuman things around us, and not liking what they see. It is not necessary for me to recount the story as they see it here; nor shall I quarrel with their judgment that much of what is going on is wrong. The question is, By what ethics is it to be judged and by what ethics should we redirect our conduct?

We have had a number of calls for a "new ethics" in recent times, and today we are again told that we need a new one for dealing with the environment. "New lamps for old" is once more the cry. Actually, however, there is another possibility that should be explored first, namely, that our old ethics, or at least its best parts, are entirely satisfactory as a basis for our lives in the world, the trouble being only that not enough of us live enough by it enough of the time—that is, that what we need is not a new ethics but a new "moral rearmament," a revival of moral dedication. One might agree that our prevailing treatment of nature is wrong, and that we need important changes in our actions, laws, and practices, and yet argue that what is wrong is not due to our ethics but to our failure to live by it. After all, a lot of us do act out of thoughtlessness, self-interest, or disregard for the requirements or ideals of morality, and the present status of environmental matters may reflect an inadequacy, not in our ethics, but in our morals. I believe myself that there is much to be said for this line of thought, and that a good deal of what is needed would come about if enough people could be persuaded to be really moral by standards that are already widely accepted. However, I am not here concerned to try to show that what we need is not a new morality but only a new devotion to one we already have, especially since John Passmore has already so ably discussed the question "whether the solution of ecological problems demands a moral or metaphysical revolution."[2] What interests me now is a systematic rather than a historical question, not asking what ethical lamps are old and what new, or trading old lamps for new, but finding out what lamp is best, that is, throws the most moral light on ecological problems. Actually, though this is sometimes forgotten by recent writers in their eagerness to sell us a new "ecological ethics," every ethics that is at all complete is or includes an ethics of the environment, since every such ethics, new or old, tells us, at least indirectly, what we may or may not, should or should not do about plants, lakes, minerals, etc.; therefore, the main question is not which are old and which new, but which is the most satisfactory. However, while I shall be dealing with this question, I shall not try to answer it by proposing a certain specific ethics and applying it to environmental problems. Rather I shall address myself to a more general preliminary issue that is being much discussed in recent ecological literature, namely, the question which general *type* of ethics is most adequate.

I

Much of the recent discussion of this question has been too simplistic, proceeding as if there are only two contestants, our "old" type of ethics, with what it says or implies about the environment, and some "new" proposed and properly ecological ethics. Thus, for example, Holmes Rolston III, in a very helpful, perceptive, and stimulating article, talks as if the issue is between a humanistic or anthropological ethics and a planetary or ecosystemic one.[3] Actually, however, there are at least eight different types of "ethics *about* the environment," to use his phrase, that need to be distinguished, described, and compared as to their relative merits, his two falling respectively under what I shall call 2 and 5. I shall first indicate briefly what these eight types of ethics are and then proceed by describing them more fully and commenting on them.

It is generally thought that what Clarke calls "rational creatures" are moral *agents* and all of my types of ethics can agree about this. What they differ about is about what kinds of beings are or should be taken to be moral *patients*. Roughly the issue here is the question what kinds of beings we have duties *to*. More accurately, in G.J. Warnock's words, it is this: "What . . . is the condition of moral *relevance?* What is the condition of having a claim to be *considered* by rational agents?"[4] The point is that, in every ethics whatsoever, there are certain sorts of facts about certain sorts of things that are the ultimate considerations in determining what is morally good or bad, right or wrong, and the question now is: What sorts of things are such that certain sorts of facts about *them* are the final determinants, directly or indirectly, of moral rightness or virtue? For present purposes, this is the main issue distinguishing different types of ethics, not the usual issues between teleological and deontological ethics or between an ethics of virtue and an ethics of duty.

1. The first of my types of ethics is ethical egoism, which holds that, basically, it is certain facts about an agent himself, e.g., facts about what is in his own interest, that determine what is right or wrong, good or bad, in what he is or does. For it, an agent is or should be his own sole patient, perhaps not proximately but at least ultimately.

2. A second family of positions consists of various forms of humanism or personalism, views holding that what matters morally is finally only what happens to human beings or to persons. Clarke takes such a view, as does Kant when he maintains that "Our duties toward animals are merely indirect duties toward humanity."[5] These views are not in any proper sense egoistic, since they insist that *all* persons or *all* human beings are to be considered in morality, but they do also insist that, ultimately, only persons or only humans are to be considered.

3. The third type of ethics contends that the class of moral patients must be extended to include not only human beings and/or persons but all consciously sentient beings. This is Warnock's position when he answers the question, "How far down the scale, so to speak, of the brute creation should moral relevance be taken to extend?" by saying that "it extends just as far as does the capacity to suffer."[6]

4. The next type of ethics maintains that the range of moral patiency or relevance should be taken to extend even further, namely, to include whatever is *alive*, flora as well as fauna. An example is Albert Schweitzer's well-known ethics of "reverence for life."

A man is truly ethical only when he obeys the compulsion to help all life which he is able to assist, and shrinks from injuring anything that lives. He does not ask how far this or that life deserves one's sympathy as being valuable, not . . . whether and to what degree it is capable of feeling. Life as such is sacred to him. He tears no leaf from a tree, plucks no flower, and takes care to crush no insect.[7]

5. Another type of ethics goes even further, holding that in some sense *everything* is to be considered as morally relevant, directly and not just indirectly. What matters ultimately is everything, not just what is personal, human, conscious, or alive. Such views will be spelled out and illustrated later.

They are the best candidates for being "new."

6. One might think there are no other possibilities, but, alas, there are. Of these, one is a certain kind of theistic ethics, namely, a theistic ethics in which God is conceived of as transcendent (and not just as immanent) and then is held to be, ultimately, the one and only moral patient, the only being that finally matters morally. On such a view it is, in the end, only certain sorts of facts about God that determine what is morally right or wrong, good or bad. Theists need not take such a view, but they may and, as we shall see, sometimes do.

7. It is also possible to combine two or more of the above (pure) types of ethics. For example, one might, in a way, combine a humanistic ethics of type 2 and a theistic ethics of type 6 by saying that the moral law has two basic and coordinate parts: to love the Lord thy God with all thy heart and to love thy neighbor as thyself.

8. As my final type of ethics I shall list a type of view that is sometimes suggested in recent environmental literature but may have an ancestry in the Stoic maxim, *Naturam sequere*, namely, views that tell us to let nature alone, not to interfere with it, to cooperate with it, to follow or imitate it, etc. For all such views there is such a thing as nature and its ways, and the natural is the right and the virtuous both in general and in ecological matters.[8]

II

As I said, any ethics of any of these types is relevant to our problem, since it includes, at least by implication, certain instructions (directions, permissions, or prohibitions) about how we may or should treat the environment. In this sense, all of them are ecological or environmental ethics; that is why I have put all eight families of them on the stage (which is not often enough done). It is, however, not possible to study them all here in any detail. I shall therefore, not look further at such combination ethics as belong to 7, except to point out, first, that some such combination ethics may be more plausible than any pure one; second, that just because they combine two or more basic ethical norms, they may be faced by a problem of possible conflict between them, as pure forms of ethics are not; and third, that some proponents of "new" ecological ethics seem actually to be subscribing to what I am calling a combination of it with an older one. Rolston appears to do so, for example, when he writes

> As a partial ethical source, [this eco-systemic or planetary environmental ethics] does not displace functioning social-personal codes, but brings into the scope of ethical transaction a realm once regarded as intrinsically valueless and governed largely by expediency. The new ethical parameter is not absolute but relative to classical criteria. Such extension will amplify conflicts of value, for human goods must now coexist with environmental goods. In operational detail this will require a new casuistry. Mutually supportive though the human and the ecosystemic interests may be, conflicts between individuals and parties, the rights of the component members of the ecosystem, the gap between the real and the ideal, will provide abundant quandaries.[9]

I shall also not say much about an ethics of type 8. Such literally naturalistic ethics flourished in the heyday of evolutionism and appear to be surfacing again in our present upsurge of ecologism (which is itself in considerable part a revival of evolutionism). They were acutely and interestingly dealt with by J.S. Mill and Henry Sidgwick in the nineteenth and again by Basil Willey and others in the twentieth century, and I could at best add but little to their reflections.[10] As for ethical egoism—it has been much discussed in other contexts and, to my mind, satisfactorily disposed of.[11] Even it has an environmental ethics of a sort, namely, that it is morally permissible for an individual to treat his environment, including other individuals as well as plants, animals, rocks, etc., in any manner he pleases, provided only that doing so is not contrary to his own interest. That this is the rational way for an

individual to live with the rest of his world may be true, though I hope not, but that whatever is to one's own interest is morally permissible, no matter what it may be, is simply paradoxical. In any case, ethical egoism is almost universally opposed by ecological moralists, as might be expected; it is, in fact, the type of ethics that many of those who "exploit" and "violate" the environment live by and might appeal to in their own defense. Here, like the environmentalists, I shall assume that it is mistaken. It should be pointed out, however, that it is logically possible for an ethical egoist to argue that it is to an individual's own interest, carefully considered, to behave toward his environment in precisely the ways in which environmentalists desire him to. In other words, an egoist can come out exactly where the "planetary altruist" comes out. The trouble is that, given his premises, he can just as well come out at an entirely different place and claim to be equally moral.

This brings us to theistic ethics of type 6. If they conceive of God as a person, then they agree with ethical egoism and what I call personalism in holding that only persons are moral patients; these views differ only, but of course importantly, about which persons they regard as morally considerable. In any event, views that regard only God as ultimately morally relevant, and only certain facts about him as finally morally determinative, may take various forms: (i) A theist who believes that God can be harmed, benefited, or lied to by us may hold that, basically, all that matters morally is whether we are benefiting God, harming him, being honest or just to him, etc. (ii) One who rejects this conception of God may contend instead that all that matters morally is whether or not we are obeying his commands, doing what is dear to him, or loving what he loves (whatever it may be that he commands or cares about). This is a more common view among theologians than (i); it is held, for example, by theological voluntarists. (iii) Another possibility for theists is to maintain that what matters basically in morality is whether we are working to promote "the glory of God," if we may assume that doing this is not reducible to living by (i) or (ii). This view has sometimes been ascribed to, and apparently subscribed to by, Calvinists. (iv) A type 6 theist can insist that the whole law and the prophets, morally speaking, is to love the Lord thy God with all thy heart, and with all thy soul, and with all thy mind, and with all thy strength. And then he may put under loving God as much of what is called for by (i), (ii), and (iii) as he sees fit; he may also put under it loving one's neighbor as oneself. What he cannot say is that love of neighbor is another commandment "like unto" love of God, if this means that the former is independent of or coordinate with the latter. To affirm this is to hold a view of type 7, combining 2 and 5, as I indicated earlier.

These forms of theistic ethics can readily generate conclusions dealing with the environment, excepting possibly the first. For example, they can argue that God commands us to care for all his creatures, including plants, rocks, and lakes; that God cares for all of these creatures, and so we should too; or that respecting the heavens is a way of joining them in declaring the glory of God. They deserve more attention than they can be given here. I shall only say now that there are problems about all of them, and that, in addition, they all make ethics dependent on theology in ways that, along with other moral philosophers (as well as some theologians), I find troubling and wish to avoid.[12]

III

We come now to the types of ethics I mainly wish to study and assess. Let us begin with those of type 2. Here we must first distinguish between personalism and humanism.[13] Personalism holds that the class of moral agents and the class of moral patients both coincide with that of persons. For us the main point about it is that it insists that all persons and only persons matter morally; nothing else matters morally unless it bears on the lives of persons in one way or another. Personalism need not hold that all human beings are persons, nor that all persons are human beings. If fetuses, neonates, and imbeciles are not persons, then, even if they are human, personalism maintains that they have no more moral status than brute animals, plants, or rocks, unless it is as potential persons. Humanism can agree that all and only persons are moral agents, but it equates the class of moral *patients* with that of human beings, not with that of persons. Thus it will hold that nonhuman persons, if there are any, are not moral patients and have no moral claims, and that fetuses, newborn babies, imbeciles, and idiots, if they are human, have status as moral patients, even if they are not persons. Both personalism and humanism contend of course, that brute animals, plants, air, rocks, etc., have no moral status, except indirectly via their relations to persons or humans respectively.

Ethics of both kinds can be aretaic or deontic, as well as utilitarian or deontological. Clarke and Kant are deontologists, but personalists and humanists can also be utilitarians. On the question whether what is morally right or good is what is conducive to the greatest balance of good over evil in the community of humans or persons, humanists and personalists can take either side; also people on either side can be either deontologists or utilitarians.

We need not discuss here the relative merits of humanism and personalism. Our question is whether or not any such ethics will do as an environmental ethics. Now, such an ethics may take the line that any kind of treatment of animals, plants, or inorganic objects and substances is morally permissible, or that no way of treating them is morally either obligatory or wrong. Then it would not require, but it would permit, a ruthless and exploitative approach to the environment of the kind that has been causing so much agitation recently. More plausibly, it might maintain that some ways of treating animals, plants, etc., are morally right or wrong, though they are so only because through them persons or human beings are or will be gainers or losers, directly or indirectly, sooner or later. And then it might go on to defend the practices that have been characteristic of the industrial and technological revolutions of recent times as being necessary to or at least not inconsistent with the welfare of humans and/or persons. On the other hand, however, it might argue, depending on the evidence available, that the present and future well-being of persons and/or human beings requires all the measures of conservation, antipollution, etc., that environmentalists support. There are so many ways in which nature is important to us and our successors, economically, aesthetically, cognitively, and psychically, that the case for such measures can be made very plausible indeed, without giving up the premises of humanism or personalism. In effect this is sometimes recognized by new ecological moralists, for example, by Rolston when he says, borrowing from Réné Dubos and Paul Shepard,

It is only as man grants an intrinsic integrity to nature that he discovers his truest interests . . . biotic-environmental complexity is integrally related to the richness of human life. . . . Without oceans, forests, and grasslands, human life would be imperiled. . . . For maximum noetic development, man requires an environmental exuberance. . . . Remove eagles from the sky and we will suffer a spiritual loss.[14]

It may even be that "when people everywhere come to view the native black bear as an indicator of environmental health, a symbol of wilderness, there will be more hope for bears and people alike."[15]

Such claims ring a bell for a birdwatcher like me, but they are compatible with a type 2 ethics. Therefore, as I said, it is possible to argue persuasively, on humanist and personalist grounds, for all of the measures and practices desiderated by environmentalists. What then is wrong with humanism and personalism? They are alleged to embody a kind of "anthropological egoism" and "human chauvinism,"[16] but I am not impressed

by these charges. The ascription of egoism to an ethics of type 2 is misleading. Such an ethics is in no way a form of ethical egoism; it can take the form of the law of love, the Golden Rule, Kant's second version of the Categorical Imperative, or utilitarianism. In any case, labeling it "species egoism" or "species chauvinism" does nothing to show that it is morally inadequate; in fact, it has no moral force unless it is presupposed that such an ethics is unacceptable from the moral point of view. But since that is precisely the question at issue, using such pejorative labels is simply begging the question and handing out a red herring.

I agree, however, that humanism and personalism are not morally adequate. Like Warnock, I believe that there are right and wrong ways to treat infants, animals, imbeciles, and idiots even if or even though (as the case may be) they are not persons or human beings—just because they are capable of pleasure and suffering, and *not* just because their lives happen to have some value to or for those who clearly are persons or human beings.[17]

IV

If what I have just said is correct, then we must prefer an ethics of type 3 to one of type 2 on simple moral grounds, independently of any findings of ecological science. Clearly an ethics of type 3 will also give us a somewhat better basis for arguing for conservation, antipollution laws, etc., than will any ethics of type 2. The really interesting question at this point, then, is whether we should move on to an ethics of type 4 or type 5. An ethics of type 4 holds, it will be recalled, that we should have respect for persons, human beings, animals, and plants just because they are alive. It is therefore reasonable to think that it will provide an even better basis for conservation, etc., than an ethics of type 3.[18] The difficulty about it, to my mind, is that I can see no reason, from the moral point of view, why we should respect something that is alive but has no conscious sentiency and so can experience no pleasure or pain, joy, or suffering, unless perhaps it is potentially a consciously sentient being, as in the case of a fetus. Why, if leaves and trees have no capacity to feel pleasure or to suffer, should I tear no leaf from a tree? Why should I respect its location any more than that of a stone in my driveway, if no benefit or harm comes to any person or sentient being by my moving it?

An ethics of type 4 strikes me, consequently, as merely an implausible halfway house between one of type 3 and one of type 5, and this leads me to think that our crucial choice in a quest for an environmental ethics is between a type 3 ethics and a type 5 one, not between one of type 2 and one of type 5, as Rolston and others tend to assume. The rest of this essay will be devoted to this issue. Should we opt for an ethics of type 5 rather than one of type 3? I have my doubts. But first we must get clearer about the nature of a type 5 ethics and about the forms it may take—clearer than we can get just by reading its recent proponents.

V

Type 5 covers a variety of views, all of them denying what those of types 1 to 4 (and 6) affirm. Now, ethics of these other types all assert that what is morally right or wrong, good or bad, is ultimately to be determined, solely and wholly, by looking to see what happens to persons, human beings, sentient creatures, or living things. Ethics of type 5 (pure ones) hold that this is not so; for them, in making moral judgments on what we do or are, we must consider what happens to other things as well, in fact, we must consider *everything*, and we must consider everything as such and not merely because of some relation it may have to what is alive, sentient, human, personal, or divine. What is alive, sentient, human, personal, or divine is not all that matters morally. Everything matters. Everything is a moral patient.

But everything may be viewed either distributively or collectively, and so two some-

what different kinds of type 5 ethics are possible. In the first, the world is viewed as made up of a number of things, and they are thought of separately and considered as moral patients in themselves, even those that are not alive, sentient, human, personal, or divine. All of them, taken distributively, are morally relevant as such. Rolston seems to think in this way when he describes his proposed ethics as "recognizing the intrinsic value of every biotic component."

Consider how slowly the circle [of "persons"] has been enlarged fully to include aliens, strangers, infants, children, Negroes, Jews, slaves, women, Indians, prisoners, the elderly, the insane, the deformed, and even now we ponder the status of fetuses. Ecological ethics queries whether we ought again to universalize, recognizing the intrinsic value of every ecobiotic component.[19]

The other kind of "planetary altruism" is more properly "holistic" or "ecosystemic" and is the favorite of our new ecological moralists. It involves thinking of everything as forming a system or Whole, and then considering the system or Whole as what matters morally. Thus, what makes our actions or traits morally right or good is the character of their effects on the system. What happens to persons, sentient beings, etc., is not morally relevant as such but only because of its bearing on the character of the Whole. As Rolston puts it (for he seems to like this way of thinking too, without distinguishing it from the first): "The focus does not only enlarge from man to other ecosystemic members, but from individuals of whatever kind to the system. . . . here the community holds values."[20]

Such a holistic ethics seems to be envisaged in T.B. Colwell's talk about "the balance of Nature," as well as in Rolston's about "maximizing the ecosystem." A nice example of it is Aldo Leopold's affirmation: "A thing is right when it tends to preserve the integrity, stability, and beauty of the biotic community. It is wrong when it tends otherwise."[21] Even better, because much clearer, is C.D. Broad's, made well before the rise of our current environmentalism, if we take it as speaking, not just of a society of minds, but of the whole "community" of nature.

I think that, in the case of a community of interrelated minds, we must distinguish between the total goodness in the community and the total goodness of the community. The latter depends partly on the former, partly on the way in which the former is distributed among the members of the community, and partly on certain relations between the members. What we ought to try to maximize is the total goodness of the whole community of minds, and it is conceivable that we may sometimes have to put up with less total goodness in the community, than might otherwise exist, in order to accomplish this.[22]

Broad is here espousing a teleological ethics, but it is not clear that a holistic ethics must be teleological in the sense of maximizing the intrinsic value of the whole. It might be that other features of the system, such as its balance or integrity, are to be considered independently of any value they promote, and a holism so maintained might well be called deontological. It might hold, for example, that the universe constitutes a cosmos with a certain kind of order or plan, and that human beings should copy its order in their lives or fit themselves into its plan.

Holists, as far as I can see, may be atheistic or theistic. Sometimes they come close to pantheism, and I suppose that a pantheistic view in which God is not conceived as a person but is identified with the universe would be a holism of type 5, though it might perhaps be put under type 6 with equal justice for all.

VI

What are we to think of these two sorts of type 5 ethics? Take first the nonholistic ones. These entail believing that there are, at least *ceteris paribus*, morally right or wrong ways of treating rocks, air, etc., considered simply as such, independently of any relation they may have to living, sentient, or conscious beings, human or nonhuman. I

find this belief incredible when it is thus openly formulated, just as earlier I found it incredible that we should give moral consideration to beings that are alive but without any conscious experience. If possible, it is even harder to believe. If we owe no moral consideration to things that are merely alive, why should we accord it to things that are not even alive? It will be replied that both things that are merely living and those that are unliving have a variety of values—they are interesting to watch and study, they are beautiful to contemplate, it may heal us to be with them, etc.—and these values are not just instrumental or utilitarian, they are "inherent."[23] All this is true, as any good birdwatcher knows, but still the reply misfires. For even these inherent values are values that the things in question have in relation to us, for example, on being contemplated by us; they are not values those things have in and by themselves, and so it does not follow that we owe those things moral consideration as such. It may follow that it is morally wrong for me to do certain things to such beings, but this will follow only because we conscious ones will be losers if I do them. The substance of the reply is correct, but it is compatible with an ethics of type 3 or even 2.

Another possible reply involves an appeal to metaphysics. According to some metaphysicians, all things consist of minds, monads, or spirits, even plants and inorganic objects. These minds are not all conscious, and presumably those that make up plants and rocks are not, but still they are minds (for there is such a thing as unconscious mind), and consequently we owe them moral consideration, even if we need not give them equal consideration with minds of other kinds. To this reply I can only say once more that I see no reason why we should extend the range of moral relevance to minds that are unconscious; even if it makes sense to say that they have feelings or thoughts, why should we care what their feelings or thoughts are if they are unaware of them? How can I visit good or evil upon them, lie to them, etc., if they know not what they do, feel, or think? I should also point out, of course, that, while I find the type of metaphysics here appealed to attractive, it is a rather speculative foundation on which to build one's ethical house.

What about a holistic ethics of type 5? First, I wish to point out that a holist might believe that the Whole is itself a person or at least a mind (God, the Absolute, etc.). If he does this, however, then he shares with views of types 1, 2, 3, 4, and 6 the belief that finally what matters is only mind, life, or personality and has not wholly dissociated himself from such "egoism" or "chauvinism." Be this as it may, we must now review the arguments for holism. One is precisely the claim that all the other types of ethics are guilty of a kind of species-egoism or chauvinism; they all "discriminate" against something. This claim can, of course, also be used in favor of a nonholistic type 5 ethics. I have already dealt with it, however, in expounding and discussing ethics of types 2 and 3. Here I only wish to add that at least some ecological moralists of type 5 may be more justly charged with egoism than those of type 2. This comes out nicely in Rolston's essay. Like many other environmentalists he does not hesitate to pin the labels of "egoism" and "chauvinism" on humanistic ethics. But, again like many of his allies, he also makes much of the "coincidence of human and ecosystemic interests," as we have already seen. In all honesty, he recognizes that doing this is "ethically confusing," but adds that it is also "fertile." Then he writes:

To reduce ecological concern merely to human interests does not really exhaust the moral temper here, and only as we appreciate this will we see the ethical perspective significantly altered. That alteration centers in the dissolution of any firm boundary between man and the world. Ecology does not know an encapsulated ego over against his environment. Listen, for instance, to Paul Shepard: "Ecological thinking, on the other hand, requires a kind of vision across boundaries. The epidermis of the skin is ecologically like a pond surface or a forest soil, not a shell so much as a delicate interpenetration. It reveals the self ennobled and extended, rather than threatened, as part of the landscape, because the beauty and complexity of nature are continuous with ourselves." Man's vascular system includes arteries, veins, rivers, oceans, and air currents. Cleaning a dump is not different in kind from filling a tooth. The self metabolically, if metaphorically, interpenetrates the ecosystem. The world is my body.

This mood frustrates and ultimately invalidates the effort to understand all ecological ethics as disguised human self-interest, for now, with the self expanded into the system, their interests merge. One may, from a limited perspective, maximize the systemic good to maximize human good, but one can hardly say that the former is only a means to the latter, since they both amount to the same thing differently described. We are acquainted with egoism, égoïsme à deux, trois, quatre, with familial and tribal egoism. But here is an égoïsme à la système, as the very etymology of "ecology" witnesses: the earth is one's household. In this planetary confraternity, there is a confluence of egoism and altruism.[24]

There it is, all eloquently laid out. Reading it, however, one suspects that such enthusiasm for the interests of the Whole depends on two premises: one, that one's self is at least a part of the Whole so that its interests cannot be wholly lost in those of the Whole in any case; the other, that, praise be, it turns out that one's self and the Whole are or may become one so that one cannot lose at all by being planetarily "altruistic." If this be not egoism, make the least of it! I do not mean that we are incapable of loving the system disinterestedly; I believe we can, and just for that reason am unhappy with those who insist that there is no call for such love after all.

As I said earlier, however, the real question is whether it is clear, from the moral point of view, that we must consider everything in trying to determine what moral judgments to make. Now, as I also said, I can see that we ought to consider animals that are capable of pleasure and pain, as well as human beings and/or persons. I cannot, however, see in the same way, at least not without further argument that we ought morally to consider unconscious animals, plants, rocks, etc. I also cannot see at all directly that we ought to consider the Whole as such, at least not if the Whole is not itself a conscious sentient being. But perhaps there are further arguments to lead me and others like me out of darkness into light.

Here again much may be said by holists about the balance, beauty, integrity, etc., of the Whole, but once more it may be replied that these values are or may be viewed as inherent values the Whole has as an object of contemplation or study by beings capable of contemplation and study, that is, as values it has, not in or by itself, but in relation to minds like ours. If this is so, then such considerations give us no reason for relinquishing views of types 2 or 3. Even if beauty and other such qualities of nature are not dependent on the reaction of some observer, not just in the eye of the beholder, it may still be true that there is a moral call to do something about them only if and insofar as doing this enriches the lives of such observers, present or future.

Writers like Rolston make much of the recent findings of ecological science. These show, they claim, that nature is a homeostatic system with a *nisus* (nice word!) for balance, equilibrium, and wholeness, and they conclude that we ought to protect, preserve, and cooperate, or even to affirm, admire, and love. Now, I cannot try to determine what ecological science does or does not show. There is a question, however, whether from its facts, whatever they are, one can infer any ethical conclusions. Can one infer an Ought from an Is? There has been much debate about this. I do not think such an inference can be claimed to be logical, except perhaps in certain uninteresting cases. But I do believe that, given certain Ises, some Oughts become more reasonable than others, and this may be all that "ecologically tutored" moralists would wish to claim for their ethics. In any case, Rolston for one is rather careful about this, being well aware of the problem. He argues, as I understand

him, that, being ecologically informed about the Ises of nature, one just naturally frames new evaluations, new judgments of what is good or bad, and then just as naturally moves on to espouse a new holistic Ought.

The transition from "is" to "good" and thence to "ought" occurs here . . . but is an evaluative transition which is not made under necessity . . .. What is ethically puzzling, and exciting, . . . is that here an "ought" is not so much derived from an "is" as discovered simultaneously with it. . . . the sharp is/ought dichotomy is gone; the values seem to be there as soon as the facts are fully in.[25]

It is hard to know what to say about this. Again, it rings a bell in me; I do believe, as Rolston does, that we shape our values in great measure by our conception of the universe we live in. I have, however, not yet heard the knell that summons me to heaven or to holism. Perhaps I am simply obdurate, but, for instance, I am more troubled than Rolston is by the fact that "ecosystems regularly eliminate species."[26] Nature wiped out the dinosaur. Yet I am supposed to draw the conclusion that I ought to help preserve endangered species. But if nature herself extinguishes them, why should not I? In fact, even if I do it, it is only nature doing it through me, since I am a part of nature. Thus viewed, the dispatch of a species "by human whim" does not seem to be of as different an order "from their elimination by natural selection" as Rolston thinks.[27] Anyway, he allows that we need not simply maintain the status quo in nature; we must promote its integrity, stability, and beauty, but we may be creative and innovative about this, even interfering with and rearranging "nature's spontaneous course."[28] But if our art may improve on nature in this way, then, even though it may learn a great deal from the science of ecology, we may still wonder whether it can learn anything that it cannot learn if it proceeds from an ethics of types 2 or 3. Even if it proceeds from such a base, it might still find that, at least among other things, it should promote the integrity, stability, and beauty of nature.

At any rate, I am not yet convinced that the findings of ecological science make a holistic ethics of type 5 more reasonable than one of type 3 or even 2. I am also not convinced that a concern, say, for the integrity, stability, and beauty of the Whole is a *moral* one if or insofar as it goes beyond a concern about the lives of the persons and consciously sentient beings that are involved. This, however, raises questions of an order we cannot take up here. Another ground for a holistic ethics, of a sort very different from the science of ecology, is mystical experience, which is supposed to witness to the fact that all being is one, and a word must be said about it. If a mystic identifies the one reality with God, then he is a pantheist of the sort described before. But he need not do this; in fact, as the example of Schopenhauer shows, he may even be an atheistic pessimist ending up with an ethics of resignation, hardly what an environmentalist is looking for. What worries me about mysticism, apart from my having doubts about its theory of knowledge, is its insistence that, ultimately at least, all the differentiation and variety of nature is mere appearance and unreal. This makes it hard to see how there can be any reason for treating it in one way rather than another, as any ethics seems to require. What, for instance, does it matter whether I appear to wipe out passenger pigeons or not, or humans for that matter, if I do not really change anything by doing so? Maybe the moral of mysticism is that one should not do anything—or even appear to do anything—except to contemplate the One, but, once more this moral will hardly give aid and comfort to an environmentalist, not even if all he wants to do is to *watch* the *show.*

To my mind, the strongest argument for a holistic ethics of type 5 is suggested by what Broad says in the passage quoted earlier, if we apply it to a community of interrelated entities, such as "the biotic community" or "ecosystem" is supposed to be, instead of to

one of interrelated minds. Then the argument will be (a) that such a community has or may have a value that is not *reducible* to the value in or of the lives or beings of the entities that make it up, though it may *depend* on the value in or of the lives or beings of those entities and on the way in which this is distributed; and (b) that we ought to try to maximize the value of the community even if this involves lessening the value in or of the lives or beings of its constituents. Both of these theses have been much debated, and it is hard to show that they are false. But it is certainly not clear that they are true. I see how a community can have an *instrumental* or even an *inherent* value (in the sense indicated earlier) that is not reducible to those of its members. Perhaps even the *moral* goodness or virtue of a state is not reducible to that of its members, as Plato thought, though this is more doubtful. I do not see, however, how anything can have *intrinsic* value except the activities, experiences, and lives of conscious sentient beings (persons, etc.). Thus I also do not see how a community can have intrinsic value over and above that contained in the lives of its members, unless it is itself a conscious sentient being or mind—something I find hard to believe. As for (b)—if what I have just said is true, then (b) simply does not make sense.

It has been held that there are intrinsically good things that do not fall within the lives of any persons or sentient beings and whose value does not rest on any relation they have or may have to the lives of such beings. Thus, G.E. Moore once held that a beautiful world would be intrinsically good even if there were no minds or sentient beings to contemplate or enjoy it, and W.D. Ross believes that a state of affairs in which happiness is distributed in proportion to merit or virtue is as such intrinsically good.[29] If there are such "impersonal" goods or values, then a holist can reply to what I have just said by contending that a certain kind of ecosystemic Whole is one of them, perhaps the greatest or most inclusive of them all, and should therefore be kept or brought into existence.

If he holds that it should be our sole ultimate end, he will be a holist of an "extended ideal utilitarian" kind. I do not find this line of thought convincing. Even if a world can be beautiful apart from any beholder, I cannot see that it would be intrinsically good if it contained and occasioned no enjoyment whatsoever. It might be "inherently" good, that is, such that the contemplation of it would be intrinsically good, but that is not a point in favor of a type 5 ethics. I would say the same thing about the alleged intrinsic value of any pattern of distribution of happiness or "personal" goods or about that of any ecosystemic Whole that is not itself a conscious sentient being. As for the claim that they are nevertheless intrinsically good or good as ends, this seems to me, at this point, to be just another way of insisting that they ought to be preserved or promoted for their own sakes. I can discern no *other* sense in which they are intrinsically good, nor do I see that they are intrinsically good in *this* sense. For to say that they are intrinsically good in the sense that they ought to be taken as ends is to assert precisely what is at issue.[30]

VII

Our review of the various possible types of ethics about the environment is now complete. Like our ecological moralists, I find ethical egoism, humanism, and personalism morally inadequate. Unlike them, however, I see no convincing reason for going beyond an ethics of type 3 unless we move to a theistic one of type 6, which I have doubts about, or to a combination ethics of type 7. Rolston asks, "After the fauna, can we add the flora, the landscape, the seascape, the ecosystem?" and votes, somewhat speculatively, to accept the challenge. I see the challenge, but my vote remains no. As he says,

Much of the search for an ecological morality will . . . remain . . . "conservative," where the ground is better charted, and where we mix ethics, science, and human interests [I would add some animal interests] under our logical control.[31]

This does not mean that I think we should not share the environmentalist's concern for the flora, the landscape, the seascape, or the ecosystem. I believe we should, but, as I said, I also believe that a type 3 ethics provides an adequate basis for justifying and directing that concern, at least if it is informed by the facts of ecological history and science, as I agree it should be.

An ethics of type 3, like those of type 2, can be either teleological (e.g., utilitarianism) or deontological, and either aretaic or deontic; and it remains, of course, to see which form is most satisfactory from the moral point of view and to work out its environmental implications. On the first of these questions I have said something elsewhere, though, unfortunately, without any explicit reference to animals.[32] The second task must be left to others.

Footnotes

1. See D.D. Raphael, ed., *British Moralists* (Oxford: Clarendon Press, 1969), I: 207–12.

2. John Passmore, *Man's Responsibility for Nature* (New York: Charles Scribner's Sons, 1974), p. x.

3. Holmes Rolston III, "Is There an Ecological Ethic?" *Ethics* 85 (1975): 103ff. Later references to Rolston are to this article.

4. G.J. Warnock, *The Object of Morality* (London: Methuen and Co., 1971), p. 148. I take the term "moral patient" from Warnock.

5. T. Regan and P. Singer, eds., *Animal Rights and Human Obligations* (Englewood Cliffs, NJ: Prentice-Hall, 1976), pp. 122f.

6. Ibid., 151f. Note that then "the object of morality" is not merely "the amelioration of the *human* predicament."

7. A. Schweitzer, *Civilization and Ethics*, 3d ed. (London: A.C. Black, 1949), p. 344. See also M. de Montaigne, *Essays* (New York: Modern Library, 1933), p. 384f.

8. Such a view is suggested by T.B. Colwell, Jr., "The Balance of Nature: A Ground for Human Values," *Main Currents in Modern Thought*, 26 (1969): 50.

9. 105f. See also pp. 93, 97. On the whole, however, I shall take Rolston as proposing a type 5 ethics.

10. See J.S. Mill, "Nature," *Three Essays on Religion*, 3d ed. (London: Longmans Green, 1874), pp. 1–65; H. Sidgwick, *The Methods of Ethics*, 7th ed., (London: Macmillan and Co., 1907), pp. 80–83; B. Willey, *The English Moralists* (London: Methuen, 1964), pp. 73–90. See also A. Flew, *Evolutionary Ethics* (London: Macmillan and Co., 1967).

11. For more on egoism, see W.K. Frankena, *Ethics*, 2d ed. (Englewood Cliffs, NJ: Prentice-Hall, 1973), pp. 17–23.

12. I say something about these matters in ibid., pp. 28ff., 102.

13. There are other senses of these terms; my uses of them here are simply for present purposes.

14. Rolston, "Is There an Ecological Ethic?" p. 104. Remember, e.g., how Heidi's grandfather learned from the eagle.

15. George Laycock, *Audubon* 79 (May 1977).

16. E.g., Rolston, "Is There an Ecological Ethic?" p. 103.

17. See Warnock, *Object of Morality*, pp. 148–51.

18. I do not mean to imply that the fact that an ethics provides a better basis for conservation, etc., is much of an argument in its favor. To do this would be like picking out a certain particular cart and then looking for a horse to put it before. One must, in a fundamental sense, have one's ethics first, before one can decide, on moral grounds, for or against conservation, etc. Even so, however, it is also true that one cannot be satisfied with one's ethics unless one is satisfied with its environmental implications.

19. Rolston, "Is There an Ecological Ethic?" p. 101. In fairness, it should be observed that proponents of type 5 ethics of this (or even of the next) kind are probably not insisting on the moral relevance or considerableness of literally everything, e.g., dirt, junk, decayed vegetation, useless cars, etc., and perhaps artifacts generally. I owe this point to a conversation with Nicholas P. White.

20. Ibid., p. 106.

21. A. Leopold, "The Land Ethic," *A Sand County Almanac* (New York: Oxford University Press, 1949), pp. 201–6. See Colwell, "The Balance of Nature."

22. C.D. Broad, *Five Types of Ethical Theory* (New York: Harcourt Brace and Co., 1930), p. 283.

23. "Let us call those values which objects have by their capacity to contribute directly to human life by their presence, *inherent* values. And let us call the mere usefulness of an object for the production of something else which is desirable, an *instrumental* value of it. An art-object . . . has inherent value . . . the painter's brushes . . . have a value which is instrumental only." C.I. Lewis, *The Ground and Nature of the Right* (New York: Columbia University Press, 1955), p. 69. Cf. my *Ethics*, p. 81.

24. Rolston, "Is There an Ecological Ethic?" p. 104.

25. Ibid., p. 101f. For more discussion see my *Ethics*, pp. 97–102.

26. Rolston, "Is There an Ecological Ethic?" p. 102.

27. Ibid., p. 102.

28. Ibid., p. 106.

29. See G.E. Moore, *Principia Ethica* (Cambridge at the University Press, 1903), pp. 83f.; W.D. Ross, *The Right and the Good* (Oxford: Clarendon Press, 1930), pp. 27, 138.

30. For some discussion, see R.B. Brandt, *Ethical Theory* (Englewood Cliffs, NJ: Prentice-Hall, 1959), pp. 303f., 317, 355f., 395f.; Frankena, *Ethics*, pp. 42f. and chapter V.

31. Rolston, "Is There an Ecological Ethic?" p. 109.

32. Frankena, *Ethics*, chs. 2–3, 4. On a subject related to this one see my "The Ethics of Respect for Life," in Owsei Temkin, W.K. Frankena, and S.H. Kadish, *Respect for Life in Medicine, Philosophy, and the Law* (Baltimore: Johns Hopkins University Press, 1977), pp. 24–62.

Review Questions

1. What is ethical egoism?
2. Explain humanism or personalism.
3. Why is it rejected by Frankena?
4. Explain the third type of ethics.
5. Explain Schweitzer's "reverence for life."
6. Why doesn't Frankena accept it?
7. What is "holistic ethics?"
8. What criticisms does Frankena make of this sort of ethics?
9. Explain theistic ethics.
10. Explain naturalistic ethics.

Discussion Questions

1. Do you agree that ethics of type 3 is acceptable or not? Explain your answer.
2. Do you prefer one of the other types of ethics over type 3 ethics? Which one? Explain your choice.

Problem Cases

1. Suppose a farmer raises chickens on his farm. They are well fed; they have plenty of room; they have a comfortable place to sleep; in short, they are well cared for. Each year the farmer kills some of the chickens quickly and with little pain. Then he eats them. He replaces the chickens killed with other chickens so that the chicken population remains stable. Does this farmer do anything that is morally wrong or unjust or not? Explain your position.

2. The proposed Dickey-Lincoln Dam on the St. John River in Maine will produce hydroelectric power, provide recreational opportunities (boating and fishing), and will increase real estate values. Environmentalists who are opposed to the project point out that it would drown more than half the population of furbish louseworts, a rare relative of the snapdragon. This type of plant is in danger of becoming extinct. But it seems to have little or no commercial value; it is not pretty or beautiful. Should this dam be built or not? Defend your position.

Suggested Readings

Feinberg, Joel. "The Rights of Animals and Unborn Generations." In W. Blackstone, ed., *Philosophy and Environmental Crisis.* Athens: University of Georgia Press, 1974, pp. 48–68.

Francis, Leslie Pickering and Norman, Richard. "Some Animals Are More Equal Than Others," *Philosophy* 53 (October 1978): 507–527.

Leopold, Aldo. "The Land Ethic." In *A Sand County Almanac.* New York: Oxford University Press, 1966, pp. 217–241. Leopold's view is discussed in the reading.

McCloskey, H.J., "Moral Rights and Animals," *Inquiry* 22 (Spring-Summer 1979): 25–54.

Safoff, Mark. "On Preserving the Natural Environment," *Yale Law Journal* 84 (December 1974): 205–267. Safoff proposes a nonutilitarian rationale for preserving the natural environment.

CHAPTER 8

Nuclear War

BASIC CONCEPTS

THE EFFECTS OF NUCLEAR BOMBS
Jonathan Schell

THE CHALLENGE OF PEACE
The National Conference of Catholic Bishops

DISARMAMENT AND ARMS CONTROL
The Harvard Nuclear Study Group

SOME PARADOXES OF DETERRENCE
Gregory S. Kavka

PROBLEM CASES

SUGGESTED READINGS

Basic Concepts

WAR SCENARIOS

Discussions of nuclear war often include scenarios, possible ways in which nuclear weapons might be used. Of course these are hypothetical, but they could become actual very quickly with present-day missiles.

There are two main scenarios: MAD (mutual assured destruction) and limited or tactical war. The MAD scenario dates back to the Eisenhower-Dulles era, and it remains dominant in nonmilitary thought. This plan calls for massive first strikes (called preemptive first strikes) and massive retaliations against civilian populations. There might be more flexible responses against lesser strikes, but these are very likely to escalate into massive strikes; there would be no way to limit the exchange. Such an exchange, in which both sides use thousands of nuclear warheads (the U.S. and Russia together have about 50,000 nuclear warheads with more being built every day) would involve enormous losses on both sides. Neither side could really be said to "win" such a war. Although it is believed that no rational leader or group would intentionally start such a war, there is still the possibility of threatening such an attack for political or military gain. For example, when President Kennedy ordered a naval blockade of Cuba in 1962 in order to halt the Soviet deployment of intermediate range missiles, he was tacitly threatening to use nuclear weapons if the Soviets did not withdraw.

Current military thinking places more emphasis on the limited use of nuclear weapons to counter setbacks in conventional military battles, and thereby win the conflict. A possible conflict that is often discussed, and is being carefully planned for on both sides, is a Soviet invasion of West Germany. The Soviets have forty-seven divisions at full strength stationed within quick striking distance of the West German frontier. These

troops might be committed to a sneak attack, a blitzkrieg, on West Germany. Led by tanks, the troops could quickly cross the border and overrun the surprised NATO forces. With their conventional forces overrun, the NATO leaders would be left with only one option besides surrender, and that is to use tactical or intermediate-range nuclear weapons. Currently 572 Pershing II and cruise missiles are being deployed in Europe to defend against a Russian attack, and these could be used to destroy the attacking forces.

THE FIRST–USE POLICY

The current policy of the NATO Alliance is to initiate the use of nuclear weapons, if necessary, to turn back a conventional Soviet attack against Western Europe. Nuclear weapons are viewed as a way of balancing numerically superior Warsaw Pact ground forces.

But this policy has dangers. What would the Soviets do if the NATO forces began the use of nuclear weapons? The Soviets have about 243 SS–20 intermediate-range missiles (with 729 warheads), and they could be used to respond to the NATO's first use of nuclear weapons; they could even be launched as soon as there is a warning of a nuclear attack. If the Russians did respond with nuclear weapons, they could easily devastate Europe even if they hit only military targets.

To prevent the Soviets from using their missiles, or to retaliate against them for their attack on West Germany, the U.S. might launch a preemptive strike using their accurate land-based missiles. The U.S. has about 1,000 ICBMs (inter-continental ballistic missiles) carrying about 2,000 warheads, and 100 more MX missiles (which are first-strike weapons) are in the planning stages. A first strike against the Soviets would be risky, of course, for as soon as they had a warning of a U.S. missile launch, the Soviets would be tempted to launch their own ICBMs (they have about 1,400 ICBMs with around 6,000 warheads). As the military strategists say, the Soviets would have to "use 'em or lose 'em." No doubt they would choose to use their weapons in a first-strike situation, and the result would be a nuclear holocaust.

THE EFFECTS OF NUCLEAR WAR

In his book, *The Fate of the Earth,* Jonathan Schell vividly describes the effects of an air burst of a one-megaton bomb—a bomb equal in explosive yield to a million tons of TNT. There is initial radiation, an electromagnetic pulse, a thermal pulse, a blast wave, initial radioactive fallout, and mass fires. The electromagnetic pulse would produce widespread damage to solid-state electrical circuits; this means, for one thing, that unshielded defense communications would be disrupted and electronic guidance systems on missiles would not work properly. Schell also describes some little-known global effects of nuclear bombs: delayed or worldwide radioactive fallout lasting millions of years, dust in the stratosphere cooling the earth's surface and producing a nuclear winter, and destruction of the layer of ozone that shields the earth from ultraviolet radiation. He emphasizes that a nuclear holocaust in which ten thousand megatons are detonated would probably make life on earth impossible except in the ocean. The United States would become a "republic of insects and grass."

MORAL ISSUES

Is nuclear war ever morally justified? In their Pastoral Letter, "The Challenge of Peace," the U.S. Catholic Bishops condemn any use of nuclear weapons, even in retaliation against attack. Their main reason for this condemnation is that nuclear war, whether offensive or defensive, limited or all-out, inevitably results in the killing of innocent noncombatants and "No Christian can rightfully carry out orders or policies deliberately aimed at killing noncombatants." The Bishops also evaluate current

strategies of deterrence, and make some recommendations for arms control.

The Harvard Nuclear Study Group has a different perspective. They claim that disarmament is "inherently unstable" and not in a nation's best interests. They accept the common view that arms are necessary to deter aggression and to project political influence. Nevertheless they allow that some kind of arms control might contribute to three dimensions of stability: deterrence, arms-race stability, and crisis stability. Using these criteria, as well as negotiability and possible verification, they critically discuss a number of proposals including arms reductions, freezes, force restructuring, and stabilizing measures.

Gregory S. Kavka raises further problems about deterrence strategies. He contends that the standard view of deterrence, including the view that nuclear weapons are necessary for deterrence, results in serious moral paradoxes. Each of these moral paradoxes of deterrence calls into question a plausible and widely accepted moral principle. The first paradox denies the Wrongful Intention Principle that it is wrong to intend to do what one knows to be wrong. The second paradox denies the truth of the Right-Good Principle that doing something is right if and only if a morally good man would do the same thing in the given situation. The third paradox denies the Virtue Preservation Principle that it is wrong to deliberately lose or reduce one's moral virtue. Kavka grants that act-utilitarians and Extreme Kantians can easily dismiss these moral paradoxes of deterrence. But he thinks that their extreme conceptions of morality are too one-sided. One stresses act evaluation and the other agent evaluation, but an acceptable morality must accommodate the valid insights of both act- and agent-oriented perspectives. But then one is confronted with the moral paradoxes of deterrence, and Kavka, for one, does not see any satisfactory way out of them. It seems that either our moral principles or our use of deterrence strategies must give way.

JONATHAN SCHELL
The Effects of Nuclear Bombs

Jonathan Schell is a writer. His book The Fate of the Earth originally appeared in The New Yorker.

Schell describes the effects of an air burst of a one-megaton bomb (initial radiation, electromagnetic pulse, thermal pulse, blast wave, radioactive fallout, and destruction of the ozone layer), and he speculates about the effects of a nuclear holocaust on individual life, human society, and the earth as a whole.

Whereas most conventional bombs produce only one destructive effect—the shock wave—nuclear weapons produce many destructive effects. At the moment of the explosion, when the temperature of the weapon material instantly gasified, is at the superstellar level, the pressure is millions of times the normal atmospheric pressure. Immediately, radiation, consisting mainly of gamma rays, which are a very high-energy form of electromagnetic radiation, begins to stream outward into the environment. This is called the "initial nuclear radiation," and is the first of the destructive effects of a nuclear explosion. In an air burst of a one-megaton bomb—a bomb with the explosive yield of a million tons of TNT, which is a medium-sized weapon in present-day nuclear arsenals—the initial nuclear radiation can kill unprotected human beings in an area of some six square miles. Virtually simultaneously with the initial nuclear radiation, in a second destructive effect of the explosion, an electromagnetic pulse is generated by the intense gamma radiation acting on the air. In a high-altitude detonation, the pulse can knock out electrical equipment over a wide area by inducing a powerful surge of voltage through various conductors, such as anten-

nas, overhead power lines, pipes, and railroad tracks. The Defense Department's Civil Preparedness Agency reported in 1977 that a single multi-kiloton nuclear weapon detonated one hundred and twenty-five miles over Omaha, Nebraska, could generate an electromagnetic pulse strong enough to damage solid-state electrical circuits throughout the entire continental United States and in parts of Canada and Mexico, and thus threaten to bring the economies of these countries to a halt. When the fusion and fission reactions have blown themselves out, a fireball takes shape. As it expands, energy is absorbed in the form of X-rays by the surrounding air, and then the air re-radiates a portion of that energy into the environment in the form of the thermal pulse—a wave of blinding light and intense heat—which is the third of the destructive effects of a nuclear explosion. (If the burst is low enough, the fireball touches the ground, vaporizing or incinerating almost everything within it.) The thermal pulse of a one-megaton bomb lasts for about ten seconds and can cause second-degree burns in exposed human beings at a distance of nine and a half miles, or in an area of more than two hundred and eighty square miles, and that of a twenty-megaton bomb (a large weapon by modern standards) lasts for about twenty seconds and can produce the same consequences at a distance of twenty-eight miles, or in an area of 2,460 square miles. As the fireball expands, it also sends out a blast wave in all directions, and this is the fourth destructive effect of the explosion. The blast wave of an air-burst one-megaton bomb can flatten or severely damage all but the strongest buildings within a radius of four and a half miles, and that of a twenty-megaton bomb can do the same within a radius of twelve miles. As the fireball burns, it rises, condensing water from the surrounding atmosphere to form the characteristic mushroom cloud. If the bomb has been set off on the ground or close enough to it so that the fireball touches the surface, in a so-called ground burst, a crater will be formed, and tons of dust and debris will be fused with the intensely radioactive fission products and sucked up into the mushroom cloud. This mixture will return to earth as radioactive fallout, most of it in the form of fine ash, in the fifth destructive effect of the explosion. Depending upon the composition of the surface, from forty to seventy percent of this fallout—often called the "early" or "local" fallout—descends to earth within about a day of the explosion, in the vicinity of the blast and downwind from it, exposing human beings to radiation disease, an illness that is fatal when exposure is intense. Air bursts may also produce local fallout, but in much smaller quantities. The lethal range of the local fallout depends on a number of circumstances, including the weather, but under average conditions a one-megaton ground burst would, according to the report by the Office of Technology Assessment, lethally contaminate over a thousand square miles. (A lethal dose, by convention, is considered to be the amount of radiation that, if delivered over a short period of time, would kill half the able-bodied young adult population.)

The initial nuclear radiation, the electromagnetic pulse, the thermal pulse, the blast wave, and the local fallout may be described as the local primary effects of nuclear weapons. Naturally, when many bombs are exploded the scope of these effects is increased accordingly. But in addition these primary effects produce innumerable secondary effects on societies and natural environments, some of which may be even more harmful than the primary ones. To give just one example, nuclear weapons, by flattening and setting fire to huge, heavily built-up areas, generate mass fires, and in some cases these may kill more people than the original thermal pulses and blast waves. Moreover, there are—quite distinct from both the local primary effects of individual bombs and their secondary effects—global primary effects, which do not become significant unless thousands of bombs are detonated all around the earth. And these global primary effects produce innumerable secondary effects of their own throughout the ecosystem of the earth as a whole. For a full-scale holocaust is more than the sum of its local parts; it is also a powerful direct blow to the ecosphere. In that sense, a holocaust is to the earth what a single bomb is to a city. Three grave direct global effects have been discovered so far. The first is the "delayed," or "worldwide," fallout. In detonations greater than one hundred kilotons, part of the fallout does not fall to the ground in the vicinity of the explosion but rises high into the troposphere and into the stratosphere, circulates around the earth, and then, over months or years, descends, contaminating the whole surface of the globe—although with doses of radiation far weaker than those delivered by the local fallout. Nuclear-fission products comprise some three hundred radioactive isotopes, and though some of them decay to relatively harmless levels of radioactivity within a few hours, minutes, or even seconds, others persist to emit radiation for up to millions of years. The short-lived isotopes are the ones most responsible for the lethal effects of the local fallout, and the long-lived ones are responsible for the contamination of the earth by stratospheric fallout. The energy released by all fallout from a thermonuclear explosion is about five percent of the total. By convention, this energy is not calculated in the stated yield of a weapon, yet in a ten-thousand-megaton attack the equivalent of five hundred megatons of explosive energy, or forty thousand times the yield of the Hiroshima bomb, would be released in the form of radioactivity. This release may be considered a protracted afterburst, which is dispersed into the land, air, and sea, and into the tissues, bones, roots, stems, and leaves of living things, and goes on detonating there almost indefinitely after the explosion. The second of the global effects that have been discovered so far is the lofting, from ground bursts, of millions of tons of dust into the stratosphere; this is likely to produce general cooling of the earth's surface. The third of the global effects is a predicted partial destruction of the layer of ozone that surrounds the entire earth in the stratosphere. A nuclear fireball, by burning nitrogen in the air, produces large quantities of oxides of nitrogen. These are carried by the heat of the blast into the stratosphere, where, through a series of chemical reactions, they bring about a depletion of the ozone layer. Such a depletion may persist for years. The 1975 N.A.S. report has estimated that in a holocaust in which ten thousand megatons were detonated in the Northern Hemisphere the reduction of ozone in this hemisphere could be as high as seventy percent and in the Southern Hemisphere as high as forty percent, and that it could take as long as thirty years for the ozone level to return to normal. The ozone layer is crucial to life on earth, because it shields the surface of the earth from lethal levels of ultraviolet radiation, which is present in sunlight. Glasstone remarks simply, "If it were not for the absorption of much of the solar ultraviolet radiation by the ozone, life as currently known could not exist except possibly in the ocean." Without the ozone shield, sunlight, the life-giver, would become a life-extinguisher. In judging the global effects of a holocaust, therefore, the primary question is

not how many people would be irradiated, burned or crushed to death by the immediate effects of the bombs but how well the ecosphere, regarded as a single living entity, on which all forms of life depend for their continued existence, would hold up. The issue is the habitability of the earth, and it is in this context, not in the context of the direct slaughter of hundreds of millions of people by the local effects, that the question of human survival arises.

Usually, people wait for things to occur before trying to describe them. (Futurology has never been a very respectable field of inquiry.) But since we cannot afford under any circumstances to let a holocaust occur, we are forced in this one case to become the historians of the future—to chronicle and commit to memory an event that we have never experienced and must never experience. This unique endeavor, in which foresight is asked to perform a task usually reserved for hindsight, raises a host of special difficulties. There is a categorical difference, often overlooked, between trying to describe an event that has already happened (whether it is Napoleon's invasion of Russia or the pollution of the environment by acid rain) and trying to describe one that has yet to happen—and one, in addition, for which there is no precedent, or even near-precedent, in history. Lacking experience to guide our thoughts and impress itself on our feelings, we resort to speculation. But speculation, however brilliantly it may be carried out, is at best only a poor substitute for experience. Experience gives us facts, whereas in pure speculation we are thrown back on theory, which has never been a very reliable guide to future events. Moreover, experience engraves its lessons in our hearts through suffering and the other consequences that it has for our lives; but speculation leaves our lives untouched, and so gives us leeway to reject its conclusions, no matter how well argued they may be. (In the world of strategic theory, in particular, where strategists labor to simulate actual situations on the far side of the nuclear abyss, so that generals and statesmen can prepare to make their decisions in case the worst happens, there is sometimes an unfortunate tendency to mistake pure ratiocination for reality, and to pretend to a knowledge of the future that it is not given to human beings to have.) Our knowledge of the local primary effects of the bombs, which is based both on the physical principles that made their construction possible and on experience gathered from the bombings of Hiroshima and Nagasaki and from testing, is quite solid. And our knowledge of the extent of the local primary effects of many weapons used together, which is obtained simply by using the multiplication table, is also solid: knowing that the thermal pulse of a twenty-megaton bomb can give people at least second-degree burns in an area of 2,460 square miles, we can easily figure out that the pulses of a hundred twenty-megaton bombs can give people at least second-degree burns in an area of 246,000 square miles. Nevertheless, it may be that our knowledge even of the primary effects is still incomplete, for during our test program new ones kept being discovered. One example is the electromagnetic pulse, whose importance was not recognized until around 1960, when, after more than a decade of tests, scientists realized that this effect accounted for unexpected electrical failures that had been occurring all along in equipment around the test sites. And it is only in recent years that the Defense Department has been trying to take account strategically of this startling capacity of just one bomb to put the technical equipment of a whole continent out of action.

When we proceed from the local effects of single explosions to the effects of thousands of them on societies and environments, the picture clouds considerably, because then we go beyond both the certainties of physics and our slender base of experience, and speculatively encounter the full complexity of human affairs and of the biosphere. Looked at in its entirety, a nuclear holocaust can be said to assail human life at three levels: the level of individual life, the level of human society, and the level of the natural environment—including the environment of the earth as a whole. At none of these levels can the destructiveness of nuclear weapons be measured in terms of firepower alone. At each level, life has both considerable recuperative powers, which might restore it even after devastating injury, and points of exceptional vulnerability, which leave it open to sudden, wholesale, and permanent collapse, even when comparatively little violence has been applied. Just as a machine may break down if one small part is removed, and a person may die if a single artery or vein is blocked, a modern technological society may come to a standstill if its fuel supply is cut off, and an ecosystem may collapse if its ozone shield is depleted. Nuclear weapons thus do not only kill directly, with their tremendous violence, but also kill indirectly, by breaking down the man-made and the natural systems on which individual lives collectively depend. Human beings require constant provision and care, supplied both by their societies and by the natural environment, and if these are suddenly removed people will die just as surely as if they had been struck by a bullet. Nuclear weapons are unique in that they attack the support systems of life at every level. And these systems, of course, are not isolated from each other but are parts of a single whole: ecological collapse, if it goes far enough, will bring about social collapse, and social collapse will bring about individual deaths. Furthermore, the destructive consequences of a nuclear attack are immeasurably compounded by the likelihood that all or most of the bombs will be detonated within the space of a few hours, in a single huge concussion. Normally, a locality devastated by a catastrophe, whether natural or man-made, will sooner or later receive help from untouched outside areas, as Hiroshima and Nagasaki did after they were bombed; but a nuclear holocaust would devastate the "outside" areas as well, leaving the victims to fend for themselves in a shattered society and natural environment. And what is true for each city is also true for the earth as a whole: a devastated earth can hardly expect "outside" help. The earth is the largest of the support systems for life, and the impairment of the earth is the largest of the perils posed by nuclear weapons.

The incredible complexity of all these effects, acting, interacting, and interacting again, precludes confident detailed representation of the events in a holocaust. We deal inevitably with approximations, probabilities, even guesses. However, it is important to point out that our uncertainty pertains not to *whether* the effects will interact, multiplying their destructive power as they do so, but only to *how*. It follows that our almost built-in bias, determined by the limitations of the human mind in judging future events, is to underestimate the harm. To fear interactive consequences that we cannot predict, or even imagine, may not be impossible, but it is very difficult. Let us consider, for example, some of the possible ways in which a person in a targeted country might die. He might be incinerated by the fireball or the thermal pulse. He might be lethally irradiated by the initial nuclear radiation. He might be crushed to death or hurled to his death by the blast wave or its debris. He might be lethally irradiated by the local fallout. He might be burned to death in a firestorm. He might be injured by one or another of these effects and then die of his wounds before he was able to make his way out of the devastated zone in which he found himself. He might die of starvation, because the economy had collapsed and no food was being grown or delivered, or because existing local crops had been killed by radiation, or because the local ecosystem had been ruined, or because the ecosphere of the earth as a whole was collapsing. He might die of cold, for lack of heat and clothing, or of exposure, for lack of shelter. He might be killed by people seeking food or shelter that he had obtained. He might die of an illness spread in an epidemic. He might be killed by exposure to the sun if he stayed outside too long following serious ozone depletion. Or he might be killed by any combination of these perils. But while there is almost no end to the ways to die in and after a holocaust, each person has only one life to lose; someone who has been killed by the thermal pulse can't be killed again in an epidemic. Therefore, anyone who wishes to describe a holocaust is always at risk of depicting scenes of devastation that in reality would never take place, because the people in them would already have been killed off in some earlier scene of devastation. The task is made all the more confusing by the fact that causes of death and destruction do not exist side by side in the world but often encompass one another, in widening rings. Thus, if it turned out that a holocaust rendered the earth uninhabitable by human beings, then all the more immediate forms of death would be nothing more than redundant preliminaries, leading up to the extinction of the whole species by a hostile environment. Or if a continental ecosystem was so thoroughly destroyed by a direct attack that it could no longer sustain a significant human population, the more immediate causes of death would again decline in importance. In much the same way, if an airplane is hit by gunfire, and thereby caused to crash, dooming all the passengers, it makes little difference whether the shots also killed a few of the passengers in advance of the crash. On the other hand, if the larger consequences, which are less predictable than the local ones, failed to occur, then the local ones would have their full importance again.

Faced with uncertainties of this kind, some analysts of nuclear destruction have resorted to fiction, assigning to the imagination the work that investigation is unable to do. But then the results are just what one would expect: fiction. An approach more appropriate to our intellectual circumstances would be to acknowledge a high degree of uncertainty as an intrinsic and extremely important part of dealing with a possible holocaust. A nuclear holocaust is an event that is obscure because it is future, and uncertainty, while it has to be recognized in all calculations of future events, has a special place in calculations of a nuclear holocaust, because a holocaust is something that we aspire to keep in the future forever, and never to permit into the present. You might say that uncertainty, like the thermal pulses or the blast waves, is one of the features of a holocaust. Our procedure, then, should be not to insist on a precision that is beyond our grasp but to inquire into the rough probabilities of various results insofar as we can judge them, and then to ask ourselves what our political responsibilities are in the light of these probabilities. This embrace of investigative modesty—this acceptance of our limited ability to predict the consequences of a holocaust—would itself be a token of our reluctance to extinguish ourselves.

There are two further aspects of a holocaust that, though they do not further obscure the factual picture, nevertheless vex our understanding of this event. The first is that although in imagination we can try to survey the whole prospective scene of destruction, inquiring into how many would live and how many would die and how far the collapse of the environment would go under attacks of different sizes, and piling up statistics on how many square miles would be lethally contaminated, or what percentage of the population would receive

first-, second-, or third-degree burns, or be trapped in the rubble of its burning houses, or be irradiated to death, no one actually experiencing a holocaust would have any such overview. The news of other parts necessary to put together that picture would be one of the things that were immediately lost, and each surviving person, his vision drastically foreshortened by the collapse of his world, and his impressions clouded by his pain, shock, bewilderment, and grief, would see only as far as whatever scene of chaos and agony happened to lie at hand. For it would not be only such abstractions as "industry" and "society" and "the environment" that would be destroyed in a nuclear holocaust; it would also be, over and over again, the small collections of cherished things, known landscapes, and beloved people that made up the immediate contents of individual lives.

The other obstacle to our understanding is that when we strain to picture what the scene would be like after a holocaust we tend to forget that for most people, and perhaps for all, it wouldn't be *like* anything, because they would be dead. To depict the scene as it would appear to the living is to that extent a falsification, and the greater the number killed, the greater the falsification. The right vantage point from which to view a holocaust is that of a corpse, but from that vantage point, of course, there is nothing to report.

Review Questions

1. Describe the effects of an air burst of a one-megaton bomb.
2. What would happen in a nuclear holocaust?

Discussion Questions

1. Can you think of any circumstances in which a nuclear holocaust would be morally justified?
2. The U.S. presently has about 9,000 H-bombs with more being made every day, and about 20,000 smaller A-bombs like the one dropped on Hiroshima. Russia has about 240 medium-sized cities and perhaps a few hundred military targets such as air bases and missile sites. Why do we need so many bombs? Why are we building more and more?

THE NATIONAL CONFERENCE OF CATHOLIC BISHOPS
The Challenge of Peace

*Following a general meeting of the U.S. Catholic Bishops in November,
1980, a committee of Bishops was appointed to draft a Pastoral Letter on
War and Peace. The third draft of the Pastoral Letter was approved by
the body of Bishops during the plenary assembly in Chicago on May 3,
1983.*

*The Bishops condemn any use of nuclear weapons, even in retaliation.
Their reason for this condemnation is that nuclear war in any form kills
innocent noncombatants and this is always morally wrong. The Bishops
also evaluate current strategies of deterrence, and make specific recommendations for arms control.*

THE USE OF NUCLEAR WEAPONS

Establishing moral guidelines in the nuclear
debate means addressing first the question of
the use of nuclear weapons. That question
has several dimensions.

It is clear that those in the Church who
interpret the gospel teaching as forbidding
all use of violence would oppose any use of
nuclear weapons under any conditions. In a
sense the existence of these weapons simply
confirms and reinforces one of the initial
insights of the non-violent position, namely,
that Christians should not use lethal force
since the hope of using it selectively and
restrictively is so often an illusion. Nuclear
weapons seem to prove this point in a way
heretofore unknown.

For the tradition which acknowledges
some legitimate use of force, some important
elements of contemporary nuclear strategies
move beyond the limits of moral justification. A justifiable use of force must be both
discriminatory and proportionate. Certain
aspects of both U.S. and Soviet strategies fail
both tests as we shall discuss below. The
technical literature and the personal testimony of public officials who have been closely
associated with U.S. nuclear strategy have
both convinced us of the overwhelming

probability that major nuclear exchange
would have no limits.[1]

On the more complicated issue of "limited" nuclear war, we are aware of the extensive literature and discussion which this topic has generated.[2] As a general statement, it
seems to us that public officials would be
unable to refute the following conclusion of
the study made by the Pontifical Academy of
Sciences:

*Even a nuclear attack directed only at military
facilities would be devastating to the country as a
whole. This is because military facilities are
widespread rather than concentrated at only a few
points. Thus, many nuclear weapons would be
exploded.*

*Furthermore, the spread of radiation due to the
natural winds and atmospheric mixing would kill
vast numbers of people and contaminate large
areas. The medical facilities of any nation would
be inadequate to care for the survivors. An objective examination of the medical situation that
would follow a nuclear war leads to but one
conclusion: prevention is our only recourse.*[3]

Moral Principles
and Policy Choices

In light of these perspectives we address
three questions more explicitly: (1) counter

population warfare; (2) initiation of nuclear war; and (3) limited nuclear war.

Counter Population Warfare Under no circumstances may nuclear weapons or other instruments of mass slaughter be used for the purpose of destroying population centers or other predominantly civilian targets. Popes have repeatedly condemned "total war" which implies such use. For example, as early as 1954 Pope Pius XII condemned nuclear warfare "when it entirely escapes the control of man," and results in "the pure and simple annihilation of all human life within the radius of action."[4] The condemnation was repeated by the Second Vatican Council:

Any act of war aimed indiscriminately at the destruction of entire cities or of extensive areas along with their population is a crime against God and man itself. It merits unequivocal and unhesitating condemnation.[5]

Retaliatory action whether nuclear or conventional which would indiscriminately take many wholly innocent lives, lives of people who are in no way responsible for reckless actions of their government, must also be condemned. This condemnation, in our judgment, applies even to the retaliatory use of weapons striking enemy cities after our own have already been struck. No Christian can rightfully carry out orders or policies deliberately aimed at killing noncombatants.[6]

We make this judgment at the beginning of our treatment of nuclear strategy precisely because the defense of the principle of noncombatant immunity is so important for an ethic of war and because the nuclear age has posed such extreme problems for the principle. Later in this letter we shall discuss specific aspects of U.S. policy in light of this principle and in light of recent U.S. policy statements stressing the determination not to target directly or strike directly against civilian populations. Our concern about protecting the moral value of noncombatant immunity, however, requires that we make a clear

reassertion of the principle our first word on this matter.

The Initiation of Nuclear War We do not perceive any situation in which the deliberate initiation of nuclear warfare, on however restricted a scale, can be morally justified. Non-nuclear attacks by another state must be resisted by other than nuclear means. Therefore, a serious moral obligation exists to develop non-nuclear defensive strategies as rapidly as possible.

A serious debate is under way on this issue.[7] It is cast in political terms, but it has a significant moral dimension. Some have argued that at the very beginning of a war nuclear weapons might be used, only against military targets, perhaps in limited numbers. Indeed it has long been American and NATO policy that nuclear weapons, especially so-called tactical nuclear weapons, would likely be used if NATO forces in Europe seemed in danger of losing a conflict that until then had been restricted to conventional weapons. Large numbers of tactical nuclear weapons are now deployed in Europe by the NATO forces and about as many by the Soviet Union. Some are substantially smaller than the bomb used on Hiroshima, some are larger. Such weapons, if employed in great numbers, would totally devastate the densely populated countries of Western and Central Europe.

Whether under conditions of war in Europe, parts of Asia or the Middle East, or the exchange of strategic weapons directly between the United States and the Soviet Union, the difficulties of limiting the use of nuclear weapons are immense. A number of expert witnesses advise us that commanders operating under conditions of battle probably would not be able to exercise strict control; the number of weapons used would rapidly increase, the targets would be expanded beyond the military, and the level of civilian casualties would rise enormously.[8] No one can be certain that this escalation would not occur, even in the face of political efforts to keep such an exchange "limited." The chances of keeping use limited seem remote, and the consequences of escalation to mass destruction would be appalling. Former public officials have testified that it is improbable that any nuclear war could actually be kept limited. Their testimony and the consequences involved in this problem lead us to conclude that the danger of escalation is so great that it would be morally unjustifiable to initiate nuclear war in any form. The danger is rooted not only in the technology of our weapons systems but in the weakness and sinfulness of human communities. We find the moral responsibility of beginning nuclear war not justified by rational political objectives.

This judgment affirms that the willingness to initiate nuclear war entails a distinct, weighty moral responsibility; it involves transgressing a fragile barrier—political, psychological, and moral—which has been constructed since 1945. We express repeatedly in this letter our extreme skepticism about the prospects for controlling a nuclear exchange, however limited the first use might be. Precisely because of this skepticism, we judge resort to nuclear weapons to counter a conventional attack to be morally unjustifiable.[9] Consequently we seek to reinforce the barrier against any use of nuclear weapons. Our support of a "no first use" policy must be seen in this light.

At the same time we recognize the responsibility the United States has had and continues to have in assisting allied nations in their defense against either a conventional or a nuclear attack. Especially in the European theater, the deterrence of a *nuclear* attack may require nuclear weapons for a time, even though their possession and deployment must be subject to rigid restrictions.

The need to defend against a conventional attack in Europe imposes the political and moral burden of developing adequate, alternative modes of defense to present reliance on nuclear weapons. Even with the best coordinated effort—hardly likely in view of contemporary political division on this question—development of an alternative defense position will still take time.

In the interim, deterrence against a conventional attack relies upon two factors: the not inconsiderable conventional forces at the disposal of NATO and the recognition by a potential attacker that the outbreak of large-scale conventional war could escalate to the nuclear level through accident or miscalculation by either side. We are aware that NATO's refusal to adopt a "no first use" pledge is to some extent linked to the deterrent effect of this inherent ambiguity. Nonetheless, in light of the probable effects of initiating nuclear war, we urge NATO to move rapidly toward the adoption of a "no first use" policy, but doing so in tandem with development of an adequate alternative defense posture.

Limited Nuclear War It would be possible to agree with our first two conclusions and still not be sure about retaliatory use of nuclear weapons in what is called a "limited exchange." The issue at stake is the *real* as opposed to the *theoretical* possibility of a "limited nuclear exchange."

We recognize that the policy debate on this question is inconclusive and that all participants are left with hypothetical projections about probable reactions in a nuclear exchange. While not trying to adjudicate the technical debate, we are aware of it and wish to raise a series of questions which challenge the actual meaning of "limited" in this discussion.

• Would leaders have sufficient information to know what is happening in a nuclear exchange?

• Would they be able under the conditions of stress, time pressures, and fragmentary information to make the extraordinarily precise decision needed to keep the exchange limited if this were technically possible?

• Would military commanders be able, in the midst of the destruction and confusion of a nuclear exchange, to maintain a policy of "discriminate targeting"? Can this be done in modern warfare, waged across great distances by aircraft and missiles?

• Given the accidents we know about in peacetime conditions, what assurances are there that computer errors could be avoided in the midst of a nuclear exchange?

• Would not the casualties, even in a war defined as limited by strategists, still run in the millions?

• How "limited" would be the long-term effects of radiation, famine, social fragmentation, and economic dislocation?

Unless these questions can be answered satisfactorily, we will continue to be highly skeptical about the real meaning of "limited." One of the criteria of the just-war tradition is a reasonable hope of success in bringing about justice and peace. We must ask whether such a reasonable hope can exist once nuclear weapons have been exchanged. The burden of proof remains on those who assert that meaningful limitation is possible.

A nuclear response to either conventional or nuclear attack can cause destruction which goes far beyond "legitimate defense." Such use of nuclear weapons would not be justified.

In the face of this frightening and highly speculative debate on a matter involving millions of human lives, we believe the most effective contribution or moral judgment is to introduce perspectives by which we can assess the empirical debate. Moral perspective should be sensitive not only to the quantitative dimensions of a question but to its psychological, human, and religious characteristics as well. The issue of limited war is not simply the size of weapons contemplated or the strategies projected. The debate should include the psychological and political significance of crossing the boundary from the conventional to the nuclear arena in any form. To cross this divide is to enter a world where we have no experience of control, much testimony against its possibility, and therefore no moral justification for submitting the human community to this risk.[10] We therefore express our view that the first imperative is to prevent any use of nuclear weapons and our hope that leaders will resist the notion that nuclear conflict can be limited, contained, or won in any traditional sense.

Deterrence In Principle and Practice

The moral challenge posed by nuclear weapons is not exhausted by an analysis of their possible uses. Much of the political and moral debate of the nuclear age has concerned the strategy of deterrence. Deterrence is at the heart of the U.S.-Soviet relationship, currently the most dangerous dimension of the nuclear arms race.

The Concept and Development of Deterrence Policy The concept of deterrence existed in military strategy long before the nuclear age, but it has taken on a new meaning and significance since 1945. Essentially, deterrence means "dissuasion of a potential adversary from initiating an attack or conflict, often by the threat of unacceptable retaliatory damage."[11] In the nuclear age, deterrence has become the centerpiece of both U.S. and Soviet policy. Both superpowers have for many years now been able to promise a retaliatory response which can inflict "unacceptable damage." A situation of stable deterrence depends on the ability of each side to deploy its retaliatory forces in ways that are not vulnerable to an attack (i.e., protected against a "first strike"); preserving stability requires a willingness by both sides to refrain from deploying weapons which appear to have a first-strike capability.

This general definition of deterrence does not explain either the elements of a deterrence strategy or the evolution of deterrence policy since 1945. A detailed description of either of these subjects would require an extensive essay, using materials which can be found in abundance in the technical literature on the subject of deterrence.[12] Particularly significant is the relationship between "declaratory policy" (the public explanation of our strategic intentions and capabilities) and "action policy" (the actual planning and targeting policies to be followed in a nuclear attack).

The evolution of deterrence strategy has passed through several stages of declaratory policy. Using the U.S. case as an example, there is a significant difference between "massive retaliation" and "flexible response," and between "mutual assured destruction" and "countervailing strategy." It is also possible to distinguish between "counterforce" and "countervalue" targeting policies; and to contrast a posture of "minimum deterrence" with "extended deterrence." These terms are well known in the technical debate on nuclear policy; they are less well known and sometimes loosely used in the wider public debate. It is important to recognize that there has been substantial continuity in U.S. action policy in spite of real changes in declaratory policy.[13]

The recognition of these different elements in the deterrent and the evolution of policy means that moral assessment of deterrence requires a series of distinct judgments. They include: an analysis of the *factual character* of the deterrent (e.g., what is involved in targeting doctrine); analysis of the *historical development* of the policy (e.g., whether changes have occurred which are significant for moral analysis of the policy); the relationship of deterrence policy and other aspects of *U.S.-Soviet affairs;* and determination of the key *moral questions* involved in deterrence policy.

The Moral Assessment of Deterrence The distinctively new dimensions of nuclear deterrence were recognized by policymakers and strategists only after much reflection. Similarly, the moral challenge posed by nuclear deterrence was grasped only after careful deliberation. The moral and political paradox posed by deterrence was concisely stated by Vatican II:

Undoubtedly, armaments are not amassed merely for use in wartime. Since the defensive strength of any nation is thought to depend on its capacity for immediate retaliation, the stockpiling of arms which grows from year to year serves, in a way

hitherto unthought of, as a deterrent to potential attackers. Many people look upon this as the most effective way known at the present time for maintaining some sort of peace among nations. Whatever one may think of this form of deterrent, people are convinced that the arms race, which quite a few countries have entered, is no infallible way of maintaining real peace and that the resulting so-called balance of power is no sure genuine path to achieving it. Rather than eliminate the causes of war, the arms race serves only to aggravate the position. As long as extravagant sums of money are poured into the development of new weapons, it is impossible to devote adequate aid in tackling the misery which prevails at the present day in the world. Instead of eradicating international conflict once and for all, the contagion is spreading to other parts of the world. New approaches, based on reformed attitudes, will have to be chosen in order to remove this stumbling block, to free the earth from its pressing anxieties, and give back to the world a genuine peace.[14]

Without making a specific moral judgment on deterrence, the council clearly designated the elements of the arms race: the tension between "peace of a sort" preserved by deterrence and "genuine peace" required for a stable international life; the contradiction between what is spent for destructive capacity and what is needed for constructive development.

In the post-conciliar assessment of war and peace, and specifically of deterrence, different parties to the political-moral debate within the Church and in civil society have focused on one aspect or another of the problem. For some, the fact that nuclear weapons have not been used since 1945 means that deterrence has worked, and this fact satisfies the demands of both the political and the moral order. Others contest this assessment by highlighting the risk of failure involved in continued reliance on deterrence and pointing out how politically and morally catastrophic even a single failure would be. Still others note that the absence of nuclear war is not necessarily proof that the policy of deterrence has prevented it. Indeed, some would find in the policy of deterrence the driving force in the superpower arms race. Still other observers, many of them Catholic moralists, have stressed that deterrence may not morally include the intention of deliberately attacking civilian populations or noncombatants.

The statements of the NCCB/USCC over the past several years have both reflected and contributed to the wider moral debate on deterrence. In the NCCB pastoral letter, *To Live In Christ Jesus* (1976), we focused on the moral limits of declaratory policy while calling for stronger measures of arms control.[15] In 1979 John Cardinal Krol, speaking for the USCC in support of SALT II ratification, brought into focus the other element of the deterrence problem: the actual use of nuclear weapons may have been prevented (a moral good), but the risk of failure and the physical harm and moral evil resulting from possible nuclear war remained. "This explains," Cardinal Krol stated, "the Catholic dissatisfaction with nuclear deterrence and the urgency of the Catholic demand that the nuclear arms race be reversed. It is of the utmost importance that negotiations proceed to meaningful and continuing reductions in nuclear stockpiles, and eventually to the phasing out altogether of nuclear deterrence and the threat of mutual-assured destruction."[16]

These two texts, along with the conciliar statement, have influenced much of Catholic opinion expressed recently on the nuclear question.

In June 1982, Pope John Paul II provided new impetus and insight to the moral analysis with his statement to the United Nations Second Special Session on Disarmament. The pope first situated the problem of deterrence within the context of world politics. No power, he observes, will admit to wishing to start a war, but each distrusts others and considers it necessary to mount a strong defense against attack. He then discusses the notion of deterrence:

Many even think that such preparations constitute the way—even the only way—to safeguard peace in some fashion or at least to impede to the utmost in an efficacious way the outbreak of wars, especially major conflicts which might lead to the ultimate holocaust of humanity and the destruction of the civilization that man has constructed so laboriously over the centuries.

In this approach one can see the "philosophy of peace" which was proclaimed in the ancient Roman principle: Si vis pacem, para bellum. Put in modern terms, this "philosophy" has the label of "deterrence" and one can find it in various guises of the search for a "balance of forces" which sometimes has been called, and not without reason, the "balance of terror."[17]

Having offered this analysis of the general concept of deterrence, the Holy Father introduces his considerations on disarmament, especially, but not only, nuclear disarmament. Pope John Paul II makes this statement about the morality of deterrence:

In current conditions "deterrence" based on balance, certainly not as an end in itself but as a step on the way toward a progressive disarmament, may still be judged morally acceptable. Nonetheless in order to ensure peace, it is indispensable not to be satisfied with this minimum which is always susceptible to the real danger of explosion.[18]

In Pope John Paul II's assessment we perceive two dimensions of the contemporary dilemma of deterrence. One dimension is the danger of nuclear war, with its human and moral costs. The possession of nuclear weapons, the continuing quantitative growth of the arms race, and the danger of nuclear proliferation all point to the grave danger of basing "peace of a sort" on deterrence. The other dimension is the independence and freedom of nations and entire peoples, including the need to protect smaller nations from threats to their independence and integrity. Deterrence reflects the radical distrust which marks international politics, a condition identified as a major problem by Pope John XIII in *Peace on Earth* and reaffirmed by Pope Paul VI and Pope John Paul II. Thus a balance of forces, preventing either side from achieving superiority, can be seen as a means of safeguarding both dimensions.

The moral duty today is to prevent nuclear war from ever occurring *and* to protect and preserve those key values of justice, freedom, and independence which are necessary for personal dignity and national integrity. In reference to these issues, Pope John Paul II judges that deterrence may still be judged morally acceptable, "certainly not as an end in itself but as a step on the way toward a progressive disarmament."

On more than one occasion the Holy Father has demonstrated his awareness of the fragility and complexity of the deterrence relationship among nations. Speaking to UNESCO in June 1980, he said:

Up to the present, we are told that nuclear arms are a force of dissuasion which have prevented the eruption of a major war. And that is probably true. Still, we must ask if it will always be this way.[19]

In a more recent and more specific assessment Pope John Paul II told an international meeting of scientists on August 23, 1982:

You can more easily ascertain that the logic of nuclear deterrence cannot be considered a final goal or an appropriate and secure means for safeguarding international peace.[20]

Relating Pope John Paul's general statements to the specific policies of the U.S. deterrent requires both judgments of fact and an application of moral principles. In preparing this letter we have tried, through a number of sources, to determine as precisely as possible the factual character of U.S. deterrence strategy. Two questions have particularly concerned us: (1) the targeting doctrine and strategic plans for the use of the deterrent, particularly their impact on civilian casualties; and (2) the relationship of deterrence strategy and nuclear war-fighting capability to the likelihood that war will in fact be prevented.

Moral Principles and Policy Choices

Targeting doctrine raises significant moral questions because it is a significant determinant of what would occur if nuclear weapons were ever to be used. Although we acknowledge the need for deterrent, not all forms of deterrence are morally acceptable. There are moral limits to deterrence policy as well as to policy regarding use. Specifically, it is not morally acceptable to intend to kill the innocent as part of a strategy of deterring nuclear war. The question of whether U.S. policy involves an intention to strike civilian centers (directly targeting civilian populations) has been one of our factual concerns.

This complex question has always produced a variety of responses, official and unofficial in character. The NCCB Committee has received a series of statements of clarification of policy from U.S. government officials.[21] Essentially these statements declare that it is not U.S. strategic policy to target the Soviet civilian population as such or to use nuclear weapons deliberately for the purpose of destroying population centers. These statements respond, in principle at least, to one moral criterion for assessing deterrence policy: the immunity of noncombatants from direct attack either by conventional or nuclear weapons.

These statements do not address or resolve another very troublesome moral problem, namely, that an attack on military targets or militarily significant industrial targets could involve "indirect" (i.e., unintended) but massive civilian casualties. We are advised, for example, that the United States strategic nuclear targeting plan (SIOP—Single Integrated Operational Plan) has identified 60 "military" targets within the city of Moscow alone, and that 40,000 "military" targets for nuclear weapons have been identified in the whole of the Soviet Union.[22] It is important to recognize that Soviet policy is subject to the same moral judgment; attacks on several "industrial targets" or politically significant targets in the United States could produce massive civilian casualties. The number of civilians who would necessarily be killed by such strikes is horrendous.[23] This problem is unavoidable because of the way modern military facilities and production centers are so thoroughly interspersed with civilian living and working areas. It is aggravated if one side deliberately positions military targets in the midst of a civilian population. In our consultations, administration officials readily admitted that, while they hoped any nuclear exchange could be kept limited, they were prepared to retaliate in a massive way if necessary. They also agreed that once any substantial numbers of weapons were used, the civilian casualty levels would quickly become truly catastrophic, and that even with attacks limited to "military" targets, the number of deaths in a substantial exchange would be almost indistinguishable from what might occur if civilian centers had been deliberately and directly struck. These possibilities pose a different moral question and are to be judged by a different moral criterion: the principle of proportionality.

While any judgment of proportionality is always open to differing evaluations, there are actions which can be decisively judged to be disproportionate. A narrow adherence exclusively to the principle of noncombatant immunity as a criterion for policy is an inadequate moral posture for it ignores some evil and unacceptable consequences. Hence, we cannot be satisfied that the assertion of an intention not to strike civilians directly, or even the most honest effort to implement that intention, by itself constitutes a "moral policy" for the use of nuclear weapons.

The location of industrial or militarily significant economic targets within heavily populated areas or in those areas affected by radioactive fallout could well involve such massive civilian casualties that, in our judgment, such a strike would be deemed morally disproportionate, even though not intentionally indiscriminate.

The problem is not simply one of producing highly accurate weapons that might minimize civilian casualties in any single explo-

sion, but one of increasing the likelihood of escalation at a level where many, even "discriminating," weapons would cumulatively kill very large numbers of civilians. Those civilian deaths would occur both immediately and from the long-term effects of social and economic devastation.

A second issue of concern to us is the relationship of deterrence doctrine to war-fighting strategies. We are aware of the argument that war-fighting capabilities enhance the credibility of the deterrent, particularly the strategy of extended deterrence. But the development of such capabilities raises other strategic and moral questions. The relationship of war-fighting capabilities and targeting doctrine exemplifies the difficult choices in this area of policy. Targeting civilian populations would violate the principle of discrimination—one of the central moral principles of a Christian ethic of war. But "counterforce targeting," while preferable from the perspective of protecting civilians, is often joined with a declaratory policy which conveys the notion that nuclear war is subject to precise rational and moral limits. We have already expressed our severe doubts about such a concept. Furthermore, a purely counterforce strategy may seem to threaten the viability of other nations' retaliatory forces, making deterrence unstable in a crisis and war more likely.

While we welcome any effort to protect civilian populations, we do not want to legitimize or encourage moves which extend deterrence beyond the specific objective of preventing the use of nuclear weapons or other actions which could lead directly to a nuclear exchange.

These considerations of concrete elements of nuclear deterrence policy, made in light of John Paul II's evaluation, but applying it through our own prudential judgments, lead us to a strictly conditioned moral acceptance of nuclear deterrence. We cannot consider it adequate as a long-term basis for peace.

This strictly conditioned judgment yields *criteria* for morally assessing the elements of deterrence strategy. Clearly, these criteria demonstrate that we cannot approve of every weapons system, strategic doctrine, or policy initiative advanced in the name of strengthening deterrence. On the contrary, these criteria require continual public scrutiny of what our government proposes to do with the deterrent.

On the basis of these criteria we wish now to make some specific evaluations:

1. If nuclear deterrence exists only to prevent the *use* of nuclear weapons by others, then proposals to go beyond this to planning for prolonged periods of repeated nuclear strikes and counterstrikes, or "prevailing" in nuclear war, are not acceptable. They encourage notions that nuclear war can be engaged in with tolerable human and moral consequences. Rather, we must continually say "no" to the idea of nuclear war.

2. If nuclear deterrence is our goal, "sufficiency" to deter is an adequate strategy; the quest for nuclear superiority must be rejected.

3. Nuclear deterrence should be used as a step on the way toward progressive disarmament. Each proposed addition to our strategic system or change in strategic doctrine must be assessed precisely in light of whether it will render steps toward "progressive disarmament" more or less likely.

Moreover, these criteria provide us with the means to make some judgments and recommendations about the present direction of U.S. strategic policy. Progress toward a world freed of dependence on nuclear deterrence must be carefully carried out. But it must not be delayed. There is an urgent moral and political responsibility to use the "peace of a sort" we have as a framework to move toward authentic peace through nuclear arms control, reductions, and disarmament. Of primary importance in this process is the need to prevent the development and deployment of destabilizing weapons systems on either side; a second requirement is to insure that the more sophisticated command and control systems

do not become mere hair triggers for automatic launch on warning; a third is the need to prevent the proliferation of nuclear weapons in the international system.

In light of these general judgments *we oppose* some specific proposals in respect to our present deterrence posture:

1. The addition of weapons which are likely to be vulnerable to attack, yet also possess a "prompt hard-target kill" capability that threatens to make the other side's retaliatory forces vulnerable. Such weapons may seem to be useful primarily in a first strike;[24] we resist such weapons for this reason and we oppose Soviet deployment of such weapons which generate fear of a first strike against U.S. forces.

2. The willingness to foster strategic planning which seeks a nuclear war-fighting capability that goes beyond the limited function of deterrence outlined in this letter.

3. Proposals which have the effect of lowering the nuclear threshold and blurring the difference between nuclear and conventional weapons.

In support of the concept of "sufficiency" as an adequate deterrent, and in light of the present size and composition of both the U.S. and Soviet strategic arsenals, *we recommend:*

1. Support for immediate, bilateral, verifiable agreements to halt the testing, production, and deployment of new nuclear weapons systems.[25]

2. Support for negotiated bilateral deep cuts in the arsenals of both superpowers, particularly those weapons systems which have destabilizing characteristics; U.S. proposals like those for START (Strategic Arms Reduction Talks) and INF (Intermediate-range Nuclear Forces) negotiations in Geneva are said to be designed to achieve deep cuts;[26] our hope is that they will be pursued in a manner which will realize these goals.

3. Support for early and successful conclusion of negotiations of a comprehensive test ban treaty.

4. Removal by all parties of short-range nuclear weapons which multiply dangers disproportionate to their deterrent value.

5. Removal by all parties of nuclear weapons from areas where they are likely to be overrun in the early stages of war, thus forcing rapid and uncontrollable decisions on their use.

6. Strengthening of command and control over nuclear weapons to prevent inadvertent and unauthorized use.

These judgments are meant to exemplify how a lack of unequivocal condemnation of deterrence is meant only to be an attempt to acknowledge the role attributed to deterrence, but not to support its extension beyond the limited purpose discussed above. Some have urged us to condemn all aspects of nuclear deterrence. This urging has been based on a variety of reasons, but has emphasized particularly the high and terrible risks that either deliberate use or accidental detonation of nuclear weapons could quickly escalate to something utterly disproportionate to any acceptable moral purpose. That determination requires highly technical judgments about hypothetical events. Although reasons exist which move some to condemn reliance on nuclear weapons for deterrence, we have not reached this conclusion for the reasons outlined in this letter.

Nevertheless, there must be no misunderstanding of our profound skepticism about the moral acceptability of any use of nuclear weapons. It is obvious that the use of any weapons which violate the principle of discrimination merits unequivocal condemnation. We are told that some weapons are designed for purely "counterforce" use against military forces and targets. The moral issue, however, is not resolved by the design of weapons or the planned intention for use; there are also consequences which must be assessed. It would be a perverted political policy or moral casuistry which

tried to justify using a weapon which "indirectly" or "unintentionally" killed a million innocent people because they happened to live near a "militarily significant target."

Even the "indirect effects" of initiating nuclear war are sufficient to make it an unjustifiable moral risk in any form. It is not sufficient, for example, to contend that "our" side has plans for "limited" or "discriminate" use. Modern warfare is not readily contained by good intentions or technological designs. The psychological climate of the world is such that mention of the term "nuclear" generates uneasiness. Many contend that the use of one tactical nuclear weapon could produce panic, with completely unpredictable consequences. It is precisely this mix of political, psychological, and technological uncertainty which has moved us in this letter to reinforce with moral prohibitions and prescriptions the prevailing political barrier against resort to nuclear weapons. Our support for enhanced command and control facilities, for major reductions in strategic and tactical nuclear forces, and for a "no first use" policy (as set forth in this letter) is meant to be seen as a complement to our desire to draw a moral line against nuclear war.

Any claim by any government that it is pursuing a morally acceptable policy of deterrence must be scrutinized with the greatest care. We are prepared and eager to participate in our country in the ongoing public debate on moral grounds.

The need to rethink the deterrence policy of our nation, to make the revisions necessary to reduce the possibility of nuclear war, and to move toward a more stable system of national and international security will demand a substantial intellectual, political, and moral effort. It also will require, we believe, the willingness to open ourselves to the providential care, power, and word of God, which call us to recognize our common humanity and the bonds of mutual responsibility which exist in the international community in spite of political differences and nuclear arsenals.

Footnotes

1. The following quotations are from public officials who have served at the highest policy levels in recent administrations of our government: "It is time to recognize that no one has ever succeeded in advancing any persuasive reason to believe that any use of nuclear weapons, even on the smallest scale, could reliably be expected to remain limited." M. Bundy, G.F. Kennan, R.S. McNamara, and G. Smith, "Nuclear Weapons and the Atlantic Alliance," *Foreign Affairs* 60 (1982):757.

"From my experience in combat there is no way that [nuclear escalation] . . . can be controlled because of the lack of information, the pressure of time and the deadly results that are taking place on both sides of the battle line." Gen. A.S. Collins, Jr. (former deputy commander in chief of U.S. Army in Europe), "Theatre Nuclear Warfare: The Battlefield," in J.F. Reichart and S.R. Sturm, eds. *American Defense Policy,* 5th ed., (Baltimore: 1982), pp. 359–60.

"None of this potential flexibility changes my view that a full-scale thermonuclear exchange would be an unprecedented disaster for the Soviet Union as well as for the United States. Nor is it at all clear that an initial use of nuclear weapons—however selectively they might be targeted—could be kept from escalating to a full-scale thermonuclear exchange, especially if command-and-control centers were brought under attack. The odds are high, whether weapons were used against tactical or strategic targets, that control would be lost on both sides and the exchange would become unconstrained." Harold Brown, *Department of Defense Annual Report FY 1979* (Washington, D.C.: 1978).

Cf. also: *The Effects of Nuclear War* (Washington, DC: 1979, U.S. Government Printing Office).

2. For example, cf.: H.A. Kissinger, *Nuclear Weapons and Foreign Policy* (New York: 1957), *The Necessity for Choice* (New York: 1960); R. Osgood and R. Tucker, *Force, Order and Justice* (Baltimore: 1967); R. Aron, *The Great Debate: Theories of Nuclear Strategy* (New York: 1965); D. Ball, *Can Nuclear War Be Controlled?* Adelphi Paper # 161 (London: 1981); M. Howard, "On Fighting a Nuclear War," *International Security* 5 (1981):3–17.

3. "Statement on the Consequences of the Use of Nuclear Weapons."

4. Pius XII, "Address to the VIII Congress of the World Medical Association," in *Documents,* p. 131.

5. *Pastoral Constitution, # 80.*

6. Ibid.

7. M. Bundy, et al., "Nuclear Weapons," cited; K. Kaiser, G. Leber, A. Mertes, F.J. Schulze, "Nuclear Weapons and the Preservation of Peace," *Foreign Affairs* 60 (1982):1157–70; cf. other responses to Bundy article in the same issue of *Foreign Affairs.*

8. Testimony given to the National Conference of Catholic Bishops Committee during preparation of this pastoral letter. The testimony is reflected in the quotes found in note 61.

9. Our conclusions and judgments in this area although based on careful study and reflection of the application of moral principles do not have, of course, the same force as the principles themselves and therefore allow for different opinions.

10. Undoubtedly aware of the long and detailed technical debate on limited war, Pope John Paul II highlighted the unacceptable moral risk of crossing the threshold to nuclear war in his "Angelus Message" of December 13, 1981: "I have, in fact, the deep conviction that, in the light of a nuclear war's effects, which can be scientifically foreseen as certain, the only choice that is morally and humanly valid is represented by the reduction of nuclear armaments, while waiting for their future complete elimination, carried out simultaneously by all the parties, by means of explicit agreements and with the commitment of accepting effective controls." In *Documents,* p. 240.

11. W.H. Kincade and J.D. Porro, *Negotiating Security: An Arms Control Reader* (Washington, DC: 1979).

12. Several surveys are available, for example cf.: J.H. Kahin, *Security in the Nuclear Age: Developing U.S. Strategic Policy* (Washington, DC: 1975); M. Mandelbaum, *The Nuclear Question: The United States and Nuclear Weapons 1946–1976* (Cambridge, England: 1979); B. Brodie, "Development of Nuclear Strategy," *International Security* 2 (1978):65–83.

13. The relationship of these two levels of policy is the burden of an article by D. Ball, "U.S. Strategic Forces: How Would They Be Used?" *International Security* 7 (1982/83):31–60.

14. *Pastoral Constitution, # 81.*

15. United States Catholic Conference, *To Live in Christ Jesus* (Washington, DC: 1976), p. 34.

16. John Cardinal Krol, "Testimony on Salt II," *Origins* (1979):197.

17. John Paul II, "Message U.N. Special Session 1982," # 3.

18. Ibid., # 8.

19. John Paul II, "Address to UNESCO, 1980," # 21.

20. John Paul II, "Letter to International Seminar on the World Implications of a Nuclear Conflict," August 23, 1982, text in *NC News Documentary,* August 24, 1982.

21. Particularly helpful was the letter of January 15, 1983, of Mr. William Clark, national security adviser, to Cardinal Bernardin. Mr. Clark stated: "For moral, political and military reasons, the United States does not target the Soviet civilian population as such. There is no deliberately opaque meaning conveyed in the last two words. We do not threaten the existence of Soviet civilization by threatening Soviet cities. Rather, we hold at risk the war-making capability of the Soviet Union—its armed forces, and the industrial capacity to sustain war. It would be irresponsible for us to issue policy statements which might suggest to the Soviets that it would be to their advantage to establish privileged sanctuaries within heavily populated areas, thus inducing them to locate much of their war-fighting capability within those urban sanctuaries." A reaffirmation of the administration's policy is also found in Secretary Weinberger's *Annual Report to the Congress* (Casper Weinberger, *Annual Report to the Congress,* February 1, 1983, p. 55): "The Reagan Administration's policy is that under no circumstances may such weapons be used deliberately for the purpose of destroying populations." Also the letter of Mr. Weinberger to Bishop O'Connor of February 9, 1983, has a similar statement.

22. S. Zuckerman, *Nuclear Illusion and Reality* (New York: 1982); D. Ball, cited, p. 36; T. Powers, "Choosing a Strategy for World War III," *The Atlantic Monthly,* November 1982, pp. 82–110.

23. Cf. the comments in Pontifical Academy of Sciences "Statement on the Consequences of the Use of Nuclear Weapons," cited.

24. Several experts in strategic theory would place both the MX missile and Pershing II missiles in this category.

25. In each of the successive drafts of this letter we have tried to state a central moral imperative: that the arms race should be stopped and disarmament begun. The implementation of this imperative is open to a wide variety of approaches. Hence we have chosen our own language in this paragraph, not wanting either to be identified with one specific political initiative or to have our words used against specific political measures.

26. Cf. President Reagan's "Speech to the National Press Club" (November 18, 1981) and "Address at Eureka College" (May 9, 1982), Department of State, *Current Policy* # 346 and # 387.

Review Questions

1. What is the nonviolent position?

2. Why is using nuclear weapons against population centers always wrong?

3. Why can't any Christian rightfully carry out orders or policies deliberately aimed at killing noncombatants?

4. Why can't the deliberate initiation of nuclear warfare ever be justified?

5. Why can't a "limited nuclear exchange" be justified?

6. What are the "two dimensions" of deterrence?

7. Explain the "strictly conditioned moral acceptance of nuclear deterrence."

Discussion Questions

1. "It is not morally acceptable to intend to kill the innocent." Can you think of any exceptions to this principle? What are they?

2. Is nuclear deterrence as a policy or strategy morally acceptable or not? Explain your view.

3. Do you agree with the specific recommendations made by the Bishops? Why, or why not?

THE HARVARD NUCLEAR STUDY GROUP
Disarmament and Arms Control

Reprinted by permission of the authors and publisher from *Living with Nuclear Weapons* by the Harvard Nuclear Study Group, Cambridge, MA: Harvard University Press. Copyright © 1983 by the Harvard Nuclear Study Group.

The Harvard University Nuclear Study Group includes: Albert Carnesale, Professor of Public Policy and Academic Dean of Harvard's John F. Kennedy School of Government; Paul Doty, Director of the Center for Science and International Affairs and Mallinckrodt Professor of Biochemistry, Harvard University; Stanley Hoffmann, Chairman of the Center for

European Studies and Douglas Dillon Professor of the Civilization of France, Harvard University; Samuel P. Huntington, Director of the Center for International Affairs and Clarence Dillon Professor of International Affairs, Harvard University; Joseph S. Nye, Jr., Professor of Government, Harvard University; and Scott D. Sagan, Staff Director of the project, and Ph.D. candidate in the Department of Government, Harvard University.

The Group claims that disarmament is "inherently unstable" and not in the nation's best interests. They accept the common view that arms are necessary to deter aggression and to project political influence. Still they grant that some kind of arms control might contribute to deterrence, arms-race stability, and crisis stability. Using these criteria, as well as negotiability and possible verification, they critically examine a number of proposals for arms reductions, freezes, force restructuring, and stabilizing measures.

DISARMAMENT AND DISTRUST

Successful efforts at disarmament are extremely rare, but there have been some. An outstanding example was the reduction of naval forces on the Great Lakes during the nineteenth century. Naval battles in the War of 1812 against Great Britain proved the importance of naval control of the Lakes. Both sides threatened to build more ships in the period following the war. A treaty concluded in 1817, still in force today, limits navy ships to sizes smaller than the existing fleets. As a result the U.S. and British fleets were dismantled, the threat of a future war was removed, and a major step was taken on the road that has produced the longest, enduring demilitarized border in modern history.

One reason that successful disarmament efforts are rare is that they require a degree of political accommodation that is difficult to achieve. Unless some political trust exists, efforts to disarm prove fruitless. Such trust is difficult to build, but not impossible—witness the peaceful relations between France and Germany today in contrast with the past. But political accommodation and trust are built slowly and this makes complete disarmament—as contrasted with more limited arms control—a long-term rather than an immediate prospect.

Complete disarmament would require some form of world government to deter actions of one nation against another. In a disarmed world, without such a government armed with sufficient force to prevent conflict between or among nations, differences in beliefs and interests might easily lead to a renewal of war. But any world government capable of preventing world conflict could also become a world dictatorship. And given the differences in ideology, wealth, and nationalism that now exist in the world, most states are not likely to accept a centralized government unless they feel sure of controlling it or minimizing its intrusiveness. A weak central machinery would be ineffective. And even a strong one—assuming governments would agree to set it up—could still be faced with breakdown. It is worth remembering that the central government of the United States fell apart in the mid-19th century, leading to a horrible civil war. Such a breakdown of authority in a world government would not only lead to bitter power struggles for domination of the world government in order to advance one or another national group, but could also lead to massive warfare. Individual nations would rearm. And those who could, would race to make nuclear weapons.

Disarmament would leap into the unknown; each state would accept it only if the dangers it feared could be ended or if it thought that the danger of nuclear holocaust outweighed the risks involved in nuclear disarmament. Despite the present costs of national military forces and arms competition, despite the limited gains which the threat to use force now brings, and despite the enormous risks such uses may entail, most nations still see a clear national advantage in having such forces. They provide the possibilities of deterring aggression and of projecting political influence. Disarmament would not necessarily ensure a state's position in the international contest between states. It would not necessarily ensure a state's security. Nor would disarmament guarantee that the funds saved from weapons would necessarily be devoted to raising the living standards of poor peoples. As a result, governments, even in this dangerous nuclear world, have preferred a combination of arms, self-restraint, and arms control to complete disarmament.

Ironically, while complete disarmament may be a worthy long-term goal, trying to achieve it before the requisite political conditions exist could actually increase the prospects of war. If the political pre-conditions of trust and consensus are missing, complete disarmament is inherently unstable. In a disarmed world, the first nation to acquire a few arms would be able to influence events to a much greater extent than it could in a heavily armed world. Nuclear weapons greatly magnify this effect.

On a cold January day in 1977, a little boy listened to President Carter aspire in his inaugural speech to remove nuclear weapons from the face of the earth. "Daddy, do you think he really means it?" the boy asked. "Yes," his father replied. After a moment's thought the boy responded. "Daddy, don't you think we should hide at least one?" The boy had a point. While mistrust exists, there will be strong temptation to hedge one's bets. Moreover, nuclear weapons can be easily hidden or quickly reinvented. At high numbers, even hidden bombs do not matter. But if the numbers are few and political mistrust persists, rumors of hidden bombs or fears of their reinvention by any number of nations could lead to the worst kind of nuclear arms race—a crash program

of rearmament with few of the safety features that are built into existing weapons.

ARMS CONTROL

Therefore, when the consequences and risks of complete world disarmament are examined it appears that it does not guarantee peace and security if attempted before the political conditions are right. But nuclear arms races do not guarantee peace and security either. Instead they can guarantee enormous destruction if war occurs either by design, or more likely through accident, miscalculation, or misunderstanding. With no safe port in complete nuclear disarmament or in unrestricted competition, mankind has been compelled to seek safety by using arms control to lower the risks that nuclear weapons impose on peace and security.

"Arms control" has to a large extent replaced "disarmament" in the specialist's vocabulary since about 1960, but as long as disarmament is not taken to mean complete disarmament, the terms overlap. Arms control includes a wider range of actions than the removal of arms. For example, it includes steps that improve stability and help avoid accidents. Some "arms control" agreements reduce armaments; but not all do.

A common criticism of arms control and disarmament is that they mistake the symptoms for the disease. Since the origins of conflict do not reside in the weapons, its cure should not be sought in their restraint. But this is only a partial truth. The easy recourse to weapons in times of stress or panic does increase the likelihood of their use. This problem is ever so much larger in the Nuclear Age.

The parallel can be seen with handguns. Clearly they are not the sole or even the primary cause of murders, but where they are not generally available to the adult population, there are fewer murders, as in Britain, Japan, and the Soviet Union. Where guns are widely available, as in the United States, and much more so in Lebanon, murder is considerably more common. In daily life or international politics the proper control of arms, whether they are symptoms or not, can lower the risk of their being used.

Arms control alone is not enough. It is also important to attack the sources of conflicts. The ultimate hope for peace clearly lies with improving international relations to the point where conflict does not threaten to erupt into war and reconciliation replaces aggression. Whether the world eventually reaches this goal or not may depend on the combination of arms control with effective deterrence over the next decades.

DIFFICULTIES
CONFRONTING
ARMS CONTROL

During the past three decades the military establishments of the United States and the Soviet Union have become, by most counts, the most powerful and most expensive institutions ever created. It is no wonder that they are difficult to change. Such enormous bureaucracies often resist the changes that arms control initiatives attempt to introduce. The Arms Control and Disarmament Agency of the U.S. government is funded at an annual cost of less than the cost of the least expensive fighter aircraft! Ideally, arms control and security policy should go hand in hand. But in reality many arms control initiatives do not survive the raised eyebrows of the defense community and defense decisions may therefore ignore their arms control implications.

This uneven situation would ordinarily suppress most arms control initiatives were it not for heads of governments. It is chiefly by this route that arms control has had a role. Even so, its role is precarious and vulnerable to the changing views of successive administrations. Nevertheless, at least in democracies, polls show recurrent public support for efforts at arms control. When presidents ignore these opinions, they do so to their own political peril.

Another difficulty encountered by arms control is the unusual U.S. constitutional clause on the ratification of treaties. The United States alone among industrialized Western countries requires a two-thirds majority in the Senate to ratify treaties. This means that a minority, one that often represents much less than one-third of U.S. voters and one motivated by diverse interests, can block ratification. The role of arms control would have been much greater in the last decade if ratification required only a majority vote.

These examples, which do not exhaust the list, illustrate why arms control is often harder to accomplish than it would first appear. Two more problems deserve special attention: conflicting views about Soviet conceptions of arms control and the special limits that may be set by verification.

SOVIET ARMS CONTROL POLICY

Arms control negotiations have been a constant ingredient of Soviet-American relations for a quarter of a century. There is ample evidence that the Soviet Union, like the United States, has been motivated by an interest in preserving and managing the strategic relationship. Not only does this make for diminished risks and greater effectiveness in both sides' military planning, but it has also helped establish the Soviet Union's claim to co-equal status with the United States. As might be expected in a country that has steadily increased its military spending for two decades and where the defense programs are insulated from fluctuating public attitudes, Soviet arms control policy has been tightly integrated with Soviet military policy.

The substance of the Soviet Union's arms control positions can be summarized as follows. Until about 1960 the Soviet Union was in such an inferior position strategically that it resisted Western arms control initiatives for the understandable reason that agreements would freeze them in perpetual inferiority. However, they camouflaged this negative position by campaigns for general and complete disarmament and offers to ban weapons first and work out verification later. Nevertheless, from 1959 through the 1960s a number of agreements were negotiated that prohibited nuclear deployments in Antarctica, space, and the seabed, banned nuclear tests in the atmosphere, and created a Non-Proliferation Treaty. With the approach to parity in the 1970s it became possible to open up negotiations in the domain of central strategic forces.

The Soviet approach was limited by their concept of deterrence, which emphasizes that whichever side can deliver the greatest blow first is likely to remain in a dominant position thereafter. This explains the Soviet preoccupation with land-based, highly controlled, large ICBMs rather than bombers. Hence a main Soviet arms control objective has been to retain these forces and to ensure their modernization. They have resisted American efforts to use arms control to encourage greater Soviet reliance on their submarines (which they have regarded as an area of American advantage). At the same time, they have stressed a number of measures that do not reduce their central forces, such as a series of bans and limitations on new weapons or weapons in the planning stage. The successful treaty limiting antiballistic missile defenses was of this sort.

Another Soviet preoccupation has been with the concept of equality. Not only has the symbol of equality with the U.S. been important to them, but they have argued that "equal security" requires more than an equal number of weapons. They use the term to justify claims of compensation for geographical handicaps, for nuclear weapons in Europe, and for British, French, and Chinese nuclear forces. They are less open to U.S. claims that they have a geographical advantage because of their proximity to Europe. This complicates efforts to negotiate reductions that maintain rough "parity."

The Soviets, like the U.S., often use arms control proposals as propaganda weapons; with no effective public opinion at home,

this is far easier for them to manage than for democracies. The extent to which the Soviet Union publicizes its role in negotiations seems to tell something about the seriousness with which it wants a compromise agreement. The negotiations of SALT I and SALT II were generally carried out with considerable privacy until the late stages. This seems to apply to the START negotiations as well. However, the INF negotiations have been carried out in public view almost from the beginning. One of the Soviet objectives in these negotiations is to split Western Europe from the United States and thereby halt or limit the deployment of intermediate-range forces. But if this tactic fails, an agreement may be possible.

What does the Soviet record tell us about the outlook for future arms control agreements? The picture is mixed. On the one hand, the proposals of the Reagan administration would cut deeply into the Soviet land-based missiles. These forces have been sacrosanct in the past. The "deep cuts" approach runs counter to the Soviet penchant and tradition for slow increments of change. In a period of political transition, Soviet leaders often find it especially hard to move in radical directions. Yuri Andropov, was a product of this system and was beholden to military support in attaining his position of leadership. Not surprisingly, the Soviets had only offered proposals for more modest reductions and restrictions on new systems of interest to the U.S.

On the other hand, changes do occur in international politics. There are several possible catalysts for change in the Soviet situation. Andropov came into office in 1982 at the age of 68. With only a few years to leave his mark, he may have wished to move faster in arms control negotiations. More important, he faced serious political and economic problems: a decreasing Soviet work force; minority pressures for larger roles; a chronically incompetent agricultural system; inadequate consumer goods production; unrest in Eastern Europe; and most of all, a shrinking growth rate that does not provide the base it once did for the Soviet military machine. Together, these pressures may induce a more active search for maintaining the military competition with the West at lower levels of risk and expenditure.

VERIFYING ARMS CONTROL AGREEMENTS

Given the distrust between East and West, only arms control agreements that are verifiable are likely to be negotiated and ratified. How severe will this limitation be?

In the 1950s, the West routinely proposed, and the Soviet Union routinely rejected, measures to monitor arms control and disarmament agreements that involved on-site inspection, that is, provision for the physical inspection of a country's weapons and facilities by foreign experts. Until technology developed that permitted states to monitor one another at a distance, nuclear arms control was not possible. The absence of acceptable verification measures prevented the negotiation of limits on strategic weapons systems. When President Eisenhower proposed, in 1955, his Open Skies arrangement whereby the United States and the Soviet Union would exchange military blueprints and open one another's airspace to airborne reconnaissance the Russians rejected it, but in 1956 the U.S. began carrying out aerial reconnaissance photography anyway, using the U–2 aircraft. By January 1961, the first successful photo-reconnaissance satellite was launched. Such satellites have continually improved, and the level of detail gleaned by modern satellite scanners is, by all accounts, quite remarkable. In addition to photography, satellites have infra-red sensors (which work at night and through clouds) and listening devices for monitoring radio transmissions from Soviet missile tests.

The U.S. employs a variety of means, besides satellites, to determine the size of Soviet forces as well as verify Soviet compliance with arms control treaties, including large radars in the Aleutians, a space-tracking ship, line-of-sight radar stations around the

Soviet periphery, and over-the-horizon radars. In combination, these systems provide detailed information on Soviet missile tests and weapons deployments. The Soviet Union has similar ships and satellites, which are collectively referred to as "national technical means" of verification.

But even such sophisticated measures as these cannot be all-seeing. There are aspects of the weapon systems production cycle that remain difficult to monitor by national technical means. The production of individual bombs, warheads, and missiles takes place in secrecy and production rates can only be inferred from scrutiny of what comes to the factories. If small changes in numbers of weapons are important, this process may be far too crude to be adequate.

It was the revolution in verification technology in the 1960s that made the more ambitious efforts of the Strategic Arms Limitation Talks possible. Of necessity the SALT process reflected the limitations of verification technology. Only delivery vehicles that were large enough to spot from space (for example, ICBM silos) or that, if mobile, could only operate from relatively few, known bases (heavy bombers and strategic submarines) could be verified. It was possible, however, to set limits on warheads and bombs, which were too small to be verified directly, by agreeing to somewhat arbitrary counting rules. A missile was counted as having the maximum number of warheads ever tested on that missile, rather than the actual number deployed (which might be much less). In this way verification was extended to what could not be seen.

While the Soviets have elaborate surveillance equipment, their interests in verification are less than those of the United States because of the very different nature of the two societies. The high level of reporting from American congressional hearings, media coverage, leaks to newspapers, and the likelihood that any violation of an agreement will find its way into newspapers make verification much easier for the Soviet Union. Hence exacting verification procedures are seen by the Soviets as something they "give" to the United States. At the same time, the Soviet Union is extremely secretive about military matters, a tradition with deep roots in the history of a frequently invaded Russian state. Many of the verification measures proposed by the U.S. look like espionage measures to the Soviets. Over the years, negotiations helped convince the Soviets that such procedures are not a cover for espionage but are an essential requirement for ratifiable arms control measures. Yet in each instance procedures must be justified in minute detail and negotiated in ways that minimize intrusiveness.

It should be remembered that the vast system of monitoring and intelligence collection that the United States must use for verification is needed whether arms control agreements exist or not. Indeed, arms control agreements, especially SALT II, have greatly increased our knowledge of the Soviet nuclear arsenal; both sides have promised not to interfere with each other's surveillance devices, and both have agreed that certain activities will not be concealed but will remain open to monitoring. Hence the verification of future agreements will have a broader foundation on which to build. Moreover, improvements in verification technology continue and it is reasonable to expect that capabilities that were not possible in the past will exist in the future.

When matters of national security are at stake, both the government and the public wish to know for certain whether agreements are being kept. But in daily life we know that we must live with some uncertainty. Verification of arms control agreements is no different; some risks are inevitable. But an untrammeled arms race also creates risks. Risks must be balanced and judgments made about adequacy. Verification must be adequate enough so that a Soviet violation of an agreement large enough to threaten our security could be detected in time for us to be able to make a sufficient response. Ironically, some of these judgments are easier to make at cur-

rent high levels of weaponry than would be the case if there were deep reductions in numbers.

Much of the U.S. internal debate during the SALT II negotiations and ratification hearings focused on such judgments. Although the verification of some treaty provisions was seen to be less adequate than others, the trade-offs made between uncertainty and the importance of the item to be limited was generally agreed to be prudent.

Nevertheless, the new weaponry scheduled for deployment in this decade raises new problems. Cruise missiles will present a special challenge to verification. They are small and can be easily changed from conventional to nuclear warheads. The focus may have to be on restricting the ships and planes and geographical regions of their deployment. Close monitoring of both sides' production plants may also help. Mobile ICBMs will require special measures as well. As greater emphasis shifts to the number of warheads and the ability to reload missile launchers, further measures will be required. In each case difficult judgments of two sorts will have to be made: what kinds of violations have significant adverse consequences on American security, and what is the probability that such violations could be detected. If one insists on absolute certainty in verification, then very little can be verified and arms cannot be controlled. On the other hand, if verification procedures are absent or lax, cheating may occur and confidence will be lost in the other side's compliance. The task is to find the right middle ground.

Verification procedures in future agreements will be subject to even greater scrutiny for two reasons. First, the Soviet Union refused to cooperate with American efforts to discover if an outbreak of anthrax in a Soviet city was a violation of the Biological Weapons Convention of 1972. Second, there is increasing evidence of the use of poison gas by the Soviet forces in Afghanistan and by the military forces they support in Cambodia. In the latter case there is a technical loophole in that the countries allegedly under attack were not themselves parties to the Geneva Protocol that prohibits such use. Those conventions did not have the elaborate verification provisions and procedures that the SALT treaties have. Soviet actions have therefore reinforced the importance of having such provisions in any future arms control agreements.

Despite all these difficulties, however, over the past twenty-five years there has been a gradual improvement in Soviet willingness to provide information, even to negotiate details of on-site inspections in the 1976 Threshold Test-Ban Treaty, and to permit the discussion of such requirements. It has been a slow process but it should not go unnoticed.

THE ROLE OF PUBLIC OPINION

Arms control has tended to succeed in the United States in periods of significant public involvement and concern. The 1963 Test-Ban Treaty and the 1972 ABM Treaty both were achieved during such periods. One of the most interesting developments of the early 1980s was the remarkable rise of public interest and public protest in the area of nuclear policy. Failure of the U.S. to ratify SALT II, after a similar failure to ratify two treaties negotiated in 1976 to further limit nuclear tests, suggested to the public that arms control was not working, and that the principal diplomatic lever for controlling the arms competition was stuck. The 1980 election was filled with rhetoric about rearmament. Concern in Europe about these events and the plans to deploy new nuclear weapons helped to stimulate mass movements. A year-long series of pronouncements by the U.S. president and his secretaries of state and defense that reflected a preoccupation with improving U.S. nuclear war-fighting capability and a new level of hostility toward the Soviet Union followed. This was accompanied by rapidly increasing military budgets.

As budgets and rhetoric escalated, so did the memberships and the influence of public and professional groups opposed to nuclear war. Physicians' groups, some dating from the campaign against nuclear testing two decades earlier, were particularly effective in reminding Americans of the horrible human suffering and death that would accompany nuclear war. Because of this revival of public interest in arms control, the current nuclear freeze movement, the careful examination of the moral basis of nuclear policy by the U.S. Catholic bishops, and intensified support for arms control in the scientific and professional community came into being.

The nuclear freeze movement began in the spring of 1980 with a call for bilateral, verifiable freeze on the production, testing, and deployment of all nuclear weapons systems in the U.S. and the USSR. Its aim is to prevent further development or deployment of counterforce and other destabilizing weapons, and to stabilize the current balance so that reductions can go forward. Various freeze resolutions were supported by the electorates in eight (of nine) states where it appeared on the ballot in November 1982. Public opinion polls at the end of 1982 showed the freeze idea appealed to some three-quarters of the public if it is verifiable and would grant no significant advantage to the Soviet Union. The same polls showed overwhelming opposition to unilateral disarmament and considerable mistrust of the Soviet Union.[1]

Earlier freezes suggested by Presidents Johnson and Carter did not have any obvious drawing power, nor have the various moratoria proposed by the Soviet Union. But with the combination of the seemingly bellicose pronouncements of the early Reagan administration and the belief that arms control was not being seriously pursued, the freeze movement took hold with the public. Considering the difficulty of any treaty of substance gaining the two-thirds Senate vote needed for ratification, this degree of public arousal may turn out to be an essential requirement for any future arms control agreement.

In Europe, the anti-nuclear opposition has focused on deployment of new NATO missiles and is strongest in northern Europe and among the Protestant churches. By contrast, in the U.S. the initiative from the religious sector has come from the Catholic bishops. This has taken the form of a well-planned, deliberate debate.

A further indication of the spread of concern is seen in the mobilization of support for arms control in the scientific community. Not only are activist scientists busy refining freeze proposals, but the establishment itself is involved. For the first time the National Academy of Sciences passed virtually unanimously a resolution urging intensified efforts at the negotiating table and adherence to the still unratified treaties. A carefully crafted statement by the presidents of scientific academies and other leading scientists on these matters was presented to Pope John Paul II in September 1982. It urged curbing "the development, production, testing and deployment of nuclear weapons systems and their reduction to substantially lower levels," claiming that "the sole purpose of nuclear weapons, as long as they exist, must be to deter nuclear war," and calling upon all nations "never to be the first to use nuclear weapons."

This brief overview cannot convey the full extent of the diversity and vigor of the new public engagement in nuclear policy. Like public involvements in the past, this one may be changed or move in new directions. But it seems likely that this new force will prove durable enough to affect government policies . . ..

THREE MORAL DILEMMAS

As long as nations have fought wars efforts have been made to place moral restraints on the violence unleashed. Medieval writers on the subject sought to encourage what they called a just-war theory. Justice in warfare required several conditions: a good cause (for example, self-defense rather than aggression); some proportion between the ends

sought and the means used; and keeping the distinction between civilians and combatants, between innocent bystanders and soldiers fighting a war. Nations at war have never been able to follow this moral distinction with complete success, but many have tried. The history of warfare contains many stories of statesmen, generals, even common foot soldiers attempting to spare civilian lives even in the midst of fighting. Such actions are efforts to maintain a sense of the moral world even in the hell of war.

Have nuclear weapons made such efforts futile and destroyed the just-war tradition?

Not completely, although they have shaken some of its assumptions. Aggression can still be condemned, and in principle one can conceive of small-scale use of very low-yield nuclear weapons that would do less destruction than conventional bombs (thus meeting the criterion of proportion), and allow discrimination between enemy soldiers and civilians. The key question, however, is whether the violence would remain at that level. Once the nuclear threshold has been crossed, will conflict escalate to large-scale nuclear war where the distinction between civilians and soldiers is lost in blind ferocity, and all sense of proportion is obliterated? No one knows. And therefore, however just the cause involved, unintended consequences could transform a limited nuclear use into a highly immoral action. Certainly it is hard to envisage any circumstances in which a nuclear war that would destroy the societies in conflict would be morally justifiable.

The Catholic bishops of the United States are addressing these issues. One of the dilemmas they have discussed is whether it can ever be moral to initiate the use of nuclear weapons, even if a conventional war is being lost. If one believes that escalation is unlikely to be controlled and that a full-scale nuclear exchange would be immoral, can initiating the use of nuclear weapons ever be morally justified?

The dilemma arises because it is not known whether, in a conventional war, the

use of nuclear weapons in an extremely limited fashion, to destroy a Soviet radar site for
example, would be more likely to lead to
nuclear escalation or to stop the conventional war. If initiating the use of nuclear weapons led to escalation, the action would have
been immoral. But if it led to a quick end of
the conventional war in Europe, might not
the action be seen as moral? Perhaps. But
every effort would have to be made to keep
close control of the risks (i.e., small weapons;
no delegation of authority to dispersed military units; continual communications with
the Soviet Union; a clear idea of how to
terminate the conflict, etc.). Even then, giv-
en the enormous cost of the unintended
consequences, and the uncertainty about
reaching the intended ones (a quick de-esca-
lation or end of violence), such an action
could only be a last resort. What morality
and prudence dictate is "no early use" of
nuclear weapons as policy and strategy, and
a highly selective and limited use if it should
come to that; indeed, morality and prudence
suggest that were deterrence to fail, one
should have the means to carry out an alternative, non-nuclear strategy.

This brings us to the second dilemma that
the bishops have raised: Can it be right to
have nuclear forces and a targeting doctrine
that deliberately aim at civilians? The bishops believe not. Many others differ over this
issue. Some have argued that assured destruction is an immoral doctrine because it
rests on the deterrent threat of disproportionate damage to civilians and industry.
The American government does not aim its
weapons at the Soviet population per se, and
ever since the 1950s our doctrine has in
practice involved military targets. But many
people also powerfully argue that counterforce targeting is immoral because it makes
nuclear weapons seem more usable and requires ever more war-fighting capabilities;
there is no limit on the number of targets
and weapons, thus the insatiable needs of
the nuclear arsenal will compete with other
moral claims on the resources of our society.
Moreover, destruction of large parts of civil-

ian society is an unavoidable part of any
large-scale strategic nuclear war.

Targeting certainly raises an important
moral issue. But it is not the theology of
"counterforce versus countercity." The issue is whether our strategy and arsenal can
reduce the prospect of war in a time of
crisis. Since the moral claims for deterrence
rest on averting large-scale nuclear war, the
truly immoral behavior is to have nuclear
force and doctrines that invite preemptive
attack by one's opponent or by oneself. For
example, a force that is highly lethal and
highly vulnerable at the same time will
tempt a political leader to "use it or lose it"
at a time of crisis. Even an invulnerable but
complete counter-silo capability may incite
one's opponent to use his vulnerable missiles
against some enemy targets before the missiles are lost. Morality is not just about
choices at a time of crisis; it can also be
about averting terrible choices at a time of
crisis. The crucial moral question about
force posture and targeting doctrine therefore is: How can our current actions ensure
that even in a deep crisis no general on
either side can persuasively argue that it is
imperative to launch his nation's strategic
forces because they might otherwise be lost?

A third dilemma raised by the bishops'
letter concerns neither the use nor the specific targets of nuclear weapons, but the
morality of deterrence itself. It can be called
the "intentions versus consequences" dilemma: Is it justifiable to threaten a nuclear
attack that might destroy innocent civilians
if the intention is to deter nuclear war altogether? Even if the consequences of the
threat are moral—if deterrence works, in
other words—is making the threat itself
morally acceptable? Some theologians who
stress the importance of intent believe it is
not, and that therefore the whole motion of
nuclear deterrence is morally unsound.
They argue that it is wrong to threaten what
it is wrong to do. Others would place more
stress on consequences. For example, we
may believe it is wrong to kill another person, but believe it moral to threaten to kill

someone who is about to attack our children if such a threat would deter the act.

Most people judge the morality of actions on their intentions and their consequences. Moreover, in deterrence our intentions are not to do evil. Our threat is intended to avoid both the horrible outcome of nuclear war and aggressive behavior by the other side. Our intent in making the threat is not immoral, and the consequences depend in part upon the intentions of the other side. On the contrary, to remove the threat altogether—because it is evil to threaten to kill entire populations, or to threaten to attack military targets with weapons that are likely to be neither discriminating nor controllable—might indeed have disastrous moral effects, if it incites one's adversary to take greater risks, and thereby made war more likely.

While we differ with some details raised by the bishops' arguments about nuclear weapons, we are sympathetic to their overall conclusion that nuclear deterrence is morally tolerable as long as there is no acceptable alternative means to prevent a feared action and the intent is to avert the greater evil of nuclear war. We agree with the bishops that nuclear deterrence is only conditionally moral; the condition being that we make genuine efforts to reduce dependence on nuclear deterrence over the long run. To resort to nuclear deterrence in order to protect low stakes is a morally and politically nasty bluff. To resort to nuclear deterrence to protect *high* stakes makes political and moral sense only if the credibility of the threat is enhanced by the availability of non-nuclear weapons, which may make the actual execution of the threat unnecessary.

Those who disagree with this position would argue that deterrence implies some risk of nuclear war, and that nothing is worth nuclear war, particularly if it would end life on earth. This might be obvious if a breakdown of deterrence would really end life on earth. Trust in the existence of future generations pervades our daily life. We seek to preserve the environment, to save

money, to raise children properly, all the time assuming that life will continue to exist. But a nuclear war between the superpowers today would most likely not end all human life on earth. A critical moral goal should be to avoid passing that awful threshold.

Of course that is not enough. The current inventors of 50,000 weapons could wreak indescribable devastation. Even if its use would not end human life, it would destroy the human society we now know and cherish. But that does not mean one could not imagine a moral use of nuclear weapons. Suppose a nuclear war were limited, and the alternative was to succumb to a Hitler-type domination of the world in which tens of millions of innocent people would be exterminated without war. Many people would think such a war worth fighting. Fortunately, that is not our current situation.

Even if one believes that nothing is worth fighting nuclear war, it does not follow that nothing is worth the risk of nuclear war. Imagine, for the purposes of argument, a tiny risk of a nuclear war occurring in the first place, and only a small risk of it escalating to a large scale if it did break out. But imagine that the threat of that risk helped to prevent large-scale conventional war that would cost tens of millions of innocent lives as occurred in the Second World War. Would it be immoral to rely on a small risk of nuclear war to avoid the higher probability of large-scale conventional war? We think not—so long as efforts are made to keep the risks as low as possible, and so long as one realizes that this is only an interim solution. A complacency that led one to relax about the dangers of relying on nuclear deterrence could become the source of great immorality. But so also would a utopianism that could raise both nuclear and conventional risks.

In short, nuclear deterrence can be tolerated, but never liked. Deterrence can be seen as a necessary evil. Because it is necessary, one cannot abandon it carelessly; because it is evil, one must strive to rely on it less . . . ..

Footnote

1. Lou Harris Associates Polls.

Review Questions

1. Why is successful disarmament so rare?

2. What are the problems with complete disarmament?

3. What are the advantages of arms control?

4. Explain the Soviet position on arms control.

5. How can an arms control agreement be verified?

6. State the nuclear freeze proposal.

7. Explain the just war theory.

8. What are the three moral dilemmas raised by the U.S. Catholic Bishops?

Discussion Questions

1. Does the just war theory apply to nuclear war or not? Defend your answer.

2. Can a "limited" nuclear war be justified? How?

3. Is the risk of nuclear war justified? Explain your view.

4. Is nuclear deterrence a "necessary evil" or not? Explain your answer.

GREGORY S. KAVKA

Some Paradoxes of Deterrence

Gregory Kavka, "Some Paradoxes of Deterrence," *The Journal of Philosophy*, vol. LXXV, no. 6 (June 1978), pp. 285–302. Reprinted with permission.

Gregory S. Kavka is Associate Professor of Philosophy at the University of California, Irvine. He has written articles on political philosophy, ethics, and decision theory.

Kavka argues that the standard view of deterrence results in serious moral paradoxes that challenge three widely accepted moral principles: the Wrongful Intention Principle, the Right-Good Principle, and the Virtue Preservation Principle. Kavka does not see any entirely satisfactory way out of these moral paradoxes of deterrence; it seems that either our moral principles or our use of deterrence strategies must give way.

Deterrence is a parent of paradox. Conflict theorists, notably Thomas Schelling, have pointed out several paradoxes of deterrence: that it may be to the advantage of someone who is trying to deter another to be irrational, to have fewer available options, or to lack relevant information.[1] I shall describe certain new paradoxes that emerge when one attempts to analyze deterrence from a moral rather than a strategic perspective. These paradoxes are presented in the form of statements that appear absurd or incredible on first inspection, but can be supported by quite convincing arguments.

Consider a typical situation involving deterrence. A potential wrongdoer is about to commit an offense that would unjustly harm someone. A defender intends, and threatens, to retaliate should the wrongdoer commit the offense. Carrying out retaliation, if the offense is committed, could well be morally wrong. (The wrongdoer could be insane, or the retaliation could be out of proportion with the offense, or could seriously harm others besides the wrongdoer.) The moral paradoxes of deterrence arise out of the attempt to determine the moral status of the defendant's *intention* to retaliate in such cases. If the defender knows retaliation to be wrong, it would appear that this intention is evil. Yet such "evil" intentions may pave the road to heaven, by preventing serious offenses and by doing so without actually harming anyone.

Scrutiny of such morally ambiguous retaliatory intentions reveals paradoxes that call into question certain significant and widely accepted moral doctrines. These doctrines are what I call *bridge principles.* They attempt to link together the moral evaluation of actions and the moral evaluation of agents (and their states) in certain simple and apparently natural ways. The general acceptance, and intuitive appeal, of such principles, lends credibility to the project of constructing a consistent moral system that accurately reflects our firmest moral beliefs about both agents and actions. By raising doubts about the validity of certain popular bridge principles, the paradoxes presented here pose new difficulties for this important project.

I

In this section, a certain class of situations involving deterrence is characterized, and a plausible normative assumption is presented. In the following three sections, we shall see how application of this assumption to these situations yields paradoxes.

The class of paradox-producing situations is best introduced by means of an example. Consider the balance of nuclear terror as viewed from the perspective of one of its superpower participants, nation N. N sees the threat of nuclear retaliation as its only reliable means of preventing nuclear attack (or nuclear blackmail leading to world domination) by its superpower rival. N is confident such a threat will succeed in deterring its adversary, provided it really intends to carry out that threat. (N fears that, if it bluffs, its adversary is likely to learn this through leaks or espionage.) Finally, N recognizes it would have conclusive moral reasons *not* to carry out the threatened retaliation, if its opponent were to obliterate N with a surprise attack. For although retaliation would punish the leaders who committed this unprecedented crime and would prevent them from dominating the postwar world, N knows it would also destroy many millions of innocent civilians in the attacking nation (and in other nations), would set back postwar economic recovery for the world immeasurably, and might add enough fallout to the atmosphere to destroy the human race.

Let us call situations of the sort that nation N perceives itself as being in *Special Deterrent Situations* (SDSs). More precisely, an agent is in an SDS when he reasonably and correctly believes that the following conditions hold. First, it is likely he must intend (conditionally) to apply a harmful sanction to innocent people, if an extremely harmful and unjust offense is to be prevented. Second, such an intention would very likely deter the offense. Third, the amounts of harm involved in the offense and the threatened sanction are very large and of roughly similar quantity (or the latter amount is smaller than the former). Finally, he would have conclusive moral reasons not to apply the sanction if the offense were to occur.

The first condition in this definition requires some comment. Deterrence depends only on the potential wrongdoer's *beliefs* about the prospects of the sanction being applied. Hence, the first condition will be satisfied only if attempts by the defender to bluff would likely be perceived as such by the wrongdoer. This may be the case if the defender is an unconvincing liar, or is a group with a collective decision procedure, or if the wrongdoer is shrewd and knows the defender quite well. Generally, however, bluffing will be a promising course of action. Hence, although it is surely logically and physically possible for an SDS to occur, there will be few actual SDSs. It may be noted, though, that writers on strategic policy frequently assert that nuclear deterrence will be effective only if the defending nation really intends to retaliate.[2] If this is so, the balance of terror may fit the definition of an SDS, and the paradoxes developed here could have significant practical implications.[3] Further, were there no actual SDSs, these paradoxes would still be of considerable theoretical interest. For they indicate that the validity of some widely accepted moral doctrines rests on the presupposition that certain situations that could arise (i.e., SDSs) will not.

Turning to our normative assumption, we begin by noting that any reasonable system of ethics must have substantial utilitarian elements. The assumption that produces the paradoxes of deterrence concerns the role of utilitarian considerations in determining one's moral duty in a narrowly limited class of situations. Let the *most useful* act in a given choice situation be that with the highest expected utility. Our assumption says that the most useful act should be performed whenever a very great deal of utility is at stake. This means that, if the difference in expected utility between the most useful act and its alternatives is extremely large (e.g., equivalent to the difference between life and death for a very large number of people), other moral considerations are overridden by utilitarian considerations.

This assumption may be substantially weakened by restricting in various ways its range of application. I restrict the assumption to apply only when (i) a great deal of *negative* utility is at stake, and (ii) people will likely suffer serious injustices if the agent fails to perform the most useful act. This makes the assumption more plausible, since

the propriety of doing one person a serious injustice, in order to produce positive benefits for others, is highly questionable. The justifiability of doing the same injustice to prevent a utilitarian disaster, which itself involves grave injustices, seems more in accordance with our moral intuitions.

The above restrictions appear to bring our assumption into line with the views of philosophers such as Robert Nozick, Thomas Nagel, and Richard Brandt, who portray moral rules as "absolutely" forbidding certain kinds of acts, but acknowledge that exceptions might have to be allowed in cases in which such acts are necessary to prevent catastrophe.[4] Even with these restrictions, however, the proposed assumption would be rejected by supporters of genuine Absolutism, the doctrine that there are certain acts (such as vicarious punishment and deliberate killing of the innocent) that are always wrong, whatever the consequences of not performing them. (Call such acts *inherently evil.*) We can, though, accommodate the Absolutists. To do so, let us further qualify our assumption by limiting its application to cases in which (iii) performing the most useful act involves, at most, a small *risk* of performing an inherently evil act. With this restriction, the assumption still leads to paradoxes, yet is consistent with Absolutism (unless that doctrine is extended to include absolute prohibitions on something other than doing acts of the sort usually regarded as inherently evil).[5] The triply qualified assumption is quite plausible, so the fact that it produces paradoxes is both interesting and disturbing.

II

The first moral paradox of deterrence is:

(P1) There are cases in which, although it would be wrong for an agent to perform a certain act in a certain situation, it would nonetheless be right for him, knowing this, to form the intention to perform that act in that situation.

At first, this strikes one as absurd. If it is wrong and he is aware that it is wrong, how could it be right for him to form the intention to do it? (P1) is the direct denial of a simple moral thesis, the Wrongful Intentions Principle (WIP): *To intend to do what one knows to be wrong is itself wrong.*[6] WIP seems so obvious that, although philosophers never call it into question, they rarely bother to assert it or argue for it. Nevertheless, it appears that Abelard, Aquinas, Butler, Bentham, Kant, and Sidgwick, as well as recent writers such as Anthony Kenny and Jan Narveson, have accepted the principle, at least implicitly.[7]

Why does WIP seem so obviously true? First, we regard the man who fully intends to perform a wrongful act and is prevented from doing so solely by external circumstances (e.g., a man whose murder plan is interrupted by the victim's fatal heart attack) as being just as bad as the man who performs a like wrongful act. Second, we view the man who intends to do what is wrong, and then changes his mind, as having corrected a moral failing or error. Third, it is convenient, for many purposes, to treat a prior intention to perform an act, as the beginning of the act itself. Hence, we are inclined to view intentions as parts of actions and to ascribe to each intention the moral status ascribed to the act "containing" it.

It is essential to note that WIP appears to apply to conditional intentions in the same manner as it applies to nonconditional ones. Suppose I form the intention to kill my neighbor if he insults me again, and fail to kill him only because, fortuitously, he refrains from doing so. I am as bad, or nearly as bad, as if he had insulted me and I had killed him. My failure to perform the act no more erases the wrongness of my intention, than my neighbor's dropping dead as I load my gun would negate the wrongness of the simple intention to kill him. Thus the same considerations adduced above in support of WIP seem to support the formulation: If it would be wrong to perform an act in certain circumstances, then it is wrong to intend to perform that act on the condition that those circumstances arise.

Having noted the source of the strong feeling that (P1) should be rejected, we must consider an instantiation of (P1):

(P1') In an SDS, it would be wrong for the defender to apply the sanction if the wrongdoer were to commit the offense, but it is right for the defender to form the (conditional) intention to apply the sanction if the wrongdoer commits the offense.

The first half of (P1'), the wrongness of applying the sanction, follows directly from the last part of the definition of an SDS, which says that the defender would have conclusive moral reasons not to apply the sanction. The latter half of (P1'), which asserts the rightness of forming the intention to apply the sanction, follows from the definition of an SDS and our normative assumption. According to the definition, the defendant's forming this intention is likely necessary, and very likely sufficient, to prevent a seriously harmful and unjust offense. Further, the offense and the sanction would each produce very large and roughly commensurate amounts of negative utility (or the latter would produce a smaller amount). It follows that utilitarian considerations heavily favor forming the intention to apply the sanction, and that doing so involves only a small risk of performing an inherently evil act.[8] Applying our normative assumption yields the conclusion that it is right for the defender to form the intention in question.

This argument, if sound, would establish the truth of (P1'), and hence (P1), in contradiction with WIP. It suggests that WIP should not be applied to *deterrent intentions*, i.e., those conditional intentions whose existence is based on the agent's desire to thereby deter others from actualizing the antecedent condition of the intention. Such intentions are rather strange. They are, by nature, self-stultifying: if a deterrent intention fulfills the agent's purpose, it ensures that the intended (and possibly evil) act is not performed, by preventing the circumstances of performance from arising. The unique nature of such intentions can be further explicated by noting the distinction between intending to do something, and desiring (or intending) to intend to do it. Normally, an agent will form the intention to do something because he either desires doing that thing as an end in itself, or as a means to other ends. In such cases, little importance attaches to the distinction between intending and desiring to intend. But, in the case of deterrent intentions, the ground of the desire to form the intention is entirely distinct from any desire to carry it out. Thus, what may be inferred about the agent who seeks to form such an intention is this. He desires *having the intention* as a means of deterrence. Also, he is willing, in order to prevent the offense, to accept a certain *risk* that, in the end, he will apply the sanction. But this is entirely consistent with his having a strong desire not to apply the sanction, and no desire at all to apply it. Thus, while the object of his deterrent intention might be an evil act, it does not follow that, in desiring to adopt that intention, he desires to do evil, either as an end or as a means.

WIP ties the morality of an intention exclusively to the moral qualities of its object (i.e., the intended act). This is not unreasonable since, typically, the only significant effects of intentions are the acts of the agent (and the consequences of these acts) that flow from these intentions. However, in certain cases, intentions may have *autonomous effects* that are independent of the intended act's actually being performed. In particular, intentions to act may influence the conduct of other agents. When an intention has important autonomous effects, these effects must be incorporated into any adequate moral analysis of it. The first paradox arises because the autonomous effects of the relevant deterrent intention are dominant in the moral analysis of an SDS, but the extremely plausible WIP ignores such effects.[9]

III

(P1′) implies that a rational moral agent in an SDS should want to form the conditional intention to apply the sanction if the offense is committed, in order to deter the offense. But will he be able to do so? Paradoxically, he will not be. He is a captive in the prison of his own virtue, able to form the requisite intention only by bending the bars of his cell out of shape. Consider the preliminary formulation of this new paradox:

(P2′) *In an SDS, a rational and morally good agent cannot (as a matter of logic) have (or form) the intention to apply the sanction if the offense is committed.*[10]

The argument for (P2′) is as follows. An agent in an SDS recognizes that there would be conclusive moral reasons not to apply the sanction if the offense were committed. If he does not regard these admittedly conclusive moral reasons as conclusive reasons for him not to apply the sanction, then he is not moral. Suppose, on the other hand, that he does regard himself as having conclusive reasons not to apply the sanction if the offense is committed. If, nonetheless, he is disposed to apply it, because the reasons for applying it motivate him more strongly than do the conclusive reasons not to apply it, then he is irrational.

But couldn't our rational moral agent recognize, in accordance with (P1′), that he ought to form the intention to apply the sanction? And couldn't he then simply grit his teeth and pledge to himself that he will apply the sanction if the offense is committed? No doubt he could, and this would amount to trying to form the intention to apply the sanction. But the question remains whether he can succeed in forming that intention, by this or any other process, while remaining rational and moral. And it appears he cannot. There are, first of all, psychological difficulties. Being rational, how can he dispose himself to do something that he knows he would have conclusive reasons not to do, when and if the time comes to do it? Perhaps, though, some exceptional people can produce in themselves dispositions to act merely by pledging to act. But even if one could, in an SDS, produce a disposition to apply the sanction in this manner, such a disposition would not count as a *rational intention* to apply the sanction. This is because, as recent writers on intentions have suggested, it is part of the concept of rationally intending to do something, that the disposition to do the intended act be caused (or justified) in an appropriate way by the agent's view of reasons for doing the act.[11] And the disposition in question does not stand in such a relation to the agent's reasons for action.

It might be objected to this that people sometimes intend to do things (and do them) for no reason at all, without being irrational. This is true, and indicates that the connections between the concepts of intending and reasons for action are not so simple as the above formula implies. But it is also true that intending to do something for no reason at all, in the face of recognized significant reasons not to do it, would be irrational. Similarly, a disposition to act in the face of the acknowledged preponderance of reasons, whether called an "intention" or not, could not qualify as rational. It may be claimed that such a disposition, in an SDS, is rational in the sense that the agent knows it would further his aims to form (and have) it. This is not to deny the second paradox, but simply to express one of its paradoxical features. For the point of (P2′) is that the very disposition that *is* rational in the sense just mentioned, is at the same time irrational in an equally important sense. It is a disposition to act in conflict with the agent's own view of the balance of reasons for action.

We can achieve some insight into this by noting that an intention that is deliberately formed resides at the intersection of two distinguishable actions. It is the beginning of the act that is its object and is the end of the act that is its formation. As such, it may be assessed as rational (or moral) or not, according to whether either of two different acts promotes the agent's (or morality's) ends. Generally, the assessments will agree. But, as Schelling and others have noted, it may sometimes promote one's aims *not* to

be disposed to act to promote one's aims should certain contingencies arise. For example, a small country may deter invasion by a larger country if it is disposed to resist any invasion, even when resistance would be suicidal. In such situations, the assessment of the rationality (or morality) of the agent's intentions will depend upon whether these intentions are treated as components of their object-acts or their formation-acts. If treated as both, conflicts can occur. It is usual and proper to assess the practical rationality of an agent, at a given time, according to the degree of correspondence between his intentions and the reasons he has for performing the acts that are the objects of those intentions. As a result, puzzles such as (P2′) emerge when, for purposes of moral analysis, an agent's intentions are viewed partly as components of their formation-acts.

Let us return to the main path of our discussion by briefly summarizing the argument for (P2′). A morally good agent regards conducive moral reasons for action as conclusive reasons for action *impliciter*. But the intentions of a rational agent are not out of line with his assessment of the reasons for and against acting. Consequently, a rational moral agent cannot intend to do something that he recognizes there are conclusive moral reasons not to do. Nor can he intend conditionally to do what he recognizes he would have conclusive reasons not to do were that condition to be fulfilled. Therefore, in an SDS, where one has conclusive moral reasons not to apply the sanction, an originally rational and moral agent cannot have the intention to apply it without ceasing to be fully rational or moral; nor can he form the intention (as this entails having it).

We have observed that forming an intention is a process that may generally be regarded as an action. Thus, the second paradox can be reformulated as:

(P2) There are situations (namely SDSs) in which it would be right for agents to perform certain actions (namely forming the intention to apply the sanction) and in which it is possible for some agents to perform such actions, but impossible

for rational and morally good agents to perform them.

(P2), with the exception of the middle clause, is derived from the conjunction of (P1′) and (P2′) by existential generalization. The truth of the middle clause follows from consideration of the vengeful agent, who desires to punish those who commit seriously harmful and unjust offenses, no matter what the cost to others.

(P2) is paradoxical because it says that there are situations in which rationality and virtue preclude the possibility of right action. And this contravenes our usual assumption about the close logical ties between the concepts of right action and agent goodness. Consider the following claim: *Doing something is right if and only if a morally good man would do the same thing in the given situation.* Call this the Right-Good Principle. One suspects that, aside from qualifications concerning the good man's possible imperfections or factual ignorance, most people regard this principle, which directly contradicts (P2), as being virtually analytic. Yet the plight of the good man described in the second paradox does not arise out of an insufficiency of either knowledge or goodness. (P2) says there are conceivable situations in which virtue and knowledge combine with rationality to preclude right action, in which virtue is an obstacle to doing the right thing. If (P2) is true, our views about the close logical connection between right action and agent goodness, as embodied in the Right-Good Principle, require modifications of a sort not previously envisioned.

IV

A rational moral agent in an SDS faces a cruel dilemma. His reasons for intending to apply the sanction if the offense is committed are, according to (P1′), conclusive. But they outrun his reasons for doing it. Wishing to do what is right, he wants to form the intention. However, unless he can substan-

tially alter the basic facts of the situation or his beliefs about those facts, he can do so only by making himself less morally good, that is, by becoming a person who attaches grossly mistaken weights to certain reasons for and against action (e.g., one who prefers retribution to the protection of the vital interests of innocent people).[12] We have arrived at a third paradox:

(P3) In certain situations, it would be morally right for a rational and morally good agent to deliberately (attempt to) corrupt himself.[13]

(P3) may be viewed in light of a point about the credibility of threats that has been made by conflict theorists. Suppose a defender is worried about the credibility of his deterrent threat, because he thinks the wrongdoer (rightly) regards him as unwilling to apply the threatened sanction. He may make the threat more credible by passing control of the sanction to some *retaliation-agent.* Conflict theorists consider two sorts of retaliation-agents: people known to be highly motivated to punish the offense in question, and machines programmed to retaliate automatically if the offense occurs. What I wish to note is that future selves of the defender himself are a third class of retaliation-agents. If the other kinds are unavailable, a defender may have to create an agent of this third sort (i.e., an altered self willing to apply the sanction), in order to deter the offense. In cases in which applying the sanction would be wrong, this could require self-corruption.

How would a rational and moral agent in an SDS, who seeks to have the intention to apply the sanction, go about corrupting himself so that he may have it? He cannot form the intention simply by pledging to apply the sanction for, according to the second paradox, his rationality and morality preclude this. Instead, he must seek to initiate a causal process (e.g., a reeducation program) that he hopes will result in his beliefs, attitudes, and values changing in such a way that he can and will have the intention to apply the sanction should the offense be committed. Initiating such a process involves taking a rather odd, though not uncommon, attitude toward oneself: viewing oneself as an object to be molded in certain respects by outside influences rather than by inner choices. This is, for example, the attitude of the lazy but ambitious student who enrolls in a fine college, hoping that some of the habits and values of his highly motivated fellow students will "rub off" on him.

We can now better understand the notion of "risking doing X," which was introduced in section I. For convenience, let "X" be "killing." Deliberately risking killing is different from risking deliberately killing. One does the former when one rushes an ill person to the hospital in one's car at unsafe speed, having noted the danger of causing a fatal accident. One has deliberately accepted the risk of killing by accident. One (knowingly) risks deliberately killing, on the other hand, when one undertakes a course of action that one knows may, by various causal processes, lead to one's later performing a deliberate killing. The mild-mannered youth who joins a violent street gang is an example. Similarly, the agent in an SDS, who undertakes a plan of self-corruption in order to develop the requisite deterrent intention, knowingly risks deliberately performing the wrongful act of applying the sanction.

The above description of what is required of the rational moral agent in an SDS leads to a natural objection to the argument that supports (P3). According to this objection, an attempt at self-corruption by a rational moral agent is very likely to fail. Hence, bluffing would surely be a more promising strategy for deterrence than trying to form retaliatory intentions by self-corruption. Three replies may be given to this objection. First, it is certainly *conceivable* that, in a particular SDS, undertaking a process of self-corruption would be more likely to result in effective deterrence than would bluffing. Second, and more important, bluffing and attempting to form retaliatory intentions by self-corruption will generally not be mutual-

ly exclusive alternatives. An agent in an SDS may attempt to form the retaliatory intention while bluffing, and plan to continue bluffing as a "fall-back" strategy, should he fail. If the offense to be prevented is disastrous enough, the additional expected utility generated by following such a combined strategy (as opposed to simply bluffing) will be very large, even if his attempts to form the intention are unlikely to succeed. Hence (P3) would still follow from our normative assumption. Finally, consider the rational and *partly corrupt* agent in an SDS who already has the intention to retaliate. (The nations participating in the balance of terror may be examples.) The relevant question about him is whether he ought to act to become less corrupt, with the result that he would lose the intention to retaliate. The present objection does not apply in this case, since the agent already has the requisite corrupt features. Yet, essentially the same argument that produces (P3) leads, when this case is considered, to a slightly different, but equally puzzling, version of our third paradox:

(P3*) In certain situations, it would be morally wrong for a rational and partly corrupt agent to (attempt to) reform himself and eliminate his corruption.

A rather different objection to (P3) is the claim that its central notion is incoherent. This claim is made, apparently, by Thomas Nagel, who writes:

The notion that one might sacrifice one's moral integrity justifiably, in the service of a sufficiently worthy end, is an incoherent notion. For if one were justified in making such a sacrifice (or even morally required to make it), then one would not be sacrificing one's moral integrity by adopting that course: one would be preserving it (132–133).

Now the notion of a justified sacrifice of moral virtue (integrity) would be incoherent, as Nagel suggests, if one could sacrifice one's virtue only by doing something wrong. For the same act cannot be both morally justified and morally wrong. But one may also be said to sacrifice one's virtue when one deliberately initiates a causal process that one expects to result, and does result, in one's later becoming a less virtuous person. And, as the analysis of SDSs embodied in (P1') and (P2') implies, one may, in certain cases, be justified in initiating such a process (or even be obligated to initiate it). Hence, it would be a mistake to deny (P3) on the grounds advanced in Nagel's argument.

There is, though, a good reason, for *wanting* to reject (P3). It conflicts with some of our firmest beliefs about virtue and duty. We regard the promotion and preservation of one's own virtue as a vital responsibility of each moral agent, and self-corruption as among the vilest of enterprises. Further, we do not view the duty to promote one's virtue as simply one duty among others, to be weighed and balanced against the rest, but rather as a special duty that encompasses the other moral duties. Thus, we assent to the Virtue Preservation Principle: *It is wrong to deliberately lose (or reduce the degree of) one's moral virtue.* To many, this principle seems fundamental to our very conception of morality.[14] Hence the suggestion that duty could require the abandonment of virtue seems quite unacceptable. The fact that this suggestion can be supported by strong arguments produces a paradox.

This paradox is reflected in the ambivalent attitudes that emerge when we attempt to evaluate three hypothetical agents who respond to the demands of SDSs in various ways. The first agent refuses to try to corrupt himself and allows the disastrous offense to occur. We respect the love of virtue he displays, but are inclined to suspect him of too great a devotion to his own purity relative to his concern for the well-being of others. The second agent does corrupt himself to prevent disaster in an SDS. Though we do not approve of his new corrupt aspects, we admire the person that he *was* for his willingness to sacrifice what he loved— part of his own virtue—in the service of others. At the same time, the fact that he succeeded in corrupting himself may make

us wonder whether he was entirely virtuous in the first place. Corruption, we feel, does not come easily to a good man. The third agent reluctantly but sincerely tries his best to corrupt himself to prevent disaster, but fails. He may be admired both for his willingness to make such a sacrifice and for having virtue so deeply engrained in his character that his attempts at self-corruption do not succeed. It is perhaps characteristic of the paradoxical nature of the envisioned situation that we are inclined to admire most the only one of these three agents who fails in the course of action he undertakes.

V

It is natural to think of the evaluation of agents, and of actions, as being two sides of the same moral coin. The moral paradoxes of deterrence suggest they are more like two separate coins that can be fused together only by significantly deforming one or the other. In this concluding section, I shall briefly explain this.

Our shared assortment of moral beliefs may be viewed as consisting of three relatively distinct groups: beliefs about the evaluation of actions, beliefs about the evaluation of agents and their states (e.g., motives, intentions, and character traits), and beliefs about the relationship between the two. An important part of this last group of beliefs is represented by the three bridge principles introduced above: the Wrongful Intentions, Right-Good, and Virtue Preservation Principles. Given an agreed-upon set of bridge principles, one could go about constructing a moral system meant to express coherently our moral beliefs in either of two ways: by developing principles that express our beliefs about act evaluation and then using the bridge principles to derive principles of agent evaluation—or vice versa. If our bridge principles are sound and our beliefs about agent and act evaluation are mutually consistent, the resulting systems would, in theory, be the same. If, however, there are underlying incompatibilities between the principles we use to evaluate acts and agents, there may be significant differences between moral systems that are *act-oriented* and those that are *agent-oriented*. And these differences may manifest themselves as paradoxes that exert pressure upon the bridge principles that attempt to link the divergent systems, and the divergent aspects of each system, together.

It seems natural to us to evaluate acts at least partly in terms of their consequences. Hence, act-oriented moral systems tend to involve significant utilitarian elements. The principle of act evaluation usually employed in utilitarian systems is: in a given situation, one ought to perform the most useful act, that which will (or is expected to) produce the most utility. What will maximize utility depends upon the facts of the particular situation. Hence, as various philosophers have pointed out, the above principle could conceivably recommend one's (i) acting from nonutilitarian motives, (ii) advocating some nonutilitarian moral theory, or even (iii) becoming a genuine adherent of some nonutilitarian theory.[15] Related quandaries arise when one considers, from an act-utilitarian viewpoint, the deterrent intention of a defender in an SDS. Here is an intention whose object-act is anti-utilitarian and whose formation-act is a utilitarian duty that cannot be performed by a rational utilitarian.

A utilitarian might seek relief from these quandaries in either of two ways. First, he could defend some form of rule-utilitarianism. But then he would face a problem. Shall he include, among the rules of his system, our normative assumption that requires the performance of the most useful act, whenever an enormous amount of utility is at stake (and certain other conditions are satisfied)? If he does, the moral paradoxes of deterrence will appear within his system. If he does not, it would seem that his system fails to attach the importance to the consequences of particular momentous acts that any reasonable moral, much less utilitarian, system should. An alternative reaction would be to stick by the utilitarian principle of act evaluation, and simply accept (P1)–(P3), and related oddities, as true. Taking this line would require the abandonment of the plausible and familiar bridge principles that contradict (P1)–(P3). But this need not bother the act-utilitarian, who perceives his task as the modification, as well as codification, of our moral beliefs.

Agent-oriented (as opposed to act-oriented) moral systems rest on the premise that what primarily matters for morality are the internal states of a person: his character traits, his intentions, and the condition of his will. The doctrines about intentions and virtue expressed in our three bridge principles are generally incorporated into such systems. The paradoxes of deterrence may pose serious problems for some agent-oriented systems. It may be, for example, that an adequate analysis of the moral virtues of justice, selflessness, and benevolence, would imply that the truly virtuous man would feel obligated to make whatever personal sacrifice is necessary to prevent a catastrophe. If so, the moral paradoxes of deterrence would arise within agent-oriented systems committed to these virtues.

There are, however, agent-oriented systems that would not be affected by our paradoxes. One such system could be called Extreme Kantianism. According to this view, the only things having moral significance are such features of a person as his character and the state of his will. The Extreme Kantian accepts Kant's dictum that morality requires treating oneself and others as ends rather than means. He interprets this to imply strict duties to preserve one's virtue and not to deliberately impose serious harms or risks on innocent people. Thus, the Extreme Kantian would simply reject (P1)–(P3) without qualm.

Although act-utilitarians and Extreme Kantians can view the paradoxes of deterrence without concern, one doubts that the rest of us can. The adherents of these extreme conceptions of morality are untroubled by the paradoxes because their viewpoints are too one-sided to represent our moral beliefs accurately. Each of them is closely attentive to certain standard principles of agent *or* act evaluation, but seems too little concerned with traditional principles of the other sort. For a system of morality to reflect our firmest and deepest convictions adequately, it must represent a middle ground between these extremes by seeking to accommodate the valid insights of both act-oriented and agent-oriented perspectives. The normative assumption set out in section I was chosen as a representative principle that might be incorporated into such a system. It treats utilitarian considerations as relevant and potentially decisive, while allowing for the importance of other factors. Though consistent with the absolute prohibition of certain sorts of acts, it treats the distinction between harms and risks as significant and rules out absolute prohibitions on the latter as unreasonable. It is an extremely plausible middle-ground principle but, disturbingly, it leads to paradoxes.

That these paradoxes reflect conflicts between commonly accepted principles of agent and act evaluation is further indicated by the following observation. Consider what initially appears a natural way of viewing the evaluation of acts and agents as coordinated parts of a single moral system. According to this view, reasons for action determine the moral status of acts, agents, and intentions. A right act is an act that accords with the preponderance of moral reasons for action. To have the right intention is to be disposed to perform the act supported by the preponderance of such reasons, because of those reasons. The virtuous agent is the rational agent who has the proper substantive values, i.e., the person whose intentions and actions accord with the preponderance of moral reasons for action. Given these considerations, it appears that it should always be possible for an agent to go along intending, and acting, in accordance with the preponderance of moral reasons thus ensuring both his own virtue and the rightness of his intentions and actions.

Unfortunately, this conception of harmonious coordination between virtue, right intention, and right action, is shown to be untenable by the paradoxes of deterrence. For they demonstrate that, in any system that takes consequences plausibly into account, situations can arise in which the rational use of moral principles leads to certain paradoxical recommendations: that the principles used, and part of the agent's virtue, be abandoned, and that wrongful intentions be formed.

One could seek to avoid these paradoxes by moving in the direction of Extreme Kantianism and rejecting our normative assumption. But to do so would be to overlook the plausible core of act-utilitarianism. This is the claim that, in the moral evaluation of acts, how those acts affect human happiness often is important—the more so as more happiness is at stake—and sometimes is decisive. Conversely, one could move toward accommodation with act-utilitarianism. This would involve qualifying, so that they do not apply in SDSs, the traditional moral doctrines that contradict (P1)–(P3). And, in fact, viewed in isolation, the considerations adduced in section II indicate that the Wrongful Intentions Principle ought to be so qualified. However, the claims of (P2) and (P3)—that virtue may preclude right action and that morality may require self-corruption—are not so easily accepted. These notions remain unpalatable even when one considers the arguments that support them.

Thus, tinkering with our normative assumption or with traditional moral doctrines would indeed enable us to avoid the paradoxes, at least in their present form. But this would require rejecting certain significant and deeply entrenched beliefs concerning the evaluation either of agents or of actions. Hence, such tinkering would not go far toward solving the fundamental problem of which the paradoxes are symptoms: the apparent incompatibility of the moral principles we use to evaluate acts and agents. Perhaps this problem can be solved. Perhaps the coins of agent and act evaluation can be successfully fused. But it is not apparent how this is to be done. And I, for one, do not presently see an entirely satisfac-tory way out of the perplexities that the paradoxes engender.

Footnotes

1. *The Strategy of Conflict* (New York: Oxford, 1960), chs. 1–2; and *Arms and Influence* (New Haven, CN: Yale, 1966) ch. 2.

2. See, e.g., Herman Kahn, *On Thermonuclear War*, 2nd ed. (Princeton, NJ: University Press, 1960, p. 185; and Anthony Kenny, "Counterforce and Countervalue," in Walter Stein, ed., *Nuclear Weapons: A Catholic Response* (London: Merlin Press, 1965), pp. 162–164.

3. See, e.g., note 9, below.

4. Nozick, *Anarchy, State, and Utopia* (New York: Basic Books, 1974), pp. 30/1 n; Nagel, "War and Massacre," *Philosophy and Public Affairs*, 1 (Winter 1972): 123–144, p. 126; Brandt, "Utilitarianism and the Rules of War," ibid. 145–165, p. 147 especially note 3.

5. Extensions of Absolutism that would block some or all of the paradoxes include those that forbid intending to do what is wrong, deliberately making oneself less virtuous, or intentionally risking performing an inherently evil act. (An explanation of the relevant sense of "risking performing an act" will be offered in section IV.)

6. I assume henceforth that, if it would be wrong to do something, the agent knows this. (The agent, discussed in section IV, who has become corrupt may be an exception.) This keeps the discussion of the paradoxes from getting tangled up with the separate problem of whether an agent's duty is to do what is actually right, or what he believes is right.

7. See *Peter Abelard's Ethics*, D.E. Luscombe, Trans. (New York: Oxford, 1971), pp. 5–37; Thomas Aquinas, *Summa Theologica*, 1a2ae. 18–20; Joseph Butler, "A Dissertation on the Nature of Virtue," in *Five Sermons* (Indianapolis: Bobbs-Merrill, 1950), p. 83; Immanuel Kant, *Foundations of the Metaphysics of Morals*, first section; Jeremy Bentham, *An Introduction to the Principles of Morals and Legislation*, ch. 9, secs. 13–16; Henry Sidgwick, *The Methods of Ethics* (New York: Dover, 1907), pp. 60/1, 201–204; Kenny, pp. 159, 162; and Jan Narveson, *Morality and Utility* (Baltimore: Johns Hopkins, 1967), pp. 106–108.

8. A qualification is necessary. Although having the intention involves only a small risk of applying the threatened sanction to innocent people, it follows, from points made in section IV, that forming the intention might also involve risks of performing *other* inherently evil acts. Hence, what really follows is that forming the intention is right in those SDSs in which the composite risk is small. This limitation in the scope of (P1') is to be henceforth understood. It does not affect (P1), (P2), or (P3), since each is governed by an existential quantifier.

9. In *Nuclear Weapons*, Kenny and others use WIP to argue that nuclear deterrence is immoral because it involves having the conditional intention to kill innocent people. The considerations advanced in this section suggest that this argument, at best, is inconclusive, since it presents only one side of a moral paradox, and, at worst, is mistaken, since it applies WIP in just the sort of situation in which its applicability is most questionable.

10. "Rational and morally good" in this and later statements of the second and third paradoxes, means rational and moral in the given situation. A person who usually is rational and moral, but fails to be in the situation in question, could, of course, have the intention to apply the sanction. (P2') is quite similar to a paradox concerning utilitarianism and deterrence developed by D.H. Hodgson in *Consequences of Utilitarianism* (Oxford: Clarendon Press, 1967), ch. 4.

11. See, e.g., S. Hampshire and H.L.A. Hart, "Decision, Intention and Certainty," *Mind* LXVII.1, 265 (January 1958): 1–12; and G.E.M. Anscombe, *Intention* (Ithaca, NY: Cornell, 1966).

12. Alternatively, the agent could undertake to make himself into an *irrational* person whose intentions are quite out of line with his reasons for action. However, trying to become irrational, in these circumstances, is less likely to succeed than trying to change one's moral beliefs, and, furthermore, might itself constitute self-corruption. Hence, this point does not affect the paradox stated below.

13. As Donald Regan has suggested to me, (P3) can be derived directly from our normative assumption: imagine a villain credibly threatening to kill very many hostages unless a certain good man corrupts himself. I prefer the indirect route to (P3) given in the text, because (P1) and (P2) are interesting in their own right and because viewing the three paradoxes together makes it easier to see what produces them.

14. Its supporters might, of course, allow exceptions to the principle in cases in which only the agent's feelings, and not his acts or dispositions to act, are corrupted. (For example, a doctor "corrupts himself" by suppressing normal sympathy for patients in unavoidable pain, in order to treat them more effectively.) Further, advocates of the doctrine of double-effect might consider self-corruption permissible when it is a "side effect" of action rather than a means to an end. For example, they might approve of a social worker's joining a gang to reform it, even though he expects to assimilate some of the gang's distorted values. Note, however, that neither of these possible exceptions to the Virtue Preservation Principle (brought to my attention by Robert

Adams) applies to the agent in an SDS who corrupts his *intentions* as a chosen *means* of preventing an offense.

15. See Hodgson, *Consequences*. Also, Adams, "Motive Utilitarianism," *The Journal of Philosophy*, LXXIII, 14

(Aug. 12, 1976): 467–81; and Bernard Williams, "A Critique of Utilitarianism," in J.J.C. Smart and Williams, *Utilitarianism: For and Against* (New York: Cambridge, 1973), sec. 6.

Review Questions

1. What is a Special Deterrent Situation?

2. Is the balance of nuclear terror such a situation?

3. What is the first moral paradox of deterrence?

4. Does it apply to the strategy of nuclear deterrence?

5. What is the second paradox?

6. And the third paradox?

7. Why isn't simply bluffing a good strategy?

8. Are nations who threaten nuclear war corrupt?

9. Are they irrational?

10. What are the three "bridge principles?"

Discussion Questions

1. Is there any acceptable way to avoid these moral paradoxes of deterrence? Explain your answer.

2. Which is better—giving up deterrence strategies or giving up the three moral principles they conflict with?

Problem Cases

1. The standard nuclear freeze proposal is this: "There should be a bilateral and verifiable freeze on the testing, production, and deployment of nuclear weapons and of missiles and of new aircraft designed primarily to deliver nuclear weapons." Notice that submarines are not mentioned; the new Trident submarines would be allowed. But the production of 100 MX missiles with ten warheads each, 100 B–1 bombers, thousands of cruise missiles, more warheads, and the development of anti-ballistic missile systems would be stopped. These items are expected to cost about $200 billion over six years. Referendums in support of the freeze proposal have won in several

states, and opinion polls show that the majority supports it. Should the freeze proposal be passed by Congress or not? Explain your position.

2. The current policy calls for the NATO Alliance to initiate the use of nuclear weapons if there is a conventional Soviet attack against Western Europe. Suppose that the Soviets invade West Germany, and suppose that it looks as though their numerically superior ground forces will prevail over the NATO forces. Should the NATO Alliance be the first to use nuclear weapons in this case or not? Defend your answer.

Suggested Reading

Kavka, Gregory S., "Doubts About Unilateral Nuclear Disarmament," *Philosophy and Public Affairs* (Summer 1983): 255–260. Kavka replies to Lackey's article; Kavka is opposed to unilateral nuclear disarmament by the U.S.

Lackey, Douglas P., "Missiles and Morals: A Utilitarian Look at Nuclear Deterrence," *Philosophy and Public Affairs* (Summer 1982): 189–231. Lackey gives utilitarian arguments in favor of unilateral nuclear disarmament by the U.S.

Schell, Jonathan. *The Fate of the Earth*. (New York: Avon Books, 1982). A very well-written account of the horrors of nuclear war. Schell argues that our deterrence strategy is contradictory.